Emotional Intelligence

Emotional Intelligence
Science and Myth

Gerald Matthews, Moshe Zeidner, and Richard D. Roberts

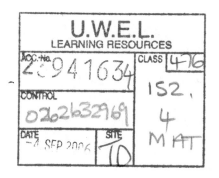
A Bradford Book
The MIT Press
Cambridge, Massachusetts
London, England

First MIT Press paperback edition, 2004
© 2002 Massachusetts Institute of Technology

This book was set in New Baskerville on 3B2 by Asco Typesetters, Hong Kong, and was printed and bound in the United States of America.

Library of Congress Cataloging-in-Publication Data

Matthews, Gerald.
  Emotional intelligence : science and myth / Gerald Matthews, Moshe Zeidner, and Richard D. Roberts.
      p.   cm.
  Includes bibliographical references and index.
  ISBN 0-262-13418-7 (alk. paper), 0-262-63296-9 (pb)
  1. Emotional intelligence. I. Zeidner, Moshe. II. Roberts, Richard D. III. Title.
BF576 .M28 2003
152.4—dc21   2002066034

10   9   8   7   6   5   4   3

This book is dedicated to Diana Ciupka, with love and appreciation of your understanding; Eti Zeidner, the very embodiment of emotional intelligence; Patricia Roberts; and Marie Benevides

Contents

Foreword   xi
Robert J. Sternberg
Preface   xv

I
Conceptualizations and Measurement   1

1
Introduction   3

Historical and Sociocultural Context of Emotional Intelligence   3
Conceptions of Emotional Intelligence   9
A Research Agenda for Emotional Intelligence   21
Chapter Synthesis and Preview   28

2
Toward a Science of Emotional Intelligence   31

Toward a Psychometrics of Emotional Intelligence   32
Toward a Theory of Emotional Intelligence   47
Integrating Theory and Psychometrics: Differential Psychology and Emotional Intelligence   57
Emotional Intelligence in the Real World: Practical Applications   74
Conclusion: Toward a Science of EI   79

3
Understanding the Intelligence Component of Emotional Intelligence   81

Why Mess with Intelligence?   81
The History of Intelligence   83

The Concept of Intelligence   86
Structural Theories of Intelligence   91
System Models of Intelligence   115
Conclusions   129

4

Emotions: Concepts and Research   133

Conceptualizing Emotion   134
Categories and Dimensions of Emotion   140
Sources of Emotion   150
The Natural Ecology of Emotions   159
Functions and Behavioral Consequences of Emotion   164
Conclusions   171

5

Psychological Assessment and the Concept of Emotional Intelligence   175

Psychometric Issues Revisited   176
Performance Measures of Emotional Intelligence   180
Self-Report Measures of Emotional Intelligence   205
Overlap of Emotional Intelligence with Personality   223
Conclusions   226

II

Individual Differences in Emotion and Adaptation   231

6

The Biological Science of Emotional Intelligence   233

The Neuroscience of Emotion   234
Subcortical Control of Emotion: The Amygdala   238
Frontal Control of Emotion   242
Functions of Emotion   248
Conclusions on Biological Models and Emotional Intelligence   253

7

Cognitive Models of Emotion and Self-Regulation   255

Cognitive Origins of Emotion   256
Cognitive Architectures for Emotional Intelligence in Action   259

Self-Regulative Models of Emotional Intelligence   270
Criticisms of the Cognitive Approach   277
Conclusions   280

8

Emotional Intelligence, Coping, and Adaptation   283

Stress and Coping: The EI Perspective   286
Emotional Intelligence and the Psychological Theory of Stress   295
EI, Coping, and Adaptation to Stressful Encounters   303
Coping and Self-Regulative Processes   314
Conclusions   316

9

Personality, Emotion, and Adaptation   321

Personality and Emotion: A Cognitive-Adaptive Perspective   326
Negative Emotionality   330
Social Competence and Extraversion   342
Prosocial and Antisocial Behavior   350
Self-Control, Conscientiousness, and Impulsivity   361
Conclusions   368

III

Applications   371

10

The Clinical Psychology of Emotional Maladjustment   373

Diagnostic Categories for Emotional Disorders   374
Abnormal Personality and Emotional Disorder   383
Alexithymia   387
Pathological Processes   400
Therapy for Emotional Pathology   412
Conclusions   416

11

Development and Schooling of Emotional Intelligence   419

Origins and Development of Emotional Intelligence   420
Schooling Emotional Intelligence   442

Desired Features of EI Intervention Programs and Future Research   460
Conclusions   464

12

Emotional Intelligence, Work, and the Occupational Environment   467

Emotions and the Workplace   467
The Role of EI in Career and Occupational Assessment   477
EI and Coping with Occupational Stress   488
Conclusions   504

IV

Conclusion   511

13

The Science, the Myth, and the Future of Emotional Intelligence   513

Psychometric and Conceptual Issues   516
Theoretical Issues   531
Applied Issues   539
The Science and Myth of Emotional Intelligence   544

Appendix A: A Review and Critique of Social Intelligence   551
Appendix B: A Review of Sundry Other Performance Measures of Emotional Intelligence   563
Appendix C: A Review of Sundry Other Self-Report Measures of Emotional Intelligence   577
Notes   587
References   591
Index   683

Foreword
Robert J. Sternberg

Emotional Intelligence: Science and Myth is, in many respects, a tour de force with regard to the analysis of the literature on emotional intelligence. I do not claim to know all of the literature in the field, but I am unaware of any book that is as extensive, intensive (i.e., in-depth), and unified in tone and voice as is this book. It is hard to imagine anyone interested in emotional intelligence not reading the book, and I suspect that even those quite knowledgeable about the field will learn a lot from reading it. The book covers the waterfront—from the nature of intelligence, to the nature of emotion, to various theoretical attempts to understand the interface between intelligence and emotion, to diverse attempts to measures skills at this interface, to equally diverse attempts to provide training that increases these skills. Because the book covers not only theory, measurement, and training, but also specific applications to clinical, educational, and occupational settings, the book will be of interest to practitioners as well as scientists. The book will be tough slogging for laypeople, but laypeople with some understanding of psychology and statistics will find the book rewarding, if challenging.

Matthews, Zeidner, and Roberts are certainly correct that part of the interest in emotional intelligence derives from a reaction to Herrnstein and Murray's somewhat narrow and pessimistic evaluation of intelligence in *The Bell Curve* (1994), but I suspect that this field would have evolved in much the same way as it has even if Herrnstein and Murray's book had never been written. Emotional intelligence is of such great interest in its own right that it no doubt would attract attention regardless of what other views and books were around.

Matthews, Zeidner, and Roberts wisely point out that, in some sense, the field has bifurcated origins. The scholarly field of emotional intelligence got off the ground with the publication of Salovey and Mayer's initial article on the construct (1990). Although there were earlier references to the term, Salovey, Mayer, and their colleagues certainly provided the first clearly delineated theory and the first systematic program of research. The popular field of emotional intelligence got off the ground with the publication of Goleman's (1995) book, which created widespread lay and scientific interest in the construct. Goleman's work does not represent a systematic scientific program of research, at least in the usual sense of the term, in that there appear to be no refereed published studies where hypotheses are predictively tested against data. But it has stirred the imaginations of many people.

I can find little to quibble about in the authors' analysis of the existing literature. It seemed, for the most part, reasonable and carefully thought through. I share their profound skepticism of much of the popular movement. The positive side of the movement is that it helps broaden our concept of intelligence and get us away from the common fixation on IQ-based or IQ-related measures. The negative side of the movement is that it is often crass, profit-driven, and socially and scientifically irresponsible. The same people who criticize the conventional psychometric testers for potentially making a mess out of the lives of people who have potential but do not score well on conventional tests do much worse in promoting what, for the most part, are largely unvalidated or poorly validated tests of emotional intelligence. But some of the tests do have scientific bases and at least some reasonable data to support their use. The analyses of the authors of this book should be very helpful to consumers in deciding on which tests have greater merit.

The arguments of the authors leave one concerned that there is no equivalent to the Food and Drug Administration for educational and organizational tests and instructional programs. We would not want drugs to go to market that are essentially untested and that have only their promoters' claims to back them up. Yet we routinely rely on such claims to buy educational and organizational products and services. People's lives may be affected in much the same way that their lives can be affected by drugs, but in this case, they have not even the appearance of protection. As the authors of the book point out, the only solution is *caveat emptor*: buyer beware.

I share the concerns of the authors of this book with respect to personality-based theories and measures of emotional intelligence, because, at least to date, it is unclear that they have adequate discriminant validity with respect to existing theories and measures of personality, especially those that derive from five-factor theory. I am more sanguine than the authors of this book with respect to the abilities-based approach. Although there are still many unanswered questions and many psychometric issues that need to be resolved, when one considers that the Salovey-Mayer article was published just a little over a decade ago, what is amazing to me is that the theory and measures have advanced as far as they have, not that they are still lacking in some respects. I suspect that over time this approach will be vindicated. The value of a detailed and careful analysis such as that provided in this book is to show what aspects are most in need of further research.

In sum, I found this book to be tremendously helpful to me in learning about and understanding the field of emotional intelligence as it currently stands. I am confident that other readers will feel the same way.

References

Goleman, D. (1995). *Emotional intelligence.* New York: Bantam.

Salovey, P., & Mayer, J. D. (1990). Emotional intelligence. *Imagination, Cognition, and Personality, 9,* 185–211.

tackling conceptual issues, we have recently been actively involved in analyzing data on hundreds of people given prominent measures of EI, personality, and intelligence. These data, woven into our exposition, represents cutting-edge empirical research and helps bring into sharp relief the prospects and limitations of the concept of EI.

This book differs in various respects from existing volumes. The majority of books on emotional intelligence are targeted towards the general public; the few scientific books that exist are slanted towards promoting the concept of EI. There are edited books that present a variety of divergent perspectives and viewpoints, but these generally fail to present a critical and integrated exposition of the topic. Our book is the first to present a scientifically grounded critique of the basic assumptions of EI research. We point out fundamental weaknesses of the concept, as well as possibilities for developing the concept rigorously. The book will also be the first volume to challenge the current popularity of emotional intelligence in applied settings.

The target audience for this book is students and professionals in psychology, education, and the health and welfare sciences. Because EI has recently been touted as an important component of success in business, it should also find a readership with students and professionals in management, human resources, and industrial relations. Given the widespread public interest in the topic and the extensive coverage of EI by the media, the book should be of considerable interest to the lay public as well. The book hopes to make a contribution to scientific psychology, has relevance to clinical, occupational, and educational psychology, and seeks to present a distinctive and potentially controversial point of view on a topic of general public concern.

We have sought to capitalize on our joint experience of working on empirical research in many of the areas germane to EI. Gerald Matthews is a cognitive scientist who works on information-processing models of personality, stress, and mood in both theoretical and applied contexts. Moshe Zeidner is an emotions researcher who has studied cognitive-affective interaction, test anxiety, and educational applications of differential psychology. Richard Roberts is a hard-core intelligence researcher and expert in psychometrics. Although all three of us have spent considerable time researching in the United States, there is a decidedly international flavor to our current collaboration. Matthews (the United States, but formerly from Scotland), Zeidner (Israel, but formerly of the United States), and Roberts (Australia) bring some differing perspectives to a construct alleged to have universal application.

Organization and Structure of the Book

A scientific account of emotional intelligence requires the following. First, it is necessary to have a clear conceptualization of what emotional intelligence means, and this leads to having an adequate methodology for assessment of the construct that discriminates EI from other, seemingly analogous, concepts. Second, we require a theoretical account of EI that grounds the construct in psychological processes and parsimoniously explains how EI may influence adaptive functioning in the real world. Third, we must explore its use (and potential abuse) in a variety of applied settings. Applied utility is not necessarily a defining quality of EI, but if the construct is as far-reaching as claimed, it should have significant ramifications for psychological practitioners. To address the foregoing issues systematically, the chapters are arranged to reflect four broad but overlapping issues.

Part I, "Conceptualizations and Measurement," surveys some basic issues in research on EI and provides a conceptual framework for reviewing the evidence interrelating emotion and ability constructs. Chapter 1 provides a broad overview of the construct of emotional intelligence. More specifically, this chapter delineates the historical and sociocultural backdrop for the emergence of EI, highlights reasons for the salience and recent widespread interest in the construct of EI, and surveys early and contemporary conceptions of EI. In addition, this chapter provides a research agenda for a science of EI based on the three pillars of measurement (psychometrics), theory development, and practical applications. Chapter 2 lays out a chart for this scientific enterprise, reviewing the psychometric and theoretical principles to be followed and setting out a cognitive science framework for understanding emotional function. The chapter also differentiates personality and ability models of EI and raises the key issue of how EI should be located within the existing science of differential psychology. Its final part reviews some of the practical benefits that may ensue from a valid theory of EI. Chapters 3 and 4 respectively provide the conceptual framework for understanding the two grand constructs that serve as building blocks for the hybrid concept of emotional intelligence: emotion and intelligence. Chapter 3 reviews a number of definitions of intelligence and presents the key issues, concepts, and controversies that a century of research on intelligence has given us. We present a number of formal structural models of intelligence and discuss the implications that emerge from these models for the concept of EI. Chapter 4 discusses ways of understanding emotion that might provide a basis for understanding EI. This chapter presents a number of conceptual issues generated by a century of scientific attempts to understand emotion. Historical perspectives on emotions (e.g., centralist versus peripheralist theories) lead into an account of possible sources and functions of emotions. Here we also review empirical studies using measures of emotional state to investigate the causes and consequences of emotion. Chapter 5 delineates major issues in defining and assessing EI. The chapter summarizes the criteria that the concept of EI should satisfy (construct validity, reliability, etc.) and critically assesses the success of self-report and performance-based tests in meeting these criteria. It provides a comprehensive review of contemporary assessment procedures and their limitations. A major limitation is the overlap of self-report tests with existent personality constructs.

Part II, "Individual Differences in Emotion and Adaptation," discusses the theoretical basis for attempting to classify people in terms of competence in handling emotional events. Chapter 6 discusses the biological substrata for adaptation and EI. This chapter discusses various facets of the biology of emotion, including animal models, neuropsychology, and evolutionary biology. Both subcortical and cortical emotion systems of the brain may provide a physical substrate for EI. However, biological models are limited by their lack of engagement with real-world human behavior and by their neglect of cognitive control. In chapter 7 we present the implications for EI of key cognitive models of emotion (appraisal theory, network, attentional, and self-regulatory models of emotion). We argue that the cognitive approach is more successful than biological models of emotion in explaining emotion-behavior links. However, there are difficulties in linking EI either to individual differences in information processing or to self-regulation. We conclude that, despite various difficulties, it is possible that EI relates to an emotional executive system that may have a neurological basis in the frontal lobes. However, much work remains to be done before such a view is credible. The next two chapters focus on the adaptive benefits that might result from individual differences in emotion-regulation processes. Chapter 8 focuses on emotional intelligence and the psychological theory of stress. We present and review various hypothesis regarding the causal mechanisms relating EI to adaptive coping. Chapter 9 discusses personality traits as adaptive specializations and uses the cognitive-adaptational framework as a basis for reviewing key dimensions of personality, with focus on the Five-Factor model.

Part III, "Applications," is devoted to examining the value of using notions of EI to guide practical interventions in various applied settings. Chapters 10, 11, and 12 discuss the potential importance of EI in clinical, occupational, and educational settings, and examine evidence on applications purporting to be based on EI. Chapter 10 discusses the nature and origin of clinical disorders related to dysfunction of negative emotions (anxiety, depression, and anger) and links EI to the extensively researched construct of alexithymia. It also looks at the potential for targeting therapeutic techniques at EI. Chapter 11 discusses major sources of emotion and stress at the workplace and reviews the empirical research on ways of coping with stress at the workplace. In addition, we examine the role of EI in three major applied areas: occupational assessment, prediction and selection, and coping with stress. We also present empirical evidence on the effectiveness of EI interventions. Chapter 12 begins with an account of factors contributing to the origins and development of emotional competence during childhood, including biology, primary socialization, and related factors (personal experience, peers, teachers, media, etc.). It then discusses current attempts to cultivate and school EI in educational settings. We describe and critically evaluate selected educational programs for affective education and present criteria for the development of EI intervention programs. Together, the three chapters provide a critical perspective on whether the concept of EI provides for coherent, theory-driven interventions, or whether it simply relabels practices that are already well-established.

Part IV, "Conclusions," summarizes the implications of our review for the role of EI as a scientific construct. The concluding chapter attempts to present a balanced discussion of the unique strengths and weaknesses of the EI construct, shedding light on both the scientific and mythical facets of the construct. The chapter also delineates priorities and directions for future research.

We are grateful to a number of colleagues and friends for their support. We wish to thank Robert Sternberg for offering us considerable social support and for graciously agreeing to write the foreword to this book. Thanks go to the following individuals for reading and commenting on earlier versions of various parts of this manuscript: Elizabeth Austin, Aaron Ben-Ze'ev, Nathan Brody, Ian Deary, Norm Endler, Adrian Furnham, Andrew Hawkins, Richard Lazarus, Jack Mayer,

Joseph McGrath, Reinhard Pekrun, Dino Petrides, Carolyn Saarni, Peter Salovey, Klaus Scherer, Miri Sharf, Keith Topping, and Adrian Wells.

This has been a challenging, thought provoking, and rewarding collaborative experience, and we hope readers will find it helps to better integrate current EI theory, research, and interventions. We will be rewarded if this book advances our psychological knowledge of emotional intelligence and assists in understanding adaptive coping in circumstances that provoke emotion.

Preface

Emotional intelligence (EI) has recently emerged as a key construct in modern-day psychological research, appearing as one of the most widely discussed aspects of intelligence in the current literature. EI refers to the competence to identify and express emotions, understand emotions, assimilate emotions in thought, and regulate both positive and negative emotions in oneself and others. The construct has matured and subsequently gathered international media attention ever since its inception in the 1980s. Researchers claim to have made important strides toward understanding its nature, components, determinants, effects, developmental track, and modes of modification. EI research has prospered in part because of the increasing personal importance of both intelligence and healthy emotions for people in modern society. It has even been claimed that EI predicts important educational and occupational criteria above and beyond those predicted by general intellectual ability.

Although first mentioned in the psychological literature nearly two decades ago, it is only in the past five years that emotional intelligence has received widespread public attention. Daniel Goleman's book on the topic appeared on the *New York Times* Best-Sellers List in 1996, the same year in which a *Time Magazine* article was devoted to detailed exposition of the topic. More recently, the influential e-zine *Salon* devoted a lengthy article to discussion of its application (both potential and realized) in the work force. Moreover, the last year or so has witnessed a plethora of trade texts dealing with self-help and management practices, assessment, and other practical applications implicit in the concept of emotional intelligence. Popular interest notwithstanding, scientific investigation of a clearly identified construct of emotional intelligence is sparse. Although several measures have been (or are currently being) designed for its assessment, it remains uncertain whether there is anything to emotional intelligence that psychologists working within the fields of personality, intelligence, and applied psychological research do not know already. Moreover, the media hype and vast number of trade texts devoted to the topic often subsume findings from these fields in a faddish sort of way, rather than deal directly with the topic as defined by its chief exponents.

Like many of our professional colleagues, our initial reaction to emotional intelligence was skeptical. It seemed to be a creation of the popular self-help movement, dressed up with some psychological terminology: a myth for our times rather than serious science. As differential psychologists, we found it hard to accept that a century of research on ability and personality could somehow have failed to notice such an important feature of the psychological landscape. Subsequently, we became aware that, beyond the media spotlight, cautious, systematic research was taking shape. Some researchers were developing tests for EI and attempting to validate them. Others were working with seemingly related constructs such as emotional knowledge, emotion perception, and emotional awareness. These various strands of research were reviewed in Bar-On and Parker's *Handbook of emotional intelligence* (2000). Like the editors of this volume, we detected a genuine sense of discovery among the researchers involved. As Bar-On and Parker (2000) also pointed out, the basic idea of emotional intelligence has been current for many years, in guises such as social intelligence. Perhaps EI was not just a popular fad, but the apotheosis of some longstanding, but hitherto poorly articulated, concerns of psychology. Because of the upsurge of interest in the topic over the past years, the time seemed ripe for a comprehensive critical review of EI.

This book sets out to examine the burgeoning research on the nature, components, determinants, and consequences of EI. It aims to shed light on the scientific status and validity of the construct of emotional intelligence by critically assessing the state of the art in EI theory, research, assessment, and applications. This book represents an even-handed attempt to disentangle factual, scientific evidence for the construct of emotional intelligence from accounts that are grounded in anecdotal evidence, hearsay, and media speculation. In doing so, we highlight the extent to which empirical evidence supports EI as a valid construct, and debunk some of the more extravagant claims appearing in the popular media. We attempt also to integrate understanding of EI with existing knowledge, theory, and practice in the areas of intelligence, emotion, personality, and applied psychology. In addition to

I

Conceptualizations and Measurement

1

Introduction

The jury is still out as to whether or not there is a scientifically meaningful concept of emotional intelligence.

S. Epstein

Historical and Sociocultural Context of Emotional Intelligence

What is the secret of human happiness and fulfillment? Philosophers, prophets, and other sages have debated this question since ancient times without arriving at a satisfactory resolution. The advance of psychology in the last century has raised the hope of a scientific answer. Perhaps, systematic, empirical study of human success and failure will tell us how we should live. Recently psychologists have proposed that understanding the emotions of oneself and others is the key to a satisfying life. Those people who are self-aware and sensitive to others manage their affairs with wisdom and grace, even in adverse circumstances. On the other hand, those who are "emotionally illiterate" blunder their way through lives marked by misunderstandings, frustrations, and failed relationships. A scientific understanding of this emotional intelligence may allow us to train our emotional skills so that we can live more fulfilling and productive lives. In this book, we examine this emerging science and assess critically the likelihood that it offers a genuine path toward personal and social development, as opposed to a myth of self-actualization unsupported by empirical evidence.

Emotional intelligence (EI) is a relatively new and growing area of behavioral investigation, having matured recently with the aid of lavish international media attention. EI refers to the competence to identify and express emotions, understand emotions, assimilate emotions in thought, and regulate both positive and negative emotions in the self and in others. The construct has received widespread, international attention, both within secular and academic circles, ever since its inception in the 1980s. Subsequently, researchers have purportedly made important strides toward understanding its nature, components, determinants, developmental track, and modes of modification.

Although first mentioned in the psychological literature nearly two decades ago, it is only in the past five years or so that emotional intelligence has received widespread public attention. Daniel Goleman's book on the topic appeared on the *New York Times* Best-Sellers List in 1995, the same year in which a *Time Magazine* article was devoted to detailed exposition of the topic (Gibbs, 1995). More recently, the influential e-zine *Salon* devoted a lengthy article to discussion of its application (both potentially and realized) in the work force. Moreover, the last year or so has witnessed a plethora of trade texts dealing with self-help and management practices, assessment, and other practical applications implicit to the concept of emotional intelligence.

Few fields of psychological investigation appear to have touched so many disparate areas of human endeavor, since its inception, as has emotional intelligence. Seemingly acknowledging this fact, the American Dialect Society selected it among the most useful new words or phrases of the late 1990s (American Dialect Society, 1999; see also Mayer, Salovey & Caruso, 2000). Indeed, for a concept that up until 1995 had received short shrift, the impression that the subdiscipline devoted to the study of emotional intelligence is a pivotal area of contemporary psychology appears difficult to dispute. Thus, emotional intelligence has been touted as a panacea for modern business (Druskat & Wolff, 2001) and the essential but often neglected ingredient in the practice of nursing (Bellack, Morjikian, Barger et al., 2001), law (Silver, 1999), medicine (Carrothers, Gregory & Gallagher, 2000), and engineering (Marshall, 2001). In some commentators' eyes, emotional intelligence even provides the medium by which educational reform can and finally will reach its full potential, across primary, secondary, and tertiary levels of schooling (e.g., Arnold, 2000; Bodine & Crawford, 2000; Hargreaves, 2000; Ormsbee, 2000).

Popular interest notwithstanding, scientific investigation of a clearly identified construct of emotional intelligence is sparse. Although several measures have been (or are currently being) designed for its assessment, it remains uncertain whether there is anything to emotional intelligence that psychologists working within the fields of personality, intelligence, and applied psychological research do not know already. Moreover, the media hype and vast number of trade texts devoted to the topic often subsume findings from these fields in a faddish sort of way, rather than deal directly with the topic as defined by its chief exponents. This approach has arguably led to obfuscation, misunderstanding, and wildly outlandish claims.

The popularity of emotional intelligence

The idea that people differ in EI has prospered because of a number of converging factors, including contemporary cultural trends and orientations. To begin with, EI has been the target of widespread interest owing to the increasing personal importance attributed to emotion management for people in modern society. It is believed that EI can be trained and improved in various social contexts (educational, occupational, and interpersonal) and that personal and societal benefits will follow from investment in programs to increase EI. There is currently a growing impetus towards the provision of personal, educational, and workplace interventions that purport to increase EI.

Furthermore, EI has been commonly claimed to play an important role in modern society by determining real-life outcomes above and beyond the contribution of general intellectual ability and personality factors (e.g., Goleman, 1995; Saarni, 1999). Thus, EI is claimed to be positively related to academic achievement, occupational success and satisfaction, and emotional health and adjustment (Elias, Zins, Weissberg, Frey et al., 1997). EI, in fact, has been claimed to be even more important than intellectual intelligence in achieving success in life (Goleman, 1995).

A subtext in the claimed importance of EI to success in modern society is that the benefits of general (cognitive) intelligence are overstated, and emotional intelligence may often be more important than conventional IQ. Accordingly, EQ has become fashionable in part because it seems to reduce the predominance and importance typically accorded to intellectual intelligence. A possible related factor underlying the popularity of the EI construct is antagonism (warranted or unwarranted) toward the concept of intellectual intelligence and its measurement. Substantial numbers of people are antagonistic to intelligence tests, perhaps because many have been subjected to the misuse and misinterpretation of the results of IQ tests. There is sometimes even antipathy to people with high IQs in Western society, exemplified by the way that television programs relentlessly mock academically gifted children as nerds lacking elementary social skills, quite at variance with reality (see Zeidner & Matthews, 2000). Goleman (1995) himself makes considerable play of anecdotal accounts of how high-IQ adults may be socially inept. Thus, many people resent the excessive import attributed to scholastic IQ in modern society (Epstein, 1998). From grade school on, people with high IQ tend to be viewed negatively, particularly if they are studious and highly successful at school, university, and work. As a result, any view that deflates the importance of IQ finds a receptive audience, and there is excessive enthusiasm for questionable views about the nature of other attributes that are labeled as forms of intelligence, including EI (Epstein, 1998).

Thus, the appeal of EI reflects both positive and negative cultural mores. On the positive side, the construct emphasizes the value of nonintellectual abilities and attributes for success in living, including emotional understanding, awareness, regulation, adaptive coping, and adaptive adjustment. EI has driven home the notion that, while the road to success in everyday life is determined partly by intellectual ability, there are a host of other contributing factors, including social competencies, emotional adjustment, emotional sensitivity, practical intelligence, and motivation. EI also focuses attention on character and aspects of self-control, such as the ability to delay gratification, tolerate frustration, and regulate impulses (ego strength). On the negative side, writings on EI place greater emphasis on the importance of emotional abilities than on intellectual intelligence—an outcome that is congenial to the personal profiles and worldviews of many.

Emotional intelligence: a rebuttal to **The Bell Curve***?*

Another attractive feature of EI, and a plausible reason for the immediate acceptance and widespread and often uncritical embracing of the construct, is that it countered the pessimism contained in Richard Herrnstein and Charles Murray's (1994) book, *The Bell Curve*. In contrast, EI offers hope for a more utopian, classless society, unconstrained by biological heritage. Herrnstein and Murray's (1994) monumental, though contentious, work is a lengthy tome combining a review of the intelligence field with implications for informing public policy on class in the United States. This book argued for the importance of intelligence in understanding social class in modern societies. Intelligence was touted as the best predictor of success in various spheres of life, including educational, occupational, and social contexts. The authors implied that individuals who were born into economically and educationally advantaged family backgrounds also inherited higher intelligence when compared to their lower-class counterparts. This differential distribution of intelligence in sociocultural groups was claimed to determine, in large part, the differential chances of various social groups for educational and occupational success. The approach espoused by the authors conveyed a rather pessimistic message for an egalitarian society and offered little hope for the future of those individuals destined to be born into lower-class families or those coming from ethnic-minority backgrounds.

When Goleman published his best-selling book *Emotional Intelligence*, the author implied that it served as an egalitarian rebuttal to Herrnstein and Murray's arguments, which were widely seen as supporting the entrenchment of a cognitive elite (Goleman, 1995, p. 34). In contradistinction to IQ, EI was believed to offer much hope for individuals characterized by low levels of cognitive ability. The appeal of the EI construct lies in part in the view that the competencies underlying EI can be learned, and this offers a more optimistic message for society's future than the views presented in *The Bell Curve*. In contrast to general intelligence, which was differentially distributed across sociocultural groups, EI was assumed to be more equally distributed, thus holding considerable hope for a more egalitarian society. Furthermore, whereas general ability was viewed as a rather stable and immutable psychological trait, and relatively impervious to environmental experience and training, EI was believed to be more amenable to intervention and learning (Goleman, 1995). From this perspective, the cultural value of emotional intelligence was egalitarian, for anyone could learn and cultivate it. For the skeptical, however, it suggested a dumbed-down picture of the future, in which reason and critical thinking no longer mattered and people were sized-up by their emotional expressiveness. In this context, emotional intelligence was suggestive of a kinder, gentler, intelligence—an intelligence anyone can have.

Diminishing the great divide between rational thought and emotions

Furthermore, EI has gained prominence because it represents additional present-day cultural values (Salovey, Woolery & Mayer, 2001). The hybrid term "emotional intelligence," combining emotion and intelligence, could well be considered an oxymoron by some. This assertion follows from the fact that emotions commonly convey the idea of irrational passions, whereas intelligence is best characterized by a high degree of reasonableness and rational thought. Indeed, the relationship between intellect and emotion has traditionally been viewed as one involving a conflict between two different psychological forces. Throughout Western history, reason has generally been valued over blind passion, as illustrated in a quotation from Marcus Aurelius, who was influenced by Stoic philosophy:

Let no emotions of the flesh, be they of pain or of pleasure, affect the supreme and sovereign portion of the soul [i.e., reason]. See that it never becomes involved with them: it must limit itself to its own domain, and keep the feelings confined to their proper sphere.   (Meditations, V, 26)

Currently, the pendulum has swung toward a view that the intellect has been over-valued, at the expense of emotions, leading to lack of self-understanding and impoverished shallow social relationships. Thus, the interest generated by the EI construct is part of the current zeitgeist of modern Western society, which is increasingly recognizing the importance of emotions. Indeed, the battle between heralding the importance of emotions and denying their important role is a longstanding one in Western thought (see Salovey, Woolery & Mayer, 2001, for an extensive historical discussion). Seemingly, philosophers and psychologists have relied on a glorified analytic intelligence throughout much of Western history (Salovey, Bedell, Detweiler & Mayer, 2000). A contrasting zeitgeist, is suggested by talk-show host Oprah Winfrey (who is evidently no Stoic):[1]

Never again will I do anything for anyone that I do not feel directly from my heart. I will not attend a meeting, make a phone-call, write a letter, sponsor or participate in any activity in which every fiber of my being does not resound yes. I will act with the intent to be true to myself.

To paraphrase, emotion provides the ultimate validation of action: if it doesn't feel good, don't do it. There is no place here for the use of reason to guide action in the face of doubts and misgivings, or to examine one's emotional reactions critically and analytically.

The past few years have seen a flight from the rigors of intellect, coupled with a renewed appreciation of the emotional side of one's persona and the legitimization of emotional expressiveness. The 1960s ushered in a period of social turmoil, which upset Western assumptions about the primacy of the intellect, generating both critical thought and a decade-long emotional rebellion against the forces of rationalism. There was growing awareness of the failings and injustices of society, such as prejudice and discrimination toward sociocultural minority groups, international hostilities and war, environmental pollution, and inequitable treatment of women. These problems highlighted unmet emotional needs that seemed interwoven into the very fabric of society. The sixties generation witnessed the rise of the civil-rights

movement, student activism in opposition to the Vietnam War, new social movements (hippies and yuppies), and the rise of the women's-
rights movement. Uncontrollable feelings of anger, contempt, anxiety,
and depression against society's injustice could no longer be interpreted
as an irrational defect in human nature, but rather had to be interpreted as a consequence of, and a message about, a faulty and oppres-
sive society. The feelings of these oppressed groups were signals of
how various groups of people were (mis)treated before society could or
would correct inequities. In this context, EI refers to social justice, and
a resolution of the long war fought between emotion and rationality
throughout human history.

Conceptions of Emotional Intelligence

The sometimes wildly extravagant claims with respect to the usefulness
of EI raise an important series of issues that challenged us throughout
the writing of this book. What does a given researcher mean when she
uses the term "emotional intelligence"? To what extent is the concept
of EI used consistently by its various proponents? Does EI ever denote a
logically coherent scientific construct? Given the ease with which the
definition of EI may be shaped to fit different interests and areas of application, EI may be *the* most protean of all known psychological constructs. Thus construed, researchers promoting EI may build a virtual
Tower of Babel. Each claim, then, would likely be unsubstantiated in the
face of new evidence; misunderstandings would constantly perpetuate
themselves; and little scientific progress toward understanding its nature, consequences, or determinants would occur. We note, even at this
early stage, that protean definitions of EI are easily located in the research literature (see Roberts, 2001), perhaps in reflection of "some
aspects of present-day zeitgeists" (Mayer, Salovey et al., 2000, p. 97).
Nevertheless, EI remains a viable field of scientific study, and several
contemporary researchers have attempted to develop validated tests for
assessment of EI (e.g., Bar-On, 1997; Mayer, Caruso & Salovey, 2000).
Beyond test development, there remains an urgent need for the application of strict, logical principles in formulating the scientific boundaries and delimiting conditions of EI (see Davies, Stankov & Roberts,
1998; Roberts, Zeidner & Matthews, 2001).

In the passages that follow, we provide an overview of concepts and
models underlying EI, which we discuss throughout the present book
in more elaborate detail. This approach sets the stage for appreciating

both scientific and sensationalized claims (often of mythological proportions) surrounding contemporary conceptualizations of EI. Before this undertaking, however, some introduction to the historical background in which EI has emerged would seem prudent.

The origins of emotional intelligence

The history of research into human intelligence has raised a number of concepts that bear more than passing semblance to EI, including most especially the concept of social intelligence, which we take up in chapters 2 and 3. However, the first formal mention of emotional intelligence appears to derive from a German article entitled (and we translate here) "Emotional Intelligence and Emancipation," published in the journal *Praxis der Kinderpsychologie und Kinderpsychiatrie*, by Leuner in 1966. The article describes adult women who, because of hypothesized low emotional intelligence, reject their social roles. In the article, Leuner suggests that the women's difficulties stem from being separated at an early age from their mothers. The treatment used by the author to improve deficits in EI appear extreme and ill contrived by today's standards—the women were administered the hallucinogenic drug LSD-25 while undergoing psychotherapy (see Mayer, Salovey et al., 2000).

The first time that the term "emotional intelligence" appears to be used in an English treatise is in an unpublished doctoral dissertation by Payne (1986). Parenthetically, given widespread interest in EI, Payne may well go on to be one of the most cited authors never to have made it through the peer-review process. In something of a visionary statement, Payne advocated the fostering of EI in schools by liberating emotional experience through therapy. Much of Payne's thesis is polemic in nature. For example, he also foreshadows an age where emotion and intelligence are integrated into the educational system, and governments are responsive to the feelings of the individual (see also Mayer, Salovey, et al., 2000). Early references to EI generated little interest. Indeed, it is only in very recent years that scientific articles on the topic have appeared in any number (see figure 1.1).

Daniel Goleman and the popularization of emotional intelligence

In a strict historical account of EI, one might turn at this point to discuss the ability models of Jack Mayer, Peter Salovey, and colleagues, since they were the first to publish scientific articles in peer-reviewed journals. Another researcher, whose work is discussed subsequently, Reuven Bar-On, claims to have used a related concept—emotional quotient—still

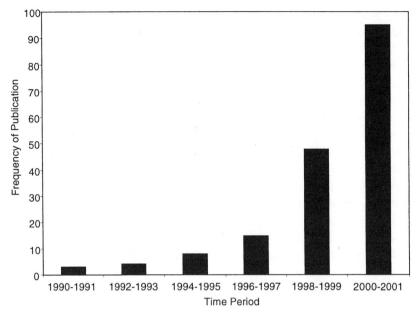

Figure 1.1
Frequency distribution of EI publications from 1990 to 2001.

earlier, but this was in an unpublished doctoral dissertation that has proven difficult to track down (see Bar-On, 2000). Even so, Daniel Goleman (1995, 1998, 2001) has clearly been the most influential in bringing this concept to the masses. Because his impact on the field has assumed epic proportions (see Gibbs, 1995), it is to consideration of his conceptualization of EI that we now turn.

Goleman's (1995) definition of emotional intelligence is sweeping and open to the criticism that it is overinclusive. Consider, for example, the definition that in many ways introduces the original (and most controversial) aspects of his best-selling book. "Emotional intelligence [includes] abilities such as being able to motivate oneself and persist in the face of frustrations; to control impulse and delay gratification; to regulate one's moods and keep distress from swamping the ability to think; to empathize and to hope" (Goleman, 1995, p. 34).

Goleman invokes qualities here that the trained psychologist would recognize as longstanding concerns of the field of personology, or the study of personality traits (see Maddi, 1996; Matthews & Deary, 1998). He seems also to refer to Judeo-Christian ethical values, a Pandora's box that the scientist should perhaps forbear to open. Seemingly acknowledging this fact, after leading the reader through various ramifications of the aforementioned definition, Goleman (1995) pronounces, almost defiantly, "There is an old-fashioned word for the body of skills that emotional intelligence represents: character" (1995, p. 34). A question then immediately springs to mind (and we return to it at a number of points in the present book): Is EI simply an old wine, which has been well marketed in a new bottle? Interestingly, over a century of research has also shown that the relationship between personality and intelligence is modest at best (see, e.g., Ackerman & Heggestad, 1997). If this is the case, Goleman's definition necessarily *precludes* thinking about EI, as akin to traditional forms of human cognitive abilities. Indeed, Goleman almost seems to define EI by exclusion—that is, EI represents all those positive qualities that are *not* IQ. Consequently, we suggest that a natural tension exists between his definition and several others that have been offered in the literature.

Another point of critical interest concerning Goleman's definition of EI is the extent that traits, which themselves might be thought of as functionally independent, are all assumed to cluster together to define this one construct called EI. The implication is, after all, that EI constitutes a general factor representing individual differences in the efficiency of handling emotionally laden information. If it is a general factor, then the personal qualities composing it should correlate positively and moderately with each other (see Roberts, Zeidner, et al., 2001; also chapter 5 below). However, consider hope and impulse control. It seems illogical to assume that these are in any way related. Thus, one can hope and still control one's impulses, or one can hope and have poor impulse control—that is, hope and impulse control appear unrelated and it is questionable whether they form part of the same, unitary construct.

Ultimately, Goleman's conceptualization of EI rests on other aspects of what is known today of cognition, personality, motivation, emotions, neurobiology, and intelligence, rather than on this (problematic) definition in isolation. For this reason, some commentators refer to it as a "mixed model" of EI, in that it captures diverse psychological phenomena that embody both cognitive and noncognitive processes (see, e.g., Mayer, Caruso, et al., 2000). Goleman (2001) rejects this characterization, claiming that EI is pure ability, although, somewhat confusingly, he elsewhere seems to suggest that personality traits "drive" emotional competencies (Boyatzis, Goleman & Rhee, 2000). Goleman appears willing to make strong claims with little (or scant) empirical backing. Consider, for example, Goleman's (1998, p. 34) frequently cited claim that EI has higher predictive validity for performance in the workplace than traditional measures of intelligence (e.g., Druskat & Wolff, 2001). (Subsequently, Goleman, 2001, has argued that EI is most predictive within a specific job category or profession.) There is no published study actually indicative of this trend, and the commissioned, unpublished investigation that Goleman (1998) cites in support of this claim does not actually include any measures of EI (see chapter 12). At a conceptual level, Goleman relies on varied models gleaned from established areas of psychology, especially those relating to the neuroscience of emotion. However, his treatment of these models is uncritical, and he appears unaware that results from animal studies may not generalize to humans. Many distinguished emotion theorists (e.g., Lazarus, 1991, 1999) believe that emotion is only indirectly linked to brain systems, and psychological accounts have greater explanatory power. We return to these issues in chapters 7 and 8.

In recent times, Goleman (1998, 2001; see also Boyatzis et al., 2000) has attempted to deflect some of the aforementioned criticisms of his model and has even suggested that it meets "criteria for a 'pure' (ability) model" (2001, p. 14). He suggests that the competencies associated with EI relate to four domains, defined by whether competence relates to (1) self versus other, or (2) recognition versus regulation. The two aspects of self-competence are thus self-awareness and self-management, and competence with others breaks down into social awareness and relationship management. A questionnaire measure, the Emotional Competence Inventory (ECI) assesses 20 aspects of competence from an organizational perspective, with generally good reliability (see Boyatzis et al., 2000). Theoretically, the competencies are clustered into four groups similar to the domains described by Goleman (2001). However, a table provided by Boyatzis et al. (2000) suggests that empirical studies fail to confirm the theoretical grouping, and results also appear to differ from study to study. Little of this research has appeared in the peer-reviewed psychological literature, and we are unable to evaluate whether it meets accepted psychometric standards. Goleman's empirical research, in collaboration with Boyatzis and others, seems to lag that of other researchers on the assessment of EI, though it may represent a promising future development.

There are further issues regarding Goleman's attempts to conceptualize EI that appear problematic. Consider, for example, the following quote, where, in a linguistic sleight of hand that fails to match either data or theory (not to mention accepted standards of logical inference), he commingles personality, ability, and motivational constructs to explain why EI rightfully constitutes a legitimate form of intelligence:

> I would agree with Mayer and Salovey's (2000) critique that a "warm and outgoing nature" is not an EI competency. It could be a personality trait. However, it might also be a reflection of a specific set of EI abilities—chiefly, the ability to relate positively to others, which are products of the empathy and social-skills clusters of competence. Likewise, optimism, while it can be seen as a personality trait, also refers to specific behaviors that contribute to the competence I label "achievement drive." (Goleman, 2001, p. 4)

These comments fail to clarify how EI relates to existing psychological constructs. Goleman (2001) also attempts to distinguish EI as a potential for learning practical skills from emotional competence as the extent to which that potential has been translated into effective on-the-job capabilities. The ECI then assesses competence rather than EI, for which Goleman fails to provide an independent measure. Goleman has little to say on several major issues. For example, are the dimensions of EI the same as those of emotional competence? What is the magnitude of correlation between potential and actual competence? What are the learning processes that translate potential into competence? To what extent do individual differences in competence reflect learning history rather than potential? A figure provided by Boyatzis et al. (2000) confuses the issue further, by showing competence as directly driven, through causal paths, by neurological, motivational, and value-based antecedents, with no reference to potential or EI at all. In discussing this figure, Boyatzis et al. claim, "These causal links do not imply determinism but forms of association and disposition" (2000, p. 359). Causality can, of course, be a philosophically difficult concept, but the statement here seems less than lucid.

One final comment on Goleman's conceptualization of EI is in order. It has been suggested that his model of EI simply represents a journalist distilling scientific information for the consumption of the populist, rather than a legitimate scientific theory (see Mayer, Salovey, et al., 2000). Goleman states otherwise, as have the vast majority of scientists who now work within the area of EI (in our experience, peer-reviewed publications on EI invariably cite Goleman's name). Consider, for example, Goleman's preface to his second book: "I've also gone back to my professional roots as an academic psychologist, conducting an exhaustive review of research.... And I've performed or commissioned several new scientific analyses of data" (1998, p. 5).

For us, Goleman's work is of interest primarily as a source of ideas. His conceptualization of EI and its biological and psychological roots appears at present to be too open-ended and loosely specified to constitute a good scientific theory, although in the future it may develop to the point of being empirically testable.

Reuven Bar-On and the operationalization of emotional intelligence

While Goleman's name is rightfully associated with the popularization of EI, equally influential has been the work of Reuven Bar-On (1997, 2000), who has constructed the first commercially available operational index for the assessment of EI. Notably, Bar-On's conceptualization of EI is not that far removed from Goleman's, in that he appears to invoke clusters of established personality traits. Thus, Bar-On characterizes EI as "an array of non-cognitive capabilities, competencies, and skills that influence one's ability to succeed in coping with environmental demands and pressures" (1997, p. 14). (It is a little unclear what it means for a skill to be noncognitive: see Anderson, 1996.) The self-report instrument designed to assess each of these underlying components, the Emotional Quotient Inventory (EQ-i), provides the medium for understanding his model of EI more fully. Bar-On's research (1997, 2000) has been directed almost exclusively toward validating this instrument against other criteria.

The EQ-i assesses five broad subtypes of EI. Each of these higher-order components is measured by various subcomponents defined by pools of items, and the subcomponents are subsequently summed together to create each higher-order construct. The first is *intrapersonal intelligence*, which is composed of emotional self-awareness, assertiveness, self-regard, self-actualization, and independence. The second is *interpersonal intelligence*, which comprises empathy, interpersonal relationship, and social responsibility. The third higher-order construct of the EQ-i is *adaptability*, which divides into problem solving, reality testing, and flexibility. Fourth is *stress management*, which comprises stress tolerance and impulse control. Finally, the EQ-i contains measures of *general mood*, which is composed of happiness and optimism. In a twist likely to confuse users of his instrument, Bar-On (2000) has recently argued that this final component should be viewed as a "facilitator" of EI, rather than a higher-order construct that provides understanding of EI.

Bar-On (1997, 2000) reports a series of validation studies that are quite impressive in scope. The EQ-i has been normed in a large, diversified North American sample ($N = 3,831$), and the scales seem to be statistically reliable in North American and other samples worldwide. It has been correlated with a wide range of existing personality and other theoretically relevant constructs, such as coping. There is also some evidence, from single studies, that the EQ-i predicts other criteria, such as academic success in university students, presence of clinical disorders, and response to a treatment for alcoholism. The predictive validity of the EQ-i seems promising, but there is the potential problem of overlap with extant personality constructs. The reader familiar with psychological assessment may at this point have noticed concepts (indeed, measures) that closely resemble those of well-established personality questionnaires. For example, the widely used California Psychological Inventory (CPI) includes scales measuring, among other personality constructs, responsibility, tolerance, empathy, flexibility, self-control, intellectual efficiency, psychological mindedness, self-acceptance, and social presence (Hogan, 1987). Hence, it is not clear whether the EQ-i measures any construct that is not already captured in existing personality measures (see Davies et al., 1998; Mayer, Salovey, et al., 2000; Newsome, Day & Catano, 2001). Predictive validity may simply be a consequence of the EQ-i functioning as a proxy measure of personality. Relabeling products that vary little in content is common in the world of marketing, but it is not the proper stuff of psychological science. On the other hand, the EQ-i may indeed be measuring qualities beyond personality as currently understood. In chapter 5 we will look in more detail at Bar-On's operationalization of EI, and the extent to which data suggest that it measures something more than existing personality constructs.

Putting the intelligence into emotional intelligence: The Mayer-Salovey-Caruso conceptualization of EI

While Goleman appears to have popularized the concept of EI, he freely admits in his first, best-selling book that the work of Jack Mayer, Peter Salovey, and colleagues (among them David Caruso) has been most influential in its scientific genesis. Indeed, these researchers were not only the first to publish extensive accounts of EI in peer-reviewed psychological journals (Mayer, DiPaolo & Salovey, 1990; Salovey & Mayer, 1990), they also remain the most prolific protagonists of EI in the scientific literature (see, e.g., Mayer, Caruso & Salovey, 1999, 2000; Mayer & Cobb,

2000; Mayer & Geher, 1996; Mayer & Salovey, 1993, 1995, 1997; Mayer, Salovey & Caruso, 2000a, 2000b; Salovey, Bedell, Deitweiler & Mayer, 1999, 2001; Salovey, Mayer, Goldman, Turvey & Palfai, 1995).

Arguing that other conceptions of EI are misleading, these researchers suggest that their specific "use of the term stresses the concept of an intelligence that processes and benefits from emotions. From this perspective, EI is composed of mental abilities, skills, or capacities" (Mayer, Salovey, et al., 2000b, p. 105). In support of this derivation, they have developed an extensive conceptual model and several operational indices. It is to their conceptualization of EI that we now turn.

A major assumption of the Mayer-Salovey-Caruso model is that EI should resemble other forms of ability in terms of concepts, assessment vehicles, developmental trajectories, lawful phenomena associated with patterns of interrelationships with other measures, and further empirical instantiations. Essentially, under this framework, EI represents an intelligent system for the processing of emotional information, and as such, it should resemble central parts of traditional, well-established intelligence systems. According to Mayer and Mitchell (1998), an intelligence system consists of a capacity for inputting information and a capacity for processing information, through both immediate manipulation of symbols and reference to expert knowledge. EI cuts across the cognitive and emotional systems and is at one time unitary and multidimensional, being subdivisible into four branches. The first branch, *emotional perception/identification*, involves perceiving and encoding information from the emotional system. The second branch, *emotional facilitation of thought*, involves further processing of emotion to improve cognitive processes with a view to complex problem solving. The third branch, *emotional understanding*, is in some ways the obverse of the second: it concerns cognitive processing of emotion. The fourth and final branch, *emotion management*, concerns the control and regulation of emotions in the self and others (Mayer, Salovey, et al., 2000). Inside a systems theory account, this final branch likely entails additional aspects, including metacognitive and other response mechanisms that translate intelligent processes into action.

The theoretical underpinnings surrounding each of these branches are quite complex and we return to them at several points in this book. For example, such a system implies a hierarchical structure, where emotion management would be closer to a general factor of EI than lower-level processes like emotion perception. Nevertheless, without any measurement operations, principles, and procedures for assessing these branches, these constructs would remain theoretical abstractions with little utility. To allay this criticism, Mayer, Caruso, and Salovey (1999) have embarked on an ambitious undertaking: to derive a measure that objectively captures salient features of each of the four branches. To combat the problems that are endemic to self-reported EI, they suggest that performance-based measures, akin to those found in the intelligence literature, are requisite if EI is to be considered a legitimate form of intelligence. The end-result is the Multifactor Emotional Intelligence Scale (MEIS), to which, because it is so pivotal to empirical understanding of EI, our attention now turns. (A revised but basically similar measure, the Mayer-Salovey-Caruso Emotional Intelligence Test [MSCEIT]—see Mayer, Caruso, et al., 2000—has yet to be used extensively in research.)

The MEIS contains 12 subscales, with anywhere from 2 to 4 of these measures providing a particular branch score, and a linear composite of all 12 subtests providing a global index of general EI (see chapter 5). Each of the actual subtests contains stimuli that yield, according to its creators, objective indices of performance (Mayer, Caruso, et al., 2000). These stimuli include pictures of faces, passages of music, abstract designs, short stories/vignettes, and clusters of trait terms, all of which are rated for emotional valence, most generally on a five-point rating scale. For example, in one of the subtests devoted to emotional perception/identification, complex, abstract figures are rated for the level of happiness, fear, sadness, and so forth that they convey to the respondent. Three different scores are derived: (a) *consensus*, where the individual receives credit for an item on the basis of the proportion of all previous individuals answering in that particular fashion; (b) *expert*, where the individual is given credit for an item on the basis of proportions provided by a small panel of experts; and (c) *target*, where the respondent is given a score on the basis of observed correspondence with the emotional intentions of the person creating the item. Note that because only a small number of subtests provide conditions appropriate for target scoring, it is seldom discussed in the literature (see, e.g., Carriochi et al., 1999; Mayer, Caruso, et al., 2000; Roberts, Zeidner, et al., 2001).

Having thus operationalized the Mayer-Salovey-Caruso model, a pivotal feature of the MEIS is that it allows multivariate, empirical studies to be conducted in order to ascertain whether a strict ability conceptualization of EI is scientifically tenable. Mayer, Caruso, et al. (1999, 2000) claim to have established a number of conditions under which EI parallels traditional, psychometric intelligence. Specifically, they demonstrate, first and foremost, that the vast majority of the scales composing the MEIS are reliable, i.e., measure the underlying concepts consistently (see further discussion of reliability below). Second, they claim "findings with the MEIS are supportive of the four-branch model of intelligence.... There is an overall emotional intelligence that can be broken down into several subsidiary groups of skills" (Mayer, Caruso, et al., 2001, p. 333). This finding is consequential because, in the intelligence literature, established cognitive abilities correlate together to reveal similar stratified clusters of constructs (see, e.g., Carroll, 1993; Horn, 1999; Roberts & Stankov, 1999; see also chapter 3). Third, data collected by Mayer and colleagues reveals that the MEIS correlates with other ability measures, but not too highly so as to suggest that it is merely repackaging older intelligence constructs (compare self-reported EI and personality). This condition is crucial to the claim that EI is a form of intelligence: in what is often considered a lawful phenomenon, all forms of cognitive ability correlate positively with one another (see, e.g., Guttman, 1992). Fourth, adults outperform adolescents on the MEIS (Mayer, Caruso, et al., 1999)—a finding that, it is claimed, parallels data obtained with all traditional intelligence measures. Finally, the authors present some data demonstrating the predictive validity of the MEIS (i.e., that it modestly predicts other criteria, such as self-rated empathy and parental warmth).

The Mayer-Salovey-Caruso model is to be applauded for its attempt to measure EI as a construct distinct from existing personality dimensions, and for the sophistication of its account of what it means to be emotionally intelligent. However, the difficulties of such an enterprise are considerable. It must be established that the test has good measurement properties—that it measures some underlying construct accurately, and that subtests are properly distinguished. There is a special problem for tests of EI in that the researcher must decide how items are to be scored (i.e., which answers are correct and which are wrong). Often, the emotionally intelligent response to a real-life problem is unclear, or depends on the exact circumstances. We have recently published a large-scale study of the MEIS that suggests some measurement problems in this regard (Roberts, Zeidner, et al., 2001). At this early stage of research, there is also rather little evidence on predictive validity. In addition, there are conceptual issues concerning how well the components of EI described by Mayer, Salovey, and colleagues relate to what is already understood about intelligence and emotional functioning. The MEIS and MSCEIT deserve a special status as the most original and intriguing tests of emotional intelligence yet devised. We will examine their status as psychological tests in chapter 5, and we refer to the underlying conceptualization of EI provided by Mayer, Salovey, Caruso, and colleagues throughout the book.

Other conceptualizations of emotional intelligence

Since the success of Goleman's book, there has been a proliferation of academic books, doctoral dissertations, websites, scientific articles, and further popular accounts dealing with EI. To do all of these ideas justice inside the present volume would require, even at this early stage of concept development, more pages than any self-respecting publisher would allot. Our impression is that many of these works are of little scientific value and create the impression that the authors are merely jumping on the EI bandwagon. There are also several self-published books, with at least one instance where the author has been quoted as discovering the very concept of EI itself (see *The Age*, March 11, 2000)!

In chapter 5 we review various other conceptualizations or empirical findings that have made it through the peer-review process or have scientific credibility from other sources. For example, Cooper (1996) has recently conceptualized emotional intelligence as comprising emotional awareness of self and others, interpersonal connections, resilience, creativity, compassion, and intuition (to name but a few abilities) and developed an operational index: the EQ Map. Indeed, it is worth noting that many alternative conceptualizations of EI are tied to a proliferation of instruments that have recently been developed (e.g., Schutte, Malouff, Hall, Haggerty, et al., 1998). We also address, at various points in the book, some concepts that predate EI but are conceptually linked to it, such as empathy and alexithymia (i.e., diminished verbal expression of emotion).

Summary

A basic problem in developing conceptualizations of EI is that psychology already has some understanding of both intelligence and personality traits linked to emotional functioning. A theme we will develop is that existing conceptualizations of EI tend to neglect what is already known about the two main ingredients of EI: emotions and intelligence. To rectify this imbalance, coverage of these two critical psychological constructs constitutes a major undertaking of the present volume. In addition, the onus is on proponents of EI to show that the wine and the bottles are new: To what extent is EI independent of established psychological constructs and processes? We have already indicated possible overlap with personality traits, and we will review both empirical and conceptual literature relevant to this assertion in subsequent chapters (chapters 5 and 9). The possible redundancy of EI with respect to existing constructs is not merely of theoretical importance; it also impacts directly upon various proposed applications of EI. Extensive research has demonstrated how psychological constructs like intelligence and personality impinge, for example, on education, work, and quality of life.

At this point in our exposition, a mission statement would appear in order. We have seen that writings on EI are a confusing mixture of unsubstantiated opinion and hyperbolic claims, together with serious, but still preliminary, research grounded in psychological theory and careful test development. Rather than uncritically accept what advocates of EI have given us thus far, much of which appears to be of mythical status, we aim throughout this book to separate science from pseudoscience, fact from fiction, unfettered speculation from contemporary psychological theories and real data.

Applying such standards, we may find that there is a basis for a compelling, scientifically valid model of EI. On the other hand, if scientific standards suggest otherwise, we may be forced to conclude that EI does not exist. Intermediate positions are also possible; for example, there may be distinct abilities for emotion-regulation, which, in turn, are likely to be of less import than IQ. To realize our mission, we review and critically appraise information from a broader array of psychological disciplines pertinent to the concept of EI than has been attempted up until the present point in the brief history of this concept. In addition to research on EI measures such as the MEIS, we will also focus on conventional intelligence (IQ), biological and cognitive models of emotion, personality theory, and applied efforts to improve emotional functioning in clinical, occupational, and educational settings. In the next section we introduce principles that the concept of EI should adhere to if it is to lead to good science.

A Research Agenda for Emotional Intelligence

Emotional intelligence and individual differences

It is often said (e.g., Revelle, 1995) that there are three aspects of human nature: how all people are alike, how some people are alike, and how all people are unique. Thus, we could see EI as any of the following:

1. A general quality of human beings, that is, a faculty for handling emotional encounters possessed by every normal person

2. A quantitative spectrum of individual differences in EI, such that people can be rank-ordered in terms of how much EI they possess

3. A qualitative, fine-grained account of how the individual person manages emotion, which provides no direct basis for comparison between people

In this book we will be concerned primarily with the second option, EI as an individual difference construct. The third option is important at a case-study level, for example, in clinical psychology, but studies of idiographic emotional function cannot support a science based on general nomothetic principles. Identifying a general faculty of EI is scientifically important, and there may be specific biological and psychological systems that support emotion regulation. Studies of abnormality may contribute to isolating such systems; for example, the finding that damage to the frontal lobes of the brain leads to impairments in emotion regulation (Bechara, Tranel & Damasio, 2000) implies a role for this brain area in all persons. At this time, though, it is difficult to construct a coherent account akin to the psychology of other basic faculties, such as, say, perception, motivation, or emotion itself. There are two significant barriers to such a generalized account of EI. First, EI is believed to have some inertia or resistance to change. We have no validated experimental procedures for raising or lowering EI, while leaving other faculties unchanged. By comparison, we can readily change motivation, through incentives, or emotion, through mood induction, for example. Thus, the primary raw material for studying EI is at present the differences between people, rather than their commonalities. Second, there is convincing evidence that other faculties have a universal quality derived from either inherited biology or commonalities in learned adaptations to the universal problems faced by all humans, such as seeking food, shelter, and companionship. For example, although there are important cultural differences in causes and consequences of emotion, it appears that emotions have similar personal meanings, and elicit similar response tendencies, in all cultures (e.g., Scherer & Wallbott, 1994). It is unclear whether there are similar universals of EI, in that much of what constitutes appropriate behavior during interpersonal reaction is culturally determined.

Indeed, a focus on individual differences may contribute to understanding EI in the more generalized sense. Research on conventional intelligence is instructive. "Intelligence" is notoriously hard to define, and there is still no good general definition of what it means for some autonomous system (whether human, animal, or artificial) to possess intelligence (see, e.g., Sternberg, 2000). However, research on individual differences in intelligence, though initially lacking conceptual clarity, succeeded in identifying a measurable quality that relates to other important qualities of the person, such as their educational and occupational success. Studies of the biological and psychological correlates of intelligence provide a network of interrelationships that tell us about the nature of what is being measured. The essence of this *operational definition* of intelligence is that understanding proceeds through measurement. Reliable measurement of some quality of the person is the necessary precursor to defining that quality in terms of its relationships with other constructs. Conventional intelligence tests (IQ tests) have sufficient power to predict other personal qualities that we can say that they define an important attribute of the person that relates to intelligence, as popularly understood. Rocket scientists obtain high scores on the tests; intellectually challenged people, having substantially impaired cognitive skills in everyday life, do not.

None of this is to say that intelligence is *only* what is measured by IQ tests. It is frequently argued that there are additional intelligences, such as musical intelligence, that do not relate to IQ (Gardner, 1983). There have also been attempts to operationalize social intelligence, which may overlap with EI (see chapter 3). Some authors (e.g., Carroll, 1993) see different varieties of intelligence hierarchically, with general intelligence as superordinate to other more specialized forms, whereas others, such as Howard Gardner, would give multiple intelligences equal weight.

In sum, it may be impossible to capture all the various facets of intelligence. Just as it is impossible to prove a negative statement, so too it may never be possible to draw a line under established dimensions of intelligence and definitively state that there are no more to be found. However, the systematic search for reliable and significant dimensions provides the most promising technique for understanding constructs of intelligence, potentially including EI. Within such an approach, we need three contexts for understanding the concept of emotional intelligence:

• A psychometric context that concerns operationalization and measurement of EI

• A theoretical context that links measurements of EI to psychological processes

• An applied context that describes how emotionally intelligent behavior may be trained, facilitated, or otherwise influenced in the service of real-world problems

It is to preliminary discussion of these three contexts, which would help to provide a viable model of EI, that our attention now shifts.

The psychometric context

Logically, it might seem that theory should precede measurement. However, in common with many individual difference constructs, including IQ, the road to understanding EI has started from attempts to develop a satisfactory operational definition of the construct. That is, researchers have begun with some initial description or *conceptualization* of the qualities associated with EI and attempted to develop reliable and valid tests for these qualities. Broadly, EI may be conceptualized as a spectrum of levels of ability, perhaps following a normal bell curve, as IQ does. We need tests of EI that pick out the emotional geniuses and the emotionally challenged at the ends of the spectrum, and discriminate different levels of ordinary EI in the middle part of the range. Developing such tests places EI within the sphere of *differential psychology* (i.e., the psychology of individual differences).

The major tool of differential psychology is *psychometrics*, measurement of the mind and/or its constituent mental processes (derived from the combination of two Greek words "psyche" and "metre"). Statistical techniques (many of which were developed by the early differential psychologists, such as Galton, Spearman, and Pearson) provide the psychometrician with an impressive array of procedures for understanding individual differences. One of the subtleties of this field is that we can test whether an instrument is an accurate measuring device without knowing exactly what it is that is being measured. Measurement accuracy is referred to as *reliability* or internal consistency. For example, for a test made of multiple items, scores on the different items should be intercorrelated if they relate to some common underlying quality. Similarly, different tests of EI should be highly correlated, just as two thermometers should show similar temperature readings; if not, one or both must be a poor instrument. Only when reliability is established—that is, the test measures some quality accurately—can we ask what is being measured. This latter process relates to the notion of *validity*: a test for EI should predict criterion variables, such as real-life outcomes believed to reflect EI, including measures of life success and satisfaction.

Further progress requires a brief digression to introduce the single most important statistic of differential psychology, the *correlation coefficient*. One of the most important issues that the psychometrician is called upon to solve is determining the degree that psychological tests are linearly associated. Various measures of statistical association and dependence are available (Carroll, 1961), although far and away the most frequently used measure is the Pearson correlation coefficient (denoted r). This coefficient provides an indication of the degree to which two variables assess the same thing (i.e., the same underlying individual-differences construct). A value of 1.00 indicates perfect correlation (i.e., identity), and a value of -1.00 indicates that the two variables are entirely opposite qualities. Between these limits, the correlation coefficient indicates the degree to which there is similarity or overlap in the individual-differences constructs under investigation (Carroll, 1993), with a zero value indicating that there is no linear association at all. Correlations must be calculated and interpreted with caution; they are subject to various biases and open to different interpretations (see Cronbach, 1990).

Existing differential psychology offers a blueprint for identifying intelligence-related constructs through test development and statistical analyses in which calculations of various correlations feature prominently. In chapter 2 we discuss this blueprint at length, along with the statistical and conceptual instruments that can guide us through uncharted territories, to discover whether indeed there is any substance to EI.

The theoretical context

To understand what is being measured with a given test of a psychological construct, we require a theory. For the most part, existing EI "theory" is primarily structural and descriptive in nature. That is, the theory is little more than a list of qualities deemed central, and does not go much beyond the initial conceptualization. Structural approaches of this kind were very prevalent in early studies of differential psychology. In recent work, however, such approaches are often criticized for providing description rather than explanation. Understanding EI in more depth entails identifying psychological processes that control the outcome of emotionally significant encounters. Perhaps the emotionally intelligent person has a brain that handles signals of threat and challenge more effectively than the brain of someone low in EI. Alternatively, EI might relate to the information-processing routines that encode emotional information and analyze its implications for response (i.e., to efficient "emotional software"). Goleman (2001) provides a somewhat speculative account of links between neocortical and limbic systems of the brain that may support EI. Salovey et al. (1999), on the other hand, relate EI to cognitive processes such as coping and rumination. However, process accounts of EI are in their infancy and, in our view, fail to make sufficient contact with existing theory. Furthermore, accounts of what it means to be emotionally intelligent at any given time require supplementation with developmental accounts of how emotional competence is acquired in childhood.

We will explore a possible conceptualization of EI as an index of the person's overall *adaptive competence* in encounters that provoke emotion (Matthews & Zeidner, 2000). Perhaps the emotionally intelligent person is someone who sizes up encounters quickly and accurately, and chooses a strategy for dealing with the encounter that is effective in maximizing personal gains, while maintaining good relationships with the other persons involved. Such a definition has several potential advantages. First, it distinguishes EI, as an underlying latent ability, from the outcomes of emotional events. If EI is no more than a running index of success or failure, the concept has no explanatory power. Second, the definition relates EI to handling personally significant events, rather than to some abstract quality detached from the external world. Third, it highlights EI as a moderator of process and change. The emotionally intelligent person is not just successfully adapted but *adaptable*, in the sense of being competent to deal with new challenges. The cognitive and biological processes that control adaptation may operate differently in high- and low-EI persons, and are of prime interest in theory development. Theory should also explain factors controlling long-term developmental changes in EI. Fourth, it links EI to the person in his role as an active agent, attempting to take charge of situations and deal with them proactively as well as reactively. One of the essential elements of theory is how the person controls and regulates emotional events.

At the same time, there are also significant difficulties in developing a conceptualization of this kind, notably that individual differences in adaptability may be as hard to conceptualize and assess as EI itself (see Matthews & Zeidner, 2000). In attempting to relate EI to adaptation, we will review the adaptive processes specified by existing biological and cognitive models. The fundamental question is whether there are individual differences in some configuration of adaptive processes that might be identified with EI. Conversely, we might find that individuals differ more in style of adaptation than in overall efficiency. Different persons may be better at satisfying different adaptive goals. For example, one person might find fulfillment through career success, and another person through raising children, and their competencies in handling emotion might reflect these different orientations.

The applied context

A central element underlying EI is the impetus to improve emotional functioning in real life. Individuals may enjoy happier, more fulfilled lives if they have better awareness and control of their own emotions and those of others. Organizations benefit from the increased productivity, teamwork, and organizational commitment of emotionally intelligent persons. Society, in general, gains from alleviation of problems that may result from poor emotion-management skills, such as violent crime, drug abuse, and some forms of mental illness. Goleman looks forward "to a day when education will routinely include inculcating essential human competencies such as self-awareness, self-control and empathy, and the arts of listening, resolving conflicts, and cooperation" (1995, p. xiv).

As in the case of theory, there is a considerable body of existing knowledge that is not always adequately acknowledged by proponents of EI. Clinical psychology offers a plethora of therapeutic techniques for improved emotion management, especially in the fields of anxiety and mood disorders. For example, cognitive-behavioral therapies aim to correct faulty cognitions that generate negative emotions inappropriate to the person's actual life circumstances. Occupational psychology offers stress-management techniques and programs for motivational enhancement. Dealing with the emotional problems of students has been a central part of educational and school psychology since the beginnings of these disciplines. Again, we must ask what research on EI can add to these efforts, other than a cheerleading function that raises a flag for the importance of emotion in real life. There are two tentative answers. First, "emotional dysregulation" may define a specific set of problems that have not been sufficiently recognized in existing practice. Emotion dysregulation may be distinct from other sources of emotional problems, such as oversensitivity to threat (in clinical anxiety) or poor social skills (in occupational psychology). Writers such as Goleman (1995) tend to cluster together different sources of emotional dysfunction, but perhaps a more differentiated view would pay practical dividends. Second, practitioners in applied fields may have been improving EI without realizing it. Perhaps a common element overarches good clinical, occupational, and educational practices, which, in turn, raises EI. If so, an explicit understanding of EI as a focus for real-world interventions may improve existing practice and suggest new techniques for hitherto intractable problems.

Summary

In sum, we have argued that the research needed to build a science of EI has three pillars: reliable and valid measurement, process-based theory, and practical application. It would be a mistake to construct any of these supports without considering the very extensive theoretical and applied research already dealing with emotional aptitudes and competencies. Thus, it needs to be demonstrated that tests of EI measure something new, i.e., that EI is distinct from existing dimensions of individual differences. Similarly, a theoretical account of EI must differentiate the biological and cognitive processes supporting emotional competence from those processes that are known to underpin existing personality, emotional, and intelligence dimensions. Finally, claims concerning the importance of EI in applied domains also hinge on a demonstration that is distinct from concepts, procedures, and techniques that are more fully understood.

Chapter Synthesis and Preview

We have seen that current conceptions of EI have both strengths and weaknesses. On the positive side, there are promising descriptive accounts of attributes of EI, such as self-awareness, empathy, and effective coping skills. Inside the academic community, we sense a genuine excitement surrounding the possibility that psychologists may have overlooked or underestimated a major personal quality. Educationalists also appear much enamored with the EI concept, since it raises the possibility of using emotional skills as tools for tackling social problems such as violence, drug addiction, and social alienation. There are also various measures of EI and its constituent attributes that have sufficient reliability and validity to justify their use as research instruments, notably the MEIS/MSCEIT (Mayer, Salovey, et al., 2000) and the EQ-i (Bar-On, 1997).

On the negative side, there are significant problems in the conceptualization and assessment of EI. We cannot even be sure that different measures of EI are assessing the same underlying construct. The personal attribute that is the target of measurement efforts is hazily defined, largely in terms of everyday "implicit" qualities, rather than constructs explicitly derived from psychological theory. Distinguishing EI from intelligence, personality, and emotion itself also presents serious conceptual and empirical problems.

Earlier in the introduction we tendered a mission statement—that this book would attempt to separate the scientific aspects of EI from those that appear more ephemeral, market-driven, and pseudoscientific. The research agenda that we have outlined serves to provide us with both general principles and a logical structure to achieve this goal. In the remainder of the first part of this book we draw together some of these basic conceptual and assessment issues. Our aims include clarifying the underlying psychology of emotion and intelligence, reviewing the success of empirical studies of EI to date, and identifying some possible developmental antecedents. In the second part we move on to a detailed evaluation of the status of EI as an index of individual differences in emotional adaptation, covering biological and cognitive processes in emotion, stress and coping processes, and personality theory. In the third part we look at whether research on EI adds to existing practical techniques for enhancement of emotional functioning in clinical, occupational, and educational arenas. Our conclusions reflect an integration of our analyses of issues pertaining to measurement, theory, and application.

Prior to embarking upon our journey of critically evaluating these relevant literatures, we try to attune the reader more fully to major issues, concepts, terminology, and procedures embedded inside our attempt to develop a scientific account of EI. In what we see as a companion chapter to this introduction, we will focus upon the standards one might expect of theory, research, and practice in the area, taking pains carefully to delineate all assumptions. Psychometric and philosophical concepts will be clearly laid out, and some overarching principles explained. In short, while the context of EI has been set in the present chapter, chapter 2 will introduce the scientific frames of reference that are essential to a full appreciation of the content, scope, and vision of the current volume.

2

Toward a Science of Emotional Intelligence

The Temple of Science is a multi-faceted building.
Albert Einstein

In the introductory chapter, we pointed out the need to develop a comprehensive science of emotional intelligence in order to sift valid knowledge from speculation and fancy. Although some promising beginnings have been made (e.g., Bar-On, 1997; Mayer, Salovey, et al., 2000), no existing work is entirely satisfactory. However, the reader should not think badly of the pioneers of EI research, since the topic presents special problems in methodology and conceptualization. We have seen that assessment may be based either on supposedly objective tests, similar to IQ tests, or on self-report measures that resemble personality questionnaires (at least superficially). It is perhaps not surprising that the convergence between different methods appears modest (see Bar-On, 2000).

Theory also presents a major challenge. A basic problem is that definitions of EI often appear overinclusive, touching on existing constructs that reflect a bewildering array of theoretical notions. We could see EI as a property of anything from basic neural processes controlling sensitivity to emotional stimuli to high-level cognitions of the meaning of events. Not only may EI be conceptualized at different levels of abstraction from physical reality, but it may also relate to multiple constructs within each level of abstraction. For example, at the level of brain (neurophysiological) systems, EI may be influenced by both subcortical emotion centers, such as the amygdala, and cortical systems, such as the prefrontal cortex. Again, there is a risk of a Tower of Babel, with multiple theories of EI making little contact with one another and researchers prone to talking at cross-purposes. Failure to develop a coherent theory will also impede attempts to develop an applied science of improving EI.

Consequently, any report card on the state of EI research needs to begin with an account of how models of EI are to be judged: psychometrically, theoretically, and in terms of real-world applications. In this chapter we set out problems in developing the science of EI and some possible solutions. We also discuss, in some detail, important concepts from the fields of psychology, philosophy, and cognitive science, to give the reader a solid background for appreciating a variety of scientific issues that we grapple with throughout the book. We will address conceptual and measurement issues first, followed by a review of theoretical perspectives. The emphasis is on establishing principles and criteria that may be used in developing and evaluating a scientific account of EI. A more detailed review of evidence is a task for later chapters. We move then to discuss that domain where theory and psychometrics meet, differential psychology, focusing in particular on how this has shaped knowledge of personality, intelligence, and group differences. Finally, we discuss the role that EI currently plays in applied psychological settings.

Toward a Psychometrics of Emotional Intelligence

Determining whether or not EI is a measurable quality of the human organism is pivotal to a scientific account of the construct. First, as discussed in the previous chapter, much EI research proceeds via operational definition, with the aim of developing a test with good measurement properties. Second, the focus needs to be on conducting further empirical research to develop a more articulate theory of the biological and psychological processes that support the construct assessed by the test. The field of psychological assessment, which has a rich research history, provides a series of psychometric principles for determining whether a test indeed has good measurement properties. Importantly, psychological assessment, unlike the relatively fledgling field to which the study of EI belongs, is *relatively* uncontroversial. Thus, a good deal of expert consensus has now been reached on how to establish the worthiness of a psychological test (see, e.g., Anastasi & Urbina, 1997). In fact, we can see psychometrics in both outcome and process terms. Established knowledge provides some criteria for deciding whether or not a test is acceptable. However, especially in dealing with a novel construct like EI, it is important to look at the process by which psychometricians, starting with little more than a hopeful idea, eventually arrive at a reliable and valid test. Briefly, a very informal road-map of how to arrive at a good test involves the following:

• Identifying and conceptualizing several distinct qualities of the human organism, which may cluster together to define a meaningful, scientific construct

• Checking that the source of this clustering is not some trivial artifact, such as a response bias, the particular measurement operations and methods employed to assess the construct, or other extraneous factors

• Checking that the cluster of qualities represents a new, rather than existing, scientific construct

• Establishing that the construct has some predictive validity, in other words, that the test relates to other psychologically meaningful or practically useful criteria

In this section, we first outline a destination—the desiderata for a good test of EI. Next, we look at some of the roadblocks that may be encountered en route. At the beginnings of the enterprise there are difficulties associated with sampling items to be included in tests. One of the early forks in the path concerns whether EI is to be assessed by an objectively scored test, similar to an IQ test, or by self-report, similar to a personality questionnaire. Both routes have pitfalls: uncertainty over how to achieve genuinely objective scoring in the former case, and avoiding deliberate or unconscious bias in response in the latter case. Further down the road, once we have a reliable test that predicts interesting criteria, there are additional problems related to the distinctiveness of the test from existing measures.

Criteria for reliability and validity
Using internationally acclaimed opinion and research from this field (e.g., Anastasi & Urbina, 1997; Gregory, 1996; Murphy & Davidshofer, 1998; Psychological and Educational Testing Standards, 1985), the ideal EI test should minimally satisfy each and all of the following four criteria:

Content validity   A psychometrically valid test of EI is required to cover a representative sample of the domain that it was designed to assess. The issue here is one of *conceptualization*; deciding a priori what qualities should be assessed as components of EI and what qualities should be excluded from EI. For example, if a test is to serve as a measure of emotion perception, then its developers need to ensure that major aspects of emotion perception are covered by the test items, ideally in the correct proportions. According to existing research, such a test (actually subtests, since emotion perception may be thought of as a higher-order construct) should probably cover the perception of emotions in faces, music, abstract designs, human interaction, and colors (to name but a few areas that have established literatures surrounding them). Moreover, test developers should not focus exclusively on one type of perception (e.g., happiness) to the exclusion (and detriment) of other basic emotions (e.g., fear, anger, sadness, disgust, surprise, and so forth).

Content validity is difficult to ascertain when the candidate psychological test measures an ill-defined trait (Gregory, 1996). Interestingly, one of the primary methods used for ascertaining content validity in the past has been the consensual judgment of experts in the field, so that content validity can actually be quantified (see, e.g., Hambleton, 1984; Lawshe, 1975; Martuza, 1974). To date, it is curious that such techniques have not been utilized with the myriad psychological tests supposedly assessing EI that have appeared recently on the market.

Reliability For EI to exist as a scientifically meaningful individual-difference construct, people must differ reliably across its major dimensions. In particular, should a person taking an EI test obtain a below-average score on one occasion, then that same person should get a below-average score when given the same test again some time in the future. This is termed the test-retest reliability of a measure. If performance is inconsistent (especially across all individuals tested), then what is being measured is unstable, and consequently of questionable utility. Another important form of reliability involves determining the extent to which responses that people give on items correlate with other items of the same test (i.e., internal-consistency reliability). For example, if each item in a test of emotional regulation is measuring emotional regulation, then responses to each item should correlate (in a meaningful and statistically significant manner) with responses to all the other items of this test.

Predictive validity and usefulness EI measures should predict important practical outcomes of emotional life—if not, the test is of little use. These might include how well people deal with stress, how effective they are at maintaining intimate relationships, how respected they are by their peers, and how well they deal with others in emotional turmoil (Ciarrochi, Chan, Caputi & Roberts, 2001). In organizational psychology, in particular, the extent to which a given psychological test satisfies this criterion has, in recent years, become one of the hot topics of that field (see, e.g., Schmidt & Hunter, 1998).

Construct validity Construct validation is the process of testing whether or not a test actually measures some theoretical construct or trait (Anastasi & Urbina, 1997). The critical point is that "no criterion or universe of content is accepted as entirely adequate to define the quality to be measured" (Cronbach & Meehl, 1955), especially when the construct is complex, multifaceted, and theory-bound, as EI appears to be. As such, the demonstration of construct validity rests on a systematic program of research using a number of diverse procedures. To successfully evaluate the construct validity of a test, a variety of evidence from numerous sources should be accumulated. Indeed, studies pertaining to content and predictive validity are merely supporting evidence in the cumulative quest for construct validation. Note also that these theorists often see construct validation as a process without end—that all studies should continue to provide construct validity, but that no study represents an endpoint in this process. As a corollary, only when studies of a test consistently lead to negative outcomes should the wider psychological community reject it.

Although construct validity is a lengthy and complex process, each empirical procedure is designed to answer a crucial, specific question. The main issue is this: "Based on the current theoretical understanding of the construct which the test claims to measure, do we find the kinds of relationships with non-test criteria that the theory predicts?" (Gregory, 1996, p. 119). For example, it has been proposed that cognitive abilities increase (systematically) from early childhood through to adolescence and adulthood. Any new measure of cognitive abilities should reflect this developmental trend. Tests for EI might be required to pass some of the same empirical tests as cognitive ability measures; for example, a similar developmental trend has been seen as critical (see Mayer, Caruso, et al., 1999, 2000). Other tests may be unique to EI; for example, some researchers have contended that females might have greater emotional competence than males, and so construct validation of measures involves examining gender differences.

In addition, one of the most important forms of construct validation involves *convergent* and *discriminant* validity (Campbell & Fiske, 1959). A test should correlate highly with other variables that theory specifies should relate to the underlying construct (convergent validity). Thus, alternate tests of EI should intercorrelate highly. Conversely, the test should not correlate highly with theoretically unrelated variables (divergent validity). If it does, the test may be measuring something other than the construct targeted for measurement, and it may indeed be *redundant* with existing measures. This issue is critical to EI research, and we will return to issues of similarity and distinctiveness shortly.

A final comment is that construct validity of EI requires engagement with existing research on emotional competence. The complexity of this research field is such that construct-validity research might be directed toward many different subdisciplines and criteria, ranging from neural processes to high-level cognition. One of the difficulties of EI research is that it is unclear what kind of theory is required to support construct validity. We return to the issue of what a theory of EI should look like in the next section.

Beginning the psychometric journey: Sampling issues

Finding the Eldorado of EI requires a starting-point for the quest. People have many qualities and attributes: how do we decide which ones to investigate in order to find clusters of qualities that might define EI? The problem is one of *sampling* personal attributes and abilities. It is possible to begin the search somewhat blindly. We could write a list of behaviors and actions related to emotion, devise tests for each behavior, and then investigate the interrelationships between test scores. If our sampling of behaviors is sufficiently extensive, we should find a cluster of intercorrelated EI tests distinct from clusters of other dimensions related to emotion. Indeed, Binet's pioneering work on cognitive intelligence, lacking a clear definition, proceeded in much this way (though guided by Binet's insight and lay conceptions of intelligence). By contrast, some of the initial work on personality traits used an explicit *sampling strategy*, using the corpus of personality-descriptive words in English as the initial basis for generating personality attributes (Cattell, 1944).

Unfortunately, EI presents more severe sampling problems than both intelligence and personality, for the following reasons:

Item content   Both intelligence and personality research began with a sense of the type of item appropriate for the domain concerned, such as personality-descriptive words. Intelligence research rests, broadly, on the belief that human beings are in part rational. People make judgments about the correctness of beliefs and actions, and provide reasoned accounts for why a belief is right or wrong. Narrowly, human rationality provides a basis for constructing problems that can be answered correctly or incorrectly, with some rationale for one answer being correct, the rationale perhaps taken from some formal system such as logic or mathematics. Even with a very limited understanding of the psychology of intelligence, the pioneers in this area were able to construct prototype tests on this basis by writing items that tested the ability to answer right-or-wrong questions. In the case of EI, it is unclear what a prototypical EI item should look like. We probably cannot locate EI from simple personality descriptions, or we would already have discovered EI as a standard component of personality. There are many problems or questions we could devise that would have some emotional content, but how do we decide which ones are likely to require EI to answer? Does giving dictionary definitions of emotion names constitute EI? Does a good memory for emotional stimuli constitute EI? Does the ability strongly to experience emotions constitute EI? One could argue the merits of each suggestion on intuitive grounds, but there are no pre-existing standards for making this decision.

Rationality and emotion   Beyond immediate sampling difficulties, there are problems associated with the lack of rationality, of emotional reactions, to events. Of course, emotions can be linked to rationality or irrationality in the sense that an emotion may be more (or less) appropriate to circumstances (see Ben Ze'ev, 2000, for a conceptual analysis of emotion and rationality). Happiness is normally a rational reaction to praise from a friend; anger is not. However, happiness is not a rational response to praise in the sense that (under the assumptions supporting standard arithmetic) $2 + 2 = 4$ (Zeidner, Matthews & Roberts, 2001). In certain circumstances, the emotional response to sincere praise might be different; the recipient might feel ashamed if they had just betrayed their friend in some way. The correct or appropriate emotional response depends on contextual factors. If a person receives unmerited praise from a friend, should he or she feel embarrassment because the praise is undeserved, annoyance because the friend's perceptions are inaccurate, anxiety over future repercussions, or gratitude because the friend is trying to be emotionally supportive? The person's cultural and personal values provide guidelines, for example, in how much honesty is valued over pleasantness, but there is no calculus of human relations that supplies a definitive answer. Hence, it is difficult to pose problems, especially those related to emotions, that admit of only a single correct answer.

Self-reflexiveness   Although conceptions of EI differ, a common theme is that, at least in part, EI is once removed from emotion itself. To be emotionally intelligent is not to experience only positive emotions, but to manage emotional experience in order to facilitate personal gains and interpersonal interaction. Such a position is plausible, but leads to difficulties in assessing emotion management independent of the emotion itself. It is relatively straightforward to measure anger proneness (e.g., Spielberger et al., 1983), but harder to assess whether the person typically manages anger to produce desirable consequences. Compounding the problem is the likelihood that style of emotion management and the actual emotion expressed are reciprocally related. Failure to deal successfully with irritating events is liable to provoke further frustration and anger, for example. Conversely, it is probably easier to "be in touch with" one's emotions if those emotions are predominantly positive. Indeed, as we shall see, measures of EI are frequently correlated with measures of dispositional emotion, such as (low) depression. It is open to debate whether such correlations reflect simply the positive outcomes of high EI or rather a failure to tease apart EI measures from emotion per se.

There is no simple solution to these sampling problems. Possibly, an intuitive approach to sampling, through normal processes of test refinement, will eventually lead to a good EI measure (which, in turn, would inform the theory of EI). However, our analysis points to various pitfalls along any route taken, pitfalls that need to be avoided. These include failure to sample some or all of the components of EI, the lack of a rationale for scoring items as correct or incorrect, and the danger of confounding (low) EI with negative emotion. For these reasons, we emphasize in this book the importance of using existing research on ability and on emotion to guide research on EI. In particular, quite a lot is known about the psychological and biological systems that support emotion. It follows that EI is a property either of these systems themselves or (in line with the self-reflexiveness principle described earlier) of higher-level systems that regulate the operation of lower-level systems directly controlling emotional experience and response.

Scoring issues in self-report and performance-based assessment

A further issue in developing an initial test is item scoring. How do we decide whether the person's response to a test item is emotionally intelligent or not? Resolving this issue depends, in part, on which of the two types of EI measure is being used (i.e., a performance test, like the MSCEIT, or a self-report questionnaire, like the EQ-i). A performance test has responses that can be evaluated against objective, predetermined scoring criteria. A self-report questionnaire, on the other hand, asks people to report on their own level of functioning. For example, in assessing emotion perception, the researcher may have an individual identify whatever emotions are present in a passage of music (performance) or else ask them to judge how good they are at recognizing emotions in musical excerpts (self-report). In either case, the emotionally intelligent response must be specified, but the principles for so doing are different. Performance testing requires criteria for rating *responses* (i.e., selecting answers) that are more or less intelligent (e.g., criteria for deciding whether an emotion is actually present in a passage of classical music or not). Self-report assessment specifies, in advance, the qualities of EI, as written into the questionnaire items, and scoring simply depends on the match between self-report and the target qualities. There are five major differences between performance and self-report measures:

Maximal versus typical performance   Performance tests assess actual EI, whereas self-report measures assess perceived EI. This distinction has been summarized elsewhere as indicating that performance tests are indicative of maximal attainment, whereas self-report measures assess typical attributes (Cronbach, 1970).

Internal versus external appraisal   Unlike performance measures, self-report measures require people to have insight into their own level of EI. Unfortunately, people may not have an accurate understanding of either their academic or emotional intelligence. It is questionable whether items asking participants to self-appraise intellectual ability (e.g., "I am an extremely intelligent person") would make for a valid measure of general intelligence. Indeed, past research has found only modest correlations between self-rated and actual ability measures (see, e.g., Paulhus, Lysy & Yik, 1998). Similarly, Ciarrochi, Deane, and Anderson (2001) found that self-reported emotion perception is unrelated to how people actually perform in recognizing emotions. Extending this line of reasoning, some commentators have questioned the usefulness of self-reports in the assessment of EI (see Salovey, Woolery & Mayer, 2001).

Response bias A major difficulty with self-report measures is that people can distort their responses in order to appear better (or worse) than they actually are, consciously or unconsciously. The problem is especially acute for self-reports of ability: individuals in the lower quartile on several abilities have been shown to grossly overestimate their performance and ability (Kruger & Dunning, 1999). Performance-based tests are free of such bias. Response bias in questionnaire measures of EI is discussed in further detail below, but we should be especially wary of the capacity of low-EI individuals to recognize their deficiencies.

Practical considerations Performance measures generally are more time-consuming to complete, are more difficult to score, and require more detailed instructions and greater training for the test giver to administer the test competently, than self-report measures. These various disparities occur because self-report measures allow people to summarize their level of EI in a few concise statements (e.g., "I am in touch with my emotions"). Performance measures, on the other hand, require a substantial number of observations before EI level can be ascertained with any degree of accuracy. It has been reported, for example, that it takes about 2 minutes to complete an emotion perception questionnaire, whereas it takes about 15 minutes to complete a performance measure of emotion perception alone (see, e.g., Ciarrochi, Chan, Caputi & Roberts, 2001; Garcia & Roberts, 2001).

EI: Personality or intelligence? Self-report measures of EI tend to be related to well-established personality traits and in particular the various factors comprising the Big Five Factor model (see, e.g., Davies et al., 1998; Dawda & Hart, 2000; McCrae, 2000). Performance measures of EI, on the other hand, tend to be less related to personality measures, sharing overlap instead with traditional intelligence measures (see, e.g., Ciarrochi, Chan & Caputi, 2001a; Roberts, Zeidner, et al., 2001). It would appear that for EI to be considered a type of intelligence, performance methods should be favored over self-report. We reserve a more detailed examination of this claim for our review of individual tests in chapter 5.

Pitfalls of self-report assessment: Response bias

The self-perceptions assessed by questionnaire may not be particularly accurate, or even available to conscious interpretation, being vulnerable to the entire gamut of response sets and social desirability factors afflicting self-report measures, as well as deception and impression management (see Furnham, 1986). In order to combat these types of problem, self-report measures can include scales that measure the amount people are distorting or are otherwise open to the effects of socially desirable responding (e.g., Bar-On, 1997). To counteract this criticism in other fields where self-reports are used, researchers have also compared self-assessed responses to reports provided by a respondents' peers (see, e.g., Costa & McCrae, 1992a). Validation studies of this type have yet to be systematically conducted by researchers employing self-report EI assessment. The ECI (Boyatzis et al., 2000) has the capacity for self and other rating, but there appear to be no data in the public domain on the comparability of the two measures.

Two types of problem may arise. First, especially in practical situations, people may deliberately lie. An applicant for a job requiring counseling skills may be reluctant to admit to lack of empathy or interpersonal skills. Ironically, the more the public acceptance of EI, the greater the motivation to fake high EI is likely to be. Second, response bias may reflect not deliberate deception, but lack of awareness of one's own shortcomings. Paulhus and John (1998) identify two self-deceptive tendencies towards self-enhancement, which they link to power and approval motives, respectively. The first self-favoring tendency is an egoistic bias toward exaggerating one's social and intellectual status. The person has unrealistically positive self-perceptions with respect to qualities such as dominance, courage, and ability. The second tendency is a moralistic bias, associated with overestimation of socially desirable traits, such as agreeableness and dutifulness, and denial of socially unacceptable behaviors. Scales for social desirability (e.g., Crowne & Marlowe, 1964) may assess this source of bias.

The dangers of contamination of self-report measures of EI by these two biases are evident. Some elements of EI relate to a sense of self-empowerment (e.g., assertiveness and self-regard, on the Bar-On, 1997, scales), and might be open to contamination by egoistic self-bias. The respondent might be big-headed and narcissistic rather than emotionally intelligent. Other elements of EI relate to social conformity, such as the Bar-On (1997) social-responsibility and impulse-control dimensions.

Moralistic bias might elevate scores here. Bar-On (1997) wisely included scales for positive and negative impression management on the EQ-i. Some of the correlations between negative impression management and the other EQ-i scales are disconcertingly high (e.g., $r = -0.69$ with problem solving, and $r = -0.50$ with stress tolerance), although Bar-On claims that such scales may be assessing unconventional behavior rather than impression management. In addition, both positive and negative bias scales seem to relate to moralistic rather than egoistic bias, and so the possible role of egoism as a bias factor is unknown. Bar-On's (1997) attempt to tackle the response-bias problem is laudable, but this appears an area requiring extensive research.[1]

Pitfalls of ability assessment: Expert versus consensus scoring

As previously noted, the two primary techniques for scoring ability tests of EI, such as the MEIS and MSCEIT, are *consensus* and *expert* scoring (Mayer, Caruso, et al., 1999, 2000). The emotional intelligence of a response is assessed with respect either to the group consensus or to the correct response identified by experts. The use of multiple scoring methods in objective assessment of EI contrasts with the scoring of conventional intelligence tests. Standardized intelligence tests require the application of a true veridical criterion against which one judges a response as correct or incorrect (see, e.g., Guttman & Levy, 1991; Most & Zeidner, 1995; Zeidner & Feitelson, 1989). Of course, there can be room for debate over the correct answers to some IQ test items, but there is generally a clear rationale for the correct answer, and little dispute among experts in the field. For EI to be assessed as a mental ability, it must be possible to categorize answers to stimuli assessing various facets of feelings as correct or incorrect (Mayer & Salovey, 1997). Ideally, therefore, a true and unequivocal veridical standard against which to judge responses is required.

The rationale for expert scoring is that psychologists versed in EI can set those standards. However, some forms of EI test appear to be more open to this procedure than others. We have suggested previously that processes at different levels of abstraction from raw sense data may separately contribute to EI. Mayer, Salovey, and Caruso (e.g., 2000a, 2000b) propose four branches of EI, spanning a continuum of abstraction, from lower-level or basic skills of perception and appraisal of emotion to higher-level synthetic skills for emotion management that integrate lower-level skills. It seems plausible that lower-level skills might be assessed objectively. For example, the extensive research literature on facial expression as a universal indicator of emotion (e.g., Ekman, 1999) might support objectively scored tests of identification of facial emotion, because an expert can unequivocally identify the emotion expressed by a face. Likewise, information-processing tasks, such as deciding that two words or faces expressed related emotions, could be constructed.

However, expert scoring of more abstract, higher-level qualities, such as managing the emotions of oneself and others, seems more problematic. Certain emotional reactions may be assessed, according to logically consistent criteria, only by reference to personal and societal standards. For example, the emotionally intelligent response to being insulted or mocked by a coworker depends on contextual factors such as personal and cultural norms for behavior, the individual's position in the status hierarchy, and the presence of other individuals (see Roberts, Zeidner, et al., 2001). In different circumstances, it might be appropriate to make a joke of the situation, ignore the insult, confront the other person, or discuss the incident with him at a subsequent time. Furthermore, as we shall discuss further in looking at adaptation (see chapters 8 and 9), multiple criteria for deciding whether the response is effective may conflict (e.g., preserving self-esteem, maintaining good relationships with others, advancing in one's career).

Experts may indeed have more knowledge than lay persons, but this expertise is limited. First, research on emotion typically reveals only statistical, rather than directly contingent, relationships; for example, being insulted typically (but not, invariably) leads to anger. Second, there are multiple domains of expertise leading to conflicting viewpoints. A psychologist's expert judgment might differ from that of experts in other relevant fields. As Roberts, Zeidner, et al. (2001) point out, the solutions to a child's emotional problems proposed by a cognitive therapist, an evolutionary psychologist, a psychoanalyst, a social worker, a high-school teacher, and a gender-studies professor would likely differ drastically.

The basis for consensus scoring is the view that the pooled response of large normative samples is accurate (Legree, 1995; Mayer, Caruso, et al., 1999). The idea seems to be that, if we ask respondents about typical emotional encounters, the group as a whole has sufficient expertise for the modal response to be correct. It is argued too that both evolution and culture tend to select emotionally correct responses, through natural selection or some cultural analogue (Mayer, Caruso, et al., 2000). However, there are serious concerns about bias in consensus judgment. There is a traditional British belief that a stiff upper lip is the best response to emotional problems, that is, to endure the problem without talking about it. However, research on emotional disclosure (e.g., Pennebaker, 1997) suggests that this belief is incorrect (although it might prove to be consensual among Britons of a certain age). Similarly, cultural consensus taken at different historical times might link emotional problems to evil spirits, excess black bile, or the Oedipus Complex. It would be foolhardy to suppose that current Western culture has a perfect clarity of emotional vision denied to our ancestors.

There are also concerns about the validity of consensus judgments that cross gender and cultural boundaries. In some respects, consensus scoring addresses the problem of cross-cultural differences in appropriate emotional behaviors, in that responses can be judged against the consensus for the respondent's culture. Sacrificing a pig might be an appropriate response to emotional difficulty in some cultures, but we might worry about a native New Yorker who indulged in such behavior. The difficulty here is that people around the world increasingly live in multicultural societies with a variety of social norms, with the result that the normative values applied vary from setting to setting. The prototype for shifting norms is gender relations. On the assumption that there are differences between men and women in norms for emotional behavior, EI resides in applying the correct norm at the correct time. Jokes acceptable in a single-sex locker room are inappropriate in the workplace, for example. Gauging responses against some averaged norm from a mixed sample of men and women fails to address this need for flexibility and context sensitivity. There is also a risk that within-sex norms might simply indicate extent of agreement with gender-based prejudices.

A final problem with consensus scoring is that is likely to be more effective in assessing "emotional stupidity" than emotional intelligence. Consensus is likely to be more accurate for questions that test whether a person would avoid a grossly incorrect response (e.g., spitting at one's friend) than questions that test the more delicate problems raised by everyday social interaction. In intelligence testing, it is usual to select items with a graduated series of difficulties so that the test discriminates between individuals equally well at all levels of intelligence. Item analyses may be conducted to ensure that the probability of correct response increases with overall test score. The issue of sampling items so that EI is reliably assessed across its full range seems to have been entirely ignored in the literature, although it is a traditional concern of intelligence-test research (see Nunnally, 1978). Consensus scoring is likely to lead to special problems at the top end of the scale, especially in distinguishing the "emotional genius" from the normally functioning, emotionally intelligent person. If a test item asks about an especially difficult emotional encounter, by definition, only a relatively small percentage of exceptionally gifted persons will answer correctly, meaning that the consensual answer will certainly be incorrect. For example, on a four-choice test, if 10% of respondents answer correctly, at least 30% will check the most popular, incorrect choice. Consensual scoring will then artifactually reduce the EI score allotted to the correct responders.

Distinctiveness of EI from intelligence and personality

Thus far we have discussed some of the difficulties encountered in the early stages of test development. Now presume that you have an EI measure that adequately covers the content domain, is reliable, and is useful in predicting important, practical outcomes. In principle, this measure should also relate to other measures of analogous psychological constructs (similarity or convergence), but also not relate too highly with measures that are clearly irrelevant (distinctiveness or divergence). Two tests correlate or overlap if they have similar items and a person scoring highly on one test also tends to score highly on the second test (and this trend is repeated over numerous observations). For example, an arithmetic test and a test of algebra should overlap. However, an arithmetic test and a comprehension test should also overlap (because they are both dependent on educational opportunities, genetic influences, and so forth), but not too as great an extent. Indeed, research in the intelligence realm consistently shows these patterns of relationships with both similar and disparate abilities (see, e.g., Carroll, 1993; Horn, 1998; Roberts, Goff, Anjoul, et al., 2001).

Whenever an EI measure has large overlap with another non-EI measure (e.g., coping with stress), then, it might be argued, the EI measure in question is really just another measure of the non-EI construct (in this case, coping). Generally, a test should not be labeled as a measure of EI when really it is a measure of some other, well-established personality trait or related individual-difference variable (representing a failure of divergent validity). If this practice were repeated throughout the scientific community, thousands of new (but redundant) tests would flood the market each year. Even worse, two scientists might be studying exactly the same underlying psychological construct and not realize it, because they have given different names to the same test and assumed incorrectly that they have measured different empirical entities. Some overlap between EI and other psychological constructs is acceptable.

For example, self-esteem has been linked to management of aversive affect (Smith & Petty, 1995), and so it may make theoretical sense for a test of EI to contain a subtest that measures self-esteem. The scientist-practitioner must be careful, however, to identify how her EI measure overlaps with preexisting instruments. If it turns out that the test measures *no more than* self-esteem, the test is redundant.

In any attempt to evaluate the distinctiveness of EI, it needs to be ascertained how much EI overlaps with existent measures of both intelligence and well-established personality dimensions such as those encapsulated under the Big Five model: neuroticism, extroversion, openness, agreeableness, and conscientiousness (see below). The extent of overlap between personality and EI will be a major theme of chapter 5. Equally, of course, with so many measures of EI welling up from the testing community in recent times, there is a need to demonstrate similarity and convergent validity. Failure to find correspondences between tests for different aspects of EI might be a consequence of assessing a collection of unrelated and possibly rather narrow abilities (see Davies et al., 1998). Evaluation of convergent validity is difficult because these tests have a relatively recent history and there is a dearth of the large-scale, carefully controlled multivariate investigations required. Nevertheless, we will evaluate the information at hand in chapter 5.

Psychometrics and EI: A summary

We have seen that the assessment of EI presents various psychometric problems, some shared with personality and intelligence, and some unique to the construct itself. *Content validity* is a difficult area, given disputes over the definition and conceptualization of EI and attendant sampling difficulties. *Reliability* of published tests normally ranges from fair to good, but they are potentially misleading, given the difficulties noted in scoring performance-based items and discriminating EI from impression management in questionnaire response.

Evidence on *predictive validity* appears to be accumulating steadily, as we will see in chapter 5. Thus far there is nothing to support the more grandiose claims made for EI, and there is a notable lack of studies using experimental paradigms. Too high a proportion of EI research simply involves correlating questionnaires with other questionnaires. Establishing *construct validity* may be the most important issue of all, but one which is hampered by the theoretical uncertainties, already alluded to, and potential difficulties relating to both convergent and divergent validity.

Toward a Theory of Emotional Intelligence

In line with the research agenda established in the introductory chapter, we now consider how we might build on existing research so as to work towards a theory of what it means to be emotionally intelligent and to establish construct validity. We begin with the conceptualization of EI as a competence for successful adaptation to emotional events, introduced in chapter 1, and then review some of the philosophical and conceptual problems that must be addressed in order to transform the initial conceptualizing into an adequate and testable scientific theory. One of the salient features of emotion is its complexity (Ben Ze'ev, 2000). Indeed, there is a turf-war aspect to emotion research, as various disciplines, including philosophy, sociology, neuroscience, and cognitive psychology, attempt to place their own particular concerns at the center of the field. The assessment and understanding of emotion raises some difficult conceptual and philosophical issues, such as the mind-body problem, the nature of consciousness, and the causal status of emotion, that we will address in chapter 4. At this stage we sidestep the nature of emotion to argue that fundamental to EI is some theory of individual differences in adaptive processes that are concomitants of emotional experience, which may be conceived in biological or cognitive-psychological terms. We will argue that we may need different levels of understanding emotional competence, and we outline a multilevel cognitive-science framework that allows EI be defined at different levels of understanding, each of which are addressed in later chapters of this book, especially in part II.

Adaptational processes as the basis for EI

For the most part, existing EI theory is primarily structural and descriptive in nature. As we shall demonstrate later in this chapter, contemporary differential psychology complements structural description with *process-based* accounts that specify how intelligence and personality relate to the operations on sense data performed by neural and cognitive systems. This more fine-grained approach is essential to understanding how individual difference factors influence the person's interactions with the external environment.

What kind of process-based theory would tell us about the nature of EI? Very broadly, the essential process is that of *adaptation* (Zeidner & Matthews, 2000). By "adaptation" we mean the processes that support the person's attempts to fulfill personal goals and to minimize harm from external events, within a changing external environment (cf. Lazarus, 1991). Adaptation can be a slippery concept, and we must be clear from the outset about the sense in which we are using this term. An alternative meaning, from evolutionary psychology, is an inherited biological mechanism that enhanced fitness to survive or reproduce within the prehistorical period that natural selection produced the human genotype (Tooby & Cosmides, 1992). In this book, we separate an adaptation as it may be observed empirically from the source of that adaptation, which may be inherited or learned. Within this context, the term "adaptation" does *not* imply an inherited mechanism. Adaptive processes also differ in time-span, ranging from the milliseconds taken to encode a stimulus to the years taken to shape enduring personal dispositions.

As discussed in chapter 1, EI may be conceptualized as an index of the person's overall aptitude for success in adaptation to encounters that provoke emotion. However, such a broad definition is useful only if we can identify the specific processes that support adaptation. In fact, adaptive processes may be found at different levels of biopsychological organization and conceptualized in biological or cognitive-psychological terms. Some processes, like the startle response to an unexpected stimulus, are directly controlled by neural circuitry that is relatively well understood. Others, such as the appraisal processes that support evaluation of the personal significance of events, may relate to discrete information-processing routines or to high-level cognitive processes that do not map onto the biological substrate in any simple fashion. Perhaps persons high and low in EI differ in how major brain systems respond to motivational stimuli, or in the interpretations they place on events.

Once we start to look at EI in this more fine-grained way, we no longer occupy terra incognita. Quite a lot is known about both the biological basis (e.g., Rolls, 1999) and cognitive basis (e.g., Lazarus, 1999) of emotion. The map is dense with brain systems, neurotransmitters, memories, and appraisal processes. There are many controversies about the nature of emotion (see chapter 4), but it is unlikely that current biological and cognitive theory has entirely overlooked some key EI process, anymore than the early European cartographers of North America could ignore the Great Lakes or Rocky Mountains. Hence, if EI exists, we should be able to link it to the processes specified by existing biological and cognitive models. One of the tasks of this book is to review this existing theory and evaluate whether it describes promising candidate processes as the basis for EI.

One barrier to progress is that emotion, as a term used ordinarily to describe subjective feelings, is uniquely difficult to conceptualize in scientific terms. A prelude to discussing emotion and adaptation is to outline some of the philosophical and conceptual difficulties that arise from treating "emotion" as a scientific construct, akin to "gravity" or "electricity" in the physical sciences. A further barrier is the complexity of both biological and cognitive models of emotional function. The brain appears to be modular, in that it comprises many distinct sub-systems operating in parallel. Localizing any form of intelligence entails either picking out one essential module that has some overall regulatory role or accepting that the intelligence may be distributed across many modules. In the case of emotion, several biological theorists, notably Panksepp (1998), have argued that there are separate brain systems for different basic emotions. One possibility is that structures in the frontal lobe of the brain regulate all these multiple systems. Alternatively, properties of the different systems, such as their reactivity to stimuli, may be correlated. Similarly, cognitive theories of emotion, such as that of Lazarus (1991, 1999), discriminate emotions on the basis of appraisals and action tendencies. Again, we must find some common element or identify some superordinate regulatory system.

Another barrier concerns the nature of individual differences in adaptation itself. A good theory requires a description of individual differences in biological and/or cognitive processes *and*, as a logically separate issue, an account of how individual differences in processing govern individual differences in adaptation to emotional encounters. Thus, it is essential that outcomes of encounters can be categorized in terms of some spectrum of success and failure. As discussed in chapter 8, assessment of adaptive success is hard, because there are different criteria for success that may conflict (Zeidner & Matthews, 2000). This conceptualization also assumes that persons adept in handling one type of encounter are skilled in dealing with other types of situations too, which may not be correct. We will argue that a multilevel cognitive-science framework that differentiates multiple levels of explanation is required both to describe the different levels of biological and neural process to which EI may be linked and to explore whether individual differences in these processes control adaptive success in emotional situations.

A cognitive-science framework for understanding emotional competence
In the light of the discussion so far, a cynic might say that, in the spirit of Humpty Dumpty in *Alice through the Looking Glass*, "Emotion means what

we choose it to mean." In the current book, we cannot take the conceptual analysis of emotion much further, although we will subsequently discuss some specific theories of emotion in more detail (see chapters 4, 7, and 8). However, for clarity, we must describe our own conceptual perspective, although other approaches may be equally viable. The conceptual model underpinning much of our discussion of emotion and EI has been described as the "classical theory of cognitive science" (Pylyshyn, 1984, 1999). It derives from Alan Turing's pioneering work on artificial intelligence and is best known from its application to cognitive functions such as language, memory, and thought (e.g., Pylyshyn, 1984). However, it appears also to provide a fresh perspective on emotion (Matthews, 1997a, 2001). The classical theory accepts that a phenomenon as complex as emotion may require multiple levels of description, and different levels of description may be appropriate for different aspects of emotional functioning.

According to cognitive-science theory (Newell, 1982; Pylyshyn, 1984), cognitive phenomena are open to three complementary types of explanation (see figure 2.1). Each level of explanation makes different assumptions about the nature of the correspondences between the phenomenon to be explained and qualities of the cognitive system. The first is the *biological* level, which describes the neural hardware supporting processing in terms of physical and chemical processes. Individual differences in emotion might reflect variation in brain functioning, as proposed by biological theories. We might say that emotion corresponds to the level of activity of a specific brain system, such as the amygdala, or to the availability of a neurotransmitter, such as the endorphins, which are thought to control happiness. Empirical studies of emotion aim to show how brain function controls behavior using evidence from studies of neuropsychology, psychoactive drugs, and learning in animals.

The second level of explanation is described by Pylyshyn (1984) as the *symbolic* level. This refers to the formalized computational operations that constitute the software of the mind, and the software facilities, such as memory space and communication channels, that support processing. Events are represented as data in some abstract code, as a computer represents information as variables. It is assumed the mind has an "instruction set" of permitted operations performed on codes, such as a comparison of two codes that outputs a code for "same" or "different." All types of information-processing, both conscious and unconscious, possess this computational nature, although there may be some division of the processing system into different processing units or modules,

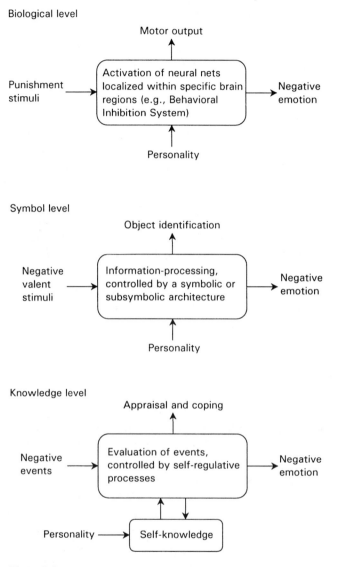

Figure 2.1
Three levels of explanation for emotion within cognitive science.

perhaps using different codes or "programming languages." Descriptions of multiple processors and the flow of information between them are referred to as *cognitive architecture*. In this case, we might say that emotion corresponds to some subset of processing operations. Appraisal theory, for example, binds emotion to computations that perform stimulus evaluation, such as encoding a threat value for the stimulus. Emotion might correspond to one out of several processing units, such as a processor that computes the overall status of some ongoing plan (Oatley & Johnson-Laid, 1987). The aim of research at this level is to develop a detailed computational model of emotional behavior that could be expressed as a computer simulation.

Pylyshyn (1984) labels the third level of explanation the *semantic* level, in that it refers to the personal meaning of otherwise arbitrary processing codes. It is also called the *knowledge* level (Newell, 1982), because it refers to the person's knowledge of how to obtain personal goals. More generally, this level explains behavior on the basis of intentions, motivations, and self-referent knowledge of how to attain goals. It is compatible with transactional theories of emotion (Lazarus, 1991), which see emotion as signaling the state of ongoing person-environment interaction. The overall relational meaning is not dependent on any specific set of computations. In other words, cognitive science distinguishes cognition, in the sense of information-processing, from cognition, in the sense of personal understanding. The knowledge-level (as we shall call it) is similarly compatible with Ben Ze'ev's (2000) position that intentionality is central to emotion, which entails knowledge, evaluation, and motivations related to some other object (often a person). Research at this level aims to analyze the rationality of emotions: how emotions relate systematically to the person's goals, values, and beliefs.

The interrelationships between levels is a matter of debate (see Bechtel, 1988; McCauley, 1996). One view (e.g., Fodor, 1974) is that levels are *strongly autonomous*. Concepts in neuroscience and cognitive psychology may be incommensurable; for example, it may be impossible to link concepts such as that of breaking a promise to brain states. In this case, the three levels of explanation would represent separate fields of inquiry. Alternatively, all of psychology may eventually be reduced to neural-level accounts (see Churchland, 1996). An intermediate position, *explanatory pluralism*, is favored here. That is, we will always need theories at different levels, but partial integration and mutual influence will develop. Indeed, some of the most exciting research in the fields of emotion and personality uses constructs that appear to bridge the levels

(Matthews, 1997a, 2000). Choice of strategy is now seen as one of the primary variables mediating the behavioral effects of stressors (Matthews, Davies, Westerman & Stammers, 2000). Strategy use may be addressed both in terms of information-processing descriptions and in terms of personal meaning and coping, thus bridging cognitive-architectural and symbolic levels. Likewise, neural net models of emotion and cognition (e.g., Matthews & Harley, 1996; Siegle & Ingram, 1997) may serve to bridge cognitive-architectural and neural levels of description. Matthews (1997a) speculates that evolutionary psychology may eventually link knowledge-level accounts to neural function, through specifying how personal motivations are shaped by natural selection. The ladder of explanation may then be reconceptualized as a circle, as shown in figure 2.2.

It follows that different perspectives on emotion may be accommodated within a common framework. We can establish *correlations* between indices of emotion and constructs at all three levels, i.e., the presence of an emotion allows us to statistically predict the person's brain states, information processing, and personal meanings. The nature of *necessary correspondences* between emotion and constructs at different levels is more difficult. For example, we might suppose that emotion fundamentally corresponds to brain activity; that is, a person, say, is anxious if and only if a certain set of neurons is active (an isomorphism between brain states and emotion). Correlations between cognitive constructs and emotions follow from brain states being statistically correlated with information processing, although, in the classical theory, there is no isomorphism between constructs at the different levels. However, one feature of the theory is that no level should be given primacy. Cognitive constructs can be just as real as biological ones (Sperry, 1993). By way of analogy, a description of the logic of a computer program is just as real (and often more useful) than a description of the electric currents in silicon transistors when the program is run. Equally, we could see emotion as corresponding directly to information processing or knowledge-level constructs, with biological correlates of emotion representing the role of brain function as an imperfect reflection of cognition. Empirical research does not allow a definitive resolution of such issues (see, however, chapters 6 and 7 for further discussion), but we will tend to favor a position corresponding to Lazarus's (1991) theory. Within this perspective, emotion is viewed fundamentally as a property of knowledge-level personal meaning and intentionality.

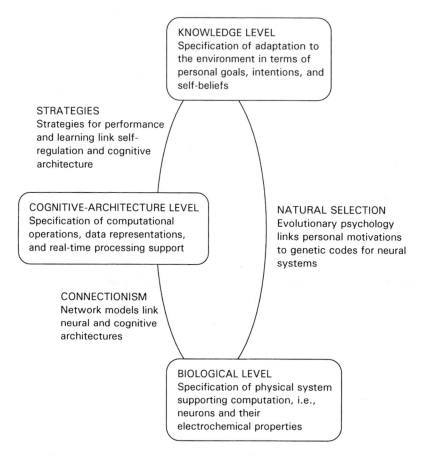

Figure 2.2
The circle of explanation: constructs bridging the three levels of explanation in cognitive science (Matthews, 1997a).

Conceptualizing emotional intelligence

The cognitive science framework apprises us that there are three levels of process which may relate to EI: neural processes, information processing, and knowledge-level processes such as evaluation and coping (Lazarus, 1991). *Emotions* may be seen as indicators of these underlying processes, rather than as causal agents themselves, although it is open to question which level of process directly corresponds to emotion. *Emotional intelligence* is then a quality of processing, which refers to whether the processing supporting emotion is adaptive or maladaptive. Depending on the context, processes at all three levels may control adaptation.

Consider, for example, a person run over by a car. This person might be slow to activate a biologically preprogrammed instinctive leap to safety, she might fail to compute the trajectory of the vehicle successfully, or she might fail to realize that her mortal enemy was driving the vehicle. In the second part of this book, we will look at whether research identifies a coherent set of individual differences at each level. Are there some people whose brains equip them for handling emotional encounters? Do some people possess information-processing routines that are especially efficient in performing computations on emotional data? Are some people especially skilled in evaluating the emotional significance of encounters, and choosing the most appropriate coping strategy?

Common sense might suggest that in normal social interaction, knowledge-level analysis of how we should conduct ourselves to fulfill our goals, in the light of our assessment of other people's motivations and beliefs, may be the most important level. Conceivably, though, purposive evaluation and action is an indirect expression of constructs at lower levels (i.e., the efficiency of cognitive and neural architecture). The cognitive-science framework implies that it is contentious to assert that EI refers to the management of emotion, as the term "emotion" is ambiguous in its referents. Does handling anger entail managing biology (e.g., suppressing some noncognitive primal rage), managing processing (e.g., through full analysis of the anger-provoking stimulus), or managing self-knowledge (e.g., through reflecting on personal consequences of responding with aggression)? We will devote a significant amount of space in chapters 6 and 7 to reviewing theories at the different levels, and this review will in turn provide a solid conceptual basis for addressing such issues.

The cognitive-science framework is useful also in addressing the self-reflexive nature of EI. That is, the concept implies some separate system that takes emotional state as input and operates upon it, influencing both the emotion and its impact on behavior. For example, an angry person may evaluate his anger as inappropriate for the situation and adopt a strategy of suppressing impulsive response. This statement describes self-reflexivity at the knowledge level. At the information-processing level, there may be architecture for self-regulation, which describes how information about current emotional states are encoded and fed into processes that compute responses to this information. For example, according to attributional theories of emotion, an unexplained emotional state may elicit a search for possible causes of the emotional state. That is, information-processing has a *metacognitive* aspect, concerned with processing internal state. At the brain level, it has been proposed that the prefrontal cortex operates as an executive control system that regulates the behavioral consequences of emotion generated within more primitive brain systems, such as the amygdala (Rolls, 1999). In other words, there is likely to be a control structure *within* each level, and understanding EI entails understanding how this control structure separates emotion-related processing from regulatory routines. (It is important to distinguish *levels of explanation* from *levels of control*, within each level of explanation).

Current theory of EI is often rather vague about such issues. For example, Mayer, Salovey, and Caruso (2000) identify EI with faculties that include emotion identification and management. Emotion management is operationalized, in their MEIS and MSCEIT tests, as making judgments about the appropriate responses to emotional events, which appears to be a knowledge-level faculty. Emotion identification is operationalized as the ability to judge the emotional content of stimuli such as faces and stories. It is unclear whether responses, on the test reflect the operations of (1) a brain process that assigns emotions to stimuli, without use of symbolic representations, (2) computations performed on a symbolic representation of the stimulus, or (3) a knowledge-level evaluative process, which weighs up the "personal meaning" of the stimulus.

The difference between (2) and (3) is this: The former case might refer to some analysis of the content of, say, a story: does it have a happy ending or not? The latter case refers to the personal significance of the story: an unhappy story might have a personal resonance that transforms reading it into a positive experience. Furthermore, it is unclear whether the processes controlling responses on the test are representative of responses to similar stimuli found in real-world environments. For example, in processing facial emotion, we typically make use of contextual information as well as the face itself. A sad face will be evaluated differently depending on whether it belongs to a clown, to a movie villain, to an over-sensitive child, or to a friend who has just lost her job.

The cognitive-science framework is also important for understanding how EI might be represented as dispositions resembling personality traits, such as hardiness, self-control, and empathy (e.g. Bar-On, 1997). Recent analyses of personality show that such qualities are expressed simultaneously at different levels. For example, resilience under stress might reflect insensitivity of brain systems for anxiety, or information-processing routines that bias stimuli toward being interpreted as challenging rather than threatening, or a sense of personal agency that supports adaptive coping in stressful situations. We will examine how the personality traits conceptually and empirically linked to EI relate to processing and adaptation in chapter 9.

Theory and EI: A summary

Current accounts of EI are ambiguous in their referents to processing. EI could be variously conceptualized in terms of neural, information-processing, or self-knowledge theory. One of the main tasks of this book is to examine theories of emotion and assess whether existing research is compatible with there being some general competence for emotional adaptivity at one or more levels of explanation. In doing so, we must distinguish the processes that support emotion from the value of processing to adaptation. This approach entails addressing EI primarily as an individual-difference construct, i.e., by seeking systematic individual differences in emotion-related processes that promote successful adaptation (or maladaptation). For example, an appraisal process that outputs exaggerated threat values might be maladaptive if it causes chronic and unrealistic anxiety. In reviewing relevant theory, it is useful to distinguish adaptive processing operations over shorter and longer time periods. At the shortest periods of duration, we are concerned with the processing lasting for seconds or minutes, which might influence the outcome of a single encounter. We discuss theories of biological and cognitive processes of this kind in chapters 6 and 7. In the medium-term, adaptation concerns coping with life events over periods of weeks or months (see chapter 8). Over longer periods, we are concerned with the styles of adaptation indexed by the personality traits that overlap with EI, discussed in chapter 9.

Integrating Theory and Psychometrics: Differential Psychology and Emotional Intelligence

A major purpose of the current chapter is to acquaint the reader with terminology and concepts central to our entire exposition, while simultaneously raising issues that guided our writing of the present book. In so doing, we hope also to have justified the need for the present volume and set forth a number of guiding principles for establishing a systematic, scientific agenda for EI research. However, thus far we have referred to both intelligence and personality constructs, without giving many details of these two fields of psychological inquiry. Clearly, having some rudimentary understanding of these individual-difference constructs is important in the context of arguments we will make throughout the current volume. Further, understanding major issues in these fields may help the reader understand more fully what standards are minimally expected of a science of EI. For this purpose, it is to discussion of differential psychology that we first turn, since it is from this scientific discipline that the specialist fields of intelligence and personality were spawned.

The two branches of psychology

Differential psychology is sometimes seen as one of the two major branches of empirical psychology—the other being experimental psychology. The experimental approach is to examine group trends in order to derive general principles, so individual differences are treated as random statistical error in statistical analyses. Cronbach (1957) famously lamented the lack of contact between psychological theories based on psychometrics and theories based on experimental studies, and called for their integration. Research on human emotions has been hampered by this methodological fracture. There has been important work on individual differences in states of emotion and mood (e.g., Thayer, 1989), and on related personality traits (e.g., Spielberger, 1972). However, historically, human emotions have been studied predominantly using experimental paradigms that neglect individual differences and measurement issues. At least part of the current interest in EI stems from its potential for integrating experimental and individual-differences approaches (see Roberts, Zeidner, et al., 2001).

In contrast, two fields of immense relevance to appreciating the empirical and conceptual significance of EI use the methodologies, statistical techniques, and theoretical rationales that are endemic to differential psychology. The first subdiscipline is the study of intelligence, or more correctly (because "intelligence" does justice to neither the complexity nor controversies still rife in the field) human cognitive abilities. The second subdiscipline is the field of personality. Notably, this field has, in recent times, undergone something of a paradigm shift, moving away from the psychodynamic theorizing of Freud, Jung, Adler, and their followers to focus primarily on *traits*: stable dispositions that index key personal qualities such as extraversion-introversion, and emotionality. Importantly, trait theories use all the methodological and conceptual architectures associated with differential psychology (Matthews & Deary, 1998). The psychological reality of traits is no longer in doubt, although, for a complete account of personality, we also need to look to the social-psychological approach and the idiographic approach (i.e., at the level of the individual person). In the passages that follow, we briefly introduce some of the major concepts and theories associated with these two fields.

Intelligence

Overview General intelligence refers to a person's overall capacity for adaptation through effective cognition and information processing. It may be seen as a general competence of the mind (mental ability) or of higher-order faculties such as understanding, reasoning, problem-solving, and learning, especially of complex, structured material (cognitive ability). However, the concept of general intelligence says little about the more specific competencies that compose it. Thus, psychologists have sought to partition the domain of intelligence into more manageable chunks, including less narrow (but still broad) categories of abilities (e.g., crystallized intelligence) or more specific abilities (e.g., verbal comprehension). These various levels of conceptualization have led to taxonomic models, most often derived from factor-analytic techniques, which have recently been synthesized inside Carroll's (1993) three-stratum model. Carroll found, after reanalysis of virtually all data sets collected in the twentieth century, a hierarchy of structures (see also Roberts, Goff, Anjoul, et al., 2001). Primary mental abilities clustered to define broad cognitive abilities, and broad abilities clustered to define general intelligence. We discuss this model, along with the empirical evidence supporting it, more fully in chapter 3.

This synthesis aside, there has been over a century of debate on the concept of intelligence and the appropriate means to assess this construct. As stated by the APA Task Force on Intelligence (APA Public Affairs Office, 1997), it is generally (though not universally) agreed that the conventional psychometric approach has successfully identified a reliable quality of the individual that predicts important real-world criteria. It is seen as the most influential and most systematically researched approach, although other conceptions of intelligence also have much to offer. The literature also contains criticisms of the notion that there is a consensual definition of intelligence shared by most psychologists (see various chapters in Sternberg, 2000a), especially in view of cultural differences in conceptions of intelligence (see Sternberg, 2000b). The supremacy of conventional, cognitive intelligence has also been challenged by recent suggestions that there are many different kinds of intelligence (e.g., Gardner, 1983).

Notably, Gardner's (1983) model includes abilities such as kinesthetic intelligence, musical intelligence, and in recent instantiations, even moral intelligence (see Gardner, 1999). Interestingly, there is scant empirical evidence for many of these constructs, and recent studies have suggested that kinesthetic intelligence, for example, overlaps, factorially at least, with measures of spatial abilities (see Roberts, Pallier, Stankov & Dolph, 1997; Stankov, Segiova-Cajic & Roberts, 2001). Inside Gardner's model, despite claims that he has made to the contrary, it also appears difficult to assume that the same criterion for inclusion holds true for all intelligence constructs. Thus, many psychometricians would concur that the defining attribute of a cognitive ability test is that there is one correct answer based on logical, empirical, semantic, or even normative criteria (Guttman, 1965a; 1965b; Nunnally, 1978; Zeidner & Feitelson, 1989). However, the psychometric criteria developed in studies of cognitive ability may not be applicable to certain domains of intelligence, such as practical intelligence (see, e.g., Sternberg, Wagner, Williams & Horvath, 1995; Wagner & Sternberg, 1985). In short, it is arguably premature to abandon EI on these grounds alone, especially since some commentators have sought to broaden the frames of reference of human cognitive abilities, often with some level of success (see, e.g., Hedlund & Sternberg, 2000).

Other studies have sought to identify biological and cognitive processes that may support individual differences in intelligence-test performance. It is now well-established that intelligence is partly inherited, and partly shaped by the environment (Brody, 1992). The influence of genes on intelligence implies an influence of individual differences in neural function, and some correlations between brain functions (e.g., cerebral glucose metabolism) and measured IQ have been established empirically (e.g., Vernon, Wickett, Bazana & Stelmack, 2000). It is an open question whether intelligence is fundamentally a biological construct, which could be directly linked to such neural properties, or whether intelligence is fundamentally psychological, with individual differences in neural functioning exerting an indirect effect on the development of cognitive functions that are the more direct determinant of intelligence. Sternberg (1977, 1985) pioneered an important strand of research when he investigated how IQ was expressed in individual differences, specifically in the encoding and reasoning processes that support performance of test items. Working memory, a key construct in cognitive psychology defined as information processing integrated with short-term retention of information, appears to be especially highly correlated with intelligence (Kyllonen & Christal, 1990). Other researchers have linked IQ to various other high-level processes supporting reasoning (Lohman, 2000) and, intriguingly, to rather low-level psychophysical functions, such as line length and pitch discriminations (Deary, 2000). In general, the picture that emerges is that intelligence relates to individual differences in a variety of neural and cognitive-psychological functions, and it is a matter of debate which are most closely and directly related to intelligence as operationally defined. Some authors (e.g., Neubauer, 1997) have seen overall speed of information-processing as central to IQ, whereas others (e.g., Roberts & Stankov, 1999) reject this view and emphasize higher-level processing components.

EI and intellectual intelligence: Complimentary or strange bedfellows? How might EI relate to existent intelligence theory? At a psychometric level, there are two broad possibilities. First, we might see EI as a further element of the hierarchical structure described by Carroll (1993). Perhaps EI should be seen as a distinct collection of abilities that are modestly correlated with some of the other cognitive ability factors subsumed under a top-level, general, factor. The theory of fluid and crystallized ability (Gf/Gc) proposed by Cattell (1987), Horn (1988), and their associates (see Horn & Noll, 1994; Horn & Stankov, 1982) is arguably the most efficacious empirically based psychometric model of intelligence (see Roberts & Stankov, 1999; Stankov, Boyle & Cattell, 1995). It has been speculated that within this theory, EI will constitute an additional aspect of (possibly one or more constructs underlying) crystallized ability (Gc)—a conglomerate of primary abilities that all appear to derive from acculturated learning experiences. This assertion is based on the assumption that the appraisal, expression, regulation, and utilization of emotion develops through experience and social interaction in much the same way as do other psychological processes comprising Gc (see Davies et al., 1998). Consistent with this suggestion, the MEIS appears related, modestly, to Gc but not to Gf (Ciarrochi et al., 2000; Roberts, Zeidner et al., 2001). On the other hand, the EQ-i seems to be unrelated to cognitive intelligence scales (Bar-On, 2000).

We might also expect to see process-level correlates of EI that resemble those supporting Gc, distinguished perhaps by their emotional content. For example, EI might correlate with more rapid processing of emotional stimuli. Similarly, there may be overlap in underlying brain systems. For example, frontal-lobe function has been implicated in both intelligence (Duncan et al., 1996) and the regulation of emotion (Damasio, 1994), though the specific brain areas may differ. Alternatively, in line with Gardner's (1983) analysis, EI might be psychometrically at the same level as cognitive intelligence and other multiple intelligences, with no necessary link to IQ. Likewise, there may be unique cognitive and neural processes supporting EI. In fact, attempts to define aspects of intelligence related to everyday social interaction have quite a long history and may prefigure EI. Because this literature is relevant, we move now to examine conceptual linkages between EI and some pre-existing constructs identified within disparate models of intelligence.

Social intelligence and related constructs   As alluded to previously, many commentators suppose that EI derives from the broader construct of *social intelligence* (e.g., Bar-On, 2000). Thorndike (1920) distinguished three broad classes of intelligence: (a) abstract/scholastic—the ability to understand and manage ideas; (b) mechanical/visuospatial—the ability to understand and manipulate concrete objects; (c) social—the ability to understand and manage people and act wisely in social contexts. Social intelligence was defined as "wisdom in social contexts"; in practice, the study of how people made judgments regarding others and the accuracy of such social judgments. Another model of historical interest, Guilford's (1967, 1985) Structure of Intellect Model, classified mental abilities in terms of operations, such as cognition and memory; content (figural, semantic, symbolic, or behavioral); and products, such as relations and systems. Emotional intelligence involves the processing of both information that refers directly to emotion (e.g., one's own mood) and information on behaviors that have emotional connotations (e.g., violent behaviors). Intelligence in understanding behaviors and their significance already appears in Guilford's Structure of Intellect Model, in the guise of cognition of behavioral content (e.g., ability to identify internal status of individuals, interpretation of consequences of social behavior, and so forth). In fact, the test items designed to gauge behavioral cognition, constructed by Guilford's team (e.g., O'Sullivan, Guilford & deMille 1965), are reminiscent of current behavioral measures of EI (see chapter 3).

Contemporary differential researchers remain interested in social facets of ability and, conversely, social psychologists have become more interested in cognitive determinants of person perception (Mayer & Geher, 1996). Despite considerable interest and numerous attempts to define and measure social intelligence over the past eight decades or so, these attempts have proven problematic (for a review, see Kihlstrom & Cantor, 2000). While defining social intelligence seemed easy enough, the measurement of the construct proved to be an almost insurmountable task. The inability to discriminate between general and social intelligence, coupled with difficulties in selecting validation criteria, led to a decline in research focusing on social intelligence as a distinct intellectual entity, until the recent upsurge of interest in EI.

The concept of EI also strongly overlaps with Gardner's (1983) notion of *personal intelligence*, which comprises two subtypes. *Intrapersonal intelligence* involves the abilities to access one's own feeling life, to identify, label, and discriminate among one's feelings, and to represent them symbolically. These abilities resemble several of those taken to define EI by Mayer, Salovey, and Caruso (2000). *Interpersonal intelligence*, on the other hand, involves the ability to discern the moods, intentions, and desires of others. As suggested earlier, current conceptualizations of EI generally focus on managing the emotions both of self and of others. Thus construed, EI appears to overlap with Gardner's notion of personal intelligence, subsuming both intrapersonal and interpersonal forms of intelligence.

In attempting to locate these "intelligences" within the traditional psychometric domain, Carroll (1993) suggests that interpersonal intelligence is a specialized type of acquired knowledge (i.e., Gc ability). However, Gardner's intrapersonal intelligence—"access to one's own feelings"—finds no counterpart in Carroll's taxonomic model. Elsewhere we have argued that this situation may have arisen because adequate assessment of this type of ability has never appeared in the extant factor-analytic literature (Roberts, Zeidner, et al., 2001). Nevertheless, certain theoretical issues and data sets becoming available that speak to this issue more directly and that require careful consideration in the chapters that follow.

Trait models of personality
Overview   Personality traits may be defined as stable, dispositional characteristics that influence behavior across a variety of different situations; typical examples are extraversion-introversion, emotionality, and sensation seeking (see Matthews & Deary, 1998, for a review). They are typically distinguished from abilities as representing *styles* of behavior, rather

than efficiency of performance output. Some authors (e.g., Wechsler, 1958) have used "personality" as an umbrella term to cover both intelligence and qualitative style of behavior, but we will not adopt this usage.

The scientific study of traits began in the early years of the twentieth century and has been preoccupied with two questions. The first issue is how many different traits should be distinguished from one another. Answers to this question have ranged from three to more than thirty. However, there are now signs of some limited consensus on the dimensional structure of personality. As with ability theory, trait psychologists typically adopt hierarchical models, with a level of 20–30 relatively narrow primary factors supporting a superordinate level of broader secondary factors or superfactors. The dominant view is that there are five robust superfactors: the Big Five (Costa & McCrae, 1992a; Goldberg, 1993; de Raad, 2000) of extraversion, neuroticism, conscientiousness, agreeableness, and openness (sometimes also known as intellect or even culture). Costa and McCrae (1992c) have proposed four ways in which the five factors are basic:

Heritability   Like cognitive abilities, personality traits are partially inherited, and hence biologically based, although the environment explains a greater part of the variation in personality than in intelligence (Brody, 1992; Loehlin, 1992).

Consensual validation   The five factors relate to psychologically meaningful constructs that emerge from various approaches to personality.

Cross-cultural invariance   The five factors are *universal* in that, it is claimed, they appear in all cultures, although debate continues on how closely personality models correspond to one another cross-culturally (e.g., de Raad, 2000).

Predictive utility   The five factors provide "added value" in that they predict a variety of characteristics over and above the trait itself. For example, knowing that a person is extraverted not only tells us that she is lively and sociable but also allows us to predict both her leisure and vocational interests, her risk of various mental disorders, and her performance on laboratory tasks.

The second issue is the theoretical basis for traits: what underlying processes are responsible for individual differences in personal characteristics? Here the dominant paradigm has been neuroscientific models, reflecting the influence of DNA on personality. Eysenck (1967) proposed that traits were controlled by individual differences in the excitability of key brain systems. Extraversion, for example, was thought to relate to a circuit controlling arousability of the cerebral cortex in response to stimuli. There is an extensive psychophysiological literature that provides partial support for such hypotheses (Matthews & Gilliland, 1999; Zuckerman, 1991). In recent years there has been growing interest in cognitive psychological accounts of personality traits, which may be related to individual differences in processing and evaluating events and in choice of action (e.g., Matthews, Schwean, et al., 2000).

Because of the aforementioned features, we turn now to examine the Five Factor Model (FFM) in a little more detail. Certainly, there are various other alternative models of personality superfactors, notably Eysenck and Eysenck's (1985) three-factor model, discriminating extraversion, neuroticism, and psychoticism, which is a worthy competitor to the FFM. However, as Zuckerman (1998) has pointed out, there is some convergence between different models, and there is nearly universal consensus on extraversion and neuroticism as basic personality dimensions. The FFM has also been used as the basis for several studies linking EI scales to personality (e.g. Davies et al., 1998; Dawda & Hart, 2000; Roberts, Zeidner, et al., 2001), and for conceptual analysis (McCrae, 2000). Consequently, we will use this model as the basis for discussing personality, acknowledging that other conceptions also have significant merit.

The Five Factor Model and emotional intelligence   The FFM has two converging bases. First, analyses of personality-descriptive words in English (and other languages) suggest that the domain of personality descriptors is almost completely accounted for by five robust factors (Digman & Inouye, 1986; Goldberg, 1993; Tupes & Christal, 1961). In short, the Big Five Factors appear to be embedded in natural language. Second, factor-analytic studies of personality questionnaires frequently demonstrate the five factors (e.g., McCrae & Costa, 1989, 1992, 1995). Thus, the modern personality researcher has been urged "to adopt the working hypothesis that the five-factor model of personality is essentially correct in its representation of the structure of traits and to proceed to its implications for personality theory and its applications throughout psychology" (McCrae & John, 1992, p. 176). The model has been criticized both by proponents of alternative dimensional schemes (e.g., Eysenck, 1992; Zuckerman, Kuhlman, Joireman, Teta & Kraft, 1993) and by those who doubt the validity of reducing personality to a small number of superfactors (Block, 1995). The coherence of the openness dimension has been a particular point of contention (Saucier, 1997). However, over the last decade or so, the FFM has won a remarkable degree of acceptance as a basic paradigm for trait psychology.

The basis for the Big Five in psychological processes is receiving increasing attention, although there is much more evidence relating to extraversion and neuroticism than to the remaining three factors. In this volume we will adopt the view that traits are supported by multiple processes, represented at different levels of abstraction (Matthews, 1997; Matthews, Schwean et al., 2000; Zeidner & Matthews, 2000). Indeed, consistent with the cognitive-science framework outlined previously for EI, these personality traits appear underpinned by individual differences in neural function, information-processing, and high-level cognitions of personal meaning. For example, extraversion-introversion relates to arousability of the neocortex and subcortical reward systems; information-processing routines influencing attention, memory, and language use; and a tendency to evaluate situations as challenging and calling for direct action. The different component processes associated with a trait may be seen as supporting a common adaptation, handling demanding social environments in the case of extraversion (see, e.g., Matthews & Dorn, 1995). The adaptive qualities of traits linked to EI are discussed further in chapter 9.

Table 2.1 shows how the Big Five relate to narrower, primary personality traits in Costa and McCrae's (1992a) model. The extraversion factor of the FFM closely parallels the dimension of extraversion-introversion in the Eysenckian framework (see, e.g., Eysenck & Eysenck,

Table 2.1
Trait facets associated with the five domains of Costa and McCrae's Five Factor Model of personality

Factor	Trait facets
Neuroticism	Anxiety, angry hostility, depression, self-consciousness, impulsiveness, vulnerability
Extraversion	Warmth, gregariousness, assertiveness, activity, excitement-seeking, positive emotions
Openness	Fantasy, aesthetics, feelings, actions, ideas, values
Agreeableness	Trust, straightforwardness, altruism, compliance, modesty, tender-mindedness
Conscientiousness	Competence, order, dutifulness, achievement striving, self-discipline, deliberation

1985). On the basis of conceptual analysis, McCrae (2000) has argued that certain dimensions of Bar-On's EQ-i, by their very nature, will share overlap with this dimension (in particular, the subscales assessing assertiveness and optimism). The neuroticism dimension contrasts people described as emotional, anxious, and highly strung with those seen as unemotional, calm, and comfortable with themselves. Based on these capsule descriptions alone, one might suspect a close relationship with EI, although the similarity of the constructs has tended to escape the notice of commentators (cf. McCrae, 2000). Agreeableness is a dimension best perceived as interpersonal in its manifestation, containing aspects of sympathy, compassion, and generosity. Notably, Bar-On's EQ-i contains measures of empathy and interpersonal relationships, which McCrae's (2000) conceptual analysis suggests share correspondence with facets of the disagreeable-agreeable dimension (trust and tendermindedness, respectively). Davies et al. (1998) found that a number of other measures of EI shared close correspondence with agreeableness. The major aspects of conscientiousness include accomplishment, organization, scrupulousness, and responsibility (see, e.g., Krause, Roberts, et al., 2001). McCrae's (2000) analysis suggests that problem-solving and social-responsibility from the EQ-i should conceivably share overlap with conscientiousness. Interestingly, this dimension is also represented (near verbatim in several instances) in Goleman's (1998) emotional competence clustering of EI. Although openness may be the least understood of the five (see, e.g., McCrae, 1996), the open individual is generally "more willing to entertain novel ideas and unconventional values ... while [the individual] low in Openness tends to be conventional in behavior and conservative in outlook" (Costa & McCrae, 1994). Openness is also the trait most related to cognitive intelligence, correlating around $r = 0.30$ with crystallized intelligence (Ackerman & Heggestad, 1997). McCrae (2000) has argued that this personality dimension will share the strongest (and most robust) relationship with EI.

Conceptual analysis suggests considerable overlap between EI and the robust, established personality dimensions of the FFM. We will postpone review of links obtained empirically until chapter 5, but at this stage two general observations are useful. First, questionnaire measures of EI, such as Bar-On's (1997) EQ-i, resemble personality questionnaires in item content and, not surprisingly, correlate much more substantially with existing personality constructs than quasi-objective tests like the MEIS. Second, there are broad correlations between self-report EI and personality, as suggested by conceptual analyses. For example, the EQ-i is substantially correlated with low neuroticism, agreeableness, conscientiousness, and extraversion, although, perhaps surprisingly, its correlations with openness are modest (Dawda & Hart, 2000). The empirical and conceptual overlap between EI and personality represents a considerable challenge, and will be discussed further especially in chapters 5 and 9.

Emotional intelligence at the crossroads of intelligence and personality

Locating EI within the existing science of differential psychology requires it to be triangulated with respect to both intelligence and personality (and perhaps motivational dispositions, such as achievement motivation). Recent years have seen increasing interest in the relationship between personality and intelligence (see Saklofske & Zeidner, 1995; Sternberg & Rungis, 1994; Zeidner & Matthews, 2000). Although correlations between ability and personality constructs are frequently near zero (Ackerman & Heggestad, 1997), there may be some constructs, such as openness, that straddle both domains. Another such construct is *ego resiliency* (Block & Kremen, 1996), which relates to capacity for dynamic control of the environment, and correlates with IQ. The ego-resilient person experiences self-esteem, zest for life, and harmony with others. Like openness and ego-resiliency, "emotional intelligence appears as a variable on the boundary between personality and cognition" (McCrae, 2000, p. 268).

Personality-intelligence overlap may also be identified at the level of component processes (Matthews & Dorn, 1995; Zeidner & Matthews, 2000). Some specific processes may contribute to both personality and intelligence constructs, although the constructs concerned are largely independent and relate to different configurations of process. For example, impaired working memory is a feature of both neuroticism and low intelligence. Cognitive intelligence is occasionally linked, modestly, to processes more usually seen as an aspect of personality, such as coping (Haan, 1977) and resistance to trauma (McNally & Shin, 1995). Individual differences in information-processing may feed into not just intellectual abilities and acquired knowledge and skills, but also into processes supporting adaptation to other real-life challenges (Ackerman, 1996; Matthews & Dorn, 1995). For example, a good short-term memory for verbal material may influence acquisition of conversational skills and bias personality development toward extraversion (Matthews & Dorn, 1995). At the process level, then, the question is whether emotional competence is constructed from some of the same building blocks as intelligence and personality. Processing components that support accurate judgment of emotion or reasoning about emotions might contribute to both cognitive and emotional intelligences.

A significant obstacle to placing EI within the existing framework of differential psychology is lack of convergence between different EI measures. Bar-On (2000) refers to an unpublished finding that the correlation between the EQ-i and MSCEIT is only 0.46, a significant association, but much less than would be expected for two measures of the same underlying construct. Likewise, the MEIS predicts cognitive intelligence but the EQ-i does not, and the EQ-i is considerably more strongly associated with personality traits than the instruments devised by Mayer, Salovey, and Caruso, i.e., MEIS, MSCEIT (see Roberts, Zeidner et al., 2001). In sum, research on emotion intelligence must be integrated with current understanding of differential psychology at both psychometric and process levels, but the field also needs to resolve conflicts between different brands of EI.

Group differences in emotional intelligence: An uncharted domain?

Perhaps the most controversial issue associated with the study of human individual differences, if not psychology in general, is exploration of so-called group differences. In an age where political correctness is sacrosanct, the scientist is left with a research agenda that is bound to place them in a difficult position—to study specific populations, impartially, in order to communicate knowledge that may reduce inequalities. But at the same time, in drawing attention to these differences, the scientist is left open to charges of racism, sexism, ageism, and the like, particularly if even the most qualified of statements is treated unfairly in the media. Conversely, several researchers working within this area appear to have gone beyond the data. As one commentator, addressing the special case of intelligence testing, has remarked "of all the contentious issues thrown up ... few have aroused more bad feeling and generated more shoddy argument than the suggestion that different groups may differ in average IQ" (Mackintosh, 1998, p. 143).

It is perhaps necessary at this point to list some of the group differences appearing in the literature on intelligence, personality, and emotions, since these serve to inform us of group differences one might wish to explore in EI. Because this is a complex and controversial area we refrain from specifying the nature of these differences; fearing that to do them justice would require extensive, balanced treatment moving us too far afield (see, however, Mackintosh, 1998). For cognitive abilities, among the most salient differences would appear those exhibited between ethnic (or racial) groups, gender, specific age groups, and social class. In the area of personality, both age and gender have also been the target of extensive research, with some evidence also for ethnic differences in a personality dimension referred to as individualism-collectivism (see, e.g., Hui & Triandis, 1986). Emotions appear to be subject to complex developmental trajectories and differential effects related to gender (see, e.g., Saarni, 2000), and, in cross-cultural studies, there emerges a picture of universality of basic emotions, tempered by important cultural differences.

In many instances, the interpretation of group differences, their magnitude, and likely causative factors generally remains a matter of ongoing debate. For example, as noted in the introductory passages of the current book, a considerable amount of the momentum afforded to EI has arisen from a book that focuses, quintessentially, on group differences in intelligence—*The Bell Curve.* That differences in measured intelligence exist between ethnic (or racial) groups is, for many authors, an issue not so much of contention, but of careful, balanced interpretation (Mackintosh, 1998). For example, in a recent study, Roberts, Goff, et al. (2001) demonstrated that the intelligence test that gave rise to group differences in Herrnstein and Murray's major study, was a measure of crystallized intelligence, rather than the general factor. Thus conceived, the gap between ethnic groups in the United States is likely an environmental effect that could conceivably be reduced via interventions targeted towards acquired intellectual skills. In addition, many group differences may be peculiar to particular epochs in human history. For example, among the earliest documented group difference studied, was the observation that children living in the city obtained higher scores on intelligence tests than those living in rural areas (Thomson, 1921). Thomson speculated that this result might be attributed to the fact that the intelligent often moved from the country to town to take up financially rewarding forms of employment. Recent studies suggest that the size of this difference has declined dramatically in the United States, at least, such that these differences no longer approach statistical significance (Kaufman & Doppelt, 1976; Reynolds, Chastain, Kaufman & McLean, 1987).

Plausibly, because research into EI remains in its infancy, there are relatively few studies that explicitly investigate group differences in this psychological trait. This shortcoming makes definitive comments concerning group differences problematic. However, a handful of recent studies may be brought to bear on certain group differences, while some important principles from differential psychology suggest likely group differences in EI. In the passages that follow, we comment briefly on group differences in EI in light of these literatures. Because the most relevant data on group differences derive from operational indices, we also cover these issues in some depth, later, in chapter 5.

EI and gender differences With respect to gender, it is clear that different operational indices and indeed conceptualizations of EI lead to notably different hypotheses, conjectures, and/or empirical findings regarding group differences. For example, Goleman (1995) devotes an entire chapter to discussing emotional differences between the sexes. (Interestingly, Goleman uses these differences to explain rising divorce rates, suggesting "antidotes to marital disintegration are a small remedial education in emotional intelligence" [1995, p. 147]). His argument is simple: "Women, on the average, experience the entire range of emotions with greater intensity and more volatility than men—in this sense, women *are* more emotional than men" (1995, p. 132, italics his). Thus, Goleman would have us believe that women have higher EI than men—although it is unclear how heightened emotional experience represents an ability. In contrast, citing his normative sample, Bar-On (2000) notes no differences between males and females regarding overall emotional and social competence, though both gender groups do show slight differences (in their favor) in some domains. (Females score higher on interpersonal skills, men score higher on stress management and adaptation). In fact, existing personality data (e.g., Feingold, 1994) suggest that women score higher on some of the personality traits linked to EI, especially agreeableness and its components such as trust and tender-mindedness. Men, on the other hand, score higher on others, such as emotional stability, and there is no gender difference on still other relevant traits, such as conscientiousness and impulsivity. Objective indices of EI further muddy the waters. Using consensual scores, we found that a sample of females scored higher on the vast majority of subtests comprising the MEIS, with this trend actually reversed when expert scores were analyzed (Roberts, Zeidner, et al., 2001).

EI and ethnic differences As for gender differences, the available information on ethic differences in EI is both scant and contradictory. Inside Goleman's (1995) conceptualization, there is clearly an implicit assumption that citizens of diverse, racial and cultural origins can possess

EI, in equal measure. Supporting this proposition, Bar-On (2000), in examination of a North American sample, claims that there were no significant differences on social and EI between various ethnic groups administered the EQ-i. However, using the MEIS, we (Roberts, Zeidner, et al., 2001) discovered a rather unusual phenomena. Using consensual scores there appeared no difference between ethnic groups, and yet when expert scoring was used Whites outperformed minority groups on many of the sub-scales.

EI and age differences   Perhaps the most prolific area of research into group differences in intelligence focuses on cognitive aging. Interestingly, this area has turned up a number of interesting findings, including the fact that not all cognitive abilities show equal levels of improvement (or decline) over the life-span (see, e.g., Stankov, 1988). Similarly, there is evidence for a phenomenon known as *cognitive dedifferentiation*. Simply put, this refers to the fact that during childhood and late adulthood, abilities tend to cluster together more to define a general factor than through the middle period of life when cognitive abilities diverge to form separate broad abilities. This information clearly should inform research programs examining EI, though so far the types of investigation carried out to examine age differences has been both meager and contradictory. Bar-On (2000), for example, claims relatively small differences across the life-span, whereas Mayer, Salovey, et al. (1999) claim that increasing age differences are required of the MEIS, if it measures a legitimate form of intelligence. In providing preliminary data, they compared a sample of adolescents with a population of university students; two samples too close in age to make definitive statements.

EI and social class   Among the earliest documented of the various group differences studied, was the observation that children of "superior" social class outperformed children of "inferior" social class on measures of general intelligence (see, e.g., Terman & Merrill, 1937). These social class differences appear to have remained with us to the present point in time (see Mackintosh, 1998; Mascie-Taylor & Gibson, 1978; Waller, 1971). It is something of a curious oversight, especially given that the impetus of Goleman's (1995) book rests on its rebuttal of *The Bell Curve*, that no study, to our knowledge, has systematically examined EI in relation to socioeconomic status. Unfortunately, despite extravagant claims to the contrary, it remains entirely possible, given close links that we have already alluded to in respect of crystallized intelligence, that EI is positively associated with social class.

Group differences: A cautionary note   There would appear an urgent need for further research exploring group differences in EI. This appeal is nontrivial; in no small measure, the attraction of EI rests upon its inherent idealistic vision of an egalitarian society, but the data so far derived on group differences provides no definitive answers. Indeed, it remains entirely plausible that the abuses, with which intelligence tests have been subjected, could similarly be perpetuated with tests of EI— that some researcher could demonstrate (sincerely or otherwise) the existence of an "emotional" elite. While we hope that history does not repeat itself, we also feel compelled to call for balanced scientific studies of group differences, which demonstrate the qualities of EI that its major proponents would have us accept.

Differential psychology and EI: A summary
Differential psychology provides both a prototype of science, to which EI researchers might aspire, and a set of personality and intelligence constructs with which EI should *not* overlap substantially. The measures designed to assess both intelligence and personality subscribe to high psychometric standards, and within the tri-level cognitive science framework, the mechanisms underlying intelligence and personality constructs may be specified at various levels of explanation. It does not appear fancifully idealistic, therefore, to construct a science of EI that also meets these theoretical and psychometric criteria.

In terms of conceptual overlap, certain models of EI appear to share much in common with social intelligence, which in turn has been shown to share too much conceptual overlap with crystallized intelligence to constitute an independent domain of scientific inquiry. We note here, however, that no empirical data has yet been collected demonstrating the correspondence between EI and social intelligence, leaving this something of a speculative argument. Nevertheless, in those instances where conceptualizations of EI appear independent of intelligence, aspects of the Five Factor Model of personality may likewise explain much of the variation in what is claimed to be emotional intelligence. Our foray into discussion of group differences highlights inconsistencies in the various models of EI proposed. We also trust that it has alerted the reader to a number of empirical issues that seemingly have been ignored by proponents of EI, although they appear in large measure to account for its popularity.

Emotional Intelligence in the Real World: Practical Applications

It is largely because proponents of EI claim that this construct has real-world relevance that it has gained such widespread acceptance in both the academic and general community. Because this claim is central to understanding the scientific, social, and political value of EI, this exposition now turns to examination of proposed practical applications of EI. There is actually a paucity of studies measuring the practical utility of EI in various applied settings. This fact notwithstanding, in recent years, there has been increasing interest in applying this construct in educational, occupational, and clinical settings (Salovey, Woolery & Mayer, 2001). In part, this constitutes the zeitgeist that is EI. In the passages that follow, we discuss potential application of the EI construct in resolving real-world problems that are endemic to each of these three fields.

Clinical settings

EI is commonly held to play an important role in clinical applications. To begin with, EI is often viewed as a prerequisite for any form of change in behavior following psychotherapy. Thus, before a person is able to regulate, control, modify, or manage her emotion, she must first be open to the experience of emotion, be able to identify and discriminate among emotions, and to regulate emotions. The ability to understand and analyze emotions translates into the ability to understand one's self and one's relation to the environment better, which may foster effective emotional regulation and greater well being (Salovey, Bedell, Detweiler & Mayer, 2000).

Not only is EI viewed as a prerequisite to therapy, but high EI individuals would also be expected to be more amenable to treatment and more successful in achieving their therapeutic goals. Bar-On (1997) cites some preliminary research suggesting that individuals high in EI have greater reported gains in psychotherapy. Salovey, Bedell, et al. (2000) maintain that being able to recognize emotions and then modify the type of thoughts that lead up to an emotional reaction (i.e., emotion identification and assimilation components of EI) are central goals of treatment. Thus viewed, therapy requires helping a client to learn to discriminate between emotions; not only their own emotions but also those of others. Understanding emotions and using them to work through difficult situations in therapy is an important EI skill that may be taught. Whether it is the shoulder of a friend to cry upon or the pages of a notebook to write on, expressing emotions is a skill that appears integral to becoming an emotionally intelligent individual. Moreover, a disproportionate number of individuals suffering from clinical problems and disorders, all of whom typically show deficits in processing emotional information and in self-control, may be deficient in EI. Further still, EI is said to be applicable to a broad range of emotional problems embedded in both interpersonal and intrapersonal competencies (Salovey, Bedell, et al., 2000). Individuals who are best able to accurately perceive, understand, and empathize with other's emotions may be able to respond to their social environment and build a supportive social network that makes them less vulnerable to emotional disease.

A basic theme found in the EI literature is that emotionally intelligent individuals recognize and pursue the most effective means of coping, as discussed further in chapter 8. Thus, it is assumed that individuals skilled at regulating emotions should be better able to repair their emotional states by using pleasant activities as a distraction for negative affect. In particular, emotional disclosure, less rumination, increased social support, and so forth, are among the ways high EI individuals are said to manage to stay on top of life (Salovey, Bedell, et al., 2000).

It has also been conjectured that EI measures may be particularly useful for psychodiagnostic purposes. Thus, Mayer, Salovey & Caruso (2000) suggest that ability-based measures of EI may yield useful information in clinical settings about client's emotional resources and potential functioning. EI measures have been proposed to be helpful to clinicians in sizing up a client's emotional abilities, assessing what they know about emotions; whether or not they are able to identify their own and others emotions accurately; and whether the client has effective emotion management strategies available to them. Mayer and coworkers (2000) envision a time when clinicians will be able to enhance their prediction of a client's therapeutic progress, based in part on their level of EI.

Whereas psychologically handicapped individuals have been viewed as deficient in EI, psychotherapists have been viewed as experts in EI. Thus, psychotherapists trained in recognizing and interpreting emotions are called in to correct poor emotional education (Mayer & Salovey, 1997). Psychotherapists are trained in empathic listening, reflection of feelings, and searching for lost emotions that need to be constructed.

For instance, if a therapist sees a client who is abused, but yet denies anger, the therapist may inquire if the emotion is still there and help the individual to channel it positively for the purpose of self-protection and placing limits on other's appropriate behavior.

Occupational settings

A bewildering array of emotional and social competencies has been claimed to be critical precursors for success in occupational settings (see, e.g., Carson & Carson, 1998; Cooper & Sawaf, 1997; Goleman, 1999; Weisinger, 1998). These relevant competencies include emotional awareness (possessing psychological insights, recognizing and understanding sentiments in self and others), empathy (being attuned to social cues, recognizing and responding to the needs of others), and emotion regulation (being able to delay gratification, stifle impulses and bounce back from anxiety/depression). Goleman (1999) lists some 25 different competencies necessary for effective performance in the workplace, with different competencies believed to be required in different professions.

These issues notwithstanding, EI has been claimed to validly predict a variety of successful behaviors, on the job, at a level exceeding that of intelligence (see, e.g., Cooper & Sawaf, 1997; Weisinger, 1998). EI is claimed to predict occupational success because it influences one's ability to succeed in coping with environmental demands and pressures (Bar-On, 1997). Recently, the use of EI measures for career selection and placement purposes has become a common practice in many organizations in the Western world. Indeed, more and more companies are starting to realize that EI-related skills are a vital component of any organization's management philosophy. To this end, EI appears useful when evaluating ongoing functioning and the well being of employees at critical stages of their career (selection, placement, training, and promotion). It has also been claimed that EI is valid for gauging the impact and intervention effectiveness of organizational change and restructuring (Bar-On, 1997). For this reason, the past decade has witnessed a proliferation of programs designed to promote emotional skills and competencies in the occupational environment.

The ability to read people has been claimed to be an important ingredient in management effectiveness (Goleman, 1995, 1999). Indeed, managing people requires both technical, as well as, emotional, skills. Thus conceived, emotional knowledge and skills may provide new information on high-performance individuals and teams. Furthermore, individuals interested in encouraging managers in corporate settings to cultivate a broader range of skills than those relevant to technical aspects of one's job, have seized on EI as *the* construct capturing these diffuse competencies (Cooper & Sawaf, 1997; Goleman, 1999; Weisinger, 1998). Nevertheless, extant research strongly supports two basic findings. First, for most jobs, general intelligence is the single, strongest predictor of objective performance indicators, such as productivity. Second, the value of personnel to the organization depends not just on objective performance but on qualities such as personal reliability and integrity and ability to work with others.

Educational settings

Current attitudes to education in the developed world reveal a paradox. On the one hand, there is an increasing emphasis on objective performance and examination success, with some evidence of rising standards. On the other hand, educators have become increasingly concerned by the incidence of behavioral problems, and a perceived loss of values and self-control, highlighted by the recent outbreak of school shootings in the United States. It is claimed that such problems reflect a failure to train students in the social and emotional skills thought to underlie EI. Thus, an increasing number of educators and psychologists believe that children's emotional learning should be given serious consideration and promoted in schools (Elias et al., 1997).

It has been argued that EI plays a major role in the development of emotional and social skills prerequisite for school learning and adjustment (Eisenberg, Cumberland & Spinrad, 1998). Inside this cocoon of optimism, EI has also been claimed to be of prime importance for academic success and productive experience in the school setting (Elias et al., 1997). Similarly, EI programs are claimed to favorably influence academic achievement; improving children's academic achievement scores and school performance (Goleman, 1995).

It is commonly held that it may be possible to educate those who are low in emotional competencies to improve their abilities to better recognize their feelings, express them, and regulate them (Mayer & Geher, 1996). Consequently, even if the socialization of emotions in the child's early familial (or social environment) was not entirely optimal, there is some possibility for remedial learning in the schools to take place. In short, schools can correct some of the deficits in emotional learning (Mayer & Geher, 1996). Thus, the idea that social and emotional problems of young people can be addressed through school-based intervention programs became popular among educational reformers during the past decade or so.

In schools, the popularity of programs designed to encourage socio-emotional learning or character education (Cohen, 1999a, 1999b; Elias et al., 1997) has led to the search for a unifying idea bridging interest in the development of morality and acquisition of social problem-solving skills. For some, EI has provided this unifying framework. Indeed, a wide array of curricular-based programs seeks to educate children about the value of EI and foster the development of specific emotional competencies, e.g., recognition of emotions in self and others, empathy, conflict resolution (see Cohen, 1999). These programs include many different components. For example, one program includes instructions in identifying and labeling feelings, expressing feelings, assessing intensity of feelings, impulse control, reduced stress, understanding perspective of others, verbal communication skills, using steps for problem solving, and having a positive attitude towards life.

Applications of EI: A summary
A major impetus for EI has been its proposed relevance to solving real-world problems that currently plague Western society. Clearly, proponents of EI have discovered one of (if not) *the* most important psychological construct(s), of all time, if it can be demonstrated that raising EI will help improve the quality of the individual's private and occupational life, and reduce crime and interpersonal strife. More importantly, perhaps, what EI offers through educational interventions is the hope of a more egalitarian and utopian society. Ranged against these promises are some grounds for skepticism. The literature discussed above touches on three broad areas of applied psychology, which have rich research histories: clinical, organizational, and educational psychology. In fact, applied psychologists have accumulated quite a good deal of information on the effects of intelligence, personality, and affect on specific issues endemic to these three fields. The prevailing wisdom is that there is no magic bullet for defeating emotional problems, but that different problems, require different solutions. It remains to be established that interventions that directly target EI add to existing interventions. Furthermore, EI may be a source of confusion rather than assistance. The lack of conceptual clarity in defining EI means that different programs purporting to raise EI may be addressing, in fact, different psychological qualities. The lack of a strong theoretical basis for EI renders the development of such programs problematic, in any

case. If EI in fact overlaps considerably with existing intelligence and personality constructs, then reference to EI may obscure which of these multiple, independent constructs is actually relevant to the problem at hand. There is a considerable dissonance between the grandiose claims made for EI, and the limited and preliminary nature of the relevant scientific research. In part III of this book, we will evaluate where the potential value of applications based on EI lies, between two polar extremes. At best, EI may provide a rationale for a fresh approach to old problems that will dramatically improve over existing solutions. At worst, we might be drawn to reframe certain analogies we have made in these introductory chapters. For example, rather than an old wine in a new bottle, EI might more appropriately be considered a psychological form of snake oil.

Claims concerning the importance of EI in applied domains hinge on a demonstration that is distinct from concepts and practical interventions that are more fully understood. In evaluating the potential of EI, we address three areas of application. In a chapter on clinical issues, we examine whether or not individuals exhibiting a variety of clinical syndromes (e.g., alexithymia, various personality disorders) may be characterized as lacking in EI. In this chapter, we also examine the degree to which theories of EI add anything new to existing cognitive-behavioral and psychobiological treatments for such disorders. In a chapter devoted to issues underlying organizational psychology, we will consider whether programs said to raise EI may enhance both objective performance and other aspects of behavior in the workplace. In a chapter devoted to education and EI, we examine the role of cognitive and emotional intelligence in the classroom, the success of "emotional literacy" programs, and the extent to which EI should be an explicit focus for intervention.

Conclusion: Toward a Science of EI

Much work remains to be done before EI can be seen as an established construct like cognitive intelligence or the Big Five personality factors. In this chapter, as well as introducing these fields of psychological inquiry, we have mapped some of the steps to be taken in developing a scientific account of EI. At the psychometric level, it is essential to devise reliable tests that correlate highly with one another (convergent validity), and less strongly with known, individual difference constructs (divergent validity). Barriers to this research program include difficulties in deciding on the appropriate content for tests and scoring problems. Performance-based tests suffer from lack of explicit veridical criteria for correct responses to items, whereas questionnaire, self-assessments are open to response bias. There is a growing literature on the predictive validity of measures for EI, but a potential problem is lack of distinctiveness from existing constructs, especially for questionnaire measures. Correlations with external criteria may be a consequence of confounding of EI scales with personality and intelligence. Some of these difficulties may be addressed using normal psychometric techniques, such as writing better items or including additional items to counter reliability problems. Other difficulties may be more entrenched and intractable (e.g., scoring problems). The problem to which we turn in the next two chapters is the neglect of the existing research literatures on intelligence and emotion. We will review evidence-based conceptions of intellectual and emotional function, and consider how they constrain the nature of any additional emotional intelligence. The final chapter in part I then addresses empirical studies of existing tests of EI.

A major element in redressing psychometric shortcomings is the development of a stronger theoretical rationale to guide item selection, scoring, and discriminations between EI and other aspects of individual differences. However, theory development is especially challenging because of the conceptual indeterminacy and complexity of emotion, emotion-regulation, and adaptation. It is unlikely that EI, if it exists, is a property of some single key neural or cognitive process. Instead, it may be distributed across a variety of processes, at different levels of abstraction. We presented a cognitive science framework that permits accounts of EI in terms of neural processes, the constraints on information-processing set by the cognitive architecture, and high-level cognition and self-knowledge. Interlevel constructs such as strategy use and neural nets may also have explanatory potential. There is a plethora of biological and cognitive theory that is potentially relevant to EI. We return to this topic in part II of the present book. We also highlighted the promise of EI for practical, real-world interventions, but at this early stage of research this promise is yet to be unrealized. In part III we look at whether it is realistic to expect EI research to provide a panacea for psychological problems, within the arenas of clinical, occupational, and educational psychology.

3

Understanding the Intelligence Component of Emotional Intelligence

Abilities are analogous to the elements in the periodic table: Some, like fluid intelligence, are obviously important as carbon or oxygen; others are more like the rare earth elements whose importance have not always been appreciated or become apparent—their possible importance is unpredictable

John B. Carroll

Why Mess with Intelligence?

As we noted from the outset, the concept of emotional intelligence has gained a great deal of scientific credibility by linking concepts underlying the study of emotions (and emotionality) with those comprising the investigation of human cognitive abilities (i.e., intelligence). These two main ingredients of EI have sometimes been placed at opposite ends of a behavioral continuum. This dichotomy arose, in particular, from Western philosophical traditions that often predated modern psychology, and viewed reason and intellect as opposing forces to supposedly nonrational phenomenon like passion, intuition, feeling, and emotions (see chapter 1). Belabored by these traditions, the study of emotions appears, to some, as a 'soft' branch of psychology. In contrast, intelligence research, by virtue of its focus on understanding rational reason, appears among the most hard-core and/or scientific of the psychological disciplines.

Philosophical influences aside, the study of intelligence has flourished, certainly in giving to society the intelligence test, which many commentators see as the most practical contribution made to humanity by all of psychology (e.g., Anastasi & Urbina, 1997). Two lines of converging evidence support this assertion. First, standardized tests of intelligence are widespread across the Western world, influencing individual life decisions. For example, in the United States alone, performance on the Armed Services Vocational Aptitude Battery (one of many thousands of standardized intelligence tests) is a major determinant in the career choices of over 1.3 *million* people per annum (Kaplan & Saccuzzo, 1997). Second, various meta-analyses (a statistical procedure that summarizes data obtained across many, different studies) have indicated that measures of intelligence predict job and academic performance particularly well. Indeed, these instruments appear better for this purpose than any other measure of psychological, sociological, or demographic significance (see, e.g., Herrnstein & Murray, 1994; Hunter, 1986; Hunter & Hunter, 1984; Hunter & Schmidt, 1996; Schmidt & Hunter, 1998; Schmidt, Ones & Hunter, 1992).

Findings on normal (nonclinical) emotional functioning, while often useful and certainly making valuable contributions to scientific knowledge per se, seem not to have had anywhere near the same impact on society. In part, this is because the constructs studied in this psychological domain, as we have seen, do not lend themselves easily to a universally agreed upon series of measurement operations. In contrast, it would appear that there is a consensus on how to best determine an individual's intelligence level. Equally important, many of the major figures in intelligence research (see below) have pioneered various multivariate statistical procedures, giving this field a rigorous methodological apparatus to address issues of major theoretical and practical importance.

Inside this context, the conceptual pairing of emotions and intelligence might be construed as an attempt to greater legitimize the field of emotions and enhance its impact on society (see Stankov, 2001a). This assumption certainly seems feasible and not without justification given the many claims concerning measures of EI and their utility in clinical, organizational, and educational settings as valid selection devices (see part III). But in so doing, it is important to bear in mind that the study of intelligence has a rich history that should not be ignored. It seems curious that major efforts to introduce the concept of EI have often neglected systematic examination of the intelligence literature, arguably re-inventing (or worse still, ignoring) a wheel that is scientifically and conceptually sophisticated. For example, Goleman's (1995) influential book on EI pays only rather minor lip service to intelligence research. Indeed, only a handful of intelligence theories are discussed and among these, certain (e.g., Gardner, 1983) are quite controversial and not so widely accepted as he appears to construe (see, e.g., Carroll, 1993, p. 641). Indeed, with the possible exception of Mayer, Salovey, Caruso, and colleagues, the intelligence component of EI receives short shrift in leading reviews and empirical research devoted to the topic.

The purpose of the present chapter is to fill in a conceptual void in the emotional intelligence literature. In particular, we wish to provide the reader with a balanced (and mature) account of major issues, concepts, findings, consensus, and controversies that over a century of research into cognitive abilities has given us. Central to this exposition are a number of formal, structural models of intelligence that have been put forward to account for the available empirical data. Each model has important implications as to whether EI might constitute a legitimate domain of scientific inquiry. Both unique and congruent features of these cognitive ability models are emphasized. To this end, structural, experimental, genetic, and developmental data are examined in relation to testable predictions made by each model. We will also determine whether the available evidence points to the efficacy of one theory of cognitive abilities over all others. Implications that ensue for the concept of EI from each model are also discussed. Later in the chapter, we explore several other theories of intelligence, which are theoretical (rather than, structural) in scope. We also advise the reader to supplement this chapter with the exposition of social intelligence provided in appendix A.

A brief outline of the history and conceptual underpinnings of "intelligence" precedes a formal evaluation of the various models. An attempt is made to provide a working definition of the concept of "intelligence," one that may guide the decision of which structural theory of cognitive abilities (among several viable alternatives) is to be preferred. Historical and conceptual issues of relevance to the study of EI, which we carry through the remainder of this chapter, are also highlighted.

The History of Intelligence

Overview and leading figures

The history of research into human cognitive abilities and intelligence testing makes for a fascinating read. One hears stories of fabricated data (see, e.g., Hearnshaw, 1979), documented racist conclusions and eugenic implications (see, e.g., Gould, 1997), rising intelligence scores (e.g., Flynn, 1987), and policy recommendations (e.g., Browne-Miller, 1995). Its characters and events often seem more fictional, more soap-like, than real. It is beyond the scope and requirements of the present book to touch upon this history in any great depth. The interested reader can consult any of several histories on cognitive abilities, including books and articles written specifically on the topic (or books that are part of longer treatments of intelligence theory). Among several that we believe do justice to this topic's complex tapestry are Carroll (1982, 1993), DuBois (1970), Gregory (1996), Fancher (1985), Mackintosh (1998), Robert Thorndike and Lohman (1990), and Sokal (1987).

Nevertheless, it is necessary to touch on the contributions of three figures that have influenced theoretical, methodological, and pragmatic developments in the discipline.[1] The first is Sir Francis Galton (1869, 1879, 1883, 1908), who pioneered attempts to relate chronometric measures (derived from timed performance) and anthropometric indices (representing physical attributes of humans) to intellectual ability (as represented by position in society). Galton also introduced the concept of correlation to the study of individual differences, conceived the idea of percentiles, and drew attention to the typical Gaussian normal distribution (i.e., bell curve) that measures of cognitive ability form. His influence is still felt today, through these statistical techniques and especially in the cognitive-correlates approach. In this approach, tasks from experimental cognitive psychology, with rich theoretical architectures, are used to provide greater insight into performance on intelligence tests (e.g., Jensen, 1998; Matthews & Dorn, 1989; Roberts & Stankov, 1999; Sternberg, 1977; Widman & Carlson, 1988).

A second major figure is Alfred Binet. Along with Theophile Simon (1905a, 1905b, 1916/1983), Binet, after a period of investigating (and becoming increasingly frustrated with) simple tasks analogous to those used by Galton, essentially created the modern intelligence test. Charged to produce a selection device for the determination of intellectually disabled children in Parisian schools, Binet and Simon concluded that tests comprising more complex tasks, analogous to mental activities required in school, were more promising measures of human intelligence. Since that time, virtually all attempts to measure intelligence have used the ideas and procedures pioneered by Binet within their design. Indeed, one of the leading contemporaneous intelligence tests (i.e., Stanford-Binet Intelligence Scales—Revision IV) still carries his name (see Thorndike, Hagen & Sattler, 1986).

The final figure in this historically influential triptych (see figure 3.1) was Charles Spearman (1904), who developed the procedure of factor analysis. Spearman was also the first individual to attempt to model and provide a series of theories to explain intelligence. Here we refrain from

Figure 3.1
Three pioneers of the science of intelligence: Galton, Binet, and Spearman.

discussing his contributions too much, since his model remains as alive and well today as in the past. As such, it is covered in detail later in this chapter. Nevertheless, his attempt to provide a taxonomic model describing intelligent behavior, through the process of factor analysis, has influenced the science of human cognitive abilities immensely. Indeed, several commentators have argued that attempts to provide structural models of intelligence remains among the field's most important undertakings (see, e.g., Hunt, 2001).

History lessons for the study of emotional intelligence
As we have demonstrated from the outset, systematic research into EI is a little over a decade old. In contrast, the concept of intelligence has been around for over a century, during which period a corpus of scientific research has accumulated to better understand its structure, processes, and mechanisms. What is particularly interesting, however, is that the types of issues that dogged the early pioneers of intelligence seem to be among those providing the most serious challenges to researchers interested in EI. For example, as was the case for Binet, two different ways of assessing EI (self-report versus performance-based indices) confronts the scientist (or practitioner) interested in measuring this construct (see chapter 5). Issues pertaining to the structure of EI, like those that confronted Spearman, are currently at the fore, though given nowhere near the importance they might rightfully be afforded (see Roberts et al., 2001b). It would also not seem too fanciful to assume that with advances in the measurement of EI, establishing the cognitive

correlates of EI (which dominate modern approaches to intelligence and may be traced to Galton) will drive future research in the field.

From the history of intelligence testing there is also a lesson to be learned by those peddling the virtues of EI tests as selection devices in educational, clinical, and organizational settings. In the early days of psychometric testing, flagrant abuses were commonplace. For example, immigrants to the United States, landing on Ellis Island in the early 1900s, were often classified as "feebleminded" (with all the resulting social stigma attached), based on scores obtained with the newly emerging intelligence test (see, e.g., Gelb, 1986; Gould, 1981; Gregory, 1996). With the benefit of hindsight, this was essentially because at the time, researchers poorly understood cognitive abilities, and especially the conditions under which they should be assessed and the actual domains that should be assessed. It is to be hoped that the use of EI measures in contemporary society will be treated with great sensitivity until when our knowledge concerning this construct is more fully formed.

The Concept of Intelligence

Definitions: A critique

The concept of intelligence, like that of much psychological terminology, means something far more precise than the way in which it might be used by the average person on the street. Unfortunately, while scientific concepts should ideally remain free of social values, intelligence is something that remains prized in many cultures. Hence, while dictionary definitions might do injustice to the technical distinctions that the specialist wishes to make, they are nonetheless suggestive of the source of this concept's value-laden connotations.

In a culture where knowledge equates with status, if intelligence is taken to mean "the ability to learn and know; understanding; intellect; mind" (Barnhart et al., 1974, p. 1088), then to be labeled intelligent is highly desirable. Psychologists are seldom able to escape populist notions once they invoke terminology such as "aptitude," "general ability," "IQ," and the like. All too often the results from psychological experiments are used to encourage views in which the central premise is that the possession of high intelligence is a necessary prerequisite for life success (e.g., Herrnstein & Murray, 1994).

Allowing that popular notions of intelligence are too subjective, is it possible to find within the psychological (or educational) literature a meaning that stands up to empirical and/or philosophical scrutiny?

Seemingly from several conferences, spanning some 70 years and attended by large numbers of luminaries in this area (e.g., Jensen, 1987a, 1987b; Sternberg & Berg, 1986; Sternberg & Detterman, 1986; E. Thorndike et al., 1921), there appears more controversy than consensus. One possible reason for this unusual state of affairs may be that few psychologists have attempted to understand the nature of human intelligence, yet all too many have wanted to join in the discourse surrounding it. The possibility has been expressed that psychometricians are "more interested in finding large correlations and making practical predictions with their IQ tests than in advancing our scientific understanding of intelligence itself" (Jensen, 1980, p. 688).

A brief examination of various definitions of intelligence offered by prominent psychologists working in the area illustrates its elusive character. For instance, Charles Spearman (1923, 1927) had taken it to mean "the eduction of relations and correlates," in the process emphasizing the notion of "mental energy." Philip Vernon (1950), on the other hand, believed that intelligence equates with "all-round thinking capacity" or "mental efficiency." Further still, David Wechsler (1974), who developed one of the most popular psychometric measures, defined intelligence as "the aggregate or global capacity of the individual to think rationally, to act purposefully and to deal effectively with his/her environment."

An operational definition has also been put forward, which essentially maintains that intelligence is what intelligence tests test (Boring, 1923). Each of these definitions (and several others offered as alternatives) seems to contain serious flaws. For instance, in Spearman's (1927) account it would appear unsound to pre-suppose the existence of some force that lies behind or explains behavior (Ryle, 1949), while in Wechsler's (1974) account the criteria only obscure a precise conceptualization of intelligence. The meaning of "to act purposefully" or "to think rationally" varies as a function of the individual, situation, or culture and concurrently introduces the problems of teleology. Finally, the operational definition suffers since it begs the question, What is an intelligence test? (see, however, Hunt, 2001, for an interesting, alternative perspective).

Intelligence and definitional controversies
In light of this problem of definition, several commentators have argued that the concept of intelligence should be rendered obsolete (e.g., Ceci, 1990; Ceci & Liker, 1986, 1988; Howe, 1988a, 1988b, 1990a, 1990b; see

also Eysenck, 1988; Howard, 1993; Sternberg, 1988, for alternative views). In perhaps the most vitriolic of these critiques, Michael Howe (1990a, 1990b) argues that intelligence is a word that may be used to *describe* certain classes of behavior but which at all costs should *not* be invoked to *explain* behavior. For Howe, intelligence serves two important descriptive functions and nothing more. Thus, the word "intelligence" exists as a label, firstly, identifying concern with various psychological capacities that help an organism adapt to its environment and secondly, indicating how well a person deals with certain cognitive problems. When used as an explanatory construct, Howe argues, "intelligence" is either reified or misused relying on a linguistic sleight-of-hand whereby the descriptive function that it serves forms the basis of explanation.

Importantly, Howe concedes, "The absence of logical grounds for assuming that intelligence must have a conceptual status other than that of a descriptive or labeling construct does not justify our ruling out the *possibility* that there might still exist a quality of intelligence which can help to account for people's abilities" (1990a, p. 491). To this end, he examines the empirical evidence for intelligence, suggesting that this research remains flawed both methodologically and in the interpretation of results. While a critique of Howe's arguments is outside the scope of the present book (see, however, Nettelbeck, 1990) it is clear that his criticisms concerning the empirical status of intelligence rest on the assumption of a single, general factor. This factor, known as psychometric *g* (see, e.g., Spearman, 1904), which we review later in this chapter, nonetheless has a status that, in and of itself, is largely questionable. It is doubtful whether many of the empirical problems Howe raises apply equally well, if at all, to a multidimensional model of human cognitive abilities.

Similar attacks on the concept of intelligence have been made by Stephen Ceci (1990), often with the support of interesting empirical data. For example, Ceci and Liker (1986, 1988) have demonstrated that a group of highly successful gamblers, betting on harness racing, used amazingly complex algorithms, indeed, ones educated mathematicians might struggle to develop. One might expect these individuals to have high IQs and yet their measured general intelligence was in the average range. Without going into details, the arguments subsequently put forward by Ceci and colleagues, to downplay the importance of intelligence, contain certain logical problems (see, e.g., Brody, 1992; Detterman & Spry, 1988; Flynn, 1999). We would argue most importantly that Ceci's arguments are rendered less convincing by the proposition, argued in this chapter, that intelligence is a multifaceted construct.

Intelligence as prototype and implicit theories

Ulric Neisser (1979) offers an alternative approach to dealing with the lack of consensus surrounding the meaning of the concept "intelligence." Using principles derived from cognitive psychology, Neisser asserts that a person's intelligence is mainly a function of their resemblance to prototypically intelligent individuals. For Neisser, no single definition of intelligence is adequate "because no single characteristic defines the prototype" (1979, p. 218). While Neisser's dissertation challenges conventional attempts at defining intelligence, it is also possible to interpret his ideas as supporting a view whereby intelligence is perceived as something that is multidimensional rather than unidimensional.

Using Neisser's (1979) approach, Robert Sternberg and colleagues (Sternberg, Conway, Ketron & Bernstein, 1981) obtained a list of behaviors judged by people as "ideally intelligent," which they factor analyzed (in a fashion similar to lexical analysis of the Big Five). These "ideally intelligent" behaviors fall into three distinct classes that Sternberg and colleagues have labeled problem solving ability, verbal ability, and social intelligence/competence. Using data obtained from listing prototypes, there is no evidence for sets of independent "factors" corresponding to each individual's notion of intelligence nor indeed is there evidence for a single general construct of intelligence.

In light of the above, it is important to note that a theme emerging in some commentators' writing, is that the notion that a single factor, psychometric g, is an extremely naive conceptualization of intelligence. Certainly, several authors argue, a general factor conceptualization of intelligence is of little (at best, minor) empirical or theoretical worth (e.g., Detterman, 1982; Horn, 1985; Roberts, Goff et al., 2001; Stankov, 2001b). The available empirical evidence (to be examined shortly) largely supports the view that "intelligence" is composed of several broad factors of ability. If this is the case, intelligence has not been defined adequately, because there are in fact not one but several different types of abilities. Indeed, since empirical data suggests that these cognitive abilities are relatively structurally independent of one another, it appears that each requires its own, separate conceptualization.

Problems defining intelligence and its implications for emotional intelligence

If there was an agreed consensus on the precise, scientific meaning of "intelligence," the conceptual pairing of emotions and intelligence could be accepted or rejected on a priori grounds. That no singular definition of intelligence suffices suggests that there is likely to be a good deal of debate in the scientific literature surrounding the use of the term "emotional intelligence" now, and in the future. Moreover, if intelligence is best conceived as a multidimensional entity, then one of these multidimensional components *could* be the influence of emotions on cognitive behavior, something we might subsequently label emotional intelligence.

An interesting issue emanating from the preceding discussion is that despite differences in emphasis, many commentators equate intelligence with the ability of the organism to *adapt* to its environment (e.g., Howe, 1990a; Sternberg, 1985; Thorndike et al., 1921; Wechsler, 1981). We have already linked EI to adaptation in chapter 2 and will return to it again in the next chapter, and in part II of the present volume. Moreover, one of the chief methodologies employed in the measurement of EI, as we have seen, uses consensus-based scoring. This form of scoring (or close derivatives) has had great survival value, witnessed in chronicles from the first century of our era (e.g., gladiators in the Coliseum) through to the present day, where many political leaders are elected through consensual processes.[2] In using this scoring procedure, the ecological validity of performance-based approaches to the assessment of emotional intelligence should not be underestimated (Roberts, Zeidner et al., 2001).

The research conducted by Sternberg et al. (1981), which derives from Neisser's idea of intelligence as prototype, also suggests there may be some psychological utility to the concept of EI. Central to this research, is the distinction between explicit and implicit theories of intelligence.[3] Clearly, the importance of the former is self-evident to developing scientific models of intellectual functioning. However, Sternberg et al. (1981) argue, "Implicit theories are (also) interesting ... because these theories may suggest aspects of intelligent behavior that need to be understood but are overlooked in available explicit theories of intelligence" (1981, p. 38). On the basis of data obtained by Sternberg et al., because social intelligence was conceptually (and factorially) distinct from other forms of cognitive ability, it appears extant explicit theories have erred in not considering it a crucial component of intelligence. Significantly, as noted in chapter 2, a number of theories of EI view it as a component of social intelligence (see, e.g., Goleman, 1995; Mayer et al., 1999; Salovey et al., 2000).

Of course, proponents of EI, who suggest it is separate from (or indeed more important) than social intelligence (e.g., Bar-On, 1997), would have to account for the fact that implicit theories fail to uncover an independent EI construct. On the other hand, critics of EI, so defined, might use this investigation to buttress arguments against EI. In short, the evidence to date from research into implicit theories could be used to either confirm or reject the existence of EI; this research is far from definitive. There is another intriguing issue associated with implicit theories, which we believe might be worthwhile investigating empirically and which might bring into question the efficacy of this approach to understanding the concept of intelligence per se. Given the widespread popularization of EI by the media during the past five years it is entirely possible that a study of implicit theories conducted *today* might yield an independent construct that we would label EI. Clearly, it is questionable whether a science of human cognitive abilities should focus on what might simply be a media invention.

The definitional issues touched on in the preceding passages also have clear implications for an important aim of the current chapter. In the search for an efficacious model of intelligence, a *crucial* prerequisite would appear to be the formulation and establishment of broad factors of ability within any given theory. Thus, while single factor models are considered in the preceding review of structural models of intelligence, the *explicit* reliance on explanation of intelligent behavior in terms of a general factor is seen as a major shortcoming of such theories.

Structural Theories of Intelligence

Spearman's theory of psychometric g
Overview Perhaps the most famous theory of intelligence is that offered by Spearman (1904, 1923, 1927) who proposed that there are two factors underlying mental test performance: a general factor (g) and specific factors (s).[4] Since specific factors are unique to performance on any cognitive test, whereas the general factor permeates performance on all intellectual tasks, Spearman postulated that g alone is of psychological significance. Individual differences in general mental ability, Spearman hypothesized, are the result of differences in the magnitude of mental energy invested in any given task. Throughout his writings, Spearman suggests that such individual differences must ultimately be understood in terms of the variation in people's abilities to use three "qualitative principles of cognition": apprehension of experience, eduction of relations, and the eduction of correlates.[5]

It is worth noting that these three principles, in the strict sense of the term, constitute an attempt to provide a *cognitive* model to intelligence long before cognitive psychology had actually become a legitimate psychological discipline (see Spearman, 1923). Thus, Spearman speculated that the ability to educe relations and correlates represented a form of mental processing with identifiable neurophysiological substrates that were largely inherited. A particular strength of these three laws of "noegenesis" is that they provide important guidelines for test construction. The Raven's Progressive Matrices Tests, for example, were constructed on the premise that the eduction of relations and correlates is central to intelligent behavior (J. C. Raven, 1938; J. C. Raven, Court & J. Raven, 1979).

The equivocal nature of Spearman's theory of g   Support for Spearman's theory is claimed to occur whenever there is positive manifold among cognitive test intercorrelations and a large first principal component (see, e.g., Jensen, 1993a). However, as Horn (1985) argues, the first principal component is no more than a good weighted linear combination of the abilities of a test battery and as such does not represent any test of a single factor model. Different collections of ability tests may yield different principal components, since no one intelligence test provides a representative sample of the known abilities that might legitimately constitute the domain of intelligence. There can be no singular *g* because this varies from occasion to occasion, depending on the arbitrary collection of tests chosen by the experimenter (e.g., Horn, 1985; Humphreys, 1979; Stankov, 2001b; Thomson, 1939/1948).

In a similar vein, some researchers have suggested that the reasons for measures of people's performance correlating positively on any two tasks may be the result of any number of attributes, in isolation or combination (e.g., Howe, 1990a). This possibility is a particularly difficult problem for any single factor theory of intelligence to counter, especially as the derivation of a general factor initially involves comparing correlation coefficients between each pair of test scores.

Of perhaps greatest concern to proponents of single factor theory, though, is the vast literature from diverse areas of psychology that suggests that different cognitive abilities have different construct validities. Particularly pertinent is research emanating from cognitive processing science, developmental psychology, neurology, and behavioral genetics that attest to this phenomenon (see, e.g., Horn, 1985, 1986, 1988, 1989; Horn & Hofer, 1992; Stankov, Boyle & Cattell, 1995). We take this argument up in some detail later in this chapter when discussing hierarchical models of intelligence.

Of some additional significance is the fact that studies designed as specific tests of Spearman's theory often suggest that it cannot account for differences in human intellectual capacity. For instance, Rimoldi (1948) concludes that more than one common factor accounted for his data, designed specifically to provide a general factor. This result has been replicated in several studies with different tests and populations, using a variety of statistical techniques, including both confirmatory and exploratory factor analysis (e.g., Botzum, 1951; Cohen, 1959; Corter, 1952; Martin & Adkins, 1954; McArdle & Horn, 1983).

In juxtaposition to the criticisms given above, it would be remiss not to acknowledge Jack Carroll's *Human cognitive abilities: A survey of factor-analytic studies* (1993). In some 477 data sets that Carroll reanalyzed (representing the major research conducted in the psychometric tradition during the twentieth century) there is evidence for a general intelligence factor. However, as Horn (1998) has argued, the most tenuous factor within this three-stratum model is undoubtedly the highest order construct (i.e., *g*). In support of this assertion, Horn (1998) notes a number of theoretical and practical difficulties for the general factor, which have seemingly passed critical attention. Most damning is Horn's (1998) contention that, of the 33 separate analyses conducted by Carroll (1993) in support of psychometric *g*, the factor derived from one analysis turns out to be conceptually dissimilar to those of further analyses.

To highlight the impact of Horn's argument, consider how psychometric *g* has been conceptualized within the wider scientific literature. Certain researchers suggest that fluid intelligence (a construct we discuss shortly that derives from incidental learning and is tied to reasoning) is analogous to the general factor (e.g., Gustafsson, 1984). Others, however, claim that "verbal/math [a very different construct, related more to crystallized intelligence, also described below] ... is frequently considered the avatar of *g*" (Stauffer, Ree & Carretta, 1996, p. 199 [brackets ours]; see also Herrnstein & Murray, 1994; Matarazzo, 1972). These seemingly contradictory positions may be reconciled by the fact, mentioned earlier, that the meaning of the general factor can be made to vary considerably depending on the mix of psychometric instruments used in a given study. Thus, commentators equating *g* with verbal/math do so simply because they have extracted the general factor from tests where these concepts are heavily assessed. Other commentators (examining a very different selection of tests) will link it to processes like reasoning (if there is an overabundance of reasoning tests) or sometimes sensory processes (if, say, there are a large number of visualization measures) (Stankov, 2001b). In short, the confusion generated by these varying conceptualizations of the *g* construct seems difficult to reconcile with its reputed sound, scientific status.

Neo-Spearmanian approaches to psychometric g

Overview   Despite the lack of empirical data supporting Spearman's *g*, features of this theory are endorsed either implicitly or explicitly in several contemporary models of intelligence (e.g., Belmont, Butterfield & Ferretti, 1982; Jensen, 1985a, 1985b, 1992b, 1993a). In the case of implicit attempts at retaining *g*, the terminology has been replaced with concepts such as "Executive Functioning" (see Belmont et al., 1982). Detterman (1982) argues that such constructs nonetheless assume that a unitary process circumscribes performance on all cognitive tasks. In turn, individual differences are responsible for manifest differences in this process.

A more explicit attempt to retain the essential aspects of psychometric *g* has been that made by Arthur Jensen and his collaborators. These researchers have retained not only much of Spearman's terminology but also the spirit of his many research proposals (e.g., Jensen, 1985b, 1987c, 1987d, 1987e, 1992b, 1998; Kranzler & Jensen, 1994; Jensen & Weng, 1994). Consideration is given to Jensen's application of this particular theory, since a considerable body of present-day research in the field of human intelligence assumes the efficacy of this model as a given.

The contribution of Arthur Jensen   Jensen (1970, 1974) originally endorsed a theory in which a distinction was made between level 1 and level 2 abilities. In this theory, level 1 abilities require minimal mental transformation and manipulation when compared to level 2 abilities. The usefulness of this theory has increasingly been shown to be questionable (see Horn & Stankov, 1982; Stankov, 1987a; Stankov, Horn & Roy, 1980). Subsequently, Jensen (1980) appears to have abandoned this model in favor of a neo-Spearmanian approach.

Throughout more contemporary writings, Jensen (e.g., 1980, 1982, 1985b, 1987e, 1990, 1992c, see also Jensen & Weng, 1994) provides several reasons for moving to posit a new theory of general intelligence. These arguments have been systematized in a book (Jensen, 1998) and numerous research articles. Some of the more crucial arguments presented by Jensen, include the following:

The existence of positive manifold   A particularly robust finding in intelligence research acknowledges that intelligence tests, almost without exception, correlate in a lawful fashion. "The fact that, in large unre-stricted samples of the population, the correlations are virtually always *positive*" means "that the tests all measure some common source of vari-ance in addition to whatever else they may measure" (Jensen & Weng, 1994, p. 232).

The stability of g across test batteries   Jensen (1992b, 1998) claims that however *g* is extracted from a correlation matrix (i.e., whichever method of factor analysis is used), the coefficient of congruence (a measure of how similar constructs are) between factor solutions remains high (see also Jensen & Weng, 1994). The astute reader will note that this claim is clearly at odds with the previously elucidated diversity of definitions of *g*, and Horn's (1998) critique of Carroll's (1993) attempts to uncover a general factor.

The practical utility of g in the real world is great   Jensen argues that it is psychometric *g* that is the chief "active ingredient" responsible for cognitive tasks having both practical and concurrent validity in real-life situations (Jensen, 1987b, 1992b, 1993c, 1998; see also Jensen & Weng, 1994).

Psychometric g has meaningful, yet independent, empirical correlates   One of the major features of *g*, according to Jensen, is the fact that it cor-relates with "a number of variables which themselves have nothing to do with psychometrics or factor analysis" (1992b, p. 278). Behavioral variables identified by Jensen (1992b) include decision time, inspection time (two constructs, deriving from experimental cognitive psychology, which emphasize the primacy of mental speed), and musical tests. Non-cognitive variables, suggested in Jensen's (1992b) exposition, include heritability coefficients, inbreeding depression, average evoked poten-tial, the rate of glucose metabolism in the brain, speed of neural and synaptic transmission, head and brain size.

It is worth noting that Jensen (1992b) prefaces his empirical instantia-tion of *g* with the following:

In recent years, the study of general mental ability, or *g*, has begun to look as a science should. Along with the increasing realization of the tremendous impor-tance of this subject, there has been an unusually rapid growth of theoretical and experimental research, both psychometric and experimental. What seems most significant for the development of a science of human abilities is that all this activity by numerous investigators has not only resulted in the discovery (and re-discovery) of many phenomena importantly related to our understanding of *g*, but key findings have been replicated repeatedly in different laboratories around the world. It is most gratifying to see various items of empirical evidence already fitting together with the kind of consistency and coherence that signify scientific progress. (1992b, p. 271–272)

A critical appraisal of Neo-Spearmanian approaches   The question remains as to whether Jensen's (1992b, 1998) assertions regarding the study of general mental ability are as unequivocal as he would have the reader believe. We might also wonder whether the scientific community as readily endorses his claims as would appear from the previous quote. While a comprehensive critique of Jensen's postulations concerning evidence in support of *g* is outside the scope of the present volume, it is difficult to reconcile Jensen's alleged key points with empirical findings in both the experimental and psychometric literature. Consider for example, each of the following:

1   The so-called lawful principles underlying g are problematic   Guttman (1992) provides a controversial and disputatious critique of Jensen's attempts to apply Spearman's principles (Roskam & Ellis, 1992a), which has stimulated considerable debate (Gustafsson, 1992a, 1992b; Jensen, 1992c, 1992d; Loehlin, 1992a, 1992b; Roskam & Ellis, 1992a, 1992b; Schönemann, 1992a, 1992b). In his critique, Guttman provides compelling evidence that suggests that neither positive manifold nor the invariance of *g* is as unequivocal as Jensen has claimed. Indeed, positive manifold need not mathematically imply *g*. Moreover, a large number of noncognitive variables (e.g., athleticism, absence of neuroticism and psychosis, openness) each correlate positively with intelligence tests yet do not represent a functional unity (Roberts, Pallier & Goff, 1999).

Guttman (1992) has also alerted the reader to certain anomalies that exist between Spearman's research program and hypotheses put forward by Jensen. For example, Guttman (1992) notes that Spearman (1927) held little hope for mental speed measures (like decision and inspection time) providing any meaningful account of the existence of a general factor. Guttman (1992) has also queried the extent to which Spearman had suggested differences between racial groups might be predicted by a general intelligence factor. However, Jensen (1985b, 1988, 1993b, 1998; see also Braden, 1989) has published several papers examining racial differences, explicitly alluding to the "Spearman hypothesis." (Note also that Herrnstein and Murray's *Bell Curve* (1994) similarly assumes the efficacy of *g* as a given.)

2 The general factor does not account for all that much variance in a test battery   As Carroll (1992) argues, the first principal component, at best, may account for no greater than 50% of the common factor variance observed in cognitive test performance, a figure that Stankov (2001b) has argued undoubtedly represents an upper limit. Whether this figure is construed as satisfactory would seem largely arbitrary. Even so, a substantial percentage of variance, which is neither specific nor error variance, remains unaccounted for in the presence of a general factor (see, e.g., Carroll, 1993; Gustafsson, 1992a, 1992b; Roberts, Pallier et al., 1999). In short, no self-respecting researcher can assume that cognitive abilities entail only the general factor—to do so would be akin to religious dogma, rather than adopting a proper scientific stance.

3 The predictive utility of g per se in several fields appears open to question   The predictive validity of *g* has been questioned extensively in the literature involving cognitive aging (e.g., Horn, 1987; Horn & Hofer, 1992; Horn & Noll, 1994; Stankov et al., 1995). Gustafsson (1992a, 1992b) makes a similar point regarding hypothesized racial differences in psychometric *g*, where, if group factors are considered, a noticeably different picture emerges. We might also add that meta-analyses supporting the validity of intelligence tests for job selection *assume* (perhaps incorrectly) that all tests measure the same general factor. It is actually an open empirical question whether classes of tests defining broad cognitive abilities might have different validity coefficients.

4 General intelligence is (questionably) determined by a small selection of tests   Jensen (e.g., 1979, 1992b, 1998) has often asserted that *g* may only be extracted from a large (in principle, infinite) and varied battery of intelligence tests. However, in practice, the empirical research involving behavioral and non-cognitive variables often uses a small number of tests, indeed most commonly a single index (most often the Raven's Progressive Matrices Tests [see Roberts & Stankov, 1999]). Whether conclusions may be applied to psychometric *g*, from tests assumed to have a high *g*-loading (and it is not a given that this is true of the Raven's tests) remains contentious (e.g., Carroll, 1993; Stankov et al., 1995).

5 The empirical correlates of g are sometimes problematic   Almost all of the behavioral correlates of *g*, which Jensen (see above for references) suggests as indicative of the importance of general mental ability, have been questioned in the literature. For example, inspection time research has been criticized on methodological, conceptual, and theoretical grounds (e.g., Levy, 1992, Stankov et al., 1995). Similarly, Stankov, and Roberts (1997) have questioned the pivotal assumptions under which decision time per se has been linked to general intelligence, recently supporting these propositions with data (Roberts & Stankov, 1999). Interestingly, these authors show that measures of mental speed correlate meaningfully with some (but not all) cognitive ability factors—a proposition that is immediately at odds with the concept of a single, general intelligence.

Evidence for the noncognitive correlates of psychometric *g* is equally equivocal. In particular, Jensen claims, "Persons' rates of glucose metabolism by the brain while taking a highly *g*-loaded test ... is correlated (negatively) with the persons' test scores" (1992b, p. 281). Jensen bases this proposition on a study, involving Positron Emission Tomography, conducted by Haier and colleagues (see Haier, Siegel, Nuechterlein, Hazlett, Wu, Paek, Browning & Buchsbaum, 1988). An attempt at replicating the Haier et al. findings (Haier, Siegel, Tang, Abel & Buchsbaum, 1992) met with mixed results (see Stankov & Dunn, 1993), while earlier findings presented by Metz, Yassillo, and Cooper (1987) lend themselves to a somewhat different interpretation. With regard to the genetic correlates of *g* postulated by Jensen (1992b), different perspectives have been offered in the literature (e.g., Carroll, 1993, p. 658ff.; Cattell, 1963). Similarly, correlations between many of the noncognitive variables (e.g., head size) and *g* seldom exceed 0.30 (e.g., Jensen & Sinha, 1992); and even this modest correlation may represent an upper limit. Therefore, whether or not these constitute meaningful dimensions of individual differences in intelligence remains, for many commentators, equivocal (e.g., Stankov et al., 1995; Willerman, 1991).

Psychometric g and its implications for emotional intelligence
It is worth noting that a strict Spearmanian (and, for that matter, neo-Spearmanian) account of human intelligence would render the concept of EI quite problematic, perhaps even nonsensical. By definition, EI requires the presence of at least one other intelligence (e.g., something we might call, rational intelligence) for the qualifier (i.e., emotional) to have currency. This notion is clearly inconsistent with a single-factor intelligence model. Equally disconcerting, the three "qualitative principles of cognition" (also known as the noegenetic laws) do not seem relevant to emotional life. Although such principles could conceivably be used to construct tests where "conventional" (e.g., verbal) stimuli are replaced with emotions,[6] the principle of "the indifference of the indicator"

becomes important. This principle acknowledges that it is not so much whether an item is given in verbal, numerical, or spatial form that determines what construct is being measured, but rather the underlying processes that are being assessed. By extension, constructing a test with emotional content using noegenetic principles means this should de facto remain a "pure" measure of intelligence (see, e.g., Horn, 1985, see also our discussion of fluid and crystallized intelligence concepts).

Notably, available research suggests that prevailing EI tests tend *not* to be heavily *g*-loaded, perhaps even violating the phenomenon of positive manifold. For example, Davies et al. (1998) found that certain self-report measures of EI share *negative* correlations with traditional psychometric tests (including the ASVAB). Similarly, Ciarrochi et al. (1999) found performance-based measures of EI sharing near zero (sometimes, negative) correlations with the Raven's Progressive Matrices Test. In light of the robustness of positive manifold, within the extant literature on cognitive abilities, these violations might be construed as definitive evidence—whatever EI is, it is not an "intelligence."

Lessons from history also do not seem out of place here. Spearman (1927) talked openly of emotional content, choosing to list it along with other aspects of psychological character that he designated as components of the concept of will. This observation aside, later research in Spearman's laboratory, at the University of London, did examine a concept bearing close similarities to contemporary notions of EI—something termed "the psychological ability." This construct was thought to involve the "ability to judge correctly the feelings, moods, [and] motivations of the individual" (Wedeck, 1947, p. 133). Wedeck (1947) operationalized the psychological ability through a number of tests, which look remarkably similar to contemporary performance-based measures of EI (e.g., pictures portraying the facial expressions of laughter, doubt, vexation, etc). Based on a large-scale study, Wedeck argued that the psychological ability exhibited some distinctiveness from verbal and non-verbal intelligence tests. Carroll's reanalysis of this data set, however, indicated that "all tests ... had substantial loadings on a second-order general factor" (1993, p. 527). Carroll suggests two reasons for this outcome, which are worth keeping in mind, particularly for future reference. In particular, (a) psychological-ability tests relied too heavily on verbal content, and (b) general intelligence appears the essential component in the acquisition of psychological ability.

One final comment concerns the fact that the *Bell Curve* relies, for its impact, on the assumption that general intelligence is paramount

(Herrnstein & Murray, 1994). Goleman (1995) uses this work as a starting point to promote the virtues of EI. Indeed, he contends that his book, *Emotional Intelligence*, represents a rebuttal to the claims made by Herrnstein and Murray about differences in intellect and its implications for social class. Demonstrably, there appears sufficient lack of consensus concerning the status of general intelligence among researchers within the differential psychological community to call into question many claims made within the *Bell Curve* (e.g., Hunt, 2001; Roberts, Goff, et al., 2001). That is, one might question the central propositions of the *Bell Curve* without recourse to an EI concept that remains to be substantiated in empirical work.

Thurstone's model of primary mental abilities

One of the major differentiating features of multivariate models of intelligence is the number of factors considered necessary to provide an understanding of intelligent behavior. In a significant departure from Spearman, Louis Thurstone (1931, 1935, 1938, 1944; see also L. Thurstone & T. Thurstone, 1941; T. Thurstone, L. Thurstone & Standskov, 1955) proposed and later verified that there exist certain primary mental abilities, which collectively make up intelligence. In total, these abilities are thought to replace the notion of psychometric g (Wood, 1983). While originally finding thirteen such factors, Thurstone eventually settled on nine that he was both able to consistently validate and assign psychological labels. The factors so derived include verbal comprehension, verbal fluency, number facility, spatial visualization, memory, inductive reasoning, deductive reasoning, practical problem reasoning, and perceptual speed. These factors are not ordered in any particular way and are thus of equal importance in detailing the structure of intelligent behavior (for this reason, Thurstone's model is sometimes called an oligarchic theory). To measure each of these constructs, Thurstone devised a battery of tests that he labeled the Test of Primary Mental Abilities.

It is interesting to note that since Thurstone's initial formulations, at least forty primary mental abilities have been identified (and replicated) within the literature (e.g., Ekstrom, French & Harman, 1979; French, Ekstrom & Price, 1963; Hakstian & Cattell, 1974). This figure is not conclusive since, for example, Stankov and colleagues (e.g., Danthiir, Roberts, Pallier & Stankov, 2001; Roberts, Pallier, Stankov & Dolph, 1997; Stankov & Horn, 1980; Stankov et al., 2000) have located primary factors tied to various sensory modalities. Thus, in perhaps one of the most extensive reviews of the psychometric literature to date, Carroll (1993, p. 626) suggests somewhere between 65 and 69 primary mental abilities. On these grounds alone, Thurstone's original theory seems overly simplistic. Equally, it appears extremely difficult to envisage how all of these abilities might form an internally consistent, coherent, and empirically founded theory of intelligence (Horn & Hofer, 1992). In fact, it would be difficult to construct studies that adequately take into account each of these abilities. As a consequence, theoreticians have advocated moving up the ladder of abstraction from a model postulating primary mental abilities to a theory incorporating second-order factors (e.g., Cattell, 1941, 1971; Horn, 1982, 1987). In such theories, primary abilities represent components of broader, more meaningful, constituents of intelligent behavior.

Within this context, it is interesting to note that even Thurstone (1947) was forced to acknowledge the existence of factors beyond primary mental abilities. This reconceptualization was largely forced by the observation that some primary mental abilities share substantial correlation with one another (see Carroll, 1993, p. 638). Recent analysis of large data sets, using both exploratory and confirmatory factor-analytic techniques (e.g., Carroll, 1989, 1993; Gustafsson, 1989; Roberts, Goff et al., 2001), supports the existence of cognitive factors broader than primary mental abilities.

Emotional intelligence and primary mental abilities

Three features of the scientific investigation of primary mental abilities are directly relevant to research on EI. The first is that if EI is to be accepted as a major form of intelligence, by definition, it should comprise three (or more) interrelated primary mental abilities (e.g., Carroll, 1993), where emotional processes are engaged and of utmost importance. Interestingly, the vast majority of attempts to operationalize EI have thus far postulated such primary abilities (in the process reinventing terminology by referring to these as 'branches'), without perhaps appreciating the logic underlying this approach (see chapter 5). Secondly, there may be but one factor of EI, while other postulated emotional constructs are already taken up by existing individual differences (particularly intelligence and personality) constructs. This would render EI a primary mental ability of relatively *minor* importance. Indeed, Davies et al. (1998) alert the reader to this possibility, since emotional perception alone, in their study of a variety of putative indices of EI, seemed to represent a coherent and conceptually independent domain of individual differences. Finally, it would not seem too fanciful that the approach that should guide preliminary investigations into EI (should it exist) should resemble that pioneered by Thurstone and his predecessors. In short, a science of EI might begin by specifying the number, type, and range of primary *emotional* abilities. Thus far, this disciplined scientific approach to understanding EI has not been forthcoming.

Guilford's Structure of Intellect Model

Overview   While the number of factors in Thurstone's original theory is large, Guilford and his associates (e.g., Guilford, 1967, 1982; Guilford & Hoepfner, 1971) take a more extreme view in positing that some 150 factors comprise intelligence. Accordingly, for Guilford, every mental task involves three "ingredients": an operation, a content, and a product. There are five kinds of operations in this model, five types of content, and six varieties of products. The "structure of intellect" has subsequently been symbolized as a rectangular prism composed of 150 smaller prisms (see figure 3.2). Each dimension of this prism corresponds to one of the three "ingredients" (i.e., operation, content, and product) with each of the 150 possible combinations of these three categories forming even smaller rectangular prisms. An early appeal of this model was its ability to incorporate both "creativity" and social intelligence (what Guilford calls behavioral cognition [see O'Sullivan, Guilford & deMille, 1965]) into its structure—psychological dimensions that few models of intelligence include. In addition, the facets of Guilford's system provide useful guidelines for test construction (Humphreys, 1962).

Critique   Guilford and his associates have subsequently devised batteries of tests that measure many of the factors suggested by the model. Prior to his death, Guilford claimed to have demonstrated the existence of 105 of the possible 150 factors postulated by the model (see, e.g., Guilford, 1982). However, as it appears that some factors are represented by no more than a single test, their validity would seem doubtful. The model is further weakened by studies that demonstrate that even these factors are not well defined by the tests designed to measure them— they possess poor factor replicability (see Brody & Brody, 1976). Furthermore, the evidence for independence and breadth of processing in certain Guilfordian constructs is largely unconvincing (see, e.g., Horn, 1970; Horn & Cattell, 1966; Horn & Knapp, 1973, 1974; Undheim & Horn, 1977). Using confirmatory factor analysis, Kelderman, Mellen-

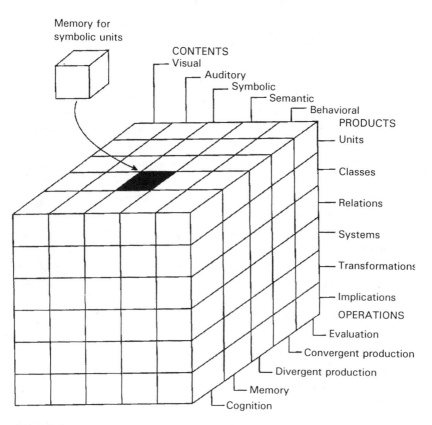

Figure 3.2
Guilford's Structure of Intellect Model.

bergh, and Elshout (1981) were unable to find, in seven of Guilford's studies, one data set fitting the proposed orthogonal model (Brody, 1992, p. 29ff.; see also Kyllonen, 1994).

Largely because of these many and varied criticisms, including the use of a subjective factor analytic technique known as Procrustean analysis, Guilford (1981, 1985) later modified his theory to include second- and third-order factors. Pairs of dimensions, and dimensions defined each higher-order construct, respectively. In this hierarchical arrangement, there are thus 85 second-order factors and 16 third-order factors. However, Brody (1992, p. 32ff.) questions the utility of this model on several grounds. Since the derived hierarchical factors are based on poorly defined first-order factors, it is difficult to envisage how these higher-order factors could, in any way, be valid. In addition, the limited data cited by Guilford in support of this revised model is (at best) only weak since factor loadings used to support claims often barely approach levels of significance.

Implications of the Structure of Intellect Model for emotional intelligence

The criticisms given above render Guilford's structure of intellect model highly problematic. Indeed, for some commentators this proposition is overly euphemistic. Carroll, for example, suggests Guilford's model "be marked down as a somewhat eccentric aberration in the history of intelligence models; that so much attention has been paid to it is disturbing, to the extent that textbooks and other treatments of it have given the impression that the model is valid and widely accepted, when clearly it is not" (1993, p. 60). Nevertheless, some psychologists have viewed the inclusion of a concept analogous to social intelligence, as a major strength of the structure of intellect model (see, e.g., Sternberg, 1985). Given that certain commentators posit close links between social and emotional intelligence, we provide a detailed exposition, of the behavioral-knowledge facet of Guilford's model in appendix A.

Hierarchical theories of human cognitive abilities

In the contemporary literature, the most influential and widely employed models of intelligence would appear to involve a hierarchical arrangement of factors (e.g., Cattell, 1971; Cronbach, 1970, 1990; Horn, 1976; Snow, 1978; Vernon, 1950, 1965). Such models seem to provide the most promising and parsimonious way of conceptualizing human ability (e.g., Marshalek, Lohman & Snow, 1983; Messick, 1992; Roberts & Stankov, 1999; Snow, Kyllonen & Marshalek, 1984; Sternberg, 1985). They also appear to be best supported by the available evidence from both exploratory and confirmatory factor analyses of large data sets (Carroll, 1988, 1993; Gustafsson, 1984, 1999; Roberts, Goff et al., 2001; Undheim & Gustafsson, 1987). Often in hierarchical theories of intelligence, but not always, a general mental ability is posited that accounts for performance on a variety of psychological tasks. Below this construct are the all important group factors, the definitions of which vary from theory to theory. Each of these factors may in turn, be divided into narrower more sharply focused factors—the previously elucidated primary mental abilities. At the lowest level are numerous factors that remain test-specific.

The first mention of a multifactor theory of intelligence can be traced to the Spanish physician Juan Huarte, who in the late 1500s listed a number of natural abilities and aptitudes that interacted with training and climate (Detterman, 1982). The first formal hierarchical model of intelligence (representing an elaboration of Spearmanian theory) derives from Holzinger's (1938) suggestion that group factors exist that are intermediate in generality between the general and specific factors. There have been several subsequent variations on this theme. For instance, Cyril Burt (1940) proposed a five-level hierarchic model, with human mind at the apex and sensation at the base. A more elaborate hierarchical model was that provided by Phillip Vernon (1950), who firstly defined *g* and then proceeded to define two broad ability factors, which he labeled verbal-education ability and practical-mechanical-spatial ability. Although Vernon proposed that these group factors could be further differentiated into narrower group factors, these appear rather unimportant in his theory.

However, it would appear that the most fully developed hierarchical model of intelligence is that proposed by Raymond Cattell (1941, 1963, 1971, 1987), John Horn (Cattell & Horn, 1978; Horn, 1968, 1970, 1979, 1985, 1988, 1989, 1998; Horn & Cattell, 1966), and several associates (Hakstian & Cattell, 1978; Horn & Donaldson, 1980; Horn & Stankov, 1982; Roberts & Stankov, 1999; Stankov & Horn, 1980). Based initially on Hebb's (1942, 1949) distinction between intelligence A and intelligence B, the theory of fluid and crystallized ability lists among its attractions a relative independence from the general intelligence factor. Another defining feature of the theory is the manner in which it not only takes into account, but also actually predicts, findings pertaining to individual differences across diverse areas of the discipline of psychology.

The theory of fluid and crystallized ability

Overview In the theory of fluid and crystallized ability (henceforth referred to as Gf/Gc theory), there is considered to be enough (factorial) structure amongst primary mental abilities to define several distinct types of intelligence. Though researchers sometimes calculate a higher-order factor within this paradigm, this is most often considered a means of assessing the general organization of behavior (Horn, 1985; Roberts, Pallier et al., 1999).

Empirical evidence, from several lines of inquiry, support the distinctions between factors of this theory (e.g., Boyle, 1988; Boyle, Stankov & Cattell, 1995; Cattell, 1987; Horn, 1976, 1985, 1988, 1998; Horn, Donaldson & Engstrom, 1981; Horn & Hofer, 1992; Stankov et al., 1995). Data have shown that these broad factors (1) involve different underlying cognitive processes (e.g., Fogarty & Stankov, 1988; Horn, 2001; Roberts & Stankov, 1999; Stankov, 1988a, 1988b; Stankov, Roberts & Spilsbury, 1994; Stankov & Roberts, 1997), (2) share different predictive validities (e.g., O'Toole & Stankov, 1992), (3) are differentially sensitive to intervention (e.g., Stankov, 1986; Stankov & Chen, 1988), (4) appear to be subject to different sets of learning and genetic influences (e.g., Horn, 1985, 1987; Horn & Hofer, 1992; Horn & Noll, 1994).

The most compelling evidence for the distinctions between these constructs comes from factor analytic and developmental research (e.g., Stankov et al., 1995). Consideration of a wide body of data within these fields verifies the presence of seven broad second-order factors. Besides fluid (Gf) and crystallized (Gc) ability, there is broad visualization (Gv), broad auditory function (Ga), short-term acquisition and retrieval (SAR), tertiary storage and retrieval (TSR), and the broad speediness function (Gs). In isolation, each construct represents a broad organization of ability that involves mental processes, for which each factor is purported to have a neurophysiological counterpart (see, e.g., Horn, 1998; Roberts, Goff et al., 2001; Stankov, 2001b).

Carroll's (1993) previously mentioned reanalysis of several hundred data sets from psychometric studies conducted this century supports the presence of each of these seven factors. As testament to this assertion, we present his three-stratum model in figure 3, noting any differences between this model and Gf/Gc theory are particularly subtle (see Roberts, Goff, et al., 2001). However, at least two other factors have tentatively been suggested in recent elaboration's of Gf/Gc theory (see, e.g., Horn, 1998). The first is broad quantitative ability (Gq), which Horn (1988) claims might constitute a meaningful, second-stratum factor. The second construct is correct decision speed (CDS), a factor that Horn and Hofer conceptualize as the "complement of the time it takes to produce answers to questions or problems which all subjects attempt" (1992, p. 62). Moreover, an implicit assumption of Gf/Gc theory is that additional factors corresponding to sensory modalities other than vision and audition (e.g., tactile-kinesthetic), will be isolated sometime in the future. Indeed, preliminary investigations by Stankov and associates (see, e.g., Danthiir, Pallier, Stankov & Roberts, 2001; Roberts, Stankov, Pallier & Dolph, 1997; Stankov, Seizova-Cajic & Roberts, 2000) have found evidence for independent primary mental abilities in the tactile, kinesthetic, and olfactory domains. However, because studies involving these sensory processes remain sparse, these new abilities have yet to reach the status of other broad cognitive abilities.

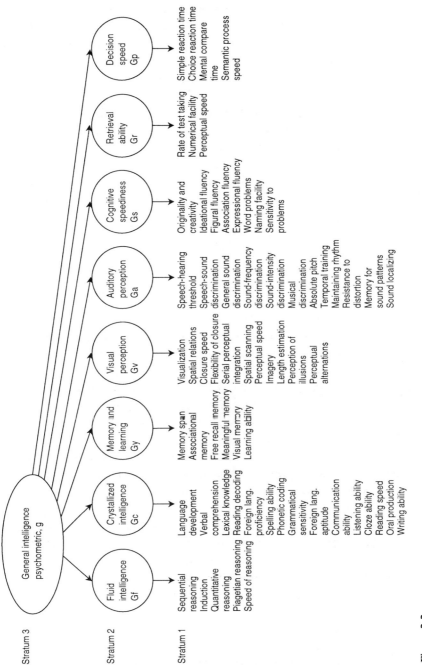

Figure 3.3
Carroll's (1993) three-stratum model of mental abilities.

Within Gf/Gc theory, each of the factors is deemed structurally equivalent. However, most researchers (largely because of historical precedent) have focused attention upon fluid and crystallized abilities (which, in principle, share important common features). Processes of perceiving relationships, logical reasoning, abstraction, concept-formation, problem solving, and the like, for instance, characterize both of these broad cognitive abilities. Moreover, both fluid and crystallized intelligence can be measured by speeded or power tests with material that can be presented in any of the following three forms: pictorial-spatial, verbal-symbolic, or verbal-semantic.

The main distinguishing feature between Gf and Gc is the amount of formal education and acculturation that is present either in the content of, or operations required during, tests used to measure these abilities. It is well established that Gf depends to a much smaller extent on formal education experiences than does Gc (e.g., Horn, 1979, 1985, 1998; Horn & Hofer, 1992; Horn & Noll, 1994). Equally, the available evidence tends to suggest that Gf has greater genetic concomitants than does Gc, although this is not conclusive (see, e.g., Horn, 1985, 1998; Horn & Hofer, 1992; Horn & Noll, 1994).

Gf and Gc also show distinct developmental trends during adulthood. Thus, while Gc remains constant or shows slight increment over the course of an individual's life span, Gf generally declines as a function of age (see Botwinick, 1978; Horn, 1978, 1979, 1988; Stankov, 1988b, 1994). These different developmental trajectories appear a function of the proposed information-processing mechanisms underlying the Gf/Gc distinction. Thus, Gf appears dependent on the capacity of working memory (e.g., Kyllonen & Christal, 1990; Myors, 1984; Myors, Stankov & Oliphant, 1989). Gc, on the other hand, is thought to depend on long-term memory store and the organization of information within that store (Stankov et al., 1995). Research suggests that working memory deteriorate with age as a function of neurological decay, while long-term store is less prone to such effects. The concerned reader, who might be over 26 years of age, when fluid intelligence first begins to decline, should note the effects are rather gradual. In any event, the improvement witnessed in the individual's crystallized intelligence tends to be nature's compensation.

The presence of broad abilities other than Gf and Gc, indicates that performance on all cognitive tasks depends not only on "higher" mental processes, but also on processes often viewed as "lower" level functions. These functions include visual and auditory perceptual processes;

represented by the factors of broad visualization (Gv) and broad auditory perception (Ga), respectively. Generically, these factors provide information about the fundamentals of cognitive processes employed when an individual is required to perform any given psychological test. These factors remain sufficiently different and independent from Gf and Gc to define factors in their own right (Horn & Stankov, 1982; Stankov & Horn, 1980). Their separate existence indicates that some people are more efficient at processing information that is auditory in nature, while others are more efficient at processing information through the visual medium (Stankov et al., 1995).

The two memory abilities (SAR and TSR) share similar roles in cognitive functioning. Essentially, they reflect storage areas that are useful for the operation of Gf and Gc, respectively. They also indicate the relative independence of memory from the "higher" mental processes of fluid and crystallized intelligence.[7] Finally, the role of the broad speediness (Gs) construct reflects individual differences in the speed of mental operations—some people are very fast, others quite slow in performing certain intellectual activities. Confirmation of the independence of Gs again occurs through factor analysis; it does not share substantial correlation with Gf, Gc, perceptual processes, or either type of memory ability.

In addition to Carroll's (1989, 1992, 1993) meta-analysis, the evidence for the independent factors underlying Gf/Gc theory is persuasive. Thus, Woodcock's (1990) study of 6,359 participants, spanning a range from childhood to old age, found convincing evidence for the range and breadth of abilities provided by this theory. More recently, Roberts, Goff et al. (2001) used confirmatory factor analysis to recover the structure suggested by Gf/Gc theory, in a sample of nearly three thousand military enlistees.

Further instantiation of the validity of Gf/Gc theory comes from the literature on aging where there has been some controversy regarding the effects of age on intellectual functions. Previously, researchers argued for no decline in intelligence with age (e.g., Baltes, Reese & Lipsitt, 1980), largely because they assumed a single factor model of intelligence. This is contradictory to an established empirical fact—as one becomes older, scores on verbal tests (e.g., vocabulary) tend to improve, while scores on culture-fair tasks (like the Raven's Progressive Matrices Tests) decline. Gf/Gc theory, on the other hand, predicts this finding. Subsequently, the literature on cognitive aging predominately employs the Gf/Gc model (see, e.g., Fry & Hale, 1996; Salthouse, 1998). Indeed, attempts to account for the cognitive processes underlying developmental trends in separate domains of task performance is currently one of the most lively research topics in the emerging field of gerontology (e.g., Lindenberger & Baltes, 1997; Salthouse, 1998; Stankov, 1988b).

Gf/Gc theory: A critique It would be remiss to suggest that Gf/Gc theory has not undergone any substantive criticisms. For instance, Humphreys (1967) reanalyzed a study conducted by Cattell (1963) on 13- to 14-year-old children, arguing that the data supported a general factor. Gustafsson (1984, 1988), on the other hand, concluded that while there is evidence for second-order factors postulated by Gf/Gc theory, there is also evidence for a superordinate *g* that is indistinguishable from a second-order Gf factor. Notwithstanding, both of these studies involve data collected on young children. A corollary of Gf/Gc theory is that there is a causal link between Gf and Gc (see Cattell, 1963). Accordingly, "fluid ability is a necessary condition for the development of crystallized ability" (Brody, 1992, p. 20). It is also possible that differentiation of cognitive abilities does not take place until young adulthood (e.g., Bayley, 1949; Garrett, 1946; also Horn and Hofer, 1992, for an alternative view). Certainly more attention needs to be devoted to this topic before generalizations can be made across samples of widely differing age. When both of these features are considered, it would appear that neither the Humphreys nor Gustafsson study is at odds with Gf/Gc theory; rather, they support Cattell's (1963) causal analysis of the relationship between Gf and Gc.

In light of this argument, an attempt to replicate Gustafsson's (1984) findings with an adult sample failed to provide evidence for his conjecture that *g* and Gf are indistinguishable (Waldman, Bouchard, Lykken & McGue, 1993). Similarly, when adults' performance on the various subtests of the WAIS is considered, the superordinate *g* appears more closely related to Gc than Gf. For example, Matarazzo (1972) has shown that the Vocabulary test (a reliable indicator of crystallized intelligence) has the highest loading on the first principal component extracted from the Wechsler Adult Intelligence Scales. Since the apex of an intelligence hierarchy appears to be dependent upon either the test battery or sample studied, its utility (other than as an index of behavioral organization) appears questionable (see Carroll, 1993).

Gf/Gc theory and emotional intelligence
The theory of fluid and crystallized intelligence is a notably dynamic structural model, willing, as it were, to accept additional constructs into

its hierarchical family of concepts, providing that the evidence for them is overwhelming. Until such time, researchers working within this tradition remain decidedly cautious. For example, available research does suggest that tactile and kinesthetic primary mental abilities have been isolated (e.g., Stankov et al., 2000). However, in this case, the lack of differentiation of these abilities from measures of broad visualization, and failure to uncover multiple primary mental abilities to ensure its breadth, means that they have yet to be included within the full-blown model. In the case of placing EI within the Gf/Gc hierarchy, systematic empirical studies devoted to uncovering structural relationships between primary abilities, their developmental track, predictive validities, cognitive correlates, and their relationship to extant constructs would appear requisite.[8]

Since one of the first empirical investigations into EI was, by in large, conducted inside Gf/Gc theory (Davies et al., 1998), a series of more definitive statements are also possible. Many critics have taken from that study the more negative aspects—the fact that evidence for measures of EI forming a coherent empirical domain was not particularly compelling (see, e.g., Salovey et al., 2000). However, there is a positive message in the Davies et al. (1998) study: that emotion perception plausibly constitutes a legitimate primary mental ability. Davies and colleagues then moved to suggest there was an urgent need for further research to determine the place of emotion perception within a hierarchical model of intelligence. Thus far, this particular suggestion has been rather neglected.

Nevertheless, if EI is granted the status of a cognitive ability construct, perhaps within Gf/Gc theory, then it may constitute an additional primary mental ability contributing to overall crystallized ability. This assertion is based on the assumption that the appraisal, expression, regulation, and utilization of emotion (a core definition of EI; see Salovey & Mayer, 1990) develops through experience and social interaction. As explicated earlier in this section, these highly acculturated psychological processes also comprise Gc, making this an obvious candidate for circumscribing EI (see Davies et al., 1998). Data collected by Roberts, Zeidner, et al. (2001) support this proposition, at least in the special case of performance-based measures of EI, which consistently show highest correlation with crystallized intelligence indices.

Recent extensions of Gf/Gc theory also have interesting implications for the concept of EI. One of the most interesting would appear Ackerman's (1996, 1999) reconceptualization of Cattell's investment theory

(Cattell, 1987), which captures four major components: intelligence as process (which is linked to Gf), personality, interests, and intelligence as knowledge (which relates to Gc). This so-called PPIK theory acknowledges close links between personality and intelligence as knowledge. In particular, the Big Five trait of openness and typical intellectual engagement (a construct that relates to long-term academic and occupational performance, taking place in a "typical" environment) both appear related to measures of crystallized ability. PPIK theory also acknowledges weak (or near zero) correlations between personality and intelligence as process. Under the PPIK model and consistent with arguments made for performance-based measures, it is likely self-report indices of EI will thus correlate meaningfully with intelligence as knowledge (Gc), but not intelligence as process (Gf). This follows from the fact that self-report measures of EI appear to capture salient aspects of Openness (see chapter 2).

These facts aside, it is non-incidental to determining the status of EI within Gf/Gc theory that its originator, Raymond Cattell, was involved as much in the scientific investigation of both personality and motivation, as he was in cognitive abilities. Another history lesson is perhaps pertinent here. For Cattell, emotions appeared more closely related to motivational (rather than ability) constructs and he believed these could be assessed in a relatively objective manner. For this purpose, he devised the Motivational Analysis Test (see Cattell, Horn, Sweeney & Radcliffe, 1964) and it is perhaps curious that any attempts to measure individual differences in emotionality have ignored both this instrument and its accompanying findings. Conceptually, for Cattell, emotions may influence human cognitive abilities, but they are clearly not the same things as the various broad ability constructs.

While we reserve the next chapter for more detailed discussion of the conceptual status of emotions, consider recent research examining emotion control, which would appear in the spirit of Cattell's views of the motivational value of emotions. Emotion control involves efforts to minimize performance anxiety, worry, frustration, and other distractions that the learner encounters during the difficult and demanding initial stages of skill acquisition (Kanfer & Heggestad, 1999; Zeidner, 1998). Learners with high levels of emotion control can maintain motivation and resist being sidetracked by self-blame (or the anticipation of negative consequences) for performance errors, when in the midst of task practice or training. Learners with low levels of emotion control, on the other hand, compound the difficulty of learning a new task by being distracted by worry and anxiety (stress-related processes that reduce the individual's available cognitive resources when performing a given task). Kanfer and Ackerman (1990, 1996) have developed a set of training modules for emotion control, which involve teaching the learner not to become anxious during the early stages of skill acquisition on a complex task (an air traffic control simulation). They found that this intervention was successful, particularly for low ability trainees, who improved early full-task transfer of performance.

One final comment concerning the status of EI within Gf/Gc theory is in order. It should not go unnoticed that there is no mention of social intelligence within this theory, largely because the available evidence is contradictory (see appendix A). Instead, researchers, working within this tradition, tend to ascribe the label social competence to many of the phenomena that might otherwise be assigned to social intelligence (see, e.g., Schneider, Ackerman & Kanfer, 1996). The distinction between ability and competence is more than a purely linguistic device. Competence appears a broader concept than intelligence, involving a "generative capability in which cognitive, social, and behavioral skills must be organized and effectively orchestrated to solve innumerable purposes" (Bandura, 1990, p. 315). Reflecting this breadth, Schneider et al. define social competence as "socially effective behavior and its cognitive, affective, and conative antecedents" (1996, p. 471). Notably this definition refrains from linking social competence to ability (or intelligence) conceptions per se, with notions of self-concept exerting important influences on the individual's perceived levels of competence (Markus, Cross & Wurf, 1990). This viewpoint, while certainly at odds with commentators who see social intelligence as a traditional form of cognitive ability (see chapter 2), is more consistent with how social competence is assessed: through self-report methodologies.

Recently, frustrated by the failure of this distinction to be applied to the emerging domain of EI, Stankov (2001b), a leading researcher in Gf/Gc theory, has been moved to suggest, "In the absence of a demonstration that whatever is measured by the alleged tests of emotionality is indeed akin to intelligence, it would be more appropriate to talk about 'emotional awareness', 'emotional competence', or 'emotion perception' rather than 'emotional intelligence' in future. The removal of 'intelligence' from the title is likely to lead to a dissipation of much of the current enthusiasm. In reality, this may benefit serious workers in the field" (2001b, p. XX).

Structural theories and emotional intelligence: Concluding comments

Our critical review of the various structural theories of intelligence, which are based upon psychometric science, brings into sharp focus obstacles which proponents of EI must traverse if they wish to demonstrate that EI is a scientifically valid, ability construct. For example, it must be shown that there are a number of primary emotional abilities that cluster together to define a higher-order construct. Otherwise, EI is rendered a relatively trivial primary mental ability. Assuming this is possible, structural independence from other forms of cognitive ability would appear a necessary and sufficient condition for this new broad cognitive ability. Developmental, cognitive, neuropsychological, and genetic evidence are then requisite before we can feel comfortable building a scientific model of EI. We return to explore these issues in chapter 5, noting here that the preliminary data are equivocal in many of these respects.

This relatively staid position is perhaps the most optimistic vision for EI inside the preceding review—that over time it will assume the conceptual status of a broad cognitive ability like fluid or crystallized intelligence. A more pessimistic account is also possible. It is quite clear, in the search for intelligence factors, that there are instances where similar concepts to EI appear in the literature. The claim that EI is somehow new, and that we anoint it with special status until such time that it matures, represents then nothing more than a smokescreen. Indeed, it would appear that concepts resembling EI have been rendered redundant (or otherwise cast as alternative, but by no means trivial, psychological mechanisms). We provide detailed discussion of potential overlap with one such construct, social intelligence, tracing its rather patchy history, in appendix A.

Our review of structural theories has also argued that among several alternatives, the most viable would appear the theory of fluid and crystallized intelligence. It is ironic (perhaps even sinister) that so little of the discourse on the conceptual status of EI, by its proponents, seems constrained to single factor conceptions of intelligence. This viewpoint impoverishes the concept of intelligence, at the same time giving EI greater currency than is apparently warranted. Within Gf/Gc theory, for example, it is certainly possible to modify some classes of broad cognitive abilities (see, e.g., Stankov, 1986), rendering Goleman's (1995) comments concerning the immutability of intelligence a straw man. Note that this state of affairs would *appear* reinforced by individuals working within the intelligence area, when books like *The Bell Curve* tout the virtues of general factor theories. (Interestingly, it turns out that neither Richard Herrnstein nor Charles Murray had particular specialist expertise in differential psychology: Herrnstein, now deceased, was better known for his research on learning theory, while Murray is actually a political scientist!)

Related to the preceding arguments, there has been a push recently to examine psychological concepts in relation to both broad cognitive abilities and primary mental abilities. In determining the psychological correlates of intelligence, ranging from biological mechanisms to measures of metacognition (e.g., Roberts & Stankov, 1999; Stankov & Crawford, 1997; Stankov & Dunn, 1993), misleading findings will ensue if not referenced to cognitive strata. Indeed, Carroll goes further, arguing that the overly simplistic cognitive approach is "likely to be unsuccessful because the 'correlates' that it claims to find are difficult to interpret if they are not referred to a broader theory. It is likely to be misleading because it may not correctly identify the locus or source of a correlate" (1993, p. 647). Recent research conducted with EI measures, which we review in chapter 5, appears to suffer from this shortcoming and it may certainly lead to confusion. For example, one series of researchers have demonstrated that the performance-based MEIS does not correlate with intelligence (using a measure of fluid intelligence; see Carriochi et al., 1999). On the other hand, another group of researchers has shown that it does (using a measure of crystallized intelligence; see Mayer, Caruso, et al., 1999). Outside the context of Gf/Gc theory, these findings would be difficult to reconcile. Inside Gf/Gc theory, these findings are consistent, suggest precise cognitive mechanisms that might underpin ability-based models of EI (e.g., long-term store), the form of developmental trajectories, and so forth.

System Models of Intelligence

Two contemporary theorists—Howard Gardner and Robert Sternberg—have proposed intelligence models that attempt to be fairly encompassing in dealing with both the internal and external world of the human being. Because such theories view intelligence as a complex system, they are often referred to as system models, a point of departure that we use now to demarcate them from structural models covered earlier in this chapter. Interestingly, such system models, in expanding notions of the proper subject matter of intelligence, include concepts that other theories of human cognitive abilities, particularly structural models, would not view as intelligence. Perhaps because of their more expansive breadth, EI researchers appear to have embraced systems theory accounts of intelligence more fully than they have structural theories, the latter of which, as we have demonstrated, are strongly entrenched in psychometric science. Thus, one will find *no* mention in Goleman (1995) of any of the preceding corpus of scientific literature on human cognitive abilities, though it is clearly pertinent. Instead, Goleman (1995) presents Gardner's theory as a particularly influential account of contemporary knowledge concerning human cognitive abilities. Consequently, it is to discussion of Gardner's systems model that we first turn, though we also consider Sternberg's (1995) triarchic theory of intelligence, since its focus, in particular, on practical intelligence, overlaps with aspects of EI (see Hedlund & Sternberg, 2000).

Gardner's Theory of Multiple Intelligences

Arguing that contemporary models of human intelligence are overly restrictive in their subject matter, Gardner (1983) has developed a theory of multiple intelligences (see also Chen & Gardner, 1997). This model is not based on factor-analytic evidence but rather on Gardner's analysis of information derived from a number of sources, including domains where extraordinary degrees of talent/giftedness, or deficits in brain-damaged individuals, occur. In all, Gardner requires a number of different criteria (from among eight possibilities) to be fulfilled in order for an intelligence to be considered a candidate concept under his theory. (We return to discussion of each of these criteria shortly.) Because of its intuitive appeal, the theory has attracted considerable attention in the popular press. The underlying message—that there is more than a single, general factor of intelligence—also found ready acceptance amongst educationalists and psychometricians who had become increasingly disenchanted with single factor models of intelligence.

In all, there are seven, independent types of intelligence within Gardner's theory. Below, we list each type of intelligence, along with a brief description intended to capture the most salient aspects of each construct. We also make some comments concerning possible overlap with concepts already discussed. Note that each of the seven intelligences derives from Gardner's subjective classification of human abilities using what he believes to be important scientific criteria. The staunch critic might construe this as a form of factor analysis, without the use of statistics!

Linguistic intelligence   This ability is used by the reader uses in coming to terms with the content of the current book. The three authors writing this book also had to exhibit this ability, as would any individual who embarks on writing a poem, novel, or paper. Linguistic intelligence is also required to understand spoken words. One may note parallels to ability constructs already discussed inside structural models of intelligence (e.g., Gc, verbal comprehension), a point we shall return to shortly.

Spatial intelligence   This ability helps the individual to read a map, to get from one place to another along the shortest route, and to play platform video games effectively. There is obvious overlap between this concept and broad visualization (Gv), with high levels evidenced in the great paintings of the world.

Logical-mathematical intelligence   This ability is used to solve mathematical problems, to balance a company's books, to solve complex mathematical proofs, and to perform statistical analyses. Curiously, despite empirical evidence demonstrating independence between reasoning processes and mathematical ability (i.e., Gf and Gq appear factorially distinct, see discussion of Gf/Gc theory), Gardner also sees logical reasoning as a core component of this intelligence.

Musical intelligence   This ability is evidenced when singing a song, composing a piece of music, or playing a musical instrument. Musical intelligence might also come into play whenever an individual appreciates the structure of a particular piece of music. Again, there appears overlap with this concept and another emanating from the theory of fluid and crystallized intelligence—broad auditory reception (Ga).

Bodily kinesthetic intelligence   This intelligence is hypothesized to be quite diverse, apparently being demonstrated when one dances or plays *any* sport. It has no counterpart in structural models of intelligence, though as we have mentioned, attempts have been made to examine the relationship between tactile-kinesthetic processes and more traditional forms of cognitive ability (e.g., Roberts, Pallier, et al., 1999). Unfortunately, in terms of Gardner's model and the hypothesized independence of the multiple intelligences, tactile-kinesthetic processes appear to share much in common with spatial intelligence, at least from a psychometric perspective (Stankov et al., 2001).

Interpersonal intelligence   This ability is used whenever we relate to other people, such as trying to understand what another person is feeling after they have been insulted. Interpersonal intelligence more generically covers the individual's attempts to understand another person's behavior, motives, and/or emotions. Interpersonal intelligence is obviously related to aspects of EI, a point that has often times been acknowledged (e.g., Davies et al., 1998; Goleman, 1995), and which we will take up shortly.

Intrapersonal intelligence   This intelligence is used to help us understand ourselves. Gardner assumes that this concept forms the basis for understanding who we are, what makes us tick, and what drives us. Intrapersonal intelligence also informs us how we can change ourselves into becoming a more fulfilled person given the constraints of our abilities and interests. Again, as might be expected of one of the two so-called "personal" intelligences, this construct has also been related to EI.

Gardner acknowledges that one can never develop "a single irrefutable and universally acceptable list of human intelligences" (1983, p. 60). On what basis, then, did he choose this particular subset of seven intelligences? The answer lies in some eight criteria, which we turn now to discuss in the passages that follow.

Potential isolation by brain damage   Accidents can result in lesions in certain parts of the brain or, worse still, lead to the destruction of certain parts of the brain. The sub-discipline of neuropsychology is concerned with studying patients with such damage. Certain groups of patients can be helpful in isolating portions of the brain that are responsible for particular mental functions. The individual lacking a part of the brain should not be able to perform a cognitive function that is supposedly located in the damaged portion. The aim of such studies is to localize brain functions and indeed there is considerable evidence that some functions are localized. For example, speech and language functions appear to reside in the left cerebral hemisphere, while tasks that call upon visual and auditory perceptual abilities are localized in the right hemisphere. Based on such findings, Gardner contends that multiple intelligence exist because we have multiple neural modules. The modularity of intelligences, in turn, suggests that a person's ability in one area does not predict their ability in another (Gardner, 1983).

The existence of idiot savants, prodigies, and other exceptional individuals
Idiot savants may perform very poorly on typical IQ tests, yet show exceptional capabilities in certain domains. Some of them can play passages of classical music without peer; others can reproduce faultless imitations of classical paintings; while others can carry out incredibly involved mathematical calculations in an amazingly short period of time (e.g., Sloboda, Hermelin & O'Connor, 1985). Similarly, prodigies have extraordinary gifts in one area, with normal abilities in all others. Both groups seem to have some rather specific area of cognitive functioning that is highly developed relative to other areas of functioning. Gardner believes that these high levels of performance are again indicative of separate, modular intelligence systems. Moreover, the existence of idiot savants and prodigies in a given area provides increased evidence for the existence of that particular form of intelligence.

An identifiable core operation or set of operations   Gardner believes that each of the seven intelligences should have its own distinctive set of operations, which may be used in the execution of that intelligence. For example, musical intelligence has as its core operation the ability to discriminate tones according to pitch. Linguistic intelligence, on the other hand, is supposed to contain four different core operations including rhetorical ability, memory ability, explanatory abilities, and the ability to understand the meaning conveyed by language. Thus, if we can identify the complete set of operations or some core operation, the case for the existence of that particular type of intelligence is strengthened.

A distinctive developmental history along with a definable set of expert end-stage performances   One way of separating a given intelligence from any other is to show a pattern of development throughout childhood that is distinctive with respect to that intelligence. Some types of intelligence appear to develop gradually, while other types show spurts of development at a particular age. Indeed, Gardner suggests that the fact that one domain of human capability develops more quickly (or slowly) than another, supports the notion of separate multiple intelligences.

An evolutionary history and evolutionary plausibility   The origins of each of the intelligences, according to Gardner (1983), must go back many millions of years. However, we know very little about their evolutionary history. Nevertheless, the plausibility of a specific intelligence may be enhanced if it can be shown that there are antecedents to its present stage. For example, Gardner claims that bird song might be seen as a forerunner of musical intelligence.

Support from experimental psychological tasks Experimental psychological investigations that point to different patterns of stimuli leading to distinctive reactions in the organism also demonstrate the distinctiveness of the intelligences. For example, manipulations of the properties of visual stimuli lead to changes in performance on spatial tasks, while changes in auditory stimuli lead to changes in performance on musical tasks; suggesting that these may be two distinct types of intelligence.

Susceptibility to encoding in a symbol system In Gardner's opinion, each of the intelligences should have its own distinctive, culturally predetermined symbol system. For example, in the case of linguistic intelligence, the symbol system consists of the formal rules of language. Similarly, in musical intelligence, the symbols are musical notes, while for logical-mathematical intelligence it is logical or mathematical notations. Gardner's argument rests here on the assumption that symbol systems have developed because separate intelligences had to have a means of expressing themselves.

Support from psychometric findings In addition to all the above criteria, Gardner claims that patterns of intercorrelations among psychological tests and factor analysis also support the theory of multiple intelligences. To get around some conflicting evidence, Gardner points out that the intelligence tests that have been used in psychology are based on paper-and-pencil formats of presentation and therefore some of the important types of intelligence might have been missed. He also points out that many psychometric tests are designed to measure not one but several types of intelligence simultaneously and therefore they do not always test what they are claimed to test.

A critique of Gardner's theory

In Gardner's view, all seven intelligences are independent in the sense that they satisfy each of the criteria listed in the preceding passages. In reality, however, the intelligences must interact with one another whenever a task requires the use of more than one type of intelligence. Moreover, for some types of intelligences, only a couple of criteria appear relevant, for other types, all criteria appear equally important. It is necessary to note that because the choice of different criteria were subjective and because these criteria were based on subjective evaluation of evidence, the whole theory might be considered an idiosyncratic view of what constitutes the major abilities.

It is perhaps necessary to highlight these criticisms with a few examples. First of all, concerning modularity, a major problem with Gardner's view is that, although there are some tasks that are appear localized, performance on many psychological tests cannot be linked to any particular site in the brain. Second, there are certainly some candidate processes, like olfaction, which should seemingly be added to this list (i.e., olfactory intelligence), more especially given that recent evidence suggests the existence of a separate memory system for odors (Danthiir et al., 2001). In addition, how might Gardner's theory account for the fact that measures of tactile and kinesthetic performance correlate so highly with measures of visualization? Indeed, this appears a finding that sports psychologists must certainly have preempted given the suggested benefits of visual imagery to elite athletes. Equally, how would Gardner (1983) reconcile the fact that mathematical abilities appear to be structurally independent from measures of logical reasoning (see Horn & Noll, 1994), when clearly they appear to constitute the same construct (i.e., logical-mathematical reasoning) inside his theory?

Indeed, comparisons of Gardner's theory with structural models leave the reader to ponder both considerable overlap and a number of potentially serious omissions. For example, the first four types of intelligence in Gardner's list have counterparts in contemporary structural models, and appear more clearly specified therein than he often leads his readers to believe. But what of replicated cognitive abilities, which do not have counterparts in Gardner's theory of multiple intelligences? Among primary mental abilities, concepts such as Word Fluency, Inductive Reasoning, Memory, and Perceptual Speed cannot be classified inside his system, not to mention the fact that higher-order memory and mental speed constructs are not even entertained.

A further limitation of Gardner's theory concerns the potential proliferation of intelligences. Assuming bodily kinesthetic intelligence is a distinct domain, do we take it that one should also distinguish tennis intelligence, athletic intelligence, football intelligence, dance intelligence, and golf intelligence? If not, one might assume that an individual who turns out to be highly proficient at football might equally have turned that talent to performing in a classical ballet production? Similarly, the concept of musical intelligence conceals differences between writing a musical score for the symphony and being able to play in a highly successful rock band without any formal training. Indeed, differences have even been documented between people's ability to play various musical instruments (Judd, 1988). It is questionable also whether some of these aptitudes are as important to real life as the cognitive intelligences. Certainly, being unable to appreciate music detracts from the quality of life, but low musical intelligence does not disrupt everyday functioning as subnormally low general intelligence does.

Emotional intelligence and the personal intelligences

Within his theory, Gardner identifies the personal intelligences as being "of tremendous importance in many, if not all, societies of the world—forms that have, however, tended to be ignored or minimized by nearly all students of cognition" (1983, p. 241). Gardner's personal intelligences, as we have noted at several points, clearly overlap with EI. Indeed, part of Gardner's definition of personal intelligence focuses specifically on the processing of affective information. Recall for an earlier point in this exposition that interpersonal intelligence includes the ability to understand other people and know what they feel. Intrapersonal intelligence, on the other hand, involves access to one's own feeling life, the capacity to effect discriminations among these feelings, and draw upon them as a means of guiding behavior. Attempting to locate these "intelligences" within the traditional psychometric domain, Carroll (1993) suggests that interpersonal intelligence is a specialized type of acquired knowledge (i.e., Gc ability). However, Gardner's other personal intelligence—"access to one's own feelings"—finds no counterpart in Carroll's account. Gardner would likely argue that this situation has arisen because adequate assessment of this intelligence has never appeared in the available psychometric literature.

To what extent is Gardner correct in asserting that the personal intelligences have "tended to be ignored or minimized by nearly all students of cognition" (1983, p. 241)? We would argue quite emphatically that this assertion is wholly misleading. As we demonstrate in appendix A, considerable attention has been devoted to the concept of social intelligence—the idea that politicians, clergyman, and counselors may be exceptionally good in dealing with interpersonal relationships. Indeed, much work on social intelligence has been carried out over the past 80 years and despite considerable efforts, it has proved difficult demonstrating its structural independence. Unfortunately, different putative indices of social intelligence tend to go together with other factors such as verbal comprehension and inductive reasoning. In terms of Gardner's criteria, at the very least, it can be said that the psychometric conditions for the existence of this multiple intelligence do not appear convincing.

Indeed, one might speculate which of the criteria for multiple intelligence might legitimately apply in the context of these personal intelligences. While history gives us exemplars of individuals who are extremely gifted in their interpersonal skills (e.g., Gandhi), it also the case that these individuals possessed high levels of linguistic intelligence, without which their contributions might not have gone on record. It is also extremely unlikely that there is the special case of an idiot savant, with advanced social skills, functioning below average on IQ tests—the expression of interpersonal intelligence would appear dependent on language (which most IQ tests assess).

Another problem for positing modularity for the personal intelligences is the observation that disorders of emotional or social competence appear as a symptom of frontal damage (see chapter 6). However, damage in this area, and especially the prefrontal cortex, is also associated with measures that Gardner would ascribe as indices of logical-mathematical intelligence (see, e.g., Duncan, Burgess & Emslie, 1995; Duncan, Emslie, Williams, Johnson & Freer, 1996). Furthermore, the evolutionary antecedents of the personal intelligences would appear questionable (Mackintosh, 1998). Thus, most primatologists agree that even monkeys (apparently the most social of all nonhuman primates) do not have a theory of mind (which would allow them to understand that other monkeys have emotions, hopes, beliefs, etc [see, e.g., Seyfarth & Cheney, 1997]).

Sternberg's triarchic theory

Sternberg (1985) has also emphasized a departure from traditional conceptualizations of intelligence. In particular, he defines intelligence as "purposive adaptation to, and selection and shaping of, real-world environments relevant to one's life" (1985, p. 45). By recourse to various analogies, Sternberg shows that "academic" intelligence, as assessed by psychometric tests, is imperfectly related to the ability to function intelligently in everyday life. For example, he gives anecdotal evidence of academically intelligent individuals who do not function well in academic settings because of emotional difficulties (see Brody, 1992). On this basis he goes beyond IQ to emphasize different aspects of intellectual functioning, prominent of which have included concepts that are not all that dissimilar from EI (e.g., tacit knowledge, practical intelligence). Before discussing these concepts, however, it would appear necessary to give the reader a brief overview of his systemic theory, which he refers to as a triarchic theory of human intelligence (Sternberg, 1985).

As the name suggests, Sternberg's triarchic theory of intelligence consists of three parts (also known as subtheories). In its entirety, the theory acknowledges that the term "intelligence" has many meanings. Three senses of "intelligence" are developed within this theory. We highlight these, along with the further subcomponents making up each so-called subtheory, in the passages that follow.

1   Intelligence and the internal world of the individual   This part of triarchic theory, also known as the *componential* sub-theory, refers to states and processes that underlie intelligent thought. Sternberg proposes three types of components, which essentially represent information processing mechanisms that appear in theories emanating from cognitive psychology:

1.1   Performance components   For analogy items (e.g., red is to stop as green is to ?), these include cognitive processes such as inference, mapping, encoding, and so forth. Other types of intelligence test items may have different sets of performance components. A possible criticism of these performance components is that there are a potentially infinite number of these processes. Thus, it is not known which are the most important, nor whether we should focus on narrow, atomistic processes or processes that are broad in scope.

1.2   Metacomponents   These are higher-order, executive processes, that are used to plan what one is going to do, to monitor the ongoing process, and to evaluate it after it is done. Metacognition, involves, for example, recognizing the existence of a problem, selecting a set of appropriate lower order components, choosing a strategy into which to combine performance components, monitoring solution processes, and evaluating the adequacy of a solution.

1.3   Knowledge acquisition components   These are used to learn how to do what the metacomponents and performance components eventually do. They include sifting relevant from irrelevant information (selective encoding) and combining the selected information to form an integrated and plausible whole (selective combination and comparison).

These knowledge acquisition components are important in acquiring higher vocabulary.

2 Intelligence and experience According to Sternberg (1985) intelligence is, best measured by, processes involving tasks and situations that are relatively novel and/or are in the process of becoming highly automatized. Two aspects of this *experiential subtheory* are emphasized inside triarchic theory:

2.1 Ability to automatize information processing It is claimed that the ability to automatize a particular process is a major aspect of intelligence. The process of reading, for example, can be highly practiced and automatized and more intelligent people seem to be faster readers. Experiments with the acquisition of various skills (e.g., chess playing) show that people who score high on intelligence tests acquire these skills more rapidly than people with lower measured intelligence.

2.2 Ability to deal with novelty Intelligent people can solve tasks that are non-entrenched and that have not been attempted previously. According to Sternberg, novel tasks make demands on a person's intelligence, which are quite different from those tasks in which automatic procedures have been developed. Inside triarchic theory, relatively novel tasks—such as visiting a foreign country, learning a new language, or mastering a new topic, like psychometrics—demand more of a person's intelligence. Sternberg also points out that novelty is a characteristic of many tests of fluid intelligence.

3 Intelligence and the external world of the individual The role of environment in intelligence is emphasized here, placing Sternberg in opposition to many of the so-called hereditarians, especially proponents of psychometric *g* (e.g., Jensen). It is argued that intelligence is not an aimless (or random) mental activity that happens to involve certain components of information processing and certain levels of experience. Rather, intelligence may be defined in terms of behaviors that are relevant to one's life. It is proposed that intelligent behavior is directed towards certain goals. There are three such goals within this, the *contextual sub-theory* of the triarchic model:

3.1 Adaptation to environment Intelligence involves adaptation to (i.e., achieving a good fit between oneself and) the environment. Environments differ, therefore although the same components may be involved the instantiations of these processes (i.e., behavioral manifestations) may differ across cultures. Thus, tests of intelligence that are adequate in one context may not be so in another context. In addition, entirely different abilities may develop in different cultures (e.g., spatial abilities among the Eskimos, Australian aborigines, and Polynesian navigators). Sternberg points out that one remarkable difference between Western and non-Western cultures involves perceptions of the role of time in our everyday lives and the need to schedule our activities into time slots. These differences between environments can influence the way people define intelligence. It also influences what one might believe to be adaptive behavior.

3.2 Shaping of the environment If adaptation is not possible, intelligent behavior often results in an attempt to *shape* and *change* that environment. In science, for example, scientists that are the leaders in the field tend to set new paradigms, they shape the environment. Those who follow them resort to adaptation. The difference, of course, is not in their use of shaping alone but rather rests in a combination of their willingness to do it, along with their skill in doing it.

3.3 Selection of new environment If adaptation and shaping fail, intelligent behavior is often indicated by leaving one environment and choosing another. Job selection to suit one's goals and skills is a typical example. There are many examples where selection of a new environment is the most intelligent course of action. Sternberg mentions 'the fate of the quiz kids'. As children, these individuals were selected for radio and TV shows based upon intellectual and personality traits. Almost all of them had exceptionally high IQs, typically well over 140 on standard measures of intelligence. Their adult lives, however, appear rather devoid of high achievement. Those who did achieve more than the rest, appear to have been able to find out what they were good at and pursue this activity relentlessly. The less successful ones could not find any one thing that interested them.

The main point of Sternberg's contextual sub-theory is that the expressions of intelligence can differ widely across individuals and groups, such that intelligence cannot be understood independently of the ways in which it is manifested. People mastering their environment seem to be able to capitalize upon their strengths and to compensate for noteworthy weaknesses. According to Sternberg, what is adaptive differs by degree, both across people and across situations, and therefore intelligence is not quite the same thing for different people and for different situations.

Triarchic theory: A critique

Sternberg's triarchic theory represents an ambitious attempt to reconcile psychometric (note his references to fluid and crystallized intelligence), information-processing, cultural, and lay (i.e., implicit) conceptions of human cognitive abilities. Some notions contained inside his subtheories may, however, be criticized on philosophical grounds. Metacognitive processes, for example, invite the idea of an homunculus (a person inside your head, à la Woody Allen's *Everything You Wanted to Know About Sex But Were Afraid to Ask*, who controls your actions), although progress is being made in developing a rigorous cognitive psychology of metacognition (e.g., Nelson & Narens, 1994). Moreover, the central tenets of triarchic theory are sometimes difficult to refute. In Sternberg's own words: "The breadth of the systems theories is a problem because it is difficult to disconfirm theories that are so broad. A sound theory should be specific enough that it could clearly be disproved, if evidence against it were to be found. Perhaps systems theories are so general that they incorporate almost anything under, say, 'adaptation to the environment'" (1995, p. 396).

Indeed, we would argue that while triarchic theory represents a bold step in the right direction for establishing a model of intelligence that combines many aspects of scientific knowledge, available empirical evidence supporting all facets is scant. Carroll (1980, 1993), for example, has called for Sternberg's data on analogy tasks to be factor-analyzed to show the generality of performance components over different tasks. We might also question where concepts, that are clearly part of the cognitive ability realm and of some importance both conceptually and practically (e.g., broad auditory reception and the broad memory factors), might fit inside triarchic theory.

Triarchic theory and practical intelligence: Implications for emotional intelligence

Criticisms aside, triarchic theory appears to have broaden the conceptualization of intelligence to include in particular, practical intelligence (e.g., Sternberg, 1993; Sternberg et al., 1993, 1995, 2000). Focusing in particular on the contextual sub-theory, Sternberg and colleagues argue that while academic intelligence is useful in the classroom, it is practical intelligence that helps us to solve problems occurring in everyday life (especially work). According to Sternberg and colleagues, practical intelligence is especially dependent on acquired "tacit knowledge," which is procedural rather than declarative, informal rather than formal, and generally learned without explicit instruction. In short, tacit knowledge is reflected in knowing what to do in a given situation, and getting on and doing it. It occurs without ever necessarily being taught what to do, how to do it, or being able to articulate why you are doing it.

Sternberg and colleagues have studied tacit knowledge in disparate populations, ranging from business managers and university professors to North American and rural Kenyan children (Hedlund & Sternberg, 2000). Tacit knowledge tests generally involve the presentation of a set of problem scenarios (often encountered by the person inside their cultural context), with the participant required to rate the quality (or appropriateness) of a set of responses to these situations. The set of ratings the individual generates for all scenarios is used to assess tacit knowledge within that domain. These tests (like measures of EI) do not lend themselves to veridical scoring. Thus, tacit knowledge tests have been scored in one of three ways: by correlating participants responses with an index of group membership (expert, intermediate, novice), by judging the degree that the participants' response meets professional standards (or norms), or by computing the difference between participants responses and some expert prototype.

It is worth noting that tacit knowledge tests have low (but positive) correlation with measures of traditional academic intelligence (Gc, in particular). These tests also appear unrelated to personality constructs, with the possible exception of measures of agreeableness (see, e.g., Wagner & Sternberg, 1985, 1990). They also appear to have considerable utility. For example, in a study of business managers, tacit knowledge scores correlated in the range of 0.20 to 0.40 with criteria such as salary, years of management, and whether the manger worked for a Fortune 500 company (Wagner & Sternberg, 1985). Importantly, tacit knowledge measures also appear to possess incremental predictive validity, over and above measures of academic intelligence (Hedlund & Sternberg, 2000).

Practical, social, and emotional intelligence share a focus on acquired knowledge (both declarative and procedural), flexible cognitive-retrieval mechanisms, and problem solving that does not lend itself to one correct solution (Jones & Day, 1997). Recently, Hedlund and Sternberg (2000) argue that the main distinguishing feature between each concept lies in the content of the knowledge, and the types of problems, emphasized. For them, "Unlike many approaches to understanding social and emotional intelligence, the tacit-knowledge approach ... limits the definition of practical intelligence to cognitive ability (such as knowledge acquisition) rather than encompassing an array of individual differences variables" (Hedlund & Sternberg, 2000, p. 157).

Moreover, the tacit knowledge approach is not limited to a specific domain of performance, but rather is relevant to understanding problems of a practical, social, or *emotional* nature.

Indeed, inside the tacit knowledge approach, three categories of tacit knowledge directly impinge upon social and emotional intelligence: managing self, managing others, and managing tasks (Wagner & Sternberg, 1986). Tacit knowledge about managing oneself refers to knowledge about self-motivation for dealing with everyday tasks, while tacit knowledge about managing others refers to knowledge about how to deal with one's interpersonal relationships. Tacit knowledge about managing tasks refers to knowledge about how to perform specific tasks, including planning activities, monitoring progress, and evaluating outcomes. Overlap between EI and tacit knowledge is non-incidental and yet tacit knowledge tasks appear to have construct and predictive validity, where this is questionable for many measures of EI. Given this imbalance, it is tempting to conclude that further research should focus more on understanding practical intelligence over and above EI.

Conclusions

In chapter 2 we argued that establishing the validity of any personal trait requires both a strong measurement model, and a conceptual and theoretical rationale that links the trait to neural and cognitive processes. In this chapter, we have examined the extent to which aspects of conventional intelligence meet these criteria. So far as psychometrics are concerned, we have seen that intelligence has progressed beyond Spearman's notion of the "positive manifold," and a single underlying general intelligence. Messick (1992) has summarized some of the strengths and weaknesses accompanying multivariate theories of intelligence and models espoused by Gardner (1983) and Sternberg (1985). He concludes that the available evidence supports the efficacy of the theory of fluid and crystallized intelligence, noting that neither of these systems models is necessarily at odds with the general tenets of this structural theory. Further, Stankov et al. (1995) have highlighted some of the conceptual similarities that Gf/Gc theory shares with other psychometric approaches (e.g., Guttman's [1992] radex model). Inasmuch as Carroll's (1993, p. 639ff.) three-stratum model also shares correspondence with Gf/Gc theory, salient features of this structural model may extend to parallels with a wide range of 'intelligence' theories (e.g., Royce & Powell, 1983). We have found that theories that neglect measurement specification of this type, such as Gardner's (1983) multiple-intelligence theory, are correspondingly weak.

Hence, it makes no sense to operationalize EI as a construct entirely detached from existing measurement frameworks for ability. The handful of studies that correlate EI scales with intelligence tests (with varying results) have so far done little to place EI within the wider psychometric context, as we shall discuss in chapter 5. A concept such as EI (perhaps better labeled as "emotional competence") could be accommodated inside the theory of fluid and crystallized intelligence. In principle, EI might be defined as either a higher- or lower-stratum ability. To establish EI as a broad, higher-level ability, perhaps on a par with Gc and Gf, would require that multiple primary emotional abilities were identified. These abilities would need to be psychometrically and conceptually distinct from existing constructs, but sufficiently intercorrelated to support a distinct high level factor. Alternatively, EI might be construed as a narrower, primary ability that might be subsumed under higher-order abilities. Indeed, existing tests of EI might refer to several distinct primary abilities that do not, in fact, cohere around a higher-order intelligence. For example, emotion perception, which may be represented by a distinct primary (Roberts et al., 1998), might be grouped with other visual perception abilities that support a higher-order perceptual factor such as Gv. Social intelligence, if conceptualized as a set of acquired, largely language-based skills, might be a subcomponent of Gc. Existing research on EI has yet to address these issues in any systematic way.

At the theoretical level, research on mental ability has provided a wealth of detail on how cognitive ability is related to psychological processes. Sternberg's (1985) triarchic theory is an exemplary model of how an ability may be linked to information-processing, real-world adaptation and cultural-bound conceptions (although some of its specific propositions may be incorrect). We might also wish to add a biological substrate to this account. Indeed, intelligence may be conceptualized within the three-level cognitive science model as a property of neural systems, computational function, and real-world adaptation (Matthews, 1997). Gf/Gc theory may offers an overarching framework for relating psychometrically defined constructs to these levels of theoretical understanding (see also Mackintosh, 1998). Although each of the current authors has been actively involved in such research, we have refrained from discussing these efforts at length for fear that they will take us too far afield. Nevertheless, a brief detour is perhaps in order to demonstrate, with specific examples, the types of correspondence herein asserted.

Recently, Roberts and Stankov (1999) examined a number of processing speed indices that support fluid but not crystallized intelligence. Attentional mechanisms that are linked to cognitive complexity are critical. Computational models focusing on more specific cognitive mechanisms, such as lexical-access speed (the speed of retrieving information about words, stored in long-term memory), on the other hand, share more in common with crystallized intelligence (Hunt, 1978). At the neurophysiological level, Gc and Gf may be differentiated in terms of the brain systems that support these computational functions. In addition, operation of computational modules may be modulated by motivational influences that serve to press intellectual functions into the service of real-world adaptation (Zeidner & Matthews, 2000). It is our contention that biological and computational models of the future will look towards structural models emphasizing the diversity of processing functions supporting intelligence, resulting in more successful application of 'reductionist' scientific frameworks (Stankov & Roberts, 1997).

As we have noted, acknowledging the breadth of intelligence offered by a multidimensional model of intelligence must also inform our understanding of EI. Research is needed to probe the neuropsychological, computational, and high-level cognitive concomitants of EI scales, together with their genetic and developmental antecedents. We note that this undertaking must be shaped by what is currently known from research devoted to emotions, discussed in the next chapter. Unfortunately, as we will see, current conceptualizations of EI fail to make adequate contact with existing psychometric ability models, or with the psychological theory of emotion, and related fields such as personality, motivation, and neuroscience. Nevertheless, our current understanding of EI, must, of necessity, be shaped by those attempts made so far to assess and validate the construct, which are reviewed in chapter 5.

4

Emotions: Concepts and Research

We know too much and feel too little. At least, we feel too little of those creative emotions from which a good life springs.

Bertrand Russell

We cannot hope to understand EI without a clear conception of emotion. As noted in chapter 2, emotion is a complex and much-disputed psychological faculty. The science of emotion is hampered by the subjective nature of felt emotional states, and so there is an underlying problem of how to link this elusive quality of felt experience to physical reality. Researchers have variously tried to link emotion to brain structures, or to more abstract psychological constructs such as cognitions and self-regulative state. It is important also to understand the function of emotion in supporting adaptation to a changing world and how emotions may sometimes be maladaptive rather than adaptive.

We begin this chapter by reviewing the main conceptual issues surrounding emotion, which originate in prescientific philosophical attempts to understand emotion and continue to shape contemporary discourse concerning both emotion and EI. Next we will look at attempts to differentiate and measure basic categories and dimensions of emotion: the source material on which EI operates. We will review possible sources of emotion, paying attention in particular to the tension between biological and cognitive accounts and placing theoretical accounts of emotion within an ecological framework that sees emotions as arising out of the interplay between person and environmental demands. Finally, we will consider functional accounts that see emotion as a concomitant of adaptation, and outline the consequences of emotion for real-world behavior. If we know what emotions are for, perhaps EI relates to how well emotions achieve their intended purpose.

We will conclude that emotion is a complex, diffuse concept that may be expressed differently at different levels of abstraction. Emotional intelligence does not leap out at us as a necessary concomitant of emotion theory. Instead, we must search for some competence in emotion-regulation that is distinct from emotion itself and from other outcomes of the adaptive process. Where we choose to look for this competence depends on our theory of emotional functioning. Plausible cases might be made that EI is variously a property of brain physiology, the cognitive architecture, or high-level self-knowledge, but existing data do not clearly point to any of these sources as the site of EI.

Conceptualizing Emotion

Philosophical perspectives on emotions

Although we all experience emotions, they appear among the most difficult elements of psychology to conceptualize scientifically. The backdrop to the science of emotion is a long history of philosophical debate, often entwined with religious and ethical issues (Lyons, 1980, 1999). Three interlocking topics, in particular, have contemporary resonance. The first is the mind-body problem. Lyons (1999) identifies a dualist strand of thought, originating with Plato and continuing through Thomas Aquinas and Descartes, that distinguishes an immaterial soul that inhabits a physical body. As Lyons states: "Theoretically speaking, emotions could no longer be seamlessly psychosomatic. A mediaeval philosopher-theologian had to choose whether to place emotions in the soul or the body" (1999, p. 26). Emotions might variously be seen, for example, as a largely undesirable consequence of animal-like physiology or as an expression of higher, immaterial, levels of being. Descartes's resolution of the problem was (crudely put) to identify emotion with the soul's consciousness of bodily reactions to events. The alternative, Aristotelian view (and also held by the Stoics) was that body and mind were expressions of the same basic stuff (monism). Aristotle and later monists, such as Spinoza, saw emotion as a concomitant of beliefs and desires, which colored awareness of somatic reactions. These issues are mirrored by contemporary debate over whether emotions are primarily a quality of brain (neuroscience) or mind (psychology).

The second issue is the relationship between emotions and consciousness. Common sense would tend to identify emotions as conscious feelings, and some modern authors (e.g., Ben Ze'ev, 2000; Ryle, 1949) have pointed to the absurdity of positing unconscious, unfelt feelings. Cartesian approaches too see emotion as intrinsically conscious, reflecting but detached from somatic reactions. On the other hand, if emotion is seen as a quality of body rather than of soul, consciousness may provide only an indirect expression of emotion. Lyons, discussing Aquinas, states, "Emotions were viewed as felt bodily tendencies or desires, and only impinged upon the soul and its cognitive, evaluative and volitional life in so far as these bodily desires were reflected upon by humans. Sometimes our emotions remained wholly bodily or sensory" (1999, p. 26). In contemporary research, the issue is whether conscious feeling states *are* emotions, or partial expressions of some underlying, unconscious system (a view that resonates with psychoanalytic theory).

The third issue is the causal place of emotions. Do emotions have direct consequences, or is emotion simply a concomitant of other physical or mental processes that are the true causal agents? In Aquinas's view, for example, emotions correspond to bodily impulses, and so have a motivating force. Descartes, however, saw emotions as an end point, arrived at after interaction between body and soul had already organized the appropriate somatic and behavioral responses. Contemporary researchers are wary of assigning a direct causal role to a subjective feeling. Indeed, the traditional behaviorist view is that emotions are just froth on the surface of consciousness, with no causal implications at all. Others see emotions (conscious or unconscious) as directly linked to causal systems. One view is that cognition and emotion are separate though interacting systems in such a way that emotion is somehow non-cognitive in nature (Izard, 2001; Zajonc, 1980). To the extent that emotion is identified with system functioning (which is not fully accessible to consciousness), emotion may be seen as a description of a causal agent.

Conceptual issues in contemporary theories of emotion

We turn our attention now to examine contemporary ways of understanding emotion, which might provide a conceptual basis for EI. Unfortunately, theories of the psychology of emotion give us a variety of somewhat incompatible approaches to the subject. Emotion has been variously related to a set of largely independent (i.e., modular) brain systems, to a central executive control system residing in the frontal cortex, to dimensions of subjective experience measured by questionnaires, and to information-processing routines for self-regulation. Many conceptions of emotion necessarily give us many conceptions of EI.

From a scientific standpoint, a central problem is the subjective nature of emotions. Although emotions have physical counterparts such as facial expressions, brain activity, and characteristic behaviors, emotions are defined primarily by labels that we attach to conscious awareness: feelings of joy, sadness, anger, and so forth. Consciousness is a difficult thing to build into a scientific theory. It is not a physical component of the brain, nor an aspect of behavior, nor an element of computation. Psychological science has a materialist basis, and so it is an enigma why any material object, including the brain, has any awareness at all. The broad answer to the problem, for psychologists, is to see emotions as *corresponding to* some underlying process or system, which can be described in materialist terms. Emotions might represent a type of learning, specific brain systems, properties of information-processing software, and so forth. In very general terms, the scientific issue then is the nature of the correspondence. If a person is in a given emotional state, can we infer that the brain is *necessarily* in some physical state, or that particular computations are being performed? We should distinguish a direct correspondence (a one-to-one mapping or isomorphism) from a statistical correlation between emotion and a property of physical reality. For example, a brain system might typically be active while an emotion is experienced, without the system being necessary or sufficient for the emotion to occur.

Researchers differ sharply in their conceptions of the correspondences between emotion and physical reality. The first fissure between theorists concerns the centrality of subjective experience. Biological theorists, especially (e.g., Damasio, 1999; Panksepp, 1998), are inclined to downplay subjective emotion. For them, emotion is fundamentally a state of specific neural systems, activated by motivationally significant stimuli, and so is a latent construct, which is difficult to observe directly. The activity of the system is expressed through various responses that may dissociate somewhat, including autonomic nervous system activity, behaviors, and subjective feelings, which are conceptually distinct from emotion (Damasio, 1999). Conversely, emotion may be seen as a subset of conscious experience. This approach is identified with operationalization of emotion through self-report measures. There is a large literature on the measurement of emotion and feeling states, that uses standard psychometric techniques to identify and validate dimensions of feeling (Mackay & Cox, 1980). Validated measures of subjective emotions such as anxiety and depression (e.g., Spielberger, 1972) can then be treated as constructs in their own right, rather than as pale reflections of some deeper, but unmeasured, emotion system.

Second, there is contention over the relationship between emotion and other basic psychological categories of cognition and motivation. No self-respecting researcher, to our knowledge, denies some overlap between emotion and the other categories. Emotions are typically associated with evaluations of personal significance, and with motivations to act. Fear correlates with evaluations of personal threat, and the inclination to run away or escape the feared object, for example. However, two views of the inter-relationships between cognition, motivation, and feeling may be distinguished. Traditionally, emotion, motivation (or "conation"), and cognition make up a three-fold classification of the mind (e.g., Hilgard, 1980; Mayer, Frasier Chabot & Carlsmith, 1997). In other words, emotion represents a distinct system, which is separate from motivation and cognition, though interacting with them. According to Mayer et al. (1997), EI describes how emotion may facilitate cognition, and cognition may facilitate intelligence.

Given separate domains, there are various conceptions of the inter-relationships between them. One view is that emotions are chained to motivations and cognitions. Below, we describe basic emotions theory that assigns each major emotion a characteristic motivation and cognition, such as the impulse to flee, and the thought of danger, in the case of fear (Plutchik, 1980). A more subtle view is that emotions represent a high-level integration of other domains. As Lazarus puts it, "emotions ... express the intimate personal meaning of what is happening in our social lives and combine motivational, cognitive, adaptational, and physiological processes into a single complex state that involves several levels of analysis" (1991, p. 6).

An alternative view posits that emotion represents a complex of more basic components: cognition, evaluation, motivation, and feeling (Ben Ze'ev, 2000).[1] This perspective gives us a broader conception of EI, in that it may have cognitive, motivational, and feeling elements. According to Ben Ze'ev (2000), EI relates to the interplay between emotion (in this broad sense) and intellectual thought. He discriminates between modes of evaluation characteristic of the emotion and the intellect, respectively: "schematic" evaluation, which is spontaneous and content-specific, versus "deliberative" evaluation, which is more stable and concerned with generalizable principles. In a sense, emotion and intelligence refer to different styles of cognition. Lazarus (1991) makes a somewhat similar point in arguing that Zajonc's (1980) supposedly distinct emotion and cognition systems may relate to different modes of information processing.

A third source of discord refers to the extent to which feeling states are free-floating, as opposed to grounded, in some specific interaction with the external environment. A distinction is often made between *emotions* and *moods* (e.g., Ortony & Clore, 1989; Parkinson, 1996). An emotion is transient and tied to a particular stimulus or event. It is often said to reflect the person's cognitions of the event, and so emotions may be quite complex and differentiated. Moods, however, are more free-floating and need not refer to any particular object. They may also persist longer than emotions, although they may be brief, in duration. Moods are more easily reduced to a small set of basic dimensions than are emotions. It is sometimes said that emotions may be more intense than moods, which tend to reside in the background of awareness (e.g., Simon, 1967). (*Affect* is a useful as an umbrella term for describing feeling states that take in both emotions and moods, although there is some variability in usage in the literature.) Much emotion theory is quite explicitly concerned with emotions as grounded in specific interactions with the environment. However, this theoretical stance jars with the actual content of emotion measures, which often assess general feelings, rather than feelings *about* some event.

Multiple conceptions of emotion

Unfortunately, the answers to traditional philosophical questions about emotion are unresolved, such that we are left with a variety of incompatible definitions. We can choose to define emotion as a high-level mental property (e.g., Lazarus, 1991) or as an attribute of physiological functioning (Damasio, 1999). We can choose to identify emotions with parts of conscious experience or with latent systems whose state may be unconscious. We can link emotions to psychological or physiological systems with causal force, or we can downgrade emotions to epiphenomenal froth. Conceptual analysis may provide some answers (e.g., Ben Ze'ev, 2000), but there is little that is definitive in the empirical evidence to constrain choices one way or the other. Generally, it is useful to apply the three-level cognitive science framework described in chapter 2 (Pylyshyn, 1999). Depending on the research context, it may be useful to see emotion as a property of brain systems or information-processing or, as in Lazarus's (1999) conception, abstracted personal meanings that do not map onto neural or cognitive architectures in any simple way (we will tend to favor the Lazarus conception in this book).

In this section we have been able only to convey the flavors of the different conceptual approaches. However, it may be useful to distinguish two families of emotion theory, which are sometimes conflicting and sometimes complementary. The first type of theory starts with a conceptual analysis of emotion, distinguishing emotions from other aspects of mentation (i.e., mental life), and attempting to delineate defining features of both emotion, in general, and specific emotions. Naturally, different instances of theory differ in fundamental issues relating to definition, consciousness, and causality. The common theme, though, is that emotion is a latent construct, which may be distinguished from the subjective feelings that are one of several manifest expressions of emotion. This approach may be worked out in terms of cognitive psychology (Lazarus, 1991), neuroscience (Panksepp, 1998), or philosophical-conceptual terms (Ben Ze'ev, 2000). The implications of the model may be explored empirically through studies of various types of response, including self-report, overt behavior, and physiology.

The second approach starts with an *operationalization* of affect, for example, through a questionnaire that measures the intensity of feelings such as depression and happiness. Research then focuses on explaining the causes and consequences of the constructs indexed by the questionnaire, so that the subjective feeling is foregrounded. Mood research is usually of this kind. Thayer (1989, 1996), for example, has identified energy and tension, as two fundamental aspects of mood, and explored their antecedents and psychological consequences in empirical studies. However, there is no reason why more specific emotions cannot be grounded in the same operational approach, and some authors (e.g., Izard et al., 1993), have developed self-report emotion measures. Whereas the first approach addresses emotion primarily as a universal psychological quality, the second is especially concerned with *individual differences*: why people are more or less emotional than one another and the behavioral consequences of this variation across individuals.

Both approaches may inform understanding of EI. On the one hand, we need a general understanding of what it means to be emotionally intelligent (i.e., what the underlying competencies are that support adaptive functioning in emotional encounters). Conceptual models of emotion should tell us something about how emotions may be linked to more (or less) adaptive behaviors and outcomes. On the other hand, we have identified individual differences as central to EI. The move to quantify EI, through tests such as the MSCEIT and Bar-On scales, assumes that some people are more emotionally intelligent than are other people. If so, a central task for research is to inter-relate individual differences in EI to individual differences in affective functioning, measured by subjective measures of emotions and other states, and by objective measures of behavior and performance.

Categories and Dimensions of Emotion

Thus far, we have looked at some broad conceptual issues generated by over a century of scientific attempts to understand emotion. However, we do not typically experience some undifferentiated emotion. Instead, we feel the specific emotions of anxiety, happiness, shame, and so forth, perhaps reflecting a few basic underlying emotions just as the color spectrum is based on three primary colors (Plutchik, 1980). If emotions are differentiated in this way, is it really sensible to refer to some intelligence controlling management of these very different experiences? Thus, we look next at how emotions are differentiated and categorized by psychologists. Investigation of individual differences necessitates a good operationalization of emotion, that is, reliable and valid scales that represent a focus for research linking emotion scales to causes and consequences. In fact, dimensional approaches to emotion have been surprisingly controversial, reflecting the rift between more conceptually driven and more data-driven theories indicated above. Lazarus (1991) argues that dimensionalizing emotion obscures the distinct relational themes to which each emotion relates, according to his theory. On this view, emotions are to be seen as discrete states, rather than points in a multidimensional continuum, although the strength of the emotion may vary continuously. The structure of emotions may be different within persons than between persons, a point obscured by dimensional analyses (Pekrun, personal communication). We will survey the distinctions made between basic categories or dimensions of emotion, although we will find that the dimensional approach, with its basis in differential psychology, is more immediately productive for studies of EI.

Categories of basic emotion

Evidently we experience different emotions: joy, shame, anxiety, pride, disgust, and so on. The idea of EI seems to require some unity of handling these different emotions. It does not logically follow that a person good at handling fear, for example, is also good at handling rage. Former president Bill Clinton is widely perceived as a good communicator who connects emotionally with voters, but also as a man poor at dealing with lustful passions. We need some conception of what are the basic emotions, how people differ in emotional experience, and how we can conceptually unify people's handling of qualitatively different types of emotion. A more subtle issue of the same kind is how emotional states are related to other aspects of mental state, especially motivations and cognitions. A student agonizing over a difficult exam paper may also be experiencing thoughts of the consequences of failure and motivations to escape the threatening situation. If the student fails the paper, should we attribute their adaptive failure specifically to their anxious emotion, or to their distracting thoughts or to their lack of commitment to apply effort to the task at hand? In the latter cases, perhaps we are dealing not with EI, but cognitive or motivational aspects of adaptation. There is an extensive empirical literature differentiating different dimensions of emotion (most simply, positive and negative emotions), and we will now review it.

Many of the principal theories of emotion attempt to draw up lists of *basic emotions* on rational grounds, with the aim of distinguishing qualitatively different categories of emotion that may correspond to fundamental adaptive functions. This approach goes back to Descartes (see Lazarus, 1991, p. 79), who listed wonder, love, hatred, desire, joy, and sadness as basic. One modern approach is to distinguish emotions that are cross-culturally universal, that may also be found in higher animals, and that correspond to some evolutionary challenge. Plutchik (1980) claims that fear, anger, joy, sadness, acceptance, disgust, anticipation, and surprise are primary emotions that are associated with characteristic stimulus events, inferred cognitions, behaviors, and adaptive effects (see table 4.1). Ekman (e.g., 1993) on the basis of universal facial expressions, picks out happiness, fear, surprise, anger, distress and disgust, and contempt, although he cautions that there may be other basic emotions that do not have a unique facial signal; especially positive emotions such as amusement, contentment, and pride in achievement. Oatley and Johnson-Laird (1996) differentiate emotions on the basis of their function in signaling the status of plans for goal achievement: four potentially "acausal" free-floating emotions of happiness, sadness, anger, and fear; and five necessarily object-related emotions of attachment, parental love, sexual attraction, disgust, and personal rejection. Panksepp's (1998) list is based on discrimination of mammalian brain systems for

Table 4.1
Characteristics of eight primary emotions (Plutchik, 1980)

Feeling state	Stimulus event	Inferred cognition	Behavior	Adaptive effect
Fear, terror	Threat	Danger	Running away	Protection
Anger, rage	Obstacle	Enemy	Biting, hitting	Destruction
Joy, ecstasy	Potential mate	Possess	Courting, mating	Reproduction
Sadness, grief	Loss of valued person	Isolation	Crying for help	Reintegration
Acceptance, trust	Group member	Friend	Grooming, sharing	Affiliation
Disgust, loathing	Gruesome object	Poison	Vomiting, pushing away	Rejection
Anticipation	New territory	What's out there?	Examining, mapping	Exploration
Surprise	Sudden novel object	What is it?	Stopping, alerting	Orientation

fear, rage, expectancy (behavioral facilitation), and, similar to Oatley and Johnson-Laird, systems for more complex social behaviors such as maternal nurturance. Hence, basic-emotions theories offer a "syntax" for understanding emotions whose "semantics" or adaptive meanings may be quite different.

We could compile other lists, but their general style should now be apparent. Although the distinctions between emotions seem sensible, and categorization of some kind is essential, basic emotions have basic problems (see also Ben Ze'ev, 2000, for a conceptual critique). First, different theorists disagree on the criteria for deciding what is basic. What appears basic may differ depending on whether we look at brain systems, at facial expressions or at personal meanings of emotions. If different brain and mind systems were closely aligned, the problem would disappear, because different criteria would be equivalent. Unfortunately, this is not the case: the mappings between different emotional systems are not clear-cut. In fact, data on cross-system correlations of emotional indices suggest that links are weak (e.g., Eysenck, 1997). Second, most basic emotion systems emphasize evolved functionality; emotions correspond to specific adaptive tasks linked to evolutionary challenges. Unfortunately, there is no definitive way of deciding what the key adaptive challenges actually are. Should we see parental love as a subcomponent of acceptance/affiliation? Should we distinguish specific fears from one another and from anxiety (given that phobias may be biologically based)? Rational considerations do not provide clear answers to such questions. Third, it is unclear that there is any simple mapping between emotions and adaptive challenges. For example, joy may be felt not just in the context of sexual reproduction (as table 4.1 has it), but also in situations involving escape from danger, friendship, nurturance and personal accomplishment. The attempt to limit emotions to specific adaptive contexts often seems forced. Fourth, it is unclear too whether, as Plutchik (1980) suggests, some emotions are primary, and others are secondary, perhaps being blends of primaries. Panksepp (1994), for example, downgrades the status of both low-level, reflex-lie responses such as startle and disgust, and 'higher sentiments' found only as subjective states in humans. Conversely, Ekman claims that all emotions are basic: "There may be some characteristics that are very important for one emotion and of little significance for another. It may never be possible to have an adequate comprehensive theory of emotion. Instead we may need to have a separate theory for each emotion, to best capture its uniqueness" (1994, p. 19).

Dimensions of mood and affect

Alternatively, we can investigate the structure of emotional experience in empirical data, using a dimensional approach to operationalize affect. Techniques such as factor and cluster analysis may indicate how many dimensions we need to differentiate to account for most of the reliable variation in emotion. Strictly, this research usually addresses mood rather than emotion; it is easier to measure feeling states persisting for a few minutes than it is to measure transient states closely tied to changing external events. Various methods, some quite sophisticated psychophysically, have been used in mood assessment (Mackay & Cox, 1980). There are reliable and valid questionnaires for many emotions/mood states, of which the best known are probably the Spielberger scales for anxiety, anger, depression, and curiosity (e.g., Spielberger et al., 1999). Also widely used are adjective checklists, on which people rate how well mood descriptors such as "tense" and "calm" apply to their current feelings (e.g., Matthews, Jones & Chamberlain, 1990; Thayer, 1989).

Most researchers agree that there are only a few dimensions of mood (see Thayer, 1989, for a review). In contrast to basic emotions, these dimensions are *bipolar*, contrasting opposite qualities, such as a continuum of states from happiness to sadness. The structure may be as simple as two dimensions: one for positive affects and one for negative affects (Watson & Clark, 1992). Thayer (1989, 1996) offers a similar scheme for self-report arousal distinguishing energetic arousal (vigor versus tiredness) and tense arousal (nervousness versus calmness). Two-dimensional models may be a little too austere. Wundt (1905) distinguished pleasantness-unpleasantness, relaxation-tension, and calm-excitement as fundamental. There is modern factor-analytic data favoring a scheme of this kind (Adan & Guardia, 1997; Matthews et al., 1990), separating the overall pleasantness of mood (or hedonic tone) from two Thayer-like subjective arousal dimensions. Schimmack and Grob (2000) used structural equation modeling to show that dimensions of positive and negative affect are inadequate to explain variance in mood; a three factor-model distinguishing pleasure, wakefulness and tension performed better. There may also be additional dimensions relating to social feeling states such as dominance (Sjoberg et al., 1979). Dimensional models of this kind have proved very useful for organizing empirical data on the biological and cognitive antecedents of mood, and on their psychological consequences (Thayer, 1989).

Studies of mood are challenging to most basic emotions models. One the one hand, they highlight dimensions that basic emotion theories neglect, such as the energy-tiredness spectrum that is fundamental to the Thayer (1996) and Matthews et al. (1990) models. On the other hand, they suggest that some of the distinctions made are too fine-grained to be very distinctly represented in people's experience. Fear, anxiety, anger, and unhappiness may be conceptually distinct, but in actual fact, they tend to co-occur. Anger, for example, is experientially different from other negative emotions, but aversive events often provoke both anger and sadness (Berkowitz, 1993). State anger is almost indistinguishable from state anxiety and depression measured by Spielberger's STPI (Zeidner, unpublished). Watson and Clark (1993) show that the correlation between anxiety and depression measures is often as high as those between alternate measures of anxiety or of depression; that is, there is a lack of discriminant validity.

There are several possible explanations for the mismatch between concepts and data. First, basic emotions research misses an essential level of organization of human feeling states, in terms of two or three dimensions of mood or basic affect. It follows that there is no simple isomorphism between dimensions of basic affect and the more differentiated categories of emotion evident in brain systems, facial expressions, and personal meaning. Second, there may in fact be isomorphism (or nearly so) between moods and underlying systems. Watson and Clark (1992), for example, relate positive and negative affect to brain systems for reward and punishment, implying that these systems are more basic than the multiple systems identified by Panksepp (1998) and others.

Third, there are questions over the interrelationship of moods and emotions. Previously, we referred to the view that emotions must refer to some object (Clore & Ortony, 2000), so that free-floating moods do not qualify as emotions, and identified some difficulties for this conceptualization. This analysis leaves open the question of why attachment of contextual information to a feeling state apparently changes dimensionality. It is unclear too how we could operationally distinguish, say, anxious emotion from anxious mood. For example, state anxiety, as measured by the Spielberger scale, is usually seen as an emotion, but it correlates highly with tense arousal, conceptualized as a mood (Thayer, 1989). Clore and Ortony also point out that the contextual information that anchors affect to an object is not necessarily consciously accessible, so, presumably, what appears to be a free-floating mood might actually be an emotion.

A reasonable solution to such difficulties is to identify a small number of dimensions of 'basic affects' that contribute to both mood and emotion states. Conventional scales do a good job of measuring these affects (see Matthews & Deary, 1998, for a review), and the empirical literature (reviewed below) shows how these basic affects align with psychological functioning. Within the universe of affect, there may be continuous rather than discrete differentiation, such as temporal persistence, intensity, richness of associative links with representations of events, and accessibility to consciousness of contextual information. "Mood" and "emotion" might be better seen as rather loosely defined terms that signal the extent of explicit linkage of the feeling state to precipitating events. Subsequently, we will focus on affective states in general, using the terms "mood" and "emotion" in a non-rigorous way as labels for the different research traditions in the area. Thus, experiments on affect are rarely looking at affect alone, but at complexes of affect, motivation and cognition related to the person's interactions with the external environment.

Overlap between affect and other domains

To operationalize emotion and mood, it is required that questionnaire items refer to the *short-term* experience of *affect*. However, if these constraints are relaxed, considerable overlap between affective dimensions and other individual difference factors is found. At the level of transient states, affect is entangled with constructs from other domains of experience, especially motivation and cognition. Work on anxiety states shows the importance of distinguishing affective (tension) and cognitive (worry) components of states (Sarason et al., 1986; Zeidner, 1998). Matthews et al. (1999) developed and validated a comprehensive questionnaire, the Dundee Stress State Questionnaire (DSSQ), for assessing subjective states in performance settings. They found that the mood dimensions identified in earlier work (Matthews et al., 1990) correlated with dimensions related to motivational and cognitive experience.

Factor analysis of the ten scales produced a three-factor solution stable across different samples, and at different times of assessment, which is shown in table 4.2. The first factor (task engagement) brings together Thayer's energy dimension with task motivation and concentration (i.e. a complex of affect, motivation, and cognition). The second factor (distress) links mood dimensions of tension and unpleasant mood to cognitions of lack of control and confidence. The third factor (worry) is exclusively cognitive, relating to self-focused attention, low self-esteem, and intrusive thoughts, i.e., "cognitive interference" (see Sarason, 1984). These factors appear to be differentially sensitive to different sources of stress, and show different patterns of correlation with

Table 4.2
Three higher-order dimensions of subjective state (Matthews et al., 1999)

	Task engagement	Distress	Worry
Subjective states	Energetic arousal (affect)	Tense arousal (affect)	Self-focused attention (cognition)
	Task interest (motivation)	Unpleasant mood (affect)	Low self-esteem (cognition)
	Success strivings (motivation)	Low confidence (cognition)	Thoughts about current task (cognition)
	Concentration (cognition)		Thoughts about other concerns (cognition)
Cognitions	Challenge	Threat	Avoidance coping
	Task-focused coping	Emotion-focused coping	Emotion-focused coping
	Low avoidance coping		
Transactional meaning	Commitment to effort	Mitigation of overload	Self-reassessment

personality measures and with performance (Matthews et al., 1999). They also relate to different patterns of cognition of external demands, representing different meanings of the person-environment transaction (Matthews, Schwean et al., 2000; see also chapter 8).

Long-term stabilities in response and experience define personality trait dimensions (see chapter 2). Traits may be defined by emotional qualities: Spielberger's (1972) trait anxiety dimension represents a predisposition to experience short-term anxiety states. Certain broader traits, such as those of the Five Factor Model, have a pronounced affective component. Neuroticism and extraversion are sometimes said to relate to negative and positive affective vulnerability respectively (Watson & Clark, 1992), although this view is over-simplified (Matthews, Derryberry & Siegle, 2000). This dispositional basis for emotion provides one avenue for linking EI to established personality constructs. We discuss personality further in chapter 9. For now, we simply note that variability in emotional response overlaps with stable personality traits.

Implications for emotional intelligence

The data reviewed show that the dimensional structure of affect is complex. Basic emotions theories tend to assume a series of isomorphisms between emotions and other categories of functioning. Typically, each emotion is said to align with its own characteristic cognitions, motivations, and behaviors. However, empirical data (e.g., Matthews et al., 1999) show that the affective psyche simply cannot be partitioned into these neat boxes. Empirically, we seem to find a different organization of subjective experience at different levels of generality. At the lowest level, there may be fifteen (Lazarus, 1991) or more, basic emotions. However, the covariance of these emotions suggests a higher-level organization in terms of only two (Watson & Clark, 1992) or three (Matthews et al., 1990) fundamental dimensions. Above this level, there is a further structural description in terms of complexes of affect, motivation, and cognition. Behavioral consequences of emotion may, therefore, be intrinsic to the specific emotion (e.g., guilt and restitution), or a product of fundamental mood states (e.g., mood-congruence effects), or a consequence of affective-cognitive-motivational complexes, which are associated with changes in coping (Matthews, Schwean, et al., 2000). EI cannot be defined with reference to emotion alone.

The discrimination of different categories or dimensions of affect is challenging to the concept of EI. If, as in basic emotions theory, we have multiple, independent systems supporting different emotions, where is the common element that might relate to EI? A hot-tempered person might have some deficiency in an anger system, but normal functioning of other emotional systems. Such a modular view of emotional functioning is antithetical to the concept of EI as a general faculty for handling emotion. The existence of different levels of structural description is similarly problematic: is EI tied to the handling of very specific emotions, or to higher-level constructs? The view of emotion as strongly modular is countered to some extent by the clustering together of specific emotions around basic affects, but it is unclear whether, for example, people might have separate emotional intelligences for handling positive and negative affects.

Similarly, dispositions to experience positive and negative emotion may constitute major elements of stable personality. Crudely, we might relate high EI to the disposition to experience high positive affect and low negative affect. Such a state, as well as being preferred by people, is also the polar opposite of the maladaptive states of low positive affect and high negative affect seen in emotional disorder (Watson & Clark, 1993). Consistent with this view, Bar-On's EQ-i scale relates quite strongly to personality dimensions associated with high negative affectivity and low positive affectivity (e.g., Dawda & Hart, 2000), as further discussed in chapter 5. However, although well-adapted people may tend to enjoy more pleasant emotions, we may not be able to link emotional states to adaptive outcome in any simple way. Negative emotions may sometimes be adaptive and positive emotions counter-productive. In fact, as discussed further in chapter 8, assessment of the adaptive significance of emotions requires a transactional perspective (Lazarus, 1991), that evaluates the emotion in the context of some person-environment interaction. Negative emotions may sometimes be an entirely appropriate reaction to challenges such as being demeaned (anger) or threatened (anxiety).

A further limitation of EI as an emotional disposition is that this view neglects the self-reflexive aspects of the person's experience of emotions. Salovey and Mayer (1997) emphasize *self-regulatory* functions of EI: the person's metaexperience of their own emotions and active control of personal emotion. In this conception, EI is at one remove from emotion itself. Intelligence resides not so much in the emotions one experiences, as in how these emotions are handled. Consistent with this position, Mayer, Salovey, Gomberg-Kaufman, and Blainey (1991) have shown that individual differences in mood-regulation strategies, such as taking planned action and suppression, are psychometrically distinct from the moods themselves.

Sources of Emotion

To understand how EI regulates emotional response, we must understand the sources of emotions, and how the genesis of emotions is modulated by the physiological and/or psychological processes that support EI. Does EI reside in some especially adaptive configuration of the brain systems that generate emotion? Or is EI a quality of biases in information-processing that filter experience of emotive events to select the essential information for maintaining emotional awareness and effective action? Or does EI relate to self-knowledge, in the sense of understanding how to manage emotional response in the course of seeking worthwhile and attainable goals? We also need to understand how EI relates to the processes that may support individual differences in emotion as a disposition, i.e., what makes a person dispositionally cheerful or morose. In this section, we review theories of the origin of emotions, and what they tell us about the nature of adaptive emotional functioning.

Historically, debates on the source of emotions have addressed the issue of whether emotions are *centrally* or *peripherally* generated. The question is whether emotions are a direct reflection of some brain system, or whether emotions are constructed in some more indirect way from the cues provided by peripheral signals such as a racing heart. The centralist view gains credence from evidence that emotions are influenced by damage to certain brain areas and by drugs such as cocaine and heroin that affect neurochemistry. On the other hand, the peripheralist view is supported by studies showing that, within some limits, the way we experience bodily activity seems to feed into emotional experience (Parkinson, 1985). Traditionally, theories of emotion have been rooted in biology. Theorists from Charles Darwin onwards have been struck how emotions seem to be linked to bodily responses. However, as we saw in chapter 2, it is important to distinguish cognitive from neural level explanations. The postwar years have seen an explosion of interest in relating emotion to the functioning of the "software" or information-processing programs supported by the brain. In this section, therefore, we will distinguish the more traditional centralist and peripheral positions, before considering how the distinction is represented in cognitive models, and the implications of these conceptions of emotion for EI.

Emotion and central brain systems

The development over time of the debate between centralists and peripheralists tells us much about the conceptual difficulties of contemporary emotion theory. Centralist thinking can be traced back to Darwin's view that emotions are concomitants of physiological reactions; crying when sad, for example, evolved from the response of the eye to a foreign body. His studies of emotions aimed to show that emotional responses were innate, appearing reflexively to trigger stimuli of evolutionary significance (although he allowed for partial repression of behaviors by exercise of will). In other words, emotions are part of an integrated biological response and are rigidly tied to other components of that response. Modern centralism is usually traced to twentieth-century studies that link emotion to specific brain systems. Cannon (1927) proposed that the thalamus is the seat of the emotions. Events activate this structure, which outputs emotion and physiological change concurrently. (Contemporary studies de-emphasize the thalamus in favor of other brain areas). At around the same time, Hans Selye (1936) proposed a centralist theory for the longer-lasting negative emotions associated with chronic life disturbance. He borrowed the term "stress" from material engineering to refer to the progressive changes in behavioral and physiological function observed in animals subjected to various noxious agents, including disease, toxins and trauma. A "General Adaptation Syndrome" described the progression of the stress response from initial alarm to eventual exhaustion and breakdown of bodily systems, expressed in psychosomatic and psychiatric illnesses. He saw these changes as controlled by a "hypothalamo-pituitary axis," which influences other organs through the autonomic nervous system and hormone secretion (Selye, 1975).

In the postwar period, centralist models of emotion were boosted by work on nonspecific arousal of the cerebral cortex. The idea of linking emotion to some sort of general excitation of the brain lurked at the back of many of the early theories. Darwin (1890) referred to an excess of "nerve-force" as a driver of emotion. In the 1940s, Moruzzi and Magoun (1948) seemed to have provided a measure of nerve-force by placing electrodes on the scalp and measuring the spontaneous electrical activity of the cerebral cortex of the brain (the electroencephalogram or EEG). They noted that the waveforms they observed corresponded to the activity of the subject. States of mental activity and emotional excitement were associated with small-amplitude, high-frequency waves, termed beta waves (frequency > 13 Hz), whereas more relaxed but still wakeful states were linked to higher-amplitude, slower waves called alpha waves (8–13 Hz). Drowsiness and sleep (with the exception of "dreaming" rapid-eye-movement sleep) were linked to still slower waves.

The continuum of activity evident in the EEG came to be described as "arousal" or "activation" (Duffy, 1962), as though the brain were a kind of light-bulb whose luminance varied with the current it would support. Emotion could then be seen as a concomitant of cortical arousal. Hebb (1955), for example, suggested that moderate levels of arousal generated positive emotion, whereas high levels produced agitated, negative emotion. It has often been assumed that moderate levels of arousal are preferred. Arousal theory has tended to fall out of favor in more recent cognitive neuroscience work, which emphasizes the roles of multiple activating systems associated with different brain areas and neurotransmitters (e.g., Parasuraman et al., 1998). Nevertheless, the idea of generalized energizing systems remains influential.

Contemporary studies emphasize more specific brain systems believed to have evolved to handle motivationally significant stimuli. These include evolutionarily relatively primitive systems, such as the amygdala, and areas in the frontal lobes of the cerebral cortex, whose development is an especially human characteristic. Evidence for the role of these systems in emotion comes from studies of experimentally induced brain lesions in animals, and accidental damage in humans. Links between the various neurotransmitters of the brain and emotion are also important (Panksepp, 1985). The general position is that various brain systems analyze incoming stimuli for reward, punishment and other motivational implications, and concurrently produce both emotion and physiological change. Individual differences in these brain systems may support personality traits such as anxiety, neuroticism, and extraversion (Zuckerman, 1991). Perhaps some individuals are fortunate enough to possess brains that accentuate the positive and screen the negative aspects of life, conferring desirable qualities such as optimism, confidence, and motivation that support EI.

Areas of the frontal lobe, such as prefrontal cortex, may of particular importance as a higher-order system that regulates the functioning of other, more primitive emotion systems (e.g., Damasio, 1994; Rolls, 1999). Damage to these areas produces disruption of emotional function, with symptoms such as mood swings, impulsivity, and inappropriate emotion, coupled with difficulties in personal and social decision making (Bechara et al., 2000). As we shall discuss in chapter 6, the frontal lobe may support an emotional executive system as a prime candidate for a neurological basis for EI.

Emotion as awareness of peripheral response

The contrary, peripheralist perspective, is generally attributed to William James and Carl Lange. This perspective, although still rooted in biology, emphasized a more psychological basis for emotion, from an essentially Cartesian standpoint (Lyons, 1999). James saw emotion as a kind of perception based on awareness of signals from peripheral bodily organs, such as the heart and skin. Common sense suggests that if we meet a bear, this event causes a state of fear, and so we run away. James turned common sense on its head by proposing that the threatening event elicits preorganized bodily reactions. These include what we now call autonomic nervous system responses such as accelerated heart rate, trembling, shallow breathing, facial expression, and behaviors such as flight. Awareness of these responses IS emotion: running away precedes fear. Similarly, we do not weep because we are sorry; we are sorry because we weep.

James (1890) rejected the attempt simply to list emotions and their physical concomitants. He stated, "The merely descriptive literature of the emotions is one of the most tedious parts of psychology. And not only is it tedious, but you feel that its subdivisions are to a great extent either fictitious or unimportant, and that its pretenses to accuracy are a sham." He suggests instead that by posing causal rather than descriptive questions we reach a deeper level of inquiry. His analysis of causality suggests that emotional expressions are not as strongly coupled to physiology and behavior as a taxonomic approach would suggest. As Lange (1885/1912) pointed out, joy can be associated with talkative or dumb behavior, and grief can lead to restless lamentation or to sitting bowed down and mute. In other words, the *construction* of the emotion from its physical basis allows from some slippage in its expression, and we need a psychology of emotion separate from biological underpinnings.

Peripheralism fell out of favor in the first part of the twentieth century, due to difficulties identified by Cannon (1926) and others, including the slow response of peripheral systems. However, Schachter and Singer (1962) revived interest in the link between peripheral somatic response and emotion. Their study suggested that it was the person's interpretation of the bodily signs of arousal that generated emotion, rather than central brain activity. Commentators have identified various theoretical weaknesses in the Schachter and Singer position, together with failures to support predictions in subsequent empirical studies (e.g., Leventhal & Tomarken, 1986; Reisenzein, 1983). Causal attributions of arousal feedback may amplify emotion, as the theory predicts, but there is no evidence that peripheral arousal is the principal cause of emotion.

The principal legacy of the Jamesian tradition is continued interest in the role of feedback from physiological systems in producing emotion (e.g., Damasio, 1994; Heilman, 2000), although, in general, central brain systems seem to be more strongly implicated (e.g., Marshall & Zimbardo, 1979). However, James' work was important also for introducing psychology as well as physiology into emotion research, albeit in a rather limited way (see Plutchik, 1994). By contrast with Darwin's fixed response patterns, James referred to the individual's personal idiosyncrasies, memories, and associations as shaping the emotion. As Markus has commented, "From James' chapter on emotions, it is evident that feelings are not pure bodily states. What is experienced depends on the nature of the 'I' doing the experiencing" (1990, p. 182). The nature of the self is a major focus of the cognitive conceptions of emotion, which we will discuss next.

Emotion and cognition

During the 1960s, the cognitive revolution led to a fundamental re-examination of every area of psychology. The idea that mental processes can be compared to symbolic computer programs (see chapter 2) allowed theorists to detach emotion from some immediate biological substrate. In the 1960s, Richard Lazarus (e.g., Lazarus & Alfert, 1964) conducted experiments using stimuli liable to make any male volunteer acutely uncomfortable; films of the ceremonial incision of the penis and scrotum performed by a primitive culture as a rite of passage for adolescents. Using films of this type, Lazarus found that both subjective distress and autonomic nervous system responses (skin conductance) depended on the orientation given to the subject and their strategy for dealing with the distressing material. For example, distress was reduced using a denial instruction emphasizing that the incisees welcomed the operation, or when participants made efforts to detach themselves from the content of the film. Such findings indicate the importance of the appraisal of events, and of the strategies adopted for coping with them. The cognitive approach was also bolstered by clinical studies suggesting that emotional disorders derived from maladaptive cognitions

(Beck, 1967; Ellis, 1962). These theorists pointed to the role of faulty knowledge and styles of interpreting events as the underlying source of cognitions.

Cognitive theories can be expressed in both centralist and peripheralist terms, which may be complementary. They are centralist to the extent that information processing directly outputs emotional states. Simon (1967), for example, suggested that emotions reflect interruptions to ongoing behavior. As discussed further in the next chapter, it has also been argued that appraisal processes generate emotion. Evaluating an event as a threat (consciously or unconsciously) may necessarily produce anxiety, and anxiety may require a prior threat appraisal. As with biological centralism, we have a concept of emotion as a necessary concomitant of a central (cognitive) process. However, there is not necessarily any simple one-to-one mapping between specific cognitions and emotions. Averill (1980), for example, makes an important distinction between what he calls "prereflective" and "reflective" experience. Prereflective awareness is the raw stuff of experience, generated, presumably, by unconscious analysis of events, and common to animals and humans. Reflective experience refers to the subsequent, meaning-based reconceptualization of experience. According to Averill, "The emotions are often considered to be the epitome of prereflective or lived experience.... But that is not the case. Emotional experiences are reflective, the product of second-order monitoring" (1980, p. 316).

Transactional theories (Lazarus, 1991) see emotion as an index of some abstracted personal meaning. Specific information-processing routines, such as a threat appraisal, may feed into the personal meaning, but do not rigidly determine it. Instead, the emotion reflects a construction of meaning based on the various cues provided by analysis of the eliciting event. Transactional theory is discussed further in chapters 7 and 8. Similar concepts are expressed in contemporary work by *self-regulative* theories of emotion (see Boekaerts et al., 2000), which see emotion as arising out of the cognitive control of meeting personal goals. These theories suggest that emotions may relate to "knowledge-level meanings" that do not map in any simple way onto either neural or computational processes. It is tempting to use Averill's (1980) term "constructivism" for this perspective, but its association with social psychology is misleading for the present purpose. A better term is *evaluative* models of emotion (see Ben Ze'ev, 2000), to signal that (1) emotions reflect evaluation and interpretation of physiological and psychological cues, (2) emotions are intimately linked to personal meaning (Lazarus,

1991), and (3) emotions reflect preexisting memories (e.g., schemas) that shape the process of interpreting the state of the self.

Averill (1980) was also an important pioneer of the social-psychological understanding of emotion. Events are understood, in part, on the basis of their fit with social norms: people react with negative emotion when others violate these norms (which, of course, vary from culture to culture). Other social-psychological work emphasizes the role of emotions in controlling social interaction, in signaling social intentions to other people, using "feeling rules" that define the emotional significance of events, appropriate expressions of emotion, and appropriate social behaviors (Hochsbert, 1979; Levy, 1984). Such an approach leads to radical social-constructivist approaches, which state that emotion is not a property of the individual, but of a discourse between individuals, actively constructed and negotiated during social interaction (see Harré & Gillett, 1994).

Sources of emotion: Implications for emotional intelligence
These different conceptions of emotion suggest differing views of EI as a quality of adaptive functioning. In the centralist tradition, emotion may be an integral part of either a biological state, such as the level of activity of some brain system, or of a cognitive state, such as a set of codes representing an appraisal. To borrow a philosophical term, this is as an "essentialist" view of emotion, which has a fixed nature, derived from its lockstep relationship with neural or information processing. In terms of the three-level cognitive science framework, there may be an isomorphism between the emotion and some pattern of activity within either the neural or the cognitive architecture. In this case, EI may be a quality of the underlying neural or cognitive substrate. There are several ways such an idea could be developed.

Emotional intelligence as (lack of) deficit   To the extent that individual differences in EI reflect suboptimal functioning of central brain systems for emotion, we might think in terms of "emotional stupidity" rather than "emotional intelligence." Deficit in EI might, at the extreme, reflect actual organic damage to central brain systems. Patients with lesions of ventromedial frontal cortex show pronounced deficits in social decision-making, deficits that Bechara et al. (2000) have linked to the loss of EI. Variation in EI in normal groups might reflect non-clinical levels of deficit; for example, impulsivity might be attributed to a less than optimal frontal emotion system. The test of individual differences

in face perception included in the MSCEIT suggests a place for this model in the Mayer-Salovey-Caruso model of EI. The deficit position could be developed both in neurological terms, as here, or in terms of impairments in information processing without direct reference to the biological substrate.

Emotional intelligence as environmental tuning   A more subtle idea concerns how central systems might operate across a range of environmental contingencies. For example, a threat detection system (whether conceived neurally or cognitively) should produce a response scaled to different levels of environmental threat. To take a cognitive example, Williams et al. (1988) proposed that state anxiety influences a threat-detection processor that attaches a threat value to each incoming stimulus. High anxiety led, in effect, to over-estimation of threat, so that the person was prone to overreact to minor hazards. Conversely, low anxiety might be associated with potentially dangerous neglect of threat. In general, emotional states seem to signal how the person is tuned to respond to significant events (Matthews, Pitcaithly & Mann, 1996). A simple model might attribute EI to moderate levels of sensitivity of motivational systems.

An alternative instantiation might recognize some degree of bias as adaptive—in particular, a moderate degree of optimism. People seem to differ in their dispositional level of happiness (Diener, 2000), so perhaps one aspect of EI is simply the biasing of central systems to output more happiness than sadness. It is also widely believed that high self-esteem is intrinsically beneficial, although one view that is gaining ground is that self-esteem is more beneficial when won through striving wholeheartedly for worthwhile ends, rather than derived from praise unrelated to actual behavior (Dweck, 2000). The view that a positive bias is adaptive seems, at least implicitly, to be part of Bar-On's (2000) conception of EI in that he includes scales for optimism and happiness as part of his questionnaire. According to Bar-On, "It is this positive mood which fuels emotional energy required to increase one's motivational level to get things done" (2000, p. 383). The conceptual relationship between affect and motivation is not very clear here, but the point seems to be that happiness is not just an outcome of good adjustment, but a motivating force, and so dispositional happiness is seen as a cause rather than an effect of EI.

Alternatively, emotions may relate to knowledge-level personal meanings. If so, both efficiency and bias of the interpretive process might serve as a basis for EI. However, by contrast with the previous hypotheses, we cannot describe efficiency and adaptive bias in terms of some preset hardware or software configuration. The most efficient understanding of an emotional situation may be dependent on personal goals and the environmental context for attaining those goals.

EI as effective interpretation of emotional situations   Some people may be more efficient at interpreting emotional cues in the light of personal motivations than others, i.e., in reading the true personal significance of an encounter and acting accordingly. The link between alexithymia and low EI (Parker, 2000) implicates difficulties in generating internal representations of emotion that facilitate adaptation to external demands. Qualities such as appraisal of emotions and social skills that are frequently found as components of self-reports of EI (Petrides & Furnham, 2000b) relate, at least loosely, to this concept. The Mayer-Salovey-Caruso conceptualization of EI includes branches for assimilating and understanding emotions, which might also be related to the more effective extraction of personal meaning. However, their scales assess abstract understanding, e.g. of the meaning of emotion words, without reference to personal goals and context, an ability which may be of limited relevance to real-world adaptation (Zeidner, Matthews & Roberts, 2001).

EI as adaptive bias in problem evaluation   Another possibility is that high EI is associated with biases in evaluating the problem at hand that generate more adaptive emotions concurrently with promoting effective action. For example, in transactional stress theory (Lazarus, 1991), one process that feeds into both emotion and coping is secondary appraisal of one's competence to cope with demanding situations. People who are high in self-efficacy, in that they have confidence in their coping ability, appear to deal with stress more effectively (Bandura, 1997). So perhaps EI relates to self-serving biases in interpretation of situational cues that maintain self-confidence and application to solving the problems of daily life. Even if there is no bias within the cognitive architecture, the emotionally intelligent person may be able, to use a sports term, to "find a way to win," i.e., to commit their capabilities resourcefully in meeting the needs of the situation. Bar-On (1997), for example, includes self-regard as a component of EI. He believes that having a strong sense of identity is a prerequisite for emotional awareness.

The protean nature of EI thus derives, in part, from the different ways in which emotions may be generated, which lead to rather different conceptions of the nature of adaptive emotional responses. EI theorists are prone to draw upon constructs at different levels of abstraction, avoiding a rather clear conceptual decision. On the one hand, EI might be defined in terms of a specific level of analysis, e.g., as a physiological property of the frontal lobes, or as a set of high-level strategies for self-regulation. On the other hand, EI might somehow be distributed over different levels, appearing in different guises in neurophysiological function, in information processing and in strategy choice. Substantiating either conception of EI requires investigation at the process level, an enterprise we review in part II of this book.

The Natural Ecology of Emotions

Central to the concept of EI are its benefits in everyday life, so we need to consider the relationships between emotional response and behavior and adaptation in real-world encounters. In this section, we review the origins of emotions within an ecological perspective, and, in the next section, we consider how emotions may facilitate or impede effective response in real life. Emotions are experienced within a natural ecology of ongoing person-environment interaction (Lazarus, 1991). That is, emotions are generated by the processes discussed in the previous section within the framework of a self-regulative feedback loop whereby the person attempts to change the external world so as to maintain some ideal state (including, but not limited to, a preferred emotional state). Emotions signal both the demands placed upon the person, and the person's style of action upon external reality. In this section we briefly survey the factors that drive emotional experience in the real world. We will also consider how emotional intelligence might be linked to real-world adaptation.

Antecedents of mood and emotion

One of the defining operational characteristics of mood is its changeability over time spans of minutes or hours (Zuckerman, 1976). An affect measure that fails to change is more like a stable personality characteristic. In fact, it is generally straightforward to show that mood measures show only modest test-retest reliabilities at time intervals of a day or more; moods fluctuate. For example, Matthews et al. (1990, 1999) found 1-day test-retest correlations of about 0.40 for fundamental mood dimensions, for individuals assessed in the same setting. This correlation is sufficiently low to imply that moods are not just driven by immediate situational factors; presumably, changing the situation at re-test would give lower correlations still. Hence, a major research goal is to determine the factors that influence mood variability. Although affective states fluctuate, they do so about different baseline values; some people are more dispositionally cheerful than others, although everyone has happy and unhappy moments. These baseline values relate to personal-ity, as discussed in chapter 9. Personality also relates to the amount of variability about the baseline (Hepburn & Eysenck, 1989); some people experience mood swings, whereas others are more stable (Larsen, 1987). In the remainder of this section, we focus on determinants of change in level of affect, leaving aside personality for the time being.

Two basic methods are used to investigate antecedents of mood and emotion. The first is experimental. In the laboratory, we can manipulate various stimuli, and assess affective change. Much of this work is con-cerned with stress factors such as loud noise, but positive stimuli such as comedy videos are also used. Occasionally, naturalistic experiments are run, such as allowing subjects to "find" a coin or receive a small gift (e.g., Isen, Daubman & Nowicki, 1987). The second method is correla-tional: in essence, to observe moods and their concomitants in diary studies of real life, which afford linkages between mood and real-life events.

Both methods have limitations. The artificial stimuli and procedures of experimental studies may not be ecologically valid. Another common objection is that moods in the laboratory may be much weaker than those experienced in real life. It is true that life-or-death situations can-not be simulated, but data show that this objection is probably over-stated. For example, Matthews et al. (1999) found that elevation of tense arousal was of similar magnitude (about 1.2 standard deviations) during a real university examination and during a time-pressured laboratory working memory task. Affect is not necessarily closely scaled to the ob-jective significance of events. Certainly, experimental studies are essen-tial for isolating specific influences on mood, and attempting to tease apart biological and cognitive influences. The disadvantage of diary studies is the lack of control over events, and the respondent's aware-ness of events. If a correlation between a particular event and mood is found, it is difficult to isolate the critical aspect of the event or of the person's reaction to it. However, such studies are essential in linking affect to everyday functioning, and providing evidence on antecedents of affect that may converge with evidence from experimental studies.

A review of the various influences on affect established by empirical science is beyond the scope of this book (see Thayer, 1989, 1996). But, very broadly, we can discern at least five types of causal factor:

Biological agents Evidently, drugs affect mood, as shown in numerous double-blind studies, providing evidence on the central brain systems involved. Drug action in real-world settings is not just a matter of pharmacology. Subjective effects of drugs such as alcohol, caffeine and nicotine vary somewhat with expectancies, the ambient environment, and the person's intentions in taking the drug (Kirsch & Weixel, 1988; Matthews, Davies et al., 2000). Various other factors presumed to have a strong biological component include physical activity (e.g., exercise), illness, and nutrition, although it is likely that cognition has moderating effects.

Biological rhythms There are powerful circadian rhythms, especially in energetic arousal, driven by "brain clocks" or oscillators, and entrained to external cues indicating time of day (Adan & Guardia, 1993). Another important biological rhythm is the female menstrual cycle, whose notorious effects on mood (premenstrual tension) probably reflect both variation in hormone levels and in expectancies and attributions (Asso, 1987).

Cognitions The role of cognition is shown most directly by autosuggestion studies, in which verbal techniques are used for mood induction. The Velten technique requires the participant to read aloud a series of self-descriptive statements, such as "I feel really depressed." Hypnosis may also be effective in changing mood, at least in suggestible individuals. These techniques produce change in objective performance as well as subjective mood (Larsen & Sinnett, 1991). Experimental studies also show that mood change induced by stressors is substantially mediated by the person's appraisals of the source of demand and their coping strategies (Matthews, Derryberry, et al., 2000). Beyond experimental studies, many everyday stressors seem to have an important cognitive component. Effects of loud noise on affect depend on cognitive factors like perceived utility of the noise source (military aircraft noise fails to disturb true patriots) and perceived controllability (Jones, 1984). There is also an expansive literature suggesting that affective consequences of major and minor life events are mediated by cognitive factors (Lazarus

& Folkman, 1984). Cognitions also drive emotions linked to *feedback from action*. Within the dynamic system described by Lazarus, the person's appraisal of the results of their own actions feeds back into emotional experience.

Social interaction   Diary studies demonstrate the importance of social factors in everyday mood. Social activities are broadly associated with more positive moods, but arguments are a potent source of negative affect (Watson & Clark, 1988). Social support from others tends to protect against negative mood in response to adverse events. In part, cognitive models explain the influence of social factors. For example, in anger and aggression, the person's appraisals of hostile intentions of another person appear to be critical (Dodge, 1991). Social interaction may perhaps have emergent properties that are difficult to explain in information-processing terms, as explored by constructivist models. Certainly, feedback processes are critical to the emotive aspects of emotional encounters. Social motivations may also be important, such as the person's desire to express an emotion appropriate for the social context (Parkinson, 1996).

Mood-regulation   Critical to understanding moods is that people voluntarily seek to change moods they dislike or consider inappropriate for their current activity. Table 4.3 lists strategies identified by Thayer (1996), in order of efficacy (according to self-report, which may not be

Table 4.3
Six strategies for mood management, ranked according to their perceived successfulness (Thayer, 1996)

Rank	Strategy	Examples
1	Active mood management	Relaxation, stress management, engage in cognitive activity, exercise
2	Seeking pleasurable activities and distraction	Engage in pleasant activities such as humor or a hobby
3	Withdrawal, avoidance	Be alone, avoid person or thing causing bad mood
4	Social support, ventilation, and gratification	Call or talk to someone, engage in emotional activity
5	Passive mood management	Watch TV, drink coffee, eat, rest
6	Direct tension reduction	Take drugs, drink alcohol, have sex

veridical). In other words, we have a dynamic, feedback-driven process where mood states operate as both input and output variables. Mood-regulation is an element of coping. The person evaluates their mood state against contextual standards, and chooses to repair negative moods or maintain positive affect. Strategies used may involve biology (taking drugs), cognition (attention to positive self-statements), or social interaction (seeking social support). It is simplistic to see these efforts as entirely homeostatic (i.e., aimed at tension-reduction). Apter (1982) discusses how, in certain "paratelic" states of mind, the person actively seeks vivid experience and excitement.

Implications for emotional intelligence

We have seen that one aspect of EI is the person's tendency to experience 'appropriate' emotions that match the demands of the situation, facilitating rather than impeding effective management of the external world. Indeed, Lazarus (1991, 1999) proposes that emotions describe a relation between person and environment. The picture emerging from empirical research is that affective states register a complex interplay between the objective environment, intra-personal biological and cognitive factors, and social interaction. Affective states appear to be determined by multiple, qualitatively different factors, which, in turn, makes it difficult to pinpoint EI. We could variously see EI as a property of brain systems, cognitions, social skills, or acquired coping strategies, such that each of these sources might deliver maladaptive emotion. It is difficult to see any conceptual unity here. Furthermore, the sensitivity of emotion to environmental factors raises problems in attributing maladaptive emotion to the person factor of EI rather than to the situation. A person who appears low in EI may simply be in a particularly difficult life situation, which admits no easy solutions.

Major life events do not necessarily elicit extremes of mood and emotion (Folkman & Lazarus, 1984). People appear to regulate their exposure to the environment to minimize strong emotion (especially negative emotion). Typically, people choose not to take on challenges far beyond their capabilities. We have seen that Salovey and Mayer emphasize self-regulation of emotion as critical to EI, and especially to mood-regulation as an influence on emotional state. Perhaps, individual differences in response to life events are controlled by EI in the guise of effective self-control of emotions. However, this view may be too narrow, in that the person's skills in regulating life experiences so as to avoid disruptive emotions may be as important as their regulation of the emotions themselves. EI may relate to choosing attainable goals, to recognizing one's limitations and to seeking out supportive environments and people, processes that promote adaptation without acting directly on the person's emotional state.

Even when people are exposed to major adverse events, such as natural disasters, it seems that only a minority develop severe post-traumatic stress symptoms (Bowman, 1997; Rubonis & Bickman, 1991). The resilience of the human spirit in adversity might be attributed to EI, in the sense of effective assimilation of traumatic events into conscious experience, as described by theories of traumatic stress (e.g., Foa & Riggs, 1995). On the other hand, external factors such as the severity of the event, availability of social support and culture-bound scripts for handling trauma also contribute to maladaptive emotional response. Just as some of the "practical intelligence" of a society resides in its technology for enhancing intellectual function (e.g., books and computers), so too emotional adaptation may reflect whatever support the harmed person may find in the outside world. A central problem in investigating EI in real-world contexts is to distinguish person and situation factors (and their interaction) in the genesis of adaptive emotions.

Functions and Behavioral Consequences of Emotion

It seems unlikely that emotions are simply an accident or a curiosity. Most theories address the question of what emotions are actually *for*? To answer this question, we also have to address the behavioral consequences of emotion, and their consequences for adaptation. Ideally, a theory of emotion would describe (1) how emotion influenced action and (2) how these behavioral effects of emotion subserved some adaptive goal. Crudely, for example, fear increases the likelihood of a person running from a source of danger, a response that serves to preserve personal safety. If we know what emotions achieve for the person, perhaps we can relate EI to success or failure in obtaining the benefits of emotions.

Functions of emotion
As discussed in previous chapters, a theory of EI requires some conception of adaptive success and failure, and criteria for passing judgment on whether or not a person has successfully managed an emotion-provoking encounter (see also chapter 8). We may take both a long and short view of the functionality of emotions. Evolutionary psychology,

following on from Darwin, sees emotions as the legacy of natural selection operating in the Pleistocene era, when our species separated from its lower primate precursors. Hence, we might expect that emotions will sometimes conflict with adaptation to modern cultures and technology. In many countries, spiders are nonexistent (or trivial) sources of threat, so phobic responses to house spiders will simply be disruptive, however adaptive they might have been in earlier environments. Other adaptive challenges, such as handling conflict with other people and seeking a mate, may not have changed so much, with emotions playing the same roles as in prehistory. The evolutionary perspective does not mesh straightforwardly with EI. Is the high EI person simply the evolutionary success story, and the low EI person the misfit, with little chance of passing on his or her genes? Or is the emotionally intelligent person someone who can transcend their evolutionary heritage and disregard or otherwise manage dysfunctional emotional impulses incompatible with contemporary culture?

Over the shorter time scales that characterize the emotions of the individual human, we must seek different answers (evolutionary psychology is notoriously vague about "proximal" mechanisms for behavior). For example, self-regulative theories propose that emotions signal the status of personal goal-satisfaction. In this case, EI might reside in self-knowledge and understanding of personal motivations, as a product of culture and personal history as much as evolved predispositions to specific trigger stimuli. Yet another approach would be to emphasize the communicative functions of emotion. In turn, this would give us a social-psychological perspective on EI, perhaps as the ability to read and express emotions accurately.

Consequences of emotions

If emotions are adaptive, than the emotion has, through natural selection and/or learning, the function of promoting some desired outcome. Clearly, emotions may have a range of consequences, some unintended. We might distinguish *direct* and *indirect* consequences of emotion. A direct consequence would reflect the adaptive purpose of the emotion, such as, in the case of fear, a mobilization for flight (a biological preparedness) or readiness to compete in a high-stakes sporting encounter (a culturally influenced, acquired personal meaning). An indirect consequence would be an outcome unrelated to adaptive function, such as the distraction that may result from anxiety, or the health problems that may follow from chronic stress.

In assessing how well a person has handled an encounter, we need to look at the full range of outcomes. If we are to describe a person as "emotionally intelligent," we need to be sure that apparent success in handling encounters is not canceled out by some indirect cost or harm in other areas of functioning, or, conversely, that there are not hidden benefits to apparently unsuccessful behaviors. For example, the tennis player John McEnroe was notorious for temper tantrums on court—apparently an instance of poor self-control and low EI. However, as Murgatroyd (1983) has pointed out, his emotional immaturity did not seem to impair his performance. Murgatroyd believed that fits of temper were a strategy for self-motivation that aided his successful playing career, with the desirable side effect of raising McEnroe's profile among the public.

These perspectives have been taken up by EI theory. Bar-On (1997), for example, has developed several scales for adaptability, such as problem solving, which point to the role of effective, goal-directed action in EI. Similarly, Mayer, Caruso, et al. (1999) have included emotion management as one of the major branches of their ability based model. One difficulty here is that EI researchers have offered little evidence from tightly controlled experimental studies on relationships between EI and objective behavior. We cannot assume that a person who claims good problem-solving skills is, in reality, an effective problem solver.

Maladaption and psychopathology
Further insight into the functionality of emotion is obtained by studying people with clinical disorders related to emotion. Perhaps, an understanding of clearly maladaptive emotions will contribute to conceptualizing EI (see chapter 10). Another issue for EI is whether the concept applies equally to normal and pathological emotion. Just as individuals of very low intelligence are described as "mentally retarded," can we identify people whose EI is so pathologically low as to cause them major life problems? Of course, negative emotion is central to many pathological conditions, especially anxiety and mood (depression) disorders. Individuals with personality disorders often seem to have various difficulties in handling emotional situations. Another element of emotional pathology of affect that Goleman (1995) emphasizes is the flatness of affect and lack of empathy seen in psychopaths, such as, in the extreme case, serial killers. There are also emotional conditions at the fringe of pathology such as alexithymia (difficulties in labeling emotion) and

anhedonia (lack of positive emotion) that might link normal and pathological emotional problems.

Such examples raise many of the questions we have already dealt with. Is dysfunction driven by biological or cognitive factors? Is emotional dysfunction a cause or a symptom of the disorder? Are these disorders simply pathological conditions, as the medical model of mental illness would suggest, or do they reflect some adaptive function in distorted form? Is there any common element to different disorders, which, conventionally, are distinct diagnostic categories with different etiologies? Do different disorders have common consequences in terms of adaptation to everyday life? The issue of whether there is a common thread of low EI to different disorders is a critical one for treatment. If we can find a common thread, then generic interventions for raising EI should contribute to therapy for a wide range of conditions. If not, then psychiatry is correct in seeking to match different treatments to the diagnostic categories.

The preceding discussion suggests that the definition and assessment of EI requires an underlying theory even more so than cognitive intelligence. IQ research can proceed empirically on the basis that right and wrong answers on the tests are clearly distinct. With EI, we do not have this simple starting point (see chapter 2). Reasonable, informed people may (and do) disagree on what constitutes successful handling of an encounter, on the nature of emotion as a scientific construct, and on the extent of commonality of behavior across different emotions. Hence, empirical studies of emotion and psychological functioning are central to understanding EI. We need an understanding of how people actually differ in emotional experience and behavior. We need to develop tools for measuring emotion in the laboratory and in the field, and to identify empirically different aspects of emotion and their psychological concomitants.

Behavioral consequences of mood and emotion

The impact of affect on behavior can be studied through experimental studies, and, trading rigor for ecological validity, through naturalistic studies of everyday functioning. Most of these studies use measures of mood, or indices of basic emotions, such as the Spielberger state anxiety scale. Mood is harder to handle within experimental studies as an independent rather than as a dependent variable, because the interpretation of mood 'effects' depends critically on our conceptual framework.

In drug studies, behavioral change would be attributed to the brain system(s) affected, rather than to subjective experience, which is epiphenomenal. In cognitively oriented mood induction studies, the mood might be seen as a marker for some change in the rules governing cognitive operation (e.g., strategies for allocating attention), or the person's self-appraisals of mood might initiate changes in task strategy. Interpretation of data is complicated by other concurrent responses to mood inductions, such as changes in motivation or cognition. It may be cognition rather than affect *per se* that drives both performance deficits (Mueller, 1992) and changes in selectivity of processing (Varner & Ellis, 1998). Again, the literature is too large to review, but we can pick out some representative findings. The behavioral consequences of anxiety, in particular, have been extensively investigated.

Change in performance efficiency   Negative moods, including depression and anxiety, are generally linked to impaired performance on demanding tasks. These effects seem to generalize to real life, although much of the applied work is concerned with trait rather than state measures. For example, evaluative or test anxiety is associated with performance deficits in examinations (Zeidner, 1998), and although dispositional negative affect is not generally related to impaired task performance (Barrick & Mount, 1991), it does seem to be a disadvantage in particularly stressful occupations (Matthews, 1999). Conversely, energetic moods are associated with performance enhancement on certain tasks (Matthews & Davies, 1998). Performance change may reflect changes in the underlying efficiency of processing (increased attentional capacity), changes in effort investment, or distraction from the task at hand, as discussed further below.

Changes in style of performance   Laboratory studies show that mood is associated with qualitative changes in information-processing. Many of these effects come under the heading of "mood congruence." There is a tendency for stimuli whose valence matches the mood to be processed preferentially. For example, anxious participants show selective attention to threat (Mathews & MacLeod, 1991), and participants in whom a positive mood has been induced sometimes show enhanced recall for positive material in memory studies (Bower, 1981). There are also effects of mood on decision-making style that may be especially important for real-world functioning.

Views of mood bias here differ somewhat. Isen (1999) concludes that positive affect promotes effective decision making through enhancing both flexibility and thoroughness. Forgas (1995), however, proposes a more complex model, within which mood has differential effects that are dependent on the type of strategy employed. In contrast to Isen (1999), he argues that negative moods are more likely to elicit effortful, thorough processing in decision making (depending on factors such as motivation and task complexity). There are also performance changes that are tied more to the arousing rather than hedonic qualities of affect. Many arousing stressors seem to narrow attention; the person focuses on high-priority task elements at the expense of low-priority ones (Hockey, 1984). In the real world, this effect may interfere with management of crises such as industrial disasters, if the person becomes locked into an incorrect diagnosis of the problem (Hartley et al., 1989).

Changes in social function As everyday experience would suggest, positive moods seem to promote prosocial interaction. Laboratory and organizational studies suggest that positive affect increases helpful, friendly, and socially responsible behavior (Isen, 1997). Effects of negative affect are predominantly deleterious. Anxiety and depression tend to be associated with negative self-beliefs that may disrupt social functioning, especially in more severe cases (Wells & Matthews, 1994). Clinical depression seems to generate dysfunctional cycles of social interaction with others. The depressed person's anticipation of negative outcomes makes him or her poor company for other people, who find their behavior and utterances unrewarding. Thus, people tend to withdraw from the depressed person, reinforcing their negative expectations (Coyne, 1975; McCann, 1990). Anger tends to elicit aggression and antisocial impulses; as Berkowitz (1993) puts it, "We're nasty when we feel bad." Berkowitz contrasts this empirically supported conclusion with the popular belief that suffering is character building (though presumably suffering might have longer-term benefits after its cessation). Prolonged stress can lead to the burn-out syndrome combining negative emotion with loss of motivation and cognitions of helplessness and overload (Maslach, 1982).

However, there may be more subtle benefits to negative moods. Tangney (1999) reviews evidence that guilt keeps people constructively engaged in relationships, through enhancement of empathy and motivating attempts at restitution, for example, whereas shame tends to lead to withdrawal or counterproductive anger. Anxiety may sometimes lead the person to seek help; for example, health anxiety may promote seeking medical advice for problems that might otherwise be neglected until too late.

In a simplistic way, it might appear that positive moods promote adaptation and negative moods tend to generate loss of processing efficiency and social dysfunction. However, there are settings within which negative moods may be advantageous, such as those requiring behavioral caution and awareness of risk. We also cannot evaluate the effects of mood on functioning in isolation from the motivational and cognitive states intermeshed with affect (Matthews et al., 1999). For example, anxiety may be more or less detrimental, or even beneficial, depending on concurrent cognitions and motivations (e.g. Eysenck, 1992).

Implications for emotional intelligence
This brief review reinforces our earlier conclusion that we cannot simply identify EI with a sunny disposition. Understanding causes of emotion requires us to discriminate multiple, independent mechanisms operating at different levels of abstraction. For example, affective change may lead both to fundamental changes in neural and cognitive processes and to higher-level, more situationally contingent "knowledge-level" changes in strategy and style of social interaction. The multiplicity of responses makes it difficult to isolate any quality of response that uniquely identifies EI. In anxiety research it is commonplace to distinguish different response domains, such as cognition, physiology, and overt behavior, that are only weakly interrelated (Eysenck, 1997). One avenue to understanding emotional control of response is to differentiate the levels of explanation discussed in chapter 2. Emotion may be simultaneously associated with neural operation, information processing, and high-level motivational change.

Broadly, the patternings of response seen at each level may align around common adaptive goals (Matthews, 2001; Matthews, Derryberry & Siegle, 2000), as discussed further in chapters 8 and 9. For example, anxiety seems to relate to physiological preparedness for flight (neural function), threat sensitivity (cognitive architecture), and strategy (active search for personally relevant threat stimuli). Similarly, energy and positive, excited emotion may be linked to muscular-skeletal activation, increased attentional resources and beliefs of self-efficacy: all qualities preparing the person for vigorous, goal-directed action. However, the different levels of response are only weakly linked. Moreover, they are not infrequently dissociated: the various subsystems controlling different aspects of response enjoy considerable autonomy. Furthermore, even a highly integrated response may be inappropriate if, for example, anxiety is generated by a nonexistent threat, or energy is expended on a point-less pursuit, such as playing a computer game. It seems that emotion is linked to multidimensional (and multilevel) patternings of response (see Hockey, 1984), whose adaptive success cannot be gauged from the response itself. Hence, although EI is presumed to function as a com-petence that influences response, the person's level of EI cannot easily be inferred from behavioral indices divorced from context.

Conclusions

Emotion may be seen as both a universal human quality and as an attribute of the individual person, operationalized through validated self-report measures. There have been conflicting approaches to under-standing emotion as a general faculty since the nineteenth-century studies of Darwin and James. On the conceptual side, perhaps the most fundamental division between theorists is the extent to which emotion is essentialist or evaluative in nature. Essentialist, centralist, or prereflec-tive conceptions of emotion are especially compatible with biological theories of emotion that see behavior as controlled by discrete brain systems shaped by natural selection to handle specific adaptive chal-lenges, such as avoiding threat, finding a mate, and raising children. A finite number of key brain systems may generate the relatively small number of basic emotions as concomitants of system activation. We might also develop a prereflective cognitive account that ties emotions to computational states such as appraisals (irrespective of whether or not computation is consciously accessible).

This view of emotions, as the outputs of largely modular systems, does not mesh well with the concept of EI, which implies some more gener-alized faculty for handling emotional encounters. However, EI might relate to some higher-order regulative system controlling multiple modules, perhaps located in the prefrontal cortex (Bechara et al., 2000). EI might also be related to sensitivity or bias of reward and or/punish-ment systems contributing to several, more distributed systems for basic emotions. Some such view seems implicit in Bar-On's linkage of EI to dispositional happiness, but we have seen that subjective well-being may not be directly associated with adaptive behavior.

Evaluative or self-reflective conceptions of emotion may provide us with the most workable rationale for EI. Even if emotions are generated initially by modular systems, an additional self-regulative system may moderate its behavioral implications or even the experienced emotion itself. In other words, emotions are constructed from cues, rather than directly output from central systems. This view of emotion appears to underpin the Salovey and Mayer conception of EI, which envisages the person as processing emotional representations in ways that may or may not be adaptive, for example, through assimilating feelings and understanding their personal implications. Bar-On (1997) also refers to seemingly evaluative constructs such as self-regard and adaptability. Developing this view of EI requires a better understanding of how we can differentiate lower-order systems, generating emotion unconsciously, from a higher-order system, the supposed site of EI, that reinterprets emotional signals as part of self-regulation.

The second strand of contemporary emotion research focuses on measurement of emotion through self-report, individual differences in emotion, and empirical studies of the causes, concomitants, and consequences of emotion. This approach encourages a view of emotion dimensions as constructs in their own right, identified with subjective feeling states, rather than as distorted reflections of underlying biological or cognitive systems. It also tends to focus on affect or mood, rather than emotion as strictly defined. Given that EI is an individual differences construct, this more empirical approach has the potential to investigate how individuals may manage emotional encounters more or less successfully. The realization of this potential faces considerable barriers though. A transactional understanding of the three-way interplay between environment, behavior, and emotion is needed (Lazarus, 1991), but this systems view may be hard to test rigorously. Affective states occur in the context of dynamic interaction between person and external environment, within which it may be hard to separate the roles of person and situation factors in contributing to emotions. To some extent, we can design studies that separate antecedents and consequences of emotional response. However, these studies show that emotion is a multilayered phenomenon, expressed at different levels of analysis that may not be readily commensurable with one another. An affective state may be accompanied by activity in specific brain systems, by changes in fundamental processing operations, and by changes in behavioral strategy and social orientations. It is difficult to say which of these levels of response is the basis for EI.

As discussed in chapter 1, fundamental to the concept of EI is the notion that people differ in some generalized competence for handling emotion. We must distinguish this competence, as a psychological construct, from the outcomes it influences, such as the person's overall happiness or life satisfaction. So far we have seen that the psychology of emotion offers two kinds of lead to pursue in tracking down the emotional-competence construct. The first possibility is to look for some quality of the central emotion system that controls how effectively they function, although in this case we face the modularity problem. The second possibility is to seek out some additional regulatory system that can be differentiated from central systems. A theory of EI would then tell us how variability in system functioning feeds into variability in emotional experience and adaptive behavior.

This chapter has covered some of the broad aspects of emotional functioning that such a theory should explain. However, it seems also that contemporary models of EI are quite promiscuous in operationalizing constructs reflecting different conceptualizations of emotion. For example, the MSCEIT includes scales for both face perception (directly controlled by central brain systems) and for emotion management (contingent upon cognitive reflection). Similarly, the EQ-i seems to assess both dispositional happiness (arguably, an output of central systems) and adaptability (dependent on higher-level cognitive functions). This mix-and-match approach has two potential shortcomings. First, it potentially confuses cause and effect; many theories (e.g., Lazarus, 1991) would see happiness as a consequence of adaptability, for example. Methodologically, predictors and criteria may be confounded. If we find that an EI questionnaire predicts well-being, it may simply reflect the inclusion of a happiness scale within the EI measure. Second, it impedes theory development, because we cannot isolate those specific elements of emotional function that may be adaptive or maladaptive. We have argued from the outset that a coherent account of EI requires that we identify a psychological competence for handling emotional encounters that is distinct from actual outcomes. In part II of this book, we shall resume our search for a theoretical basis for emotional competence.

5

Psychological Assessment and the Concept of Emotional Intelligence

Extraordinary claims require extraordinary evidence.

Carl Sagan

In psychology, as in any science, a fundamental consideration, when introducing a new construct to the field, is the establishment of a set of conditions, operations, and/or procedures allowing for the measurement (or assessment) of the hypothetical entity. Although qualitative techniques may, under certain circumstances, provide important information (Michell, 1990), quantification of the proposed construct is generally pivotal to systematic, empirical research. Indeed, measurement would appear a necessary condition for establishing a research program around which further understanding of the hypothetical entity (i.e., psychological construct) coalesces (chapter 2). The present chapter critically examines various assessment techniques and accompanying instruments, which hold the potential to unlock the scientific meaning of emotional intelligence.

In chapter 1, we highlighted the major conceptualizations of EI appearing in the literature; in particular the models put forward by Goleman, Bar-On, and the team led by Mayer and Salovey. As we noted in these passages, each of these research groups has developed psychometric instruments for the measurement of EI. A significant portion of the present chapter will thus be devoted to discussing and critically analyzing these measures. To fully appreciate these instruments, some further discussion of the conceptual background in which they emerged will also be necessary. In addition, several other researchers have developed measures that they (or others) have used as direct (or sometimes proxy) measures of EI. The conceptual background in which these types of psychological instruments have emerged also requires treatment, although we do on occasion refer the reader to accompanying appendices for expansive exposition of these tests of EI. A subsidiary aim of the present chapter, reflecting the close relationship between theory and psychometric instruments, is to provide descriptions and critical commentary on a variety of conceptualizations of EI.

Psychometric Issues Revisited

Emotional intelligence: From concept to assessment

The meaning of the term "emotional intelligence" is, as we demonstrated in chapter 1, subject to controversy. Thus, some commentators have assumed that it is a complex interaction of cognition, metacognition, emotions, mood, and personality that is applied in both interpersonal and intrapersonal situations (e.g., Bar-On, 2000; Goleman, 1995). Others have taken a more restricted view, arguing that EI is a form of cognitive ability, subject to lawful principles governing the realm of the intellect (e.g., Mayer, Salovey et al., 2000a, 2000b). Still other commentators appear to use the term in the most protean of ways, leaving EI bereft of conceptual meaning. Even allowing that consensus on the meaning of EI is possible, considerable programmatic research would be required to uncover processes responsible for manifest differences in this dimension before it constituted a working model (let alone theory) of emotional life.

In the present chapter, we begin with the important assumptions that EI is a viable scientific construct *and* that measurement is possible through a set of prespecified scientific operations. We also take the view that by critically appraising various instruments currently designed to assess EI, we may move closer to providing a model of EI that would satisfy the scientific community. This chapter is not for the faint hearted. Because psychological assessment is both a relatively benign scientific exercise and a rewarding commercial enterprise, the ensuing critical commentary is bound to engender controversy. Indeed, as we shall demonstrate, some measures of EI essentially repackage measures of other psychological processes and stamp them with the "emotional intelligence" label. We believe these particular instruments cause *more* confusion than clarity and are therefore damaging to the field. However, we will also survey other, more novel measures, which may shed light on this elusive construct.

These observations aside, it is worth noting the extent to which the various definitions and assessments of EI enjoy a symbiotic relationship. In those instances where the term EI reflects broad based emotional dispositions, the preferred methodology is that of the self-report proto-col. On the other hand, in those instances where EI assumes the status of a type of intelligence, the move has been towards the development and implementation of objective, performance-based indices. Finally, in those instances where EI takes on an all-encompassing psychological air, measurement operations (thankfully perhaps) are downplayed (or not even considered requisite).[1] Importantly, the first two approaches pro-vide a natural demarcation for the present chapter (i.e., performance-based versus self-reported EI). However, before moving to provide detailed, critical analysis of the instruments falling under these broad headings, we recapitulate the scientific principles for evaluating the effi-cacy of psychological tests discussed in chapters 1 and 2.

Psychological assessment and emotional intelligence

In chapter 1 we argued that the scientific discipline of psychometrics provides a series of *relatively* uncontroversial principles for determining what might constitute an empirically useful and conceptually justifiable measure of EI. Extending this notion in chapter 2, we maintained that the ideal test of emotional intelligence should minimally satisfy each of the following four criteria:

- Reliability
- Content validity
- Predictive validity (and usefulness)
- Construct validity

Many theorists regard construct validity as the all-encompassing, uni-fying concept for all types of validity evidence (Anastasi & Urbina, 1997; Cronbach, 1988; Guion, 1980; Messick, 1989). Within this perspective, studies pertaining to content and predictive validity are merely support-ing evidence in the cumulative, never-ending quest for construct valida-tion. Extending this notion to the special case of EI, its chief proponents might reasonably claim, in its defense, that the construct remains too new to dismiss any of its measures, out of hand, on the grounds of poor construct validity. Equally, however, preliminary evidence for construct validity would appear requisite to push the science of EI further afield.

Within this context, one of the most important construct valida-tion techniques, mentioned briefly in chapter 2, involves determining whether a test exhibits convergent-discriminant validity. For example, consistent with the structural models reviewed in chapter 3, tests in the traditional intelligence realm consistently show high correlations with tests of similar abilities, but correlate weakly with conceptually distinct qualities, such as personality. This psychometric criterion is pivotal to establishing that EI is (a) a form of cognitive ability and (b) independent (or at least psychometrically distinct) from existing, well-established constructs, like personality or cognitive abilities. There is a tension between criteria (a) and (b), because the relationship between EI and ability might turn out to be so strong that EI simply represents an old wine in a new bottle (as with social and crystallized intelligence). In fact, most conceptualizations of EI suggest that it should share some overlap with both intelligence and personality constructs, but fail to specify just how large the correlations between EI and these existing constructs should be in order for EI to remain independent of established domains of individual differences.

Thus, in any empirical attempt to evaluate the distinctiveness of EI, researchers perforce need to ascertain the magnitude of relationship between EI and existent measures of intelligence, as well as well-established personality dimensions, such as those encapsulated under the Five Factor Model: neuroticism, extroversion, openness, agreeableness, and conscientiousness (see, e.g., Costa & McCrae, 1992a). In this chapter we will focus on psychometric issues, and the extent of overlap between EI and these personality dimensions, which has proven to be an important (and at times controversial) aspect of EI research (Davies et al., 1998). We will also present data in this chapter showing that for self-assessment of EI, at least, the amount of overlap between EI instruments and personality measures can be extraordinarily high. One implication of this outcome is that personality traits conceivably be re-conceptualized in terms of emotional competence. Because this issue is both complex and controversial, we will defer discussion of this relationship (and other theoretical implications stemming from the overlap between self-report EI and personality) until chapter 9.

It is equally important to address convergent validity, and to demonstrate close correspondence between alternative measures of EI. Evidence is limited because of the relatively recent history of the vast majority of emotional intelligence tests. Nevertheless, some relevant information is starting to come to hand, often with mixed results. Thus, as we will demonstrate the correlations between EI and extant psychological constructs are sometimes very high, at other times surprisingly low, and, in certain instances, even opposite in sign to that predicted by more broadly focused theories of emotion.

Correlational data will feature largely in this chapter. The Pearson correlation coefficient (r) is sometimes a much-abused statistic, being subject to various sources of artifact and bias (McNemar, 1969), and open to different interpretations. It can be difficult to attach meaning to coefficients of different magnitude, and to decide whether a correlation is large enough to be interesting in addressing a particular problem. The issue here is one of effect size rather than statistical significance: a trivially small correlation may attain significance if the sample size is large enough. Assigning verbal labels to coefficients of different size is somewhat arbitrary (see Cohen, 1988), but to establish a consistent standard, we will consider the amount of correlation between EI and other measures as follows:

- Nonexistent or trivial (absolute value of correlation between $r = 0.00–0.09$)
- Small (absolute value of correlation between $r = 0.10–0.29$)
- Moderate or medium ($r = 0.30–0.49$)
- Large ($r = 0.50–0.69$)
- Very large ($r = 0.70–0.99$)

Providing that an EI test has small to medium overlap with another test, we can be reasonably certain that the two tests are different from each other, but related. In such instances, we might claim that the test has shown discriminant validity. A large correlation, on the other hand, calls this property into question; while a very large correlation suggests considerable redundancy. Convergent validity requires a very large correlation (e.g., as typically found when correlating two cognitive ability tests). A large correlation between two tests might suggest that further test refinement might bring about better convergence, but a correlation of less than 0.50 suggests that the prospects for attaining convergent validity are gloomy.

Clearly, assessment of whether a given EI test has predictive power over and above the other tests to which it relates can be a complex issue. Broadly, the poorer the discrimination between two tests, the less likely that predictive power will be high. However, it is possible that small overlap between a measure of EI and say a cognitive ability test will prove to explain the apparent predictive power of the EI test, disappearing when that cognitive ability is controlled. Conversely, even with large to very large overlap, it is conceivable that the EI test will remain predictive with the second test controlled. In sum, comparative tests of EI

Table 5.1
Differences between performance-based and self-report measures of EI

Performance-based EI	Self-reported EI
Maximal performance	Typical performance
External appraisal of performance	Internal appraisal of performance
Response bias minimal (or nonexistent)	Response bias may be great
Administration time long; testing complicated	Administration time short; testing easy
Abilitylike	Personalitylike

against existing personality and ability measures are essential in investigating the predictive utility of EI, although, as we shall see, this type of research has been rather sparse.

Performance Measures of Emotional Intelligence

As argued in chapter 2, performance-based measures of EI appear differentiated from self-report protocols along five dimensions. Because these are crucial to understanding how we classified the tests for this portion of our exposition, we list them again, concisely, in table 5.1. Largely because we see greater promise in these tools, this exposition focuses on performance-based tests of EI first and then moves to discuss self-report instruments. Moreover, the number of self-report tests is larger than the number of performance-based tests, with the numbers of the former evidently growing apace.

Among the most prominent of the performance-based EI tests are those developed by Mayer, Salovey, and colleagues: the MEIS and MSCEIT. However, there are also some other instruments, not necessarily designed to measure EI per se, but with some obvious correspondences to this construct, that should be considered. These include the Levels of Emotional Awareness Scale and the Interpersonal Perception Test, which we discuss briefly, with cross-references to detailed treatment in an adjunct to this chapter: appendix B. We also include several laboratory-based measures of emotion in the present review, which researchers working within the field of EI have largely ignored, believing that they too hold some promise to illuminate scientific understanding of the construct of emotional intelligence.

The Multi-Factor Emotional Intelligence Scale (MEIS)

Theoretical framework As noted in chapter 1, one of the most prominent theoretical frameworks for EI is that proposed by Mayer, Salovey, Caruso, and colleagues. Central to their mental ability conceptualization of EI are the four branches: emotional identification-perception, assimilating emotions, understanding emotions, and emotional management. Because we gave each branch passing coverage previously, and they are central to appreciating the scope (and purposes) of the MEIS, we provide additional information on the hypothesized processes captured by these branches in the passages that follow.

The verbal and non-verbal appraisal and expression of emotion in the self and others EI has been defined as "the ability to perceive emotions, to access and generate emotions so as to assist thought, to understand emotions and emotional knowledge, and to reflectively regulate emotions so as to promote emotional and intellectual growth" (Mayer & Salovey, 1997, p. 5). Inside this definitional framework, the most fundamental level of EI includes the perception, appraisal, and expression of emotions (Mayer, Caruso et al., 2000). In other words, this aspect of EI involves the individual being aware both of their emotions and their thoughts concerning their emotions. It also requires the individual to be able to monitor emotions in themselves and others, and to differentiate among them, as well as being able to adequately express emotions.

The utilization of emotion to facilitate thought and action This component of EI involves assimilating basic emotional experiences into mental life (Mayer, Caruso, et al., 2000). Utilization of emotion includes weighing emotions against one another and against other sensations and thoughts, and allowing emotions to direct attention (e.g., holding an emotional state in consciousness long enough to compare its correspondence to similar sensations in sound, color, and taste). Marshalling emotions in the service of a goal is essential for selective attention, self-monitoring, self-motivation, and so forth.

Understanding and reasoning about emotions This aspect of EI involves perceiving the lawfulness underlying specific emotions (e.g., to understand that anger arises when there is denial of justice or an injustice is performed against one's own self or close friends). This process also involves the understanding of emotional problems, such as knowing what emotions are similar and what relation they convey.

The regulation of emotion in the self and others   According to Mayer, Caruso, et al. (2000), the highest level in the hierarchy of EI skills is the management and regulation of emotions. This facet of EI involves knowing how to calm down after feeling stressed, or alleviating the stress and emotion of others. This facet facilitates social adaptation and problem solving.

Test description   The MEIS is designed to measure each of the above-mentioned branches, which are hypothesized to underlie EI (Mayer, Caruso et al., 2000). Branch 1 consists of four tests that assess the perception and appraisal of emotion in stories, designs, music, and faces (see figure 5.1 for an example). Branch 2, on the other hand, consists of two tasks that assess the ability to assimilate emotions into perceptual and cognitive processes, while branch 3 consists of four tests that assess the ability to reason about and understand emotions. Finally, branch 4 consists of two tests that assess how skilled participants are at managing their own emotions and the emotions of others. In table 5.2 we provide detailed information pertinent to each of the 12 subtests composing the MEIS.

Interestingly, in terms of both face (no pun intended!) and content validity, many of the branch 2, 3, and 4 tests are composed of short vignettes, depicting real-life episodes that are specially selected to invoke emotional responses. For instance, the Relativity Test (branch 3) measures people's ability to estimate the feelings of two characters. One test item describes two people going out on a first date and asks the participant to rate each of the respective individual's feelings about the event (and/or the other person). For example, participants must decide how likely it is that the male felt proud that the female had accepted his invitation to go out with him.

Scoring the MEIS   There is considerable difficulty in determining objectively correct responses to stimuli involving emotional content, and in applying truly veridical criteria in scoring tasks of emotional capability (see chapter 2). Proponents of EI ability measures have thus promoted three alternative scoring procedures, which are thought to discriminate right from wrong answers on tests of this type (Mayer, Caruso, et al., 2000). These are the following:

Consensual scoring   An examinee receives credit for endorsing responses that the group endorses. Thus, if the group agrees that a face (or

	Definitely not present (1)	(2)	(3)	(4)	Definitely present (5)
Anger	1				
Sadness	1				
Happiness					5
Disgust	1				
Fear		2			
Surprise			3		

Figure 5.1
A sample item adapted from the perception subtest of the Multi-Factor Emotional Intelligence Scale (Mayer et al., 2000). "Best answers" (consensual scoring) are shown. Note that the picture is of one of the authors of this book. Guess which one.

design, passage of music, vignette, and so forth) conveys a happy or sad emotion, then that becomes the correct response. This approach assumes that observations obtained from a large, representative sample of people can be pooled, then jointly used to provide reliable indicators of the various components of EI. This approach adopts a commonly accepted dictum from sociology: that there are no right or wrong "emotions" that people feel but rather correct or incorrect perception of people's emotions. Accordingly, for EI to be useful, it must reflect how emotions are perceived (and subsequently expressed) by the vast majority of individuals. For example, if the majority of people who see a

Table 5.2
Capsule descriptions of the 12 subtests composing the MEIS

Test	Task and stimuli	Response
Branch 1: Emotional identification/perception		
1. Faces	8 photos of faces, each rated for degree of anger, sadness, happiness, disgust, fear, and surprise present	Five-point scale: definitely not present (1) to definitely present (5)
2. Music	8 original musical scores rated like test 1	Like test 1
3. Designs	8 computer-generated graphic designs rated like test 1	Like test 1
4. Stories	6 narratives; participant determines characters' feelings on 7 emotion scales that vary from story to story	Like test 1
Branch 2: Assimilation of emotions		
5. Synesthesia	6 scenarios; participant is asked to imagine a feeling until they experience corresponding emotion(s)	Five-point semantic differential scale for warm–cold, yellow–purple, sharp–dull, fast–slow, dark–light, low–high, orange–blue, pleasant–unpleasant, good–bad, and sweet–sour
6. Feeling biases	4 scenarios, where participants are required to assimilate their current mood state with judgments as to how they feel about a fictional person described in the scenario	Five-point scale: definitely does not describe (1) to definitely does describe (5) for 7 trait scales (e.g., sad, trusting, etc.) that vary across scenarios

Branch 3: Understanding emotions

7. Complex Blends	8 items; participants analyze how blended emotions comprise two or more simple emotions	Multiple-choice; e.g., optimism combines which two emotions? (a) pleasure and anticipation, etc.
8. Progressions	8 items assessing people's understanding of how feelings and emotions progress and intensify over time	Multiple-choice; e.g., if you feel guiltier and guiltier, and begin to question your self-worth, you feel (a) depression, etc.
9. Transitions	4 scenarios designed to gauge understanding of how emotions follow one another (e.g., a person is afraid and later calm; *in between*, what are the likely ways the person might feel?)	Five-point scale: extremely unlikely (1) to extremely likely (5) for 6 emotion scales (e.g., fear, anger, etc.) that vary across scenarios
10. Relativity	4 scenarios depicting social encounters between two fictional persons (often in conflict); participant is asked to judge how characters are feeling	Five-point scale: extremely unlikely (1) to extremely likely (5) for 10 emotion scales that vary across scenarios

Branch 4: Managing emotions

11. Managing others	6 vignettes; participants evaluate plans of action in response to fictional persons requiring assistance	Five-point scale: extremely ineffective (1) to extremely effective (5) for 4 alternative courses of action varying across vignettes
12. Managing self	6 vignettes focusing on the self rather than others	Like test 11

particular film perceive it as sad, the emotionally intelligent response, and the one that would confer most benefits in dealing with others' emotions, is to view it as sad. This scoring ignores the expert view—it does not matter if a film critic thinks it is a happy film; what counts is the extent to which the individual matches the majority opinion. This principle is in direct contrast to traditional measures of intelligence where an objective measure of truth is considered, and may be where EI diverges from cognitive intelligence.

Expert scoring   Experts in the field of emotions (e.g., psychologists, psychiatrists, philosophers, and so forth) examine certain stimuli (e.g., a face, passage of music, or design) and then use their best judgment to determine the emotion expressed in that stimulus. Presumably, the expert brings professional savoir-faire (along with a history of behavioral knowledge) to bear on judgments about emotional meanings. The test taker receives credit for ratings that correspond to those of the experts employed, which is an attempt at an objective criteria for truth, as employed in cognitive tests of ability.

Target scoring   A judge (i.e., the test taker) assesses what a target (artist, photographer, musician, and so forth) is portraying at the time they were engaged in some emotional activity (e.g., writing a poem, playing a musical score, painting, sculpting, photography, etc.). A series of emotion rating scales are then used to match the emotions conveyed by the stimuli to those reported by the target. It is commonly held that the target has more information than is available to the outside observer (Bar-On, 1997; Mayer, Caruso et al., 2000; Mayer & Geher, 1996) and is used as the criterion for scoring judges' responses.

The assessment of EI as a mental ability depends on the presumption that answers to stimuli assessing various facets of feelings can be categorized as correct or incorrect (Mayer & Salovey, 1997). The adequacy of consensus judgments for this purpose is based on evolutionary and cultural foundations, where the consistency of emotionally signaled information appears paramount (Bar-On, 1997; Mayer, Caruso et al., 2000). However, it is unclear that veridical criteria for accuracy find ready application in the measurement of emotions. Indeed, assessment of certain emotional reactions, according to logically consistent criteria, appears unlikely through reference to personal and societal standards. For example, what is the best (or right) response to being insulted or mocked by a coworker? Clearly, this would depend on the situation, the person's experience with insults, cultural norms, the individual's position in the status hierarchy, and so forth (see Roberts, Zeidner, et al., 2001). Arguably, it would appear, at this stage, that consensual scoring by an individual's social and cultural peers is the closest approximation of a "correct" answer in performance measures of EI.

Test evaluation and empirical findings   Four studies are especially relevant to evaluation of the psychometric properties: reliability, validity, and usefulness of the MEIS. Table 5.3 contains a variety of details on

Table 5.3
Brief descriptions of the samples and designs of the four published studies examining the MEIS

Study	Sample characteristics	Measures employed
Mayer, Caruso, et al. (2000), study 1	• 503 adults from U.S. • College students = 47%; business employees = 53% • 164 male; 333 female • Mean age = 23.00 • White = 68%	• MEIS • Army Alpha (vocabulary) • Empathy (self-report) • Secondary criteria (e.g., life satisfaction, number of hours of psychotherapy, leisure pursuits)
Mayer, Caruso, et al. (2000), study 2	• 229 adolescents from U.S. • 125 male; 101 female • Mean age = 13.40 • White = 79%	• Selection of MEIS subtests: all four branch 1 subtests, synesthesia, blends, and relativity
Ciarrochi et al. (2000)	• 134 Australian university students • 31 male; 103 female • Mean age = 24.50 • Ethnic composition not reported	• MEIS • Ravens Progressive Matrices • Empathy (self-report) • Brief self-report measures of extraversion, neuroticism, openness • Secondary criteria (as for Mayer, Caruso, et al., 2000, study 1)
Roberts, Zeidner, et al. (2001)	• 704 USAF enlistees • 617 male; 76 female • Mean age = 19.80 • White = 68%	• MEIS • Army Services Vocational Aptitude Battery (ASVAB) • Big-Five Factor Measure (self-report)

each study, including brief descriptions indicating the composition of each sample examined and each of the tests employed (along with the MEIS) as part of the validation process.

Across these four studies, the MEIS yields a reliable measure of emotional perception, of understanding and managing emotions (based on all the nonperception subtests) and overall EI (which is based on all of the subtests). Several of the sub-tests, especially those related to Emotion Perception, are also reliable in their own right. Other subtests (i.e., those related to both understanding emotions [branch 3] and managing emotions [branch 4]) have less satisfactory reliabilities. For example, the internal consistency of the progressions test ranges from a disappointing 0.37 (Roberts, Zeidner et al., 2001) to an equally disappointing 0.51 (Mayer, Caruso et al., 1999). (In the Ciarrochi, Chan, and Caputi, 2000a, study, this value was 0.46.) These remarkably consistent findings are worth noting, since both of these branches are also argued to be the most important components within contemporary EI theory (see Mayer & Cobb, 1999; Mayer, Caruso, et al., 2000; Mayer, Salovey, et al., 2000).

Consensus and expert scores for each MEIS subtest also appear meaningfully correlated (see, e.g., Roberts, Zeidner, et al., 2001, where $r = 0.48$).[2] However, the magnitude of correlation for these two different scoring criteria tends to vary by branch. Thus, in the Roberts, Zeidner, et al. study the correlation between consensus and expert-based scores was relatively high for emotional understanding ($r = 0.78$), yet negligible for emotional identification/perception ($r = -0.02$). Moreover, the product-moment correlation between the consensus and expert-scored subtest strung-out-intercorrelation matrices (where all correlations between consensus and expert scores are each in turn compared) was found to be nonsignificant (i.e., $r = 0.15$, $p > 0.05$). This finding suggests weak correspondence among the pattern of intercorrelations based on these two scoring criteria, which Roberts, Zeidner, et al. have seized upon to question the psychological meaning of these scoring protocols.

An important feature of the MEIS is that the authors have constructed the test in such a fashion that empirical data captures each of the four branches. In other words, each of the sub-tests should define their respective branches. However, in the Roberts, Zeidner, et al. (2001) study, exploratory factor analysis of the MEIS subtests revealed only three interpretable factors for both consensual and expert-based scores: emotion identification, emotion understanding, and emotion management. This three-factor solution was suggested in analysis of both root-one cri-

Table 5.4

Means and standard deviations of MEIS general EI (consensus and expert) by gender and ethnic group (from Roberts, Zeidner, et al. 2001)

	M	SD	M	SD	d score
Gender	Male ($N = 617$)		Female ($N = 76$)		
Consensus	−0.22	6.82	1.51	6.59	−0.26
Expert	0.19	6.00	−1.30	6.82	0.23
Ethnic group	Majority ($N = 476$)		Minority ($N = 214$)		
Consensus	0.28	6.58	−0.63	7.12	0.13
Expert	1.16	5.86	−2.43	5.98	0.60

Notes: (1) General EI is a composite of all 12 MEIS subtests. (2) For gender, d scores = male minus female EI-score means, divided by the average standard deviation of group scores. (3) For ethnic groups, d scores = minority minus majority EI-score means, divided by the average standard deviation of group scores.

teria and the Scree plot (conventions for determining the appropriate number of factors). Any attempt to extract additional factors resulted in Heywood cases, i.e., factor loadings greater than 1.00 (see Carroll, 1993). Collectively, these findings do not support the original four-branch model of EI proposed by Mayer, Caruso, et al. (1999). Because none of the assimilation subtests shares salient loadings on any factor, these data also run contrary to a revised three-factor model later put forward by these authors (Mayer, Caruso, et al., 2000).[3]

Another issue worthy of considering in the case of the MEIS is the extent to which differing scoring protocols yield consistent information, especially with respect to important research questions such as group differences (see Zeidner, Matthews & Roberts, 2001). Table 5.4 reproduces descriptive statistics for consensus and expert-based EI by gender and ethnic group from the study conducted by Roberts, Zeidner, et al. (2001). When consensus scores are used, females scored higher than males, with this trend reversed for expert-based scoring. A similar outcome is observed for general EI as a function of ethnicity, with no real difference observed between majority and minority groups when consensus is used, but the majority group scoring higher when expert-based scoring is used. Arguably, the fact that experts were males, of Caucasian origin, reconciles these inconsistent findings.

Nevertheless, perhaps one of the greatest strengths underlying the MEIS is its distinctiveness. It has only small to medium overlap with posi-

Table 5.5

Correlations of MEIS general EI (consensus and expert) with Big Five personality dimensions and intelligence (from Roberts, Zeidner, et al. 2001)

MEIS general EI	Big Five personality dimensions					AFQT
	N	A	C	E	O	
Consensus	−.18	.24	.16	.13	.13	.32
Expert	−.02	−.03	−.02	−.03	.15	.43

Notes: (1) General EI is a composite of all 12 MEIS subtests. (2) N = neuroticism; E = extraversion; O = openness; A = agreeableness; and C = conscientiousness. (3) The Air Force Qualifying Test (AFQT) is a composite of the Army Services Vocational Aptitude Battery (ASVAB), which Herrnstein and Murray (1998) actually consider a prototypical measure of general intelligence.

tive and negative affectivity and other, well-established personality measures, such as facet scores of the Neuroticism-Extraversion-Openness Personality Inventory, Revised (NEO-PIR) (see Ciarrochi, Chan & Caputi, 2000a, 2000b). It also has small to medium (positive) overlap with verbal (i.e., crystallized) intelligence, as assessed by the Army Alpha (Mayer, Caruso, et al., 1999). This outcome is precisely what one would expect if the MEIS sub-tests are measuring a type of cognitive ability closely related to social intelligence (see chapter 3). Indeed, these relationships seem remarkably robust across studies. As testament to this assertion, again consider the study conducted by Roberts, Zeidner, et al. (2001). This investigation included, for the first time, a measure of the Five Factor Model of Personality, along with one of the most-often-used psychometric tests in the world—the ASVAB (see, e.g., Herrnstein & Murray, 1996; Murphy & Davidshofer, 1998). Table 5.5 presents correlations between the MEIS and personality so defined and the MEIS and a measure of crystallized intelligence (AFQT) that may be derived from the ASVAB (see Roberts, Goff, et al., 2001). The low correlations between performance-based EI and personality stands in contrast to self-reported EI, where these correlations can exceed 0.50, particularly for extraversion, agreeableness, and neuroticism (see Davies et al., 1998, also later in this chapter). The correlation between EI and AFQT is of sufficient magnitude to suggest that EI may represent a cluster of primary mental abilities comprising crystallized intelligence. Note however too, some problematic features again evident in these data. In particular, for personality measures, as with previous findings, different scoring procedures led to divergent outcomes.

The MEIS appears also to have some utility. People who score high on the MEIS tend to report greater life happiness, relationship success, and parental warmth. However, the correlations between the MEIS and these measures tends to be small, i.e., around 0.20 (see Ciarrochi, Chan & Caputi, 2000a; Mayer, Caruso, et al., 2000). Cobb and Mayer (2000) refer to unpublished studies showing that the MEIS is negatively related to adult 'bad behavior' such as fighting, to ratings of aggression in high school students, and to smoking and alcohol problems in students. No effect sizes are quoted by Cobb and Mayer. As part of the Ciarrochi, Chan, and Caputi (2000a) investigation, some participants were involved in a mood induction manipulation. Following positive induction (watching a short comedy film), high scorers on the MEIS showed a larger mood response and retrieved more positive childhood memories. Ciarrochi and colleagues suggest that individuals high in EI engage in behavior that tends to maintain (or increase) their positive moods, although the study offers only indirect evidence that individual differences in mood regulation mediated the observed effect. Importantly, the investigators also showed discriminant validity, by showing that the effects described were not mediated by extraversion, neuroticism, or self-esteem (although other personality confounds might also be relevant). However, the study failed to confirm predictions that high EI individuals should show smaller-magnitude negative mood inductions, and that EI test score should be associated with smaller mood-related bias in judgment. Intriguingly, IQ was more predictive than EI of judgmental bias: low IQ participants seemed to overcorrect for possible bias. In addition, low IQ participants recalled a greater number of positive memories. These findings are important in showing that MEIS score relates to individual differences in affective and cognitive response to emotional situations, and indicate the promising nature of the test in this regard. At the same time, the patchy support for predictions, and the additional role of general intelligence, suggest that the underlying processes are likely quite complex. Further progress may require some independent measure of the mood-management processes purportedly linked to emotional and cognitive intelligence.

In another study, researchers investigating the role of emotion perception in people's ability to deal effectively with life stress found further evidence for the distinctiveness and usefulness of sub-tests comprising this particular branch (Ciarrochi, Deane & Anderson, 2001). In particular, emotional perception was found to be unrelated to life stress and to measures of mental health, which is consistent with a view that EI is different from these variables (see Ciarrochi, Chan, Caputi & Roberts, 2001). A second, and somewhat counterintuitive, finding suggests that people high (and low) in emotion perception responded differently to the effects of stressors. The impact of stress on emotionally perceptive people appears stronger than on less perceptive individuals, with the former expressing higher levels of depression, hopelessness, and suicidal ideation.

Why did emotionally perceptive people appear to respond less adaptively to stress than others? Ciarrochi, Deane, and Anderson (2001) propose two hypotheses. The *insensitivity hypothesis* suggests that people with poor emotion perception successfully repress stressful thoughts (or else may ignore them altogether). This hypothesis implies that being unperceptive may be highly beneficial to the individual, in warding off the effects of stress. In contrast, the *confusion hypothesis* suggests that people who are low in emotion perception, are indeed sensitive to stress, but simply do not realize that it is impacting upon them adversely (Ciarrochi, Deane & Anderson, 2001). By definition, low perceptive people should be more confused about what they are feeling and should show less understanding of how this impinges upon their emotional life. This second hypothesis suggests that being emotionally unperceptive is detrimental to the individual because they do not know that they are feeling 'low' and thus will likely not do anything to change the situation or the circumstances. In general, research in EI, particularly that focusing on the concept of alexithymia (lack of emotionality [see discussion of the TAS-20]), is consistent with the second hypothesis (e.g., Taylor, 2000; see also chapter 11 of this book).

Summary   The research reported in the preceding passages suggests that the Multi-Factor Emotional Intelligence Scale (MEIS) is reliable, distinctive, and related to some important life outcomes. However, it does have some identifiable weaknesses. For example, it takes considerable time to administer the whole test, several subscales do not have satisfactory levels of reliability, and there is only limited empirical support for a (hypothetical) four-branch model. Moreover, scoring problems endemic to consensual, expert, and target scoring render it a more problematic objective test than its developers have indicated. The MEIS measures some quality of interest, but is that quality truly a cognitive ability? We might also wonder whether the MEIS simply represents a constellation of primary mental abilities (of an emotional nature) that are likely circumscribed by crystallized intelligence. Providing measurement problems and conceptual issues can be satisfactorily resolved, the MEIS does however, hold some promise as a psychometrically sound index of individual differences in emotionality, if not EI. Indeed, realizing psychometric problems, the test developers have constructed a revised measure—the MSCEIT (Mayer, Salovey, et al., 2000), to which attention now turns.

Mayer-Salovey-Caruso Emotional Intelligence Test (MSCEIT)

The MSCEIT is intended to as a refinement of the MEIS following empirical research in this domain. The authors also aimed to improve convenience of administration, by shortening the MEIS, without sacrificing its psychometric properties. At the time of writing, the MSCEIT had gone through two revisions: MSCEIT (Version 1.1) and MSCEIT (Version 2.0) (see Mayer, Salovey, Caruso & Sitarenios, submitted; Mayer, Salovey & Caruso, in preparation).

Test Description: MSCEIT (Version 1.1)   Like the MEIS, the MSCEIT (Version 1.1) contains 12 subscales, many of which, on first blush, appear common to both instruments. However, closer inspection reveals that all sub-tests have gone through one form of modification or another. For example, in the two tests that appear to have gone through the least extensive revisions (i.e., branch 1, measures of emotion perception: faces and designs), both stimuli and response scales have been replaced. For designs, a response scale made up of pictures of varying levels of a sad-happy face were substituted for the verbal statements aligned on a continuum. In other instances, subtests bearing common names with the MEIS (e.g., transitions) have had the response scale more significantly altered (for example, moving from a rating to multiple-choice option). Arguably, many of these tests also represent a shift in focus in task demands, since rather than representing idealized situations they now refer to specific scenarios. To give the reader a full impression of these differences we provide detailed information pertinent to each of the 12 subtests comprising the MSCEIT (Version 1.1) in table 5.6. Note that for this test, scoring is a function of consensus alone.

Several tests from the MEIS have been omitted from the MSCEIT (Version 1.1): music, stories, feeling biases, relativity, and both of the branch 4 subtests (i.e., managing others, managing self). Exactly why these tests were excluded from further consideration in the MSCEIT (Version 1.1) is not discussed in any of the available literature on this instrument. Nevertheless, cogent arguments could be mounted to

Table 5.6
Capsule descriptions of the 12 subtests composing the MSCEIT (version 1.1)

Test	Task and stimuli	Response
Branch 1: Emotional identification/perception		
1. Faces	5 photos of faces, each rated for degree of anger, sadness, happiness, disgust, fear, surprise, and excitement present	Five-point scale: no (1) to extreme (5)
2. Landscapes	5 color photographs of environment, rated like test 1	Five-point scale of cartoon faces expressing varying degree of a specific emotion
3. Designs	5 computer-generated graphic designs, rated like test 1	Like test 2
Branch 2: Assimilation of emotions		
4. Synesthesia	5 scenarios; participant is asked to imagine feeling a certain feeling (e.g., envy), and then to match this feeling to 5 sensory perceptions: cold, slow, orange, large, and sour	Five-point scale: not alike (1) to very much alike (5)
5. Sensations	5 scenarios; participants are asked to imagine feeling a string of sensations (e.g., sweet, strong, purple) and then to match these to 5 emotions: proud, content, sad, loving, and amused	Like test 4
6. Facilitation	7 scenarios; participants are asked to judge moods that assist cognitive tasks/behaviors (e.g., What mood might be helpful when generating a large number of new ideas in a group?)	Five-point scale: definitely not useful (1) to definitely useful (5) for five moods (e.g., sadness, surprise, jealousy, etc.) that vary across scenarios

Branch 3: Understanding emotions

7. Blends	13 items; participants choose combinations of emotions (e.g., Resentment, anger, anticipation, and pride are all parts of what?)	Multiple-choice, five alternatives, e.g., (a) spite, (b) rage, (c) jealousy, etc.
8. Progressions	12 vignettes assessing people's understanding of how emotions intensify over time (e.g., Michael was tired. It was late, and he received a phone call from a friend, who criticized him. . . . Michael went to bed?)	Multiple-choice, five alternatives, e.g., (a) unhappy and disappointed, (b) frustrated and angry, (c) shamed and depressed, etc.
9. Transitions	12 vignettes; participants are asked to judge likely events that would cause one feeling to change to another (e.g., A middle-aged man was fearful and then shortly thereafter felt approval. What most likely happened in between?)	Multiple-choice, five alternatives, e.g., (a) his wife kissed him lovingly; (b) an election was held and the candidate he backed won; etc.
10. Analogies	12 items; participants are asked to judge which emotion pairs are analogous (e.g., Lively is to calm as what is to what?)	Multiple-choice, five alternatives, e.g., (a) anger is to terror, (b) guilt is to disgust, etc.

Branch 4: Managing emotions

11. Emotion management	6 vignettes; participants judge actions that are likely to affect the personal feelings of the individual in a given story	Five-point scale: very ineffective (1) to very effective (5) for 5 alternative courses of action varying across vignettes
12. Emotional relationships	5 vignettes; participants judge actions that are likely to affect the feelings of other people mentioned in a given story	Like test 11

suggest that these were, in virtually all instances, precisely the tests that should have been *retained.* For example, while it seems likely the music test was the most difficult to administer in group-settings, it also gives the emotion perception factor greater generality than is now evident. In particular, a critic might now claim that branch 1 simply represents the perception of emotion in two-dimensional figural representations. In the case of stories, all three studies of the MEIS indicated that this test loaded most highly on a general EI factor. Because this construct is considered so important in performance-based models of EI, dispensing with this test is analogous to an intelligence researcher throwing out the Raven's Progressive Matrices Test (which often shares the highest loading on a general intelligence factor). Similarly, relativity has the highest loading of all non-branch-1 tests on general EI derived from the MEIS, as well as consistently adequate reliability; yet (despite these positive features) it alone has been expunged from branch 3 of the MSCEIT (Version 1.1).

In contrast, several of the tests retained in the MSCEIT (Version 1.1) and especially all of the tests assessing understanding emotions (i.e., blends, progressions, and transitions) have problematic reliabilities across the four studies of the MEIS described in table 5.3. Moreover, the test authors have, in currently making each of these tests highly dependent on verbal processing, likely created crude proxies for crystallized intelligence indices. This potential problem is highlighted in the context of the newly introduced analogies test. Although this emotional version of the test employs both consensus and expert scoring, esoteric analogies themselves can have a correct answer (if carefully constructed). Indeed, variants of the aforementioned test are frequently used as markers for the Gc factor (see, e.g., Carroll, 1993; Roberts et al., 1997).

In defense of Mayer et al. (submitted, in preparation), they have gathered data on this neoteric performance-based measure of EI. Note however we have found it difficult to directly assess some of the concerns evident from the preceding passages because of the manner in which these data are reported or the studies were designed. For example, unlike the original study examining the MEIS (Mayer, Caruso, et al., 1999), the authors have shown scant regard to demonstrating independence from existent individual difference constructs or predictive validity. Nevertheless, these data are useful in informing us of the major psychometric properties of this MEIS-derivative. For convenience, and in the interests of ready comparison, we will turn to detailed discussion of data on the MSCEIT (Version 1.1) after first discussing the tests comprising the MSCEIT (Version 2).

Test description: MSCEIT (Version 2) The MSCEIT (Version 2) represents an even greater departure from the original MEIS, with two subtests only within a given branch. Fewer items compose these subtests than in either the MEIS or MSCEIT (Version 1.1). For example, there are only four item parcels (i.e., stimuli) in faces, requiring only five (unspecified) responses, which are to be made on various rating scales. The authors have also mixed stimuli from MSCEIT (Version 1.1) to create new tests representing conglomerates of subtests within a given branch of this test of EI. In particular, pictures represents the best items from landscapes and designs, while changes incorporates progressions and transitions from branch 3 of the MSCEIT (Version 1.1). Subtests discarded from the MSCEIT (Version 1.1) include synesthesia (though it consistently demonstrates superior psychometric properties over all other branch 2 tests) and analogies (which has poor reliability, i.e., Cronbach alpha $= 0.38$) (see Mayer et al., submitted, table 1).

As for the MEIS and unlike the MSCEIT (Version 1.1), MSCEIT (Version 2) employs both consensus and expert scoring. Interestingly, the latter is based on ratings obtained from 21 members of the International Society of Research on Emotions, rather than, as in the MEIS, two of the test authors: Mayer and Caruso. Whether this change in ascertaining expert scoring gives a measure that (a) is reliable, (b) provides consistent effects (and correlates), and (c) can be defended conceptually is worth considering in light of contemporary theory and data thus far obtained.

Test evaluation and empirical findings Evaluation of both forms of this test is limited to a submitted manuscript and an (at present) unpublished test manual that Mayer, Salovey, and colleagues have prepared for Multi Health Systems Incorporated. Interestingly, Mayer, Caruso, et al. (submitted) claim the MSCEIT (Version 1.1) "approximate(s) the MEIS in reliability despite being shorter" (1999, p. 20). In fact, all of the common subtests have slightly lower reliability than the MEIS, with this assertion proving more problematic when one considers that in certain instances (specifically, progressions and blends) the subtests actually have *more* items. The reliabilities of the MSCEIT (Version 2) subtests are slightly higher than those obtained for the MSCEIT (Version 1.1), largely because the test authors have selected optimal items on the basis of psychometric analyses of the latter scale. Nevertheless, it is difficult to ignore the fact that the average reliabilities of scales, scored by consensus, has diminished relative to the original MEIS for both MSCEIT (Version 1.1) and MSCEIT (Version 2) (i.e., mean Cronbach alpha = 0.77, 0.68, and 0.71, respectively). While average reliabilities of scales, scored using expert protocols, has increased relative to the MEIS for MSCEIT (Version 2) (i.e., mean Cronbach alpha = 0.62 and 0.68, respectively), this change is not all that substantial.

Elsewhere we have argued that the reliabilities of these performance-based scales, in almost every instance, are far from optimal. This is certainly true from the perspective of making valid inferences of a practical (i.e., selecting a candidate based on a sub-test score) or scientific nature (Roberts et al., 2001; Zeidner et al., 2001). Defending themselves against this claim, Mayer, Salovey, Caruso, and Sitarenios (2001) have argued that each of the subtest (and branch) scores are of less importance than is an index of general EI. However, the appeal of tests like the MEIS and MSCEIT is that, supposedly, they capture the multidimensionality of the EI concept. In the intelligence domain, Carroll (1993) has warned researchers that all strata (or levels) of the cognitive abilities hierarchy need to be considered equally important at both empirical and conceptual levels of analysis. Furthermore, if tests such as the MSCEIT are to be used effectively in organizational, educational, or clinical settings, the most useful information may derive from considering differences between sub-test (and branch) scores. This tried-and-true approach is similar to how traditional intelligence tests, such as those developed by Wechsler, provide the most relevant information in comparing different profiles of subtest performance (and Full-Scale, Verbal-Scale, and Performance-Scale IQs) (see chapter 3).

Mayer et al. (submitted) claim that, with wider sampling of experts (i.e., the 21 members of ISRE, the premier academic society for affective science), an important advance in the MSCEIT (Version 2) is close correspondence between consensus and expert scoring. In support of this assertion, they report correlations ranging between 0.94 and 0.99 for MSCEIT (Version 2) consensus and expert scores, across all subtests, and a correlation of 0.98 for the general EI composite. On initial examination, these correlations appear impressive, representing a significant advance in establishing construct validity. There is reason to be cautious of these values, however, because of a well-known finding from psychometrics. "The highest possible validity coefficient is the square root of the product of the two reliabilities, that is [root] $(r_1 \times r_2)$" (Jensen, 1980, p. 310). This correlation can be slightly higher if the errors on the items of the two tests are correlated. Nevertheless, currently reported values seem too high in light of this principle and previous research comparing consensus and expert scores (see Roberts, Zeidner, et al., 2001).[4] In any event, this finding would appear in need of replication, preferably in a laboratory independent of Multi-Health Systems.

Even allowing that these correlations are unproblematic, there remain a number of significant, unresolved issues that Mayer and colleagues do not address in developing expert scoring protocols for the MSCEIT (Version 2). Are the leading researchers who belong to ISRE and who provide the item-weightings for expert scores still predominantly white, middle-class, Western, and highly educated? Given a relatively large pool of experts, perhaps the views of these so-called experts primarily reflect cultural consensus rather than special expertise. What is the level of interexpert agreement in judgment? Should we question the expertise of a judge who does not in fact agree with the expert consensus? ISRE is an august and distinguished scientific organization, but do a selection of its members have sufficient expertise in each of the many sub-fields of emotion to make veridical judgments outside their own specialized area? In general—and in contrast to the physical sciences—it would appear that closer attention must be afforded to the characteristics of the experts before their judgments may be accepted as valid and unbiased. Currently, scant information on the sample of experts (10 males, 11 females, of a mean age approximating 40 years, ethnicity not determined) has been provided in the available literature on the MSCEIT (Version 2) (see Mayer et al., submitted).

As final testament to the construct validity of these new performance-based measures of EI, Mayer et al. (submitted) have conducted a number of exploratory factor analyses of the MSCEIT (Version 1.1) and confirmatory factor analyses of the MSCEIT (Version 2). In each instance, there are some rather startling anomalies in the presented data. For example, a reported four-factor solution of MSCEIT (Version 1.1) (Mayer et al., submitted, table 3), purportedly uncovers a Branch 2: Facilitating Emotions factor. Closer inspection reveals that this factor is defined by a single test (i.e., sensations), with two other measures of Branch-2 (i.e., synesthesia and facilitation) sharing salient loading on Branch 1: emotional perception. Confirmatory factor analyses of the MSCEIT (Version 2) (including one-, two-, and four-factor solutions, as well as an analysis of so-called item parcels [i.e., specific subgroups of items, defined for example, by a stimulus-type]) also have problematic features. In particular, Mayer et al. (submitted) incorporate two poorly specified method factors in one analysis, without justifying (or indeed explaining) these factors. Notably, the introduction of such factors is bound to improve model fit because they increase the degrees of freedom, upon which significance tests of confirmatory factor analytic models are sensitive. Similarly, as we will argue shortly, several of the analyses reported by Mayer et al. (submitted) are questionable in light of established procedures for interpreting constructs resulting from factor analytic techniques.

While reliability, correlational, and factor analyses all constitute important forms of construct validation, there is a surprising absence of information on relationships between both forms of the MSCEIT and other variables. As explicated in chapter 2, this information is essential to establishing construct validity. The study conducted with the MSCEIT (Version 1.1) included 1,794 participants (52.4% female), ranging in age from 16 to 79 years, of diverse educational and ethnic background. The sample of 2,112 respondents used to explore the properties of the MSCEIT (Version 2), was similarly diverse, and included nearly a thousand participants from outside the United States. Not a single correlation (or test of significance) is reported between any of these demographic variables and the MSCEIT. Given the problems we have noted with respect to divergence between consensus and expert scores for gender (and ethnic) differences in the MEIS, and the proposition that EI should improve with age, this silence appears as deafening. Little independent research on correlates of the MSCEIT has yet appeared; in chapter 8 we outline unpublished data we have collected that demonstrates correlations between EI and more positive mood states in a laboratory setting.

Conceptual problems　The ensuing commentary aside, we invoke principles from psychometrics and differential psychology to provide further critical analysis of the MSCEIT, of which test users should be aware. One psychometric principle is especially pertinent. Factor analytic solutions are actually indeterminate in instances where only two tests, as in MSCEIT (Version 2), define a given latent variable. Ensuing use of factor analysis will result in so-called doublets, which are indicative of a narrower concept than the researcher might wish to ascribe (see Carroll, 1993, for detailed treatment of this issue).

Moreover, the scoring methods advocated by Mayer et al. (submitted, in preparation) leave little scope for the itemmetric analyses that are a central element of intelligence test development. Normally, items of graduated difficulty are required to ensure comparable reliability of measurement across the full range of abilities. Consensus scoring, by its nature, excludes identification of difficult items on which, say, only the 10% most able individuals pick the correct answer, and the consensus answer is incorrect. As a result, the MSCEIT (and the MEIS, for that matter) may be more effective in screening for emotional stupidity than discriminating levels of emotional intelligence at the upper end of the range (i.e., the person who is emotionally gifted).

Finally, Zeidner et al. (2001) have suggested that the most vexing issue associated with the emergence of the MSCEIT is Mayer et al.'s neglect of a standard procedure in psychological test development. Authors of well-established intelligence tests (e.g., Wechsler and Stanford-Binet scales) always show that they correlate substantially with older versions as a first step in developing revised versions (see, e.g., Anastasi & Urbina, 1998). Without such data, it is possible that what is being assessed each time is something entirely dissimilar, rendering it impossible to compile a corpus of knowledge around which a concept like EI might coalesce. To our knowledge, information on the overlap between the MEIS and MSCEIT (both versions) or between the two versions of the MSCEIT has not been collected. It is entirely plausible that with the many changes made to these various performance-based measures of EI (at the item, subtest, and scale levels—each highlighted in the section on test descriptions), entirely different concepts are being assessed. The logical implication of this proposition should not be undervalued. Until such time, as carefully conducted research establishes convergence with the MEIS, one should not make any inference from that test to the MSCEIT. Clearly, we must remain silent, therefore on how these new performance-based measures relate to other cognitive ability (or personality) constructs.

Summary   Overall, there appears much research to be conducted with these newer instruments of EI, that are likely to span many years, before we would feel comfortable that these performance-based instruments are of a quality commonly found in cognitive ability testing. Among major issues, requiring attention, would appear the relationship of the MSCEIT to the older MEIS. In addition, it is undetermined whether the MSCEIT might meet standards expected of an intelligence (e.g., moderate correlations with traditional cognitive ability tests), allegedly supported by its earlier form. The issue too of predictive validity is nontrivial: What exactly does the MSCEIT predict (over and above cognitive-ability indices)? Indeed, there would appear a doctoral dissertation (or two) contained within these projects for the avid reader intent upon an academic career in differential psychology!

Additional performance measures of EI (or closely related concepts)

In the passages that follow, we briefly discuss a range of other performance measures, which directly assess EI, emotional constructs (e.g., emotional awareness), or the related concept of social intelligence. In this section of the present chapter, we also introduce laboratory measures that might rightfully aid in providing a clearer understanding of individual differences in emotionality. Most of these objective indices may appear somewhat peripheral to EI, but each plausibly will come under close scrutiny by the research community as conceptions of EI increase in scope and sophistication in the future. We review these performance measures briefly, here, and provide additional pertinent details, including studies addressing critical features such as construct validity, in appendix B.

Direct Tests of EI   The Emotional Accuracy Research Scale (EARS) is reputedly another test for branch 1 of the Mayer and Salovey (1997) model—emotion perception (Mayer & Geher, 1996; Geher, Warner & Brown, 2001). In constituting only 96 items and resembling Stories from the MEIS, EARS conceivably represents the best one-off performance measure of general EI available in the literature. However, a critical analysis of this measure, given in appendix B, highlights further problems (of both a conceptual and psychometric nature) in the scoring of emotional items using expert, consensus, or target techniques.

Measures of emotional constructs that appear closely related to EI
Researchers have attempted to measure people's skill at expressing emotions, which plausibly represents a factor underlying EI. Equally, researchers have investigated the ability of young children to understand the meaning and content of discrete emotions exhibited, for example, in faces. We review several research findings with performance-based tests of these emotional propensities in appendix B, some of which appear promising.

Another concept that appears closely related to EI is emotional awareness, defined as an individual's ability to recognize and describe emotion(s) in the self and in others (Lane & Schwartz, 1987). In the premier objective test designed to assess this construct, the Levels of Emotional Awareness Scale (LEAS), participants are required to describe their anticipated feelings (and those of a second person) to each of twenty scenes (Lane, 2000). Each scene is followed by two questions: "How would you feel?" and "How would the other person (often a friend) feel?" Corresponding to these questions, each person's answer receives two separate scores for each emotion (or emotions) described: one for the self and one for others.

Research described in appendix B demonstrates that LEAS scores correlate with neuropsychological mechanisms known to be closely associated with emotional processing. The LEAS also predicts the accuracy of emotion recognition and people's ability to respond to aversive mood states. These findings provide preliminary evidence for both the validity and utility of this measure. However, a particularly worrying finding, which we discuss in some depth, is that LEAS scores correlate quite substantially with measures of crystallized intelligence. Moreover, the reader should note that concepts like emotional awareness, emotional expression, emotional understanding, and the like are possibly candidates for primary emotional abilities, but appear less broad than the concept of emotional intelligence per se.

Measures of social intelligence Toward the end of appendix A we discuss several of the psychometric tests developed in Guilford's laboratory, which were developed to assess concepts analogous to social intelligence. Given some conceptual and definitional overlap, it seems pertinent to ask how psychometric tests of behavioral knowledge relate to performance-based measures of EI. To our present knowledge, such research has not been conducted.

Moreover, we believe that a recently developed test of social intelligence—Interpersonal Perception Test—15 (IPT-15)—provides features which researchers might try to emulate in constructing scientifically rigorous performance-based measures of EI. For this reason, we choose to discuss it at length in appendix B, rather than along with other indices of social intelligence. The IPT-15 involves videotaped scenarios of various people engaging in social interaction (Constanzo & Archer, 1993). Participants are required to answer questions about 15 such social interactions, which have correct answers because the individuals involved in each scene are not actors, but real people doing real things. Interestingly, one study reviewed in appendix B has examined the relationship between this measure of social intelligence and several putative indices of EI, finding that these correlate near zero (Davies et al., 1998). Although these data are by no means definitive, they do question the claim that there is a strong, meaningful relationship between social and emotional intelligence.

Motivational tests measuring concepts that might overlap with EI We briefly mentioned a close relationship between certain motivational constructs studied by differential psychologists and EI in chapter 3. For example, Cattell et al.'s (1964) Motivational Analysis Test purports to assess constructs that might relate to EI, such as the self-sentiment, that refers to motives to advance in society through active regulation of the self. One motivational instrument—the Self-Awareness Questionnaire (SAQ)—was in fact, used by Davies et al. (1998) in their study of EI. In the SAQ, which is strictly speaking a quasi-objective test, participants are required to rank-order a list of ten needs or motives (e.g., sexual satisfaction, attachment to parents, social assertiveness). Participants are then required to choose from among two words (inside a list of 48 words), the word that they believe goes best with another word. For example, the test item "position PERMANENT wave" might suggest either a secure job or a hairstyle. From their responses on this latter section, participants receive a score for ten different needs, which are rank-ordered and then correlated with the self-reported list of needs. The obtained correlation coefficient represents a measure of self-insight. Thus, it is assumed that the higher the correlation between the paired-word scores and self-appraisal scores, the greater the person's insight into her/his own pattern of emotional needs (Davies et al., 1998).

In study 1 of their paper, Davies et al. (1998) found that the SAQ shared moderate correlations with a number of putative indices of self-reported EI, including moderate negative correlations with alexithymia as predicted. A subsequent exploratory factor analysis indicated that the SAQ loaded on a trait interpreted as Emotional Awareness. However, the SAQ shared near zero correlation with measures of both performance-based EI (specifically, emotion perception) and indices of fluid and crystallized intelligence. Overall, this outcome suggests that while it may be profitable to explore this type of task further, there may something uniquely different between performance, quasi-objective, and self-report measures of EI.

Social-cognitive, laboratory-based measures of EI The cognitive correlates approach involves the study of cognitive-based laboratory tasks

Table 5.7
EQ-i composite scales and subscales, with brief descriptions

Composite scale/subscale	Brief description
Intrapersonal	
Emotional self-awareness	Recognize and understand one's feelings
Assertiveness	Express feelings, thoughts and beliefs, and defend one's rights in a nondestructive manner
Self-regard	Understand, accept, and respect oneself
Self-actualization	Realize one's potential capacities
Independence	Self-directed, self-controlled, and free of emotional dependency
Interpersonal	
Empathy	Aware and appreciative of the feelings of others
Interpersonal relationship	Establish and maintain satisfying relationships characterized by emotional closeness and mutual affection
Social responsibility	Cooperative and responsible member of one's social group
Adaptation	
Problem solving	Define problems and generate potentially effective solutions
Reality testing	Evaluate the correspondence between objective and subjective reality in a realistic and well-grounded fashion
Flexibility	Adjust emotions, thoughts, and behaviors to changing conditions
Stress management	
Stress tolerance	Withstand adverse events through positive, active coping
Impulse control	Resist or delay an impulse, drive, or temptation to act
General mood	
Happiness	Feel satisfied with life, enjoy oneself, and enjoy being with others
Optimism	Maintain a positive attitude, even in the face of adversity

order to appear favorably (or unfavorably) to the person administering the test. As discussed in chapter 2, these indicators may not fully assess the egoistic and moralistic impression-management biases identified in recent research (Paulhus & John, 1998).

Test evaluation and empirical findings According to Bar-On (1997, 2000), the EQ-i and its subscales have high levels of internal consistency (across a variety of cultures), as well as high test-retest reliability over 1- and 4-month periods. These results have been replicated for each of the scales in various laboratories, by independent researchers, which is encouraging (see, e.g., Dawda & Hart, 2000; Newsome et al., 2000). Nevertheless, factor analysis of the items has provided mixed findings. For example, Bar-On's (2000) recent review of his scale, which incorporates a large-scale confirmatory factor analysis, suggests that the fifteen scales originally making up the EQ-i appear empirically *indefensible*. Instead, there appears support for only ten scales—self-regard, interpersonal relationships, impulse control, problem solving, emotional self-awareness, flexibility, reality testing, stress tolerance, assertiveness, and empathy. In a rather unusual twist, Bar-On (2000) retains, however, the five remaining scales (optimism, self-actualization, happiness, independence, and social responsibility), calling them facilitators of social and EI. Since this information has yet to filter through to test users of the EQ-i, it is probable that this unusual reformulation will lead to considerable confusion.

The scales themselves show a substantial degree of positive intercorrelation. This manifold has the advantage of supporting a general EQ factor, but some of the correlations are sufficiently high to call into question the distinctiveness of some of the scales. For example, in Bar-On's (1997) normative sample, optimism correlates at greater than 0.70 with three of the other scales, while social responsibility correlates 0.80 with empathy. Bar-On (1997) groups the scales together into five composites (intrapersonal, interpersonal, adaptability, stress management, and mood) that collectively define EQ. However, a still more economical data reduction of the EQ-i may be possible. Table 5.8 shows results from an exploratory factor analysis we conducted of the normative correlations provided by Bar-On (1997). This factor analysis extracted 3 factors together explaining 70% of the variance. The factors were permitted to correlate (oblique solution), and in fact, the first two factors correlate at 0.45, whereas the third factor correlates at less than 0.20 with both the others. Primarily, scales that relate to self-esteem, positive

Table 5.8
A three-factor solution for the EQ-i scales, based on correlational data in Bar-On (1997, p. 95), $N = 3,831$

EQ-i scale	Factor 1	2	3	h^2	α	C (%)
Emotional self-awareness	.504	.415	−.227	.618	.80	77
Assertiveness	.849	−.089	−.219	.655	.81	81
Self-regard	.853	−.014	−.054	.722	.89	81
Self-actualization	.692	.243	−.117	.675	.80	84
Independence	.812	−.179	.081	.584	.79	74
Empathy	−.091	.949	.058	.844	.75	112
Interpersonal relationship	.357	.661	−.320	.813	.77	106
Social responsibility	−.044	.877	.227	.817	.70	117
Problem solving	.564	.155	.322	.587	.80	74
Reality testing	.588	.190	.376	.703	.75	94
Flexibility	.661	.032	.223	.552	.77	72
Stress tolerance	.825	−.086	.254	.748	.84	89
Impulse control	.232	.210	.718	.732	.79	93
Happiness	.645	.298	−.200	.670	.81	83
Optimism	.799	.128	.057	.765	.82	93

Notes: The table shows factor pattern coefficients for three principal components rotated using the direct oblimin criterion. h^2 = communality. α = internal consistency (from Bar-On, 1997). $C = h^2/\alpha \times 100$.

mood, and stress resistance define the first factor: it appears to resemble (low levels of) neuroticism. Empathy and interpersonal scales define the second factor, while factor 3 is essentially defined by impulse control. The column labeled "h^2" refers to the *communality* of each scale and represents the proportion of total variance explained by all three factors. Some of the unexplained variance represents error. Harman's (1976) index of completeness, C, expresses the *reliable* variance explained by dividing h^2 by the internal consistency of the scale (α), to correct for error. It appears that, typically, 80–90% of the reliable variance of the scales can be explained by just three factors (C values > 100% presumably reflect chance fluctuations). Of course, confirmatory analyses are required to test different models against one another, but there appears to be a case that the reliable variance of the EQ-i can be attributed to just three constructs: self-esteem, empathy, and impulse control.

Bar-On (1997) reports various tests of group differences. Total EQ scores increase up to age 30 or so, and then plateau. Contrary to findings with the MEIS, there is no overall gender difference. Nevertheless, in line with existing data on personality and gender (Feingold, 1994), men tend to be higher in self-regard, adaptability, stress tolerance and optimism, whereas women are higher in interpersonal aspects of EQ (effect sizes are, however, small). Bar-On (1997) also reports data from various cross-national groups, which compared to norms for North America, suggest that EQ is especially high in Israel, and notably low in India and Nigeria. According to Bar-On, it is "relatively meaningless" to compare population means cross-nationally.[6] Internal consistency also holds up well across different cultures.

Bar-On (1997, 2000) reports an impressive array of validity data showing that EQ relates to various measures of mental health, coping, work satisfaction, and personality traits believed to relate to resistance to disorder. High total EI appears strongly related to high trait anxiety, depression, borderline personality, and emotional instability. The EI subscales show moderate to very strong relationships with high positive and low negative affectivity. In addition, each of the subscales is highly related to other measures. For example, self-regard is highly related to other measures of self-esteem, low empathy is highly related to a measure of antisocial personality, and interpersonal relationship is very highly related to a measure of warmth (see Ciarrochi et al., 2001). In studies reported by Bar-On (1997), the EQ-i has been related to people's employment status, academic success, success at fitting into a culture, prison status, and response to stress management (see also Bar-On, Brown, Kirkcaldy & Thome, 2000). However, strikingly absent from the validity data is any attempt to show that the EQ-i remains predictive when its personality correlates are controlled. By contrast with the MEIS, the EQ-i shows near-zero correlations with IQ, although Bar-On (2000) cites an unpublished study showing a correlation of 0.46 with the MSCEIT.

In one of the few independently conducted validation studies of the Bar-On scales, Newsome, Day, and Catano (2000) found that neither EQ-i total score nor factor scores predicted academic achievement or cognitive ability: the correlation between EQ-i and grade point average (GPA) in 160 Canadian college students was 0.01. By contrast, cognitive ability was the strongest predictor of GPA, with personality (introversion and self-control) making a lesser but significant contribution to predict-ing achievement. The authors conclude that there is inadequate evi-dence to justify use of the EQ-i as a selection device.

How distinctive is the EQ-i from related constructs? The measure purportedly represents a continuation and expansion of past research in the field of individual differences (Bar-On, 1997, 2000), so some overlap with existing measures is expected. However, two troublesome findings, which appear to have escaped commentators, to date, are worth mentioning. The first is unusually high correlations between a number of the EQ-i sub-scales and measures derived from the Symptom Checklist-90 (SCL-90; Derogatis, 1983), a self-report measure designed to assess the severity of psychopathological symptomatology. For exam-ple, the correlation between the interpersonal-relationship subscale of the EQ-i and the interpersonal-sensitivity scale of the SCL-90 is -0.85, while Flexibility from the EQ-i correlates $r = -0.70$ with the obsessive-compulsive subscale of the SCL-90 (Bar-On, 2000). Given likely restric-tion of range in administering the SCL-90 to samples of psychologically healthy individuals, these correlations might approach unity with suit-able corrections. Equally troublesome are reported moderate positive correlations between several EQ-i sub-scales and measures derived from an Emotional Stroop task (Bar-On, 2000). This result runs contrary to anything one might expect of an intelligence construct, since a remark-ably robust finding in the intelligence literature is that speed measures derived from such cognitive tasks correlate *negatively* with cognitive abilities. That is, high intelligence is related to faster speed of informa-tion uptake/processing (e.g., Roberts & Stankov, 1999), whereas with the EQ-i, if this finding is indeed correct, highly emotionally intelligent people take longer to process emotional information. For the present authors at least, this relationship seems counterintuitive.

These findings also call into question whether the EQ-i is too highly related to the Five Factor model of personality described in chapter 2. A recent study, by Dawda and Hart (2000), which we reproduce in table 5.9, confirms this suspicion. Average correlations approaching 0.50 were found between each of the Big Five measures (other than open-ness) and general EI, for each of the gender groups, with the correla-tion magnitudes found for neuroticism exceeding 0.60 in men and 0.70 in women. Indeed, noting the relative independence of each of the Big Five factors (e.g., Costa & McCrae, 1992), one may gain an understand-ing of how distinctive the EQ-i is likely to be in the face of overlap with personality. Squaring these correlations and then summating, one

Table 5.9
Relationships between the Bar-On EQ-i main scales and measures of the Big Five personality factors obtained by Dawda and Hart (2000) for their male and female samples

Scales	α	O	C	E	A	N
Male sample ($N = 118$)						
EQ-i total	.96	−.12	.51	.52	.43	−.62
Intrapersonal EI	.93	−.06	.54	.48	.21	−.59
Interpersonal EI	.86	−.02	.34	.55	.58	−.21
Adaptation	.87	−.15	.45	.32	.38	−.53
Stress management	.86	−.11	.32	.18	.39	−.54
General mood	.91	−.22	.40	.61	.32	−.69
Female sample ($N = 124$)						
EQ-i total	.96	.17	.33	.56	.43	−.72
Intrapersonal EI	.94	.11	.33	.51	.24	−.70
Interpersonal EI	.85	.11	.21	.51	.62	−.23
Adaptation	.86	.22	.37	.40	.40	−.58
Stress management	.81	.22	.16	.22	.38	−.58
General mood	.90	.09	.17	.64	.27	−.77

Notes: α = internal consistency (from Bar-On, 1997). O = openness; C = conscientiousness; E = extroversion; A = agreeableness; and N = neuroticism.

generally finds values close to 100% variance accounted for across almost every scale. Similarly, Newsome et al. (2000) found that EQ-i was correlated at −0.77 with the anxiety factor assessed by Cattell's 16PF questionnaire. The magnitudes of correlations between the five EQ-i composite scores and Anxiety exceeded 0.60 in all but one case. The Interpersonal composite was tolerably distinct from Anxiety ($r = -0.34$), but was substantially correlated with extraversion ($r = -0.52$). The authors conclude that the EQ-i is largely a measure of neuroticism (which is a similar construct to the Cattell anxiety dimension). Collectively, these data suggest that the EQ-i is nothing but a proxy (and likely crude) measure of the personality constructs of the Five Factor model: essentially neuroticism with an admixture of extraversion, agreeableness, and conscientiousness.

By contrast, Petrides and Furnham (in press) suggest that, despite considerable overlap, there may be some reliable variance in the EQ-i beyond that associated with the Big Five. They found correlations similar to those of Dawda and Hart between the EQ-i and the NEO-PI-R (Costa & McCrae, 1992), in a study of 166 college students. For example, EQ-i correlated at −.73 with neuroticism and .54 with extraversion. The multiple correlation for EQ-i predicted from all five factors was 0.84 (Petrides, personal communication, July 2, 2001). However, factor analysis suggested that a truncated emotional intelligence trait could be distinguished from the Big Five. That is, some of the EQ-i scales properly belong with Big Five factors. For example, stress tolerance loaded mainly on (low) neuroticism and empathy loaded highly on agreeableness. At the same time, five of the scales—assertiveness, emotional self-awareness, independence, emotion mastery, and self-regard—loaded at >.5 on a distinct factor (which might be seen as a kind of emotional self-esteem). This factor correlated positively with extraversion and conscientiousness factors, and negatively with the neuroticism factor. Petrides and Furnham (in press) conclude that EI may be a lower-level primary trait that could be placed below the Big Five in a multistratum model. In fact, the Petrides and Furnham study did not test such a model explicitly, but it represents an interesting possibility for future research. A leaner, better-defined construct might add to existing personality models, though there would be little a priori reason to refer to the trait as an intelligence.

Summary Bar-On's (1997, 2000) research is notable for its thoroughness and use of large, diverse samples in test development and validation. The EQ-i predicts various criteria, and hence is potentially useful. However, the close relationships between EQ and various measures of personality and psychopathology suggest that EI, as assessed by the EQ-i, has actually been under investigation for decades. Therefore, to fully understand the importance of the EQ-i, it is essential to understand not only research directly related to the measure, but also the research related to the earlier measures to which it is highly related. The fact that the EQ-i may represent little more than personality should be a cause of concern for those organizations prepared to employ it in personnel selection. Elsewhere, Schmidt and Hunter (e.g., 1998) have demonstrated that personality adds little, in terms of incremental validity (over general intelligence) in the selection context. It is disturbing too that the EQ-i does not show better convergence with the MEIS/MSCEIT. Not only is the correlation between the two tests only moderate, but their major correlates appear to differ. For example, the MEIS relates to measures of cognitive ability, but the EQ-i does not.

Emotional Competence Inventory (ECI)

Theoretical framework   Goleman (1998) proposed a model of EI with 25 competencies arrayed in 5 higher-order clusters. These clusters, along with the competencies comprising them, are as follows:

Self-awareness   Consists of emotional awareness, accurate self-assessment, and self-confidence.

Self-regulation   Composed of self-control, trustworthiness, conscientiousness, adaptability, and innovation.

Motivation   Defined by achievement drive, organizational commitment, initiative, and optimism.

Empathy   Consists of understanding others, developing others, service orientation, leveraging diversity, and political awareness.

Social skills   Composed of influence, communication, conflict management, leadership, change catalyst, building bonds, collaboration and co-operation, and team capabilities.

Development of the ECI (Version 1) started with a self-report competency questionnaire developed by Boyatzis, the Self-Assessment Questionnaire, and the rewriting of items to fit Goleman's (1998) theoretical model. However, following largely from cluster analyses (Boyatzis, Goleman & Rhee, 2000), these 25 competencies were collapsed into 20, with the 5 domains reduced to 4. This led to a substantial revision: the ECI (Version 2). In this reformulation optimism has been integrated with achievement drive; innovation has been collapsed into initiative; and organizational commitment has been collapsed into leadership. Collaboration and teamwork combine to form the broader construct, teamwork and collaboration, while leveraging diversity and understanding others combine to form a new construct, empathy. Finally, political awareness has been renamed organizational awareness, while emotional awareness has become emotional self-awareness. The five higher-order constructs have been reformulated as follows: self-awareness (which essentially remains as is), self-management (which represents a mix of the previous self-regulation and motivation constructs), social awareness (representing a mix of motivation and empathy), and relationship management (which is a mix of components once comprising motivation, empathy, and social skills). Clearly, the ECI (Version 2) measures a different competence-based model than that described in Goleman's (1998) *Working with Emotional Intelligence.* In any event, we present the revised model underlying the ECI in table 5.10.

Table 5.10
Revised competencies making up Goleman's (2001) EI model

	Self (personal competence)	Other (social competence)
Recognition	Self-awareness	Social awareness
	Emotional self-awareness	Empathy
	Accurate self-assessment	Service orientation
	Self-confidence	Organizational awareness
	Self-management	Relationship management
Regulation	Emotional self-control	Developing others
	Trustworthiness	Influence
	Conscientiousness	Communication
	Adaptability	Conflict management
	Achievement drive	Leadership
	Initiative	Change catalyst
		Building bonds
		Teamwork & collaboration

Test description   To our knowledge, no sample items are yet available in the published literature to give the reader a feel for the types of questions comprising each scale. Presumably, commercialization of the inventory through the Hay/McBer Group is a high priority and there may be a perception that the scales might be compromised with this information. Goleman (2001), however, does provide a series of capsule descriptions, which help to give a flavor for the content of each scale. We distill the major aspects of these capsule descriptions in table 5.11.

The ECI is a multirater instrument that provides self, manager, direct report, and peer ratings on a series of behavioral indicators of emotional intelligence, based on the emotional competencies identified by Goleman (1998). The test has a somewhat unorthodox response format, including the optional answer "I don't know", which is "read into the data as blank" (Boyatzis et al., 2000, p. 346). In the self-report format, respondents are asked to rate themselves on a seven-point Likert-type scale. Options range from "The behavior is only slightly characteristic of me (I behave this way only sporadically)" to "The behavior is very characteristic of me (I behave in this way in most or all situations where it is appropriate)." Peer-report ratings recast the scale in terms of the relevant other.[7]

Table 5.11
Capsule descriptions of the 20 competencies composing the ECI (version 2)

Scale	Capsule description
Self-awareness cluster	
Emotional self-awareness	Recognizing one's feelings and how they influence performance
Accurate self-assessment	Awareness of abilities and limitations; learning from mistakes; seeking feedback; knowing where to improve; knowing when to work with people with complementary strengths
Self-confidence	Belief in oneself and one's abilities (related to self-efficacy)
Self-management cluster	
Emotional self-control	Manifested in absence of distress and disruptive feelings
Trustworthiness	Translates into letting people know one's values, principles, intentions, feelings and acting in ways consistent with these actions
Conscientiousness	Being careful, self-disciplined, and scrupulous in attending to responsibilities
Adaptability	Open to new information; can let go of old assumptions; adaptive in how one operates
Achievement orientation	Optimistically striving to continually improve performance
Initiative	Acting before being forced to by external events
Social awareness cluster	
Empathy	Astute awareness of others' emotions, concerns, and needs
Customer service	Ability to identify client's often unstated needs and concerns and then to match them to one's own products and services
Organizational awareness	Ability to read the currents of emotions and political realities in groups
Social-skills cluster	
Influence	Can handle and manage emotions in other people and do so persuasively
Communication	Effective in give-and-take of emotional information; deals with issues straightforwardly; listens well and fully shares information; fosters open communication; receptive to both good and bad news

Table 5.11 (continued)

Scale	Capsule description
Conflict management	Able to spot troubles and take steps to calm those involved
Leadership	Possesses a range of personal skills required to inspire people to work toward some common goal
Change catalyst	Able to recognize the need for change, remove barriers, challenge the status quo, and enlist others in pursuit of new initiatives
Building bonds	Balances one's own work with carefully chosen favors; builds goodwill with people who may become crucial resources down the line
Teamwork and collaboration	Teamwork depends on the collective EI of its members. The most productive teams are those that exhibit EI competencies at the team level. Collaboration is the ability to work cooperatively with peers.

Test evaluation An indication of the internal consistency reliability of the ECI (Version 2) is given in Boyatzis et al. (2000, table 16.1b). In truth, because it may be used for high-stakes decision-making, the reliability of the self-report subscales is marginal, ranging from 0.587 (for trustworthiness) to 0.817 (for conscientiousness). However, an actual evaluation of the validity of the ECI is difficult. Almost all of the empirical studies examining this measure, emanate from working papers, unpublished manuscripts, or technical reports (or sometimes notes) (see the reference list in Boyatzis et al., 2000). Thus, we could find no factor or cluster analysis supporting the derivation of factors in the scientific literature. Nor does there appear any attempts, to date, to demonstrate convergent or discriminant validity.

Thus, of necessity, our evaluation of the ECI must rest largely on conceptual analysis. It is nonincidental that at least one of the scales (in point of fact, that competency with the highest reliability) is conscientiousness, a major factor within the Five Factor Model. A number of other competencies appear to share overlap with other Big Five constructs. For example, emotional self-control would appear the obverse of neuroticism, trustworthiness is actually a facet of agreeableness, while adaptability has the ring of openness about it. Several of the other competencies have parallels with other psychological concepts, especially those studied in the motivational (e.g., achievement orientation) and social psychological (e.g., leadership) literatures. Indeed, we note that in several instances, competencies assessed by the ECI, need not be assessed via self-report methods. For example, it is possible to assess both accurate self-assessment and self-confidence using objective techniques, within the so-called calibration paradigm. In this paradigm, the participant is asked to rate how confident they are that the answer they give, on say an intelligence test, was correct (on a percentage scale). This measure may then be compared with actual accuracy level, with complex statistical techniques available for ascertaining levels of under- and overconfidence (see, e.g., Stankov & Crawford, 1997).

Considering it assesses so many disparate concepts, it is likely that the ECI will have some utility. Even here, however, reliability is a cause for concern, as is the fact that more sophisticated techniques exist for assessing constructs comprising it. In sum, it is difficult not to be cynical of this measure, given the lack of publicly accessible data supplied by its creators and the constellation of old concepts packaged under its new label.

Schutte Self-Report Inventory (SSRI)

Test description   The Schutte Self-Report Inventory (SSRI) is based on the most recent theorizing of John Mayer and colleagues (Schutte, Malouff, Hall, Haggerty et al., 1998). The developers of this scale suggest that it provides a measure of general EI, as well as measures of four EI sub-factors. These constructs, appear similar (but not directly comparable) to processes captured by branches of the MEIS. To highlight these differences, consider sample items defining each construct, given below:

Emotion perception   For example, "I find it hard to understand the nonverbal messages of other people."

Utilizing emotions   For example, "When I feel a change in emotion, I tend to come up with new ideas."

Managing self-relevant emotions   For example, "I seek out activities that make me happy."

Managing others' emotions   For example, "I arrange events others enjoy."

Test Evaluation   The overall EI score, and the perception and managing emotion scores tend to be reliable in both adults and adolescents, whereas the utilizing emotions sub-scale exhibits relatively poor reliability (Ciarrochi, Chan & Bajgar, 2001). Regarding the distinctiveness of the SSRI, people who score high on the general EI scale also tend to score low on measures of negative affectivity and high on measures of positive affectivity (or extraversion), openness to feelings, and empathy. With individual subscales, the managing-self-emotions scale seems to be the least distinctive, having large overlap with positive and negative affectivity. In contrast, the other subscales have only small to medium overlap with affectivity and other personality variables. Moreover, the SSRI has been shown to be useful in predicting school success (Schutte et al., 1998).

Petrides and Furnham (2000a) showed that women scored more highly than men on items related to social skills, but not on overall score. Their study also included a measure that asked respondents to estimate directly various component abilities of EI: self-estimated EI correlated moderately with SSRI score. They also showed that self-estimation is biased: respondents generally tend to rate themselves as above average in ability. In addition, contrary to scale score differences men rated themselves higher than women on three of the component abilities, including "ability to understand your own emotions." A further study examining it with powerful confirmatory factor analytic statistical techniques failed to provide evidence for a general EI factor or replicable subcomponents, indicating its match to theory was less than perfect (Petrides & Furnham, 2000b). Instead, Petrides and Furnham found that the SSRI differentiated four independent factors of optimism/mood regulation, appraisal of emotions, social skills, and utilization of emotions.

Saklofske, Austin, and Minski (submitted) obtained a moderately good fit in a confirmatory factor analytic study of the SSRI for a hierarchical model that bridges the gap between single- and multiple-factor models. They extracted a general factor super-ordinate over four factors similar to those found by Petrides and Furnham (2000b). They also explored the predictive validity of the factors in a substantial sample, confirming that the SSRI correlates with indices of well-being (e.g., life satisfaction). They also showed substantial correlations with the Big Five, of which the highest was 0.51 with extraversion. In contrast to Dawda and Hart's (2000) study of the EQ-i, there were relatively modest correlations with conscientiousness (0.38), agreeableness (0.18), and neuroticism. The scale correlated more strongly, however, with openness (0.27). Furthermore, Saklofske et al. showed discriminant validity: the SSRI remained predictive of most criteria with the five personality traits statistically controlled. However, the magnitudes of the partial correlations between the SSRI and well-being criteria were small, and typically less than 0.20.

Summary The SSRI has both positive and negative features. In its favor, it appears to be more distinct from personality traits than the EQ-i, and there is some evidence for (limited) discriminant validity (Saklofske et al., submitted). It also appears to relate to a somewhat different mix of traits (i.e., more to extraversion and less to neuroticism). On the negative side, the apparent lack of convergence between self-report scales is a cause for concern, especially if the goal of this research is to provide a unified account of EI. Moreover, the predictive power of the SSRI is rather modest, and there are uncertainties over its dimensional structure, which diverges from that claimed by Schutte et al. (1998).

The Trait Meta-Mood Scale (TMMS)

Test description The Trait-Meta Mood Scale (Salovey, Mayer, Goldman, Turvey & Palfai, 1995) is based upon early notions of the cognitive model of EI put forward previously by Mayer and colleagues. It has been designed to assesses the following three constructs (Salovey & Mayer, 1990):

Attention to emotion For example, "I don't think it's worth paying attention to your emotions or moods."

Emotional clarity For example, "Sometimes I can't tell what my feelings are."

Emotion repair For example, "I try to think good thoughts no matter how badly I feel."

Test evaluation Although the attention-to-emotions and emotional-clarity subscales each have been shown to possess adequate reliability, there is something of a question mark over the reliability of the emotional-repair scale. Recent evidence also suggests that the emotion-repair and emotional-clarity subscales are not too distinct from measures of the Big Five personality factors. We reproduce this evidence, obtained by Davies et al. (1998), in table 5.12. The attention subscale appears, however, to be reasonably distinct from personality measures and also (surprisingly, given it is meant to represent a form of intelligence) cognitive-ability measures (see in particular Davies et al., 1998). These criticisms aside, the emotional-clarity scale may be useful in pre-

Table 5.12
Correlations between the Trait-Meta-Mood Scale (TMMS) and the Big-Five personality factors (from Davies et al., 1998, study 2) ($N = 300$)

TMMS subscales	α	O	C	E	A	N
Attention	.82	.25	.00	.14	.27	.05
Repair	.73	.19	.25	.29	.48	−.47
Clarity	.82	.14	.32	.23	.48	−.50

Notes: We have reanalyzed the data from Davies et al. (1998), study 2. α = internal consistency (from Bar-On, 1997). O = openness; C = conscientiousness; E = extroversion; A = agreeableness; and N = neuroticism.

dicting the extent that people dwell unproductively on sad thoughts (see Salovey et al., 1995). On the other hand, the similar concept of rumination is familiar from clinically oriented studies of personality, and there are several more extensively validated scales in this area (Matthews & Wells, in press; see also chapter 10).

Additional self-report measures of EI or closely related concepts
Commercially available tests   As noted from the introduction to this discussion, beyond tests covered herein, there is a plethora of self-report measures of EI. These include two commercially available psychometric tests based on notably more disparate models of EI than previously covered either in these passages or in chapter 1: the Constructive Thinking Inventory (CTI) (Epstein, 1998) and the EQ-Map Test (Cooper, 1996/ 1997). Arguably, these measures have not attracted as much attention as the EQ-i and SSRI in the wider scientific literature, though they do appear in populist literatures devoted to the topic of EI. Thus, we provide an extensive critical analysis of these tests (and models upon which they are based) in appendix C. Briefly, our analysis of these tests calls each measure into question. In particular, neither test appears to possess construct validity or the psychometric rigor the differential psychologist might desire.

Indeed, our analysis of these tests leads us to post a cautionary note on the commercial usage of self-report measures of EI. Many of the self-report measures of EI discussed in chapter 5 or in appendix C have found their way into corporate applications. These include use as a selection device, as aids in helping to plan individual development initiatives, and as tools around which team building, coaching, and mentoring programs might be built (see chapter 12). The number of these measures, we believe, will continue to grow apace. Thus, we would like to alert the reader to still other commercial instruments (that because of space constraints we will not discuss beyond these passages) which are available in the marketplace (but not necessarily the scientific literature).

Perforce we limited our review of self-report EI instruments (either commercial or research related) to those that are well known, established, or could be evaluated because of available research in peer-review scientific publications (or as books or book chapters). Note, however, tests such as the Emotional Intelligence Questionnaire: General and General 360 (http://www.ase-solutions.co.uk/html/business/products/eigeneral.htm) have recently found themselves into the marketplace, often with scant empirical backing. Even when these results are made available to a wider audience, the empirical support for many of these styles of instrument often appears contrived. Thus, Dulewicz and Higgs claim, "EQ and IQ is a more powerful predictor of 'success' than either measure alone" (2000, p. 341). On close inspection, this claim is highly circumspect since the measure of intelligence that they examined was self-reported. Moreover, these authors do not give detailed information on factor structure and appear to have developed scales that a psychometrician might claim have marginal reliabilities (ranging from 0.54 to 0.71 for six scales comprising the Emotional Intelligence Questionnaire).

Similarly, certain companies involved in test publishing appear to be offering information on emotional intelligence from older instruments. A case in point, is the Occupational Personality Questionnaire (Saville & Holdsworth Limited), where conglomerates of subscales can now be added to give several emotional intelligence scores. Since this instrument has been reanalyzed to show that the scales represent superfactors of the Big Five (Matthews & Stanton, 1994), the chance of it providing anything above and beyond information pertaining to personality is self-evident.

Self-report measures of emotional constructs related to EI   There are a number of self-report measures of psychological constructs such as empathy, alexithymia (see chapter 11), stress coping, and emotional control, which might clearly assess important components of EI. Indeed, some researchers have used these as proxies for the EI construct particularly when the construct was still in its infancy (see Davies et al., 1998). We review a selection of these measures briefly in appendix C. A rather consistent finding, however, mirroring problems associated with self-report measures covered in the preceding passages, is considerable overlap between these measures of emotional components and one (or more) of the Big Five personality constructs.

Overlap of Emotional Intelligence with Personality

Why overlap between emotional intelligence and personality is a problem

The preceding review of self-report measures has consistently revealed that EI relates to various aspects of personality. Two of the traits to which EI relates, neuroticism and extraversion, are often linked to emotional disposition or temperament, whereas emotionality is seen as distinct from agreeableness, conscientiousness, and openness. According to Watson and Clark (1992, 1997), neuroticism is close to negative affectivity: high trait scorers experience a broad range of negative moods, including not only anxiety and sadness but also such emotions as guilt, hostility, and self-dissatisfaction. Negative affectivity tends to be highly related to low trait self-esteem (Ciarrochi, Chan & Caputi, 2000b). Watson and Clark also link extraversion to positive affectivity, defined as a trait-sensitivity to positive events. This causes high scorers to feel joyful, enthusiastic, energetic, friendly, bold, assertive, proud, and confident, whereas those low in positive affectivity tend to feel dull, flat, disinterested, and unenthusiastic. Positive affectivity tends to have a small to moderate relationship with high self-esteem. It is probably an error to make emotional dispositions central to neuroticism and extraversion, given that their associations with emotion and mood vary according to situation and context (e.g., Brandstätter, 1994). Moreover, cognition is at least as important as emotion in defining these traits (Matthews, Derryberry & Siegle, 2000). Indeed, in controlled laboratory environments, the correlation between extraversion and positive mood may be less than 0.20 (Matthews et al., 1999). Nevertheless, EI scales may in part be assessing dispositional emotionality, which raises some difficult conceptual issues, given that we want to distinguish EI from emotion itself.

Figure 5.2, adopted from Ciarrochi, Chan, Caputi, and Roberts (2001), illustrates hypothetical relationships between self-reported EI, personality traits, and positive life outcomes. The causal explanation favored by EI theorists (e.g., Bar-On, 2000) appears to be that greater emotional competence leads to greater happiness (i.e., that EI causally precedes emotional disposition). However, there are at least three alternative

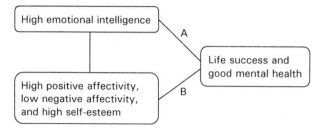

Figure 5.2
The relationship between some measures of emotional intelligence, affectivity, and life success (adapted from Ciarrochi et al., 2001).

explanations for the link between EI and personality traits linked to emotional disposition. First, personality may control the development of EI. People who experience a large number of negative emotions would find it more difficult to learn to control these emotions. For example, one item on a measure of managing self-relevant emotions might be, "I have trouble controlling my anger." If people endorse this item, is it because they have an "angry disposition" or because they lack basic skills in managing their anger? It is likely to be influenced by both factors, and existing work may not discriminate them adequately. Similarly, positive emotions may be more easily controlled than negative ones.

Second, personality is related to stability of emotion: people high in neuroticism may tend to have less stable emotional experiences (Costa & McCrae, 1992b). At one moment they may feel angry, and at another moment, sad. Such instability may make it difficult for them to have a clear understanding of what they are feeling, why they are feeling it, and how to control their feelings. A third reason for the relationship between EI and personality is that people with a "good" personality (low negative affectivity, high positive affectivity, and high self-esteem) tend to be optimistic about their abilities in general. Thus, when you ask them to evaluate how emotionally intelligent they are, they confidently say they are very emotionally intelligent, though they might not be so.

Given that self-report EI measures show moderate to strong overlap with personality, we must be careful in making drawing generalizations from the data. For example, if we find that people high in self-reported EI tend to have good mental health, we might want to conclude that it is EI that leads to superior mental health (link A, figure 5.2). However, it might be just as reasonable to argue that people high in EI have a good personality and that it is balanced personality, rather than EI, which predicts superior mental health (link B). There is certainly strong evidence that people with a good personality and high self-esteem possess some advantages in life (Watson & Tellegen, 1985), although, as we shall see in chapter 10, there are some compensatory benefits to a more pessimistic nature.

Disentangling emotional intelligence from personality measures

How can one distinguish the effects of emotional intelligence from that of personality? One way is to design an EI test that has little overlap with personality, as has been accomplished by a number of the performance measures described in this chapter. Insofar as questionnaire assessment is concerned, more systematic investigation of how the major components of EI might be integrated with existing dimensional models of personality is required. Existing accounts of EI tend to be bloated with superfluous concepts. However, further psychometric work may isolate some genuinely distinctive components such as the three factors shown in table 5.8, or the four dimensions found within the SSRI by Petrides and Furnham (2000b) and by Saklofske et al. (submitted). In any event, each of these components may be placed within models such as the Five-Factor Model. We might relate low self-esteem and alexithymia to neuroticism, interpersonal skills to extraversion, empathy to agreeableness, and self-control and motivation to conscientiousness, for example. Some components, such as optimism, which relates to low neuroticism/ high extraversion, may relate to multiple superfactors. An analysis of this kind should look at how components of EI relate to relatively narrow personality traits, as well as to broader superfactors encapsulated within the Big-Five Factor Model.

A second method involves looking at the effect of EI on outcomes while statistically controlling for personality and/or self-esteem. "Statistical control" in this case, means essentially eliminating link B in figure 5.2. This method has already been used with certain self-report measures, with some degree of moderate success. For example, Salovey, Mayer, and their colleagues (1995) found that a measure of emotional clarity from the TMMS successfully predicted ruminative thinking, even after controlling for aspects of personality (Salovey et al., 1995). Similarly, using Schutte's Self-Report Inventory (SSRI), Ciarrochi and colleagues have examined the impact of EI on various outcomes, while controlling for aspects of positive and negative affectivity. In one study, they found that adolescents who scored high in EI tended to have better social support. These same people were better at recognizing facial expressions and in engaging in behavior that would maintain good (and reduce aversive) moods (Ciarrochi, Chan & Bajgar, 2001). In a second study, Ciarrochi, Deane, and Anderson (2000) found that people who were good at managing others' emotions tended to adapt better to stress, responding with less suicidal ideation. Finally, Ciarrochi and Deane (2000) found that people high in EI had better experiences in getting help from mental health professionals. They were also more willing to seek professional help in the future. Saklofske et al. (submitted) also found that the SSRI predicted well-being indices with scores on the Big Five personality traits controlled. Taken together, these findings demonstrate that self-reported EI may have predictive power over and above major personality traits. Even so, it is unclear how these scales would perform in comparison to narrower, more specific, traits related to emotional and interpersonal functioning, such as optimism-pessimism, empathy and self-control.

Conclusions

We conclude this chapter with an outline of the accomplishments and failures of attempts to measure EI, and some reflections on future possibilities.

Measuring emotional intelligence: Promised or barren land?

Test development has been most successful with regard to *reliability*: both performance and questionnaire techniques provide internally consistent assessments. Reliabilities of subscales and components of EI are typically also high for questionnaires, but sometimes rather moderate for performance-based assessment. *Content validity* is a continuing problem. Conceptualizations of EI differ and, especially in the self-report domain, tend to be overinclusive and protean. The most satisfactory approach to date is probably Mayer, Caruso, et al.'s (2000) discrimination of four conceptually distinct branches, which inspired not just the MEIS and MSCEIT, but also Schutte et al.'s (1998) SSRI. However, there appears to have been some slippage in realizing these constructs psychometrically, with failures to reproduce the branches as factors, as hypothesized (Petrides & Furnham, 2000; Roberts et al., 2001). Furthermore, the MSCEIT seems to have lost some of the representativeness of sampling the branches that was a positive feature of the MEIS.

The *predictive validity* of EI tests is also rather unimpressive so far. Studies of the MEIS show a smattering of significant validity coefficients in the .1 to .3 range (e.g., Ciarrochi, Chan & Caputi, 2000a; Mayer, Caruso, et al., 2000), with general intelligence controlled. It is true that small validity coefficients may be theoretically interesting and, in some circumstances, practically useful (see Anastasi & Urbina, 1997). However, studies so far do not establish any dependent measure for which the MEIS should be the predictor test of choice, on the basis of comparisons between the MEIS and other tests. For example, personality scales are much more predictive of general well-being than the MEIS. The predictive validity of the MSCEIT is largely unknown, especially with the lack of information on the correlation between MEIS and MSCEIT. Other performance-based tests may have some validity in limited domains, but none have yet demonstrated strong discriminant validity with respect to other tests.

On the face of it, self-report measures have attained better predictive validity than ability tests (e.g., Bar-On, 1997). However, much of their validity is simply a consequence of their excessive overlap with existing constructs, such as the Five-Factor Model. It is entirely predictable that a proxy for neuroticism or anxiety is predictive of the same constructs as those personality dimensions (Newsome et al., 2000). Questionnaires for EI may have some discriminant validity over the Five-Factor Model (Saklofske et al., in press), but, as with performance-based measures, these scales provide only a very modest increment in predictive power, rather than a revolution in understanding individual differences. Rigorous attempts to separate what may be unique about traits for emotional intelligence from existing personality dimensions appear to be essential for further progress (Petrides & Furnham, in press).

Despite some promising advances in test development, there are also some basic problems for the *construct validity* of tests of EI, highlighted by issues relating to convergent and discriminant validity. Not only do self-report and quasi-objective performance tests fail to converge on a common construct, but there appear to be problems within each measurement approach. Performance tests are open to different scoring methods, which reflect questionable rationales, and which may disagree empirically (Roberts et al., 2001). Self-report scales appear to have some common elements, but the two leading contenders (EQ-i and SSRI) show rather different patterns of association with personality. Similarly, different tests show different relationships to IQ and demographic group. Indeed, even the two scoring systems of the MEIS appear to tell a different story regarding gender differences in EI (Roberts et al., 2001).

Divergent validity depends on the medium of assessment, being much better for performance than for self-report measures. Questionnaire scales have some modest discriminant validity with respect to existent personality scales, despite the high degree of overlap. Performance measures of EI tend not to overlap with personality, but do have small to medium overlap with traditional measures of intelligence. Thus, it is important to statistically control for intelligence when examining the effects of performance EI. Using this statistical approach, Carriochi, Chan, and Caputi (2000b) have shown that the MEIS predicts mood-management behavior. Similarly, Lane, and his colleagues (1990, 1998) have demonstrated that the Levels of Emotional Awareness Scale, a performance measure discussed in appendix B, predicts individual differences in emotional processing. While further research is required, it would appear that performance measures do have some predictive power over and above intelligence measures.

In addition to these explicit psychometric problems, there are many unresolved issues in EI research. For example, should EI be considered a type of intelligence, as opposed to a behavioral style? Mayer and his colleagues have argued that in order for EI to be a true intelligence, it should do the following:

1. Reflect performance rather than preferred ways of behaving

2. Correlate, but not too highly, with currently existing IQ measures

3. Improve during childhood to middle adulthood

4. Be predictive of emotion-related outcomes and general life satisfaction

As indicated previously, psychological models that fail to consider how EI might rightfully constitute an intelligence render the concept a euphemism rather than a precise scientific term (see Mayer & Cobb, 2000; Roberts et al., 2001).

Only the MEIS and MSCEIT appear to satisfy all of the aforementioned criteria, although there are doubts about whether agreement with consensus truly reflects objective performance. Moreover, as argued by Roberts et al. (2001), the predictive validity and theoretical basis for the MEIS/MSCEIT require much more exploration before it can be considered a legitimate measure of EI (see also Zeidner et al., 2001). The LEAS has also been shown to satisfy criteria 1 and 2, but no research has established whether it satisfies the third criterion, let alone still other criteria for designation as a measure of intelligence.

In general, the self-report measures have not been shown to influence objective performance or actual behavior (as opposed to subjective well-being). Furthermore, they do not correlate with general intelligence, so it might be argued that they do not measure a type of intelligence. Perhaps it might be better to say that these measures some assess emotional competence rather than intelligence (see, e.g., Saarni, 1999, 2000; Stankov, 2001), but even this conclusion is speculative in the absence of studies of behavioral correlates. At the least, we can conclude that the self-report measures relate to the person's experience of emotion and behavior in emotionally challenging circumstances, but they are a long way from formally satisfying the criteria for an intelligence. There is also a lack of evidence on how the behaviors, assumed to relate to self-report EI, might be adaptive in real life. It cannot be assumed, for example, that a high degree of emotional sensitivity is always in the individual's best interests. For example, it might conceivably be advantageous at times to be unaware that a person is angry with you, especially if that person's anger is transitory and detached from their behavior. We return to the adaptiveness of the traits linked to self-report EI in chapters 8 and 9.

General issues and a history lesson

There are also general issues, concerning the causal role of EI, however it is assessed, in everyday life. Many of the studies reviewed in this chapter have shown that EI relates to important behavior, but these studies not necessarily establish that EI is *causing* the behavior in question. For example, does EI leads to higher-quality friendships, or do good-quality friendships lead to higher EI? The best way to determine if EI functions as a causal variable is to train people to be more emotionally intelligent and to observe the impact of such training on behavior. This type of research has already been undertaken and has generally suggested that training young people in emotional and interpersonal competence leads to more adaptive behavior and improved mental health (Zins, Elias, Greenberg & Weissberg, in press; see also chapter 11 of this book). However, as discussed in chapter 11, these programs teach a variety of skills, and it is often unclear exactly what competences are being acquired. These results are encouraging, but we can not be certain whether it is emotional intelligence or some other skill(s) that are leading to improvement.

Research examining both intelligence and emotions has been conducted for over a century, with no evidence that this research is abating.

Thus, compared to the corpus of psychological science underlying both intelligence and emotions (with which comparisons become inevitable), EI research is in its fledgling years. Evidence presented in this chapter suggests, in certain instances and with certain tests, that EI can be measured reliably. The more promising instruments are not based upon self-report protocols, but rather represent attempts to develop objective indices of EI. In many instances, performance-based measures of EI also appear different from older, well-established measures of intelligence and personality. These measures of EI also predict important behavioral and life outcomes. The role of questionnaire-based assessment may be more to fill in some of the bricks missing from existing personality structures, rather than to construct a whole new edifice.

A lesson from history is perhaps apposite. In their attempts to develop intelligence tests, Binet and Simon (1905) toyed with many concepts that were then candidate measures for this newly evolving concept, including those using "brass instruments" experimental techniques (see, e.g., Gregory, 1996). Only when they had discarded many of those tests that were clearly inappropriate did measures of intellectual assessment progress. It seems quite likely that performance-based approaches to the assessment of EI will outlive those based on self-reports, which may be assimilated into existing personality theory. Alternatively, given the corporate sponsorship (with no particularly solid empirical basis) that many of the former measures have attracted thus far, one might wonder whether assessment of EI will follow this more scientifically driven path or rather become, like astrology and graphology, a popular superstition.

II

Individual Differences in Emotion and Adaptation

6

The Biological Science of Emotional Intelligence

The highest activities of consciousness have their origins in physical occurrences of the brain just as the loveliest melodies are not too sublime to be expressed by notes.

W. Somerset Maugham

In earlier chapters, we saw that EI may perhaps be linked to *adaptation*: the person's adjustment to external circumstances in order to minimize harm and maximize benefits. The emotionally intelligent person may be successful in adapting to circumstances that elicit emotion, either through effective regulation of emotion itself, or through application of more general coping and interpersonal skills. As discussed in chapter 2, there are two steps in developing an adaptive account of EI, and these two steps have to do with concepts at different levels of the cognitive science framework. First, the biological or cognitive processes linked to EI must be identified. What is required here is a description of how persons high or low in EI differ in neural function and/or information processing. Second, these individual differences in processing must be linked to adaptive outcomes. Not only must we show that EI is associated with individual differences in processing, but those processing differences must have significant consequences for real-world functioning. The first step might be to show that EI relates to the brain systems or information-processing routines that support accurate perception of emotion in faces. The second step would then be to demonstrate that individual differences in perception make a difference, i.e., that accurate perception leads to personal benefits. Analysis of adaptive value is essentially a knowledge-level issue; it cannot be addressed without some understanding of the person's goals and self-beliefs.

In the next four chapters, we explore EI and adaptation further, in the contexts of research on biological and cognitive approaches to emotion, coping and stress, and personality. The first two chapters aim to review what theories of emotion have to say about competence in handling emotional situations. Can we pinpoint one or more systems whose functioning directly determines whether the person is emotionally intelligent or emotionally "illiterate"? The term "system" here is deliberately ambiguous, in that the foundations for EI might be conceptualized either biologically or cognitively.

In this chapter we will first review possible biological models for EI, exploring the idea that EI might relate to neural functioning. However, we will also see that such models, at best, provide only partial explanations, and a more sophisticated understanding of emotional regulation requires models of cognitive functioning. Chapter 7 reviews evidence that EI might relate to the person's style of processing information and regulation of potentially emotional encounters. In the two chapters that conclude this part, we look at whether we can label processes for emotion as "adaptive" or "maladaptive." In chapter 8 we turn to one of the central questions arising from stress research: what works best in dealing with stress? We will examine whether coping strategies can be differentiated in terms of some continuum of adaptiveness, and whether some people have more adaptive styles of cognizing and coping with stressful events. Finally, in chapter 9 we revisit personality, focusing on theoretical rather than psychometric issues. As discussed in chapter 5, self-report scales for EI, in particular, overlap substantially with existing personality constructs. We will look at whether the (primarily cognitive) processes supporting dispositions for handling emotion can be related to individual differences in adaptive functions.

The Neuroscience of Emotion

We begin this chapter by introducing the biology of emotion and some of the cortical and subcortical brain systems that are of major importance. Developing a neuroscience of EI requires a particular focus on the functional significance and behavioral consequences of emotion. We briefly review the evolutionary psychology of emotion and its limitations, and discuss mechanisms through which neural emotion systems may affect behavior. It will be seen that, despite some impressive advances in understanding of the brain, neuroscience alone cannot tell us how emotion influences the symbolic and self-regulative processing that is critical for adaptation.

A biological basis for EI is central to Goleman's (1995) thinking, though it has not yet been taken up in empirical research using measures of EI. As discussed in chapter 1, Goleman initially sets up an antagonism between passion and reason where the higher-reasoning faculties supported by the cerebral cortex may be "hijacked" by more primitive subcortical brain systems, especially those residing in the amygdala. He then proposes that emotion and cognition can also operate synergistically in decision making. According to Damasio (1994), damage to certain brain areas associated with emotion also impairs the ability to make good life decisions, which implies that emotion is essential to rationality. Goleman's account thus reproduces the traditional ambiguity of Western culture towards emotion. On the one hand, emotions are a destructive force overriding sound judgement; on the other hand, we need to be in touch with our emotional side to manage our lives. Evidently, to reconcile these conflicting views of the functional role of emotion, a more detailed model distinguishing the different brain systems described by Goleman is required.

Biological models of emotion are currently enjoying a high profile, due in part to the new metatheory of evolutionary psychology and technological developments such as brain imaging. Biological theorists are confident in the primacy of neuroscience: "The brain states and bodily responses are the fundamental facts of an emotion, and the conscious feelings are the frills that have added icing to the emotional cake" (LeDoux, 1998, p. 302). In similar vein: "Scientific progress in understanding the root causes of human emotions will be impossible without a solid analysis of the brain mechanisms" (Panksepp, 1996, p. 33).

As scientists, we ought to be cautious about accepting such grand claims. Are these statements fair assessments of advances in neuroscience, or the rhetoric of hubris? Studies of animals, typically rats or monkeys, certainly provide powerful techniques for linking neural functioning to behavior. Researchers can make precise lesions to investigate how different brain areas influence learning and behavior in response to an emotional stimulus such as a threat. Pharmacological studies are used to investigate how neurotransmitter function controls response. At the most fine-grained level, animal studies also permit recording of single-neuron activity. Experimental studies are supplemented by ethological observations of behavior in the animal's normal environment. In principle, a detailed account of animal emotion can be provided, and generalization to human behavior may then be assessed. Animal research rests on an act of faith: that the correspondence of brain systems across rats, monkeys, and humans implies a strong correspondence in psychological functioning.

Application of physiological methods to humans is possible, but more challenging. Studies of patients whose brains have been damaged by trauma or disease allows investigation of localization of emotional experience and behavior. However, lesions are rarely as precise as those obtained from animal studies. Studies of psychosurgery performed on patients suffering from conditions such as epilepsy and intractable depression provide a kind of natural experiment on lesions in humans, but, of course, the recipients of surgery most likely have abnormal brains initially. Drug studies in humans also provide useful evidence, but the pharmacology of drugs is usually sufficiently complex that it is difficult to be sure which neural pathways are mediating any pharmacological effects. Caffeine, for instance, indirectly influences around 20 different neurotransmitter systems (Daly, 1993). Finally, biological functioning is investigated through psychophysiological recording of autonomic- and central-nervous-system activity during emotional encounters. Specifically, these recording include brain-imaging techniques such as Positron Emission Tomography (PET) and functional Magnetic Resonance Imaging (fMRI), which show levels of metabolic activity within specific brain areas. Psychophysiological techniques are invaluable in establishing correspondences between psychological and physiological functioning, but weaker in demonstrating causal effects. For example, PET and fMRI produce visually attractive brain maps suggesting localization of various functions, including emotional experience (Lane, 2000), but the great majority of studies make no attempt to link metabolic activity to behavioral outcomes. Localizing a psychological function in the brain does not explain its control over behavior.

An affective neuroscience model

Panksepp's (1998) general biological model for emotion starts from the assumption that mammalian brains support several distinct central neural control systems that handle response to motivationally significant stimuli, and concurrently generate subjective emotion. The criteria for identifying systems are as follows (Panksepp, 1982):

• The underlying circuits are genetically prewired and designed to respond unconditionally to stimuli arising from major life-challenging circumstances.

• The circuits organize diverse behaviors by activating or inhibiting motor subroutines (and concurrent autonomic-hormonal changes) that have proved adaptive in the face of such life-challenging circumstances during the evolutionary history of the species.

• Emotive circuits change the sensitivities of sensory systems relevant for the behavior sequences that have been aroused.

• Neural activity of emotive systems outlasts the precipitating circumstances.

• Emotive circuits can come under the conditional control of emotionally neutral environmental stimuli.

• Emotive circuits have reciprocal interactions with brain mechanisms that elaborate higher decision-making processes and consciousness.

There is some anatomical overlap between brain systems, in that, for example, positive and/or negative reinforcement systems will be involved (to some degree) in all emotional systems. Some neurotransmitters, such as the catecholamines typically related to arousal, participate in most emotions, whereas others, especially neuropeptides, tend to be more emotion-specific. The links between emotion and behavior are substantially based on hard-wired motor outputs. Panksepp sees a close link between rough-and-tumble play and joyfulness, energetic attacking and struggling and anger-rage, freezing or fleeing and fearfulness, plaintive crying and separation distress, and activated exploration and anticipatory excitement. The functional significance of emotions is that they constitute codes that allow the organism to respond rapidly to survival-critical situations by activating response patterns validated by natural selection. Flexibility of response is conferred by the capacity for learned activation of the emotive circuit by neural stimuli (see Miller, 1951; Mowrer, 1960), and by the rather vaguely specified role of "higher decision-making processes."

Given its modular nature, the model does not directly translate into a conception of EI. Instead, we need to identify specific structures and systems, which might contribute either to multiple systems (centralist or essentialist conception), or that might operate as a separate, regulatory system for emotion (interpretative conception). In fact, Panksepp's (1998) theory situates emotion in a variety of brain systems. These include those singled out by many biological researchers: arousal systems originating in the brainstem; subcortical forebrain structures including the hypothalamus, hippocampus, amygdala and basal ganglia;

and cortical structures such as the anterior cingulate cortex. However, beyond a general agreement that these are key sites for emotion, there are considerable differences between different researchers in how these structures relate to functional systems. Crudely, we can differentiate cortical and subcortical levels of control. Systems in the neocortex are especially concerned with "higher level" distinctively human functions such as language, thinking, and reasoning in conscious awareness and voluntary choice of action. Beneath the cortex are a group of structures traditionally described as the "limbic system," although this term is falling out of favor. These structures are presumed to function in humans much as they do in lower mammals, and to provide a level of control of emotion that, in evolutionary terms, is more primitive. Goleman's (1995) analysis attributes "emotional hijacking" to the limbic system, and emotional control and decision-making to the frontal lobes of the cortex. In the passages that follow, we will consider cortical and subcortical neural systems in more detail.

Subcortical Control of Emotion: The Amygdala

One of the more acclaimed animal models of recent years is LeDoux's (1995) account of fear, based on some very careful studies of which lesions of rat brain disrupt conditioning to fear stimuli. The key structure is the amygdala, a small but complex brain region comprising at least 13 subregions of differing function. Its role in emotion has been appreciated for quite a long time. Both lesions and electrical stimulation of the amygdala provoke emotional response. LeDoux describes a "high road" and a "low road" for fear response, as shown in figure 6.1. Fear stimuli receive early sensory analysis at pathways arriving at the thalamus. At this structure, the road forks. A direct thalamo-amygdalar pathway (the low road) permits rapid emotional response on the basis of crude, coarse-grained information, such as the outline of a snake. A slower pathway, routed via sensory cortex (the high road), permits more detailed analysis on the basis of cortical representations. These pathways are equated with unconscious and conscious fear responses. They control not just response to preprogrammed threat stimuli (unconditioned stimuli), such as snakes, but also the associative learning that confers on otherwise neutral stimuli (conditioned stimuli) the power to elicit fear responses. The amygdala also has extensive connections with various forebrain areas that (1) allow it to influence unconscious or "implicit" long-term memory for fearful events, and (2) charge explicit memories

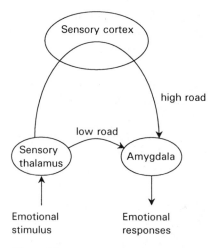

Figure 6.1
LeDoux's (1996) two amygdalar pathways for fear response.

recalled from long-term storage with emotion. According to LeDoux (1995, 1998), fear is experienced as a construct of the cortex only when the amygdalar fear circuit is active, and it is experienced through direct activation of the cortex by the amygdala, through nonspecific arousal initiated by the amygdala, and, over longer time periods, through peripheral feedback from visceral fear responses such as accelerated heart rate and stress hormones. Goleman (1995) suggests that rapid excitation of the amygdala may lead to irrational, paniclike fear responses, beyond higher-level cognitive control.

Implications for EI

Goleman (1995) cites LeDoux's work on fear extensively, because of it appears to provide the basis for his concept of emotional hijacking. Blaming surges of disruptive emotion on the amygdala defines for the organism an adaptive problem of handling its own responses. From an evolutionary perspective, it is often said that people struggle with responses tuned to the demands of the Pleistocene era, which may be inappropriate to contemporary life challenges. Hence, EI is in part the capacity to distance oneself from one's evolutionary heritage by forestalling uncontrolled emotion. However, this view of EI as conflict resolution between "higher" and "lower" brain systems is based on questionable science. Localizing fear and anxiety within the amygdala is open to question on several grounds.

Specificity of emotion   LeDoux sees the amygdala as central to systems for fear and anxiety, but this correspondence may be both too specific and too general. It is too specific in that the amygdala does much more than analyze stimuli for fearfulness. Contemporary research (reviewed by Emery & Amaral, 2000, and Rolls, 1999) confirms that the amygdala is involved in the processing of various primary reinforcers. These reinforcers include food, touch, pain, sexual stimuli, and, in primates, social behaviors such as maternal care and aggression. These different functions, might, of course, relate to different subregions of the amygdala. Generally, it seems unclear whether the amygdala should be seen as (1) the central locus of a dedicated fear system (LeDoux, 1995), (2) the site of a general system for analyzing the reinforcement value of both positive and negative stimuli (Rolls, 1999), (3) a system for emotional processing of negative stimuli (Tranel, 1997), or (4) a complex set of structures supporting multiple systems, currently poorly differentiated.

The LeDoux hypothesis may also be too general in lumping fear and anxiety together. Gray (1987; Gray & McNaughton, 1995) sees fear and anxiety as controlled by *separate* brain systems, despite their subjective similarity. Gray sees the amygdala as one of several structures supporting a system for fight (defensive aggression) or flight (fear) in response to threat. He sees the amygdala as controlling both unconditioned fight/flight and associative learning of conditioned reward and punishment signals. Anxiety, however, is an output of a separate septo-hippocampal system, which controls responses to conditioned stimuli (i.e., following on from prior "amygdalar" associative learning). This system operates to inhibit ongoing behavior while the organism processes signals of threat or nonreward based on mismatch between actual and expected stimulation. According to LeDoux (1998, p. 228), anxiety is fear in the absence of an immediate external stimulus, or fear with no opportunity to escape. Gray's view is quite different in linking anxiety to a system that functions to stop the organism in its tracks and reevaluate its behavioral priorities.

Relevance to human fear   The assumption of animal models is that brain systems identified in animals operate similarly in humans. Evidence from humans supports the place of the amygdala in fear response. For example, bilateral amygdalar lesions selectively impair processing of fear stimuli, especially recognition of facial expressions (Adolphs et al., 1994), and also memory for emotional material (Adolphs et al., 1997). Lesions also impair fear conditioning (Bechara et al., 1995). Brain-imaging studies confirm that the amygdala (along with various other structures) is active during processing of fear stimuli (Dolan & Morris, 2000). Nevertheless, there is considerable uncertainty over whether models derived from rat or even monkey studies can be applied directly to human emotion. According to two leading researchers on amygdala function in monkeys:

"While amygdala damage in monkeys produces a pronounced loss of affective behavior and a catastrophic breakdown in social interactions, comparable changes in humans are almost never reported.... Indeed, the effects of human amygdala damage often appear unremarkable" (Aggleton & Young, 2000, p. 106).

Aggleton and Young's (2000) review also points to some difficulties with the evidence in humans. Evidence on the emotionality of patients is largely anecdotal, with various reports of no overt change following lesion, increased placidity, or conversely, increased emotional lability. In humans, other temporal lobe structures appear to have a greater capacity to compensate for amygdalar damage than in animals. Hamann et al. (1996) investigated two patients with complete bilateral lesions of the amygdala, and other temporal lobe damage, whose recognition of different facial expressions was entirely normal. Rolls (1999, p. 111) points out that apparently selective effects of amygdalar damage on facial recognition may be an artifact of the facial stimuli used; some faces are more readily recognizable than others. In general, although the amygdala undoubtedly plays some role in human emotion, its function remains elusive (Aggleton & Young, 2000).

Limits on subcortical stimulus analysis   We might expect difficulties in generalizing to human fear because of the special anatomical feature of the human brain; its large cerebral cortex. Rolls (1999, pp. 102–105) points out that a critical adaptational feature of primate monkeys and, especially, humans, is the need for *view-invariant* representations. Lower animals may be able to recognize significant objects, such as foodstuffs, simply from a list of features, such as the color, size and texture of a raspberry. Primates, however, more frequently require to encode stimuli as an abstract representation of an object, that is the same irrespective of the angle from which it is viewed. For example, making and using a tool requires a view-invariant representation. Rolls argues that this level of stimulus analysis is too complex computationally to be handled subcortically; cortical processing, provided by temporal lobe cortex, is essential. Hence, the simple stimuli used in LeDoux's conditioning experiments, such as pure tones, are not ecologically valid for humans. Rolls offers a rather different view of the functional anatomy of emotion, shown schematically in figure 6.2, in which stimuli are processed to the object level within the temporal cortex, before information is sent to the amygdala, which links objects to their reinforcement values. Rolls claims that it is "unlikely that the subcortical route for conditioned stimuli to reach the amygdala, suggested by LeDoux..., is generally relevant to the learning of emotional responses to stimuli" (1999, p. 105).

Goleman (1995) wishes to attribute loss of EI to overexcitation of limbic-system structures, such as the amygdala. Of course, we cannot say that such emotional hijacking never happens. However, there are several reasons for supposing that Goleman overstates its importance. First, we have just discussed the deficiencies of LeDoux's theory of amygdalar function as the basis for human fear and anxiety. If, as Rolls (1999) indicates, the amygdala is functionally incapable of performing the discriminations central to the adaptive challenges faced by humans, it is unlikely to play a major role in controlling human fear response. Second, both Goleman (1995) and LeDoux (1998) tend to overgeneralize from studies of fear to emotion in general. We cannot assume that fits of rage or uncontrolled glee are equivalent to extreme fear and panic. Third, as discussed further below, there are alternative explanations for the experience of over-powering emotions. For example, faulty cognitions of impending disaster, which feed into heightened autonomic nervous system activity, seem to be central to panic attacks (Clark, 1985; Schmidt & Woolaway-Bickel, in press).

Frontal Control of Emotion

Areas of frontal cortex appear to be critical for human emotion. Every neuropsychology textbook relates the case of the hapless Phineas Gage, a railroad foreman who suffered massive damage to the frontal lobes when an accidental explosion propelled a 4 foot long iron rod through his skull. Although memory, language and motor skills were largely intact, Gage experienced profound personality change, becoming hostile, impulsive, and unreliable. More recent observations of emotional change, following accident or surgery, confirm these observations, although the outcomes are rather variable, including both euphoria and lack of affect (Hecaen & Albert, 1978; Zuckerman, 1990). Lesions may also lead to deficits in processing emotional information, such as facial expression (Hornak, Rolls & Wade, 1996).

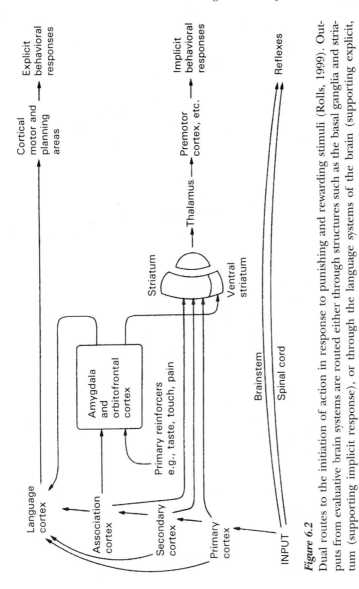

Figure 6.2
Dual routes to the initiation of action in response to punishing and rewarding stimuli (Rolls, 1999). Outputs from evaluative brain systems are routed either through structures such as the basal ganglia and striatum (supporting implicit response), or through the language systems of the brain (supporting explicit, planned response).

The frontal lobes make up a substantial part of the cortex. More fine-grained research localizes emotional control within the prefrontal cortex, and, more specifically still, within a medial part of that region called the orbitofrontal cortex (Rolls, 1999). Lesions to this area may be responsible for both anger and irritability, and for impairment in decision making, leading to impairment of social functioning (Damasio, 1994). The orbitofrontal cortex appears to control processing of the reinforcement value of stimuli, including social reinforcers. The patient appears to lack awareness of the likely consequences of his or her actions, leading Damasio (1994) to conclude that emotion is necessary for adaptive reasoning and decision making. Rolls (1999) also implicates orbitofrontal cortex in various output functions of nonverbal implicit response and of language-based explicit response, including control of autonomic and endocrine systems.

Rolls' (1999) view of the role of orbitofrontal cortex in a wider system for behavioral control is of particular interest (see figure 6.2). There is a hierarchy of information-processing systems capable of linking response to stimulus, ranging from low-level spinal cord reflexes to high-level language-based processing. The orbitofrontal cortex and amygdala are grouped together here as a common system for evaluation of the reinforcement value of stimuli. In approximate resemblance to LeDoux (1995), though de-emphasizing the role of the amygdala, Rolls provides lower and higher routes for control of action. The lower route operates on animal learning principles to produce implicit, unconscious response. Reinforcement value is computed on the basis of stimulus-reinforcement learning, current motivational state, and other factors related to the time course of reinforcement and expectations. Behaviors are then initiated via basal ganglia structures such as the striatum, based on prior instrumental learning.

The higher route operates through a symbol-manipulation system obeying a formal syntax, closely related to language (though not necessarily identical with verbal language). Symbol manipulation affords the use of multistep plans based on "if ... then ... " computations; i.e. developing appropriate actions for a variety of different contingencies as the plan is implemented. Processing models of this kind are well established as the primary basis for human skilled performance (Anderson, 1996), although Rolls does not make this connection. Symbol manipulation may reevaluate its own contents (metacognition of one's own thoughts [compare Averill's, 1980, reflective experience]), a state that

Rolls identifies with consciousness. The symbol-based system's attempts at reflection on the lower-level implicit system may lead to "confabulation" and false beliefs about this level of functioning. The symbol processing system is most likely to control behavior when there is reduced time pressure to respond, when it is advantageous to defer immediate reward for greater long-term benefits, and when the situation calls for a unique course of action. This view of behavioral control is highly compatible with theories of executive function in humans, supported by neuropsychological evidence on the role of frontal cortex (e.g., Shallice & Burgess, 1998).

It would be a mistake to see the orbitofrontal cortex as the sole frontal locus for emotion. Another key structure is the anterior cingulate, which is richly connected with both other neocortical sites and subcortical areas such as the amygdala (Vogt & Gabriel, 1993). Surgical lesions of the cingulum tend to reduce anxiety and depression (Zuckerman, 1991), and brain imaging studies (e.g., Maddock & Michael, 1997) suggest action of the left anterior cingulate when the person is presented with threatening stimuli. The anterior cingulate is also an important component of brain systems for executive control of attention (Posner & DiGirolamo, 1998). The involvement of the left anterior cingulate in both anxiety and executive control may help to explain effects of anxiety on attention (Derryberry & Reed, 1997; Matthews, Derryberry & Siegle, 2000). In fact, the functions of the anterior cingulate appear similar to those that Rolls (1999) attributes to prefrontal cortex, in controlling activation of lower-level data representations, on the basis of "conscious" expectation. Interestingly, brain imaging suggests that areas of cingulate cortex and medial prefrontal cortex are most active in response to emotive stimuli when the person is voluntarily attending to their emotional experience (Lane et al., 2000). A possible basis for distinguishing the roles of cingulate and orbitofrontal cortex is the discrimination of ventrolateral and mediodorsal pathways (Tucker et al., 1995; Lane et al., 2000). The ventrolateral pathway (including amygdala and orbitofrontal cortex) may be especially concerned with motor response to some immediate perceptual input. In contrast, the mediodorsal pathway is concerned with future planning based upon a preexisting model rather than sensory feedback. According to Lane et al. (2000), a representation of emotional state may be anatomically situated between anterior cingulate and medial prefrontal cortex, and contribute to the operation of both.

Implications for EI

EI might be attributed to some kind of higher-level integrative brain system, especially the frontal lobe systems identified by Rolls (1999) and others. Rather than link EI to emotion modules, we might see EI as residing in the higher-level executive control of emotion. Bechara, Tranel, and Damasio (2000) have shown deficits in decision making on a gambling task in patients with damage to the ventromedial frontal cortex. They link these deficits, such as risking incurring a large delayed loss for immediate benefit, to impulsiveness and inability to delay gratification. EI in this sense may be contrasted with general intelligence, in that these patients often present with normal IQ. According to Damasio's (1994) "somatic marker" theory of emotion, choosing a response option depends on activating somatic state information that attaches values to outcomes, without the need for conscious reflection. Bechara et al. attribute the failure to activate somatic state information to impairment of higher-order conditioning; for example, in gambling, the failure to associate losing cards with the negative somatic states associated with losing money. Consistent with this hypothesis, ventromedial frontal cortex patients fail to learn anticipatory skin conductance responses (SCRs) when playing with a losing deck of cards, supposedly indicating lack of the hunches or gut feelings on which people normally rely. Bechara et al. also point out that other structures such as the amygdala and somatosensory cortex also support more adaptive decision-making, but there are subtle differences in the nature of the deficit. For example, the deficit shown by patients with damage to the amygdala seems to relate to more immediate rewards and punishments; for example, they fail to show SCRs to winning and losing money. Bechara et al. (2000) conclude by linking EI to multiple emotional processes that may contribute to higher-order decision making, including perception of emotion of self and others, response inhibition and emotional conditioning. They suggest that relatively simple neural mechanisms feed into the higher level forms of emotionality described by Bar-On and Goleman.

Bechara et al.'s (2000) analysis of EI is interesting but not compelling. Generally, there is little direct evidence for the existence of somatic states as proposed by Damasio (1994). Somatic feedback does not seem to be critical for the experience of emotions (Heilman, 2000), and thus far research offers no independent means for assessment of somatic state. Even if the somatic state hypothesis is correct, it does not follow that these patient studies are relevant to variation in EI in normal, non-lesioned populations. Poor decision making may depend on factors other than lack of access to somatic-state information, such as use of inappropriate cognitive strategies. There may be faults in the algorithms used to weigh up items of evidence, rather than in the evidence itself. In normal individuals, effects of emotion on decision making are highly contingent upon the type of information-processing performed (Forgas, 1995), and the patient studies do not make contact with this important research literature. A further problem is the multiplicity of brain systems for emotion. The idea of a general factor for EI implies that the efficiencies of functioning of separate systems are correlated. It is unclear why, say, an amygdalar mechanism for primary reinforcement should correlate with a frontal mechanism for secondary reinforcement. A final comment is that the traditional view that frontal patients have intact general intelligence may be incorrect. Duncan, Emslie, and Burgess (1995) argue that crystallized intelligence tests that involve little novelty (or uncertainty over how to proceed) may indeed be largely immune to frontal damage. They showed that on a *fluid* intelligence test, Cattell's Culture Fair test, patients with frontal lesions showed deficits of 23–60 points. Hence, the jury is still out on whether there may be some commonality of neural substrate for emotional and general intelligences.

Generally, although the link between EI and brain systems for emotional regulation is plausible, there are considerable difficulties in developing this basic idea. The central issue is one of *control.* There are extensive reciprocal connections between the cortex and the subcortical systems implicated in emotion. Indeed, orbitofrontal and cingulate cortex are ideally placed anatomically to operate as gateways between the two types of structure. Beyond the issue of the role of specific structures, there is the question of how the various brain structures are coordinated and controlled so as to operate harmoniously as an integrated system. The main control issue is whether it is variation in cortical or subcortical function that actually influences emotion and behavior in typical real-world situations. Take the example of fear. Cortical control is compatible with primacy of cognition in stimulus analysis, with the amygdala generating emotional outputs under cortical control (perhaps including feedback to the cortex to produce emotional experience). The alternative position suggests emotion at the cortical level is controlled by stimulus analysis at the level of the amygdala: whatever conscious cognitions the person experiences are a post hoc gloss on decisions already taken by the lower-level system. No doubt, the truth is somewhere between the two extremes. The important point here is that we have two quite different views of human rationality. On the one hand, the individual should be conceived of as a flexible forward-planning symbol processor (though often fallible and lacking conscious insight). On the other hand, the individual appears a bundle of evolved and conditioned reflexes, with no explicit self-control. As previously discussed (e.g., chapter 4), the former perspective is more compatible with the empirical evidence on emotion and behavior.

Functions of Emotion

So far, we have discussed evidence relating to the possible localization of EI within particular areas of the brain. However, we must also look at biological bases of EI functionally. Emotional intelligence is important to the extent that it is played out in behavior, raising the question of how brain systems control emotional intelligence in action, within some demanding external environment. As described in chapter 4, a theory of emotion should describe the behavioral consequences of emotion, and the adaptive functions of such emotional influences. We saw too that existing work on EI does not offer clear answers to these questions. In this section, therefore, we consider whether biological theories can help us identify the functionality of emotions, and, hence, a biotheoretical basis for EI. Here, we step back somewhat from localization issues, and discuss in more general terms whether EI may be conceptualized as a property of whether the individual's emotions support or impede adaptive functioning. Two kinds of biological theory are relevant here. The first type of theory, evolutionary psychology, focuses on the value of these brain systems in solving generic adaptive problems such as avoiding threat and finding a mate, problems whose solution influences reproductive fitness. The second type of theory focuses on immediate behavioral consequences, in particular, the activation of specific brain systems for emotion.

Evolution of emotions

All biological theories pay at least lip service to Darwin, although, sadly, few share Darwin's concern with demonstrating in fine detail how a trait supports adaptation. The role of evolution is plain enough at a commonsense level. Obviously, flight is typically an adaptive response to fear stimuli, and nurturing behaviors are appropriate when stimuli evoke parental concern. It is a bit unclear whether evolutionary psychology, at this fairly early developmental stage, can provide insights into emotion beyond those of common sense. According to Tooby and Cosmides, "In fact, the emotions appear to be designed to solve a certain category of regulatory problem that inevitably emerges in a mind full of disparate, functionally specialized mechanisms—the problem of coordinating the menagerie of mechanisms with each other and with the situation being faced" (1992, p. 99). These authors go on to suggest that there are emotional and motivational mechanisms specifically targeted to deal with adaptive problems such as parenting, emotional communication, sexual attraction, aggression, and so on. They propose that there is an extensive set of such mechanisms, presumably far exceeding the ten or so basic emotions.

However, evolutionary psychology has tended to be more concerned with generic strategies, for choosing a mate, for example, rather than with the specific role of emotion in adaptation. For example, Buss (1999) proposes that, in the context of conflict between the sexes, emotions focus attention on events, they enhance memory storage and retrieval, and they lead to action. All this seems plausible enough, but there is little evidence that emotions actually perform these functions, when men and women conflict, that the functionality of emotion is specifically geared to the adaptive problems raised by intersex conflict, or that emotions precede rather than follow attention. In general, evolutionary psychology has been much more concerned with distal issues of how a particular strategy might be adaptive (e.g., why a man should exaggerate emotional commitment). As such, less emphasis has been placed on proximal strategy implementation issues (i.e., the specific processes supporting evaluation of potential mates, choice of strategy, choice of overt behavior, and regulation of the ongoing social encounter). Hence, evolutionary psychology is well suited towards analysis of brain emotional systems at a holistic level, but poorly equipped to differentiate the role of the multiple mechanisms (e.g., figure 6.2) identified by biological theorists. Broadly, evolutionary psychology suggests that emotions signal a particular adaptive challenge, as outlined in Panksepp's (1998) theory. So far, however, it offers few insights into the brain design evident from neuroscientific studies, other than the insights of common sense, such as fear as preparation for flight behavior.

There are also some principled reasons for caution over evolutionary explanations for human behavior. An evolved module requires either some prewired representation of the trigger stimuli that will activate it, or the capacity to learn trigger stimuli. Evidently, the ease of representation and/or learning will depend on the extent to which the trigger stimulus is defined by a consistent set of perceptual attributes. The computation that an object is a spider or snake is relatively straightforward, and so it is perhaps not surprising that people show biological preparedness to avoid these threats. Likewise, facial expressions of emotion, though complex, are consistent across time and culture, affording natural selection for specialized systems for face processing. In many cases, though, evaluation of a person or object depends on inconsistent cues, which vary from case to case and take their meaning from the sociocultural matrix. There is no reliable cue that allows us to decide whether or not someone is trustworthy, given that people are often motivated to conceal their true motivations; every society has its deceivers and manipulators of others.

Rolls (1999) points to a step function between lower animals and monkeys, in the development of a need for view-invariant representations. There may be a further step function, between monkeys and humans, in that people need what we might call "instance-invariant representations." For example, people need to recognize acts of hostility, kindness, and so on irrespective of the (culture-bound) instance of the act. Just as the rat brain is poorly equipped to process view invariance, so too may the monkey brain be poorly suited to computing instance-invariance. In evolutionary terms, perhaps less is more. The protohuman, with a set of easily activated modules for emotion, may have been at a selective disadvantage compared with protohumans, in whom control of behavior resided in more adaptable, general-purpose symbolic mechanisms for learning to recognize abstract categories of human behavior.

Consequences of emotions

Evolutionary psychology provides a picturesque backdrop but thus far few testable hypotheses about the behavioral consequences of emotion. More proximal, biological theories typically describe two mechanisms for emotion effects: (1) innate responses, such as fleeing or freezing, and (2) instrumental responses shaped by conditioning, as described in the Miller-Mowrer "two-process" theory of avoidance learning, and generalized to other aspects of emotion (Gray, 1987). The validity of animal models depends critically on the extent to which these mechanisms generalize to humans. The equation of specific emotions with specific expressive or directly functional behaviors goes back to Darwin and is forcefully promoted by Panksepp (1998), as previously discussed: animal behaviors, such as attacking, provide a direct index of emotions, such as rage. However, biological theorists are rather uncritical in assuming that emotions are as tightly mapped into behaviors in humans; as Lange (1885/1912) pointed out, people find a variety of expressions for emotion, depending on circumstances. It is generally accepted that anger is linked to an *action tendency* towards attack (Lazarus, 1991), but there is no necessary link between the action and the behavior. Anger does not inevitably lead to physical aggression (see Berkowitz, 1993). Indeed, it may be maintained internally as sullen resentment or self-blame, it may be vented harmlessly through swearing or joking, or it may be associated with delayed acts of revenge. Conversely, aggression does not always imply anger; instrumental aggression is performed simply for personal gain, without strong feelings. It seems that the fixed action patterns of animal emotion are the exception rather than the rule in human beings, although it is likely that there is some more subtle and contingent biasing of response.

The second mechanism for emotional expression is learned response to secondary (conditioned) reinforcers. As in the case of fixed response patterns, it is likely that such responses play some role in human behavior, but how much of a role? It is supposed that the motivating properties of biologically neutral stimuli reflect associative learning, and that response is shaped by instrumental learning. Both of these suppositions are of questionable applicability to humans. As the classic Lazarus (1991) studies of appraisal show, stimulus significance depends on appraisal processes more complex than simple conditioning, including reappraisal as the person evaluates their own coping capabilities. Likewise, instrumental learning is discredited as a general account of human learning: acquisition of the complex skills we require to prosper in a particular sociocultural milieu is better understood in terms of cognitive mechanisms (Anderson, 1996).

A direct demonstration of the weakness of traditional behaviorism is provided by studies of stress and human performance, briefly reviewed in chapter 4 (see also chapter 7). There is an extensive literature on how distressing events impact on this aspect of behavior (e.g., Hockey, 1984; Matthews et al., 2000), of which biological emotion theorists sometimes lack awareness. LeDoux (1998, p. 298) states, as undisputed fact, the hypothesis that moderate levels of arousal are optimal for performance. This hypothesis is wrong: it was popular forty years ago (e.g., Duffy, 1962), but, in addition to various theoretical failings, it is falsified by empirical data showing that high arousal does not necessarily lead to performance impairments (Matthews & Amelang, 1993; Neiss, 1988).

Similarly, localization of anxiety/fear within the amygdala makes almost no useful predictions about the relationship between anxiety and performance. Anxiety effects vary critically with the information-processing demands of the task, including its strategic requirements (Eysenck, 1992; Zeidner, 1998). Biological theories of anxiety lack the conceptual tools to handle these contingencies (see Matthews, 2000, for a more detailed conceptual critique).

Implications for emotional intelligence

Biological theorists have a broad consensual answer to the question of the functionality of emotions: they are concomitants of brain systems evolved to meet adaptive challenges. Most simply, high EI may reflect the extent to which systems are appropriately tuned to environmental contingencies, so that emotions and behaviors are matched to adaptive requirements. One variant of this position might be a deficit model of EI, such that low EI reflects organic deficiencies in one or more emotional brain systems. Beyond this general position, there is disagreement over the extent to which emotions are closely tied to specific response systems. Panksepp's (1998) theory, in describing multiple systems, suggests that we should address the functionality of brain emotion/motivation systems on a case by case basis, through analysis of the selective advantages of the innate behaviors elicited by biologically significant stimuli. However, this perspective is not readily compatible with the idea of an emotional intelligence generalizing across different emotions. At best, it suggests a multiple-intelligence model of emotion, with a set of independent faculties for the various basic emotions. One person might have a deficit in a fear system, leading to pathological anxiety, whereas a second person might have a deficit in a nurturance system, leading to callousness toward others. In principle, there may be many evolutionary modules, which are subject to deficits (see Tooby & Cosmides, 1992): perhaps spider phobia represents the oversensitivity of a "spider-threat-evaluation" module, for example. It seems misleading and unhelpful to refer to each such module as an intelligence. In addition, as described in this section, linking emotions to fixed action tendencies fails to explain the empirical data on behavioral consequences of emotion in humans.

Alternatively, emotions may be the conscious expression of control signals that serve to coordinate the functioning of otherwise independent systems (Tooby & Cosmides, 1992). For example, the experience of anxiety may be associated with the activation and intercommunication of multiple cortical and subcortical systems for handling threat adaptively, such as selective attention, retrieval of relevant memories and motor inhibition (e.g., Gray, 1987). Potentially, a regulative role of this kind for emotion provides a more attractive basis for EI than the hypothesis of multiple, independent modules. There may be attributes of regulation, which generalize across different emotions. A tendency towards strong control signals would force bias of multiple systems, leading to a stereotyped response likely to be maladaptive (e.g., by imposing motor inhibition when the situation called for action). In addition, the control signal hypothesis allows for the complex links between emotion and behavior revealed empirically. Furthermore, the hypothesis is compatible with the executive functions attributed to frontal areas. However, as discussed in the context of Rolls' (1999) model of frontal emotion systems, understanding control requires cognitive models of how language-based systems initiate action, and moderate the operation of lower-level systems. So far, biological research does not provide any basis for discriminating brains that are more or less adaptive in handling emotion.

Conclusions on Biological Models and Emotional Intelligence

Biological theories have made significant advances in understanding emotion. Evolutionary psychology provides a broad framework for linking human emotion to adaptive challenges common to the lower animals. Converging evidence from animal studies, human neuropsychology, and psychophysiology has generated quite good agreement on the essential brain structures, and, somewhat less consensually, on the organization of structures as functional circuits. At the same time, claims that neuroscience should provide the primary avenue toward a science of emotion are overstated. The gaping hole in contemporary biological theory is its lack of contact with empirical studies of real people experiencing real emotions while performing real activities. The claim is often made that real-world emotional functioning is simply too complex to explain, due to idiosyncratic variation in people's reinforcement history, for example. However, as discussed previously, empirical studies of emotion and performance show some clear regularities that require explanation. Despite the rhetoric of science, biological emotion theory rests on a considerable act of faith, that mechanisms relating emotion to behavior generalize wholesale from animals to humans. No doubt, there is some generalization, but the evidence indicates that it is often too weak to provide satisfactory explanations for the data. In most circumstances, the behavior of an emotional person is governed neither by a hard-wired action pattern nor by simple conditioning principles.

The traditional biological view of behavioral control is that brain, emotion, and action are *tightly coupled*; that is, a change in any one implies strongly correlated changes in the others. In the Darwinian tradition, there is a unity of function: if brain state changes, then the organism *must* feel certain emotions and *must* engage in certain behaviors. Conversely, the coupling may be weak. The brain state change may predispose emotions and actions, but there is no necessary link. Biological systems may have indirect, rather than direct, influences on emotion. We see brain evolution as creating *potentials* for experiencing emotions, but how those potentials are realized depends critically on brain "software" and cognition.

The way forward for biological theories is exemplified by the introduction of a separate language-based system into Rolls' (1999) emotion theory. Rolls caps the pyramid of behavioral control systems with a language-based system controlling behavior through symbol manipulation (i.e., cognitively). It is difficult to overstate how much this innovation of evolution changes the rules of the biological game, both directly, and indirectly, through permitting culture and contingent societal values to influence behavior. As previously discussed, a more complete account would also need to include implicit cognitive systems, and perhaps nonlanguage based explicit cognitive systems, such as one for handling imagery and visuospatial object representations (e.g., Paivio, 1986). Rolls takes the reasonable position that there is a balance between implicit and explicit control of behavior, depending on which is likely to be most adaptive. This position is fine as a general statement, but it leaves open the question of which systems actually control most of the variation in significant real-world functioning. Is the explicit system more like a sports commentator, removed from the real action, or more like a coach that intervenes periodically to call the key plays of lower-level systems?

In the next chapter, we will develop a weakly coupled position compatible with the evidence that emotion and behavior are primarily under cognitive control. This is not to say that biology is unimportant. Software requires hardware, and suboptimal processing may reflect neural impairment. Implementation of response involves subcortical systems for which nonsymbolic models may be appropriate. On rare but significant occasions, these systems may output reflexlike reactions, such as fear responses. The main point, however, is that neuroscience cannot provide more than pointers towards the nature of EI, for which we require a cognitive account, the topic addressed next.

7

Cognitive Models of Emotion and Self-Regulation

We don't see things are they are; we see things as we are.

Anais Nin

In this chapter, we review the cognitive science of emotion and its implications for individual differences in adaptability. As in the previous chapter, we examine both sources and functions of emotion, covering appraisal theories of emotion, cognitive models for emotional influence on response, and self-regulative theories. We will see that individual differences in EI do not appear to be an inevitable concomitant of either biological or cognitive theories. However, the evidence available allows us to reject some possible conceptions of EI as unlikely and, tentatively, to link EI to executive function and self-regulation.

Cognitive approaches to emotion start from the computational metaphor for brain function. As discussed in chapter 2, we can distinguish the "software" or symbolic programming of the brain from its neural hardware. We can also explain psychological functioning in terms of the person's (not always conscious) goals and beliefs about how goals may be achieved (Pylyshyn, 1999). Cognitive psychology aims to relate emotion to a cognitive architecture, i.e., a description of (1) the multiple processing units that perform mental computations, (2) the logical rules governing computation, and (3) the flow of information between processing units, and its control. Ultimately, computation depends on neurons, but understanding what the brain is doing may require the use of software-level concepts, rather than a description of physical, cellular responses. The principal technique used is *reverse engineering*. The researcher builds a computational model of the cognitive processes of interest, which is specified formally, perhaps by programming a computer simulation. The model is then tested against empirical data for its ability to explain existing data and predict interesting new findings. No computational model is perfect, but more successful models instantiate important general principles and predict a range of behavioral findings. Increasingly, cognitive research uses neuroscience techniques also. The pattern of performance deficits shown by brain-damaged patients can itself be modeled, and these models are often informative about normal information processing (Parasuraman, 1998).

Fitting emotion into the computational model of psychological function is a considerable challenge, especially as relationships between computation and emotion may be bidirectional. On the one hand, it is supposed that computations cause emotion, that fear is an outcome of calculating that a situation is threatening, for example. On the other, emotion may have various effects on the operation of the computational system, such as disrupting its functioning and changing its priorities towards processing and memorizing the emotional event. To be more exact, in line with the caveats concerning causality discussed in chapter 2, emotion is felt as a concomitant of a reconfiguration of the computational system. In either case, researchers aim to include within computational models representations of emotion and information flow between those representations and other representations. Such models may be evaluated as cognitive models normally are, i.e., by generating predictions and testing them against data. If computational models are successful and reasonable precautions are taken to eliminate methodological artifact such as demand characteristics, then it is assumed that the model captures something of the meaning of emotion in computational terms.

Cognitive Origins of Emotion

Appraisal theories of emotion

The idea that emotions reflect evaluations of the personal significance of events can be traced back to Aristotle. In more recent times, Arnold (e.g., 1960) proposed that emotions follow from a judgment of how some external "object" (e.g., a person) relates to the person. Here we have the two core assumptions of appraisal theory: (1) that emotion follows cognition, and (2) that appraisals express a *relation* between person and external environment. Smith and Lazarus's (1993) appraisal model distinguishes both molecular and molar aspects of appraisal. At the *molecular* level, specific elements of evaluation are linked to specific emotions. Smith and Ellsworth (1985) suggested that events are evaluated in terms of elements such as pleasantness, novelty, uncertainty, control, together with socially tinged elements such as responsibility. In retrospective accounts of events, these appraisal elements appear to predict the emotion experienced quite well. For example, in this study, happiness was associated with appraisals of events as pleasant, and not involving uncertainty or a need for effort. Lazarus (1991) has also distinguished *primary* appraisals of immediate personal significance (e.g., threat) from *secondary* appraisals of personal coping competence, as further discussed in the next chapter. At the *molar* level, the pattern of appraisal components associated with an emotion is termed a *core relational theme* (Lazarus, 1991), which expresses a general personal meaning central to the emotion. For example, happiness relates to success, and sadness to irrevocable loss.

Appraisal theories of the kind described have both strengths and weaknesses. On the positive side, relationships between emotion and appraisal tend to be fairly robust. Scherer (1997b) conducted a cross-cultural study of 2921 respondents in 37 countries that showed quite good consistency of results across different cultures and, overall, 40% accuracy in differentiating seven emotions using seven appraisal dimensions. Of course, these results leave substantial parts of the variation in emotion unexplained, which might be attributed to methodological limitations of retrospective studies. We note in passing that, thus far, biological researchers can only dream about predicting 30–40% of the variance in emotion from psychophysiological measures.

However, there are various criticisms of appraisal theory. Parkinson and Manstead (1992) point out that reliance of appraisal theory on retrospective reports of emotion and cognition vitiates any attempt to test a causal model. Results may also be biased by distortions of memory and the lack of attention to unconscious processes. They also question whether "dimensions of appraisal" always refer to appraisal or to other constructs such as knowledge or even outcomes of encounters. Recent work has redressed some of the problems found by Parkinson and Manstead (1992), and also identified some flaws in their critique.

Contemporary appraisal models distinguish qualitatively different appraisal processes, that serve to distinguish cogitation accessible to awareness from faster unconscious processes. Scherer (1984) suggested that stimuli undergo a series of "Stimulus Evaluation Checks" (SECs), i.e., a sequence of computations is performed for successively more abstract qualities. SECs evaluate novelty, pleasantness, goal-relevance, personal coping ability, and compatibility with personal and social norms. In a development of this theory, Leventhal and Scherer (1987) proposed that each SEC might operate at a sensory-motor level controlled by innate mechanisms, at a schematic level controlled by retrieval from memory of generalized knowledge about similar events, and at a conceptual level controlled by more abstract, reflective processes. Hence, cognitive models do not necessarily involve prolonged conscious cogitation, and emotions are probably generated by several qualitatively different types of process.

Appraisal theory also inspired empirical research that shows how such models may be tested and developed (e.g., Chwelos & Oatley, 1994). Scherer (1999) showed that variation in speed of identification of emotions presented via scenarios depended on the order in which information was presented, in a manner consistent with the SEC model. The general point here is that it is possible to write detailed specifications of how stimulus processing produces emotions and test them against performance data.

Clore and Ortony (2000) provide another account of how appraisals may operate through qualitatively different forms of information processing, through distinguishing bottom-up situational analysis from top-down reinstatement. Bottom-up processing represents an on-line computation of the personal significance of stimuli, controlled by rules operating on symbols Scherer's (1984) series of evaluation checks provides one model for how these computations might precede. Appraisals of this type may be unconscious and implicit, but they are often relatively slow and occupy conscious attention, i.e., controlled rather than automatic. Top-down reinstatement is similar to Leventhal and Scherer's (1987) schematic level, i.e., the retrieval of schematic information that provides a rapid (though error-prone) assessment of the situation by matching it to previous experience. Clore and Ortony (2000) emphasize the associative nature of the processing here: processing focuses on analyzing the superficial similarity of the current event to the prototype for past events. Although processing is associative rather than rule-based, reinstatement and on-line computation are equally cognitive. Reinstatement is controlled by computational analysis of stimulus features leading to a stimulus meaning that governs access to a meaning-based prototype.

Clore and Ortony refer to the large social psychological literature on unconscious priming, that shows how incidental exposure to primes or cues can activate complex cognitive knowledge and behavior. For example, Bargh, Chen and Burrows (1996) exposed subjects to words such as "bingo" and "Miami," with the aim of activating an old-person schema. The experiment was counted as a success, in that subjects leaving the study walked more slowly to the elevator: "Material activated in memory by incoming stimuli can be extensive and complex and can produce surprising results, regardless of whether emotion is involved" (Clore & Ortony, 2000, p. 35). Again, the Clore and Ortony theory awaits detailed testing, but it shows how, in principle, appraisal models can explain various general features of emotion such as unconscious bias of behavior and conflicts between the rule-based "head" and the associative "heart."

Implications for emotional intelligence

According to appraisal theorists, emotions are tightly coupled with specific computational operations. Analyzing a stimulus as threatening implies anxious emotion, and vice versa. The implication is that EI may be a quality of these computations of the personal relevance of the stimulus. As discussed in chapter 4, we might then conceptualize EI as either the efficiency or positive bias of these computations. The emotionally intelligent person might have more accurate evaluations of significant stimuli, or they might be biased towards evaluation of stimuli as positive rather than negative, leading to qualities such as optimism, happiness, and positive self-beliefs (see Bar-On, 2000).

However, we encounter similar difficulties to those faced in trying to link EI to neural systems for stimulus analysis. There are multiple dimensions of appraisal that vary independently (e.g., Ferguson, Matthews & Cox, 1999), so it is difficult to link EI to some single critical aspect of appraisal (see also chapter 8). A person's accuracy and bias in detecting threat tells us nothing about their orientation towards challenge, for example. Furthermore, contemporary appraisal theories propose that appraisal depends on multiple computational mechanisms, such as the different levels of Leventhal and Scherer (1987) and the bottom-up and top-down mechanisms of Ortony and Clore (2000). There is no principled basis for linking EI to one mechanism rather than another. A person might have finely tuned automatic appraisal routines but be prone to misinterpret events when using more controlled processing. Furthermore, limiting EI to appraisal also tells us little about EI in action, in the sense of coping and response on the basis of appraisals.

Cognitive Architectures for Emotional Intelligence in Action

Thus far, we have seen that computational models of appraisal aim to link emotion to specific multiple processing operations. The other face of cognitive theories of emotion is the issue of how emotion, once generated, might feed back into cognition, and so influence behavior. It is assumed that emotion corresponds to some data representation that can itself be processed. In general, cognitive theories propose that response is controlled by multiple processing systems or modules, organized so that some processes are more abstracted from sense data than others. It is likely that there are multiple sources of individual differences within the overall processing system (Matthews, 1997a). The issue for EI is whether people differ systematically in key processes linked to effective action in emotional situations. Perhaps the emotionally intelligent person is someone who, although experiencing disturbing emotions such as anxiety, nevertheless computes a response choice that will deal with the external threat. This idea corresponds to Mayer et al.'s (2000) identification of emotion-management components of EI, and to the commonsense view that dealing with potentially disruptive emotions may be more adaptive than avoiding the experience of emotion.

To develop this idea, we need (1) an understanding of how emotion influences response, and (2) an account of individual differences in the emotion-response link that provides a basis for EI. Cognitive researchers have differing conceptions of behavioral consequences of emotion. First, emotion may be seen as part of the data on which the system operates. According to Bower (1981), whose work we discuss further below, emotions are represented as concepts similar to other, nonemotional concepts. They are special only in that activation of the concept produces subjective feelings. Second, emotion may bias some of the computations performed by the system (without fundamentally altering their logic of operation). For example, anxiety might increase the threat value assigned to a stimulus (Williams et al., 1988). Third, emotion may represent some special-purpose operation within the system, such as interrupting its ongoing activity (Simon, 1967). Next, we consider these conceptions further, and discuss their implications for EI.

Emotion as data: Network models of emotion

In a classic paper, Bower (1981) proposed that emotions are represented as single concepts among an interconnected network of concepts. Network models of this kind are an important class of cognitive models, with a substantial basis in empirical research. Most simply, the idea is that each concept the person understands is represented as a single unit or node within the network, connected to other associated units. More sophisticated models also represent episodic as well as semantic memory; i.e., the network represents specific events as well as general concept knowledge. Units vary in their degree of activation; when activation reaches some threshold level, the person is consciously aware of the concept. Activation spreads between associated units, so that, for example, if a person hears a fire alarm, activating the "fire" unit, then related units such as "red," "hot," and "danger" are liable to become somewhat activated also. The person is then primed to recognize these concepts. In experimental studies, semantic priming of this kind is well documented (e.g., Neely, 1991). Emotions can then be similarly represented. For example, a unit might be connected to units for "danger" and related concepts, allowing a fire alarm to produce feelings of anxiety. (Since connections between units represent previous learning, the mechanism here is a rather simple instantiation of Clore and Ortony's reinstatement mechanism.) Figure 7.1 shows a simple illustration, in which expressive behaviors and autonomic arousal are also associated with the emotion unit (Eysenck, 1997).

Bower's (1981) model then predicts that emotions and their associated concepts should prime one another. If an emotion is induced experimentally, the person should show a general bias towards processing associated concepts, including lowered recognition thresholds (perception), selective attention, and memory. As mentioned in chapter 4, biasing effects of this kind have been widely reported. However, their

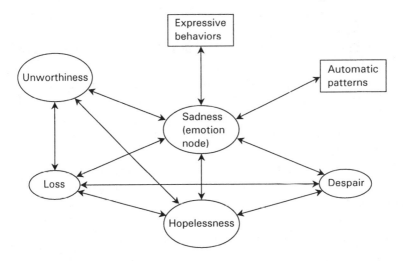

Figure 7.1
A semantic network for an emotion.

robustness varies with the nature of the task. Effects of mood on perception are relatively weak (MacLeod & Mathews, 1991), but not absent. For example, Matthews, Pitcaithly, and Mann (1996) found greater semantic priming of positive word pairs in happy subjects, at the short time intervals characteristic of associative priming. Bower's theory has been tested most extensively in studies of (1) memory and (2) judgment and decision making. The theory predicts that memory should be enhanced, first, when the person's mood at retrieval matches mood at encoding ("mood-state dependence") and, second, when the person's mood (at either encoding or retrieval) matches the content of the material learned (mood congruence).

Confirmatory results can be obtained, but outcomes vary with factors such as the strength of mood, type of memory task, and personal involvement (Eich, 1995; Ucros, 1988). Mood has fairly reliable effects on people's impressions of themselves and others, which may reflect tendencies to form and access more extensive elaborative associations for mood-congruent stimuli (Forgas & Bower, 1987). Again, there are failures of prediction. Forgas (1995) has developed a multiprocess theory that seeks to identify the circumstances under which decision making is infused by affect. The theory is too complex to review here, but processes most sensitive to mood-biasing include "heuristic processing," in which the person seeks short-cuts to a quick decision, which may include using mood as a cue, and, most importantly, "substantive processing," in which the person is forced to carry out extensive processing of some complex and/or personally relevant material. Experimental studies suggest that negative moods tend to promote substantive processing.

Network architectures have also been explored through connectionist models, which seek to explain processing in terms of the spread of activation through highly interconnected arrays of neuronlike units, sometimes called neural nets. Such models may bridge neural and cognitive-architectural levels of explanation. For example, Matthews and Harley (1993) modeled effects of subjective energy on attention in terms of its effects on level of random noise within networks for word recognition. Connectionist models also provide insight into the role of learning in linking emotion to cognition. A focal concept of connectionism is that some aspects of architecture change with learning. The mechanism for learning is that the strengths of the paths through which activation spreads from unit to unit change through processing error feedback. Beck (1967) pioneered the idea that depression results from "schemas" encoding negative self-beliefs and styles of reasoning about oneself. Building on this idea, Ingram (1984) proposed that depression derived from a "loss-associated network," within which units representing depression and units representing cognitions about current and past events become interassociated, so that the whole set of units is easily activated, leading to persevering recycling of negative thoughts and emotion. Siegle and Ingram (1997) developed a connectionist model in the same vein, within which affective and semantic features of stimuli are represented as separate but interacting sets of units. Depression was simulated through providing the network with high levels of exposure to negative stimuli. They successfully used the model to predict speed of response of depressed humans on a task requiring valence identification (i.e., whether stimuli were negative or positive). As the model predicted, depressed subjects identified negative valence faster than positive valence, but nondepressed individuals did not show this difference. In other words, the fine-grained modeling of how negative emotion is represented within a connectionist architecture helps to explain how emotion biases information processing.

In sum, the network model has been highly influential in stimulating research. However, its original prediction of a general mood-priming effect now seems simplistic, and more complex architectures such as those adopted by connectionist models seem to be required. There are also some theoretical difficulties in the network formulation (Williams et al., 1988). For example, the theory has difficulty in distinguishing feeling depressed from thinking about depression, as both involve activation of the depression node. Fortunately for psychology students, though, we can consider depression intellectually without becoming depressed. Attempts to tackle this problem (e.g., Bower and Cohen, 1982) have not been generally accepted. In dealing with empirical data, most authors have been forced to develop more complex models of processing. In other words, we need a more differentiated architecture than a single network provides. As we shall see, some authors abandoned the network concept altogether, in favor of serial-processing architectures (e.g., Williams et al., 1988), whereas others see a distinction between stimulus-driven networks and a separate, conceptually driven supervisory executive as essential (e.g., Matthews & Harley, 1996).

Emotion as bias: Attentional models of emotion

In a sense, the Bower (1981) model assigned no special status to emotions in representing them as concepts like any other. An alternative approach suggests that emotions actually influence the basic operating parameters of the network. In modeling an architecture, we need to make some assumptions about how strongly processes operate, which translate into numerical parameters within the model (Matthews & Harley, 1993). For example, if a threat appraisal leads to anxiety, we might specify a formula that links strength of anxiety to extent of threat. The parameters of the architecture may vary with emotional states and traits. Typically, this approach leads to an attentional model of emotion, i.e., that the priority afforded to different types of stimuli varies with emotion. We can develop this idea within both network and nonnetwork models. Isen (e.g., 1999) has suggested that positive and negative emotion have different effects on network function. Positive mood induction leads to enhanced cognitive flexibility, shown most directly by increased creativity in forming word associations and categorization of words. Conversely, negative mood may be associated with greater rigidity in association. Williams et al. (1988) developed a stage model of negative affects, within which state anxiety biased an early processing stage of assigning threat values to stimuli, and state depression biased a later, more conscious stage of deciding on stimulus pleasantness. Specific emotions may lead to relatively subtle changes in the operation of the basic information-processing machinery.

The main problem for models of this kind is distinguishing affect-driven changes in architecture from changes in strategy, i.e., in selection of a different sequence of computations supported by the same architecture. Models of architecture suggest that the dependence of processing on emotion is invariant. In the Williams et al. (1988) model, if the person is state anxious, he or she *must* code stimuli as being more threatening. In fact, reviews of studies of emotion and attention (Matthews & Wells, 1999; Wells & Matthews, 1994) suggest a more contingent view of the relationship between affect and attentional bias, which tends to depend on factors related to expectancy, such as prior exposure to materials, blocking of similar trials, and sufficient time to process expectancies. Personal involvement with stimuli is also an important factor (e.g., Segal et al., 1995). It is certainly possible that emotions are associated with fundamental changes in the sensitivity of processing units, with strategies functioning merely to modify architecture-based effects. We look at the alternative view, that strategy choice is the primary source of bias, below.

Emotion as a control signal: Plan-regulation

Models of cognitive architecture must specify control mechanisms for initiating and stopping activities of processors. Contemporary cognitive psychology tends to adopt one of two approaches towards control (e.g., Johnston & Dark, 1986; Matthews, Davies, et al., 2000). First, control may reflect competition between multiple processors. The stimulus that controls response may be the stimulus that activates later stages of processing most strongly, as when a surprising event captures attention. Connectionist models demonstrate how control may reflect both bottom-up activation of processing units, and the top-down influence of expectancy priming on activation (Cohen et al., 1990). Second, in contrast to such models, there may be a separate system or systems that exert control over processing. Norman and Shallice (1986) proposed a supervisory executive system that tends to be activated when tasks are difficult or novel. The executive runs "control programs" that determine and implement the most appropriate strategy for handling a challenging task, and monitor its success. It operates by biasing lower-level systems. This view of control is compatible with neuropsychological evidence suggesting that executive functions are localized in prefrontal and cingulate cortex (e.g., Posner & DiGirolamo, 1998).

We have seen already that emotion may be associated with biasing of computational operations, and so might relate to control in the first sense just mentioned, i.e., through increasing the activation of mood-congruent data representations. In addition, emotion may be related to the functioning of a separate control or executive system. Herbert Simon, one of the pioneers of the cognitive science of emotion, proposed that emotion reflects an interrupt function that reorients the person to manage some new, potentially important event. Oatley and Johnson-Laird (1987) built on this idea by proposing that emotions are the subjective experience of a control signal that propagates through the cognitive architecture. Its function is "to control the organization of the brain, to make ready mechanisms of action and bodily resources, to direct attention, to set up biases of cognitive processing, and to make the issue that caused the emotion salient in consciousness" (Oatley & Johnson-Laird, 1996, p. 363).

These authors envisage an executive system that runs plans to attain personally important goals. A monitoring system evaluates events much as specified by cognitive appraisal theories. When the probability of attaining a goal changes substantially, the monitoring system sends the emotional signal to other processors, including the executive system. Five basic emotions (see chapter 4) are linked to different types of signal, which prompt differing changes in processing. For example, attaining one of the subsidiary subgoals needed to reach a goal elicits a happiness signal that serves to maintain plan execution. Sadness, however, signals failure to attain a goal, and biases the executive system towards abandoning the goal concerned. Oatley and Johnson-Laird see the emotion signal as being evolutionarily primitive, allowing rapid coordination of separate (modular) processing systems to subserve a common adaptive goal. In other words, the Oatley and Johnson-Laird (1987, 1996) theory affords a cognitive rationale for basic emotions, as qualitatively distinct outcomes of implementing plans.

Emotion as an adaptive function

Cognitive emotion theory is compatible with biological and basic-emotions approaches in attributing broadly adaptive functions such as communication to emotion. It goes beyond such approaches in specifying and differentiating multiple functions of emotion and linking them to different components of the cognitive architecture. One of the distinctions often made (e.g., Ketelaar & Clore, 1997) is between emotion as information and emotion as motivation. The former refers to the capacity of emotion (or, rather, the signals associated with emotion) to provide information distinct from languagelike codes. The Oatley and Johnson-Laird (1996) model describes the coordinative function of emotion signals. Emotion as information may influence processing at different levels simultaneously, serving as input both to automatic biasing of discrete processors and to higher-level executive function. Ketelaar and Clore (1997) make the intriguing suggestion that emotions may signal the likely long-term outcome of encounters, based on evolved routines for evaluation of the cues provided by a situation.

Emotion as motivation refers to the power of affect to elicit behaviors that increase happiness and prevent negative affect. Again, the time factor may be important: Ketelaar and Clore (1997) argue that emotions regulate the commitment of effort to long-term strategies, such as delaying immediate gratification in favor of a long-term goal. As indicated above, it is uncertain whether emotions are rigidly tied to evolutionary imperatives. The more pertinent aspect of Ketelaar and Clore's (1997) position is that emotions may be linked to processes for weighing up the value of response choices that are distinct from conscious ratiocination (though still cognitive). The idea resembles Damasio's (1994) view that emotions facilitate social-problem solving, but Ketelaar and Clore's formulation makes more contact with the behavioral-research literature. For example, they describe how experimental inductions of guilt influence behavior in a "prisoner's dilemma" game in which the person has to decide whether to behave cooperatively or antagonistically toward (in this case) a computer opponent. Guilt (or whatever cognitions underpin guilt) tended to restrain people from taking advantage of or retaliating against their opponent.

Implications for emotional intelligence

The material just reviewed provides several possible perspectives on EI. First, suppose that emotions are "data," and individual differences in emotion reflect variation in learning experiences represented by the connection strengths within associative networks. The high EI person is one who has learned skills for handling emotional situations. Associative networks output accurate values for stimulus meaning and situationally relevant episodic and semantic memories. The situation elicits appropriate routines for action that are successfully executed. Conversely, the low-EI person misreads the situation and acts ineffectively, and may engage in dynamically maladaptive processing such as rumination. This perspective has some attractive features in capturing mastery of what Goleman (1995) calls the "social arts," such as organizing groups, negotiating solutions, making personal connections, and performing social analysis. These are learned social skills that are critical in everyday life. As Goleman (1995) also discusses, some people seem to acquire such skills more readily than others, but they may also be taught explicitly, affording the potential of high EI for everyone.

The problem with this perspective is twofold. First, as with processing routines for stimulus analysis, skills for response depend on multiple, qualitatively different processing systems. A skill may depend highly on voluntary, conscious processes, or it may be supported by automatic routines (Ackerman, 1988). The level of control at which EI might reside is unclear. Tests for EI tend to assess consciously accessible, declarative knowledge, but neglect more implicit procedural knowledge, which may actually be more important for social adaptation (Zeidner, Matthews & Roberts, 2001). Second, defining EI in terms of attributes of skill risks confusing cause and effect. Most skills are so heavily dependent upon learning and self-application (e.g., Ericsson, 1996) that assessment of skill is not very informative about initial potential for skill acquisition, the underlying competence to which EI should be related (see chapter 1). Perhaps the emotionally intelligent person was simply lucky in being well educated in emotional matters and trained in social skills commensurate with their aptitudes. To develop this position further, we would need to identify some general parameter of learning that influenced skill acquisition in a variety of emotional domains. So far, there is no hint of such a quality. In general, different aptitudes appear to control rate of learning of different types of cognitive skill (Ackerman, 1988). Another possibility is that EI reflects culture-bound knowledge of emotion, such as beliefs about how to act in specific social settings, dependent, perhaps, on the person's identification with and immersion in the culture, rather than on ability (Zeidner, Matthews & Roberts, 2001).

The second, cognitive-architectural perspective on EI is that of emotion as bias in components of the processing circuitry. Perhaps the high EI person enjoys more positive or more adaptive biases. As described in chapter 5, Ciarrochi et al. (2000a) have shown that the MEIS predicts individual differences in memory bias, although the effect seems to be complex. Again, we encounter the problem of the distributed nature of processing. Emotions are processed within a variety of discrete systems, such as perception, attention, memory, and response selection, and it is difficult to pick out a key system. Furthermore, bias results not just from "in-built" parameters of the architecture, but also from strategic choices, such as the mood-regulation strategies that Ciarrochi et al. (2000a) implicate in EI.

The third perspective, that of control signals, is interesting in that it converges with some of the biological perspectives on emotion (e.g., Rolls, 1999) in potentially linking EI to more efficient regulation of emotion. As previously discussed, perhaps the problems of modularity can be avoided if EI relates to regulation of lower-level emotion systems rather than to the systems themselves. Two problems remain. First, it is unclear what specific property of the signals might constitute the basis for EI. As previously intimated, it is hard to see how simple signal properties, such as signal strength, translate into more or less successful adaptation. Second, architectures such as that proposed by Oatley and Johnson-Laird (1987) do not in any case tell us much about adaptive success; for example, the circumstances under which it is in the organism's interest to give up a plan (accompanied by depression) or to confront obstacles (anger). To do so, we need the transactional perspective (Lazarus, 1991) that links emotion not just to architecture but to the operation of architecture within a demanding external environment.

A fourth perspective might link EI to the adaptive functions of emotion, for example, knowing when to cooperate with other people and when to compete with them. The decision-making tasks used by Ketelaar and Clore (1997) allow the costs and benefits of different strategies to be quantified. Certainly, an operationalization of EI in terms of efficiency of social decision making would be interesting, although it is likely that cognitive abilities, especially in the realm of practical intelligence (Sternberg, 1985), would also play an important role. Consonant with self-control as a core aspect of EI (Goleman, 1995), perhaps the emotionally intelligent person is effective in committing to beneficial long-term strategies, even if it conflicts with immediate interests: Ketelaar and Clore (1997) see emotions as facilitating resolution of commitment problems. The difficulty here is that the formulation seems too narrow. Perhaps there is some primary ability of effective decision making in such circumstances, but it is difficult to see its relevance to other aspects of EI, such as emotion perception and mood management. In addition, the independent assessment of the optimal solution to real-life commitment problems is not straightforward, but is dependent on personal and contextual factors. Culture and learning may shape the motivational and informational significance of emotions to the individual. For example, a person who believes that feeling guilty is a sign of weakness may not, in fact, choose to respond to guilt with prosocial behavior. Indeed, work on obsessive-compulsive disorder indicates that metacognitions of guilt influence its behavioral consequences; in this case to acting on an exaggerated sense of personal responsibility (Wells, 2000).

In summary, there are severe problems with linking EI to individual differences in parameters of the cognitive architecture, most immediately the lack of any obvious key parameter controlling all the various aspects of processing emotion-related information. Control-signal hypotheses seem more promising in potentially linking EI to some higher-level attribute of emotion regulation. Such models work well in explaining the mutual influences of emotion and cognition in laboratory studies. Linking emotion to a control signal also provides, at least in outline, a functional view of emotion as a means for coordinating multiple information processors, which is the evolutionary problem identified by Tooby and Cosmides (1992). The person's ability to use emotion as information and motivation in complex decision-making problems may provide a functional basis for EI. However, all these models tell us relatively little about the role of emotion in real-world adaptation, as the person interacts dynamically with some challenge emanating from the external environment. Our discussion of levels of explanation in chapter 2 tells us that we do not simply need more complex computational models. Instead, we need the different level of explanation afforded by the knowledge level of understanding, i.e., how behavior is shaped by personal intentions, motivations, and meaning.

Self-Regulative Models of Emotional Intelligence

At the knowledge level, we require an ecological view of the person and environment as constituting an interlinked system, as discussed in chapter 4. The best-known theory of emotion of this kind is that of Richard Lazarus (1991, 1999). Lazarus emphasizes the dynamic nature of person-environment interaction. Typically, the person's coping efforts change the nature of the challenge faced, over time, and the experience of handling the challenge changes the person's self-beliefs and coping skills. We return to Lazarus' theory of emotion in the next chapter, when we consider stress and adaptation to the challenges of the real-world. Here, we focus on the cognitive architecture that may support adaptation. As indicated in chapter 2, the key concept bridging cognitive-architectural and knowledge-level descriptions may be that of strategy. The actions of an emotional individual may be seen both as behaviors targeted towards a personal goal, shaped by self-beliefs (knowledge level), and as the computational implementation of a plan supported by the processing routines afforded by the cognitive architecture. Theories of emotion focused on strategy may allow us to explain how the personal meaning of events guides both motivated action and patterns of objective performance in emotional states observed in experimental studies.

The pioneering work on the architecture of control was the model of self-regulation proposed by Carver and Scheier (1981) and updated and further articulated in subsequent books and papers (e.g., Carver & Scheier, 1998; Carver et al., 2000). The starting point for this model is the equation of goal-directed behavior with the operation of a homeostatic feedback control system (figure 7.2). As in the classic cybernetic closed-loop control model, there is an architecture that compares ideal and actual status. If a discrepancy is detected, then behaviors intended to reduce it are initiated, leading to a change in actual status, and a further round of feedback processing and corrective action, if required. Carver and Scheier also suppose that when difficulties in reaching the required state are encountered, the person evaluates the expectancy of success and may attempt to withdraw mentally or behaviorally from the situation. Broadly, emotions are seen as signaling how the feedback system is functioning (similar to the Oatley and Johnson-Laird model previously described). For example, anxiety may be generated by difficulties

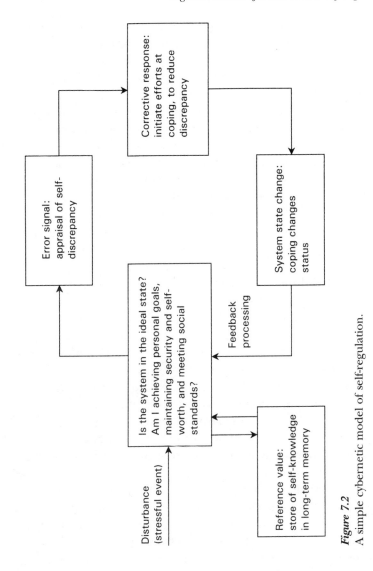

Figure 7.2
A simple cybernetic model of self-regulation.

in error correction, leading to interruption of such efforts and reassessment of whether it is worthwhile continuing them. In recent accounts (Carver & Scheier, 1998), emotion is linked not to discrepancy per se but to the rate of change of the system: anxiety may be felt when progress is too slow. By contrast in cognitive-architectural models previously discussed, emotion does not force some invariant change in processing. Instead, the nature of emotional influence on behavior is strategic. Emotion is a concomitant of flexible, contextually sensitive attempts to meet a personal goal or to withdraw from an unpromising situation.

These ideas were developed by Wells and Matthews (1994) in their Self-Regulative Executive Function (S-REF) model of negative emotion and cognition (figure 7.3). This model seeks to provide more detailed explanation for laboratory studies of emotion and performance than the Carver-Scheier model affords (see Matthews & Wells, 1999, for a review), and to explain the role of cognition in anxiety and depressive disorders (as discussed further in chapter 10). The architecture of the model comprises three levels: a set of lower-level processing networks, an executive system, and a self-knowledge level that represents self-beliefs and generic plans for coping. Consistent with an interrupt model of affect (Simon, 1967), the executive system (the S-REF) is activated by external events that generate self-discrepancy, such as threat, or by intrusions from lower-level networks, such as a somatic signal or spontaneously arising thought or image. Once activated, the S-REF supports processing directed toward discrepancy reduction by initiating and supervising coping responses, which are implemented by biasing lower-level processing networks. In other words, control of processing shifts dynamically between executive and lower-level systems, until discrepancy is resolved and the episode can finish. The S-REF operates by accessing self-relevant knowledge and modifying generic procedures for coping to deal with the immediate problem at hand, as specified by skill theory (Anderson, 1996). The influence of personality on self-regulation is mediated by individual differences in the content of self-knowledge: people differ in how they typically appraise and cope with demanding events (Matthews, Schwean, et al., 2000).

In the S-REF model, emotion signals the status of ongoing executive processing, as broadly suggested by Oatley and Johnson-Laird (1987). More specifically, emotions represent an integration of various discrete self-referent cognitions, including appraisals, choices of coping, and metacognitions (e.g., focusing attention on one's own thoughts). The

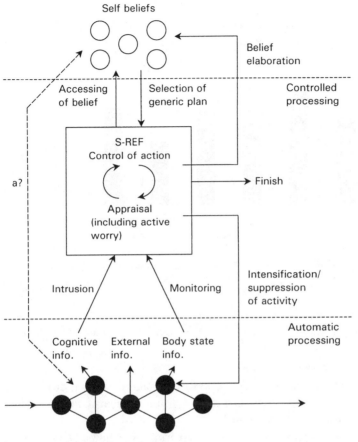

Self beliefs

Belief
elaboration

Accessing
of belief

Selection of
generic plan

Controlled
processing

S-REF
Control of action

a?

Finish

Appraisal
(including active
worry)

Intrusion

Monitoring

Intensification/
suppression
of activity

Automatic
processing

Cognitive
info.

External
info.

Body state
info.

Low-level processing units

Figure 7.3
The S-REF model of emotional dysfunction (Wells & Matthews, 1994).

different aspects of subjective state discussed in chapter 4—task engagement, distress, and worry (Matthews et al., 1999)—represent qualitatively
different states of person-environment transaction (see Lazarus, 1991,
1999). These states are more broadly defined than the specific emotions
listed by Lazarus (1991), and integrate affective, motivational, and cognitive aspects of state. Matthews et al. (1999) see task engagement as
representing a transactional theme of committing effort to a task or
activity, distress as representing a theme of overload of processing, and
worry as representing a theme of pulling back from immediate activity

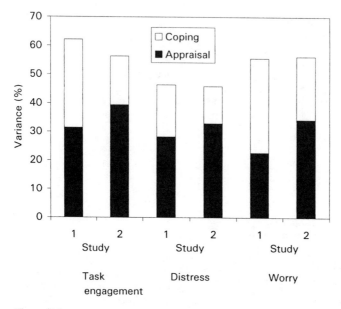

Figure 7.4
Percentages of variance in three aspects of subjective state explained by appraisal and coping, in two studies (Matthews, Derryberry, et al., 2000; Matthews & Falconer, 2000).

to focus attention on self-reflection. Task engagement includes positive affects such as energy, whereas distress subsumes negative affects such as tension, unhappiness, and anger.

To test these hypotheses, studies were run (Matthews, Derryberry & Siegle, 2000; Matthews & Falconer, 2000) in which the DSSQ (Matthews et al., 1999) was used to measure the subjective state induced by performance of high-workload, stressful tasks. Situational appraisal and coping were measured with validated scales (Ferguson et al., 1999; Matthews & Campbell, 1998) derived from stress theory (Endler & Parker, 1990; Lazarus & Folkman, 1984). Figure 7.4 shows the variance in subjective task engagement, distress, and worry explained by appraisal (at the first step of the regression) and coping (at the second step), in two studies. In study 1, university students performed a laboratory rapid information-processing task; in study 2, customer service personnel performed a simulation of their work activities. Despite differences in samples and tasks, results were similar. Both appraisal and coping made significant contributions to the regression equations, explaining about 45–60% of the variance, depending on the subjective state. In both studies, multiple predictors reached significance independently in each of the three regression equations. Despite some minor differences in detail, task engagement was consistently related to challenge appraisal, being highly focused on the task, and low avoidance coping, distress was consistently related to threat appraisal and emotion-focused coping, and worry was consistently related to coping through emotion focus. State change (including emotional change) in response to task-induced stress is quite highly predictable from assessments of how the task environment was appraised and the person's choice of coping strategies. That is, emotion and the motivational and cognitive states with which it overlaps relate to patterns of cognitive stress processes representing different modes of self-regulation.

In line with the coordinative function proposed by Oatley and Johnson-Laird (1987, 1996), the cognitive-emotional states generated by S-REF function produce a variety of consequences in parallel (Matthews & Wells, 1996). First, the person's choice of coping strategy directly impacts low-level processing operations and hence behavior (although strategies do not always function as planned). Matthews and Harley (1996) present a connectionist model illustrating how threat-monitoring intentions may influence attention on the emotional Stroop test. Second, self-regulative activity requires attentional resources and may pull resources away from other processing, leading to disruption of attention, as seen in studies of test anxiety, for example (Zeidner, 1998). Third, S-REF activity and self-focus of attention may lead to heightened awareness of discrepancy, a slippery slope leading to pathological sensitivity to threat in vulnerable individuals. Fourth, the person may modify their self-knowledge in the light of experience, either adaptively by learning generic coping skills or maladaptively by misinterpretation of stimuli or semiadaptively by learning coping skills that provide only temporary respite from the problem. Finally, Wells and Matthews (1994) attempt to specify the dynamic interactions between person and environment that may lead to pathology, such as the oversensitivity to threat resulting from coping through threat monitoring.

Implications for emotional intelligence

The idea of linking EI to self-regulation is frequently encountered. Goleman (1995), for example, describes self-control as a master aptitude. There are also advantages to linking EI to systemic functioning, rather than to specific components of the architecture. For example, this approach accommodates the contingent, context-dependent nature of links between emotion and behavior. The immediate difficulties are those of pinpointing the individual differences in function that lead to more or less successful self-regulation. Within the Wells and Matthews (1994) S-REF model, there are multiple sources of adaptive failure, including self-beliefs, metacognitions, and attentional strategies. If maladaptation is equated with low EI, then we need to find some common element to these differing aspects of processing. Wells and Matthews (1994) describe a general syndrome of self-referent executive processing of negative information, that pulls together various aspects of distress and worry, such as awareness of personal faults, excessive metacognition, self-focus of attention, negative affect and persevering worry. However, a disposition towards anxiety and pathological worry seems too narrow a basis for EI. It does not address other aspects of dysfunctional self-regulation such as lack of impulse control and coping through aggressing against others, for example. It also fails to address what might be termed the "energetics" of EI; how the person mobilizes task engagement so as to master challenging but generally positive activities. Disturbances of subjective state and emotion signal several qualitatively different types of self-regulative challenge, associated with different processing configurations. Lumping together successful coping with these different challenges as emotional intelligence seems simplistic conceptually. There is also little evidence that, for example, being able to mobilize energy and attention to deal with demanding but engaging challenges is correlated with temperance of distress reactions to overload situations (Matthews et al., 1999).

The analysis so far neglects the critical issue of whether, in some broad sense, individual styles of self-regulation may be described as "adaptive" or "maladaptive." Evidently, there are some self-regulative styles that are associated with specific pathologies, such as various anxiety and mood disorders (Wells, 1999). However, within the normal range of functioning, it is unclear that we can say, that, for example, a worry-prone person is generically maladapted. Worry may serve some useful functions such as viewing a problem from different perspectives and exploring its various implications. Furthermore, the efficacy of self-regulative routines depends on the environment within which the routine is executed. For example, self-criticism may be maladaptive in casual social interaction, in that others may not find the person rewarding company (see Coyne, 1976). However, if the person is seeking social support, negative self-statements may assist well-disposed others to help that person. In other words, the adaptiveness of the processing supporting the behavior is a property not solely of the behavior but also of the social environment as well, which controls whether the feedback the person receives is supportive or undermining.

Issues of adaptiveness are beyond the scope of cognitive-architecture models and are instead the province of knowledge-level accounts of emotion. Hence, at this stage, we cannot reach any definitive conclusion. We have seen that self-regulation appears to be a fruitful area in which to look for a psychological basis for EI. However, like any other psychological function, self-regulation is supported by a multiplicity of specific processes and higher-level configurations of processing. No single process stands out as the source of individual variability in emotional control. Unless flagrantly abnormal, a given process cannot be labeled as "adaptive" or "maladaptive" in any case. We will return to individual differences in adaptation, within the context of transactional models of stress and emotion in chapter 8.

Criticisms of the Cognitive Approach

Broadly, we favor cognitive accounts of emotion over biological ones. Cognitive models are more successful in explaining empirically observed links between emotion and behavior in humans than biological models. They provide a conceptual language for the essential role of symbolically coded meanings of events in generating emotion and supporting self-regulation. Furthermore, the acceptance of cognitive models does not imply rejection of a biological basis for behavior (Corr, 2001), and cognitive neuropsychology that integrates neural and cognitive constructs has much to offer to understanding emotion. However, in line with the critical stance of this book, it is important to look at some of the main conceptual criticisms of cognitive psychological accounts of emotion. Loosely, we can call these problem areas the three Cs: coldness, consciousness, control. All point towards possible problems in cognitive formulations, although we will argue that the problems are not fatal for cognitive theory.

The robot, the straw man, and the homunculus

"Coldness" refers to the alleged tendency of cognitive psychology to see the person as a robot without passion, feelings or personal involvement. Goleman (1995) compares the cognitive conceptualization to the characters of Spock and Data in *Star Trek*, who puzzle over emotions intellectually, in the absence of direct experience. Similarly, part of the agenda of biological theories is to counter what is seen as excessive 'cognitivism' in emotion theory. According to LeDoux (1998, p. 42), "Cognitive theories have turned emotions into cold, lifeless states of mind. Lacking sound and fury, emotions as cognitions signify nothing, or at least nothing very emotional." The rhetorical goal is to distance theory from cognitive psychology, or rather the author's (mis?)conception of cognitive psychology. However, this aim conflicts with the emerging cognitive neuroscience orientation of biological psychology itself. Even the more "subcortical" theories of emotion recognize that what brain systems do is perform computations on data (e.g., Gray, 1987, p. 300). The difference between biological and cognitive theories is in the nature of the data representations and permitted computational operations, not in some intrinsic emotionality: a collection of cells has no more sound and fury than a silicon chip. Theorists such as Damasio (1994) may be right that signals from the internal environment of the viscera play a role in emotion that cognitive theories have tended to neglect. But a signal is a signal, not an avatar mysteriously imbued with emotionality. The embodiment of emotions gets no closer to the mystery of why a physical system should feel anything at all than do cognitive models.

Consciousness is a perennial source of difficulty, and many critics of cognitive theory (e.g., LeDoux, 1995) have argued that it neglects unconscious processes. According to Parkinson and Manstead (1992), awareness of meaning does not necessarily depend on cognitive processes. They draw a parallel with the ecological view of Gibson (1979), that information is picked up directly from the in-built regularities of the environment, without need for cognitive analysis. In contemporary theory, however, this criticism is a straw man, a false representation that provides an easy target. The importance of unconscious processes is accepted by all branches of scientific psychology, and the attempt by biological theorists to link consciousness to a subset of brain processes is entirely conventional. There are many demonstrations of unconscious, implicit processing, including, most pertinently, Zajonc's (1984) observation that emotional preferences may be established for subliminal stimuli. Unconsciousness does not preclude a cognitive analysis, i.e., one based on an abstracted representation of stimulus significance, and there is much evidence from cognitive psychological studies demonstrating that exactly this type of analysis takes place, irrespective of whether the stimulus is subliminal or consciously perceived (Clore & Ortony, 2000). It might be tempting to propose a precognitive analysis of emotion that can be identified with subcortical circuits such as LeDoux's (1998) thalamo-amygdalar pathway. However, as Clore and Ortony (2000) point out, there is no particular reason to associate implicit processing exclusively with subcortical structures: some implicit computations have been localized within the cerebral cortex (Schacter, 1996). Indeed, there are probably many implicit pathways: all subcortical pathways may be implicit, but not all implicit pathways are subcortical. Hence, the suggestion that a conscious, cognitive-logical cortex is pitted against an unconscious, noncognitive, emotional amygdala (Goleman, 1995) is simply wrong. Indeed, given that consciousness is not a fundamental property of computational systems we might mix a metaphor by calling the criticism both straw man and red herring. Although philosophical difficulties concerning the nature of consciousness are likely to remain, we can, pragmatically, handle conscious emotion as a property or output of certain kinds of information-processing, that has no direct causal consequences, but may index a subset of processes of special importance in self-regulation.

Another difficulty relates to control: what are the computations that support the self-regulative operations to which emotion appears to be linked? A criticism of models of control posed from within cognitive psychology itself (e.g., Baddeley, 1986) is that control often seems to be exerted by an homunculus, a little man in the head that pulls the computational levers. In saying that a person chooses a particular coping strategy, for example, we are uncomfortably close to invoking homuncular control. The answer to the problem is the detailed specification of the information-processing supporting control (e.g., Norman & Shallice, 1986). Unfortunately, the specification of control processing is often difficult, even in highly constrained laboratory settings, though both connectionism and cybernetic, self-regulative models provide partial answers. Nevertheless, it is acknowledged that the computational basis for some of the key constructs of self-regulative theories of emotion is relatively weak: better specification of appraisal and coping is urgently required.

Cognitive models of emotional intelligence

Cognitive models offer a rich, detailed account of both computational bases for emotion, and the place of emotions in the wider person-environment system, described by self-regulative theories. These models suppose that emotion originates (proximally) from cognitions, especially appraisals, although there may be multiple evaluative routines that contribute to emotion (Leventhal & Scherer, 1987; Clore & Ortony, 2000), and processing of options for coping may make an independent contribution (Matthews & Wells, 1996). From the broad-brush perspective provided by knowledge-level accounts, emotions are caused by the dynamic operation of self-regulative control routines, as they interact with environmental contingencies (Wells & Matthews, 1994). The detailed specification of the software supporting adaptation, allows for a more contingent, Jamesian view of effects of emotion on behavior. In place of the fixed linkages between emotions and action tendencies proposed by basic emotions theory, we have a set of biases in cognition, whose consequences for behavior are contingent upon information-processing and the motivational context. Furthermore, these biases operate at different levels of processing, some of which are unconscious. Cognitive models have been considerably more successful than biological accounts in explaining the empirical data on emotion and performance reviewed briefly in the previous chapter (Matthews, 2001).

In summary, emotion is not to be identified with any specific cognitive process (if it were, the concept would be redundant). Instead, emotion serves as an integration of many processes that signals adaptive status, and supports attempts to cope with external pressures and attain personal goals. Although the experience of emotions may relate most directly to control signals generated by plan attainment (Oatley & Johnson-Laird, 1987), the diverse consequences of the control signal mean that a state of emotion is accompanied by multiple, distributed changes in information processing, supporting the functional goals subserved by the control signal. These changes may include activation of representations of personally significant events and beliefs, biases in the cognitive architecture and initiation of explicitly self-regulative processing, directed towards effective coping. A cognitive account of EI requires an analysis of how people differ in these self-regulative processing activities, but such an analysis requires the transactional approach discussed in the next chapter.

Conclusions

This chapter and the previous one have explored various possible bases for EI suggested by biological and cognitive theory. For such an important construct, EI is surprisingly elusive. The existence of EI does not follow as an inevitable consequence of any of the theories. Indeed, one of the main contributions of theory is to eliminate or discourage pursuit of some of the conceptions of EI we have explored, and we will attempt to sift these unpromising perspectives. At the same time, we have seen some pointers towards conceptions of EI that are potentially viable. We conclude our examination of processes for EI by describing some dead-ends for theorizing, together with some avenues that are promising, but have yet to be articulated in detailed and testable form.

What emotional intelligence is not

Here is a list of what emotional intelligence is not:

A property of modular brain systems for specific emotions   (e.g., Panksepp, 1998). The concept of EI is incompatible with that of separate modules for different basic emotions. Furthermore, the idea that human response in emotional states is controlled by prewired action patterns output by emotion modules is incompatible with the evidence from performance studies.

A property of subcortical brain systems such as the amygdala   The generalization of theory from animal to human models of emotions is suspect and frequently unsubstantiated by evidence. Furthermore, subcortical systems do not have the computational power to handle the adaptive challenges of being human.

Any parameter of the neural architecture   We cannot link EI to any specific aspect or parameter of the brain, such as sensitivity of brain punishment or reward systems, because, most simply, individual differences in parameters of neural function do not map onto behavior and adaptation in any simple way. The evidence shows that the tight coupling between emotion and behavior envisaged by animal models simply does not apply to humans. We may be able to localize brain structures in frontal cortex that contribute to EI, but we cannot describe the role of these structures without reference to higher levels of description.

Appraisal   EI cannot be linked to specific information-processing systems, such as those supporting appraisal, for much the same reasons it cannot be linked to modular brain systems. There is no single process or collection of processes that can support all the multifarious expressions of EI, in qualitatively different emotional states.

Emotional learning ability   If EI exists, it must relate to complex, acquired social skills for handling emotionally challenging encounters. However, skill is supported by processing at different levels of abstraction, supported by qualitatively different types of learning. There is no general ability for learning how to process emotional material that could support EI.

Any parameter of the cognitive architecture　Cognitive architectures are modular, comprising many independent processing units within a hierarchical control structure. No single lower-level module, such as an appraisal module, has sufficient control over behavior to support EI as a general quality of the person. Likewise, the higher-order systems that effect voluntary control and self-regulation are sufficiently differentiated that we cannot attribute EI to any single parameter of executive control of processing.

What emotional intelligence might be

There is converging evidence from both neuroscience and cognitive science that EI may be a quality of an executive control system for emotion regulation, supported by sites in the frontal cortex (Rolls, 1999). Lesions to areas such as orbitofrontal cortex lead to substantial deficits in social problem-solving (Bechara et al., 2000). More general control systems for attention and decision-making also reside in frontal cortex (Shallice & Burgess, 1998). From the cognitive perspective, the problems of modularity may be avoided if it is supposed that EI relates to some superordinate executive system, of the kind established by experimental studies (Wells & Matthews, 1994). The idea is also compatible with current theory linking EI to aspects of self-regulation (Mayer et al., 2000), or to effective coping (Bar-On, 2000; Salovey et al., 1999). EI may describe an executive system that makes adaptive selections of evaluative and action-oriented processing routines. Nevertheless, the executive hypothesis faces significant difficulties. Like any other cognitive system, it is supported by multiple components, and it is unclear which components are critical. Furthermore, much of the wisdom of the executive resides in its store of procedural knowledge in long-term memory (Wells & Matthews, 1994), whose quality reflects a variety of factors including exposure to supportive learning environments and transferability from past to present circumstances. Perhaps the most serious difficulty is that we cannot evaluate the adaptiveness of any item of brain software without assessment of its function within some external, demanding environment. The next chapter tackles this knowledge-level issue.

8

Emotional Intelligence, Coping, and Adaptation

Indeed, keeping our distressing emotions in check is the key to emotional well-being ...

D. Goleman

The twentieth century was variously called the age of *stress, anxiety,* and more recently, *coping* (Endler, 1996), and there is little sign of the pressures of modern life abating in the current century. Coping refers to a person's efforts to manage, control, or regulate threatening or challenging situations (Lazarus & Folkman, 1984; Lazarus, 1999). This contemporary view of stress differs from both more traditional views of stress and negative emotion in several respects. In everyday language, the word "stress" is rather ambiguous. It may refer either to a property of environments or situations, as when we say that an event such as an examination is stressful, or to a property of the person. In this latter case, "stress" describes a response rather than a stimulus (e.g., "feeling stressed out"). Furthermore, current theorizing differentiates the concept of stress from strain—the latter referring to the psychological, physiological, and behavioral impact of the person-situation interaction on the individual.

Current stress theory emphasizes that stress is more than just a stimulus. Reactions to challenging events depend on how the person interprets the demands placed upon him and on the person's active attempts at coping with demands (over time). Stress is often accompanied by physiological changes, such as autonomic arousal, and release of hormones, such as cortisol, and by subjective responses, such as emotional distress and worry (see Matthews, 2000b, for an overview). Indeed, the concept originated as a label for what was believed to be a nonspecific physiological response to various forms of harm (Selye, 1976). However, stress is more than just a response. The psychological significance of responses such as feelings of anxiety or elevated heart rate is derived from the context of the person's dynamic interactions with the external environment. In fact, there seems to be no single response that we can use as a stress index, and responses will change over time (a process) as the person attempts to deal with external demands. Stress is currently viewed as "transactional," in that stress responses reflect a developing series of transactions between person and environment that may change as the stressful encounter enfolds over time. Any evaluation of a stressful encounter must perforce consider the challenges, constraints, and affordances of a particular situation relative to one's personal resources and competencies. In fact, over the past two decades, more and more coping researchers began studying the interaction between situational factors and person variables in determining individual reactions (i.e., strain) to the person-environment stressful encounter.

Transactional stress models (e.g., Lazarus & Folkman, 1984) view stress as a multivariate process involving inputs (person and environmental variables), outputs (immediate and long-term effects), and the mediating activities of appraisal and coping processes. The relationship between appraisal, coping, and adaptational outcomes, such as psychological and physical health, has become a major concern among personality researchers (Lazarus, 1993; Zeidner & Matthews, 2000). Furthermore, handling the aversive emotions evoked in a stressful encounter may be critical to negotiating it successfully.

Importantly, the transactional approach adds to biological and information-processing accounts of emotion by relating stress to knowledge-level constructs such as personal goals and self-beliefs. Stress represents not some predefined neurological or information-processing state, but a *misalignment* between external demands and personal motivations and abilities (capacities). The person's self-beliefs are critical to this relation: stress critically depends on how the person appraises or perceives the environment and their own status as an active agent able to intervene proactively in forwarding their goals. The defining issue of this chapter is whether people can be rank-ordered in terms of their competence in *adaptive* coping (i.e., a spectrum of coping ability that might correspond to EI). As pointed out by Zeidner and Saklofske (1996), within the context of coping research, "adaptive" refers to the effectiveness of the coping process to improve outcomes for the person (e.g., emotional adjustment, physical health, sense of well-being). Deciding whether particular coping strategies, such as problem-focused, emotion-focused, or avoidance (Zeidner & Saklofske, 1996), are adaptive or not requires an examination of both personal and situational factors. The notion of effectiveness is a part of most descriptions of coping: "The prime importance of appraisal and coping processes is that they affect adaptational outcomes" (Lazarus & Folkman, 1984, p. 13). However, it is unclear (1) whether single adaptational outcomes can be scaled on some single continuum of success versus failure, and (2) whether there are consistent individual differences in success of outcome, generalizing across different types of encounter.

General intelligence (*g*) may make some contribution to adaptive coping. There is some evidence that measures of intelligence and intellectual attainment correlate with constructs related to confidence in one's own coping abilities, such as self-efficacy and ego resiliency (e.g., Block & Kremen, 1996; Zeidner, 1995; Zeidner & Matthews, 2000). The capacity for abstract reasoning may be one of various cognitive resources that facilitate real-world problem solving under pressure. Persons high on *g* may handle stress more adaptively because they manage to avoid potentially dangerous situations at the outset, perceive situations in more realistic ways, and consider a variety of coping options appropriate to the stressful context (Zeidner, 1995). At the same time, there is clearly more to successful coping than general intelligence per se. Correlations between conventional ability measures and coping scales are modest, at best, and some important correlates of EI, such as low alexithymia, are unrelated to intelligence test scores (Parker, Taylor & Bagby, 1998, 2001). EI measures may actually be superior to IQ tests in their ability to predict how successfully individuals will handle stressful environments and external pressures.

In this chapter, we explore and critically assess the prospects for establishing emotional intelligence as a novel explanatory construct in stress research. We believe that EI is of scientific interest largely depending on whether it can be identified as a coherent quality of the person that underpins adaptive coping (and other manifestations of emotion perception and regulation). We start out by presenting the proposed nexus of relationships between EI, stress, and adaptive coping, as it appears in the EI literature. Specifically, we will delineate some causal mediating variables linking EI and coping espoused by proponents of the EI construct. We aim to show that the EI literature has not been very successful at substantiating the claimed nexus of relations between EI, stress, and coping. Furthermore, the EI literature has made only occasional contact with the stress and coping literature. To rectify this condition, we attempt to validate the construct of EI within the stress and coping literature. Accordingly, we delineate and critically evaluate some potential research strategies for conceptualizing and validating the EI construct within the stress domain. One strategy we adopt is to try to discover a master process or integrated cluster of processes that controls adaptive outcome. Competence in this master process might define EI. A second strategy is to investigate individual differences in stress-related processing, in the hope that we can identify a master process that is the source of individual differences in aptitude for handling stressful events. We will conclude by adopting a critical stance, while recognizing that there is a paucity of empirical evidence on which to base definitive conclusions. Thus, while we point out potential links between EI and coping, as suggested in the EI literature, our conceptual and empirical analysis leads us to question the role of EI in the stress and coping process.

Stress and Coping: The EI Perspective

As our opening quotation suggests, proponents of EI often see effective coping as central to EI. In fact, current thinking among EI researchers (e.g., Salovey, Bedell, Detweiler & Mayer, 1999) suggests that the way people identify, understand, regulate, and repair emotions (in self and others) helps determine coping behaviors and consequent adaptive outcomes. However, there is rather little evidence to substantiate these claims.

Coping is a multidimensional construct that has traditionally been defined in the stress literature as the process of managing the external/internal demands that are appraised as taxing or exceeding a person's resources (Lazarus & Folkman, 1984). However, some EI researchers have argued that it is not just these *demands* that a person needs to cope with in a stressful encounter, but rather the *emotions* evoked by the demands with which a person actually needs to cope. Furthermore, Salovey et al. claim that more emotionally intelligent individuals cope more successfully because they "accurately perceive and appraise their emotional states, know how and when to express their feelings, and can effectively regulate their mood states" (1999, p. 161). Similarly, Bar-On (1997) includes "Stress Management" and "Adaptability" as two major components of EI. Thus, some researchers consider stress management and adaptive coping as a major component of EI (e.g., Bar-On, 1997). Others (e.g., Epstein, 1998; Salovey et al., 1999), however, view EI as a personal antecedent of adaptive coping, working through various causal factors in determining adaptive coping (which we discuss below).

EI researchers (e.g., Goleman, 1995; Salovey et al., 1999) would readily embrace the notion of adaptive coping as '*emotional intelligence in action*,' supporting mastery of emotions, emotional growth, and both cognitive and emotional differentiation, allowing us to evolve in an ever-changing world. Current thinking in the EI literature (Epstein, 1998; Salovey et al. 1999), supported only by a sparse amount of systematic empirical research, points to a number of reasons why emotionally intelligent individuals would be expected to experience less stress. These theorists would also claim that emotionally intelligent individuals cope more adaptively once stress is experienced. We turn now to delineate purported mediating mechanisms appearing in the EI literature.

Mediating mechanisms

Avoidance of stressful encounters Emotionally intelligent persons, it is claimed, may create a less stressful environment for themselves by conducting their personal and social lives in ways that produce fewer frustrating or distressing events (Epstein, 1998). Because high EI individuals would not get themselves into stressful situations to begin with, they would not need to deplete as many adaptive resources in coping with stress in their lives. Furthermore, emotionally intelligent individuals, it is claimed, may be good at identifying and thus avoiding potentially dangerous or harmful social contexts, due to more careful and effective monitoring of the emotional cues in social situations (see Epstein, 1998). At present, there is no hard empirical evidence to support this claim. In addition, adaptive success may require engaging with and successfully managing aversive environments. Studies of social anxiety suggest that avoidance of stressful circumstances undermines self-confidence and hinders the acquisition of social skills (Wells, 2000). However, even highly emotionally intelligent individuals may not always find it possible to avoid stressful situations.

Richer coping resources Emotionally intelligent individuals, it is claimed, may have richer emotional and social personal coping resources compared to their less emotionally intelligent counterparts (see Epstein, 1998; Salovey et al., 1999). Thus, when emotionally intelligent individuals compare the demands of a stressful encounter vis-à-vis their perceived resources and competencies, they tend to assess the encounter as intrinsically less stressful. In particular, EI has been hypothesized to work through the social resource of perceived social support in determining adaptive coping (Salovey et al., 1999). Accordingly, EI has been claimed to equip the individual with the necessary social skills required to build a solid and supportive social network. Thus, individuals high on EI are said to be more likely to have developed adequate social skills, to be better connected socially, and to have greater access to a wide network of social support. Social support is then accessed and utilized effectively in times of need, with emotionally intelligent individuals better able to rely on rich social networks to provide them with an emotional buffer against negative life events (Salovey et al., 2000). Hard evidence for the importance of personal resources in mediating the EI-coping interface is sparse and in further need of empirical instantiation.

Greater self-efficacy for emotion regulation   Persons high on EI, it is claimed, have a greater sense of self-efficacy with respect to regulation of emotions (Salovey, Woolery & Mayer, 2001). That is, they believe they have the wherewithal to employ the strategies necessary to repair negative moods following a stressful or traumatic encounter, as well as elicit and maintain positive moods when appropriate. Moreover, high self-efficacy is claimed to work through coping strategies to affect outcomes (Salovey et al., 2001). According to this hypothesis, individuals who can clearly perceive their feelings and believe they can repair negative moods turn their attentional resources toward coping and minimize the potentially deleterious impact of stressful events. It is further claimed that the optimistic belief system and constructive thinking patterns of high EI individuals allow them to take on challenges and risks. This follows from the fact they have confidence that things will work out well and can cope instrumentally and adaptively with stressful encounters (Epstein, 1998). Overall, there is very little evidence for the above claims, and further work is needed to support the purported role of self-efficacy as a mediating variable in the EI-coping relationship and to show that EI adds anything to existing self-efficacy constructs (e.g., Bandura, 1997).

More constructive perceptions and situational appraisals   Emotionally intelligent individuals, it is claimed, have more constructive thought patterns, and find it easier to catch and identify faulty appraisals and correct maladaptive construals (Epstein, 1998). It is said that high EI individuals become aware of their mental responses and the strong influence their cognitions have on their feelings. Therefore, they tend to more readily tune in to their stream of consciousness and more faithfully observe the procession of their thoughts. Furthermore, high EI individuals tend to interpret stressful conditions, if unavoidable, in a more benign and less stressful way, viewing them more as challenges than threats (see Epstein, 1998). It has been further claimed, but not firmly substantiated, that individuals who can make sense out of their feelings show greater rebound from induced negative mood and increased decline in rumination compared to those lower in clarity (Salovey, Stroud, Woolesy & Epel, in press). Notwithstanding claims in the EI literature, there is very little evidence in support of these claims, and the role of appraisals in mediating the EI-coping relationship has not been firmly established and is presently a hypothesis in need of future testing and research.

Adaptive regulation and repairing of emotions Clarity of emotions and repair of emotions, essential components of EI, are claimed to be essential ingredients for adaptive coping with stress (Salovey et al., 2000). Furthermore, high EI individuals are believed to be good emotional copers—not "sweating the little stuff" (Epstein, 1998). They are said to be calm, centered, and characterized by peace of mind; they are more effective in dealing with negative feeling; and they experience less stress in living than others. In particular, they are claimed to not take things personally, are not overly sensitive to disapproval or failure, and do not worry about things that are beyond control (Epstein, 1998). Those skilled at regulating their emotions, should be better able to repair their negative emotional states, by engaging in sports, self-help pep talks, or pleasant activities as a distraction for negative affect. Strategies that actively manage mood, such as using relaxation techniques and engaging in pleasant activities, appear to be more successful than more passive strategies, such as resting or taking drugs or alcohol (Thayer, 1996). Here again, future research is needed to investigate whether measures of EI are associated with the use of more effective mood-management strategies.

Emotional skills Emotionally intelligent individuals are claimed to have certain emotional skills that allow them to effectively disclose their past personal traumas (Salovey et al., 1999). Research surveyed by Pennebaker (1997) shows that the simple act of disclosing emotional experience in writing improves a person's physical and mental health, including improvement of immune functioning, decreased depression, improved grades in college students, and reduced symptoms. Cognitive housekeeping and the disclosure process restructures disturbing experiences, giving them a coherent and meaningful place in the person's life. Emotionally intelligent individuals, it is claimed, are able to strike a healthy balance between pleasant distractions from aversive events and coming to terms with their mood (Salovey et al., 2000). Furthermore, high EI individuals can reflectively engage emotions or detach themselves from emotions, depending on their utilities. Being more adept at directing their thoughts away from negative emotions, they are hypothesized to engage less in dysfunctional worry and excessive rumination. Although the evidence suggests that emotional closure is indeed salutary to one's mental and physical health (Pennebaker, 1997), little research substantiates the proposed nexus of relations between EI, emotional skills (e.g., emotional disclosure, handling worry), and effective coping.

It is evident that the scope of individual differences in coping linked to EI is very broad. Some of the mediating mechanisms (e.g., adaptive regulation and availability of emotional skills) refer directly to coping with emotion itself. Other mechanisms, such as managing exposure to stressors and more constructive appraisal and coping, are more likely to influence emotion indirectly, depending on the outcome of the encounter. It is uncertain which of these various mechanisms should relate to EI and which to other personality and ability factors, reflecting the conceptual weaknesses of EI described in the introductory chapters.

Use of effective coping strategies   EI researchers claim that emotionally intelligent individuals engage in more active coping responses to stress situations, whereas those low in emotional intelligence tend to opt for less adaptive emotion-focused or avoidance responses in stressful situations. Thus, emotionally intelligent people are said to cope more efficiently with situations once they have interpreted them as stressful (Epstein, 1988). Problem-focused coping has been associated with the competencies to clearly perceive, differentiate, and repair one's emotions. According to this line of reasoning, people need to perceive their feelings clearly in a stressful situation and believe they are capable of managing their emotions in order for them to cope adaptively.

Competence and flexibility in coping
EI might relate both to availability of more effective coping strategies and to more flexible, adaptive selection from among the person's rep-

ertoire of strategies. Recent research (Endler, Speer, Johnson & Flett, 2000) has highlighted the importance of matching coping facets to situational demands. Thus, high EI individuals should be able to cope more flexibly and less stereotypically by optimally fitting coping patterns to the cognitive and perceptual styles of the self, as well as the constraints and affordances of the situation. A body of research (Zeidner & Saklofske, 1996) suggests that in controllable situations, active and problem-focused coping is more effective and adaptive, whereas when stressors are uncontrollable, emotion-focused coping may be the only available and feasible coping response. Thus, individuals high on EI would be expected to employ problem-focused coping strategies when something can be done to alter the situation. They would also appear to prefer to use emotion-focused coping strategies when there is little that can be done to change the stressful circumstances. High EI is also claimed to lead to more effective emotion regulation, which in turn, leads to less rumination and preoccupation, along with greater clarity and organization of emotions (Salovey et al., 1999). As aptly stated by Susan Folkman, "A time-honored principle of effective coping is to know when to appraise a situation as uncontrollable and hence abandon efforts directed at altering the situation and turn to emotion-focused processes in order to tolerate or accept the situation" (1984, p. 849).

Figure 8.1 depicts, graphically, the purported nexus of relationships between EI, selected mediating variables, and coping, as it appears in

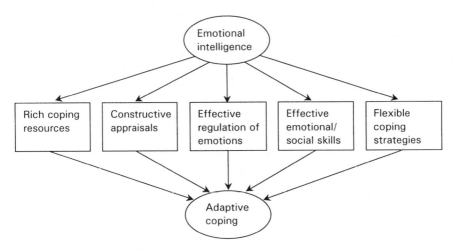

Figure 8.1
Hypothesized factors mediating the EI-coping relationship.

the EI literature. As shown in figure 8.1, EI may work through a host of personal variables (coping resources, constructive appraisals, effective emotion regulation, effective social skills, flexible coping strategies) to impact upon adaptive coping. EI researchers claim that successful coping depends on the integrated operation of rational as well as emotional competencies (Salovey et al., 2000). Accordingly, the entire hierarchy of emotional skills (i.e., basic perceptual and expressive skills, emotional knowledge, and regulation of emotions) must be developed and employed for successful regulation of emotion and coping to take place. According to these researchers, major deficiencies in basic emotional competencies will interfere with the development and implementation of more complex coping. Thus, a person who finds it difficult to identify or express her emotions may also find it difficult to seek emotional social support or ventilate feelings.

Empirical research on EI and coping

A modicum of research has been conducted linking EI components to effective coping strategies. Bar-On (1997) reports that the EQ-i correlates moderately with high task-focused coping and low emotion-focused coping. However, exactly this result would be expected based on the high correlation between EQ-i and neuroticism, which is similarly related to coping (Endler & Parker, 1990, 1999). Discriminant validity has not been established. Ciarrochi, Chan, and Bajgar (2001) report a study of the Schutte et al. (1998) EI scale in adolescents that did not address stress directly but provided some mixed findings. On the positive side, EI was related to perceived social support. The authors also found that a subscale of the EI measure, "Managing Self-Relevant Emotions," related to emotional content in stories generated by participants, depending on the type of mood previously induced, an effect attributed to use of mood-regulation strategies such as mood repair (negative mood induction) and mood maintenance (positive induction). On the negative side, EI failed to moderate emotional response to negative and positive mood inductions used in the study, so the mood management strategies attributed to EI did not appear to be effective in regulating mood in this context. Results of studies using the Multi-factor Emotional Intelligence Scale (MEIS) have been somewhat confusing. Ciarrochi, Chan, and Caputi (2000a) suggest that the MEIS indexes individual differences in mood management, but, as described in chapter 5, the evidence for this claim is somewhat indirect, and EI had no effect on negative mood response. Salovey, Stroud, Woolesy, and Epel (in press) reported that skill at repair or regulation of emotions was correlated with *active* coping in a sample of 45 college undergraduate students. However, a study on a female sample found that skill at mood repair was not meaningfully associated with active coping but rather associated with less trait and state *passive* coping (Salovey, Stroud, Woolesy & Epel, in press). These differences may well be attributed to gender differences in the EI-coping relation.

A recent unpublished study we conducted at the University of Cincinnati represents the only study to date to link the MSCEIT to coping and subjective stress response. In this study 199 college students completed six of the subtests of the MSCEIT (Mayer et al., 2001, submitted), with two subtests each for the perception, understanding, and management branches. A principal axis factor analysis identified a general factor explaining 40% of the variance, which was used as an estimate of EI. Participants were then randomly allocated to one of four conditions, a control condition (reading magazines) or one of three stress conditions validated in previous research (e.g., Matthews et al., 1999). The stress conditions were intended to elicit fatigue (vigilance task), overload of attention (time-pressured working memory task) or personal failure (impossible 9-letter anagrams). The Dundee Stress State Questionnaire (DSSQ) (Matthews et al., 1999), described in chapter 4, was administered before and after performance. Results confirmed that the three conditions induced different patterns of subjective stress response, including, in all three conditions, increases in distress of more than one SD, relative to the control condition. After performance, participants completed the Assessment of Life Events scale (ALE) (Ferguson, Matthews & Cox, 1999), as a measure of situational threat and challenge appraisal. They also completed the Coping in Task Situations (CITS) questionnaire (Matthews & Campbell, 1998), which assesses use of task-focused, emotion-focused, and avoidance strategies in performance settings. As discussed in the next section, these represent three fundamental dimensions of coping (Endler & Parker, 1990).

Table 8.1 gives correlations between the MSCEIT EI factor and the stress indices, in the whole sample. The results support Salovey et al.'s (1999) hypothesis that EI may relate to tolerance for stress, in that EI was associated with lower distress and worry, and with reduced use of emotion-focus and avoidance coping, strategies likely to be maladaptive in the performance context. Further analysis showed that when the general factor was controlled for, associations between the six subtests and stress outcome variables did not exceed chance levels. As Salovey

Table 8.1

Pearson and partial correlations between EI and neuroticism on the one hand and stress outcome and process measures on the other

	Pretask			Posttask		
	EI	EI (partial)	N (partial)	EI	EI (partial)	N (partial)
Stress state (DSSQ)						
Task engagement	.05	−.03	−.33**	.09	.06	−.13
Distress	−.30**	−.20**	.58**	.03	.04	.26**
Worry	−.31**	−.24**	.36**	−.25**	−.20**	.22**
Appraisal (ALE)						
Threat				−.12	−.08	.13
Challenge				.01	−.01	.03
Coping (CITS)						
Task focus				.05	.00	−.18**
Emotion focus				−.18**	−.12	.25**
Avoidance				−.18**	−.16*	.09

Notes: The table gives Pearson correlations between a full EI factor derived from MSCEIT subscales and stress outcome and process measures, in a study of task-induced stress (unpublished data, University of Cincinnati, $N = 199$). The table also gives partial correlations between the EI factor and stress measures, controlling for NEO-FFI neuroticism (N), and partial correlations between N and stress measures, controlling for the EI factor.
$*p < .05; **p < .01$.

et al. (1999) claim, resistance to stress relates to EI as a whole, and not to any individual branch. The study also included the NEO-FFI questionnaire, which assesses Costa and McCrae's (1992) Big Five personality traits. Previous DSSQ studies have shown that neuroticism (N) is a robust predictor of states of stress (Matthews et al., 1999). In this study, similar to other findings reviewed in chapter 5 (e.g., Roberts et al., 2001), EI was negatively correlated with N ($r = −.25$, $p < .01$), and positively correlated with agreeableness ($r = .24$, $p < .01$). Table 8.1 shows that, even with EI statistically controlled, N tended to be a stronger predictor of the stress indices than the EI factor was. However, with N controlled, some of the relationships between EI and stress indices remained significant. EI was significantly correlated with pretask and posttask worry, and it also appeared to be a more robust predictor of avoidance coping than was N. Hence, EI may be distinguished from low neuroticism as a predictor of some aspects of stress response, although its unique contribution is fairly modest. Furthermore, EI was unrelated to some key components of the stress process, such as primary appraisal, and to the positive experiences of the stressful environments represented by the DSSQ task engagement factor.

The study also aimed to test whether, as Salovey et al. (2000, p. 147) imply, EI is especially predictive of functioning in high-stress conditions; i.e., that high EI is protective in circumstances that are threatening or otherwise demanding. In fact, a comparison of correlations between EI and stress variables in the different conditions suggested that EI was no more predictive in the stress conditions than in the control condition.[1] EI also failed to predict *increases* in stress response, indexed by the DSSQ, between pretask and posttask phases of the study. Indeed, the significant pretask correlation between EI and DSSQ distress disappeared posttask. Pretask assessments, taken soon after arrival at the laboratory, are likely confounded by individual differences in activities prior to the study, whereas the posttask assessment is more reflective of stress response with environmental variation controlled. Possibly, the MSCEIT indexes greater social participation, that protects against negative moods and worries, more than it indexes basic stress processes. On the other hand, the more stable link between low EI and state worry is consistent with Salovey et al.'s (1999) identification of rumination as a process mediating EI effects, given that high worry is a direct outcome of brooding on one's problems (Matthews & Wells, in press; see also chapter 10). In conclusion, the study partially confirms a link between EI as operationalized by the MSCEIT, and stress outcomes and coping. However, it is unclear that EI is central to individual differences in adaptation to stressful environments, or that it provides a robust index of more adaptive coping.

Emotional Intelligence and the Psychological Theory of Stress

As evidenced above, a major weakness in the EI literature is the lack of systematic *empirical* work substantiating the claim that EI plays a pivotal role in adaptive coping. Although several causal mechanisms have been proposed to explain the purported link between EI and coping, very little data exists on the magnitude of the relationship between EI and coping. Such evidence as there is suggests a rather modest link and yet authors are prone to take for granted that EI may be identified with adaptive coping. Furthermore, even assuming that the evidence for a substantial association between EI and coping is forthcoming, there is little evidence for most of the claimed causal mechanisms.

A further weakness of the expanding body of research on EI is that it tends to neglect the extensive and well-established literature on stress and coping. As discussed in chapter 5, we can already measure the person's vulnerability to stress symptoms such as negative emotion and worry with a high degree of validity, by using existing personality scales (see also chapter 9). The danger is then that, in the field of stress, EI research is simply reinventing the wheel in relabeling extant stress vulnerability constructs as "emotional intelligence." Alternatively, existing stress research may actually have missed something important about individual differences, which is captured by the notion of EI. Given the dearth of empirical work, it becomes important to look at whether the concept of EI as a master faculty for adaptive coping is compatible with existing stress theory.

Transactional model of stress

To gauge whether EI offers anything new in the stress domain, we need to look in more detail at stress from the vantage of psychological theory and in particular individual differences in adaptation to demanding environments. The theoretical framework for our analysis is provided by Lazarus and Folkman's (1984), transactional model of stress mentioned previously (see figure 8.2). This theory places cognitive processes (i.e., appraisals) at the center of emotional response, and in line with our discussion of neural and cognitive bases for EI in chapters 6 and 7, we will adopt a *cognitive* orientation here. The central assumption is that stress reflects the individual's understanding of their place in the world around them, an understanding that is often imperfectly based on external reality. Stress develops from unfolding person-environment interactions that tax or exceed the person's perceived capacity to cope with environmental demands. Lazarus and Folkman distinguish *processes* such as appraisal and coping from *outcomes* such as emotional distress and health problems. The visible outcomes of stressful encounters are governed by the person's information processing of the events. If we simply say that a person who fails to cope successfully with events lacks emotional intelligence, we are falling into the trap of circular reasoning. We are saying that the person is distressed because of their lack of emotional intelligence, but we are inferring their low EI from their distressed state.

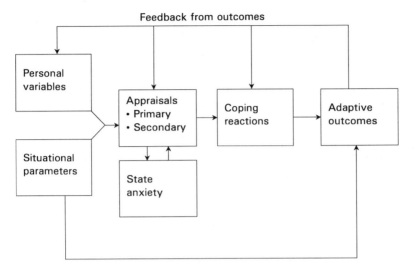

Figure 8.2
Transactional model of stress and coping.

For EI to have explanatory power, it must be distinguished from stress outcomes, as an *aptitude* or competencies that control whether or not a person handles demanding events successfully. In other words, a person's EI should tell us not just about their propensity to experience stress symptoms. It should tell us something about the underlying causes of stress vulnerability, and we should be able to measure these causal factors independently of assessments of distress. For example, if the key to emotional intelligence is good self-control (Goleman, 1995), then we should be able to assess the person's self-control under nonstressful conditions, and show that self-control predicts lower distress when the person is under pressure.

So far, we have seen that EI should be conceptualized as an *aptitude* for handling challenging situations, as opposed to an *outcome* variable, i.e., the successful resolution of emotional challenges. The aptitude increases the likelihood of a successful outcome, but it does not guarantee it, because outcome also depends on situational factors. As graphically depicted in figure 8.2, the transactional theory of stress posits that both aptitudes and situational factors operate through cognition (appraisals and threat perceptions). When a person is experiencing a stressful event (or indeed any event), processing of incoming stimuli produces appraisals.

Lazarus and Folkman (1984) distinguish *primary* and *secondary* appraisals. Primary appraisals, such as threat, loss and challenge refer to the immediate personal significance of the stimulus, whereas secondary appraisals represent the person's evaluation of how they might cope with demands. Appraisals guide choice of coping strategy. Lazarus and Folkman (1984) distinguish two broad categories of coping. *Emotion-focused* coping comprises sequences of self-referent cognitions that aim to regulate distressful emotions, channel negative affect, and reconceptualize the problem, e.g., by looking on the bright side or examining previous failures to deal with it. *Task-* or *problem-focused coping* is directed toward changing external reality, and typically refers to behaviors intended to resolve the problem. Other authors (e.g., Endler & Parker, 1990; 1999) discriminate *avoidance* of the problem (e.g., through distraction or social diversion) as a further basic type of coping. Appraisal and coping are in dynamic interaction: appraisal influences coping, but the outcomes of attempts at coping feed back into appraisal. For example, an appraisal that the problem is easily managed might elicit a *task-focused* coping strategy (e.g., increased effort in studying for an important exam). But the unexpected failure of coping efforts would revise the initial appraisal, and enhance awareness of threat and lack of personal control, possibly eliciting *emotion-focused* coping (e.g., meditation) or *avoidance* coping (going on vacation, and thus leaving the field). These three forms of coping are graphically depicted in figure 8.3.

There is extensive evidence that the nature of the situation influences appraisal and coping. Controllable situations are more likely to elicit appraisals of challenge and task-focused coping, whereas uncontrollable situations elicit threat appraisals and emotion-focused coping (Endler, et al, 2000; Wells & Matthews, 1994). Lazarus and Folkman (1984) tended to downplay the importance of stable individual differences in personality and ability. However, there is now extensive evidence that the personality factors described in a previous chapter are reliably associated with biases in appraisal and coping (Matthews & Deary, 1998). In other words, people have preferred styles of cognition, and how a person actually copes in a particular situation depends on an interaction between habitual coping preference and the situation itself.

Conceptualizing emotional intelligence within a transactional framework

The transactional model indicates how we might conceptualize EI as a causal factor promoting adaptive appraisal and coping (see figure 8.4 below). EI would operate through biasing specific processes or behaviors

Problem focused

Emotion focused

Avoidance

Figure 8.3
Illustrations of task/problem-focused, emotion-focused, and avoidance coping
strategies.

that supported coping with emotional challenge. For example, managing emotions, one of the core abilities contributing to EI, involves understanding one's feelings and managing their expression (Mayer, Salovey & Caruso, 2000; Salovey & Mayer, 1990). Such a construct might be operationalized at several conceptually distinct levels:

• The underlying *processes* which support emotional management, such as labeling somatic sensations, selecting verbal descriptors for emotions and accessing memories of personal emotional experiences

• The *behaviors* that implement emotional management, such as verbally expressing anger or avoiding a perceived threat

• The *outcomes* of instances of emotional management such as the degree of personal harm resulting from the encounter, the person's feelings of satisfaction or dissatisfaction, and physical health problems, which may develop, in the longer-term

It is expected that processes, behaviors, and outcomes are systematically related, but making the conceptual distinctions is important for clear operationalization of constructs, which in turn is required for hypothesis testing. If EI is no more than a redescription of behaviors and/ or outcomes, it is relatively uninteresting. However, the construct may be more important if it describes a systematic influence on processing that leads to more benign behaviors and outcomes.

Figure 8.4 represents a possible conceptualization of EI within a framework suggested by Lazarus and Folkman (1984) transactional model of stress, and Wells and Matthews' (1994) account of self-regulation and emotion. Emotional intelligence is seen here as a quality of the person, i.e., a set of competencies or skills for handling affectively loaded encounters, which might predict future adaptive outcomes. It is assumed that EI competencies are represented in long-term memory, although EI may change through experience and learning. In demanding or challenging environments, EI competencies influence selection and control of coping strategies directed toward the immediate situation. Regulation of coping operates in tandem with self-referent cognitions of the personal significance of events and cognitions of internal stimuli (metacognitions). The consequence of coping is a change in adaptive outcome, which may take various forms, as indicated in figure 8.4. Maladaptation might be signaled by failure to attain a significant goal, subjective distress, acquisition of self-damaging beliefs or behaviors, or health problems.

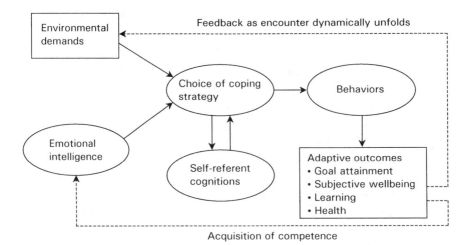

Figure 8.4
A model of the place of emotional intelligence within the transactional model of stress.

This conceptualization of EI assumes that people can be rank-ordered in terms of their personal coping efficacy, and that the rank ordering reflects the underlying competencies described as "emotional intelligence." Such a model might fail in several ways:

Competencies may be independent of each other   If EI represents a coherent psychological construct, then different competencies should be correlated. With respect to stress, the various, distinct mechanisms for adaptive coping should intercorrelate. Thus, individuals who are effective at mood-regulation should also possess a richer and more effective repertoire of coping strategies, and should be adept at handling conflictual relationships and resolving conflicts. As discussed in chapter 3, Gardner (1983), for example, identifies interpersonal and intrapersonal intelligences, and proposes that different measures of these capabilities should be positively correlated, in the same way that cognitive task intercorrelations support the construct of general intelligence. Mayer and Salovey's (1993) conception of EI subsumes these two intelligences, such that interpersonal and intrapersonal skills should correlate with one another. However, competencies identified with EI might not in fact be mutually positively correlated: a ruthless CEO might be highly effective in manipulating others to attain personal goals, but lack empathy, for example. Conceivably, handling emotive situations might be influenced by a variety of unrelated competencies. If so, "EI" (like "stress") might be a useful label for a broad area of inquiry, but the term would not identify a psychologically meaningful construct.

Adaptation may be situation-specific   People with high EI should express it in a variety of situations (see Zeidner & Saklofske, 1996). For example, individuals with good impulse control are able to resist qualitatively different impulses. Again, this is not necessarily the case: an eating disorder patient might be good at resisting all impulses except the desire to eat a lot. Similarly, an empathic individual should be effective in reading the emotions of both friends and foes, and of family and strangers. Situational generality also implies transferability of skills. One of the hallmarks of general intelligence is that cognitive skills are adapted to new problems (Sternberg, 1985): EI should be associated with a similar flexibility of application.

Adaptation may be criterion-specific   High EI is said to convey all manner of benefits: personal fulfillment, popularity, wealth, and moral virtue (Goleman, 1995). However, specific forms of coping might be adaptive with respect to some criteria but maladaptive with respect to others (Zeidner & Saklofske, 1996). Furthermore, attributes of low EI may sometimes bring adaptive benefits. Being carefree may require a certain degree of insensitivity to the problems of others, for example. People may trade off adaptive benefits against one another: smokers and drinkers may believe that enhancement of mood and social functioning more than compensates for health risks: better a short, happy life than a long, miserable one.

The key question raised by this conceptual analysis of EI and stress is whether some master process or processes controls how adaptively the person copes with demanding transactions, and supports emotional intelligence. If so, we must validate two distinct claims. First, we must show that coping strategies can be categorized in terms of how adaptive or maladaptive they are across different situations and outcome criteria. If, in general, no given style of coping is more successful than any other, we cannot describe them as more or less emotionally intelligent. If coping strategies can be rank-ordered in terms of adaptiveness, the second issue is whether individuals can be rank-ordered in terms of use of adaptive strategies. Emotionally intelligent individuals should consistently (though not invariably) use more adaptive strategies in handling a variety of different challenges. The alternative possibilities are that adaptive coping in a given situation depends either on the unique features of the situation itself, or the interaction with a variety of independent competencies (with no common element or coherence). In the remainder of this chapter we will examine the evidence on whether some coping strategies are more effective than others, and on whether some individuals consistently apply those strategies believed to more effective. We conclude with a reassessment of whether research supports the existence of an integrated set of competencies for coping with emotional challenge that generalize across situations and that are unequivocally adaptive.

EI, Coping, and Adaptation to Stressful Encounters

Current psychological writings view coping as an active process, interacting with other factors such as personality and stress management skills (Zeidner & Saklofske, 1996). The transactional model (Lazarus, 1993, 1999; Lazarus & Folkman, 1984) is consistent with a possible conceptualization of EI as an underlying competence supporting adaptive coping. Within the context of coping research, "adaptive" refers to "the effectiveness of coping in improving the adaptational outcome" (Lazarus, 1993, p. 237). Adaptive or functional coping behavior is seen as a buffer, which absorbs the impact of the stressful event and protects the person against immediate, damaging effects of stress, such as physiological disturbance and emotional distress. It also maximizes the chances of rising to the challenge and making the most of any opportunities for personal gain the situation affords. Adaptive coping serves to maintain a positive emotional state and ensures a sense of self-worth and wholeness with one's past and anticipated future. Conversely, maladaptive coping fails to resolve the situation successfully and may even exacerbate personal problems. Dealing with personal problems by risk taking (e.g., high-speed car racing) or substance abuse (e.g., alcohol) are likely to make matters worse.

Deciding on whether particular coping strategies are adaptive or not requires an examination of situational factors (e.g., nature of the stressor, degree, and chronicity), personal factors (e.g., personality and beliefs about coping resources and their effectiveness) and the nature of the adaptational outcome. Next we examine in more detail (1) what is meant by "adaptation," (2) criteria for assessment of adaptiveness, and (3) empirical studies of coping effectiveness.

Conceptualizing adaptation within the transactional model

The theoretical model or paradigm guiding research in the domain of adaptive coping (Folkman, Chesney, McKussick, et al., 1991) mainly determines defining what is an effective way of handling emotions. Psychodynamic models generally assume a hierarchy of coping and defense in which some processes are seen as superior to others. Haan (1977) categorizes ego processes as adaptive or maladaptive depending on their relative freedom from reality distortion, future orientation, and allowance for impulse gratification and expression of affect. In contrast, the transactional stress model focuses on the management of specific demands appraised as taxing or exceeding the person's resources, through cognitive and behavioral efforts (Folkman et al., 1991). The transactional model calls for a contextual definition of effectiveness in handling an emotionally laden situation (i.e., what is said, thought, or done in a specific situation). Thus, *in a given situation*, adaptive coping protects us by eliminating or modifying the conditions that produce stress or by keeping the emotional consequences within manageable bounds (Zeidner & Hammer, 1990).

The use of some strategies may impede rather than promote positive outcomes. Denial and wishful thinking might delay seeking life-saving medical attention for chest pains, and so too might the overuse of information-seeking strategies that serve as a substitute for concrete action (see Lazarus, 1993). In many instances, though, we cannot prejudge particular strategies employed in dealing with managing stressful emotional encounters as being universally adaptive or maladaptive. Rather, the concern must be for whom and under what circumstances a particular mode of coping has adaptive consequences. In more detail, the transactional model conceptualizes relationships between emotionally intelligent behaviors and outcomes, as follows:

Time-course of coping   As a stressful episode evolves and develops over time, there is a continuous interplay between appraisal, coping, and emotional and somatic responses, each fluctuating as the transaction unfolds (Lazarus & Folkman, 1984). Thus, a particular coping strategy may be more effective at one stage of a stressful encounter or in one time period than another (Auerbach, 1989). For example, whereas emotion-focused behaviors might be more adaptive following an exam, active-oriented behaviors would probably be more adaptive prior to the exam, when something could be done to change the outcomes (see Folkman & Lazarus, 1985). In addition, certain strategies found useful in one time period may not be useful in a different period. For example, resigning from a tenured position in academia on account of conflictual encounters with the dean might be a more adaptive coping strategy in time of high institutional demand for academics than in time of high unemployment, when academic positions are scarce.

Reciprocal determinism The naive view of cause and effect is that some external stressor imposes a strain on the person, but this linear causal model is simplistic, because the person's attempts at coping with the stressor influence its future impact. Hence, causal relationships among emotionally intelligent strategies and outcome indices are likely to be multidirectional rather than linear, reflecting dynamic person by situation interactions (Lazarus & Folkman, 1984; compare Endler, 2000). The idea that personal and situational factors mutually influence one another over time is known as *reciprocal determinism* (Bandura, 1986). Indices of effective behaviors, often seen as dependent variables, might also serve as independent variables in a complex process of reciprocal and unfolding transactions over time. Efforts at managing stress should not be confounded with outcomes (Lennon, Dohrenwend, Zautra & Marbach, 1990), but it must also be acknowledged that coping and outcome factors may mutually influence one another as the transaction unfolds over time.

Manifold functions of coping behaviors Each act may have more than one function, depending on the psychological context in which it occurs. Problem-focused strategies, for example, may also regulate emotion as in public speaking training that also decreases stage fright. Similarly, emotion-focused strategies (e.g., humor, relaxation exercises, tranquilizers) can have problem-focused functions if they are effective in decreasing anxiety or other aversive emotions which impedes behavioral functioning (Zeidner, 1998). It follows that current methods in stress research often fail to provide sufficient information. We may find we are comparing people who are not only grappling with different stressors and using different coping strategies, but also using the same behaviors for different purposes. It then becomes impossible to partition outcome variability among person, situation, strategy factors, and the interactions between them. The relevance of this discussion to EI research is that it may well be the specific *function* of the behavior rather than the *act* itself, which indicates whether a strategy may be emotionally intelligent.

Interactions between coping behaviors and other factors   Coping behaviors should interact with situational parameters in impacting upon both adaptive and maladaptive outcomes. For example, avoidance-type behaviors (e.g., wishful thinking, distancing, procrastination) would be ineffective when used by college students who are on probation—they should instead be attending to their study problems. On the other hand, distancing might be an adaptive response for these same individuals when confronted with a negative and unalterable situation, such as a serious illness in the family.

Context of coping: Cultural and social factors   The evaluations of effectiveness of emotional intelligent behaviors must be sensitive to broader social (Weidner & Collins, 1992) and cultural factors (Marsella, DeVos & Hsu, 1985). Preferred coping methods and perceived effectiveness must be appraised relative to a social or cultural group, values, norms, world view, symbols, and orientation. Consider the case of the mother who devotes herself to her ill parents at the expense of her newborn baby. The evaluation of this approach is not merely a scientific but also a moral matter and may differ in traditional versus modern child-centered societies. Evaluating the effectiveness of coping behaviors must be further addressed relative to people's normative response to a particular stressor. Virtually all bereaved persons manifest distress, with depression being a common feature, so that freedom from distress may not signal good coping skills. However, normative standards must be used cautiously when judging behaviors as emotionally intelligent, especially under extremely adverse conditions.

Choice of outcome criteria: What is an adaptive outcome?

Choosing criteria for adaptation is nontrivial, because conclusions about effectiveness of coping varies depending on the choice of the outcome criteria selected (Menaghan, 1982). Coping behaviors are centered and structured around certain goals, issues, and patterns of challenges referred to as "coping tasks" (Cohen & Lazarus, 1979). For example, the tasks of children of divorced parents include acknowledging the marriage breakup, disengagement from parental conflict, coming to terms with multiple losses associated with divorce, and resolving feelings of self-blame and anger (Wallerstein, 1983). Coping generally centers on five main tasks (Cohen & Lazarus, 1979): to reduce harmful environmental conditions and enhance prospects of recovery, to tolerate or adjust to negative events or realities, to maintain a positive self image, to maintain emotional equilibrium and decrease emotional stress, and to maintain a satisfying relationship with the environment. Ideally, successful coping should lead to satisfactory task completion with little additional conflict or residual outcomes while maintaining a positive emotional state (Pearlin & Schooler, 1978). However, there may be no universal criteria for assessing coping effectiveness, thus posing a serious challenge to the notion of emotional intelligence as adaptive coping in action. Indeed, a wide array of outcome criteria have proposed for judging coping effectiveness and problem resolution (Menaghan, 1982; Pearlin & Schooler, 1978; Taylor, 1986). Among the most popular are the following:

Resolution of the conflict or stressful situation   Coping with a problem should be instrumental in alleviating or removing the stressful situation, where possible (Lazarus & Folkman, 1984). This outcome is commonly viewed as the only one that will actually solve the problem for good (more or less) and obviate further investment of coping efforts to deal with the stressful situation.

Reduction of physiological and biochemical reactions   Coping efforts are judged to be successful if they reduce arousal and its indicators (e.g., heart rate, blood pressure, respiration, skin conductivity). Nevertheless, active coping itself appears to be accompanied by physiological changes such as increased catecholamine secretion. In the longer term, effective coping should be associated with better physical health (Steptoe, 1991).

Reduction of psychological distress   Adaptive coping usually involves success in controlling emotional distress, and keeping anxiety within manageable limits. However, as discussed in chapter 4, subjective stress response is multidimensional and changes in distress may be decoupled from changes in worry and in positive engagement with activities (Matthews et al., 1999).

Normative social functioning   Adaptive coping is assessed in relation to normative patterns of social functioning that reflect realistic appraisal of events. Deviation of behavior from socially acceptable norms is often a sign of maladaptive coping, although norms are also open to question, and personal and societal values may differ.

Return to prestress activities   To the extent that people's coping efforts enable them to resume their routine activities, coping may be judged effective. (Substantial life change following a stressful encounter may be a sign of successful rather than unsuccessful coping, particularly if the person's prior living situation was not in some sense ideal.)

Well-being of self and others affected by the situation   Others here include spouses, children, parents, coworkers, friends, and neighbors. Well-being might be expressed as positive affect and positive self-esteem.

Perceived effectiveness   This factor involves the respondents' claims that a particular strategy or approach was helpful to them in some way. Such testimonials, however, may have an uncertain relation to observed effects.

Judgments of the effectiveness of emotionally intelligent behaviors in action should be context-specific and related to the specific encounter. For example, relevant outcome measures of hospital patients undergoing first time coronary bypass surgery might include length of stay in hospital, progress toward walking, and pace of recovery (Carver, Scheier & Pozo, 1992). However, there are no universal criteria for assessing coping effectiveness. Indeed, the resolution of one stressful encounter might even come at the expense of another (e.g., working long hours for professional gain but contributing to marriage breakdown). Adaptation is a complex process that must be viewed as a multivariate construct and judged according to a number of criteria.

Empirical research on coping effectiveness

In spite of recent advances in theory, research, and assessment, the issue of effectiveness of various coping strategies is still open to debate (see Zeidner & Saklofske, 1996). Which coping behaviors are most effective in the short and long term, in which contexts, and for whom are questions that pose a conceptual and empirical puzzle. In fact, some coping styles thought to be adaptive are not necessarily so. The behaviors people use in stressful conditions is often conceptualized in terms of basic categories of coping, such as the task-focused, emotion-focused, and avoidance strategies previously described. There follows a brief description of research on the effectiveness of these three types of coping.

Theorists have frequently emphasized the positive effects of problem-focused strategies and negative effects of emotion-focused coping on psychological outcomes, especially when the threatening situation can be ameliorated by the individual's responses (Lazarus & Folkman, 1984). While emotion-focused behavior or avoidance may help in maintaining emotional balance, an adaptive response to remediable situations still requires problem-solving activities to manage the threat. Active behaviors are preferred by most persons and are perceived as highly effective in stress reduction (Gal & Lazarus, 1975). Active behaviors provide a sense of mastery over the stressor, divert attention from the problem, and discharge energy following exposure to threat. Active, task-focused coping relates to maintenance of task engagement in performance situations (Matthews, Derryberry et al., 2000).

Non-problem-solving strategies, such as avoidance, are increasingly used when the source of stress is unclear, there is a lack of knowledge about stress modification, or there is little one can do to eliminate stress (Pearlin & Schooler, 1978). The research evidence on the adaptiveness of avoidance behaviors is mixed. On one hand, there is a wealth of data to indicate that avoidance, in general, is positively tied to concurrent distress and may have negative consequences (Aldwin & Revenson, 1987; Billings & Moos, 1984). A review of the literature (Zeidner & Saklofske, 1996) suggested that avoidance types of coping (e.g., wishful thinking, escapism, overt effort to deny, and self distraction and mental disengagement) typically work against people rather than to their advantage. Avoidance is related to impairments of objective performance (Matthews & Campbell, 1998). On the other hand, cognitive avoidance may be an effective way to cope with short-term stressors like noise, pain, and uncomfortable medical procedures (Suls & Fletcher, 1985). Avoidance may give the person a psychological breather and an opportunity to escape from the constant pressures of the stressful situation (Carver et al., 1992). Roger, Jarvis, and Najarian (1993) claim benefits for "detached coping," which addresses the problem without the person feeling personally involved or threatened. Pearlin and Schooler (1978) found that distancing strategies were most successful for dealing with stressful impersonal situations. Furthermore, the adaptiveness of avoidance or distancing strategies may vary with specific stages of the stressful encounter. For example, for a cardiac patient, distancing may be extremely maladaptive at the early stages of the disease, when self-regulatory behaviors (diet, low salt intake, and exercise) would be most helpful, or at the stage of postoperation rehabilitation. However, distancing is adaptive immediately after cardiac surgery, where little can be done to alter the situation. Conversely, strategies by which individuals remained committed and engaged with relevant others were most successful in reducing emotional distress in more personal situations.

Some strategies appear to be inherently maladaptive in managing stress. While alcohol and drugs may provide immediate relief, ultimately the person will become worse off. Factor-analytic studies suggest a cluster of theoretically adaptive strategies: active coping, planning, suppression of competing activities, restraint coping, positive reinforcement, seeking social support, and positive reappraisal. The second cluster included denial, behavioral disengagement, focus on emotions, and alcoholism (Carver, Scheier & Weintraub, 1989). However, while some research supports the relationship between active coping and well-being (Aldwin & Revenson, 1987; Aspinwall & Taylor, 1992), the opposite effect has been reported with a focal stressor (Bolger, 1990; Mattlin, Wethington & Kessler, 1990).

Similarly, some research suggests that emotion-focused coping is maladaptive and increases stress (Folkman, Lazarus, Gruen & DeLongis, 1986). For example, habitual emotion-focused coping relates to mental disturbance, such as anxiety and somatic symptoms, and situational emotion-focused coping relates to increased emotional distress and worry (Matthews, Derryberry, et al., 2000; Matthews, Schwean, et al., 2000; see also chapter 4). There is something of a paradox in that, although the message of research on EI is that attention to emotions is important, emotion-focused coping often seems to heighten distress. On the other hand, circumstances exist in which emotion-focused strategies may be beneficial (Baum, Fleming & Singer, 1983). For instance, though keeping emotional distress within manageable bounds may reflect good adjustment, research shows that some individuals (e.g., cancer patients, spinal cord injuries) are better off, in the long run, expressing their emotions initially rather than acting restrained (Wortman, 1983). Baum, Fleming, and Singer (1983) reported that emotion-focused behaviors were adaptive in dealing with technological disaster because it increased the sense of perceived control.

Emotion-focused coping may be too broad and heterogeneous a construct to characterize the inner-directed strategies that people use to cope with stress. Emotion-focused strategies include both negatively toned strategies, such as self-blame, and strategies that, superficially, would appear beneficial such as coming to terms with an event or reappraising it as a learning experience. Endler and Parker's (1999) emotion-focused coping scale relates more to self-blame than to positive reappraisal, and several studies suggest that this style of coping relates to negative outcomes (Deary, Blenkin, Agius, et al., 1996). For example, Morgan, Matthews, and Winton (1996) found that flood victims with high scores on the Endler and Parker (1999) emotion-focus scale tended to report high levels of trauma symptoms, even with appraised severity of the flood event statistically controlled. Matthews et al. (2000) suggest that emotion-focused strategies may be functionally distinguished in terms of their intended aims. They make conceptual distinctions between *palliative* coping, intended to reduce immediate negative feelings, *self-transformation*, which aims to produce long-lasting changes in attitudes towards the problem, and *ruminative problem-solving*, which is intended to review exhaustively the personal significance of the problem. Ruminative strategies tend to backfire by generating protracted worry states, which are often maladaptive (Matthews & Wells, in press).

As discussed above, Salovey et al. (1999) claim that maladaptive coping may be a consequence of difficulties in processing emotional material, i.e., low EI. For example, rumination may be a consequence of inability to make sense of one's emotional experience. Conversely, clarity of thought and experience seems to promote well-being and active regulation of mood. Emotional disclosure and availing oneself of social support may promote adaptive self-transformation (e.g., Pennebaker, 1997). The link between problems with handling emotion and ineffective coping is supported by work on alexithymia, a personal quality associated with difficulties in describing and identifying feelings (see chapter 10). Alexithymia relates both to low EI, measured with the Bar-On scale, and to a probably maladaptive pattern of coping: low problem-focus and high emotion-focus and avoidance/distraction (Parker, Taylor & Bagby, 1998). However, direct links between EI and specific forms of effective coping have not yet been systematically demonstrated by EI researchers.

Some tentative generalizations about adaptive emotionally intelligent behaviors

Few unequivocal principles have been uncovered in three decades of coping, but we now put forward some tentative generalizations about adaptive behaviors gleaned from the coping literature (also see Lazarus' 1993 review on coping research).

Strategies work with modest effects, sometimes, with some people   Some kinds of responses to some kinds of situations and exigencies do make a difference. However, the magnitude of such differences are frequently disappointing (Pearlin, 1991), offering little justification for the power of coping in the stress outcome process. Methodological difficulties and weaknesses may account for some of these findings, which are less than robust.

Responses are not uniformly adaptive   The results of a given coping style are determined by the interaction of personal needs and preferences and by the constraints of the current situation. Adaptive coping requires a good fit between the person-environment transaction, the person's appraisal of the transaction, and the consequent coping behavior (Lazarus & Folkman, 1984; Lazarus, 1993). Hence, strategies often viewed as maladaptive (e.g., avoidance, distancing) may be adaptive under some circumstances and vice versa. Problem-focused coping is more adaptive in situations viewed as changeable whereas emotion-focused is best used in unalterable situations (Lazarus & Folkman, 1984; compare Endler, Speer, Johnson & Flett, 2000). Emotionally intelligent behaviors must also be matched to appraisals of control and personal factors (e.g., values, goals, and beliefs), and to choosing whether to stay with or abandon goals depending on circumstances.

Adaptive strategies vary between and within individuals   Task focused efforts (e.g., studying) may be activated by certain individuals upon announcement of an exam. Others procrastinate or complain about the course or instructor, yet they may use adaptive methods to manage other stressors. Person-situation interactions also occur: for example, one student uses problem-focused strategies with little skill and is less successful than another, who uses emotion-focused coping to alleviate anxiety.

Adaptive behaviors involve a flexible repertoire and combined use of coping strategies   People tend to employ both emotion- and problem-focused coping in managing most stressful events. This would appear to be functional for it allows for both the regulation of emotion and management of the stressor (Lazarus & Folkman, 1984). For example, theft of a personal possession may certainly cause anger and one may vent this in conversation with friends, while hoping for the worst to befall the culprit. At the same time, it would seem judicious report the theft to police, call the insurance company for compensation, and increase security. A large repertoire of coping resources, and flexibility and creativity in their use, may increase coping adaptiveness. A number of studies (see Mattlin et al., 1990; Pearlin & Schooler, 1978; Wethington & Kessler, 1991) suggest that having a versatile coping profile is associated with good adjustment, though the effects are rather modest. While greater flexibility may relate to better emotional adjustment (Mattlin et al., 1990), multiple coping reactions within a given period may reflect ineffective coping (Carver, Pozo, Harris, et al., 1993), because this would indicate that initial coping efforts were not effective in effectively reducing or circumventing the stressful situation.

Emotionally intelligent responses may influence some but not other outcomes
A particular behavior may differentially influence various outcomes (Silver & Wortman, 1980). Various indices are not highly correlated. Further, each coping strategy has both its benefits and costs. For example, denying the seriousness of a partner's illness may reduce emotional distress but also negatively affect the care given to the spouse.

Adaptiveness of particular strategies may vary across various phases of a stressful encounter   The relevance and effectiveness of a particular reaction to a stressful encounter varies with the phase of the stressful transaction. Denial may interfere with the early detection and treatment of breast cancer. Following diagnosis, denial of one's emotional reaction or the life threatening implications of the disease may have very different effects (Carver, Pozo, Harris, et al., 1993). Avoidance strategies may be effective for short-term stressors but nonavoidant strategies are effective for long-term stressors (Suls & Fletcher, 1985). A response positively associated with short-term well-being (e.g., maintaining hope that a husband missing in action will be found) may be negatively associated with well-being if it persists for a number of years. Continued life stressors may themselves wear down the individual and lead to the use of less effective strategies under continued stress (Aldwin & Revenson, 1987). Coping may be less effective among people exposed to a chronic difficulty than to acute stressors (see Wethington & Kessler, 1991). Thus, the power of specific strategies to promote adjustment may become weaker as stress continues. Furthermore, some situations may be so intractable that endurance is more efficacious than action.

Coping with emotional reactions may be maladaptive   The emotions provoked in oneself and others by problematic encounters may hinder adaptive coping. Difficulties in understanding emotions may elicit maladaptive rumination (Salovey et al., 1999), and emotions may prime inappropriate action tendencies, such as aggression in the case of anger (Lazarus, 1991). We might then attribute maladaptive coping to low EI, to the extent that it reflects difficulties in processing and regulating emotions. However, it is not established that difficulties in dealing with emotions are central to maladaptive coping, as opposed to being one of various contributory factors, or even a symptom rather than a cause. Rumination may be a consequence of faulty metacognitions and attention to self-referent cognitions (Wells & Matthews, 1994), rather than a direct response to emotional confusion. If a person has good problem-solving skills, unruly emotions may simply be a minor irritant, which dissipate when effective task-focused coping resolves the encounter favorably.

Coping and Self-Regulative Processes

Influences on coping: Appraisal and knowledge

Thus far, we have seen that adaptive and maladaptive coping strategies can sometimes be distinguished, in the qualified sense discussed previously. Choice of a coping strategy does not just happen of its own accord: antecedent processes and knowledge structures determine strategy selection (Matthews & Wells, 1996). These issues are addressed most directly by research on *self-regulation* (Boekaerts, Pintrich & Zeidner, 2000), following on Carver and Scheier's (1981, 2000b) pioneering cybernetic (control-theory) model, within which discrepancies between actual and preferred self-state initiate coping efforts intended to restore homeostasis, as discussed in chapter 7.

So far, the self-regulative analysis only regresses the problem one stage further back. If appraisal is a primary determinant of coping, what determines appraisal? Primary appraisal reflects multiple information-processing mechanisms within the cognitive architecture. Broadly, we can distinguish lower-level and upper-level processes in appraisal, although some authors make further subdivisions (see van Reekum & Scherer, 1997). Lower-level evaluation is bottom-up or stimulus-driven, with the result that the stimulus is evaluated with little conscious effort. Affective information is automatically processed at an early, preattentive stage of processing (Kitayama, 1997), which establishes an initial, coarse representation of stimulus significance, which feeds into subsequent attention-demanding processing. Upper-level evaluation is top-down or conceptually driven and requires controlled processing of propositions accessed from long-term memory (van Reekum & Scherer, 1997). Typically, it is intimately related to self-regulation and secondary appraisal. The Self-Referent Executive Function (S-REF) model of Wells and Matthews (1994), discussed in chapters 4 and 7, identifies this level of processing as the principal determinant of subjective stress reactions, including emotion—a position supported by the data presented in the last chapter showing that situational appraisal and coping are powerful predictors of subjective state (Matthews, Derryberry, et al., 2000). Controlled processing of stimulus significance and coping is driven by self-knowledge in long-term memory, represented as generic procedures for stimulus interpretation and action. Controlled processing compiles routines for coping that fit the immediate situation. Thus, the knowledge-level constructs of appraisal and coping are supported by various discrete information-processing mechanisms.

Sources of effective coping

As noted before (chapter 2), coping may be conceptualized both in terms of these symbol-manipulation routines, that encode demands and compute a response, and in terms of higher-level self-knowledge. Both information-processing and knowledge-level analyses suggest sources of effective and ineffective coping. Hence, coping is a complex outcome of multiple levels of appraisal and proceduralized self-knowledge. It follows that there are multiple sources of coping effectiveness, and so maladaptive coping may have various sources:

• Lower-level processing tends to misinterpret the personal significance of events. Anxiety disorders may be driven by oversensitivity in automatic threat evaluation, although the evidence is conflicting (Matthews & Wells, 1999). In addition, personal experience may lead to over-learned appraisals, which become maladaptive, as when a combat veteran misinterprets another person's movements as an immediate threat.

• Controlled processing tends to be error-prone, especially when the person's attention is overloaded. Maladaptive coping may result from misinterpretation of a complex situation, as when a pilot misdiagnoses the source of an unusual instrument reading.

• The normative self-knowledge accessed as the guide to self-regulation may be inappropriate to the situation, as when a person inadvertently transgresses the customs of an unfamiliar culture.

• The person may choose a coping strategy that they lack the skill to implement successfully. Confronting a coworker about a problem may aggravate matters unless the person has adequate social or assertiveness skills.

• The person may choose a potentially successful strategy, but fail to implement it effectively because of processing limitations. In test-anxious individuals, attempts at problem solving may be stymied by an insufficiency of attentional capacity (see Zeidner, 1998).

In summary, success or failure in coping has many sources, related to qualitatively different mental processes and structures. It seems unlikely that EI resides exclusively in any single psychological source. A person may read a situation accurately, but still fail to choose and implement an effective coping strategy. An examination candidate may know exactly what is required, but still lack the test-relevant knowledge or the verbal skills to translate that knowledge into lucid answers. Conversely, advanced behavioral coping skills may be rendered useless by a fundamental misinterpretation of the situation. The Chernobyl power plant operators were highly skilled professionally, but failed to control the nuclear reactor because they misdiagnosed the initial physical problem (Reason, 1987). It follows that there is no single EI process that controls adaptive success, analogous to the "speed of processing" factor that is sometimes (controversially) said to control general intelligence. The better-adapted person must be distinguished from the poorly adapted individual across a number of distinct processes. Processes supporting analysis and regulation of emotions, seen as central to EI (Salovey et al., 1999), might constitute a subset of these processes, but they do not support the totality of adaptation. Even a person in touch with their feelings may fail to cope successfully as a consequence of the various cognitive deficiencies listed above.

Conclusions

Successful coping with stressful encounters is central to any construct of emotional intelligence. Research on stress long predates the coining of the term "emotional intelligence." The area is complex, and no existing model fully integrates the various biological, information-processing, and self-regulative connotations of the term. However, the transactional model captures something of the underlying cognitive processes that control how demanding situations are evaluated and how the person chooses to cope with perceived demands. Unfortunately, this existing stress research does not clearly support the existence of any psychologically meaningful EI construct. Models such as that of Lazarus (1991, 1993) suggest that we can try to describe the differences between the emotionally intelligent and unintelligent in terms of high-level self-regulative processes of appraisal and coping. The process characteristics of the high-EI person should consistently promote unequivocally successful outcomes across a range of different encounters. Very approximately, successful adaptation follows from appraising oneself as competent and self-efficacious, coping through problem focus rather than emotion focus, and minimizing bouts of self-blame and ruminative worry. However, this view of EI, as a patterning of cognitive stress processes, had considerable disadvantages, since describing cognitive-stress responses in this way outweigh the advantages. It is often difficult to distinguish adaptive and maladaptive coping, in that adaptiveness is highly dependent on the criterion adopted and the situation of interest. Strategies that work in one context may fail in another, and often a strategy produces a complex mixture of outcomes operating over different time scales. Adaptive outcome is a multivariate quantity that can only be reduced to a positive or negative way at the cost of a gross oversimplification.

We saw also that deciding whether specific outcomes are beneficial or not may often be a question of personal and societal values, rather than a scientific issue. To take an extreme example, current debates over euthanasia ask whether it is better to "cope" with terminal illness through a painless death or through prolonging life despite pain and suffering. Weighing up the costs and benefits of each alternative depends almost entirely on moral judgments and ethical or religious principles. Science can provide relevant data, such as the level of cognitive functioning compatible with severe pain, but it has no criteria for making the decision. On a smaller scale, everyday life routinely throws up dilemmas concerning how we should balance our interests against those of other people, how we should balance immediate pleasure against long-term gain, and how we should balance challenge and risk against maintaining security. The value-laden nature of criteria for coping and adaptation places some constraints on any science of emotional intelligence. In principle, we might evaluate outcomes of coping against measurable criteria such as self-reported happiness, marital satisfaction, mental health, and so forth, and search for consistent individual differences in outcome. However, such an exercise addresses personal fulfillment only indirectly. Apparently, negative outcomes might be seen as the necessary price for growth, as represented by the Judeo-Christian tradition that values poverty and suffering as a path towards spiritual development.

Hence, as a science, the study of EI may potentially make statements about how individuals stack up against specific criteria. However, there is no scientific basis for making value judgments about individuals and their overall level of adaptation (with the probable exception of the maladaptiveness of mental disorder, as discussed in chapter 10). Goleman's (1995) book appears to have a subtext that promotes certain values such as emotional openness, interpersonal cooperation and commitment to civic and moral values. These are all fine qualities, but they reflect cultural norms rather than scientific principles. Those with an ethical agenda should promote it honestly, rather than disguising values as science. If, like James Dean, people choose to reject such values, we may from our particular sociocultural standpoint, find them morally deficient, but to label them as emotionally unintelligent is to confuse issues of morality with science.

At the process level, empirical studies suggest a highly differentiated view of individual differences in adaptation, which is not commensurate with the EI construct in any simple way. The various cognitive stress processes for appraisal and coping are intercorrelated, but they appear to form several distinct clusters independently related to stress outcomes. For example, it appears that the person's level of broadly adaptive cognitions (e.g., task focus) is a poor predictor of broadly maladaptive cognitions (e.g., self-critical emotion focus). Even if, rather crudely, we label processes as "adaptive" or "maladaptive," studies of individual differences fail to distinguish clearly between more or less adapted persons. Furthermore, coping seen as a knowledge-level construct is underpinned by multiple processes, operating at different levels of the cognitive architecture, which feed into adaptive outcome. When coping fails, it may either reflect architectural constraints such as insufficient attentional capacity, lack of acquired skill to handle a situation, or knowledge-level misconceptions such as under- or overestimation of personal capabilities. Grouping these sources of adaptive failure together may lack theoretical coherence. On the other hand, personality traits that relate to EI appear to relate to adaptive processes at different levels. Indeed, in the next chapter, we look at whether traits such as neuroticism can be reconceptualized in adaptive terms.

Hence, although there is only limited evidence, it seems that the EI hypothesis fails to engage with two critical aspects of stress reactions. First, *stress outcomes are often more qualitative than quantitative*. Typically, encounters may provoke a pattern of costs and benefits rather than an unequivocally positive or negative outcome. Even apparently successful coping may have costs such as loss of behavioral flexibility, fatigue, and resource depletion (Lepore & Evans, 1996). Adaptation is a multifaceted construct that may be construed differently depending on the particular situation and the criteria used for assessment of outcome. Second, *there is no single master process for stress-regulation*, and hence for emotional intelligence. Instead, the stress process is *distributed* across a diversity of functionally distinct cognitive processes. These include both processes for mood regulation, which presumably operate meta-cognitively on representations or codes for the person's appraisals of their own mood, and wider appraisal and coping processes, which might be directed toward external events and internal cognitions. It is unclear from the work of Mayer and Salovey whether they wish to restrict EI to being a property of the former or whether EI also embraces processes with a more indirect influence on emotion (Salovey et al., 1999). The scanty empirical evidence available suggests that EI scales may relate, modestly, to some of these processes, but identifying EI with some generalized coping faculty is not likely to be helpful.

In sum, notwithstanding claims of the important role EI plays in the coping process (Goleman, 1995; Salovey et al., 1999), there is presently very little empirical research on which to base firm generalizations on the role of EI in adaptive coping. Adaptation to stress seems to be dependent on several independent competencies rather than a single, underlying competence, and it should be conceptualized as a multi-variate outcome. There is little evidence from stress research to suggest that individuals without major problems in living can be differentiated on an emotional intelligence continuum. Future research would greatly benefit from empirical research on the relationship between EI and coping in general and under various environmental conditions (controllable versus uncontrollable, highly stressful versus moderately stressful, etc). Furthermore, many of the mediating factors purported to serve as causal links in the EI-coping relationship (e.g., social support, emotion disclosure, etc.) have not been empirically vindicated. Thus, systematic examination of the purported causal role of various mediating factors in the EI-coping relationship is sorely needed. A unified conceptual approach is needed for understanding the potential roles of EI in predicting an individual's responses to stress, coping behaviors, and adaptive outcomes.

9

Personality, Emotion, and Adaptation

To enjoy the things we ought and to hate the things we ought has the greatest bearing on excellence of character.
Aristotle, Nichomachean Ethics

In this chapter we turn to the role of personality factors in adaptation to the demands and challenges of real life. As in previous chapters, "adaptation" refers to the processes and strategies supporting pursuit of personal goals in a changing external environment. Previously, we have seen that mixed models of EI conceptualize EI as comprising elements of both effectiveness of adaptation (ability) and qualitative style of handling challenging encounters (personality). In this chapter we focus on EI as a personality trait, or collection of traits, as operationalized by instruments such as Bar-On's (1997) EQ-i and the Schutte et al. (1998) SSRI. The central issue is whether the styles of behavior associated with EI traits in fact confer some overall adaptive advantage in managing emotional encounters, i.e., that traits in fact function like abilities. Bar-On (2000), for example, explicitly links EI traits to social and emotional competence.

Empirically, there is often considerable overlap between personality and EI measures. Indeed, most of the variation in Bar-On's (1997) EQ-i measure is explained by existing personality traits, such as the Big Five (Dawda & Hart, 2000) and anxiety (Newsome et al., 2000). In chapter 5 we discussed the psychometric status and construct validity of questionnaire-based EI measures, concluding that they offered little that is new with respect to existing, and much more extensively validated, personality dimensions. Furthermore, the nature of structural relationships between EI traits and established personality dimensions has been neglected. It is unclear how EI and personality traits might be placed in a multistratum model of the kind common in ability research (see chapter 3). Petrides and Furnham (in press) argue that EI is a distinct primary trait that contributes to several broader traits such as those of the Five Factor Model (FFM). Conversely, EI might be seen as superordinate to dimensions such as the Big Five, as a kind of distillation of their positive attributes. In this chapter we put these important psychometric issues aside in order to explore the theoretical possibility that EI provides a new way of conceptualizing existing personality constructs. Perhaps personality theory requires a stronger focus on the role of traits in adaptive emotional functioning, supported by the cognitive stress processes discussed in the previous chapter. We examine these claims in this chapter.

Bar-On (2000) claims that emotional and social intelligence is a multifactorial array of interrelated emotional, personal, and social abilities that influence overall ability to cope actively and effectively with daily demands and pressures. It follows that the various personality traits correlated with Bar-On's EQ construct must contribute to this hypothetical overall ability. Two further issues arise. First, Bar-On is really saying that the personality dimensions related to EI have abilitylike aspects that are neglected by current differential psychology that separates personality and ability into separate domains (Zeidner & Matthews, 2000). This perspective has at least some plausibility. For example, EQ is strongly correlated with low neuroticism, which relates to hardiness during stressful encounters and resistance to clinical anxiety and depression (Eysenck & Eysenck, 1985). Perhaps we can say that neuroticism represents poor adaptation to threatening encounters, and so it should be reconceptualized as an aspect of (low) EI. However, we cannot accept this view simply on the basis of the gross characteristics of neuroticism; vulnerability to negative emotion is not synonymous with behavioral or social maladaptation. Hence, this chapter will examine the adaptive status of the personality traits related to EI. Can we really say that low neuroticism and other traits such as agreeableness and conscientiousness are straightforwardly adaptive? Perhaps their advantages are countered by adaptive costs.

A second issue is the extent to which psychometrically distinct traits are unified by commonality of the cognitive stress processes and underlying processing mechanisms discussed in the previous chapter. For example, like low neuroticism, high extraversion is an attribute of EI, but these two personality traits are largely independent from one another (Eysenck & Eysenck, 1985). If, as Eysenck and Eysenck (1985) argue, they relate to separate brain and psychological systems, then there is no basis for linking them to some overarching construct of EI. Both extra-version and emotional stability may be adaptive, but for different reasons, and often in different circumstances. The contrary argument is that there is indeed some correspondence between how extroverts and emotionally stable individuals handle demanding situations. For example, both extraversion and emotional stability (low neuroticism) tend to be associated with more adaptive patterns of coping, although the coping characteristics of the two personality dimensions differ in detail (McCrae & Costa, 1986; Endler & Parker, 1990). Similarly, Matthews, Schwean, et al. (2000) point out that both anxiety and aggressiveness are associated with distortions in cognitive appraisal, although the two dispositions relate to appraisals of personal threat and to appraisals of hostile intent in other people, respectively. Goleman (1995) considers self-control a master aptitude for EI, so perhaps we could relate the various personality dimensions to different aspects of self-control or self-regulation. Hence, this chapter will also address the basis for personality traits in styles of appraisal, coping, and self-regulation that may have common elements across different traits that are central to EI.

Questionnaire-based research on EI differs from orthodox personality theory in positing a factor that links personality constructs that are usually sharply separated. Emotional intelligence is considered to comprise such subfactors as the 15 measured by the EQ-i (Bar-On, 1997), although, as discussed in chapter 5, many of these subfactors seem too poorly differentiated in the EQ-i. The Schutte et al. (1998) instrument, although less extensively validated, is also multifactorial, although, again, the factors proposed by the test developers may not entirely correspond with those obtained empirically (Petrides & Furnham, 2000b). Thus we may distinguish different areas of personality functioning through which emotional competence may be expressed, such as stress tolerance and interpersonal sensitivity. In comparing the EI construct with established personality dimensions, we will look at four areas that conceptually appear somewhat distinct and have been related to both EI and standard personality dimensions.

"Negative emotionality" refers to vulnerability to feelings of anxiety, depression, and anger, especially in stressful circumstances. All writers on EI, including Goleman (1995), consider that high EI is protective against stress and strong negative emotion. Bar-On's (1997) model of EI refers to three composites that relate directly to negative emotion—general mood, stress management, and adaptation—which, as discussed in chapter 5, might indeed relate to a common self-esteem factor. In conventional personality psychology, neuroticism (N) is seen as the primary driver of susceptibility to negative emotion and stress vulnerability (e.g., Meyer & Shack, 1989; Matthews & Deary, 1998). Should we then reconceptualize N as low EI? We will look at the adaptive basis for N and the processes that support vulnerability to negative emotion, focusing especially on the stress and self-regulative processes discussed in the last chapter. Other Big Five dimensions, such as introversion, may make smaller contributions to negative mood (Matthews et al., 1999; Watson & Clark, 1992).

Another defining feature of EI is effective functioning in social situations. It may be important to distinguish *social competence*, in the sense of social skills and achievement of personal goals, from *prosocial behavior*, in the sense of being motivated to help others. Individuals with a Machiavellian personality (Fehr, Samson & Paulhus, 1992) are socially competent but not prosocial, in that they succeed by manipulating others. Conversely, a person might be well meaning but socially inept, like Charlie Brown in the *Peanuts* cartoon. Similarly, dominance and nurturance appear to be two independent aspects of personality in interpersonal settings (Wiggins & Trapnell, 1990). Social competence is poorly defined in Bar-On's (1997) scheme. The two most relevant subscales are assertiveness, which is classified as an intrapersonal scale (rather oddly, given that one normally asserts oneself toward other people), and problem solving, which is part of adaptation. Social skills emerged as a distinct factor in Schutte et al.'s (1998) SSRI in both independent studies of the scale (Petrides & Furnham, 2000b; Saklofske et al., submitted). Within the Five Factor Model (FFM) of personality, two dimensions stand out as predictors of social competence. Extraversion relates to qualities of self-confidence in social settings, assertiveness, and social involvement, whereas conscientiousness refers to systematic, organized efforts to succeed. Neuroticism tends to relate to lower self-appraisal of social competence and difficulties in social interaction, but we will deal with neuroticism primarily under the heading of negative emotion.

Prosocial behavior is represented in Bar-On's model by the three interpersonal subscales which appear to form a distinct sub-factor: empathy, (mutually satisfying) interpersonal relationships, and social responsibility. This element of EI is not featured strongly in the SSRI, which is only trivially correlated with agreeableness (Saklofske et al., submitted). In the FFM, agreeableness is the strongest predictor of prosocial behavior, in the form of altruism, trust, cooperation and tendermindedness, but some aspects of conscientiousness, such as orderliness are also relevant. At the opposite end of the spectrum, antisocial behavior might relate both to the cold selfishness associated with low agreeableness, and to more actively hostile and aggressive behavior.

The final area on which we will focus is *self-control*, identified by Goleman (1995) as a master aptitude for EI. This has been most studied through its absence, in the form of poor self-control, expressed as impulsivity and deviant behaviors, including criminality. It also includes poor mental self-control, expressed as delusional or bizarre beliefs. Self-control does not correspond clearly to any of the SSRI factors or the Bar-On composites: the closest EQ-i sub-scales are independence (self-directed, self-controlled thinking), which is an intrapersonal scale, reality testing (part of adaptation), and impulse control, which is part of stress management. In existing personality studies, lack of self-control may be approached both as an aspect of normal personality (primarily, low conscientiousness), and as an aspect of personality disorder (see chapter 10). Eysenck and Eysenck's (1977) psychoticism dimension combines elements of deviance and impulsivity with indifference to others' feelings. Marvin Zuckerman et al. (1991) identified as a major element of normal personality a dimension they rather inelegantly termed "P-ImpUSS," indicating psychopathy-impulsive unsocialized sensation seeking.

The remainder of the chapter is structured as follows. First, we outline a general conceptualization of personality and adaptation that relates the various expressions of personality to preparedness for acquiring skills needed for different environments and contexts (Matthews, 1999; Matthews, Schwean, et al., 2000). Next, we use this cognitive-adaptive framework as the basis for reviewing, in turn, the adaptive significance and psychological bases for traits related to the four areas of functioning just described.

Throughout, we focus primarily on the traits of the Five Factor Model (FFM), with some reference to narrower traits of particular relevance to EI, such as empathy. In reviewing evidence on traits, we will take a broad-brush approach, grouping together related traits such as anxiety, depression, and neuroticism, for example, although a more complete account would acknowledge important differences between related (but distinct) constructs. One FFM trait we are forced to neglect is openness, although it correlates moderately with crystallized intelligence (Ackerman & Heggestad, 1997), and McCrae's (2000) conceptual analysis sees it as especially relevant, owing to its place at the intersection of personality and intelligence. However, empirical data have generally shown only small correlations between openness and measures of EI (e.g., Dawda & Hart, 2000; Roberts, Zeidner, et al., 2001). We will conclude with a reassessment of whether major personality traits should be reconceptualized as aspects of EI.

Personality and Emotion: A Cognitive-Adaptive Perspective

This chapter makes use of the cognitive science framework introduced in chapter 2 to evaluate the links between personality traits and adaptation to emotional situations. Typically, a complete account of the various ways in which traits manifest themselves requires all three levels of description. Traits relate to neural functioning, as shown by psychophysiology, to the cognitive architecture, as shown by studies of performance and information processing, and to self-knowledge, as shown by studies of motivation and real-world functioning. The various levels of trait expression are unified in that they support a common adaptive goal (Matthews, 1999; Zeidner & Matthews, 2000). For example, it seems that extraversion-introversion is associated with an adaptation to social challenges (Matthews & Dorn, 1995). Extroverts engage more in social activity and appear to thrive in social settings (Furnham & Heaven, 1999). This adaptation is supported by characteristics of extraversion at different levels of description. Lower cortical arousability in extroverts may confer tolerance of the stress potentially associated with social settings (Matthews & Gilliland, 1999). Information-processing attributes of extraversion, such as enhanced verbal short-term recall and more fluent speech production, are likely to facilitate conversation with others (Matthews, 1997b). Knowledge-level attributes of extraversion such as higher self-esteem and self-efficacy appear to promote social engagement and motivate the acquisition of social skills (Matthews, 1999).

This cognitive-adaptive framework poses several key questions that may elucidate the nature of any trait, including those linked to EI. First, the concept of adaptation implies environments to which the trait is linked. People experience very different environments, making different demands and requiring different coping behaviors on a day-to-day basis. Superficially, we can divide life experience into areas such as work, leisure, and intimate relationships (e.g., Furnham & Heaven, 1999). More profoundly, environments can be differentiated on the basis of their demands on cognition (Matthews & Dorn, 1995). For example, some are characterized by high rates of information input and the risk of overload, whereas others support a lower event rate, placing demands on maintaining motivation and alertness. In the context of EI, the issue is the emotional environments to which a trait is linked. If introversion is maladaptive for handling emotion, which are the settings in which the introvert is disadvantaged?

Second, what are the skills that support adaptation in the environments of interest? The focus on fundamental information-processing models in much contemporary research has tended to divert attention from the critical role of acquired skills in real-world functioning (see Erikson, 1996). In the case of extraversion, Matthews and Dorn (1995) argue that information-processing characteristics such as verbal short-term memory are primarily an indirect rather than a direct influence on social functioning. Processing routines supporting more effective processing of speech provide a platform for acquiring skills for managing conversations with others; these skills appear shaped by culture, social norms, and the context of the conversation. Goleman (1995) is right to suggest that the skills for handling emotional encounters represent learning as well as basic aptitudes. In linking EI to personality traits, the issue is the nature of the skills linked to the trait, and their implications for adaptive success in real-life emotional environments.

Third, how do cognitive and neural architectures support skill acquisition? Traits appear to be associated with packages of stable processing characteristics, i.e., a set of multiple biases in components of the architecture, demonstrated by studies of personality and performance. The partial heritability of traits (Loehlin, 1992) implies that personality differences in cognitive architecture reflect inherited individual differences in neural architecture, presumably modified by early learning. For example, Matthews and Harley (1993) developed neural net models that may explain how extraversion influences processing of semantic content in word-recognition experiments. In other words, depending on personality, people are predisposed toward different strengths and weaknesses in information processing. These processing capabilities will feed forward into acquired expertise. Of course, general intelligence operates similarly as an influence on cognitive skill acquisition (M. Anderson, 1992; Matthews, 1997c) and is of more significance than personality for the development of intellectual skills (see Zeidner & Matthews, 2000). The issue here is how personality may influence the individual's aptitude for acquisition of skills in handling emotional situations.

Fourth, how do knowledge-level self-regulative processes control skill acquisition and execution? Effective handling of emotional encounters depends on both the availability of skills relevant to the adaptive challenge and on the individual's success in applying those skills to immediate needs. Social encounters are typically have no consistent mapping (see Shiffrin & Schneider, 1977): very often there is no fixed relation between stimulus and most adaptive response, and flexibility in response to stimuli depending on context and current personal goals is essential. If somebody insults you, you must process contextual information; if the other person is a notorious joker, then the appropriate response might be to laugh. You must also consider personal motivations; your response to an insult is likely to differ depending on whether you wish to be perceived as relaxed and laid-back, or as someone commanding respect.

More specifically, the issue is one of the transactional stress processes to which the personality trait relates (see previous chapter). Traits appear to relate to styles of appraisal and coping, and, centrally, to the self-regulative goals supported by these processes (Matthews et al., 2000). Individual differences in self-regulation are likely to influence behavior both across and within situations. In the longer term, personal motivations are likely to control interest in and exposure to particular environments, and consequently the level of skill acquired in handling those environments. The greater social skills of extroverts may reflect not just information-processing predispositions, but also the greater learning opportunities afforded by more frequent social involvement. In the short term, self-regulation influences the effectiveness with which skills are implemented; extroverts may perform more effectively in demanding social settings in part because they have coping strategies for managing social pressures that allow them to perform at full competence (Costa, 1996). In the context of EI, the question is whether relevant traits relate to patterns of coping, appraisal, and self-regulation that support the acquisition and expression of skills for handling emotional encounters.

To summarize, the view of adaptation presented here is shown in figure 9.1. It illustrates what Matthews (1999) calls the "adaptive triangle," representing a dynamic interplay between skills, self-regulation and real-world behavior. Skills are built on the foundations provided by neural and cognitive architectures. The preexisting processing attributes associated with a given trait *feedforward* into characteristic skills, which tend to promote both more effective self-regulation, and more effective functioning in the real-life environments linked to the trait (solid arrows). At the same time, there is motivationally driven *feedback* from self-regulation in acquisition and execution of skills, adaptive coping, and in learning

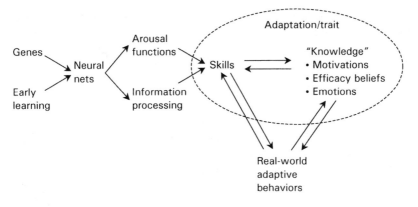

Figure 9.1
Adaptive processes supporting personality traits.

from immediate feedback from real-life performance (broken arrows). In the person successfully adapted to a particular environment, skills, self-regulation, and real-life experience are mutually supportive. In the maladapted person, difficulties at one vertex of the triangle provoke difficulties at the others, leading to a vicious circle of maladaptation, as discussed further in the next chapter. For example, deficiency in social skills may lead to lack of confidence (ineffective self-regulation) and real-life failure, blocking further development of skill (Wells & Matthews, 1994).

This model provides a framework for viewing personality traits through the lens of EI. Each of the areas of functioning identified above defines an environment (or sets of environments) to which certain traits are relevant. We will then look at (1) which traits may be adaptive or maladaptive in those environments, (2) neural and processing support for skill acquisition associated with those traits (feedforward), and (3) styles of self-regulation related to the trait (feedback). In the cases of negative affectivity and social competence, we can draw on large cognitive-psychological research literatures related to neuroticism, extraversion, and allied personality traits, so that quite a detailed picture may be presented. In the cases of prosocial behavior and self-control, individual differences in cognition have been rather neglected, and so the depiction will be sketchier. In all cases, though, we aim to evaluate whether traits, apparently adaptive for handling emotion, are truly so or whether they have hidden adaptive costs. We will also search for general properties of the multiple processes supporting acquisition of adaptive skills that might define "emotional intelligence" as a reconceptualization of personality theory.

Negative Emotionality

There is little doubt that individuals high in neuroticism and related qualities, such as trait anxiety and depression, feel that life is harder for them than those low in neuroticism.[1] At the level of self-reports, N is consistently related to negative moods, life-stress indices, social anxiety, and health problems (Matthews & Deary, 1998), and, overall, to reduced life satisfaction (DeNeve & Cooper, 2000). N correlates highly with dispositional measures of emotion such as trait anxiety and trait depression (e.g., Endler, Denisoff & Rutherford, 1998). Longitudinal studies (e.g., Ormel & Wolfarth, 1991) suggest that N is a causal factor in the future development of stress symptoms. Superficially, such findings suggest that more neurotic individuals are generally maladjusted and low in EI, in the general context of dealing with the negative side of life. However, there are reasons to be cautious about such an interpretation. First, there are two distinct ways in which N may relate to negative emotion. On the one hand, N may confer a general tendency towards negative mood irrespective of circumstances. It seems misleading to label a bias of this kind, perhaps derived from lower-level neural or cognitive functioning as lack of an intelligence. A tendency toward unhappiness does not in itself signal maladaptation, if the person is otherwise able to function effectively in society. On the other hand, N may be related to a more specific vulnerability to negative emotion in demanding circumstances, so that N may be a *moderator* of response to stressors. For example, in a diary study, Bolger and Schilling (1991) showed that more neurotic individuals showed an amplification of distress responses to minor life stressors. If N does relate to deficits in managing stressful environments, it may be reasonable to link this trait to low EI. Bar-On (1997), in fact, has it both ways: EI is said to relate both to general mood, and to stress management and adaptation.

A second difficulty is that high N frequently appears much less harmful at an objective than at a subjective level. The relationship between N and health problems often disappears when illness is evaluated objectively, to the extent that the high-N individual may simply be complaint-prone (Stone & Costa, 1991). Recent work, however, links neuroticism to some psychosomatic disorders (Deary et al., 1995), and to risk of heart disease and cancer (Amelang, 1997). Barrick and Mount (1991) performed a meta-analysis of the many studies that have linked N or similar constructs to job performance. The overall correlation, based on some 11,635 data points, was only −.07, even after correcting the correlation upwards for statistical artifacts. Although neuroticism is positively associated with (subjective) job dissatisfaction and other indices of job strain (see Tokar, Fischer & Subich, 1998, for a review), a neurotic personality does not seem to be a barrier to achievement in the real world. At the same time, carefully targeted studies may show correlations between N and job performance. Neurotic individuals are sometimes disadvantaged in especially stressful occupations such as police work (Cortina et al., 1992). In other circumstances, high N may actually be advantageous. In two studies, Mughal, Walsh, and Wilding (1996) found that high-N insurance salespersons, although experiencing greater distress, actually closed more sales, because they worked longer hours. Neuroticism may sometimes act as a spur to achievement. More neurotic workers also seem to prefer a more structured, settled career, as evidenced by greater career indecision, but greater commitment to working for one organization (Tokar et al., 1998).

One area in which high N does seem genuinely maladaptive is in relations with others. High N individuals experience poorer quality social relationships (Berry, Willingham & Thayer, 2000), and often show exaggerated negative reactions to problematic social encounters (e.g., Suls, Martin & David, 1998). N is highly correlated with social anxiety and shyness, which relate to a variety of behavioral difficulties in social interaction (Jones, Briggs & Smith, 1990). High N also relates to subjective marital dissatisfaction and to the objective likelihood of marital dissolution (Kelly & Conley, 1987).

A third issue is whether evaluations of neuroticism neglect individual differences in the type of situation that elicits negative emotion. Although N is consistently related to negative mood, the strength of the association varies with situational factors. In a diary study, Brandstätter (1994) showed that emotional stability was associated with better mood when the subject was alone or with friends, but not in family settings. To some extent, dispositions to negative affect may be context-specific. For example, there are scales that optimize prediction of negative affect in specialized environments such as test and evaluative settings (see Zeidner's, 1998, review of test anxiety research) and vehicle driving (Matthews, 2001b). Although such contextualized negative-affect measures tend to correlate with neuroticism and general anxiety, they are more predictive of affect and behavior in the context concerned (Dorn & Matthews,

1995). Endler et al. (1991) have discriminated context-specific trait anxiety dimensions related to social evaluation, physical danger, ambiguous situations, and daily routines. These traits appear to predict state anxiety in the situations to which they are matched, although it is also important to take into account how the individual perceives the situation (King & Endler, 1990). Experimental studies suggest that supposedly general trait anxiety may relate primarily to sensitivity to threats to self-worth, especially in social settings (see Eysenck, 1981).

A fourth issue is that neuroticism is associated with a variety of narrower traits with differing adaptive implications. Researchers have tried to develop traits that relate specifically to stress resistance and tolerance, such as hardiness. However, such traits are highly correlated with neuroticism, which may actually mediate these effects (Schaubroeck & Ganster, 1991). Of particular interest are traits that overlap with neuroticism, but may relate more directly to specific self-regulative processes that control the person's handling of threatening or harmful situations, discussed in the previous chapter. Although transactional stress theory defines coping as a situationally contingent process, people seem to have characteristic styles of coping that generalize across situations and are linked to personality (Matthews & Deary, 1998). Another class of trait, relates to self-referent information: either emotional (e.g., alexithymia) or cognitive processes that powerfully impact on emotional experience (e.g., self-focus of attention, optimism-pessimism dispositional worry, metacognition). For example, in experimental studies, optimism-pessimism seems to control the magnitude of negative affective response to stressors (Helton, Dember, Warm & Matthews, 2000).

To summarize, vulnerability to negative affect is influenced both by neuroticism, and by narrower dispositional traits linked to specific contexts and self-regulative processes, which are partially dissociated from N. However, individual differences in affective experience and behavior are dissociable (Eysenck, 1997). Although more neurotic individuals may have comparatively poor life experiences, they can often handle life challenges as effectively as those low in neuroticism. Neuroticism may relate to stress vulnerability within certain challenging environments. The exact nature of such environments requires elucidation, but, loosely, high N seems to be maladaptive primarily when the person faces a threat to self-worth, especially in social settings (Matthews et al., 2000). Conversely, in some work settings, high N may be associated with greater achievement (Mughal et al., 1996). Thus, it is difficult to link N to any general emotional maladaptation; rather, the high N person may be emotionally unintelligent in some settings, but intelligent in others.

Architectural foundations for neuroticism and anxiety

As we have seen, the literature on neuroticism and negative affect in the real-world is somewhat equivocal. A different perspective is provided by the very extensive literature on the relationship between traits for negative affect and performance in experimentally controlled settings. Many studies have investigated trait anxiety (Spielberger, 1972), but the overlap between trait anxiety and neuroticism is sufficiently high that results have general implications for negative affectivity.

The value of experimental studies is that they can systematically explore some of the factors that may moderate associations between negative affect and behavioral outcomes, including environmental stress, motivational pressures, and the cognitive demands of the task performed. Experimental studies build up a fine-grained picture of the behavioral benefits and costs of a particular trait, which informs understanding of the impact of the trait on real-world functioning.

In brief summary, the main features of neuroticism and anxiety traits revealed by these studies are as follows (see Eysenck, 1992; Matthews & Dorn, 1995; Zeidner, 1998, for reviews):

Impairments in attentionally demanding tasks   Anxiety is associated with wide-ranging performance deficits in tasks requiring intensive attention or a high working-memory load. Anxious individuals are more distractible and more vulnerable to performance impairment in stressful circumstances. These effects are generally attributed to states of worry that divert processing resources from the task at hand.

Compensatory motivation   Conversely, anxiety is sometimes linked to superior performance when the task is easy, or when the environment is designed to be reassuring (e.g., Sarason, 1975). Eysenck and Calvo (1992) suggest that anxiety tends to be accompanied by compensatory effort, which maintains processing effectiveness even when processing efficiency is impaired.

Selectivity of attention   Anxious individuals tend to focus attention on potentially threatening information, at the cost of neglecting neutral or positive information sources. For example, anxiety is associated with slower color-naming performance on the emotional Stroop test, and focusing of attention on spatial locations associated with threat (Mathews

& MacLeod, 1991). Conversely (although data are somewhat mixed), neurotic subjects may show enhanced processing of negative information in some paradigms (Rusting & Larsen, 1998).

Bias in judgment and evaluation   Anxiety is associated with a general tendency to make more negative judgments, especially in evaluating self-worth and personal competence, which may contribute to difficulties in social settings (e.g., Kocovski & Endler, 2000). Additionally, studies of negative mood *states* show that, under some circumstances, negative affect is associated with more cautious and more thorough decision-making (Forgas, 1995). Ketelaar and Clore (1997) suggest that negative affect may be adaptive in promoting more extensive analysis of information at hand. Conversely, happy people may be prone to mental laziness in relying on prior beliefs in evaluating stimuli or events.

As already discussed in chapters 4 and 7, performance effects of these kinds may reflect individual differences in both the cognitive architecture and in strategy, i.e., in how the person chooses to use the information-processing routines at their disposal. We saw in chapter 7 that the sources of some of these effects are controversial, for example, whether attentional bias in anxiety reflects sensitivity to threat built into the cognitive architecture or choice of strategy for monitoring for threat (Matthews & Wells, 1999, 2000). The locus of performance effects is an issue of fundamental importance, in that it controls the extent to which processing biases are an integral part of negative affectivity, as opposed to depending more contingently on style of self-regulation. We cannot present definitive answers to such questions here, although, as discussed in chapter 7, empirical studies point towards the role of self-regulative and strategic processes in generating attentional biases (Matthews & Wells, 1999). In general, we suppose that neurotic personality relates both to largely fixed properties of neural and cognitive architecture, and to acquired styles of self-regulation. In the remainder of this subsection, we will review how individual differences in architecture may feed forward in shaping skill acquisition and self-knowledge. In the next subsection, we will look at how self-regulative style may feed back dynamically into adaptation.

The neurological bases for neuroticism and trait anxiety remain something of an enigma. The leading hypotheses are that N relates to arousability of an emotionality circuit linking the limbic system and cortex (Eysenck & Eysenck, 1985), or that anxiety is associated with a septo-hippocampal system controlling behavioral inhibition in response to punishment signals (Gray, 1987; Pickering et al., 1999). However, although the trait shows substantial heritability (Loehlin, 1992), psychophysiological studies have often been disappointing (see Matthews & Gilliland, 1999, for a review), and neither hypothesis has been firmly supported. In contrast to theories that localize N and anxiety primarily in subcortical structures, more recent research has focused on the role that cortical systems may play in moderating motivation (Derryberry & Reed, 1997; Matthews, Derryberry & Siegle, 2000). Derryberry and Reed's studies focus on brain systems for attentional functions, which may be linked to trait anxiety. In experimental studies (e.g., Derryberry & Reed, 1994), trait anxious subjects are slow in a highly specialized function: the disengagement of attention from a location in space at which a threat stimulus has been presented. The disengagement function is linked by neuropsychological and brain-imaging studies to a circuit in parietal cortex (Posner & Raichle, 1994). Another specialized process related to anxiety is focusing on local details rather than on global impression, during threat detection (Derryberry & Reed, 1998), a function that may be supported by left hemisphere posterior cingulate cortex. As discussed in chapter 6, cingulate cortex is implicated in emotion regulation. *Anterior* cingulate participates in a system for voluntary control of attention (Posner & Raichle, 1994). Derryberry and Reed (1997) relate this system also to anxiety, in that anxious subjects appear to be more distractible, although the effect is nullified in those individuals who report good attentional control skills.

Interconnections between cortical and subcortical structures may also be important in neuroticism. Siegle (1999; Siegle & Ingram, 1997) has developed a neural network model of emotional information processing that focused on the rumination or persevering worry characteristic of depressed individuals. Their simulations simulate excessive rumination by (1) increasing feedback between subcortical network units representing emotion information and units representing nonemotional semantic information and (2) varying the strengths of inhibitory pathways implementing cortical control of subcortical networks. Their networks successfully model performance differences between depressives and controls in speed of performance on emotion-processing tasks.

The studies of Derryberry and Siegle are not yet definitive, because the influences of architecture and strategy remain to be discriminated formally. However, they illustrate how the neurological bases of trait anxiety and depression may be distributed across several highly specific brain systems. In part, these aspects of neuroticism may originate in relatively subtle differences in the way in which threatening or negative information is processed. Neuroticism may also affect implicit and explicit memory for emotional information (e.g., Rusting, 1999). These individual differences may in themselves be sufficiently powerful to produce the various surface manifestations of anxiety and depression, such as threat sensitivity and poor stress tolerance in the real world (see Williams et al., 1988). An alternative position is that multiple processing biases affect acquisition of skills for handling threatening and stressful situations, which are the more proximal influence on adaptation. An inbuilt difficulty in disengaging attention from sources of threat may predispose the person to acquire coping skills associated with active search for threat, as discussed in the next section.

Self-regulation

Matthews and Wells (1999) argue that many of the performance characteristics of neuroticism, anxiety and depression derive from individual differences in strategies for handling threat. Broadly, impairments in attention and working memory may be attributed to lack of attentional capacity or resources (e.g., Humphreys & Revelle, 1984). However, in the case of anxiety, there is little evidence for some general shrinkage of the resource pool. Instead, it appears that anxious individuals choose to allocate some part of their resources to processing thoughts and worries, rather than the task at hand (Eysenck, 1992; Zeidner, 1998), so that they become more vulnerable to attentional overload. Why would people choose to perform in this maladaptive fashion? Broadly, the answer relates to individual differences in the self-regulative processes described in chapters 7 and 8. The anxious person appraises threats as being especially salient, and copes through reflecting on the personal consequences of the threat (e.g., Sarason et al., 1995). There is a substantial literature relating anxiety, neuroticism, and depression to the cognitive stress processes discussed in the previous chapter. These personality traits tend to relate enhanced appraisal of threat and to coping through apparently maladaptive strategies such as wishful thinking and self-blame (e.g., Deary et al., 1996; Endler & Parker, 1990). Even with appraisal statistically controlled, neurotic individuals show higher levels of emotion-focused coping (Matthews, Derryberry et al., 2000). In the light of the evidence discussed in chapter 8, we cannot assume that the coping strategies typical of high N are globally maladaptive. However, they do seem to be damaging in potentially threatening performance environments (Matthews, 2001a).

A more fine-grained account of attentional overload is provided by the S-REF model of negative affect (Wells & Matthews, 1994; Matthews, Schwean, et al., 2000) discussed in chapter 7. Neuroticism, or trait anxiety, is associated with negative self-referent beliefs, generic procedures for coping (that incorporate negative beliefs), metacognitions that focus attention on to personal thoughts, and self-protective motivations. Negative self-knowledge increases the likelihood of self-referent executive processing, which initiates often, maladaptive coping activities such as efforts at thought-control, self-criticism, and monitoring for threat. Selection, implementation and regulation of these coping efforts diverts attentional resources from the task at hand, leading to performance impairment on tasks requiring attention or executive control. Next, we will briefly review how the S-REF model links N and allied traits to various key self-regulative functions, including appraisal, coping and metacognition.

Appraisal The negative self-appraisals typical of neuroticism have the disadvantage of activating self-referent processing, and eliciting persevering worry that interferes with attention and social interaction (Wells & Matthews, 1994). On the other hand, negative self-beliefs protect against overconfidence. A link between neuroticism and avoidance of overconfidence is suggested by work on depressive realism, the tendency for depressed individuals to more accurately perceive lack of control and to avoid the overly positive self-serving biases typical of nondepressives (Alloy, Clements & Koenig, 1993). There has been considerable debate over the real-world relevance and explanation for such effects: in line with the self-regulative account of negative affect given here, Alloy et al. (1993) suggest that depression (which correlates highly with N) is associated with control schemata that encode negative expectancies about personal control. The adaptiveness of the control schema is likely to vary with circumstances. For example, Shrauger, Mariano, and Walter (1998) found in a longitudinal study that "dysphoric" (mildly depressed) individuals were better at predicting negative future events, in their everyday lives, but nondysphoric subjects were more accurate at making positive predictions. Anxiety-prone drivers are free from the typical illusion of being superior to other drivers, which has benefits with regard to more cautious behaviors (e.g., fewer speeding citations), but costs with regard to vulnerability about personal competence and distraction from worries (Matthews, 2001b).

Coping   Although attentional bias in anxiety and related conditions is sometimes attributed to a bias in automatic processing (e.g., McNally, 1996), evidence from performance studies suggests that bias is primarily strategic (Richards et al., 1992). For example, bias tends to operate over the relatively long time intervals of greater than 500 ms typical of strategic processing (e.g., Calvo, Eysenck & Castillo, 1997). Wells and Matthews (1994) propose that attentional bias primarily reflects volitional, active monitoring for threat stimuli. The anxious person has learned to cope through scanning for potential threats, and, following detection, engaging in safety behaviors that minimize threat (Wells & Matthews, 1996; Wells, 1997). Mayne (1999) reviews data suggesting that negative emotions are associated with preventive health behaviors, care seeking, and awareness of symptoms, although chronic negative emotion carries risks associated with damaging health behaviors, such as substance abuse and overeating.

Neuroticism and anxiety may also influence task-directed effort: indeed, compensatory effort may serve to offset the detrimental effects on performance of worry (Eysenck & Calvo, 1992). According to Metcalfe (1998), overconfidence in one's performance (cognitive optimism) tends to terminate processing prematurely, before the task has been accomplished successfully. To the extent that high-N individuals show cognitive pessimism, they may be more likely to maintain task-directed effort, especially, perhaps, in low stress settings that encourage overconfidence. In social settings, the elevated levels of threat appraisal and low perceived control shown by more anxious individuals (Matthews, Schwean, et al., 2000) appear detrimental. Thus, self-denigration tends to impede social interaction and the exercise of social skills (Jones et al., 1990), and worry prevents adequate attention to managing social interaction (Wells, 2000). On the other hand, Weary, Marsh, Gleicher, and Edwards (1993) present an intriguing argument that mildly depressed (and likely neurotic) individuals are especially motivated to understand other people, and apply greater effort and attention to processing social information. Presumably, such a strategy is likely to backfire if the social information is negative.

Metacognition and self-awareness   The S-REF model emphasizes the importance of metacognition as a driver of self-referent executive functioning. Some individuals are especially motivated to examine and control their own thoughts (see Wells, 2000, for a review). Attempts at metacognitive control often have detrimental effects in perpetuating negative emotions. Heightened metacognition is a feature of anxiety disorders (Wells, 2000), and attempts to suppress negative thoughts often lead to recurrence of those thoughts subsequently (Wenzlaff & Wegner, 2000). Neuroticism and anxiety are quite substantially correlated with total metacognition, with metaworry (i.e., worry about one's own worry), and with monitoring one's mood (see Matthews, Schwean, et al., 2000, for a review). As further discussed in chapter 10, these metacognitive tendencies encourage maladaptive rumination and may contribute to the link between N and emotional pathology. Beliefs in the importance of scrutinizing one's own thoughts also lead to increased self-awareness, and self-focus of attention, an integral part of the S-REF syndrome. In stressful environments, self-focus tends to direct attention toward discrepancy between preferred and actual self-status, and to maintain ruminative worry and self-criticism, which may be maladaptive (Wells & Matthews, 1994).

Neuroticism correlates especially with public self-consciousness (Fenigstein et al., 1975), awareness of others observing oneself, which predicts a variety of stress process and outcome factors. Dispositionally socially anxious individuals are especially sensitive to being criticized or put down by others (Gilbert & Miles, 2000). A related construct is "interpersonal sensitivity," an aspect of personality characterized by excessive awareness of others (Boyce & Parker, 1989), which relates to depression, impairments in social-problem-solving skills, and low self-esteem (McCabe, Blankstein & Mills, 1999). Intriguingly, psychiatrists, who presumably benefit from an interest in others, tend to be high in neuroticism (Deary, Agius & Sadler, 1996). Generally, metacognitive tendencies appear to contribute to the difficulties high N individuals experience, in coping with threatening situations, especially when the threat is social in nature.

To summarize, figure 9.2 shows a possible adaptive basis for neuroticism and trait anxiety, in terms of the constructs of figure 9.1. More neurotic individuals develop skills in maintaining awareness of danger and personal safety. Concordant with these cognitive and behavioral skills are self-protection motives that serve to maintain a heightened sense of threat, and tendencies towards self-reflection, worry, and excessive metacognition. This self-regulative style has some disadvantages for real-world adaptation. In particular, the negative self-appraisals and emotion focused coping typical of the high-N person tends to be maladaptive under stressful or demanding circumstances calling for immediate action, because worry and self-focused attention interfere with

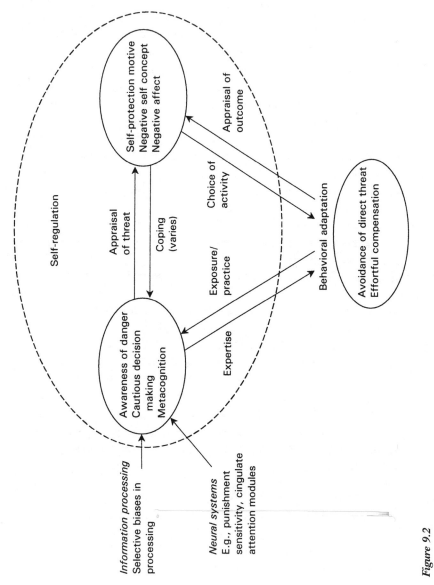

Figure 9.2
Styles of adaptive self-regulation supporting neuroticism and anxiety.

information-processing. However, it also has benefits, including maintenance of effort and task-focus in the absence of overt threat, and avoidance of potentially dangerous encounters. The positive link between N and metacognition conflicts with the view expressed in the EI literature (e.g., Goleman, 1995) that self-awareness is purely benign and contributes to EI. In fact, self-awareness is a double-edged sword. It may well contribute to personal development, but in times of crisis, emotionally intelligent behavior may sometimes reside in decisive, problem-directed action, which is impeded by awareness of the private and public self (Matthews, Mohamed & Lochrie, 1998).

Implications for emotional intelligence

The EQ-i (Bar-On, 1997) correlates between 0.60 and 0.70 with N, and so there is considerable overlap between the constructs. Perhaps N should reconceptualized as low EI in settings associated with threat, harm, and stress. However, the literature reviewed does not support this contention. Objective data suggest that individuals high in N or trait anxiety do not suffer any general life disadvantage with respect to criteria such as occupational success. However, neurotics are impaired in their ability to handle certain kinds of stressful situation, including threatening work and performance environments, and problems in intimate relationships, such as marital discord.

The research findings are somewhat paradoxical, in that N relates to heightened sensitivity to threat and yet high N individuals are often relatively poor at coping with threatening situations. One resolution is to suppose that N is associated with different strategies for dealing with threat. The high N person may be adapted for threat avoidance, through being alert to the early warning signs that a threatening situation is developing. Threat sensitivity may be supported by neural and cognitive systems for attention, and by styles of self-regulative processing that enhance threat detection, such as active monitoring for threat, and ruminating over negative consequences. In some instances, the high N person may cope through reactive aggression, fueled by negative appraisals of others, or through applying compensatory effort to prevent threatening outcomes. Conversely, the low N person is insensitive to threat, but better adapted to handling threatening situations once they develop. This style of adaption is supported by the capacity to maintain task-oriented attention in such situations.

We should be cautious about supposing that one adaptive style is intrinsically superior to another. Measured against societal values, the courage and grace under pressure of the less neurotic person seems more admirable than the avoidance tendencies of the more neurotic person. On the other hand, judged from the standpoint of the individual, walking away from impending trouble may often be more adaptive than facing unnecessary risks. Indeed, in some settings, threat sensitivity is essential.

It has been argued that, in cut-throat business environments, "only the paranoid survive" (Grove, 1996)—an exaggeration, but also a pointer towards the need for vigilance in situations where threats are often subtle or disguised. The costs of a neurotic personality seem to relate more to the detrimental effects of self-referent worry, including, at the extreme, clinical emotion disorders, than to avoidance of threat per se. In addition, there is no rigid link between neuroticism and maladaptive outcomes. Depending on cognitions, the neurotic person may be timorous, confrontational, or dedicated and hardworking. Both neuroticism and emotional stability are potentially maladaptive, but the likelihood of objective negative outcomes depends on environmental and intrapersonal moderating factors. It is true that the potential costs of a neurotic personality, such as mental disorder, are higher than the costs associated with emotional stability, such as complacency. However, it is highly misleading to equate neuroticism with a global maladaptation, and, as such, the trait should not be linked to the lack of EI.

Social Competence and Extraversion

The extraversion-introversion trait appears to overlap with many of the positive aspects of EI: assertiveness, personal warmth, social involvement, and positive emotionality (e.g., Costa & McCrae, 1992). Extroverts appear to experience greater life satisfaction and happiness (Diener, 1984; Furnham & Brewin, 1990). They also tend to be less vulnerable than introverts to stressful events (Amirkhan, Risinger & Swickert, 1995), although neuroticism appears the stronger influence in this domain. Can we then conclude that extroverts are better adapted (than introverts) to social situations and/or to the positive side of life? Should we characterize introverts as socially inept and lacking in EI? In fact, as with neuroticism, the link between extraversion (E) and superior adaptation seems tenuous when scrutinized closely. Again, the picture appears more complicated when we take into account the objective evidence, situational moderators and different facets of extraversion.

Several lines of evidence suggest that the greater happiness exhibited by extroverts is not necessarily reflected in objective indices of superior adaptation. For example, although, at the self-report level, extroverts appear to be more competent in dealing with other people at work (Costa, 1996), the overall (corrected) correlation between E and job performance in the Barrick and Mount (1991) meta-analysis was a paltry 0.10. Extraversion was more strongly related to training proficiency ($r = .26$), suggesting better adaptation to novelty. In fact, it seems that both extroverts and introverts have some strengths and some weaknesses in the workplace (see Furnham, 1992; Furnham & Heaven, 1999, for reviews), well illustrated by Furnham's (e.g., Furnham & Miller, 1997) studies of telephone sales agents. In general, extroverts are rated as better performers at this job, consistent with much evidence linking extraversion to better sales performance (Barrick & Mount, 1991). Furnham, Jackson, and Miller (1999) showed that this effect was linked to learning styles. Introverts tend to be "reflectors"; i.e., they prefer to approach their work methodically and carefully, but they also tend to be indecisive and risk-averse. In sales work, this style of performance is likely to be ineffective, but in other contexts, caution is likely to be more adaptive. For example, among university students, introverts tend to perform better, presumably because at this level, careful systematic study is essential (Goh & Moore, 1978). Furnham and Miller (1997) also found that, among young people, extroverts tend to take more periods of sick leave, a finding the authors attribute to boredom. Extroverts generally have poorer tolerance of monotony at work and a tendency to take nonpermitted absence from work in repetitive jobs (Cooper & Payne, 1967). Overall, occupational studies suggest that extroverts favor jobs that are challenging, fast-paced, and involve social contact, whereas introverts tend to prefer more routine, less socially demanding work. To some extent, these preferences are reflected in objective performance measures.

So far as social functioning outside the workplace is concerned, there is a fairly well-established relationship between extraverted personality, social participation, and positive emotion. The causal basis for positive correlations between these three constructs is unclear, but, plausibly, social engagement is partially responsible for the greater happiness of extroverts. Diary studies show that social activities are among the most powerful influences on positive affect (Clark & Watson, 1988). Furthermore, the association between extraversion and happiness is reduced when social participation is controlled (Argyle & Lu, 1990; Watson & Clark, 1992). The extraversion-happiness link does not appear to be solely socially mediated, however. Extroverts show greater sensitivity to positive mood inductions, for example (Larsen & Ketelaar, 1991; Rusting & Larsen, 1997). In addition, the relationship between extraversion and happiness is situationally moderated. An important diary study (Brandstätter, 1994) showed that the direction and magnitude of associations between extraversion and mood varied across social settings. Extroverts were happier in several contexts, such as socializing outside the home, but introverts actually experienced better moods when working alone.

Certainly, extraversion is associated with some adaptive benefits in social settings, associated with their greater dominance and influence over others. Several studies suggest differences in social skills between extroverts and introverts. For example, extroverts are more likely to initiate conversations with strangers (Argyle, Martin & Crossland, 1989), and extroverts spend more time talking and gesturing than introverts (Levesque & Kenny, 1993). Berry and Sherman Hansen (2000) suggest that extraversion is more strongly linked to verbal than to nonverbal social behaviors; as discussed below, their study suggests that agreeableness is an important predictor of nonverbal behavior. Social introversion is identified in longitudinal studies as a risk factor for clinical depression (Bartlett & Gotlib, 1988). At the same time, extraversion may have costs that balance its adaptive advantages. These include greater involvement in divorce (McCranie & Kahan, 1986), motor-vehicle accidents (Booysen & Erasmus, 1989), and delinquent behaviors (Heaven, 1996). Extroverts report more active and varied sex lives, but also a tendency toward promiscuity, which is likely to increase vulnerability to sexually transmitted diseases (Eysenck, 1976).

The downside of extraversion is often linked to impulsivity and excitement seeking, aspects of personality that we will review in more detail below. Another possible disadvantage is overconfidence, discussed in the previous section. Extraversion also correlates with narcissism, a tendency towards self-centeredness, associated with self-enhancement and egocentrism. Bradlee and Emmons (1992) found that E was the strongest predictor of dispositional narcissism (which also related to lower agreeableness and lower neuroticism). As they point out, narcissism has functional aspects such as self-sufficiency and personal agency, but it also has less desirable aspects such as inflated self-importance, exhibitionism, selfishness, and vanity. Campbell et al. (2000) link narcissism to thought distortions that serve to maintain self-enhancement and poor social relationships due to neglect of the other's needs. Their study suggested that narcissists are prone to maintain self-esteem by taking credit from a partner for a successful outcome. Closely linked to narcissism is trait self-enhancement, which relates to an egotistic style of impression management. Longitudinal and experimental studies show that individuals with this disposition tend to make a good impression initially, but lack social skills and receive progressively worse evaluations from others on repeated acquaintance (Colvin, Block & Funder, 1995; Paulhus, 1998). In the performance context, a sense of personal invulnerability is linked to failures in teamwork and increased probability of error (Helmreich, 2000). Of course, extraversion and narcissism are not the same (the correlation is about 0.40), but it appears that extraversion may sometimes be more advantageous in making first impressions than in more sustained relationships.

Architectural foundations of extraversion-introversion

There are very extensive psychophysiological and experimental literatures that suggest basic processing differences between extroverts and introverts (see Eysenck & Eysenck, 1985; Matthews, 1997b; Matthews & Gilliland, 1999, for reviews). These differences may be summarized as follows. So far as the neural architecture is concerned, there are two major hypotheses. First, extraversion is associated with lower arousability of a reticulo-cortical circuit controlling alertness (Eysenck & Eysenck, 1985; Stelmack, 1990). This hypothesis is supported by psychophysiological evidence that introverts are more readily aroused by external stimulation, and that they condition more readily to weak stimuli. Second, extraversion relates to sensitivity of a brain motivation system controlling behavioral activation in response to reward stimuli. This hypothesis can explain enhanced motor responsiveness of extroverts, their more positive moods, and, in some studies, enhanced learning in reward conditions. Indeed, there is some evidence for enhanced information-processing of positively valent stimuli by extroverts (Rusting & Larsen, 1998). The Matthews and Gilliland (1999) review concluded that both hypotheses have some merit, and extraversion-introversion may be distributed across multiple cortical and subcortical systems. However, they also point out, that, beyond simple conditioning paradigms, neither theory has been very successful in explaining behavioral data. Generally, extravert-introvert differences depend critically on the information-processing demands of the task (Matthews, 1997b), implying that the foundations of the trait are better explained in terms of individual differences in cognitive architecture. In summary, the main performance differences between extroverts and introverts (as groups representing opposite poles of the trait continuum) appear to be as follows:

Superior divided attention   Extroverts tend to be better at dual task-performance, and more resistant to distraction. These effects seem most reliable on tasks requiring verbal or symbol-based processing. It appears that extraversion is not related to overall attentional capacity, in that extroverts' performance advantage does not generalize across the full range of capacity-demanding attentional and working memory tasks (e.g., Matthews, Davies & Holley, 1990). Instead, the performance difference may be linked to superior passive short-term verbal storage (see Eysenck, 1976), or to superior skills in segregating multiple streams of verbally coded information. Extroverts are also faster at retrieving verbal information in semantic and episodic memory (Eysenck, 1981).

Superior language skills   Extroverts show greater speed and fluency of speech production, especially in informal contexts (Dewaele & Furnham, 1999). It is unclear whether this effect reflects an a priori processing advantage, or greater practice of language skills in extroverts.

Poor sustained attention   Extroverts are reliably impaired on tasks requiring sustained detection of infrequent signals (vigilance), although the effect size is moderate (Koelega, 1992). This effect is sometimes attributed to underarousal, but effects of extraversion and arousal on vigilance are distinct (Matthews, Davies & Lees, 1990). The effect may relate both to a specific impairment in sustained attention, and to perceptual abilities. Introverts tend to have lower sensory thresholds in nonstimulating conditions (Shigehisa et al., 1976).

Poorer reflective problem-solving   Several studies of problem solving show that introverts perform better, possibly because extroverts are prone to impulsive exit strategies that lead to premature termination of processing (Weinman, 1987).

Behavioral impulsivity   In some, but not all, reaction time paradigms, extroverts show a pattern of performance characterized by fast but inaccurate response (Brebner & Cooper, 1986). In signal detection studies, they tend to respond on the basis of less perceptual evidence than introverts (low-response criterion) (Koelega, 1992).

Arousal-dependence of performance   During the normal working day, extroverts tend to perform better in states of high arousal, but introverts perform better when low in arousal. This effect is often attributed to a direct effect of arousal on performance, such as the notorious Yerkes-Dodson Law. In fact, the arousal-performance relation appears to be qualitatively different in extroverts and introverts. It is also highly contingent on information-processing; tasks requiring the encoding of easily perceived stimulus attributes are most sensitive to the effect. Matthews and Harley (1993) presented evidence from semantic priming and simulation studies that extraversion and arousal conjointly affect the spreading of activation in a connectionist network. The interaction between extraversion and arousal also reverses in the evening (Revelle, 1993). Matthews and Harley (1993) argue that the time of day effect may have adaptive significance. Introverts appear to be suited to handling low arousal first thing in the morning, but extroverts are adapted to the low arousal of the evening, when social activities such as parties typically take place.

As in the case of neuroticism/anxiety, it is likely that these differences reflect both architecture and strategy. However, to the extent that extroverts and introverts differ in basic information-processing characteristics, the performance data provide some clues to individual differences in social skill acquisition (see Matthews, 1997b, 1999, for reviews). First, several of the characteristics of extraversion may support conversation skills. The extravert may be better than the introvert at retrieving topics of conversation, keeping track of utterances while speaking (i.e., dual tasks), and at speaking rapidly and fluently. Second, extraversion-introversion effects on performance seem to be moderated by temporal characteristics, with extroverts advantaged when speed is more important than accuracy, or when multiple verbal processing operations must be performed. Conversely, introverts perform better when attention must be sustained (vigilance) or when reflective thought is required (problem solving). In general, though, extroverts appear to be suited to rapid action, and introverts to tasks requiring a more cautious approach. Accordingly, military pilots tend to be extraverted, and scientists and writers are more often introverted. Third, extroverts appear to be more attentive than introverts in arousing conditions, commensurate with other evidence that extroverts are better equipped to handle stimulating environments, whereas introverts are adapted to monotony. However, as just discussed, reversal of the effect in the evening suggests that it may relate to a circadian adaptation.

Self-regulation and extraversion

In addition to feedforward from processing, extroverts and introverts differ in the self-knowledge they apply to adaptive challenges (Matthews, 1999). Extroverts are more likely to appraise events as challenging (Gallagher, 1996), and they are more likely to use task-focused coping (Deary et al., 1996; Endler & Parker, 1990), and other proactive strategies (Costa, Somerfield & McCrae, 1996). Extraversion is also associated with relatively narrow personality traits linked to style of self-regulation, including high self-efficacy, and low meta-worry (Matthews, Schwean, et al., 2000). Self-esteem is also positively correlated with extraversion, although neuroticism is a stronger predictor of low self-esteem than is introversion (Francis, 1997). Extraversion relates too to the content of self-knowledge. Generally, extroverts appear motivated towards participation in leisure activities based on social interaction, such as attending parties and playing competitive sports (e.g., Kirkcaldy & Furnham, 1991). Extraversion appears to relate to affiliative needs such as group involvement, whereas introversion is associated with needs for order and precision (Furnham, 1981). In the area of vocational choice, Ackerman and Heggestad (1997) found that extraversion related to social and enterprising interests; i.e., the application of verbal and interpersonal skills to supporting or influencing others. In other words, extroverts and introverts pursue somewhat different goals in life, supported by individual differences in self-regulation.

The knowledge-level characteristics of extraversion-introversion may be reciprocally linked to the cognitive skills supporting adaptation to challenging social environments. On the one hand, the information-processing attributes of extraversion may enhance social skill acquisition, which in turn amplifies confidence and self-efficacy in social settings and readiness to implement task-focused coping. On the other hand, self-knowledge may facilitate both competence and performance of social skills (Matthews, 1999). Extroverts' social interests lead to greater exposure to social environments and more opportunities to practice social skills, leading to greater automatization of skill and to greater explicit knowledge of social situations, affording flexibility of response. In addition, challenge and task-focus are associated with greater task engagement, motivation and energy, factors which, broadly, tend to promote superior performance and execution of skills (Matthews, 2001a). Figure 9.3 shows an adaptive triangle for extraversion: skills for handling demanding social situations cohere with self-efficacy beliefs, and behavioral adaptation to settings such as parties and high-pressure jobs.

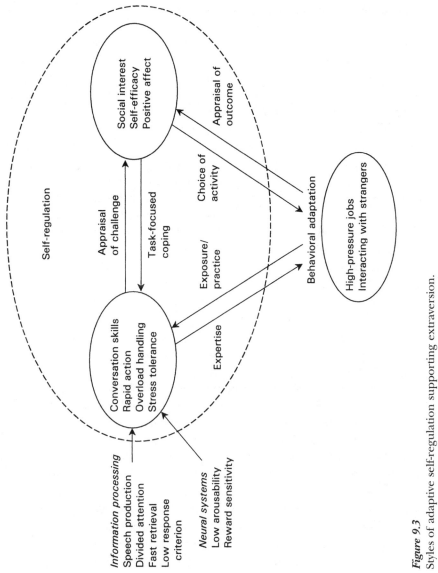

Figure 9.3
Styles of adaptive self-regulation supporting extraversion.

Implications for emotional intelligence

The evidence reviewed shows a thematic unity to the expression of extraversion in neural functioning, information-processing, self-regulation, and real-world functioning. Extroverts appear to be equipped at various levels for handling high-pressure, socially demanding environments, whereas introverts are better-suited for unstimulating environments requiring reflective thought. Evidently, extroverts are better adapted than introverts to certain social settings, but can we infer that extroverts are, therefore, more emotionally intelligent? In fact, there is little basis for such an inference. First, even within social situations, extraversion is a mixed blessing. It confers benefits with respect to influence over others, readiness to compete with others, and confidence in difficult situations, but imposes costs of recklessness, narcissism, and poor tolerance of monotony. Extraversion does not lead to major advantages in handling intimate relationships, and, via impulsivity, may even be implicated in divorce risk (see Furnham & Heaven, 1999). Second, introverts perform better in solitary and unstimulating environments, in both laboratory paradigms such as vigilance, and real-world settings such as systematic study. The ability to cope with boredom and restlessness seems no less an aspect of EI than the ability to handle high levels of social stimulation.

Finally, the cognitive characteristics of extraversion-introversion do not suggest any general adaptation to handling emotional stimuli. Extraversion is associated with a complex patterning of information processing, some components of which are advantageous and some detrimental to performance. Likewise, the self-regulative qualities of the extravert are likely to improve mood, especially in cognitively demanding circumstances, but do not link straightforwardly to adaptation. As we saw in chapter 8, the task-focused coping associated with extraversion is not a panacea for life problems, although it is likely to be advantageous in environments requiring rapid action. In sum, extraversion-introversion should be seen as an adaptive specialization, associated with level of fitness for qualitatively different environments. There is no basis for supposing that extroverts are generally better adapted than introverts.

Prosocial and Antisocial Behavior

Various personality traits contribute to the individual's propensity towards helpful and caring behavior, versus hostile, aggressive behavior. Prosocial and antisocial behavior are not entirely opposed as elements of personality, in that a person may show both forms of behavior on different occasions, but it is convenient to consider them together. The traits we have already discussed play important roles. As discussed, neuroticism is implicated in reactive aggressive acts, such as lashing out at others when unhappy. Extraversion is prosocial in that it is associated with social involvement, but antisocial in that emotionally unstable extroverts are more likely to engage in deviant behaviors than unstable introverts, whose problems tend to take the form of emotional disorder (Eysenck & Eysenck, 1985). However, the most important single trait in this area is agreeableness (A), characterized within the Five Factor Model by qualities such as altruism, cooperativeness, trust, and tendermindedness. Conversely, the low-A person tends to be cold, unsympathetic and inconsiderate (though not necessarily actively hostile). Agreeableness is substantially correlated with the Bar-On (1997) EQ-i, and components of A such as empathy and interpersonal trust are central to conceptualizations of EI. Agreeableness tends to be higher in women (Feingold, 1994), consistent with sex differences in EI (see chapter 5).

Agreeableness and social behavior

Certainly, more agreeable people are more likeable, but are they really more emotionally intelligent? Although there is much less basic science in this area, compared with work on E and N, research provides some pointers to links between agreeableness and adaptation, and to processing substrates supporting adaptation. In the workplace, although A is unrelated to job performance in general, agreeableness appears to predict performance in teams over and above cognitive ability and job-specific skills (Barrick, Stewart, Neubert & Mount, 1998; Neuman & Wright, 1999). Conversely, Barrick and Mount (1993) found that agreeableness was a predictor of poor performance in managers afforded high autonomy, and Graziano, Hair, and Finch (1997) report that high-A individuals are less competitive in group settings. It seems that less agreeable managers may have the ruthless qualities needed to succeed in a competitive business environment; Matthews and Oddy (1993) found high levels of disagreeableness in CEOs. Not surprisingly, agreeableness may also be a disadvantage in military personnel (Callister, King, Retzlaff & Marsh, 1999).

Agreeableness has some clear advantages in relationships. Generally, high-A individuals enjoy a higher quality of peer relationships (Asendorpf, 1998) and specific social interactions (Berry & Sherman, 2000).

Agreeableness is one of the most important traits that people look for in choosing a partner, and it is a strong predictor of marital and sexual satisfaction (Botwin et al., 1997). There may be costs to agreeableness in certain social settings. A diary study showed that agreeableness relates to higher levels of distress experienced following interpersonal conflict, implying that agreeableness fits better with a nonconflictual environment (Suls, Martin & David, 1998). Similarly, Barrett and Pietromonaco (1997) found that high-A individuals experience a greater decrease in self-esteem in conflict situations than do low-A persons. Another possible downside to agreeableness is that, along with neuroticism, it relates to dependency (Bornstein & Cecero, 2000), an aspect of personality disorder characterized in the *DSM*-IV by submissive and clinging behavior related to an excessive need to be taken care of.

Cognitive substrate of agreeableness

What are the psychological processes that link A to behavior? Broadly, social psychology recognizes that behavior towards others may be driven both by explicit, consciously accessible application of rules for social behavior, and by implicit, unconscious biases in cognition. A good example of rule-driven cognition is the theory of planned behavior (Ajzen, 1991). According to the theory, intentions are controlled by attitudes towards a behavior, subjective norms describing perceptions of other people's attitudes to the behavior, and perceived control over the behavior. The intention to engage in a behavior thus reflects a rational integration of these different social cognitions. For example, helping another person would be facilitated by (1) attitudes such as the belief that the person will return the favor, (2) significant others would applaud the helping effort, and (3) performing the helpful act being within the helper's capabilities. Such cognitions may be linked to A; evidence is sparse, but there are some suggestive findings.

At the level of appraisals, agreeableness relates to greater acceptance of self and others, in an experimentally controlled small group setting (Hurley, 1998), and to lower perceptions of conflict in a diary study (Barrett & Pietromonaco, 1997). More agreeable individuals see themselves as less competitive than others (Graziano, Hair & Finch, 1997). However, it is difficult to say whether these correlates of agreeableness represent biases in appraisal or reflect a different style of objective behavior. Social function is linked also to specifically social appraisals. A central appraisal process is comparison of self with others. People perform such comparisons not just for information, but as a form of mood-regulation. Downward comparison of oneself with people of inferior status may enhance one's own self-esteem and happiness. Olson and Evans (1999) quote Schopenhauer: "The best consolation in misfortune or affliction of any kind will be the thought of other people who are in a still worse plight than yourself; and this is a form of consolation open to every one."

Olson and Evans found that disagreeableness was the strongest Big Five predictor of downward comparison tendencies, implying perhaps that low-A people are more likely to take pleasure in the misfortunes of others. They also found that following upward comparison (i.e., with those of higher status), high-A individuals experienced loss of positive affect. They suggest that more agreeable persons tend to be deferential and submissive, which may increase their vulnerability to unfavorable comparisons; i.e., comparisons that the more thick-skinned, low-A individual would ignore (or avoid).

In a diary study, Berry, Willingham, and Thayer (2000) investigated links between the Big Five and accommodation style, i.e., people's self-reports of how they manage dissatisfaction with their friends, which represent a type of coping strategy. Their findings included a positive association between A and loyalty, i.e., maintaining relations despite problems, and, conversely, a negative association with exit from social interaction. Agreeableness (and other related traits) seems to affect how people choose to manage their relationships. Antonioni (1999) obtained somewhat similar findings in a study of conflict management styles: more agreeable individuals tend to use more integration and less domination in resolving conflict. However, contrary to Berry et al. (2000), agreeableness was also linked to a more avoidant style. Interestingly, extroverts also tended to adopt an integrating style, but by contrast, used fewer avoidant and more dominating conflict management styles.

In addition, social behavior may be automatically controlled, through unconscious activation of schemas that bias processing of social stimuli, for example (Wegner & Bargh, 1998). For example, behaviors such as rudeness can be primed without the person's awareness (Bargh, Chen & Burrows, 1996). Chartrand and Bargh (1999) describe the "chameleon effect" by which people tend unconsciously to mimic the movements and posture of others, behaviors that seem to facilitate social interaction. Interestingly, individuals high in dispositional empathy showed the chameleon effect more strongly. Other evidence also links agreeableness to nonverbal behavior, which is likely to be unconscious (though not necessarily so). Berry and Sherman Hansen (2000) videotaped pairs of students participating in social interaction, and used independent observers to code behaviors. They found that agreeableness related to greater visual attention, more "open" body positions, and physical orientation of the body towards the other person, and also to less frequent negative facial expressions. Visual attention and body openness mediated an association between high A and better-rated interaction quality. A may also relate to unconscious cognitive processes. Paulhus and John (1998) link agreeableness to a defense mechanism they label "moralistic bias" that denies socially deviant impulses and exaggerates moral rectitude, in the interests of affiliative motives. (They also describe an "egoistic bias" that serves power motives and may lead to exaggeration of dominance and emotional stability.) At the antisocial end of the dimension, aggression may be associated with the automatic access of confrontational behaviors in response to social problems (Rabiner et al., 1990).

Empathy

One of the key qualities of prosocial personality may be empathy, the sharing of the emotional state of another person (Eisenberg, 1989). Given that empathy requires sensitivity to others, this construct should relate to agreeableness, and indeed, the correlation between scales is about 0.40 (Shafer, 1999). Another perspective comes from developmental psychology. According to Eisenberg, Wentzel, and Harris (1998), empathy, and the related but distinct construct of sympathy, tend to relate to both dispositional emotionality, and to self-regulation (in the sense of effective self-control, discussed in the next section). This analysis appears to link empathy to neuroticism and conscientiousness, although Eisenberg's work is limited by neglect of standard dispositional measures of personality.

Empathy seems broadly adaptive, through enhancement of social interactions (e.g., Batson, 1991). Empathy is associated with altruism, though there has been controversy over whether empathy leads to true selflessness, to identification of self and other, or, as predicted by evolutionary psychology, to helping strategies that are ultimately self-serving (see Cialdini et al., 1997; Davis, 1994). There may be some costs to an empathic disposition. Simpson, Ickes, and Grich (1999) showed that anxious-ambivalent individuals, who tended to have difficulties in intimate relationships, showed higher empathic accuracy in a relationship-threatening situation. In this context, at least, empathy did not seem to be helpful. Empathy can interfere with fairness in group situations, through promoting specially favorable treatment of another person with whom one empathizes, at the expense of the group (Batson et al., 1999), or through violation of moral principles of justice (Batson et al., 1995).

Empathy is central to most conceptions of EI. At the process level, empathy should be linked to efficient analysis of the emotions of others. Mayer, Caruso, et al. (2000a) see emotion identification as a central attribute of EI. Work by Lane (2000) supports the view that there is a distinct skill for emotion recognition and description: his LEAS measure of emotional awareness (see chapter 5) predicts performance on emotion recognition tasks, and correlates with blood flow in the anterior cingulate cortex during emotion induction (see chapter 6). At the cognitive process level, Omdahl (1995) reports a series of studies using the framework of Scherer's (1984) appraisal theory, discussed in chapter 7. As well as confirming many aspects of Scherer's theory, she showed that sharing the emotions of another depends on accurate decoding of the other person's appraisals. The ability to take the perspective of another also contributed to empathy for negative emotions, but not for happiness. It is likely too that unconscious processes contribute to empathy, though there is little evidence. Plausibly, processing of nonverbal signals contributes to the sense of oneness with another person, that some authors see as central to empathy (e.g., Cialdini et al., 1997).

The individual differences in processing emotion associated with empathy should correlate with the prosocial personality traits related to EI. It is worth placing studies of empathic identification in the more general context of person perception. There is an extensive and technically sophisticated literature on the factors controlling how well one person (the judge) can evaluate the personality of another (the target), reviewed by Funder (1999). There is some uncertainty over the reliability of individual differences in judgment ability. Funder (1999) concludes that difficulties in demonstrating that judgmental ability generalizes across contexts can be attributed to methodological shortcomings. Other research (Davis & Kraus, 1997; Lippa & Dietz, 2000) suggests that the ability of individuals to judge others' personalities of traits is trait-specific (e.g., a good judge of extraversion may not be a good judge of neuroticism). Observations of this kind challenge the notion of generalized individual differences in person perception, and conflict with EI theory.

To the extent that generalized perception abilities exist, we would expect the more empathic person to judge personality and emotion more accurately. Studies of the personality of the judge have been surprisingly neglected. In reviewing studies in this area, several of which are unpublished, Funder (1999) tentatively concludes that better male judges tend to be extraverted and stable, whereas better female judges are interpersonally sensitive. It is generally supposed that women are more empathic than men, and, indeed, the largest gender difference for Bar-On's (1997) EQ-i scales is found in favor of women on the Empathy subscale. However, a recent review of the behavioral evidence (Graham & Ickes, 1997) concluded that "although the stereotype of 'women's intuition' may contain the proverbial kernel of truth, gender differences in empathic skills and dispositions appear to be small rather than large, and specific rather than general in scope" (p. 139). These authors suggest that although women are sometimes more accurate in decoding facial expressions, their advantage may be motivational rather than cognitive; perhaps machismo requires a certain amount of social insensitivity.

According to Ickes (1993), people may simply not possess good awareness of their empathic skills, a positions supported by a recent empirical study (Lippa & Dietz, 2000) finding little evidence for links between traits of the Five Factor Model and personality judgment. Davis and Kraus (1997), reviewing studies of judgments of emotions and interpersonal relationships, as well as personality, found that traits related to agreeableness (e.g., interpersonal trust) and conscientiousness (e.g., responsibility) were associated with "empathic accuracy." However, self-report measures of empathy were unrelated to empathic accuracy (a finding that does not bode well for the validity of the EQ-i Empathy scale). Self-reported social sensitivity was also unrelated to accuracy, although measures reflecting other people's judgments of the target person were predictive: "reputational social sensitivity" has some validity. Ironically, one of the traits most predictive of empathic accuracy in Davis and Kraus's (1997) meta-analysis was general intelligence, though the mean effect size was a modest 0.23. Lippa and Dietz (2000) confirmed that intelligence was more predictive of person perception than personality was.

Aggression

Insight into antisocial aspects of personality comes from work on aggression and anger. In fact, both low agreeableness and neuroticism appear to be linked to aggression, but in different ways (Caprara, Barbaranelli & Zimbardo, 1996). Neuroticism seems to relate especially to "reactive aggression"; that is aggression associated with angry emotion and with lashing out physically or verbally when provoked. Traits related to lack of self-control and impulsivity may also contribute to angry reactions, as discussed in the next section. Low agreeableness also correlates with reactive aggression, but the relation is weaker than for neuroticism. By contrast, low agreeableness, but not neuroticism, is associated with "proactive aggression"; goal-directed violent behaviors, performed to achieve some reward, that may not be associated with anger. Dispositional aggression is considered to have some basis in brain function. Animal models of aggression (e.g., Bell & Hepper, 1987) tend to distinguish various subtypes of aggression, such as predatory and irritable aggression, which may depend on different brain systems. Subtypes may show species-specificity, and are imprecisely mapped onto human subtypes such as proactive and reactive aggression. As with emotion generally, it is likely that aggressive behavior is controlled by multiple brain systems. At the subcortical level, aggression, as part of the fight-flight system, has been linked to the amygdala (Gray, 1987). It may also be associated with activity of neurotransmitters such as noradrenaline and serotonin (Zuckerman, 1999). Quay (e.g., 1993) has developed a motivational account of childhood aggression, based on Gray's (1987) theory, which proposes that aggressive children are oversensitive to reward signals and undersensitive to inhibition of behavior in response to punishment signals.

Human neuropsychological studies reviewed by Hawkins and Trobst (2000) suggest that frontal-lobe dysfunction may increase aggressiveness, though the evidence is not fully conclusive due to lack of evidence and methodological difficulties. These authors also point out that dispositional aggression correlates with poor performance on neuropsychological tests of executive function that are linked to frontal lobe function and poor impulse control. The assumption here is that performance is directly controlled by neural processes, although, as discussed in chapter 6, this is a simplistic view, that neglects the possible role of variation in cognitively mediated strategic control of performance.

So far as cognition is concerned, both reactive and proactive aggression may be linked to appraisal and coping (Matthews, Schwean, et al., 2000). Much of the work here derives from studies of children, although adult studies suggest similar conclusions. On the appraisal side, aggression is linked to cognitive distortions (Kendall, 1993) and biases in encoding and representations (Lochman & Dodge, 1994). Specifically, aggression relates to selective attention to cues for hostility, perceptions of others as cruel and malevolent, especially in emotionally reactive aggressors, and beliefs in the legitimacy and effectiveness of violence (e.g., Dodge, 1991; Pakaslahti & Keltikangas-Jaervinen, 1997). Similarly, among adults, aggressive drivers are prone to attribute hostile intentions to other drivers (Matthews et al., 1997).

Generally, reactive aggression may be linked to negative appraisals of others, but its relation with self-appraisals is more complex. One view is that positive self-beliefs (i.e., high self-esteem) reduce the likelihood of aggression (Taylor, 1989), but, somewhat provocatively, it has been suggested that it is people with very strong positive self-beliefs who are prone to aggression (Baumeister, Smart & Boden, 1996). These individuals may be prone to exposure to disconfirming social information that challenges their unrealistic views of themselves, and they use aggression self-protectively, to deny the legitimacy of the criticism. David and Kistner (2000) confirmed that children who held more positive perceptions of their social acceptance were more likely to aggress against other children. Edens (1999) found that aggressive youths were more likely to have either globally positive or globally negative self-systems; i.e., their self-beliefs were polarized and rigid. However, behavior problems were more common among those who over-estimated their personal competence.

With respect to coping, the most popular view is that aggression relates to cognitive deficiencies in social problem-solving, and in response search, response decision and enactment (Dodge et al., 1986). In part, aggressive children behave aggressively because of their appraisals that violence works. In addition, aggressive boys produce more direct action solutions in social problem solving, especially in situations perceived as hostile (Lochman & Lampron, 1986). When the task requires a reflective pause prior to response, aggressive boys still show bias in preferred solutions, but the bias appears to be reduced (Lochman et al., 1989; Rabiner et al., 1990). Generally, aggressive children seem to have a wider repertoire of aggressive "skills" in dealing with social problems (along with reduced verbal-assertion skills), and they are especially prone to access aggressive solutions on impulse. There is also a motivational component to aggression, in that aggressive children prefer to meet disruptive and confrontational goals in problem-solving. Finally, a dynamic aspect should be acknowledged. The use of aggressive coping tends to perpetuate problems, maintaining maladaptation (Blechman, Prinz & Dumas, 1995), and setting up a self-fulfilling prophecy in that aggressive behavior is likely to elicit hostility from others.

It may be simplistic to characterize aggressive coping as simply a cognitive deficit, and Björkqvist, Österman, and Kaukiainen (2000) offer a contrary view. Using instruments based on peer-estimation, they showed that social intelligence was actually *positively* correlated with all types of conflict behavior including aggression, implying that social intelligence may generally promote participation in conflict situations. However, they noted that correlations between social intelligence and use of different strategies increased with the safety of the behavior, i.e., from 0.22 for physical aggression to 0.55 for indirect aggression, and 0.80 for peaceful conflict resolution. They also investigated the role of empathy, which, in general, acts to mitigate aggressive impulses. Although empathy and social intelligence are quite strongly correlated, they differ in their relationship with aggression. With social intelligence controlled, empathy was negatively related to all forms of aggression, but positively associated with conflict resolution, providing the formulation: social intelligence − empathy = aggression. It seems that the socially intelligent but nonempathic person may cope through aggression, but cope intelligently through using violence sparingly.

Implications for emotional intelligence

Prosocial traits related to agreeableness and other traits are central to conceptions of EI. Goleman (1995) stresses the role of empathy in promoting emotional mutuality, altruism and morality, whereas Bar-On (2000) identifies interpersonal scales of empathy, social responsibility, and interpersonal relationship. However, the literature review shows that such traits are not adaptive in all situations. Although agreeableness seems to promote more positive social interactions, more agreeable individuals seem disadvantaged in competitive or conflictual situations, perhaps due to tendencies to be submissive, deferential or dependent. As Suls et al. (1998) propose, the key issue may be the fit between person and situation. Highly agreeable persons may be well suited to social environments requiring cooperation or conciliation of others, but poorly suited to taking independent, self-willed action in more competitive settings. The literature presents a similarly equivocal picture of other related traits. Like agreeableness, empathy seems to promote social interaction, but there is little evidence that dispositionally empathic individuals are actually more accurate in perceiving others. Empathy may be maladaptive in situations that require some degree of detachment from the emotions of others, such as administering justice. At the antisocial end of the scale, it is clear that an aggressive disposition is often mal-adaptive, and associated with lack of emotional intelligence. Neverthe-less, aggressive behaviors may sometimes be intelligent, in the sense of contributing to the achievement of the goals of the individual or group, and the dispositionally aggressive may develop skills in making aggres-sion work for them. The provocative findings of Björkqvist et al. (2000) appear to link aggression, especially in its more subtle forms, to social intelligence.

At the process level, we have seen that, in line with cognitively adap-tive analyses of personality (Matthews, 1999), dispositions to be prosocial or antisocial are supported by multiple mechanisms at different levels of explanation. This includes brain systems for aggression and motivation, biases in social-information processing, and self-knowledge, relating es-pecially to the social self. Evidence is insufficient for a detailed analysis of these findings. However, in general, the findings suggest that people vary in the extent to which they are prepared to process situations as requiring cooperation or competition. For example, the proactively aggressive individual appears (1) biologically sensitized to immediate reward, (2) prone to encode and represent others as hostile, (3) prone to believe that violence is a legitimate means for conflict resolution, and (4) prone to possess a wide range of skills in aggressive behavior. Gen-erally, of course, these attributes are deplorable, and frequently lead to maladaptive behavior, especially when aggression is combined with the impulsive traits described in the next section. However, it is naive to suppose that aggression never pays off. Indeed, self-controlled, verbal aggression used in winning arguments over other people in social and business settings has some degree of social acceptance. In more extreme conditions, such as a violent ghetto or during wartime, physical violence may also be adaptive for the individual.

Conversely, agreeableness may be supported by (1) brain systems for nurturance, (2) processing biases producing positive impressions of others, (3) beliefs centered around prosocial motives, and (4) skills in cooperative social interaction. Again, these qualities are likely to work together in supporting adaptation to cooperative settings, but they may be injurious when the person is in conflict with others. The low agree-able, but not aggressive, individual may be adapted to a somewhat selfish existence which may be valuable in climbing the greasy pole in politics, business or sports. Presumably, an unagreeable person coined the phrase "Nice guys finish last."

At issue here, is the value that is placed on group-oriented versus selfish behavior. Western culture is highly equivocal on this topic. On the one hand, Judeo-Christian ethics place an extremely high value on altruism, and in popular life, cooperative team players are liked and rewarded. On the other hand, economic prosperity is generally seen to depend on sometimes cut-throat competition between individuals and organizations, and competitive sports occupy a privileged place in popular culture. As a quality of the individual, we should be able to detach EI from cultural values. The emotionally intelligent person should be someone who can handle social encounters to their own advantage, irrespective of whether their motivations are socially valued. Of course, social structures are designed to reward prosocial behavior, so we might expect a bias in this direction in the emotionally intelligent. Our suspicion is that much of what is called emotionally intelligent behavior in the social domain is simply a label for socially valued behavior, irrespective of whether it benefits the individual (though it may often do so). At a psychological level, there is little evidence that agreeable behavior is intrinsically superior to disagreeable behavior, and personality research highlights a variety of social orientations, each of which may have adaptive costs and benefits, depending on circumstances.

Self-Control, Conscientiousness, and Impulsivity

Self-control is said to be central to EI (Goleman, 1995), but it is an elusive concept. The term may refer to (1) the overall operation of self-regulation, previously discussed (e.g., Carver & Scheier, 2000b); (2) specific processes such as attention focusing that optimize effortful performance of some activity (Zimmerman, 2000); (3) internalized constraints and inhibitions that are highly dependent on societal values (Megargee, 1997); (4) control of internal mental states (Pallant, 2000); or (5) inhibition of impulsive behaviors, as in studies of the capacity to delay gratification (Mischel, 1983). Self-control has both cognitive and motivational aspects. More effective self-control is believed to be promoted by self-efficacy beliefs (Bandura, 1997), perceptions of control (Alloy et al., 1993), and stable attributions of personal agency (Joseph & Kuyken, 1993). Control behaviors also depend on motivations such as the individual's need for control (Burger, 1992), proactive need for achievement or "effectance" (McClelland, 1961; White, 1959), and what Brehm (1992) calls "reactance," control motivation elicited by a threatened loss of freedom. There are large, primarily social-cognitive, literatures in these areas (see, e.g., Boekaerts, Pintrich & Zeidner, 2000; Weary, Gleicher & Marsh, 1993) that are well beyond the scope of this volume. Our concern is with personality measures that may relate to individual differences in self-control in emotional situations. Research linking personality traits to control motivations and cognitions is urgently required; for the present, the argument must be somewhat speculative.

Relationships between personality and control are untidy. Neuroticism relates to lack of perceived control, leading to stress vulnerability (Matthews, Schwean, et al., 2000). Extroverts seem to be less controlled than introverts, in the sense of being more socially expressive and verbally informal. However, in this section, we will focus on two dimensions, at opposite ends of the control spectrum, that stand out: conscientiousness (C) and impulsivity. Impulsivity is a difficult construct psychometrically, in that it appears to have different aspects (see Parker & Bagby, 1997) that may variously relate to neuroticism, extraversion, and lack of conscientiousness. Multiple traits contribute to impulsive behavior. For example, in a study of self-reported risk behaviors in adolescents, Gullone and Moore (2000) found that extraversion predicted thrill seeking, low neuroticism related to antisocial behavior, low conscientiousness was associated with reckless behavior, and, surprisingly, agreeableness was a predictor of rebelliousness—an effect attributed to sensitivity to peer pressure. There is also overlap between impulsivity and irritability, a facet of neuroticism, which may reflect overlapping genetic and environmental influences (Seroczynski, Bergeman & Coccaro, 1999). Hence, impulsivity and C should not be seen as polar opposites, in that C has central elements such as achievement strivings that have no particular relationship to impulsivity. Zuckerman et al. (1993), however, identified a complex of psychoticism, impulsivity, and unsocialized sensation seeking as a major personality dimension with a substantial negative correlation with conscientiousness. Some of the work in this area has used Eysenck and Eysenck's (1975) psychoticism scale, which predicts a variety of deviant and antisocial behaviors. In this section, we will briefly look at the relevance of C and impulsivity to individual differences in emotional adaptation.

Conscientiousness

On the whole, a conscientious disposition is beneficial, especially at work. There is a fairly substantial occupational literature that links high C to better performance in a variety of occupations (Barrick & Mount,

1991; Hogan & Ones, 1997) and occupational contexts such as teamwork (Neuman & Wright, 1999) and training (Colquitt, LePine & Noe, 2000). Ones and Viswesvaran (1997) suggest five advantages of C in the workplace: (1) spending more time on assigned tasks, (2) acquiring more job knowledge, (3) going beyond immediate role requirements, (4) setting and following goals autonomously, and (5) avoiding counterproductive behavior. Conscientious job seekers also seem to be more proactive and better prepared in seeking jobs (De Fruyt & Mervielde, 1999). High C students also perform better in academic settings in the United States (Tross et al., 2000) and Europe (De Fruyt & Mervielde, 1996), possibly owing to qualities such as drive, concentration, and personal organization (de Raad & Schouwenburg, 1996). Conscientiousness also relates to avoidance of risks, evidenced most dramatically by the greater longevity of high C individuals shown in a longitudinal study conducted by Friedman et al. (1993). Gullone and Moore (2000) found that C related to higher perception of risk, and to lower self-reported engagement in various types of risky behavior. High C may be associated with more prudent and rational health behaviors; Hampson et al. (2000), in a study of cigarette smoking, showed that perceived risk was inversely related to reduced smoking in the home in subjects high in C, but not in other individuals. We will return to individual differences in risk-taking in the context of impulsivity.

Experimental studies confirm the link between C and mechanisms such as motivation to learn (Colquitt & Simmering, 1998), and persistence on tedious tasks (Sansone, Wiebe & Morgan, 1999). Different facets of C may have somewhat different correlates. As Hough (1992) points out, some elements of C relate to achievement strivings, whereas others relate to dependability, i.e., orderliness and conformity. Achievement striving seems to be the stronger predictor of job proficiency and educational success. Two studies by Hogan et al. (1998) suggest that performance is driven by prudence (dependability) when the job offers little scope for personal advancement, but by ambition (achievement striving) when good performance is likely to lead to be rewarded. LePine, Colquitt, and Erez (2000) report an interesting experimental study that assessed effects of C on a decision-making task. Unknown to the participant, the rule for making good decisions was changed on two occasions. LePine et al. found that, whereas C was unrelated to performance prior to the change, *less* conscientious subjects performed better following the change, suggesting that C is inversely related to problem-solving flexibility. Further analysis showed that the effect was mediated by the dependability rather than the achievement striving component of C. The studies reviewed suggest that conscientiousness may relate to motivations to exert control and perhaps also to beliefs in personal control. High self-efficacy may drive the association between C and styles of appraisal and coping that may be adaptive in the work environment, such as task-focused coping (David & Suls, 1999; Deary et al., 1996).

Despite the advantages of high C, there may be disadvantages to the trait also. One risk may be that of being overcontrolled or being the control freak, who has a tendency to limit the behaviors of others. This side of conscientiousness has yet to be explored. However, the wider social-cognition literature does provide some pointers to possible risks. In a study of intimate relationships, Zak et al. (1997) showed that individuals with a high need for control were more likely to blame their partner for conflicts, and to experience less satisfaction. Some clinical studies suggest a link between conscientiousness and obsessive-compulsive disorder (Blais, 1997), and Kline (1998) has proposed that obsessionality forms a third major personality dimension (after E and N), contrasting conscientiousness and authoritarianism with traits related to psychoticism. Plausibly, conscientious individuals may be prone to maladaptive behaviors associated with obsessional personality such as preoccupations that interfere with other activities, but such relationships are yet to be demonstrated empirically.

Finally, a conscientious style of behavior entails costs associated with time and effort. Conscientious behavior, such as studying hard for examinations at university, may take months or years to pay off. There is an opportunity cost, in that the less conscientious individual is free to seek other, more immediate rewards. Although Western societies tend to be structured to reward a focus on long-term gratification, we cannot assume that delaying gratification is adaptive for every individual and in every circumstance. Indeed, if the person is not cognitively equipped for lengthy study, a more opportunistic approach may be more successful. Conscientiousness may also limit exposure to a variety of different environments, expressed by the saying "All work and no play makes Jack a dull boy." Conscientious behavior involving the sustained application of effort may also lead to fatigue, as expressed in the extreme by the Japanese concept of "karoshi": death attributed to overwork (Tsuda et al., 1993). Baumeister, Muraven, and Tice (2000) present an interesting analysis of self-control as a limited resource, which is depleted with prolonged use. The costs of depletion of self-control are countered by a tendency for self-control aptitudes to increase with frequent use, rather as exercise strengthens a muscle. Generally, some people may be grass-hoppers living for the moment, and some ants investing labor for future benefit. Certainly, as in Aesop's fable, ants may have an overall adaptive advantage, but grasshoppers have the benefits of enjoyment of leisure time, conservation of energy, and the flexibility to capitalize on unexpected opportunities.

Impulsivity

Impulsivity is broadly defined as rapid response without reflection, a definition that covers both submitting to urges, and to immediate, unplanned response to external stimuli (Lorr & Wunderlich, 1985). Often, impulsive behavior is maladaptive, and much of the interest in the concept is clinical. High impulsivity may be expressed in rather florid impulse-control disorders such as pyromania, kleptomania, various forms of deliberate self-harm, and "intermittent explosive disorder" (Hollander & Rosen, 2000). Impulsivity also overlaps with aggression, especially reactive depression, and predicts violent and suicidal behaviors (Plutchik & van Praag, 1995). However, there is a view that the clinical focus of much research has tended to neglect the role of more normal forms of impulsive behavior, which may be harmless or benign. Dickman (1990) makes an important distinction between *functional* and *dysfunctional* impulsivity. He points out that acting without forethought is sometimes ill advised and sometimes advantageous, depending on the costs and benefits of speed and accuracy in different contexts. His questionnaire measure discriminates two types of impulsive personality, that are differently related to information processing. In the normal domain, impulsivity overlaps with risk taking, which may or may not be adaptive, depending on circumstances. Broadly, impulsivity might be equated with low EI to the extent that the impulsive person behaves foolishly to relieve their emotions, as in some forms of aggression, or overvalues the excitement of a risky act, with respect to its costs in terms of potential self-injury. On the other hand, we should not equate EI with emotional dullness; the capacity for having fun may be linked to some level of risk taking and enjoyment of sensation.

There is a fairly substantial literature on biological bases of impulsivity, although much of it is clinically oriented. Human neuropsychology implicates the usual suspects, such as frontal lobes and limbic system, although the temporal lobes are also implicated (Zuckerman, 1991). The most popular biochemical hypothesis has been that impulsivity relates to low serotonergic activity, although recent work suggests this view is oversimplified: it appears that several neurochemical mechanisms may influence impulsivity, which has no unique neurobiological basis (Evenden, 1999). In personality work, two kinds of approach predominate. One is to link impulsivity to motivational systems. Gray (1991) relates impulsive personality to a behavioral activation system, associated with the basal ganglia and other structures. He claims that high impulsives are especially sensitive to reward signals. There is evidence from conditioning paradigms that impulsivity may moderate response to motivational signals (e.g., Corr et al., 1995), but the data are conflicting and provide only equivocal support for Gray's theory (see Matthews & Gilliland, 1999). Several authors in this area have concluded that cognitive factors such as expectancies must also play a role (e.g., Zinbarg & Revelle, 1989). The other approach, centered around the concept of sensation seeking (Zuckerman, 1994), focuses on the motivating properties of thrilling and exciting experiences, the acceptance of risk in the pursuit of excitement, and cortical insensitivity to high levels of stimulation.

At a psychological level, impulsivity may relate both to cognitive architecture and personal motivations. Studies using information-processing tasks have linked impulsivity to specific processes, such as faster feature comparison (Dickman & Mayer, 1988), attentional facilitation in response to reward signals (Reed & Derryberry, 1995), and difficulties in inhibiting distracting information during selective attention (Avila & Parcet, 1997). Brunas-Wagstaff et al. (1996) present data on performance of simple perceptual tasks suggesting that dysfunctional impulsivity relates to poor inhibition of competing responses, whereas functional impulsivity is associated with faster information processing. These studies overlap with the extraversion literature already discussed, with impulsivity carrying many of the same processing costs and benefits as extraversion (Revelle, 1993).

The role of impulsivity in personal motivations for risk-taking is perhaps best illustrated by driving research. Both impulsivity (Hilakivi et al., 1989) and sensation seeking (Jonah, 1997) are implicated in elevated motor vehicle accident risk and dangerous driving behaviors, consistent with a general tendency for impulsivity to relate to accidents in occupational settings (Hansen, 1989). Jonah's (1997) review suggests two possible mechanisms for sensation-seeking effects, each of which has some empirical support. First, sensation seeking may relate to overestimation of personal competence and underestimation of risk. Second, sensation seekers may perceive their driving behaviors as risky, but evaluate that risk as an acceptable price for the enjoyment of behaviors. Lajunen and Summala (1995) showed that high sensation seekers are motivated by a need to enjoy exercising their driving skills, whereas low sensation seekers are motivated to maintain safety. A further mechanism is that sensation seeking may influence style of coping with the threats and frustrations of driving. Matthews et al. (1997) found that thrill seeking was associated with a greater use of confrontational coping tactics, and reduced hazard monitoring. Thus, although neural and information processes are likely to mediate personality effects on risk taking, so too do personal goals, beliefs, and coping styles.

Implications for emotional intelligence

The literature on personality and self-control is too patchy to draw together a tightly woven skein of biological and cognitive foundations, adaptive skills, and self-knowledge as we were able to do for extraversion and neuroticism. There are many gaps in the literature, such as biological bases for conscientiousness and information-processing correlates of agreeableness. It is also unclear whether we should distinguish different aspects of dispositional self-control and impulsivity, which may have different implications for adaptation. However, a tentative sketch of the possible adaptive significance of self-control traits may be offered. The impulsivity literature in particular indicates that dispositional self-control is influenced by neural and cognitive architectures. In terms of information processing, self-control may be promoted by inhibitory attentional processes, insensitivity to reward signals, and slower execution of some stages of processing. At the knowledge level, self-control may reflect motivations toward personal achievement, social conformity, and personal integrity, willingness to defer gratification, beliefs in self-efficacy, and coping through planned, task-directed actions that may be implemented over many years. Many of these qualities are admirable, and the good citizen is typically rewarded for having them in our society. Conversely, low self-control disposes the person to clearly maladaptive outcomes such as certain personality disorders, criminality, and substance abuse.

However, it would be a mistake to see high self-control as adaptive and low-control as maladaptive. Traits such as impulsivity may bring benefits associated with opportunism: willingness to disregard social norms for personal gain, flexibility of action, and free time. To the extent that impulsives are more reward-sensitive, the less self-controlled person may have a greater capacity for enjoyment of life and perhaps (though there is no data) an ability to see opportunities for gain that the less reward-sensitive person would miss. There may also be social advantages to risk-taking behaviors, in that they afford opportunities for displaying personal courage that raise social status. Such motivations to show off play an important part in the risky driving behaviors of male teenagers. Intriguingly, lack of self-control seems to play an important part in creativity. Famous artists such as Van Gogh are often notorious for their disorganized personal lives, and yet their genius in painting seems linked to emotional sensitivity. In reviewing creativity research, Eysenck (1995) points out that creative individuals tend to be high in "psychoticism" (referring to tough-mindedness and impulsivity) and in more specific low-self-control qualities such as rebelliousness and disorderliness. At a process level, creativity may relate to low cognitive inhibition, allowing more unusual and original thought. (There is an ironic contrast here with the MEIS [Mayer, Caruso et al., 2000a], which, when consensually scored, assigns low EI to individuals making atypical aesthetic judgments.) The case should not be overstated, in that, as Eysenck points out, the artist needs some degree of ego strength and persistence in translating creative talent into finished (and saleable) works. Generally, though, high self-control may carry costs of lack of imagination and spontaneity.

To summarize, perhaps self-control is more beneficial to society at large than to the individual. Some people may simply enjoy a hedonistic, carefree lifestyle, even though it reduces their contribution to the common good. Should we label as "emotionally unintelligent" people who are unambitious and somewhat disorganized, but happy and free from major pathology or life problems? If so, we are likely to make a value judgment that goes well beyond the scientific data.

Conclusions

In this chapter we posed the question of whether established personality traits should be reconceptualized as facets of EI. We can, in a very rough and ready way, identify traits of emotional stability (low neuroticism), extraversion, agreeableness, and conscientiousness/self-control as dispositions that tend to facilitate everyday social interaction and to promote more positive emotions. However, a closer look at the data suggests that there is little to be gained by linking these dispositions to EI. First, in nonclinical populations, we cannot readily rank-order individuals in terms of level of adaptation to emotional situations. We have seen that traits balance adaptive and maladaptive aspects. For example, although neuroticism relates to various life problems, it may be advantageous in early detection and avoidance of possible threat. Extraversion relates to positive mood and social engagement, but also to narcissism and difficulties in sustaining performance. Agreeableness leads to popularity, but also to submissiveness. Self-control traits, notably conscientiousness, facilitate personal achievement and safety, but may mitigate against creativity and spontaneity. It is true that some traits, especially neuroticism, seem to carry greater risks of the serious maladaptation associated with emotional and/or personality disorders. However, such risks are an issue separate from the role of traits in normal functioning, to which we return in looking at clinical applications in the next chapter.

Second, at the process level, we find no "master processes" for EI at the trait level, just as there was no single adaptive process or process set for adaptation to stress (see chapter 8). Traits are *distributed* across many mechanisms, each imparting a small psychological bias. These biases may require description in terms of individual differences in brain function, in cognitive architecture, and in personal motivations and self-beliefs. Often, these biases are not in themselves universally adaptive or maladaptive. For example, in the case of neuroticism, sensitivity to threat is adaptive to the extent that the environment presents subtle or disguised threats that might be overlooked. Negative emotion is subjectively unpleasant, but in behavioral terms, it may be adaptive to the extent that self-protective, threat-related goals promote personal security.

According to the cognitive-adaptive analysis of personality (Matthews, 1999), the multiple psychological attributes associated with a given trait gain coherence through subserving common adaptive goals. We have seen that the established traits can be conceptualized as representing a choice of environments for which the person is best suited. Neuroticism may relate to a choice for secure environments (over those associated with danger and stress). Extroverts seem fitted to demanding social environments, whereas introverts are better suited to solitary reflection. In the case of the N and E traits, empirical evidence allows us to map out the biological bases, processing biases, and self-knowledge that come together to facilitate the acquisition of the contextualized skills needed to flourish in the preferred environment (Zeidner & Matthews, 2000). The stories for agreeableness and conscientiousness are rough drafts only, but take up the same themes. In other words, personality traits reflect not general level of adaptiveness, but a pattern of benefits and costs in engaging with the variety of environments important to human beings. Such patterns of adaptive specialization cannot meaningfully be labeled as "intelligences."

Finally, there is no general adaptation to emotional environments, as opposed to nonemotional environments. In general, traits have implications for both emotional and nonemotional functioning. Even neuroticism is closely bound up with cognitive processes such as meta-cognition and selective attention. We may infer that dealing with emotion is not a primary adaptive task for people. Instead, emotions are concomitants of what really are the fundamental adaptive issues: personal security (neuroticism), influence over others (extraversion), co-operation versus competition (agreeableness), and self-advancement within society (conscientiousness). These different challenges relate to different complexes of neural and cognitive function, and individual differences in the experience and regulation of emotion should be linked to the particular nature of the challenge, and not to some general EI. In conclusion, the reconceptualization of personality in terms of a general faculty for handling emotion is inconsistent with both empirical data and our conceptual analysis of individual differences in adaptation. On the evidence so far available, the concept of emotional intelligence does not add anything fundamental to existing personality theory, although work on EI scales may usefully focus attention on traits such as empathy and self-rated social skills. Finally, the overinclusive nature of EI obscures important differences in psychological function and adaptation between the various established traits that may influence emotional functioning.

III

Applications

10

The Clinical Psychology of Emotional Maladjustment

He who feels no compassion will become insane.

Hasidic saying

Thus far, EI research has had little impact on clinical practice. Parker (2000, p. 491) states, "When we turn to the empirical literature for evidence of the clinical importance of emotional intelligence, however, we find almost no published information." However, EI may have important clinical and therapeutic implications because (1) on theoretical grounds, emotion regulation should affect vulnerability to disorder, and response to treatment, and (2) EI overlaps with established constructs such as alexithymia that are known to be clinically significant (Parker, 1990; Taylor & Bagby, 2000). To make this case, we need to establish that the EI construct adds to existing theory and practice in clinical psychology. The place of EI in clinical psychology may be approached from two directions. First, we can examine whether existing research suggests a distinctive role for low EI as an influence on abnormality in emotion. As for normal personality, it may transpire that EI is redundant with existing constructs such as neuroticism (N), depending perhaps on the brand of EI concerned. Second, we can start from constructs close to EI, such as alexithymia, and examine their role in the etiology and treatment of pathological affect. In this chapter we use these approaches to address the following issues:

Diagnostic issues EI research supposes that emotion and its regulation can be conceptualized in some global sense, that cuts across individual emotions. Similarly, in the field of psychopathology, the construct seems to require some common abnormality that cuts across different diagnostic categories. We will begin our discussion of the clinical relevance of EI by reviewing what is meant by a disorder of the emotions.

Abnormal personality   Personality is one of the factors controlling vulnerability to clinical disorders. Individuals with very low EI may be at risk of developing disorders associated with dysregulation of emotion. We will review evidence on the structure of abnormal personality, and consider whether low EI emerges as a central dimension.

Pathological processes   There are many theories—biological, cognitive, and social—that attempt to explain why some individuals develop clinical mood and anxiety disorders. Does EI relate to abnormality in some coherent set of processes that contribute to the etiology of disorders? In line with our general orientation, we will focus on cognitive processes, acknowledging that biological factors are also important.

Alexithymia   Clinical interest in deficits in experiencing and verbalizing emotions long predates the concept of EI. As discussed in chapter 5, individual differences in alexithymia may be operationalized via questionnaire. Here, we address its clinical significance and relevance to understanding what it might mean to be low in EI.

Implications for therapy   The final issue is whether EI research suggests novel approaches to treatment of emotional disorders. There are many pharmacological and psychological treatments that work fairly well. How might therapies based on EI improve on existing clinical practice?

Diagnostic Categories for Emotional Disorders

If EI exists, we might expect to find mental disorders related to lack of EI. Conceivably, some people are so unable to make sense of emotional information that they might be unable to function as normal social beings. If so, we might contrast disorders related to emotional illiteracy with other disorders for which emotion management was not central. In this section we assess whether existing diagnostic categories for mental illness suggest the existence of *pathologically low emotional intelligence* (PLEI) as a factor in disorder.

Clinical psychology is based on a "diathesis-stressor" model. A mental disorder represents some breakdown in everyday functioning within the person's normal social environment. Breakdown may be evident in behavior, such as an attempt at suicide, or in subjective experience, such as hallucinations. Abnormalities that do not disrupt everyday social relationships or cause the person to endanger themselves or others are seen as eccentricities rather than disorders requiring clinical attention. Typically, mental disorders are an *outcome* of both internal predisposing factors, such as abnormal personality, described as a *diathesis*, and external precipitating factors or *stressors*, such as adverse life events. The most widely used classification scheme for different forms of breakdown is the *Diagnostic and Statistical Manual of Mental Disorders* by the American Psychiatric Association (*DSM-IV*). It sets out explicit criteria for diagnosing a person as suffering from various disorders; diagnosis, in turn, guides choice of therapy. The aim is to describe not just the immediate psychological state of the person, but also diathesis and stressor factors implicated in the etiology of the disorder. *DSM-IV* is *multiaxial*, in that it seeks to assess five different aspects of disorder:

• Axis I refers to the immediate, manifest disorder requiring clinical attention, such as schizophrenia, major depression, or Alzheimer's disease. Hence, it represents an outcome of pathogenic internal and external factors.

• Axis II refers to diathesis factors, i.e., abnormalities that may predispose the person to Axis I disorders. These include personality disorders, and disorders of cognitive function, such as learning disabilities, that may increase personal vulnerability.

• Axis III lists organic medical and physical disorders that should be distinguished from mental conditions. In some cases, such disorders may be a part of the diathesis.

• Axis IV describes major psychosocial stressors that the person has experienced recently, which *may* have contributed to the disorder.

• Axis V is a single 0–100 scale that purports to provide a global assessment of functioning.

How could we fit PLEI into such scheme? Evidently, Axes III and IV are irrelevant (except to the extent that low EI may precipitate stressful life events). Axis V makes no specific reference to emotion (and is of questionable validity). If EI is a causal construct, the simplest solution would be to see low PLEI as an Axis II condition that might predispose a variety of other, Axis I disorders. Unfortunately, the relationship between Axis I and Axis II diagnoses is one of the more problematic aspects of *DSM-IV*. Mental disorders tend to recur over time, so it may be hard to distinguish acute symptomatic aspects from the underlying predisposition. Conversely, when individuals with personality disorders present to clinicians, it is usually because of some distinct episode where the person has become a nuisance or danger to themselves or others, which may reflect a symptomatic outbreak overlaid on an underlying predisposition. It is difficult or impossible for the clinician to assess prior predisposition from presenting symptoms. It is not surprising that there is sometimes considerable overlap between Axis I and Axis II diagnostic criteria (Widiger and Shea, 1991), and there is no comprehensive causal framework for relating the two types of disorders.

We return to personality disorders in the next section. In the remainder of this section, we look at whether low EI has a role in diagnoses for various, mostly Axis I disorders. The issue here is whether or not PLEI maps cleanly onto diagnostic categories. If there are certain disorders to which PLEI seems central, studying these disorders may be informative about EI, and treating low EI may have therapeutic benefits. A lack of mapping would not in itself invalidate the concept of EI, but it would add to the impression that the construct is elusive and hard to define. It would also suggest that enhancing EI may not be a prime target for therapy.

Looking at *DSM-IV* criteria, a superficial observation is that emotional problems are a common criterion for many diagnoses. Of course, patients may experience negative emotions simply as a secondary consequence of their difficulties in living, but the aim of *DSM-IV* is to pick out defining features of the condition. At this level, it is difficult to confine emotional disturbance to any small number of diagnostic categories. In more detail, there are at least three ways in which PLEI might be implicated in *DSM-IV* disorders:

Disorders to which emotional symptoms are central

The mood disorders and anxiety disorders describe a group of conditions in which mood must be altered for the diagnosis to be made. We will refer to these disorders collectively as "emotional disorders." Box 10.1 summarizes some of the principal symptoms in *DSM-IV* of the disorders we will refer to in this section. Various anxiety disorders (e.g., generalized anxiety, panic disorder, phobia) require the presence of unusual or intense fear or anxiety. Negative emotions must be accompanied by other criteria for a clinical diagnosis to be made. For example, for panic disorders to be diagnosed, the patient must experience panic attacks that involve not just severe fear, but also at least four out of a list of other, mostly physical symptoms, such as chest pain, pounding heart, a choking sensation or nausea. For a major depressive episode to be diagnosed, the patient, in addition to meeting other criteria, must experience either depressed mood for most of nearly every day or marked decrease in interest or pleasure in nearly all activities. Positive

Box 10.1
Principal symptoms of some anxiety and mood disorders in *DSM-IV*

Generalized Anxiety Disorder

• For more than half the days in at least 6 months, the patient experiences excessive anxiety and worry about several events or activities.

• The patient has trouble controlling these feelings.

• Other anxiety and worry symptoms include feeling restless, tired, and irritable. May have trouble concentrating and sleeping.

• Symptoms cause clinically important distress or impair work, social or personal functioning.

Obsessive-Compulsive Disorder

• Patient must have obsessions or compulsions (or both) which cause severe distress, and interfere with social or personal functioning.

• Obsessions. Recurring, persisting thoughts, impulses or images inappropriately intrude into awareness and cause marked distress or anxiety. The patient tries to ignore or suppress these ideas or to neutralize them by thoughts or behavior.

• Compulsions. The patient feels the need to repeat physical behaviors (checking the stove to be sure it is off, hand washing) or mental behaviors (counting things, silently repeating words). These behaviors aim to reduce or eliminate distress, but they are not realistically related to the events they are supposed to counteract.

Panic Disorder (may be diagnosed with or without agoraphobia)

• The patient experiences recurrent panic attacks, defined as the sudden development of a severe fear or discomfort that peaks within 10 minutes. During this discrete episode, 4 or more of the following symptoms occur:

○ Chest pain or other chest discomfort

○ Chills or hot flashes

○ Choking sensation

○ Derealization (feeling unreal) or depersonalization (feeling detached from self)

○ Dizzy, lightheaded, faint or unsteady

○ Fear of dying

○ Fears of loss of control or becoming insane

Box 10.1 (continued)

○ Heart pounds, races or skips beats

○ Nausea or other abdominal discomfort

○ Numbness or tingling

○ Sweating

○ Shortness of breath or smothering sensation

○ Trembling

• For a month or more after at least 1 of these attacks, the patient has had 1 or more of:

○ Ongoing concern that there will be more attacks

○ Worry as to the significance of the attack or its consequences (for health, control, sanity)

○ Material change in behavior, such as doing something to avoid or combat the attacks

Posttraumatic Stress Disorder

• The patient has experienced or witnessed an unusually traumatic event that involved actual or threatened death or serious physical injury to the patient or to others, and the patient felt intense fear, horror or helplessness

• Patient repeatedly relives the event through, e.g., intrusive recollections, distressing dreams, 'flashbacks', accompanied by distress and physiological reactivity to cues that symbolize or resemble the event.

• Patient repeatedly avoids thinking about the event, and situations that recall the event

• Patient has numbing of general responsiveness; e.g., feels detached from other people

Social Phobia

• The patient strongly, repeatedly fears at least one social or performance situation that involves facing strangers or being watched by others. The patient specifically fears showing anxiety symptoms or behaving in some other way that will be embarrassing or humiliating.

• The phobic stimulus almost always causes anxiety, which may be a cued or situationally predisposed panic attack.

• The patient either avoids the situation or endures it with severe distress or anxiety.

Box 10.1 (continued)

> • Either there is marked distress about having the phobia or it markedly interferes with the patient's usual routines or social, job or personal functioning.
>
> *Major Depression*
>
> • At least one major depressive episode, i.e., in the same 2 weeks, the patient has had 5 or more of the following symptoms, occurring for most of nearly every day. Either depressed mood or decreased interest or pleasure must be one of the five:
>
> o Mood. Patient reports depressed mood or appears depressed to others.
>
> o Interests. Interest or pleasure is markedly decreased in nearly all activities.
>
> o Eating and weight. Marked change in appetite or actual weight.
>
> o Sleep. The patient sleeps excessively or not enough.
>
> o Motor activity. The patient's activity is agitated or retarded.
>
> o Fatigue. There is fatigue or loss of energy.
>
> o Self-worth. The patient feels worthless or inappropriately guilty.
>
> o Concentration. The patient is indecisive or has trouble thinking or concentrating.
>
> o Death. The patient has repeated thoughts about death, suicide or has made a suicide attempt.
>
> • Symptoms cause clinically important distress or impair work, social or personal functioning.

moods may also be a sign of pathology. Bipolar disorders are characterized by alternating episodes of depression and mania, i.e., abnormal, persistent elevation of mood.

Disorders to which nonemotional aspects of emotional intelligence are central
Many of the defining characteristics of EI refer not directly to emotional state, but to qualities related to awareness and management of emotion. In some disorders, dysfunction of these qualities is more apparent than any overall mood disturbance. Impaired self-control is one such quality. Disorders associated with poor impulse control fall under several *DSM-IV* headings, including personality disorders (e.g., antisocial personality), as discussed later, and bipolar disorder (during manic episodes).

Severely disorganized behavior is an important criterion, though not a necessary one, for schizophrenic disorders. In the disorganized type of schizophrenia, both severe disorganization and flat or inappropriate affect must be present. There is also a separate Axis I category for impulse-control disorders, which refers to conditions defined by lack of control. These include intermittent explosive disorder (episodes of disproportionate aggression), kleptomania, pyromania, pathological gambling, and trichotillomania (persistent hair-pulling and extraction). Often, these conditions are associated with anxiety before the impulsive act and relief afterwards. In children, impulsivity is a common feature of attention-deficit/hyperactivity disorder (ADHD). Another feature of low EI is interpersonal difficulties due to lack of insight into others' feelings and motives. Difficulties in relating to others are common in various mental disorders, including, as discussed in the next section, personality disorders. Axis II also includes a heading for pervasive developmental disorders in which the child fails to develop social skills, notably autistic disorder, whose diagnosis requires at least 2 indicators of impaired social interaction, such as deficiencies in use of nonverbal behavior, lack of appropriate peer relationships, and lack of social or emotional reciprocity. Social dysfunction due to inaccurate appraisal of others may also be experienced by mood and anxiety patients, and by schizophrenics.

Disorders linked to emotion by research
Several disorders are not overtly associated with emotion or emotion-regulation criteria, but are nevertheless linked to emotion by research. At the diagnostic level, it is not uncommon for various medical and psychiatric disorders to be comorbid with anxiety and/or mood disorder (Kroenke, Jackson & Chamberlin, 1997). For example, Carson et al. (2000) studied 300 patients referred to a general neurology clinic. Of these patients 140 met criteria for at least one *DSM-IV* mental disorder. These patients presented with poorer physical and somatic function, worse somatic symptoms, and more pain. Consistent with these results, neurotic personality (high N) tends to be linked to *DSM-IV* somatoform disorders, in which the patient complains of recurring physical symptoms for which no organic basis is found (e.g., Sullivan, 2000). Somatization disorder is defined entirely in terms of somatic symptoms such as pain and gastrointestinal symptoms. By contrast, hypochondriasis is defined in terms of clinically significant distress resulting from symptoms, rather than the symptoms themselves, together beliefs that one has or is developing a serious disease. Even in nonclinical samples, N is

associated with number of medical symptoms reported (Costa & McCrae, 1985) and with measures of hypochondriasis and health anxiety (Cox et al., 2000; Wells, 1994). N is also linked to some specific somatoform complaints, such as globus pharyngis, feeling a lump in the throat, in the absence of any physical cause (Deary, Wilson & Kelly, 1995). Likewise, N is also linked to psychosomatic illnesses (Kirmayer et al., 1994), in which psychological factors contribute to actual diseases such as ulcer, and it is often difficult to distinguish the psychological and medical consequences of this personality dimension. Indeed, Sullivan (2000) argues against rigid distinction of psychogenic and somatogenic symptoms, suggesting that the clinician should focus on treating the mood and anxiety disorders that may generate symptoms.

Another major classification in *DSM-IV* is for substance-related disorders. Again, criteria for substance use make no overt reference to emotion, but N tends to be elevated in chronic users of various legal and illegal substances, including alcohol (Martin & Sher, 1994) and opiate drugs (Doherty & Matthews, 1988). The causal role of N is uncertain, however, in that N scores tend to drop as alcoholism is treated, implying an effect of the disorder on personality (Shaw et al., 1997). Conversely, other evidence suggests that substance use may sometimes be a coping strategy adopted by stress-vulnerable individuals intended to neutralize the impact of some threat (Riskind, Gessner & Wolzon, 1999). Other groups of *DSM-IV* conditions known to be linked to higher N include eating disorders (Goldner et al., 1999), sexual disorders (Eysenck, 1971; Kennedy et al., 1999), and sleep disorders (Dorsey & Bootzin, 1997). Broadly, these findings suggest that the vulnerability to emotional disturbance associated with N may be expressed in a variety of disorders that are not explicitly emotional, although in some cases the causal association between negative affectivity and disorder may be complex.

Implications for emotional intelligence as a diagnostic criterion

Evidently, emotional disturbance is central to many disorders. A large proportion of mental disorders are linked to direct or indirect expression of negative affect, or to aspects of EI at one remove from emotional experience, such as self-control and interpersonal relationships. However, the diversity of mental disorders linked to emotional disturbance mitigates against any clear-cut relationship between low EI and psychopathology. Grouping together emotional disorders, impulse control disorders, autism, somatoform disorders, substance abuse, and eating, sexual and sleep disorders into a superordinate PLEI category makes little sense clinically. Despite overlaps, these conditions have distinct etiologies and require different treatments. The position that low EI is one of many factors associated with vulnerability to a range of clinical pathologies is perhaps tenable, but low EI fails to emerge from *DSM-IV* as a clear diagnostic criterion. Attributing disorders to low EI is likely to be circular, in the absence of compelling evidence that EI exists independent of diagnoses that themselves have varying degrees of reliability.

Furthermore, a more coherent set of diagnostic categories may be obtained by focusing on negative affectivity or N. Although excessive negative emotion is primarily a quality of the anxiety and mood disorders, there is considerable comorbidity between these disorders and those in which negative emotion appears to be expressed indirectly, e.g. through somatoform disorder. Anxiety and depression are also often comorbid with impulse-control disorders such as ADHD (Biederman et al., 1991), and with disorders related to poor social skills such as autism and Asperger syndrome (Green et al., 2000; Kim et al., 2000). N is elevated in children with ADHD (White, 1999), though there has been little work on autism and personality traits. Generally, it appears that N operates as a generalized vulnerability factor that may interact with other diathesis and stressor factors to produce a range of more specific pathologies, although there may be some mutual, reciprocal influence between personality and pathology over time (Widiger & Trull, 1992). However, as discussed in chapter 9, it is difficult to make the case that N should be reconceptualized as low EI, despite the substantial correlations between personality-like measures for the two constructs.

Of course, conclusions are tentative because of difficulties with *DSM-IV* and the similar World Health Organization ICD-10 scheme. There are continuing problems with validating the different diagnostic categories, as separate, unitary entities due to lack of conclusive evidence, and conceptual disagreements on how mental disorders should be distinguished from each other, and from normal functioning (Widiger & Clark, 2000). According to Farmer and McGuffin (1999), no classificatory scheme may claim validity, because the causes of most disorders are uncertain. In addition, empirical data on specific groups of disorders, notably the personality disorders, conflict with the distinctions made in *DSM-IV* (Widiger, 1997). Although anxiety and depression appear to be clinically distinct, they are frequently comorbid, and scales for the two syndromal conditions are highly correlated (Watson & Clark, 1991). It may be that a hierarchical model is required, such that anxiety and depression are lower-order dimensions linked to an overarching general negative affect factor (Mineka, Watson & Clark, 1998; Steer et al., 1995). Hence, the lack of clear PLEI conditions may be a consequence of the limitations of *DSM-IV*.

Abnormal Personality and Emotional Disorder

Low EI might emerge more clearly as a dispositional factor predisposing a variety of *DSM-IV* disorders. This hypothesis is consistent with proposals to replace categorical models of psychopathology, such as *DSM-IV*, with dimensional models (Widiger & Shea, 1991). Dimensional models emphasize a continuum of degrees of abnormality, accepting that the cut-off between normal and abnormal function is somewhat arbitrary (Matthews et al., 1998). In depression, for example, clinical patients and subclinically depressed individuals show many of the same psychological characteristics, and etiological continuity, in being associated with similar risk factors such as severe life events (Flett, Vredenburg, et al., 1997). Where discontinuity is found, it may reflect a continuum of symptom severity reaching a level at which it disrupts everyday functioning. On the other hand, we will argue below that clinical disorder may be associated with vicious circles that are qualitatively different from normal stress responses, i.e., dynamic processes that perpetuate negative cognitive and affective reactions.

The dimensional approach has been especially important in the study of personality disorders (Livesley, 1995; Widiger, 1997). Factor analyses of abnormal personality data arrive at dimensional schemes that are at variance with the *DSM-IV* Axis II diagnostic categories. *DSM-IV* recognizes that the different personality disorders have similarities, grouping them into three clusters: odd-eccentric, dramatic-emotional, and anxious-fearful, as shown in table 10.1. A case could be made that all

Table 10.1
Clusters of personality disorders in *DSM-IV*

Cluster A	Cluster B	Cluster C
Odd-eccentric	Dramatic-emotional	Anxious-fearful
Paranoid	Antisocial	Avoidant
Schizoid	Borderline	Dependent
Schizotypal	Histrionic	Obsessive-compulsive
Narcissistic		

three clusters relate to lower EI. For example, both schizoid and schizo-typal individuals tend to be socially withdrawn; schizoid persons in particular appear to have problems forming attachments and emotional connections with others. The dramatic-emotional disorders tend to be associated with impulsive behavior, and, in the case of antisocial personality, aggression towards others. Interestingly, antisocial individuals may also show some signs of EI. They are robust, socially facile and ingenious, with a superficial charm that may allow them to take advantage of other people (Brantley & Sutker, 1983). The anxious-fearful cluster tends to be associated with excessive negative emotion, and social difficulties including hypersensitivity to criticism (avoidant), lack of self-confidence (dependent) and inhibition of emotional expression (obsessive-compulsive).

However, these clusters lack conceptual coherence, and are not well supported by empirical analyses of personality disorder items (Austin & Deary, 2000; Widiger & Costa, 1994). Several researchers have, as advised by Widiger and Shea (1991), investigated dimensions of personality disorder that might have more validity than the *DSM-IV* categories. For example, Walton and Presly (1973) examined personality disorder symptoms in a large number of patients and isolated four broad personality traits: social deviance, submissiveness, schizoid/obsessional and hysterical. Widiger, Trull, Hurt, Clarkin, and Frances (1987) assessed the 81 criteria covering the personality disorders from structured interview items. The data were reduced to three dimensions: social involvement, assertion-dominance and anxious rumination versus behavioral acting out.

Perhaps the most thorough work in this area has been carried out by Livesley and his colleagues (e.g., Livesley & Schroeder, 1990). Livesley's factor analyses of a comprehensive set of items representing prototypical clinical features of personality disorder suggests around 20 basic dimensions of personality disorder. Livesley, Jang, and Vernon (1998) factor-analyzed the 18 dimensions of Livesley's Dimensional Assessment of Personality Disorder—Basic Questionnaire (DAPQ-BQ) in large samples including 656 personality disordered patients, and 939 subjects from the general population. They obtained a higher-order factor solution comprising four factors. Emotional dysregulation relates to anxiousness, emotional instability and dissatisfaction. Dissocial behavior is defined mainly by characteristics of antisocial personality such as callousness, rejection of others and stimulus-seeking. Inhibition is associated with intimacy problems and restricted emotional expression. Compulsivity contrasts high compulsivity with low passive opposition. Taken together, these studies suggest that the various aspects of abnormal personality that might be linked to abnormal personality in fact relate to several distinct constructs. It is unfortunate there is not better agreement between different studies (and *DSM-IV* categories), but qualities such as negative affectivity, antisocial personality, and social withdrawal emerge fairly consistently, albeit in somewhat different guises from study to study.

A clearer integration may be provided by studies that have factor analyzed both normal and abnormal personality scales, although some of these studies have the possible limitation of using nonclinical samples. Three studies illustrate the partial convergence obtained. Schroeder, Wormsworth and Livesley (1992) factor-analyzed together the DAPP-BQ and NEO-PI (Costa & McCrae, 1992), the standard scale for the FFM, and found five factors fairly similar to the Big Five, although NEO-PI openness failed to load heavily on any factor. In terms of the later, four-factor scheme for the DAPP-BQ (Livesley et al., 1998), the study linked emotional dysregulation to N, dissocial behavior to low agreeableness, inhibition to introversion and low openness (fairly modest links in this case), and compulsivity to conscientiousness. A later study (Jang, Livesley & Vernon, 1999) assessed normal personality the Eysenck Personality Questionnaire (EPQ), and again obtained five factors, including emotional dysregulation/N, antisocial behavior, inhibition and compulsivity. Contrary to previous results, this study found that extraversion was related to antisocial behavior, but, as Jang et al. (1999) point out, this result may reflect content differences in the EPQ and NEO-PI extraversion scales. A factor analysis based on *DSM* items for personality disorder (Austin & Deary, 2000) produced somewhat different abnormal factors, linking EPQ E to (low) social avoidance. Again, there are significant discrepancies between studies, but also some common themes. Austin and Deary's (2000) general scheme that discriminates (1) N and allied personality disorders (2) antisocial personality/low agreeableness, (3) social avoidance/introversion and (4) obsessionality/conscientiousness seems a reasonable resolution. The place of extraversion in abnormal personality is the most problematic; its sociability elements may to relate to inhibition and social withdrawal, whereas impulsivity and dominance of others may be linked to antisocial personality.

Implications: Emotional intelligence and abnormal personality

As with normal personality, the data suggest a multidimensional scheme for abnormal personality, rather than some overarching factor of impaired EI. Psychometric studies of personality disorder find independent or nearly independent dimensions that relate to different aspects of EI. For example, Widiger et al.'s (1987) dimensional model separates social behavior (social involvement and assertion dominance) from vulnerability to negative affect (anxious rumination versus behavioral acting out). Similarly, Schroeder et al.'s (1992) factor-analytic study suggests that variation in abnormal personality may correspond fairly well to the Five Factor Model. Abnormal trait dimensions related to different aspects of low EI were associated with different factors: e.g., anxiousness and social avoidance were linked to N, restricted expression and intimacy problems to a blend of introversion and low openness, and interpersonal disesteem to low agreeableness. Bundling together impulsivity, excessive negative affect and failure to connect with others as aspects of a common syndrome of low EI obscures the important differences between different aspects of personality disorder.

In addition, as at the diagnostic level, negative affectivity is strongly implicated in the personality disorders. For example, most researchers (e.g., Austin & Deary, 2000) found evidence for a general distress factor highly correlated with N, and related to the majority of disorders. Few disorders appear to be clearly distinct from N. One such disorder is antisocial personality which is consistently linked to psychoticism (O'Boyle, 1995; Austin & Deary, 2000), or, in the Five Factor Model, to low agreeableness (Schroeder et al., 1992). Within the area of antisocial personality, Hare, Hart, and Harpur (1991) have separated interpersonal and affective characteristics (e.g., lying, lack of empathy) from impulsive and unstable characteristics (e.g., impulsivity, poor behavioral control). Some authors see schizotypal personality as being largely distinct from N, but Austin and Deary's (2000) item level analysis found that the eccentric thinking aspects of this trait were related to high N. Obsessive-compulsive personality may also be somewhat distinct from N, although there is some overlap between the two constructs (Scarrabelotti, Duck & Dickerson, 1995).

Hence, N again emerges as a stronger organizing principle for abnormal personality than does EI. The dimensional analyses suggest it should be separated from other aspects of low EI such as impulsivity, interpersonal coldness, and possibly schizoid social withdrawal. At the same time, N may itself be too general a concept to guide clinical practice. Flett, Hewitt, Endler, and Bagby (1995) suggest that N should not be treated as a monolithic entity. They claim that clinical depression relates to narrower traits correlated with N such as sociotropy (dependency), autonomy, perfectionism, attributional style, and dysfunctional attitudes. Although anxiety and depression are strongly correlated, depression is more strongly elevated in children with ADHD than is anxiety (Schwean, Saklofske, Yackulic & Quinn, 1995). More-fine grained analysis of personality than afforded by general models such as the Five Factor Model is often required (Livesley & Jang, 2000). From this perspective, attempts to characterize abnormal personality as "PLEI" appear crude indeed, although, as we shall discuss, some related, but much more specific, constructs such as alexithymia may contribute to fine-grained personality assessment (Taylor, Bagby & Luminet, 2000).

Alexithymia

Alexithymia is a multifaceted construct that will be discussed at some length in this chapter because it is commonly viewed as being conceptually similar to EI (Taylor & Bagby, 2000). Although the construct emerged more than 20 years ago from earlier clinical observations, this personality trait has generated interest only recently among emotion theorists (Taylor, Bagby & Taylor, 1997). Despite some initial controversy over the concept of alexithymia, it has captured the interest of considerable numbers of clinicians, theoreticians, and researchers in various countries of the world. We begin by reviewing current conceptualizations of the construct, its etiology, correlates, and clinical parameters. We then move on to examine the conceptual similarities and differences between the two constructs and review recent research casting light on their empirical relationships.

Conceptualizations

Alexithymia is a personality construct that reflects a significant disorder of affect and encompasses a cluster of traits that reflect deficits in the experiencing, expression, and regulation of emotions (Parker, Taylor & Bagby, 1993). The term, was coined by Sifneos (1972) and stems from the Greek, literally meaning a lack of emotion (a = lack, *lexis* = word, *thymos* = emotion). The origins of the concept can be traced back at least a half century to clinical reports that observed that many patients suffering from so-called classical psychosomatic diseases show an apparent inability to verbalize feelings. Indeed, alexithymic characteristics have been reported among patients with a wide range of medical and psychiatric (Taylor, 1984). A review of the literature shows that it is implicated in somatoform disorders, eating disorders, substance abuse, panic disorder, and other illnesses (Taylor, Bagby & Parker, 1997). Ruesch (1948) noted that such patients tend to be unimaginative, use direct physical action or bodily channels for expression of emotion, and respond poorly to insight-oriented therapy. Salovey, Hsee, and Mayer (1993) have placed alexithymia at the extreme lower pole of the EI construct. According to Taylor et al. (1997), alexithymia is not a categorical phenomenon, but is best conceptualized as a dimensional construct that is distributed normally in the general population.

A review by Parker, Taylor, and Bagby (2001) shows that the salient features of the multifaceted alexithymia construct, as currently construed, include the following components: (a) difficulty in identifying and describing emotions and distinguishing between feelings and the bodily sensations of arousal, (b) difficulty in describing feelings to other people, (c) constricted imaginal processes, as evidenced by a paucity of fantasies, and (d) a stimulus-bound externally oriented cognitive style, as evidenced by preoccupation with the details of external events rather than inner emotional experiences. The salient features can be distinguished conceptually and empirically, and they are logically related (Taylor & Bagby, 2000). The ability to identify and communicate feelings to others is contingent on an ability to distinguish one's own feelings from the bodily sensations that accompany emotional states. An externally oriented cognitive style reflects an absence of inner thoughts and fantasies as well as a low range of emotional expressiveness. Because alexithymic individuals they have no words for feeling, they express their arousal in physical ways (Stephenson, 1996). Although showing expressions of anger and sadness, they actually know very little about their feelings and are unable to link them with memories, fantasies, higher level affects, or specific situations (Nemiah et al., 1976). Impairment in representing and regulating emotions cognitively is thought to render alexithymic individuals more susceptible to a variety of medical and psychiatric illnesses (Taylor et al., 1997).

Further empirical research rounds out the picture of emotional deficit. Lane, Sechrest, Reidel, Weldon, Kaszniak, and Schwartz (1996) found that alexithymia is associated with impaired verbal and nonverbal recognition of emotion stimuli. The hallmark of alexithymia, a difficulty in putting emotion into words, may be a marker of a more general impairment in the capacity for emotional information processing. This impairment is manifested through difficulties in processing both words and faces. In a study by Roedema and Simons (1999), high TAS subjects supplied fewer emotion-related words than did controls to describe their response to standardized emotion-eliciting color slides. Alexithymics also showed reduce psychophysiological responsetivity to the slides. A study of facial emotion processing (Pandey & Mandal, 1997) found that alexithymics did not differ from nonalexithymics in emotional matching and labeling tasks but had significant difficulty in verbally describing emotional expressions as evident by less duration of utterance, greater response latency and increased linguistic-type speech disruptions. This study did not suggest any deficit in recognition of emotion, but, in a doctoral study by Ovies (1998), alexithymic students made more errors when required to detect emotion in angry faces than did nonalexithymics.

Alexithymia is also associated with difficulties in discriminating among different emotional states (Bagby, Parker, Taylor & Acklin, 1993), and with a limited ability to think about and use emotions to cope with stressful situations (Parker, Taylor & Bagby, 1998; Schaffer, 1993). Beckendam (1997) found that alexithymia was associated with maladaptive styles of emotion regulation, as assessed with the ARS, in particular, sexual and aggressive fantasies and behavior, such as engaging in reckless activities and drinking alcohol.

It is generally agreed that difficulty in monitoring the feelings and emotions of *other* people is not a critical attribute in the definition of alexithymia. However, empirical studies have shown that individuals with high degrees of alexithymia experience difficulties in accurately identifying emotions in the facial expressions of others (Lane et al., 1996; Parker, Taylor & Bagby, 1993). Clinicians also report that alexithymic individuals manifest a limited capacity of empathizing with the emotional states of others (Beckendam, 1997; Davis et al., 1998; Krystal, 1979; McDougall, 1989; Taylor, 1987). These interpersonal deficits may in part be a consequence of failure to elevate emotions from a pre-conceptual level of organization to the conceptual level of mental representations. Lacking knowledge of their own emotional experiences, these individuals can't readily imagine themselves in another person's situation and are consequently unempathic and ineffective in modulating the emotional states of others. The ability to empathize with another person's emotional experience, however, might also be impaired by a difficulty in perceiving and comprehending facial and another non-verbal expressions of emotion (Parker, Taylor & Bagby, 1993).

Alexithymia may have multiple aspects. In the initial validation study of the Twenty-Item Toronto Alexithymia Scale (TAS-20), a widely used and well documented self-report measure of alexithymia (Bagby et al.,

1994a), exploratory analysis of the scale with a student sample yielded the following three-factor structure congruent with the theoretical construct of alexithymia: (a) difficulty in identifying feelings and distinguishing between feelings and bodily sensations of emotional arousal, (b) difficulty describing feelings to others, and (c) externally oriented thinking. The third factor, together with factor 2, seem to reflect the operatory thinking component of alexithymia (a cognitive style that shows a preference for the external details of everyday life rather than thought content related to feelings, fantasies, and other aspects of a person's inner experience).

Etiology

As pointed out by Taylor (1984), there have been attempts to explain the etiology of alexithymia from diverse points of view, including genetics, neuropsychological, social learning, developmental, and psychodynamic. At present, multiple factors are thought to play a role in the etiology of alexithymia (Taylor, Bagby & Parker, 1997; Nemiah, 1977), including neurobiological deficits or variations in brain organization and sociocultural influences. In the following section we focus on neurobiological, developmental and personality factors.

Neurobiological deficits   A popular etiological model of alexithymia has been the interhemispheric transfer or "functional commissurotomy" model. This model posits that alexithymia represents a deficit in the ability to transfer emotional information from the emotion centers of the right hemisphere to the language centers of the left hemisphere, i.e., via the connecting commissure. According to Taylor and Parker (2000) most cognitive tasks require a varying amount of interhemispheric cooperation. Thus, our ability to appropriately identify the affect of others and to communicate affect depends on a healthy interaction between right-hemisphere emotional perception and left-hemisphere linguistic processing and reason. In both clinical and nonclinical populations, alexithymia was found to be associated with a deficit in the bidirectional transfer of sensorimotor information between right and left hemispheres (Taylor, 2000). Alexithymics may have only a limited capacity to coordinate and integrate activity in the specialized cognitive, imaginal, and emotional processing systems of the right and left hemispheres. However, some recent research has failed to observe hemispheric specific effects (Ovies, 1998).

Lane et al. (1998) found a positive relationship between individual differences in the cognitive skill of recognizing and describing emotions in oneself in others and increased activity in the anterior cingulate cortex, when emotions were induced either by films or by recall of personal experiences. This finding led Lane, Ahern, Schwartz, and Kaszniak (1997) to speculate that alexithymia might be associated with a deficit in anterior cingulate cortex activity during emotional arousal. The anterior cingulate cortex not only plays a role in conscious experience, but also helps orchestrate autonomic, endocrine and motor responses to emotional stimuli, and so some altered functioning in this part of the brain might contribute to exaggerated arousal that could lead to somatic symptoms (see chapter 6).

Taylor and Bagby (2000) suggest a more comprehensive model in which the neural correlates of alexithymia include an interhemispheric transfer deficit, thereby reducing coordination and integration of the specialized activities of the two hemispheres, as well as that part of the anterior cingulate cortex associated with selective attention and memory. Indeed, it appears that the left hemisphere can modulate an individual's arousal response by maintaining some type of inhibitory control over the right hemisphere. Consequently, impaired interhemispheric communication could lead to extreme dominance of the right hemisphere in controlling the level of activity of the autonomic nervous system.

As pointed out by Taylor and Bagby (2000), the findings from the neurobiological studies of alexithymia are correlational only and do not imply any cause-effect relationships. Furthermore, since most of the studies can be faulted on methodological grounds, these explanations remain speculative (Taylor, 1984).

Attachment   A review of recent research (Taylor, Parker & Bagby, 1999) suggests that alexithymia is associated with insecure attachment styles, that limit the emergence of emotion representation in childhood. Insecure attachment styles are associated with inner schemata or representations that reflect failures in the integration of affective information and cognitive information (Crittenden, 1994). According to Taylor (2000), the deficits underlying alexithymia have been attributed at least in part to an arrest in emotional development during early childhood. The development of affects and affect regulating capacities is facilitated early in life by the experience of sharing emotions and the "mirroring" of affective expressions with the primary caregiver, and subsequently by engaging in pleasurable playful interactions and being taught to name and talk about feelings. Numerous studies have demonstrated that when the primary caregiver is emotionally unavailable, or when the child is subjected repeatedly to inconsistent responses because of parental "mis-attunements," the child may become behaviorally avoidant and less emotionally expressive of both positive and negative affects, and fail to learn the meaning and signal function of affects. The mothers of inse-cure avoidant infants are often low in emotional expressiveness them-selves (Bretherton, 1985). Infants who experience inconsistent responses to their affective communications develop an insecureambivalent attach-ment style, and have difficulty regulating emotional distress (Slade & Aber, 1992).

Taylor's (2000) survey of the literature suggests that, in both clinical and nonclinical adult samples, alexithymia is associated with insecure attachment styles, as measured by self-report scales. Developmental pro-cesses may interact with biological processes in a reciprocal fashion. According to Taylor and Bagby (2000), the caregiver has a regulatory influence on the maturation of parts of the brain that are involved in emotional awareness and emotion regulation (see chapter 6). Research findings suggests that the maturation of the orbitofrontal cortex occurs in stages and is dependent on the high levels of neurotransmitters that are released in the infant's forebrain by the emotion-laden interactions with the caregivers. Thus, when caregivers fail to regulate excessive levels of low emotional arousal and/or excessive levels of high negative emotional arousal, there can be permanent alternations in the mor-phological development of the orbitofrontal cortex (Schore, 1994). Ex-treme degrees of alexithymia might be a consequence of early trauma, including emotional deprivation and neglect, which appears to alter the maturation of some of the brain structures as well as the mental capaci-ties that are associated with emotional processing and EI.

Taylor (1984) points out that styles of communication are also in-fluenced by sociocultural factors, family patterns of discourse, and gen-eral intelligence. Thus, Taylor (1984) reviews studies indicating that people in developed countries may be characterized by a greater differ-entiation of emotional states than people in developing countries and that some languages impose constraints on the expression of emotion. Thus, multiple factors must be considered in research on the etiology of alexithymia.

Personality correlates   Alexithymia is related to a variety of personality variables, suggesting that it may be influenced by basic temperamental factors. A review by Taylor et al. (1997) indicates that the alexithymia construct converges with the first three dimensions of the Five Factor model of personality (see chapters 2 and 9). Specifically, alexithymic individuals show vulnerability to emotional distress (high N), low positive emotionality (low E), and a limited imagination (low O). Given these findings, Taylor et al. (1997) raise the question of whether alexithymia should be conceptualized as a unique construct with explanatory power or whether it is adequately represented by, and therefore redundant, with existing personality dimensions.

Eiden (1999) found that long-term anger and anxiety, depression, a style of coping with anger by turning it inward, and the avoidance of deep thought were the best predictors of alexithymia. Research by Newton and Contrada (1994) showed a relationship between alexithymia and repressive coping, on the basis of both psychometric and psychophysiological comparisons in 86 females. Deary, Scott, and Wilson (1997) assessed 244 respondents drawn from a range of medical and non-medical situations completed several self-report measures. Results show that two subscales from the TAS-20 had significant correlations with reported medical unexplained physical symptoms, but also with N, negative emotion health coping, anxiety, depression, general psychological distress and dysphoric mood. Finally, alexithymia has also been found to correlate significantly and negatively with measures of "psychological-mindedness," which refers to the motivation and ability to understand one's experiences in psychological terms (Bagby et al., 1994; McCallum & Piper, 2000).

Clinical parameters and interventions

Thus far, we have looked at how alexithymia may be conceptualized, and at some of the factors that may lead to alexithymia. Next, we look at the implications for clinical practice, by reviewing the role of alexithymia in psychopathology, and therapeutic methods specifically geared towards the needs of alexithymic patients. Evidence shows that alexithymia is one of several personality factors that appear to increase vulnerability to a variety of medical and psychiatric disorders involving problems in affect regulation (Taylor, 2000). These include panic disorder, PTSD, substance-abuse disorders, bingeing, hyperactivity, essential hypertension, functional gastrointestinal disorders, and a propensity to somatization. These symptoms have been conceptualized as attempts to regulate distressing and undifferentiated emotional states. The alexithymic individual's difficulties in understanding feeling states and accompanying somatic sensations may contribute to hypochondriasis and somatization disorder (Taylor et al., 1997). Lacking the ability to conceptualize emotions adequately may lead to misattribution of normal sensations to disease.

High degrees of alexithymia may also be present in a substantial number of patients with inflammatory bowel disease, essential hypertension, or functional gastrointestinal disorders. In particular, a consistent and meaningful relationship has been reported between alexithymia and essential hypertension (Taylor et al., 1997). Furthermore, alexithymia was found to be associated with maladaptive defense and coping styles (Parker et al., 1998), vulnerability to stress (Bagby et al., 1994b), and psychiatric disorders and somatic illnesses that involve problem in the modulation of distressing events (Taylor et al., 1997). Given that previous research has found alexithymia to be associated with both illness behavior and increased mortality from a variety of causes the findings raise the possibility that alexithymia might be a risk factor for both mental and physical health (Parker et al., 2001).

Treatment   Alexithymia research has its origins in clinical settings, evolving from clinical observations on clients who responded quite poorly to insight-oriented psychotherapy. Working with individuals experiencing psychosomatic disorders, Ruesch (1948) identified a cluster of personality variables in a subset of his patients, i.e., a tendency to develop dependant relationships, to engage in unimaginative thinking, and to use direct physical action for emotional expression. Taylor contends, "There is general agreement that alexithymic characteristics are difficult to modify" (2000, p. 139), but research suggests that group psychotherapy can reduce alexithymia characteristics. The specific form of therapy most appropriate for alexithymic individuals is currently debated in the literature. While Nemiah and Sifneos (1970) recommend supportive rather than interpretive forms of individual therapy, others suggest specific psychotherapeutic techniques applied to individuals or groups. The observed benefits may be related to an increase in the verbal symbolic elements of emotion representations or to enhanced connections between symbolic and subsymbolic elements, which potentially could be achieved by the specific psychotherapeutic techniques employed.

Alexithymic individuals are rarely suitable clients for traditional forms of insight-oriented psychotherapy (Taylor, 2000). Taylor (1984) cites research evidence indicating that in comparison with neurotic patients, alexithymic patients spoke less, were far less spontaneous in speech production, and were silent more, thus forcing the therapist into greater activity. Some psychoanalysts still fail to recognize the clinical features of alexithymia or low EI, and treatment can then enter a prolonged period of stagnation. Patients may complain of somatic symptoms when the therapist expects them to experience psychic distress. Premature termination of treatment is not uncommon. Krystal, who has written extensively about his experiences treating individuals with a variety of psychiatric problems (such as PTSD and substance-use disorders), suggests that alexithymia may be "the most important single factor diminishing the success of psychoanalysis and psychodynamic psychotherapy" (1982/83, p. 364), although this statement goes beyond the statistical evidence. Pierloot and Vinck (1977) compared patients who were randomly assigned to short-term psychodynamic psychotherapy or behavior therapy (systematic desensitization) and found that the dropout rate with the former treatment was related to the presence of alexithymic characteristics. These authors reported that patients with more alexithymia features are more likely to drop out from psychodynamic therapies, but in systematic desensitization they persist as well as those without these features.

Not only may traditional therapy not help, a number of clinicians have written that alexithymic individuals may actually be made worse as a result of psychotherapy (Sifneos, 1975; Taylor, 1987; Taylor et al., 1997). "Patients with active psychosomatic diseases may, instead of experiencing strong emotion, develop a serious or even life-endangering exacerbation of their illness" (Krystal, 1982/83, p. 363). Faced with the problem that conventional forms of psychotherapy might not work, or might make some clients worse, some clinicians have developed a number of therapeutic modifications for working with alexithymic clients (e.g., Krystal, 1979, 1988). Like a parent teaching the child, the therapist helps the patient to accurately label and gradually verbalize his emotions. Thus, the first step in treatment according to Krystal (1979, 1988) is to explain to the client that an important cause of their problem is a deficit in the way they understand and communicate emotional experiences. The second step in treatment is to work to improve the client's skills at recognizing and correctly labeling particular emotions,

Table 10.2
Comparison of EI and Alexithymia along key dimensions

Dimensions	Emotional intelligence	Alexithymia
Origins and context of research	Emotions and ability research—how people appraise, regulate, and use emotions	Clinical observations (medical, psychiatric)
Type of variable	Individual difference (ability/competence)	Individual difference? Personality disorder?
Recency of research	Past decade	Past 2 decades
Extent of empirical research	Sparse (several dozen publications)	Extensive (several hundred publications)
Popularity of construct	High	Low
Broader category	Social intelligence	Affect regulation disorder
Dimensionality of construct	Multidimensional	Multidimensional
Facet of personal intelligence/competence	Interpersonal and intrapersonal	Intrapersonal only
Emotional ability continuum	Entire continuum	Low end of continuum
Information processing	Cognitive processing of affective data (recognition, storage, problem-solving, decision making, etc.)	Deficit in affect processing and elevating processing from preconceptual to conceptual stage
Factor structure	3 to 4 factors (emotion perception, understanding, assimilation of emotion with cognition, emotion regulation)	3 factors (difficulty in identifying feelings, difficulty in describing feeling to others, externally oriented thinking)
Biological underpinnings	Biological determinants unclear; possible genetic factor	Neurobiological determinants attested (deficits in bi-directional transfer of information among hemispheres, anterior cingulate cortex activity)
Etiology	Primary socialization and social learning	Biology and attachment processes

Related features	Empathy, social skills, assertiveness, etc.	Limited empathic capacity, social conformity, tendency towards actions, infrequent recollection of dreams, paucity of facial expressions, stress vulnerability, etc.
Covariation with intelligence	Moderately related to verbal intelligence	Negligibly related to intelligence
Personality correlates	Unclear; a function of scoring technique	Positively correlated with N and negatively correlated with E and O; negatively correlated with psychological mindfulness
Intelligence correlates	Moderately related to verbal intelligence	Negligibly related to intelligence
Links to clinical disorders	Unclear	Widespread incidence in variety of clinical disorders: PTSD, panic disorder, drug abuse, bingeing, essential hypertension, etc.
Amenability to intervention	Good	Poor (particularly conventional psychotherapy)
Intervention focus	Socio-emotional skill training	Focus on labeling and discerning inner experiences and emotions

N = neuroticism; E = extraversion; O = openness.

differentiating one emotional experience from another, and communicating these feelings to others. Over time, alexithymic clients can learn to have a better understanding of their feelings, can learn to differentiate between different emotional states, and can develop a larger repertoire of verbal and behavioral expression for communicating information about their emotional experiences.

Emotional intelligence and alexithymia

EI and alexithymia are two conceptually similar and closely linked variables reflecting individual differences in emotional awareness, expression, and regulation, but arise from different research traditions (see table 10.2). Although less well known in the popular press than EI, the alexithymia construct has generated a far greater amount of empirical research than has the EI construct (Taylor, Bagby & Parker, 1997).

EI includes the ability to identify, label, discriminate, monitor, and regulate one's own feelings and those of others. By contrast, alexithymia is a more narrowly defined construct than EI, but one overlapping with Gardner's (1983) concept of intrapersonal intelligence—in particular, with the ability to identify, label, and discriminate among one's feelings. That is, alexithymia is conceptually similar to the lower pole of Gardner's (1983) concept of intrapersonal intelligence, but does not encompass the interpersonal intelligence facet in its domain (Taylor & Bagby, 2000), as illustrated in figure 10.1. Difficulty in monitoring the feelings and emotions of others is not included in the definition of alexithymia construct, but, as discussed above, empirical studies have shown that alexithymia relates to lack of empathy and lack of awareness of emotional states of others, difficulties that may relate back to inadequate caregiver relationships in childhood.

Recent empirical evidence suggests that alexithymia and EI are closely related and meaningfully linked constructs. Davies, Stankov and Roberts (1998) used the three-factor scales of the Twenty-Item Toronto Alexithymia Scale (TAS-20) (Bagby, Parker & Taylor, 1994a), reviewed in chapter 5, to assess the appraisal and expression of emotions in the self and the recognition of emotions in others. One of the TAS-20 factors (externally oriented thinking) correlated negatively with Mehrabian and Epstein's (1970) questionnaire measure of emotional empathy. Furthermore, in a second-order factor analysis, which included a number of different scales related to EI, the TAS-20 factor scales loaded significantly on factors pertaining to "emotional clarity" and/or "emotional awareness."

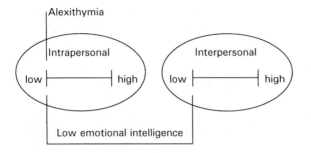

Figure 10.1
Conceptual relationship between alexithymia and Gardner's intrapersonal and interpersonal dimensions.

Parker, Taylor, and Bagby (2001) showed, in a large nonclinical sample ($n = 734$), that mean TAS-20 total scores showed a strong negative correlation with the person's score ($r = -0.72$, $p < 0.01$) on the Bar-On (1997) EQ-i questionnaire. Significant negative correlations were also obtained with all of the EQ-i subscales, including interpersonal and intrapersonal EI facets. Furthermore, they reported a structural equation analysis of the covariation between EI (represented by four EQ-i composite scores, all except stress management) and the alexithymia construct (represented by the three TAS-20 subscale scores). In a confirmatory factor analysis, the parameter estimates of correlations between the EQ-i and each of the factors of the TAS-20 proved to be significant: $-.78$ for difficulty in identifying feelings, $-.70$ for difficulty in describing feelings, and $-.55$ for external-oriented thinking. Thus, lower levels of EI and its four components were associated with higher levels of alexithymia and its salient facets. The magnitude of these correlations are uniformly moderate to large in magnitude, suggesting that alexithymia and EI are inversely related, but strongly overlapping constructs (Taylor and Bagby, in press). For each of the latent models tested, a two-factor solution was superior to one-factor solution, indicating that the construct measured by TAS-20 is also independent of the construct measured by the EQ-i.

Critique of alexithymia

Taylor et al. (1997) summarize a number of criticisms of the construct. To begin with, although there is consensus about the clinical features and definitions of the construct, there has been controversy and debate as to whether it is a clinical disorder, a stable individual difference variable or personality trait, a transient state secondary to psychological distress associated with acute illness or some other stressful situation, or a coping response to chronic illness. Some critics have argued that alexithymia can be explained merely by cultural or social class differences in emotional expressiveness or by communication difficulties specific to the patient/physician relationship. Others regard alexithymia as a defense against neurotic conflict rather than a type of deficit in affect.

Furthermore, there are several potential confounding variables in alexithymia research. For example, many of the studies have failed to control for the effects of certain biological and psychosocial risk factors, such as sex, age, SES, smoking, and alcohol use. The empirical studies of the relationship between alexithymia and somatic illness and disease are mainly cross-sectional in design. Because of the cross-sectional design of the studies, it is not possible to make causal connections between alexithymia and various illnesses and diseases. Furthermore, alexithymia might be merely a state phenomenon secondary to the emotional distress evoked by an illness or it might reflect a psychological change that occurs in response to physiological changes brought about by a somatic disease (Taylor, 2000). Finally, findings from treatment-outcome studies are preliminary and require replication with larger samples and with a variety of disorders.

Pathological Processes

Thus far, we have considered PLEI as a possible diagnostic entity, as an aspect of abnormal personality, or as a concomitant of alexithymia. A further approach is to seek out PLEI at the process level. Are some individuals deficient in dynamic adjustment to emotionally charged environmental demands? Of course, there is a huge literature on abnormality in biological, cognitive and social processes, which cannot be reviewed here. Instead, we will focus especially on cognitive processes in mood and anxiety disorders. These disorders are closely associated with negative affectivity, which, as we have seen, is central to mixed-model conceptions of EI. Their etiology reflects both biological and psychological factors, and both pharmacological and psychological therapies may be effective as treatments. We will focus on psychological factors, because, as argued in chapters 6–7, emotions map more closely onto psychological than biological constructs (whether or not psychological constructs are ultimately reducible to biological ones).

In chapter 7, we discussed some of the cognitive processes reciprocally linked to negative affect, such as biases towards negatively valenced
information in selective attention, judgment and memory. These biases
are typically stronger in clinical patients than in people who are unhappy but functioning normally, and have generated various cognitive
models of abnormality. One of the basic tenets of this research area is
that errors in cognition generate pathology (Ellis, 1962). Broadly, depression may be a consequence of inaccurate negative beliefs about
one's self-worth and future prospects, whereas anxiety reflects exaggeration of threat and personal vulnerability. Vulnerability factors may divided into those which are long-term, such as events in childhood that
lead to later vulnerability, and those which are short-term such as cognitive abnormalities that lead to pathology over a time course of, say,
a few months (see Ingram, Miranda & Segal, 1998, for a conceptual
analysis of different vulnerability factors). Here, we focus on short-term
processes of distorted self-beliefs generating abnormalities in information-
processing that lead to damaging interactions with the outside world.

There are two basic problems in specification of the causal contribution of distorted cognitions to pathology. First, it is difficult to distinguish cognitive symptoms of the disorder from underlying cognitive
factors that are genuinely causal: a cognitive *vulnerability* factor should
precede the appearance of the symptoms diagnostic of the disorder
(Ingram et al., 1998). Two complementary techniques may be used to
identify vulnerability factors. Longitudinal studies can assess the correlations between cognitive factors and symptoms over time, and test alternative models of causality. These studies have the disadvantage of
reliance on correlational data. Experimental studies can test whether
manipulations of cognition influence emotion and other symptoms,
with the disadvantage that, at least in nonclinical samples, the emotional
response may not be representative of pathological emotion. Although
both methods are imperfect, converging evidence from both sources
provides some confidence in causal models.

A second problem is that there is a multiplicity of conceptually overlapping and empirically correlated cognitive constructs that are implicated in disorder (Wells & Matthews, in press). It is often difficult to
isolate those aspects of cognition that are critical as vulnerability factors.
For example, anxiety may be linked to severity of threat appraisal, to
immediacy of threat, to lack of perceived control, and to selective attention to threat-related cognitions (e.g., Wells & Matthews, 1994). Such

constructs are correlated but discriminable. However, rather little research has attempted to test which of the various factors are critical to anxiety, and which are of secondary importance. Indeed, much cognitive research tends to focus on the one or two constructs closest to the researcher's interests, ignoring possible confounds. One necessity is a taxonomy of cognitive constructs to guide discrimination. Ingram et al. (1998), for example, distinguish cognitive products, structures and operations as the basis for theory. For example, depression might be variously attributed to irrational negative thoughts (products), to organized negative self-beliefs held in schematic form (structures) or to excessive attention to negative information (operations). Although useful for organizing a review, the weakness of such a taxonomy is that it neglects dynamic interrelationships between different types of constructs. For example, schematic structures may generate thoughts as products, and thinking may, in turn, feed back to alter the schema.

Hence, we will base a brief overview of cognitive processes on the dynamic S-REF architecture introduced in chapters 4 and 7. As previously discussed, the S-REF model (Wells & Matthews, 1994) differentiates three levels of processing that interact in normal and abnormal emotional states. The first level (lower-level networks) comprises processing networks that support a variety of involuntary, somewhat automatic processing functions on both emotional and nonemotional stimuli. The second level (self-referent executive function) implements voluntary control of processing in response to signals of threat or challenge, by modifying generic processing routines accessed from the third level (self-knowledge), such as coping strategies. These distinctions suggest conceptually different sources of pathology. First, pathology might reflect biases in computations supporting involuntary processing, as in the hypothesis that anxiety is influenced by bias in automatic registration of threat (Williams et al., 1988). Third, pathology might relate to the content of self-knowledge, such as the dysfunctional beliefs in self-worthlessness associated with depression (Beck, 1967). Second, pathology might reflect maladaptive S-REF processing configurations, such as persevering worry, that maintains the focus of attention on negative self-referent information.

We will focus on the last two sources here. In-built processing biases may well be a source of pathology, and as discussed in chapter 9, there is evidence that anxiety may be linked to multiple biases in components of attention (Derryberry & Reed, 1997). However, the empirical evidence suggests that those biases most disruptive to normal functioning, such as hypervigilance for threat, reflect strategy choice rather than the cognitive architecture (Matthews & Wells, 1999). Furthermore, the distributed nature of low-level processing across many modules makes it unpromising as a possible locale for EI. We also emphasize that self-knowledge and processing configuration are interdependent, in that, for example, S-REF operations are guided by generic plans retrieved from self-knowledge and some forms of processing will feed back into altered self-knowledge. Nevertheless, it is useful to distinguish relatively stable distortions of self-belief that refer to specific content from styles of person-environment transaction that can be abstracted from the actual content of the cognitions involved.

Dysfunctional self-knowledge in depression

The role of dysfunctional self-knowledge is best known from Aaron Beck's (1967, 1987) schema theory of depression. Beck observed that depressed patients often exhibited a pattern of distorted thinking associated with the "cognitive triad": negative beliefs about the self (e.g., worthlessness), about the world around them (e.g., nobody cares about the person), and the future (e.g., the person is doomed to fail). These negative beliefs appear to be perpetuated by errors in thinking and logic, such as overgeneralization; inferring lack of self-worth from an isolated incident of personal failure. Beck suggested that these distortions in thinking derived from a dysfunctional self-schema that maintained overly negative generic self-beliefs as representations in long-term memory. Within a diathesis-stressor framework, Beck proposed that critical incidents related to loss or failure activated the self-schema. The self-schema shapes an array of biases towards negative self-referent processing involving themes of loss, failure and deprivation, leading to the development of symptoms of depression. Subsequently, Clark and Beck (1999) have emphasized that disordered cognition is not the sole cause of depression, and biological factors are also important.

There is overwhelming evidence from both self-report and performance-based studies for the occurrence of cognitive biases and thought disorder in clinical depression (see Clark & Beck, 1999; Ingram et al., 1998, for reviews). Some of the cognitive constructs described by Beck have been operationalized as questionnaires. For example, the Dysfunctional Attitudes Scale (DAS) (Weissman & Beck, 1978) assesses irrational beliefs such as supposing that one's life is wasted unless one achieves a high degree of success. A central but problematic question is whether the various cognitive distortions seen in depressed patients represent vulnerability factors that precede the onset of illness. The simplest finding has been that measures of cognitive distortion, such as those provided by the DAS, tend to rise and fall as the clinical disorder develops and remits. Ingram et al. conclude, "An inescapable conclusion ... is that depressive cognition is largely state dependent. Little evidence was found for the existence of an enduring proximal predisposition to depression that does not change with treatment" (1998, p. 157). Several other reviews (e.g., Coyne & Whiffen, 1995) have also questioned the cognitive etiology of depression. Clark and Beck (1999) arrive at a somewhat different conclusion. While acknowledging inconsistency of results, they identify several cross-sectional and longitudinal studies that showed that high DAS scorers were more likely to develop depressive symptoms when subjected to some life stressor. They also point towards various methodological problems, such as inadequate assessment of cognition and stress, and inadequate sample sizes.

Clark and Beck (1999) also make the vital point that schemas are latent constructs, that may not influence cognition when the person is nondepressed. In other words, the DAS assesses whether dysfunctional cognitions are activated and accessible, not whether the underlying schema is dysfunctional. A latent, inactive schema may be activated through priming manipulations, such as inducing negative mood states or through presenting negative concepts as primes. These studies are more supportive of schema theory. For example, Miranda and Persons (1988) compared currently nondepressed women with and without a history of previous depression. As in other research, the two groups did not differ in DAS scores. However, when a negative mood was induced experimentally, DAS score was higher in the previously depressed group, suggesting an underlying, latent dysfunctionality consistent with schema theory. Attentional bias may be similarly latent, being dependent on priming or activation of a negative mood (McCabe, Gotlib & Martin, 2000). Ingram et al. conclude, "Although not completely uniform, results from available priming studies do support the notion that priming prior to cognitive assessment allows for the detection of depressotypic cognitive variables in individuals who are theoretically at risk, but not currently depressed" (1998, p. 169).

Another important line of evidence derives from the recent Temple-Wisconsin Cognitive Vulnerability to Depression Project, which tracked approximately 5,000 college students over a five-year period (Alloy & Abramson, 1999). These researchers defined cognitive vulnerability both in terms of the DAS, and additional vulnerability factors related to their hypothesis that hopelessness depression relates to an attributional style characterized by inferences that negative life events reflect stable, global causes such as the person's fundamental lack of worth. Initial reports on this large-scale study suggest that cognitively high-risk individuals are indeed more likely to develop clinical depression than low-risk individuals, even when never previously depressed (Alloy et al., 1999).

Vulnerability factors for anxiety

One of the unresolved issues here is the extent to which dysfunctional beliefs may increase risk of the various anxiety disorders, as well as risk of depression. Clark and Beck's content-specificity hypothesis proposes, "Psychological disorders or states can be distinguished by the form and content of their associated dysfunctional cognitions, beliefs, attitudes, and processes" (1999, p. 127). Some distortions in cognition appear to reflect the involvement of N or negative affectivity across the full spectrum of mood and anxiety disorders. For example, scores on the DAS appear to be generally elevated in states of chronic negative affect (Clark, Beck & Brown, 1989), negative self-beliefs are common to most mood and anxiety disorders (Wells & Matthews, 1994), and some commentators have questioned the cognitive discriminability of anxiety and depression (e.g., Gotlib, Kurtzman & Blehar, 1997). On the other hand, Clark and Beck (1999) cite considerable evidence in support of specific content associated with depression, related to personal loss and failure. Alloy and Abramson (1999) found that their cognitive risk index predicted onset of depression but not anxiety. However, Clark and Beck's (1999) review suggests that there is weaker empirical support for the claim that anxiety is associated with an elevated level of threat and danger cognitions, relative to depression, although, of course, anxious patients show greater concerns with threat than normal controls. Such difficulties may, in part, reflect the extensive empirical confounding between anxiety and depression. In addition, anxiety disorders may relate not so much to threat per se, but the person's metacognitive awareness of their own reactions to threat. Wells (2000) suggests that "metaworry," worry about one's own uncontrollable worries, is central to generalized anxiety disorder.

Cognitive vulnerability factors should not be restricted to explicit, declarative beliefs: latent maladaptive coping styles reflecting procedural knowledge may also lead to future pathology (Wells & Matthews, 1994). For example, a recent longitudinal study of 154 former psychiatric outpatients in Norway (Vollrath et al., 1996; Vollrath, Alnæs & Torgersen, 1998) found that coping style measures predicted clinical syndromes assessed six or seven years later. Several conditions, including anxiety, dysthymia, depression and somatoform disorder, were associated with greater use of disengagement and venting of emotions, and reduced use of active goal-oriented coping and seeking social support. Modeling of data suggested that anxiety was especially related to low active goal-oriented coping, and depression to low social support seeking (Vollrath et al., 1996). Other, process-oriented vulnerability factors may include schemas or plans controlling attentional bias, thought control strategies, and other metacognitive processing (Wells & Matthews, in press).

Awareness of somatic arousal may also be more important to anxiety than to depression; various anxious patient groups appear to have more accurate perceptions of heart rate than both normal controls and mood disorder patients (Van der Does et al., 2000). In addition, a prospective study showed that good heart rate perception predicts a poor treatment outcome for panic disorder patients (Ehlers, 1995). A more general conception is that of 'anxiety sensitivity' (Reiss & McNally, 1985); negative beliefs about the consequences of anxiety may operate as risk factor for various anxiety disorders, as when fear of fear is the source of pathology. Prospective studies suggest that anxiety sensitivity is a predictor of risk of panic attacks (Schmidt, Lerew & Joiner, 2000). The reflexive character of self-beliefs in anxiety is also represented in metacognitive theory (Wells, 2000), which as further discussed below, attributes pathology to dysfunctional beliefs about the person's own thoughts, such as appraising the content of thought as threatening and uncontrollable.

Research on cognitive vulnerability factors for specific anxiety disorders is reviewed in a recent edited volume (Alloy & Riskind, in press). An example will demonstrate how schema or self-knowledge models may be applied to specific disorders. The development of PTSD following a traumatic event such as a natural disaster or rape is associated with marked changes in personal beliefs. The world is seen as less benign and meaningful, other people are appraised as less trustworthy, and there may be a loss of self-worth (Epstein, 1991). Foa (Foa & Kokaz, 1986; Foa & Riggs, 1995) has developed an emotional-processing theory that specifies the role of dysfunctional self-knowledge in PTSD. The traumatic event elicits the development of a fear network (see chapter 7 for background on network theories) that represents information about the feared stimulus, overt responses, and interpretive information about the meaning of stimulus and response elements. The network provides a program for escape and avoidance, and commonly develops in victims. Typically, fear response dissipates over time, representing a weakening of the control of the fear network over behavior. However, fear may be pathological when the network incorporates dysfunctional elements that include maladaptive response (such as excessive avoidance behaviors), unrealistic beliefs and distortions in interpretation. Foa and her colleagues describe various cognitive vulnerability factors that increase the likelihood of a pathological network developing, especially rigid beliefs in world dangerousness and personal incompetence, factors which predict severity of trauma, and distinguish trauma victims with and without PTSD (Foa et al., 1999). Personality factors such as N are also be linked to the likelihood of dysfunctional cognitions of the traumatic event (Morgan, Matthews & Winton, 1995).

In general, PTSD appears to involve cognitive factors common to several anxiety/mood disorders, such as lack of self-worth and ineffective coping, together with factors specific to the disorder, such as beliefs about the feared event, that may be idiosyncratic to the individual person (Steil & Ehlers, 2000). A similar mixture of general and specific symptoms tend to be found for other anxiety disorders (Wells & Matthews, in press). Phobia, of course relates to beliefs about the feared object. For example, anxiety patients are generally prone to interpret ambiguous situations negatively, but social phobics are also generate especially negative interpretations of ambiguous *social* situations (Stopa & Clark, 2000). In generalized anxiety disorder (GAD), dysfunction centers on metacognitive beliefs that perpetuate worry (see Wells, 2000, for a review). Anxious and depressed individuals generally tend to show increased awareness of self-referent thoughts, and attribute greater importance to them than nonclinical samples. However, GAD is associated with especially high levels of negative beliefs about worry, and with especially high metaworry, i.e., worrying about one's own worry (Wells & Carter, 1999, 2001). Panic disorder and health anxiety are associated specifically with maladaptive beliefs about physical symptoms, focusing on imminent catastrophe such as cardiac arrest (Clark, 1986), and dysfunctional beliefs about death and illness (Wells & Hackmann, 1993), respectively. Obsessive-compulsive disorder relates to some particularly odd styles of cognition, such as thought-action fusion, in which a thought, such as harming one's child, is appraised as equivalent to actually performing the action (Rachman, 1993), and an excessively elevated sense of personal responsibility (Salkovskis, 1985), which might even make the person admit to a crime they had not committed.

Dynamic factors in emotional psychopathology

The cognitive vulnerability factors described so far refer to relatively stable features of the person's self-knowledge, that may be represented as schemas (Beck, 1967) or as generic procedures for handling external demands (Wells & Matthews, 1994). However, dysfunctional self-knowledge is harmful because of its role in shaping interaction with the outside world, and understanding these interactions requires a more dynamic perspective. The S-REF model (Wells & Matthews, 1994; Matthews & Wells, 1999) describes in more detail some of the dynamic factors that generate temporally extended patterns or configurations of processing, that may cause emotional disorders. One key process is persevering worry, i.e., prolonged but ineffective reflection on personal problems and the harm they may cause. A similar concept of *rumination* (Nolen-Hoeksema, 2000) refers specifically to persevering worry about the meaning, causes and consequences of one's distress. At one level, persevering worry is generated by dysfunctional self-knowledge, including discrepancies between preferred and actual self-status (self-discrepancies), and metacognitive beliefs to the effect that worry is a useful problem solving strategy (Matthews & Wells, in press). The concept also overlaps with transactional stress processes often associated with negative affect (see chapter 8), such as appraising the situation as hard to control, and coping through emotion-focused strategies such as self-criticism (Matthews, Derryberry & Siegle, 2000).

Critically, persevering worry reflects dynamic maladjustment, as it is a self-perpetuating vicious circle. Worry is associated with increased self-focus of attention, which leads to increased salience of self-discrepancies, which in turn maintains worry. The self-perpetuating nature of worry induces a sense of lack of control over thinking that may further strengthen self-focus (see Wells & Matthews, 1994, for a review of experimental and correlational evidence). According to the S-REF theory, the vicious circle of worry perpetuation is common to many mood and anxiety disorders. However, in line with the content-specificity hypothesis (Clark & Beck, 1999), the content of worry varies across the different disorders. In depression, for example, worry recycles cognitions of events related to personal loss (Ingram, 1984). In generalized anxiety, the person worries about their own thoughts and their uncontrollability (Wells, 2000). The limited longitudinal evidence available suggests that measures related to worry (Wells, 2000, p. 163) and rumination (Nolen-Hoeksema, 2000) are predictive of future pathology.

Wells and Matthews (1994) describe other pathological dynamics also. Many disorders are associated with coping through monitoring for external threats, as evidenced in studies of the emotional Stroop task and other attentional paradigms. However, hypervigilance for threat increases the likelihood of detecting threat, especially in conjunction with biased stimulus evaluation, which perpetuates the search strategy. In some disorders, patients attempt to suppress unpleasant thoughts. However, experimental studies (reviewed by Wenzlaff & Wegner, 2000) show that thought suppression tends to lead to a subsequent rebound of the thought, so that the strategy actually enhances thought intrusions in the longer term. Dynamic interaction with the social environment may also be critical. Some types of patient tend to engage in safety behaviors that reinforce their negative self-beliefs and prevent them from learning how to manage the feared situation (Wells, 1997). For example, social phobics may avoid other people, heightening their sense of social ineptitude and impeding development of social skills. Depression is associated with styles of interpersonal reaction that impair social exchange and cut off the depressed person from social support (Coyne, 1976). Depressives tend to be gloomy and self-preoccupied, which makes them poor company for other people, who are likely to prefer more cheerful company, enhancing the depressed person's sense of social isolation.

The obverse of pathological worry is the adaptive reconstruction of self-knowledge, such as coming to terms with a damaging event or acquiring self-regulative skills that promote effective coping with problems. For example, Foa and Kozak's (1986) concept of emotional processing of fear refers to changes to the fear network that allow it to be assimilated into normal processing. This process requires the incorporation of fear-incongruent information into the network, which requires elaboration of the memory for the traumatic event to link it with other autobiographical memories (Ehlers & Clark, 2000). Constructing a narrative for the event, either informally through talking about feelings to close confidants, or as part of a guided therapeutic intervention, appears to be effective (Foa & Rothbaum, 1998). More generally, changing metacognitions so as to evaluate negative self-referent thinking critically and realistically appears to promote normal functioning (Wells, 2000). Most people have some awareness that, under stress, their worries may become over-wrought, and acquire strategies such as distraction, positive thinking, or active problem-solving to prevent the perpetuation of worry. Anxious and depressed patients appear to be deficient in these essential self-regulative skills.

Implications for a process model of emotional intelligence

The notion of PLEI requires an underlying lack of competence in the processes controlling emotional disorders. Thus far, work on EI has provided little direct evidence on the nature of the processes that might be involved. Salovey et al. (1999) suggest that lack of coping skills may relate to ruminative coping, failure to build social support and lack of emotional disclosure. All three processes are implicated in emotional pathology, as well as the normal coping processes with which Salovey et al. are mainly concerned. We have seen that rumination appears to be a vulnerability factor for depression and anxiety disorders (Matthews & Wells, in press). Lack of social support is also a well-established vulnerability factor, although it may reflect life circumstances as well as the individual's lack of competence in forming close relationships. The depressed person's tendency to induce discomfort in others during social interaction (Coyne, 1975) may be one process supporting lack of social support. The importance of emotional disclosure comes primarily from studies of nonclinical samples showing that writing about traumatic events alleviates distress (Pennebaker, 1997). It is unclear that this procedure would be universally beneficial to patients, especially when, as in the case of some depressives, the person has developed a richly elaborated network of associations with depressogenic cognitions (Ingram, 1984). In fact, following bereavement, suppression of sadness and grief, and expression of positive emotions predict better future outcome (Bonnano, 1999). It may not be emotional disclosure per se, but the way in which emotional disclosure revises self-beliefs (positively or negatively) that is most important. Narrative construction is often beneficial to PTSD patients (Foa & Rothbaum, 1998); emotional disclosure may be beneficial to victims of trauma because it allows the fear network to be integrated with other, nonthreatening cognitive structures (Steil & Ehlers, 2000).

Evidently, Salovey et al. (1999) are right to identify the processes discussed as important for emotional well-being. However, it is not clear that, collectively, they define a distinct competence. Rumination, dysfunctional social interaction and emotional disclosure relate to different parts of the underlying architecture. According to Wells' (2000) analysis of pathological worry, rumination is driven by metacognitive self-knowledge, such as beliefs that worry is an effective technique for problem-solving. Dysfunctional social interaction is associated with the particular self-beliefs characteristic of depression, such as self-blame, possibly coupled with motives to manipulate others into providing sympathy and support (Coyne, 1976). Rumination and dysfunctional social interaction both tend to be self-perpetuating, but their dynamics are different. Rumination is prolonged, according to the S-REF theory (Matthews & Wells, in press; Wells & Matthews, 1994), by continued reactivation of negative self-beliefs, whereas dysfunctional social interaction is perpetuated by the depressed person eliciting ever more negative feedback from the other person. The pathology remedied by emotional disclosure relates to memory processes such as retrieval and elaboration (Steil & Ehlers, 2000). Hence, there is no obvious coherence, at an information-processing level, to the processes identified by Salovey et al. (1999).

At the same time, there are various pathological processes to which Salovey et al. (1999) do not refer, including depressogenic errors in reasoning and attribution, hypervigilance for threat, misattribution of physical symptoms, and obsessional thought-action fusion and responsibility cognitions. Such processes could just as easily be described as relating to low EI, but it is circular to redescribe every process shown to be pathological as emotionally unintelligent. The idea of PLEI would be more useful if EI theory specified a defined subset of pathological processes that related directly to emotion-regulation, and other pathological processes that do not. Such a demarcation would distinguish PLEI from other vulnerability factors. However, even in Salovey et al.'s (1999) conception (let alone Goleman's, 1995), the concept of EI is so broadly drawn that we cannot point to a set of non-EI cognitive vulnerability factors. The branch competences of identifying, assimilating, understanding and managing emotions appears to refer to the full set of processes that operate on negative self-referent information. It is not helpful to define PLEI as any deficiency or distortion in self-referent information processing. From this perspective, narrower concepts, such as alexithymia, that may be related to a distinct subset of damaging processing attributes may be more clinically useful.

The use of EI as a grab-bag superordinate category for maladaptive processing has two further problems. It obscures the role of cognitive content in emotional disorders. As argued by Beck and Clark (1999), content is essential in discriminating different disorders: themes of loss and inadequacy in depression, the person's own worries in generalized anxiety disorder, the feared object in phobia, and so forth. Describing a person as low in EI says nothing about the type of emotional disorder for which they are at risk. At best, PLEI represents the generalized vulnerability associated with the lower end of the negative affectivity spectrum, but, as previously argued, this vulnerability is already adequately described as high N. An additional problem is that EI obscures the essential dynamic and transactional aspects of mental disorder. As in the case of normal emotions (Lazarus, 1999), mental disorders represent a dynamic interaction between person and situation. To take an extreme example, a spider phobic would function normally in a spider-free environment. Even with more free-floating disorders, the idiosyncratic nature of disorder means that patients have more difficulties with some situations, and less with others. Attributing disorder to lack of EI neglects the role of the fit between person and environment, although a better-articulated theory of EI might overcome this difficulty.

Therapy for Emotional Pathology

If abnormally low EI or related constructs such as alexithymia play a role in the etiology of mental disorders, then treating low EI should be therapeutically effective. There is little evidence that addresses this issue directly (though see Taylor, 1987, for an account of psychodynamic therapy with alexithymic patients). In this section, we look first at how therapists and patients collaborate so as to actually change the dysfunctional self-knowledge that contributes to emotional disorder, focusing on cognitive-behavioral therapies based on the models just described. Next, we consider whether targeting low EI would enhance such therapies. Parker (2000) argues that specialized interventions are necessary for patients of below-average EI, and argues that work with alexithymics points towards the modifications to established therapies that are necessary.

Treating emotional disorders

There is a large range of therapies used for treatment of anxiety and mood disorders, including biologically based treatments such as drugs, and psychological therapies such as psychoanalysis and behavior therapy that seeks to reverse maladaptive conditioning. Here, while recognizing that various treatments may be effective, we focus on cognitive-behavioral therapies (CBTs), because of (1) their fit with our theoretical orientation and (2) their demonstrated efficacy in treating anxiety disorders in general (Clark & Wells, 1997), specific disorders such as social phobia and panic (Chambless & Gillis, 1993), and affective disorders (Scott, 1996). Although this section deals with anxiety and unipolar depression, we note in passing that cognitive therapies appear to be effective for other disorders linked to emotional dysregulation, such as somatoform disorders and impulse control disorders (see Caballo, 1998, for reviews). It appears too that cognitive therapy may be an important adjunct to pharmacological treatments for disorders believed to be primarily biological in origin, such as bipolar disorder (Ramirez Basco & Thase, 1998). Even personality disorders, long believed to be resistant to therapy, may be conceptualized at the case level in terms of core schemas; and cognitive therapies are starting to emerge (Nordahl & Stiles, 1997).

CBTs were developed in response to the perceived shortcomings of the earlier psychodynamic and behavior therapies. Pioneers of the cognitive approach such as Ellis (1962) and Beck (1967) rejected psychoanalysis because of its reliance on intuition, and the difficulty of operationalizing its key constructs to allow empirical tests of its validity. There was also increasing evidence that psychoanalysis was either ineffective (Eysenck & Rachman, 1965; Svartberg & Stiles, 1991) or was excessively lengthy and costly in regard to therapeutic benefits (Bergin & Lambert, 1978). Behavior therapies based on learning theory principles were developed in response to these shortcomings (Eysenck & Rachman, 1965). However, although more effective, they fail to recognize the key role of cognitions in assigning meaning to stimuli. CBT aims to combine the insights into the patient's inner world that are central to psychoanalysis with a focus on behavioral change, within the coherent, testable theory provided by contemporary cognitive psychology. CBT may be combined with training in specific skills, such as social skills training for depressed persons. Matthews and Zeidner (2000) discuss such interventions. They point out that although skills training is valuable, it neglects to address underlying cognitive maladaption. In any case, training a specific skill does not change any general competence in emotion regulation.

Wells' (1997) practice manual for cognitive therapy of anxiety disorders provides an excellent overview of the general approach and specific techniques. The first step is a full assessment of the patient's symptoms from interview and administration of validated psychological measures. A key aspect of the assessment is the identification of environmental triggers for anxiety, thoughts associated with the anxiety state, and emotional and behavioral responses. Early treatment sessions aim to transform this purely descriptive account into a case conceptualization based on the cognitive theory previously reviewed (e.g., Clark & Beck, 1999; Wells & Matthews, 1994). For example, negative automatic thoughts that intrude into consciousness are a source of distress for many patients. However, thoughts may have different functional significance, in indexing appraisal, coping or metacognition, for example, and so it is important to link the experienced thought to one of the several processes specified by the cognitive model (Wells, 2000). It is also important to socialize the patient, i.e., to provide him or her with a rationale for therapy that will encourage compliance. Subsequent sessions introduce various therapeutic techniques intended to reduce symptoms and, more important, to modify the underlying schema or dysfunctional self-regulative processing that is contributing to the disorder. The final sessions may also be directed towards relapse prevention, and drawing up plans for dealing with future difficulties.

The specific techniques used may be directed towards both the contents of subjective awareness, and behaviors. The therapist may deliberately evoke negative automatic thoughts, by asking the patient to imagine a worst-case scenario, for example, in order to study and treat the underlying disordered cognition. One line of treatment is through verbal reattribution, such as exposing dysfunctional metacognitions, challenging the evidence for the patient's false beliefs and generating strategies for effective coping. The aim is for the patient to restructure maladaptive schemas. However, as Wells points out, "In many instances, verbal reattribution offers only a preliminary step to cognitive-behavioural change, it is not an end in itself.... The most significant change in cognitive therapy of anxiety is usually obtained when behavioural reattribution is used" (1997, p. 78). The primary technique is the behavioral experiment, in which the patient is exposed to the feared situation and is asked to execute a disconfirmatory maneuver that will test the patient's false belief. For example, panic disorder patients may believe that their racing heart signals an impending cardiac arrest. Assuming the patient is in good health, the therapist may have the patient exercise vigorously in order to raise heart rate. The patient's subsequent failure to drop dead disconfirms the false belief and provides the basis for further verbal reattribution in dialogue with the therapist.

A key point is that the case conceptualization and treatment are structured around generic cognitive models for the various *DSM-IV* disorders, but are geared towards the idiosyncratic content of the patient's cognitions and behaviors. In depression, for example, the key problems are the patient's illogical thinking (the cognitive triad), and their failure to engage in behaviors that would support a more positive self-schema (see Beck et al., 1976; Freeman & Oster, 1998). The case conceptualization involves identifying specific events or situations that elicit negative automatic thoughts, the role that previous loss or failure experiences may have played in shaping dysfunctional cognition, and potential sources of social support. Treatment involves verbal techniques such as learning to recognize and challenge automatic thoughts, and behavioral techniques such as performing attainable tasks to counter the patient's sense of lack of self-efficacy. In each case, therapy is directed towards the specific beliefs and activities that may be problematic for the patient.

Low emotional intelligence as a target for therapy?
Loosely, it might seem that the cognitive therapist is improving the patient's EI. Evidently, patients often have difficulties with one or more of the central functions identified by Mayer, Caruso, et al. (2000a). They may misperceive emotions, as when a social phobic falsely appraises others as scornful or contemptuous. They may have problems assimilating emotion and thought, as when an obsessive-compulsive experiences thought-action fusion. They may have problems understanding emotions, as when a panic patient attributes fear to a somatic source. They may have problems in managing emotions, as when a depressive's feelings of being overwhelmed by despair lead to withdrawal from social activity. In general, cognitive therapy is geared towards a more rational understanding of life circumstances and problems, that enhances the handling of emotional situations. It has long been understood (e.g., Rogers, 1957) that empathy may enhance the therapeutic alliance the therapist builds with the client, and hence treatment outcome (Safran & Wallner, 1991).

However, the equation of adaptive personal change with increased EI is only superficially helpful, for the same reasons that it is redundant to label the full set of pathological processes as low EI. The therapist has many targets for intervention, out of the various evaluative, metacognitive, reasoning and coping processes implicated in disorder, as well as specific beliefs and skills. In fact, the challenge for the therapist is to choose *which* processes are critical in the individual case, and the EI construct is not helpful in discriminating processes at either the diagnostic or individual case level. In addition, understanding the role of environmental triggers is critical, but the theory of EI has little to say about person-situation interaction.

Parker's (2000) limited claim that treatment protocols require modification for use with alexithymic patients appears potentially more useful. As discussed previously, these patients have difficulties in identifying and communicating their emotional states (which may indeed be expressed as somatoform disorders). Hence, they respond poorly to insight-oriented psychotherapies such as traditional psychoanalysis. Parker (2000) discusses therapeutic strategies that focus on improving the patient's skills in recognizing and discussing emotions, and reviews evidence from two studies that noninsightful therapies (clinical management of cocaine abuse and behavior therapy) were more successful for alexithymics than insight-oriented therapies. The proposal that clinicians should take into account the patient's awareness of emotional states is certainly reasonable, and fits with the broader view that personality assessment may be an important element of treatment choice (Matthews et al., 1998). However, some questions remain. The CBTs previously described do not rely solely on the patient's insight. Indeed, as Wells (1997) points out, behavioral reattribution may be more important than verbal reattribution. There seems to be no reason why alexithymic patients should not benefit from CBT approaches based primarily on behavioral experiments. The patient's difficulties in reporting mental state may be a barrier to case conceptualization, but this barrier will be present irrespective of the therapeutic strategy. In sum, Parker (2000) makes some valuable suggestions for tailoring therapy to the alexithymic patient, but such modifications may perhaps be made within the existing, general framework for CBT.

Conclusions

In principle, the concept of EI has important implications for diagnosis, assessment, case conceptualization and therapy. We might be able to identify PLEI as central to certain disorders or as a vulnerability factor for multiple disorders. PLEI might be linked to a set of pathological processes, which would be a target for treatment. So far, this promise appears unfulfilled. In general, clinical disturbances of emotional function may take many forms, representing abnormality of various distinct processes. It is circular to label any manifestation of emotional dysregulation as low EI. Ideally, the theory of EI would identify a specific subset of pathological processes evident at the various levels of analysis discussed here: diagnosis, abnormal personality, and information processing. However, existing evidence does not demonstrate any distinctive, coherent quality of PLEI at any level. What the evidence does show is the pervasiveness of N or negative affectivity as a vulnerability factor for many disorders (although causality may be reciprocal). At the process level, N, as described earlier, seems to relate to a set of negative, self-referent processing biases that are generally evident in emotional disorders. Other dimensions of abnormal personality are also important, and it seems useful to discriminate N, antisocial personality, social withdrawal and obsessionality as vulnerability factors, as opposed to lumping them together as low EI.

The dimensional approach is invaluable for establishing the broad aspect of a psychopathology, but it does not fully characterize the different disorders. Understanding why a person is, say, depressed, rather than generally anxious, requires an understanding of (1) cognitive content, (2) specific abnormalities of processing, and (3) dynamic person-situation interaction. The very broad brush concept of EI fails to engage with any of these key issues. For any given disorder, work on EI has nothing to say about the specific distortions of self-beliefs typical of the disorders, about the particular patterning of cognitive bias, or about the way interaction between person and environment serves to perpetuate pathology. Hence, EI research does little to inform the practice of psychotherapy. Mood-regulation is an important concept in abnormal psychology, but its application to clinical practice requires the development of relatively narrow constructs, such as alexithymia, not some general lack of EI. Alexithymia is a condition that clinicians recognize, with implications for treatment choice. It may be a more useful construct than generalized EI precisely because it is more modest in scope, referring to a limited set of processes associated with labeling emotions. Empathy may also be a narrow construct worth further investigation. Although not central to emotional disorders, lack of empathy is an important feature of antisocial personality, and may be a suitable target for interventions for sex offenders (Geer, Estupinan & Manguno-Mire, 2000).

11

Development and Schooling of Emotional Intelligence

The temptation to form premature theories upon insufficient data is the bane of our profession.

Sherlock Holmes

In this chapter we selectively survey what we currently know about the origins, cultivation, and schooling of EI and related competencies. To this end, we examine theory and research focusing on the influence of more distal factors on the development of EI. We begin by discussing the role of biological determinants on the growth and development of EI. We then assess the role of socialization practices, concluding with a discussion of additional factors in the child's early environment (media, peers, and so forth). We then move on to discuss the role of more proximal factors on the development of EI. Accordingly, we examine some salient EI programs designed to improve emotional competencies and skills. We then discuss basic and methodological issues surrounding the implementation of current EI intervention programs. Finally, we present some general principles for conducting EI intervention program evaluation.

The reader should keep in mind three caveats when reading this chapter. First, our review of the possible role of socialization practices in the acquisition of EI competencies in children is problematic, given that the appropriate analysis of the effects of child rearing methods on children's acquisition of EI requires the use of genetically informed designs. Regrettably, studies employing such designs are preciously rare in this research domain. Thus, any links found between parental behavior and children's behavior might be mediated by genetic influences or by shared environmental influences. Only appropriate genetically informed designs can partition the observed covariation between such factors. Secondly, EI and emotional competencies are used interchangeably in this chapter, allowing us to draw freely upon the rich body of literature dealing with various emotional competencies (e.g., Denham, 1998; Saarni, 1999). Clearly, some researchers (and we count ourselves among these, conceptually) prefer to distinguish between these two constructs and not use them interchangeably. Our decision to adopt such an approach in the current chapter, however, makes the literature more amenable to extensive, critical analysis. Thirdly, we attempt to review and link under the umbrella of this chapter research from two disparate bodies of literature, i.e., research focusing on the development of emotional competencies and research focusing on the schooling and formal training of EI. These two bodies of research, focusing on informal and formal social settings, respectively, are generally treated separately in the literature and are rather difficult to integrate into one coherent picture.

Origins and Development of Emotional Intelligence

Emotional intelligence is believed to play a major role in the development of social skills and interpersonal competencies. Consequently, understanding the origins of emotional competencies would appear to be of major importance in understanding both normal and pathological behavior (Eisenberg, Cumberland & Spinrad, 1998). It is readily apparent that any systematic attempt to account for the origins and development of emotional competencies needs to consider a confluence of multiple factors interacting in complex and dynamic ways. Figure 11.1 presents a partial list of causal factors that should likely be included in any configurational model.

Biological determinants

Biological and constitutional factors are currently viewed as making an important contribution to the development of EI (Goleman, 1995a; see also chapter 6). Emotional intelligence may be construed as the repertoire of emotional competencies and skills available to an individual, at a given point in time, for coping with environmental demands and constraints. Because this behavioral repertoire is acquired, stored, and thence retrieved by a biological organism (over its entire development), it seems reasonable to assume that there is a biological substrate underlying EI.

From a biological perspective, EI may be viewed as having "survival value," facilitating the detection of threats to well-being and allowing adaptive coping in a potentially hazardous environment (Denham,

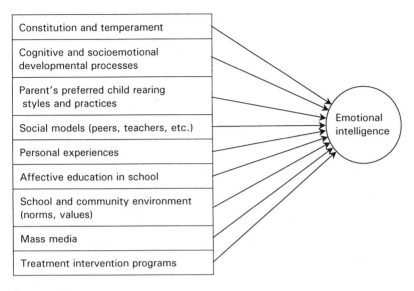

Figure 11.1
Configuration of etiological factors in the development of EI.

1998). Biological processes (autonomic and central nervous system functioning, neurotransmitter systems, and cerebral lateralization) may contribute to both expressive and regulatory facets of EI. It is now readily apparent that social, cultural, and educational experience is grafted onto the bedrock of a child's biological makeup (see Kagan, 1994). Thus, one's emotional competencies are largely determined by the way environmental forces impinge upon the developing child's biological constitution (Saarni, 1999).

Past research points to a meaningful genetic component underlying the individual differences in general intelligence (*g*), with heredity contributing between 50% to 70% of the variance in ability (Brody, 1992; Jensen, 1998). Unfortunately, available empirical data does not allow us to estimate the effects of heredity on the major components of EI. To the best of our knowledge, only one study provides evidence for the heritability of an important ingredient of emotional competency, specifically, one's tendency to react either empathically or with distress in relation to others. Thus, Zahn-Waxler, Robinson, and Emde (1992) reported that identical twins were more similar in empathic style (i.e., sympathetic or reflecting personal distress), than were fraternal twins. In turn, this suggests some degree of heritability within this component of EI. As mentioned at the outset of this discussion, until genetically informed designs are implemented, and relevant behavior-genetic data and estimates are available, it will be impossible to partition the total covariation between parental and offspring EI in order to tease apart the variance associated with genetic, shared environmental, and socialization factors.

Because EI has been conceptualized as an ability that is partly biologically determined, it has also been construed as relatively stable across developmental phases. Accordingly, it has been claimed that persons low in EI may find it difficult to learn emotional skills at a later stage of development, especially since EI is partly biologically determined (Taylor, Parker & Bagby, 1999). In fact, some authors view childhood as a critical period for shaping lifelong emotional competencies (Goleman, 1995a). The major skills thought to comprise EI may each have crucial periods for their development, extending over several years of childhood. Each period represents a window for helping the child acquire adaptive emotional skills. If missed, it makes it that much harder to offer corrective lessons later in life. Furthermore, proponents of a deterministic biological position claim that habits acquired in childhood become set in the basic synaptic wiring of neural architecture and are harder to change later in life. Thus, any attempt to seriously change or alter EI in adults might require "rewiring" of parts of the brain (see, e.g., Taylor et al., 1999).

Recent research (Halberstadt, Denham & Dunsmore, in press; Rothbart & Derryberry, 1981; Taylor et al., 1999) suggests that certain temperamental qualities (e.g., emotionality, adaptability, sociability), may impact upon the growth and development of major facets of EI (emotion regulation, coping with stress). Temperament refers to the moderately stable emotions or behavioral qualities of an individual whose appearance in childhood is influenced by an inherited biology (Kagan, 1994). Two temperamental qualities, in particular, have been implicated as determinants of emotional self-regulation (Halberstadt et al., in press). The first quality, emotional intensity (e.g., latency, threshold, and rise time of emotions) may make the child more (or less) reactive to the effects of stress. The second quality, attentional processes, may facilitate the child's efforts to cope with stress, e.g., attentional shifting or focusing, and voluntary initiation or inhibition of action (see Eisenberg & Fabes, 1995).

As cogently argued by Izard (2001), emotionality, temperament, and environment can impede or facilitate the development EI through a number of processes. For example, children who are dispositionally prone to experience negative emotions or who live in a harsh environment that frequently elicits strong negative emotions might have difficulty in regulating emotion arousal and in forming connections between these intense emotion feelings and the appropriate language for articulating them. Also, anger proneness or frequent anger experiences might contribute to externalizing aggressive behavior that is likely to elicit strong negative reactions from parents, siblings, and peers. The negative social feedback in these encounters could amplify the child's already intense anger and further impede the opportunity to acquire EI (Lochman & Lenhart, 1993).

Furthermore, recent evidence suggests that temperament and social environment contribute to the development of emotional labeling (Izard, 2001). Research on early emotional development suggests that the decoding component of emotion labeling and infants' expressive responses to the detection of emotion signals has innate determinants and is mainly a function of the emotion perception and expression systems. The emotion perception and emotion expression systems in infants are highly pre-adapted to facilitate infant-other communication (Magai & McFadden, 1995). Furthermore, early studies showed that one key component of EI, children's emotional labeling, predicted positive behavioral outcomes (e.g., peer status and academic performance), after controlling for verbal and performance components of general intelligence (see Denham, 1998, for a review). One recent study demonstrated that emotion perception (EP) and labeling had long-term predictive validity. Preschool emotion labeling predicted adaptive social behavior and academic competence four years later, when the children were in third grade (Izard, Fine, et al., 2001). High scores on EP predicted positive social behavior and low scores on EP predicted behavior problems.

The remarkable ability of young infants to perceive emotion signals, discriminate among them, and respond to them in meaningful ways suggest that emotional competence and adaptability has heritability and some independence of cognitive development (Izard, 2001). Furthermore, some newborns may be biologically predisposed to have a low threshold for arousal when confronted with social (or nonsocial) stimulation and novelty. The recent work by Buss and Plomin (1984), Kagan, Reznick, and Snidman (1987), and others is suggestive of this possibility. In the first year of life, when faced with uncertainties, these babies may evidence particular physical and physiological changes (e.g., elevated heart rate, high endorphin and norepinephrine levels) that make them very difficult to soothe. Parents, especially first-timers, may find these overly emotional infant responses to stressful circumstances personally aversive. These parents may react with insensitivity, lack of affection, nonresponsiveness, or general neglect of their babies.

Biological factors may also indirectly mediate the effects of child-rearing behaviors on emotional development, with biology partly accounting for the observed links between the emotional competencies of parents and their children (see later in this chapter). Certain parental child-rearing behaviors, often claimed to be important antecedents of EI, may largely be an adaptation on the part of parents to biologically determined temperament dispositions or other preexisting characteristics of the child (see Hock, 1992). Thus, rather than actually shaping the development of emotional competencies in their children, parents are often responding to children's biologically determined temperament and personality.

Take, for example, the case of a child with an excitable and highly emotional and expressive temperament—part-and-parcel of the child's biological repertoire. This enhanced expressiveness may try his or her parents' patience and evoke excessive control techniques, or punitive child-rearing behaviors. Indeed, a child's frequent displays of distress, in response to particular types of events, may affect a caregiver's response in a dyadic relation. The parental reactions to the child's temperament, in turn, may further strengthen the child's vulnerability to react with heightened excitability and emotionality to stressful social-evaluative situations (i.e., evaluative anxiety). Over time, this may affect the behavioral display of particular temperamental dispositions. According to this line of reasoning, the child's biology largely determines the child rearing practices of the parents, rather than the other way around. Furthermore, the fact that the children of parents who are well-regulated tend to have offspring that are well-regulated (or balanced) hints at possible intergenerational similarities in biologically based temperament. This process is graphically depicted in figure 11.2. However, as noted by Saarni (personal communication, October 20, 2001), socialization represents bidirectional influences between what an individual child brings to an interaction with parents or peers and their respective contributions. This does not necessarily mean that the effects of parental socialization practices are weakened or attenuated due to intergenerational similarities in biologically based temperament.

Not only may biology affect emotional behaviors; emotion-related behaviors may also affect biology. Thus, there is accumulating evidence that emotional interactions between infants and caretakers influence

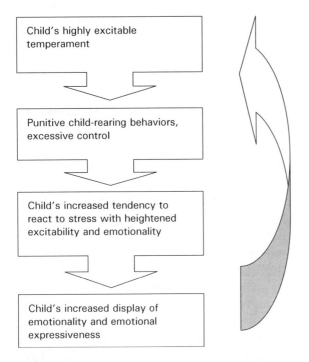

Figure 11.2
Dynamic interaction between child's temperament and parent's affective reactions.

the maturation of the brain involved in emotional awareness and regulation (e.g., Taylor et al., 1999). This interaction can lead to permanent alterations in the morphological development of the orbitofrontal cortex, which, in turn, may impact upon the capacity of the neocortex to modulate activity in the amygdala and other subcortical structures (Taylor et al., 1999). There is also evidence that severe abuse or neglect of the child can affect neocortical maturation in children and result in reduced differentiation of the left hemisphere and reversal of the normal left-right hemisphere (see, e.g., Taylor et al., 1999).

As graphically depicted in figure 11.3, human biology and human behavior show reciprocal determinism. That is, there is most likely a bidirectional pattern of effects between parents and children's emotional behavior (see Denham, 1998). Both children's and parents' temperamental traits influence the emotions they show in dyadic interaction. Accordingly, in the parent-child interaction, each dyad member's emotions influence the other's emotional responses during interaction and

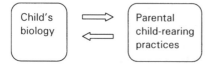

Figure 11.3
Reciprocal relationship between biological and social factors in the development of EI.

these, in turn, feed into psychosocial functioning or social emotional competence, for each.

Few would question the notion that a person's biology interacts and unites with personal experience in an enigmatic way to produce emotionally intelligent behaviors (Kagan, 1994). Thus, the family acts on the behavioral consequences of biological characteristics that combine in a seamless tapestry with the child's biology and environmental experiences and cultural surroundings. While biology predisposes us to emotional behaviors, the nature of these behaviors, the situations that elicit them, and that they are expressed, remains largely dependent on an elaborate set of social and environmental factors. We now turn to an examination of these factors in some detail in the sections that follow (see chapter 6 for a detailed discussion of the biological substrates of EI).

Socialization of emotional competencies
Family environment The family environment is commonly viewed as a major force in the socialization of emotions. The family is essentially our first school for learning emotional knowledge, competencies, and skills and is arguably the most important context in which children's emotional competencies are forged. Parents are considered to be the primary socialization agents responsible for the inculcation of emotional competencies. Accordingly, a major task of successful parenting in humans is shaping the emotional competencies of their offspring. The younger the child, the more influential the family might be (Mayer & Salovey, 1997; Saarni, 1999).

Parental socialization of emotional competencies is carried out both by acting directly on the child, mainly through the way parents regulate the children's emotions (e.g., through explicit lessons or informal conversations about emotion regulation). Parental influences may also act indirectly on the child (e.g., through the observation and modeling of other's emotional responses and competencies) (Lewis & Saarni, 1985b). In the familial context, children learn from their parents are their emotional knowledge base, as well as competence in emotion identification and regulation (Mayer & Salovey, 1997). Family socialization has been theorized to directly impact upon the child's social and emotional competency, as well as work indirectly upon socio-emotional competence, through the child's understanding of emotions and acquisition of social knowledge. The causal chain follows roughly as follows: parental socialization procedures → development of child's social knowledge → child's social competence (see Garner, Jones & Miner, 1994). However, this linear model, devoid of reciprocal effects and feedback loops, may be construed as rather simplistic or even primitive.

Different parents may have different goals in regard to the socialization of emotions in their children (Eisenberg, Cumberland & Spinrad, 1998). Thus, some parents may feel it is desirable to be in touch with one's emotions and to express them in socially acceptable ways. These parents are likely to be supportive of their children's identification and expression of both positive and negative emotions and foster these competencies in their children. Other parents may believe that negative emotions are detrimental and should therefore be controlled, repressed, or simply not expressed. These parents are likely to try to teach their children to minimize, ignore, deny, or prevent the experience and expression of negative emotion (Saarni, 1999). These children may be less aware of their negative emotions and perhaps be less able to identify them in others, thus impacting this facet of their EI.

Socialization methods   The socialization of specific facets of emotional competence has been claimed to proceed through the same mechanisms of socialization as any other set of behaviors (Lewis & Saarni, 1985). We now discuss several more common socialization mechanisms, through which parents purportedly (as well as other socialization agents, for that matter) teach their offspring emotional competencies. The behavioral principles to be discussed (see figure 11.4) below may account for the child's initial acquisition of emotionally intelligent behaviors and reactions to various situations, as well as the maintenance of these reactions over time.

Observation and modeling   Behavioral research attests to the important role that direct observation and modeling of behaviors of significant human models (e.g., parents, siblings, teachers, peers) may play in the

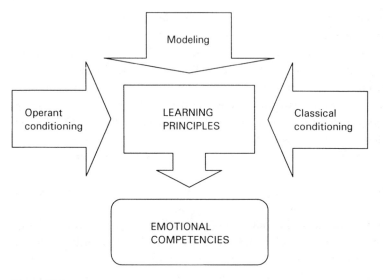

Figure 11.4
Basic learning principles shaping the growth and development of EI.

learning of social and affective responses (Bandura, 1965). In fact, much social learning is made possible by exposure to real-life as well as symbolic models who perform, intentionally or unwittingly, patterns of behaviors that may be imitated by others (Bandura, 1965). Through observation of models, demonstrating specific behaviors in a particular context, children have been shown to learn and acquire new emotional responses to specific contexts that did not previously exist in their behavioral repertoire. The observational learning of emotional patterns has not been studied much in humans, partly for methodological reasons and partly because the scientific work on observational learning took place before interest in the emotions was rekindled (Lazarus, 1991a).

Social cognitive theorists have demonstrated the pervasive effect of modeling on a variety of personal processes (Martinez-Pons, 1998/99). Modeling of emotions means teaching by example (Epstein, 1998). The basic assumption here is that a child whose parents display constructive EI-related behavior in everyday life is likely to initiate it as part of his or her own behavioral repertoire. Parents convey at least as much to their children in this way as they do by direct or indirect rewards and punishment. Thus, during the bombing of London during World War II, what most affected the children was not the actual destruction they witnessed but their parent's reactions. If the parents were calm, the children were calm. Parents who say, "Do as I say—not as I do" are fighting a losing battle. Thus, a parent who wants her child to be emotionally intelligent would do well by providing a model of emotional competency in her own behavior (Epstein, 1998).

Proponents of EI claim that children learn from role models how to process and regulate emotional information and experiences (e.g., Saarni, 1999; Salovey, Bedell, Detweiler & Mayer, 2000). The EI competencies that emerge from this learning process presumably influence how a child interacts with her peers, which, in turn, determines how successful she will be at developing a supportive group of friends. In principle, individuals high on EI have learned from exemplary role models how to process and regulate emotions, to maintain viable relations with others. This process is said to be instrumental in determining the development of a supportive group of friends. As the argument goes, those high on EI are more likely to work well within a social network and to build and maintain networks because of their social skills (Salovey, Bedell, Detweiler & Mayer, 1999).

In the dynamic process of modeling of another's emotions, the child observes and copies the parent (Lewis & Saarni, 1985). The different emotional models that children are exposed to partly account for individual differences in emotions. For example, some parents feel that it is harmful to display negative emotions (e.g., sadness or anger) and model suppression of negative emotions before their children. Other parents may have no problem at all with the open expression of negative emotions and model the open and free expression of negative emotion (Hooven, Gottman & Katz, 1995). Some parents also model techniques helpful to use in regulating emotions (e.g., problem-solving, seeking social support), whereas others model dysfunctional modes of emotional expression (e.g., explosive or abusive behavior). Indeed, infants as young as 10 to 12 months, when faced with a stranger, look to their parent's emotion-expressive behavior as a guide to their emotional reaction (Saarni, 1999). It is primarily with regard to *emotionally ambiguous* situations that the infant looks to its parents for emotionally expressive behavior for cues as to the meaning of this novel situation. Furthermore, parental displays of emotions can affect the child's arousal by contagion, vicarious processes, or through the meaning that the child attributes to the parental emotional display.

Observing their parent's particular profiles of expressed emotions may teach children which emotional displays are likely to be acceptable in specific cultural settings and social situations, and how to express them (Denham & Grout, 1993). Children who typically observe parents suppress emotional displays, in conjunction with verbal displays (e.g., "You shouldn't lose your cool when angry") are likely to internalize such strategies for use as a first resort when managing their own emotional experiences. In reviewing the development of expressiveness in infants, Malatesta concluded, "In summary, there is evidence that infants' emotional expressive behaviors are influenced by the basic learning principles of classical conditioning, operant conditioning, and observational learning" (1990, p. 41).

Some children may never have the opportunity to learn how to cope with distressing daily circumstances due to the absence of appropriate models demonstrating adaptive coping behaviors and functional emotional regulation in evaluative situations. Instead, they learn to cope with situations in a maladaptive fashion through avoidance behaviors, defensiveness, and palliative coping, which eventually interferes with their regulation of emotions. Negative emotional behaviors of parents clearly have detrimental effects on their children. Thus, a child who views temper tantrums and outbursts in her mother, father, or older brother or sister is presumably introduced to poor self-regulatory models (Salovey, Mayer, et al., 2000). Further, given that covert learning of negative affective reactions is possible, a child may learn responses that remain dormant until provided with the opportunity to be enacted in a situation, at some later time. Note that this outcome is possible even without the observer having a chance to practice the acquired responses.

Direct training, coaching, and guidance Aside from serving as meaningful models of emotional behavior for their offspring, parents also serve as formal instructors of emotional expression and regulation. Thus, parents' verbal discourse with the child, direct instruction, and emotional apprenticeship are claimed to be important factors contributing to the development of the child's emotional competencies (Thompson, 1998).

Parents who adopt an emotion-coaching philosophy are aware of the emotions in their own and their children's lives, can talk about them in a open, undifferentiated manner, and act like an emotion coach in assisting their children with negative emotions. These parents view the child's negative emotions as an opportunity for intimacy or for teaching problem-solving ability. As such, they tend to problem-solve with the child, setting behavioral limits, and discussing goals and strategies for dealing with the stressful or challenging situation that led to a particular emotion. When parents use socializing discourse (e.g., "It really hurts Danny when you knock him down") it not only imparts emotional meaning to everyday events, but also fuels the way children figure out how to feel (Denham, 1998). Parents who use formal instruction, choose learning activities for their children, believe in early timetables for children's acquisition of skills, and use drill and practice, are described as "hot-housing" (Huntsinger & Larson, 1998).

Parent-child discourse can affect emotional regulation. Parents can suggest for example, the value of distracting or pleasant imagery, comforting self-talk, redirecting thoughts and attention, using external distractors, redefining goals (or outcomes), or other specific strategies. In immediate arousal situations, parent's suggestions of this kind can provide one valuable source of exogenous management of emotions. For example, if parents see their daughter acting aggressively to her little brother, they might say, "We understand you are angry and maybe even hurt by the way you have been treated by your brother. However, hitting is no way to solve the problem. Why don't you talk things over with him. And once you have chilled out for a while, let's talk about how we can solve the problem. Eventually, you will have to talk directly with him."

Reinforcement of expressive behaviors According to learning theory, children's emotional behaviors and competencies are expected to be responsive to environmental contingencies in their early environment. Operant learning theory (see Bandura, 1976) would predict that it is children's emotional reactions (or behaviors) that are rewarded by social agents (i.e., parents, teachers, peers), and that these are reinforced and continue over time. By contrast, behaviors that go unrewarded or that are punished are predicted to become extinguished over time. Thus, through their reinforcement behaviors, parents may intentionally or inadvertently reinforce certain emotional expressions and extinguish others (see Campos & Barrett, 1984). Children who experience repeated parental reinforcement of specific emotional reactions (e.g., anger) in response to given situations (e.g., being demeaned) may strengthen and maintain these reactions over time. In turn, this enhances the probability that such responses are made the next time a similar situation is encountered. By contrast, children who suffer painful consequences for the expression of certain emotions may suppress these or similar emotions. The reinforcement value of contingencies would likely be a function of sociocultural differences within countries and between countries, as well as historical differences overtime within cultures.

The particular constellation of parenting techniques called "rewarding socialization of emotion" has been said to make a direct contribution to children's social competence (Denham, 1998). Accordingly, parental encouragement and support for children's emotions help them to express emotion acceptably and provide children with ways to deal with emotions in their peer group. By contrast, "punitive socialization" of emotion increases arousal and undermines the performance of socially competent interacting. Thus, older sibling's rewarding socialization of emotions predict teacher-rated social competence of younger brothers and sisters (Denham, 1998).

Research suggests that the emotional behaviors of young infants are responsive to environmental contingencies and can be altered on a short-term basis (Campos & Barrett, 1984). Furthermore, seminaturalistic observational studies have indicated that mothers behave in ways that can modify children's expressive behavior more permanently. For example, a review of the literature by Malatesta and Haviland (1982) suggests that the contingency of maternal facial responses to infant emotional expressions predicted increases in infant positive emotions and expressiveness from 2.5 to 7.5 months.

It is readily apparent that socialization and child-rearing practices interact with the child's development (cognitive, affective, psychomotor) in shaping emotional competencies. Thus, the ability to symbolize or label emotions involves inferential or interpretive processes that clearly depend on cognitive development. Furthermore, verbal ability is necessarily a determinant of our current measures of emotional understanding, and probably of other facets of EI as well. At the very least, the child has to have the requisite receptive vocabulary (a component of intelligence) to understand and respond to these tasks. Because emotion perception and emotion labeling abilities are fundamental to emotion communication and normal social relationships, deficits in these core abilities of EI abilities will contribute to deficiencies in other facets of EI and impede the development of social competence (Izard, 2001).

Only recently have researchers focused on pinpointing the specific mechanisms that may account for the links between parenting attributes and child-rearing practices, on one hand, and children's emotional and emotional competencies, on the other (see Mize, Pettit & Meece, 2000). Mize, Pettit, and Meece (2000) critically survey a number of these causal mechanisms with respect to children's social competence. These include the following:

- Social information-processing styles (such as hostile attributional biases)
- Internal working models and related attachment-oriented phenomena
- Emotion understanding and the motivational role of emotion in guiding behaviors
- Emotion regulation and associated processes

Unfortunately, due to methodological constraints, the current body of research does not allow us to clearly choose one mediating process over another.

Empirical evidence

We now briefly examine some of the theorizing and related empirical evidence supporting the notion that the family environment, parental child-rearing techniques and socialization practices, impact upon the development of EI. Given the rather tenuous empirical knowledge base relating directly to the origins of EI, we draw upon the related, but more established, body of developmental research focusing on the socialization of emotional competencies (Denham, 1998; Saarni, 1999). We feel justified in generalizing from this body of developmental research because the particular competencies researched in this area (i.e., emotional identification, understanding and regulation of emotions, and empathy), are precisely those most frequently subsumed under the construct of EI. Since much of the developmental literature has been recently reviewed by Saarni (1999) and Denham (1998), we suffice by selectively highlighting some of the empirical evidence that sheds light on the role of parental socialization practices on children's affective competencies.

Attachment and child-parent relationships   The quality of early attachment relations between child and caretakers has been claimed to be a crucial variable contributing to the development of prosocial behavior (Zahn-Waxler, 1991). According to attachment theorists, maternal sensitivity to the child's needs facilitates the development of a model of sensitivity to others in the child. This condition socializes the child to be empathic and sensitive to the needs of others (Taylor et al., 1999). Securely attached children are said to develop the capacity to respond empathically to others because they themselves have experienced responsive and empathic care giving. The empathic behavior displayed by their parents has satisfied the children's own needs, and provided them with the emotional resources to respond to the needs of others. These children develop internal working models of relationships that incorporate the expectancy that an individual's needs will be responded to and met.

The research literature in developmental psychopathology provides information showing the importance of the influence of parent-child relationships in the etiology of emotional dysregulation. Recent studies surveyed by Brenner and Salovey (1997) suggest that the severity, frequency, and chronicity of the child's maltreatment by caretakers are associated with the severity and frequency of dysfunctional self-regulation in elementary school aged children. Maltreated children have difficulty in coping with stress, responding with depressed affect, heightened lability, or marked anger.

Parental expressiveness and sensitivity to children's emotions   A review of the research by Salovey, Bedell, et al. (2000) suggests that the parents of emotionally intelligent individuals are emotionally responsive to their children in time of emotional need. Research by Denham and Grout (1993) suggests that those maternal aspects of expressiveness and reactions to children's emotional expressions are associated with emotional competence in preschoolers. Parent's expressive reactions to children's emotions can be important vehicles for letting children know what action tendencies are appropriate when they feel different ways can be used to respond (Halberstadt et al., in press). One study found that mother's responsiveness to children's observed emotions predicted emotional understanding in preschool children (Denham, Zoller & Couchoud, 1994). More specifically, mothers who responded by reacting with calmness and serenity to their children's distress and angry outbursts, and with happiness to children's happiness, promoted understanding of emotions in their children. Negative reinforcement of distressful emotions on the part of the parents, and ignoring a child's negative emotions, negatively predicted emotional understanding in the child. Research also indicates that the child, whose mother typically responds in an optimal way to his or her anger (i.e., calmly) is less prone to negative emotions in the preschool and responds to peer's negative emotions more prosocially (Denham & Grout, 1993).

One study reported that parents who responded sensitively to their child when emotionally distressed had children who responded positively and pro-socially to upset and anger in others (Zahn-Waxler, Radke-Yarrow & King, 1979). Furthermore, parental reactions to a child's causing harm (or distress) to another were related to later differences in the children's reparation behavior towards their victim. In addition, there is some evidence suggesting that parents might influence the development of their children's style of responding to negative affect, through the styles the parents display when they themselves are in a sad mood or disposition (Nolen-Hoeksema, 1991). Moreover, the mother's negative emotions and poor psychosocial functioning, in particular, have been shown to be negatively related to children's overall social-emotional development (Weinraub & Wolf, 1983). Unfortunately, fine-grained research on mothers and children's emotions in true-to-life naturalistic conditions is sorely lacking.

It is commonly claimed that parents fulfill emotion-specific communicative functions by showing children the emotional valence and intensity of certain experiences and by modeling the specific emotions appropriate to the situation (Zahn-Waxler, Cummings, Mcknew & Radke-Yarrow, 1984). A survey of this research suggests that emotionally non-responsive mothers (including those who express mostly negative emotions) have infants and toddlers who cope poorly with stress (Zahn-Waxler et al., 1984). These children are more aggressive, emotionally disregulated, play more immaturely, and interact less than those whose mothers show positive emotions more frequently, or are more emotionally responsive.

Research attests to the fact that sympathetic mothers tend to produce sympathetic daughters and sympathetic fathers produce sympathetic sons (Zahn-Waxler, 1991). Furthermore, data by Eisenberg, Fabes, Schaller, et al. (1991) provide support for the notion that empathic parents help their children cope effectively with aversive emotions when distressed. Thus, empathic parents were reported to have children who are relatively unlikely to experience personal distress when confronted with a sympathy-eliciting situation. Parents who encourage their children to express emotions in socially appropriate ways are also likely to have empathic children (Brenner & Salovey, 1997).

Socialization and child rearing practices   There is some evidence indicating that parental child rearing styles and practices (e.g., authoritative versus permissive; supportive versus nonsupportive; autonomous versus controlling) are associated with the development of emotional skills in the child. Thus, combined parental autonomy, encouragement, and support were reported to be positively predictive of children's self-regulation—a key facet of EI (Grolnick & Ryan, 1989). Mantzicopoulos and Oh-Hwang (1998) reported that authoritarian and neglectful parenting styles were associated with lower psychosocial competence in a group of 244 Korean and 214 American adolescents. They also found that permissive and mixed parenting styles were more advantageous to the child's well-being than either authoritarian or neglectful parenting.

Parental warmth and control have been theorized to be predictive of children's emotional competence. Data provided by Zahn-Waxler, Radke-Yarrow, and King (1979) indicate that parental control bears a nonlinear pattern of relations with emotional competence. Thus, in preschoolers moderate degrees of control were associated with optimal levels of emotional competence, whereas low and high degrees of control were both associated with lower emotional competence (Zahn-Waxler et al., 1979). Parental warmth was also shown to be positively associated with emotional competence, presumably because parental warmth and secure attachment in infancy is a precursor of later competence in social problem-solving situations in preschoolers (Zahn-Waxler et al., 1979). Furthermore, a recent review by O'Neil and Parke (2000) suggests that parents who are responsive and warm have more socially adjusted children, who are better accepted by their peers.

Research by Gottman (1997) suggest that when parents are skilled in expressing and coping with aversive emotions, such as sadness and anger, children gain emotional skills that buffer them from the negative effects of stressful events. In addition, parents' awareness of their own sadness and parents' tendencies to coach their children about their anger were found to have an impact on children's emotional regulation abilities. Specifically, children at age five whose parents possess these meta-emotional dispositions showed less physiological distress, greater ability to focus attention, and less negative playing styles. Moreover, at age eight, these variables predict children's academic achievement even when controlling for marital dissatisfaction and marital instability. However, a variety of confounding factors (intellectual, personality, etc.) may account for the covariation among the self-control and academic measures across time. A review by Denham (1998) suggests that parents who are responsive, warm, and accepting of children's emotional reactions have children who are emotionally well regulated and responsive.

Research by Shoda, Mischel, and Peake (1990) suggests that parental socialization of impulse control may affect children's emotional, social, and cognitive skills over a decade later. Thus, four-year-old children who were socialized to delay gratification by accepting two marshmallows later (rather than one right away) were found to be more socially competent. It also appeared that better managed stress, when followed up through high school, compared to those who took one marshmallow straightaway. Furthermore, those who had been able to delay gratification at age 4 were more confident, self-assured, trustworthy, dependable, willing to take the initiative, and plunge into projects at age 16. The young people who ate the marshmallow at age 4 were more likely to feel bad about themselves and to be troubled, stubborn, indecisive, easily upset by frustration, and immobilized by stress. Furthermore, those who had the skill to delay gratification had Scholastic Aptitude Test (SAT) scores that were higher at age 18, and they were more competent academically than those who acted impulsively. In fact, the children's performance on the marshmallow test was twice as powerful a predictor of their SAT scores as was their IQ. However, it appears a gross oversimplification to assume that the better all-around performance at age 18 can be attributed to the ability to delay gratification at age 4— many other factors are clearly involved (Epstein, 1998). That is, parents who trained children to delay gratification at age 4 very likely trained them to acquire other desirable attributes, such as high self-esteem and social competence. Thus, it may be these other attributes that are mainly responsible for the later success of these children. Moreover, the parents who were present when the children were 4 years of age were, in most cases, present later. Thus, it could be prolonged influence that accounts for the long-term difference between the two groups of children in observed results, not simply how they trained their children up to age 4.

The research on the role of parents in the development of children's coping strategies is rather limited (Hardy, Power & Jaedicke, 1993). The literature documents the importance of parenting in child adjustment to major life stresses, such as divorce (Hetherington, Cox & Cox, 1985) or chronic disease (McCubbin, McCubbin, Patterson, Cabule, Wilson & Warwick, 1983). Research by Finnegan, Hodges, and Perry (1994) suggests that parents' attachment processes play a key role in the development of a child's avoidant or preoccupied coping strategies, which in turn, predict the child's social adjustment during middle childhood. Further research is required on the relation between parenting and specific patterns of child coping, especially in response to daily routine stressors and hassles.

The review of the parenting literature (Hardy, Power & Jaedicke, 1993) suggests three major dimensions, which appear to be of key importance in impacting upon children's ability to cope with stress. The first dimension, parental support, is defined as behavior toward the child that makes the child feel comfortable in the presence of the parent. This confirms in the child's mind that she is accepted and approved as a person. Maternal support causes children to feel secure in times of stress and to develop a variety of effective strategies for coping with everyday stress. These children are also exposed to models of effective coping and come to understand their feelings in stress situations as well as the feelings of others. These children develop self-efficacy regarding their ability to cope with difficult situations.

The second factor, parental control, or demandingness, refers to the degree to which parents set boundaries for their children and become involved in guiding or shaping the behavior of the child within the confines of the boundaries set. Maternal control tends to show curvilinear relations with coping in children (Power & Manire, 1992). That is, mothers using moderate levels of control give their children sufficient guidelines for their behavior without either overly interfering with learning and the development of curiosity and initiative. The third factor, structure, is the degree to which parents provide a predictable organized environment for the child. A curvilinear relation was predicted between structure and adaptive coping. In one study (Hardy, Power & Jaedicke, 1993), parents who were very supportive of their children, but maintained a home environment that was not very structured had children who reported the greatest variety of coping strategies in response to everyday stress. Children in less structured homes utilized more aggressive and confronting coping methods in response to stress. The more supportive parents were of children, the more avoidant the coping strategies used, particularly in uncontrollable strategies—an adaptive coping strategy under these circumstances (Zeidner & Saklofske, 1996).

A review by O'Neil and Parke (2000), based largely on the University of California, Riverside (UCR), Social Development Project suggests that the strategies parents employ to manage children's negative emotion are associated with children's emotional reactivity, coping, and social competence. Thus, when mothers reported they encouraged the expression of negative affect when their children were upset, their children indicated that they would be less likely to use social withdrawal as a strategy to cope with emotional upset. Furthermore, mothers who expressed more awareness and sensitivity to their child's emotional state in a family problem-solving task had children who expressed their emotions more clearly. In contrast, mothers who made more attempts to regulate their children's emotional expressiveness in the problem-solving task had children who expressed less positive affect and more negative affect during the parent-child discussion task. The review suggests that fathers' regulation of emotions was only modestly related to the child's social competence. Fathers who reported being more distressed by their child's expressions of negative affect had children who were more likely to report using anger and other negative emotions to cope with distressing events. When fathers reported using strategies to minimize distressing circumstances, children were more likely to report using reasoning to cope with a distressing situation.

A number of variables may moderate the degree to which parental and child-rearing practices affect emotional competencies in the child (Eisenberg, Cumberland & Spinrad, 1998). These include the child's temperament/personality (e.g., the child's reactivity and dispositional regulatory capabilities); the type of emotion, valence, intensity, and clarity of the child's experienced and expressed emotions; the appropriateness of the child's emotional displays towards parents; the valence, type, intensity, and clarity of parent's emotion; the consistency and clarity of the parent's communication; and fit of the socialization practices to the child's sex and developmental level. Unfortunately, these hypothesized moderators have not been tested systematically.

Family discourse about emotions   The socialization technique of open family discourse about feelings and emotions enhances the child's emotional awareness and allows her (and significant others) to negotiate shared culturally relevant meanings about experience (Denham, 1998). Thus, children growing up in families in which feeling-state talk is frequent appear better at making judgments about the emotions of unfamiliar adults at six-years than children growing up in families where feeling-state talk is infrequent (Dunn, Brown & Beardsall, 1991). Family discourse may moderate the effects of negative affect on emotional competence. Thus, Salovey, Bedell, et al. (2000) suggest that the expression of negative affect in the family may lead to heightened social competence, provided that parents use the experience to initiate a conversation about how the child feels (Dunn & Brown, 1994). Children who learn to discuss negative emotions with their parents (effectively regulating these emotions) appear better able to feel sympathy for others, engage in positive behaviors, and be liked by peers/adults with whom they interact (Eisenberg, Fabes & Losoya, 1997).

Rothbart and Derryberry (1981) provided empirical evidence suggesting that parents who coached their children during emotional moments have children who are better able to physiologically self-sooth and calm themselves down. These children showed an improved ability to calm themselves down when they were upset, and were rated by their teachers as showing better peer relations. Furthermore, Gottman (1997) found that parents' awareness of their own sadness and tendencies to coach their children about their anger have a considerable impact on children's emotion regulation abilities. At age 5, those children whose parents possess these meta-emotional abilities show fewer behavioral problems, higher academic achievement in math and reading, and better physical health.

Important but neglected factors

In this section we briefly touch upon a number of important factors, which may impact upon the development of the child's emotional growth and intelligence. It is noted that the actual deployment of emotionally intelligent behaviors is highly contextually dependent. Although the variables to be discussed below are relatively unresearched, we should not be led to demote their importance in any way.

Personal experiences Aside from acquiring emotional competencies from parents and other social agents in their immediate environment, children also glean important information about emotions from their own emotional experiences. Thus, children witness emotions in themselves, think about emotion-event links, and use these relationships in their emotion-related cognitions (Denham, 1998). Young children first reflect upon, and make judgment about, their own emotions and generalize these judgments to other's feelings. Furthermore, young children build on the early understanding of basic emotional situations to create more intricate scenarios depicting particular feelings of specific persons (Denham, 1998). As pointed out by Saarni (1999), children who are impoverished in their awareness of their own emotional experiences would have parallel deficits in knowing how to respond adaptively to others experiencing similar emotions in their environment.

Peer environment   With increasing maturity, peers become a more salient influence on emotional socialization. Research by Sawyer (1996) shows that when older siblings show a rewarding socialization pattern —reacting positively to positive emotions and not showing negative reactions to negative emotions—younger siblings demonstrate more emotional knowledge. There is also some research to suggest that older siblings are particularly potent socializers of emotional knowledge. The authors hypothesize that this occurs because power amidst egalitarianism and love amidst conflict characterizes these relationships (Youngblade & Dunn, 1995). Unfortunately, very little research has focused on the socializing influence of peers and siblings on emotional competencies (Denham, 1998).

Affective environment in school and community   The overall affective environment at the school and community, to which a child is exposed, particularly if negative, may impact upon the child's emotional competence. For example, if teachers or community leaders often express anger or anxiety, children may internalize these affective states and experience them in a variety of situations (Denham & Grout, 1993). Children exposed to this sort of aversive affective environment may learn inappropriate and dysfunctional reactions to other's emotions, thus negatively impacting on their emotional development and regulation.

Teachers   Some of the most important emotional learning takes place in informal relationships between child and teacher (Mayer & Salovey, 1997). Teachers may influence the child's ability to express and regulate emotions in the following two ways: directly, by teaching and coaching, and indirectly, by observational learning or by controlling children's exposure to different situations. Thus, teachers, through their interactions with students, fellow teachers, and administrators, model for children ways how to regulate emotion appropriate in the classroom. Teachers also directly instruct students about how to manage distress. Also, in the process of designing and creating a comfortable learning environment teachers, dictate the opportunities that children have to learn about emotion regulation.

Media   Watching television or being exposed to other forms of media (movies, plays, etc.) provide children with highly salient opportunities for observational learning of emotional expression and management

(Thompson, 1990). Some TV programs designed for children (e.g., Sesame Street) present salient role models who themselves manage emotion arousal in explicit ways. Other programs, by contrast, arouse emotions directly in children and require self-management of arousal (e.g., adult programming that includes explicit violence). At present, little is known about the role of TV exposure in the development of emotional regulation.

Schooling Emotional Intelligence

This section selectively reviews what we currently know about the education and schooling of emotional competencies. EI appears being capable of being learned both inside and outside the home. Thus, having shown the various factors thought to impinge on the development of EI, the progression from the home to the school environment would appear to be a logical progression. In fact, the classroom (i.e., secondary group), being more formal in its organizational characteristics than the family (i.e., primary group), may be a particularly useful test of generalized EI skills that may be applied to other formal environments (e.g., the workplace)—perhaps with a strong implication for lifelong programs. We begin this critique by presenting a brief overview of the growth of school-based intervention programs. A number of specimen programs will be discussed in greater depth later on in the chapter.

School-based intervention programs

There is a rising tide of understanding among educators and psychologists that children's emotional learning should be given serious consideration and promoted in schools (Elias, Zins, Weissberg, Frey, Greenberg, Haynes, Kessler, Schwab-Stone & Shriver, 1997). Elias et al. (1997) call social and emotional education the 'missing piece'—that part of the mission of the school that, while always close to the thoughts of many teachers, somehow eluded them. The trend of bringing emotional literacy into schools makes emotions and social life themselves key topics for learning and discussion, rather than treating these most compelling facets of a child's life as irrelevant intrusions. In a sense, the social environment of the schools is a microcosm of the larger social system in which it is embedded. The interpersonal relationships that children establish with teachers and peers in school play a role in the acquisition of fundamental social attitudes, beliefs and values and influence children's understanding of society and their place in it.

The school setting is arguably one of the most important contexts for learning of emotional skills and competencies. In the process of emotional learning, the individual develops the aptitudes, skills, attitudes, and values necessary to acquire emotional competence. Emotional education may be provided through a variety of diverse efforts such as classroom instruction, extracurricular activities, a supportive school climate, and the involvement of students, teachers, and parents in community activities. Implicit in current work on EI is the plausible assumption that people can learn to become more emotionally intelligent. That is, emotional competencies, through systematic training and education, like most other skills, appear capable of being improved. Mayer and Geher (1996), for example, assume that it may be possible to educate those who are low in emotional competencies to improve their abilities to better recognize their feelings, express them, and regulate them. Thus, Mayer and Salovey (1997) claim that even if socialization of emotions in the child's early familial (or social environment) was not entirely optimal, the possibility remains open for remedial learning in the schools to take place to rectify deficits. However, exactly how this is to be accomplished remains unspecified.

Curricular based programs (reviewed by Cohen, 1999a, 1999b, 1999c) seek to educate children about the value of emotional competencies. They also seek to foster the development of specific skills in these areas (e.g., recognition of emotions in self and others, empathy, conflict resolution). Importantly, they can also be integrated into whatever instructional unit is currently being taught. Given that children can learn by observing and modeling real, as well as symbolic, and representational models, curriculum based emotional learning comes naturally with many of the liberal arts (e.g., literature, theater, poetry, etc). For example, children can learn much about various feelings when reading literary works that depict characters with the tendency to experience specific emotions (e.g., sadness, fear, distrust, surprise). Children can observe how characters express and display their emotions, what makes the characters feel as they do, how the characters cope in response to their feelings, and how effective are the various methods of coping employed. This form of affective learning proceeds throughout the educational system, and as the literary or artistic scenarios become more complex, so does emotional learning seeking to promote the development of social and emotional competencies.

However, the response of educators to the renewed awareness about the importance of emotional education has been mixed (Elias et al.,

1997). In the minds of many educators, the major mission of the school is to teach students academic knowledge and skills. Emotion education is often viewed with skepticism and as being outside the mandate and scope of the schools. Indeed, many an educator regards EI curricula and prevention programs as frills or as disjointed fads—"Here today, gone tomorrow" (see Zins, Elias, Greenberg & Weissberg, 2000). Opponents of EI literacy programs in the classroom further argue that school needs to concentrate efforts on academic achievement because there is simply not enough time to address other topics, regardless of their merit.

One possible reason for the upsurge in interest in social and emotional learning is the claim that emotional competencies are of prime importance for academic success. Accordingly, EI is claimed to be positively related to academic achievement and productive experience in the world (Elias et al., 1997). In fact, processes we had considered as purely cognitive or intellectual are basically phenomena in which the cognitive and emotional aspects work synergistically. Accordingly, EI programs purportedly buttress skills to listen or focus, feel committed and responsible for their work, rein impulses, and cope with upsets (Goleman, 1995a; Goleman, 1995b). Proponents of the EI construct have claimed that research has recently rediscovered what good teachers and parents have known all along. Knowledge about ourselves and others, as well as the capacity to use this knowledge to solve problems adaptively, provides an essential foundation for academic learning (Cohen, 1999a, 1999b, 1999c; Goleman, 1995a, 1995b).

Notwithstanding the potential importance of EI to intellectual attainment, several proponents of the EI construct (Goleman, 1995a, 1995b; Aronson, 2000) have made unsubstantiated (even quite fantastic) claims with respect to the predictive utility of EI in the academic domain. Thus, although most EI programs have not designated improvement of school achievement as one of their primary goals, Goleman (1995a) has argued that EI programs in fact do improve children's academic achievement scores and school performance. However, little evidence is provided in support of this claim. Furthermore, with respect to the incremental validity of EI above and beyond IQ, Elliot Aaronson, a distinguished social psychologist, writes, "Studies have demonstrated that emotional intelligence (EQ) and academic intelligence are separate qualities, and that emotional intelligence is a better predictor of success in school" (2000, p. 102). Yet Aaronson has failed to provide evidence for the foregoing claim by comparing the predictive validity of IQ and EI in predicting academic performance via appropriate statistical tests for comparing differences among validity coefficients or regression parameters (see Jensen, 1980). In fact, few studies have tested for the incremental validity of EI when IQ is held statistically constant. Thus, at present, these claims remain largely unsubstantiated.

Selective survey of specimen EI intervention programs
The programs designed to foster EI fall under the general rubric of social and emotional learning programs (SEL)—an umbrella term that provides a common framework for programs with a wide array of specified outcomes. It refers to the knowledge, skills, and competencies that children acquire through social and emotional education, instruction, activities, or promotion efforts. A broad spectrum of EI intervention programs designed to teach emotional competencies in the school are now available, including, social skills training, cognitive-behavioral modification, self-management, and multi-modal programs (Topping, Holmes & Bremner, 2000). The idea that students' emotional and social problems can be addressed through school-based intervention programs became popular among educational reformers during the last decade or so. Current interest in emotional learning was largely spurred by Goleman's book *Emotional Intelligence* (1995a, 1995b) and reinforced later with an influential book by Elias et al., *Promoting Social and Emotional Learning* (1997). The Nueva School in Hillsborough, California, was the first to start an emotional literacy program, and New Haven was the first city to implement such a program in public schools district-wide. Once established, the concept of EI has proven itself a catalyst to the thinking and planning of educators and policy makers. Thus, well over 700 school districts across the United States have expressed interest in implementing the emotional literacy approach (Goleman, 1995a, 1995b). The Collaborative for Social and Emotional Learning at the University of Illinois reports that more than 150 different emotional literacy programs are being used today by thousands of American schools. Programs seeking to inculcate emotional and social competencies go under a variety of names, such as "life-skills training," "self-science," "education for care," "social awareness," "social problem solving," "social competency," and "resolving conflicts creatively."

Most current EI programs are targeted at the general population. Accordingly, they encompass a set of skills believed to be essential for the average classroom student and not only for children who are suffering from emotional or social adjustment problems. It is still unclear, however, to what degree those students needing EI intervention the most (i.e., those characterized by maladaptive emotional responses) would profit from conventional programs requiring them to share their emotions, or feel overwhelmed by them.

Exemplary EI program: The PATH model   In order to provide the reader with a flavor for current social-emotional intervention programs, we briefly sketch the major goals, activities, and impact results of one of the most popular of this genre—the Promoting Alternative Thinking Strategies (PATH) program. The PATH program is a comprehensive affective education program designed primarily for preschool and elementary school children (K–5). The program sets out to achieve the following objectives (Greenberg, Kusche, Cooke & Quamma, 1995):

- Promote social and emotional competence
- Facilitate the development of emotional awareness
- Improve interpersonal problem-solving
- Prevent violence and aggression
- Reduce behavioral and emotional problems

PATH is divided into three major units related to core social and emotional learning competencies:

Readiness and self-control   Focuses on readiness skills and development of basic self-control.

Feelings and relationships   Focuses on teaching emotional and interpersonal understanding.

Interpersonal cognitive problem-solving   Eleven steps for formal interpersonal problem solving.

Two additional areas of focus involve building positive self-esteem and improving peer communications/relations.

We now describe in some detail the feeling and relationships unit of the PATH model, the area of focus that is most closely related to the schooling of EI competencies. This unit includes lessons focusing on 35 different affective states that are presented, and discussed, inside a developmental hierarchy. Lessons begin with the most basic emotions (e.g., happiness and anger) and then proceed to focus on more complicated feelings (e.g., pride, jealousy, and guilt). The curriculum emphasizes vocabulary for labeling and describing emotions, appraisals of basic emotions in oneself and others, and how to manage emotions (Green-berg et al., 1995). Accordingly, students are instructed in identifying and labeling feelings, expressing feelings, impulse control, understanding the perspective of others, verbal communication skills, problem-solving techniques, and cultivating a positive outlook towards life.

To give the reader a feel for the material, we move now to provide concrete examples of the type of exercises employed in this program.

Feeling faces   The feeling-faces technique engages children in making their own feeling boxes. After each emotion concept is introduced, dur-ing subsequent lessons, the children personalize their own feeling facets for that affect. As the lessons progress, the children's boxes become full of different feeling faces. The feeling faces fit into an attached strip on the child's desk that reads, "I feel...." This activity allows children to communicate feelings and with minimal difficulty to see how feelings change.

Control signals poster   The control-signals poster is designed to develop self-control, affective awareness, and beginning problem-solving skills. It is modeled on the notion of a traffic's signal and is modified version of the stop light used in Yale–New Haven Middle School Social Problem Solving Program. The control-signals poster was a red light to signal "Stop, calm down," a yellow light to signal "Go slow, think," and green light to signal "Go try my plan," and at the bottom was, "Evaluate: how did my plan work?"

Grievance mailbox   In the grievance mailbox (Aronson, 2000; Goleman, 1995a, 1995b), there is a mailbox in each classroom for student mes-sages (e.g., "Johnny won't let me join in the basketball game"). The teacher uses such a concern as a springboard for class discussion—about the vicissitudes of friendship, how it feels to be left out, how rela-tionships can change over time, how people can make friends, etc. The teacher points out that all children share such problems from time to time and they all need to learn how to handle them. As children talk about how it feels to be left out, or what they might do to be included, they have the chance to try out new solutions.

Getting lost in the mall   To foster empathy and understanding of emo-tions, children are presented with the example of a boy who separates himself from his parents in the mall (Elias et al., 1997). The class dis-cusses what the boy was feeling and how the parents felt. The class made a long list of consequences that the boy could experience as a result of leaving his parent's side and what steps the parent would have to take to find his or her son. Many children felt the need to share stories of being separated from their parents and the feelings they felt. This unit is based on an explicit model of emotional socialization that teaches children that feelings are signals that communicate useful information relating to a person's adjustment to his or her environment. Children are taught that if people learn to attend to what their feelings are telling them, the information can be beneficially utilized in making decisions. Furthermore, children are taught that it is perfectly legitimate to experience all types of emotions, although some feel comfortable and others do not.

Impact evaluation of PATH   The PATH program has been systematically tested by a series of controlled clinical studies using randomized control groups. The program was evaluated in Seattle in school grades 1 to 5. Across three studies, children in experimental groups had superior abilities to recognize emotions and social problems, increased respect for self and others, increased empathy, more effective thinking skills and solutions to social problems, and fewer aggressive and violent acts. At one-year post-intervention, students reported lower levels of negative affect and fewer conduct problems.

A study by Greenberg et al. (1995) assessed the effectiveness of a PATH program implemented in 30 second- and third-grade classrooms. This intervention was based on the ABCD (affective, behavior, cognitive, dynamic) model of development. This hybrid model stresses the developmental integration of affect, behavior, and cognitive understanding as they relate to social and emotional competence. The following five domains of emotional understanding were measured: (a) ability to discuss one's own emotional experiences, (b) cues used to recognize emotions, (c) issues regarding simultaneity of emotions, (d) display rules of emotions, and (e) whether and how emotions can change. For example, the feeling vocabulary was assessed by gauging knowledge of the total number of positive and negative feeling words students can elicit or identify (e.g., proud, guilty, jealous, nervous, and lonely). Furthermore, students were asked to respond to questions such as "Are all feelings OK?" "Can feelings change?" For both low and high risk children, intervention was effective in improving: the range of vocabulary, fluency in discussing emotional experience, efficacy beliefs regarding the management of emotions, and understanding of some aspects of emotion.

Greenberg, Kusche, Cook, and Quamma (1995) developed a longer-term PATH curriculum designed to improve emotional identification and self-regulation, along with social problem-solving skills, for first- and second-graders. Much of the curriculum focused on thinking about emotions and regulating them. Specific curricular elements included controlling emotional arousal and behavior through self-regulation ("Stopping and calming down"); and enriched linguistic experiences focused on mediating the understanding of emotions in self and others. Also included was an attempt to teach integrating emotional understanding with cognitive and linguistic skills, analyzing and solving problems, and developing positive self-esteem and effective peer relations. The intervention had extensive impact on children's understanding of emotions (greater verbal access to affect vocabulary for positive and negative emotions, understanding that people hide feelings, and understanding it is possible to change bad moods). Disappointingly, however, some more advanced aspects did not evidence change.

Some generalizations

It is beyond the scope of this chapter to extensively survey the plethora of EI intervention programs or emotion-based curricular materials available on the market today (for a recent survey of prevalent programs, see Cohen, 1999a, 1999b, 1999c). Box 11.1 briefly describes salient features (i.e., objectives, program foci and activities, EI content, assessment results) underlying the most popular and frequently referenced of these programs.

As is readily apparent from inspection of box 11.1, current EI intervention programs target a wide array of behavioral objectives. These include: improving social, communication, and life skills (problem solving strategies, assertiveness training); modifying emotional regulation and coping techniques; effective peer-relation training; fostering conflict resolution and responsible decision making skills; promoting health; preventing alcohol, tobacco, and drug use; reducing violence; developing self-esteem; and enriching linguistic experiences. Furthermore, programs vary widely with respect to their systematic coverage of the major components of EI. Whereas some programs target relatively few elements directly related to EI (e.g., Seattle Social Development Project), others (e.g., PATH) cover quite a number of important components of EI. For example, in this former program, awareness and regulation of emotions, perspective taking, conflict resolution skills, coping with stress, and several other related concepts are all subject to intervention. The behavioral objectives most frequently targeted by prevalent EI programs, as represented in box 11.1, include the following:

Box 11.1

A brief description of prevalent EI intervention programs

Promoting Alternative Thinking Strategies (PATH)

Developers   Kusche and Greenberg (Greenberg, 1995).

Target populations   Grades K-12, with emphasis on younger children.

Aims   To improve children's ability to understand, express, and regulate emotions, as well as to enhance social problem-solving skills. Much of the curriculum focuses on thinking about emotions and regulating them. Specific curricular elements include: understanding of emotions in self and others; integrating emotional understanding with cognitive and linguistic skills; controlling emotional arousal and behavior through self-regulation; developing positive self-esteem; enriched linguistic experiences; analyzing and solving problems; and promoting effective peer relations.

Focus of program   The program includes instruction in identifying and labeling different emotions (e.g., happiness and anger, pride, jealousy, guilt), expressing feelings, assessing intensity of feelings, impulse control, understanding perspective of others, verbal communication skills, coping with stress, using steps for problem solving, and having a positive attitude towards life.

Elements of EI addressed   Improving children's ability to understand, discuss, and regulate negative emotions (e.g., anger) and control impulses and empathic understanding of other's feelings.

Program assessment   An assessment reported by Greenberg et al. (1995), involving 286 kids from grades 2–3, was effective for both low and high risk special students in improving the range of vocabulary in discussing emotional experiences and efficacy beliefs regarding management of emotions and developmental aspects of some elements of emotions. Greenberg, Kusche, Cook and Quamma (1995) developed and assessed a longer-term EI curriculum for first- and second graders. The stated goal was to improve emotional identification and self-regulation for first and second graders, as well as social problem-solving skills. Much of the curriculum focused on thinking about emotions and regulating them. Among the positive outcomes observed after the 7 month intervention were: greater verbal access to affect vocabulary for positive and negative emotions; understanding that people hide feelings; and its possible to change bad moods. The intervention had an impact on children's understanding of emotions, although some advanced aspects of emotional understanding did not evidence change.

Box 11.1 (continued)

Resolving Conflict Creatively Program (RCCP)

Developers　Linda Lantieri (Aber, Jones, Brown, Chaudry & Samples, 1998).

Target populations　Grades K-12, with emphasis on elementary school.

Aims　To help children think, feel, and act adaptively in situations of interpersonal conflict by making children aware of the different choices they have for dealing with conflicts and help children develop skills for making those choices; encourage children's respect for their cultural backgrounds and those of others; make children aware of their role in creating a more peaceful world; and teach children how to identify and stand against prejudice. Activities aim to reduce youth violence by promoting constructive anger control and conflict resolution skills; to improve intergroup relations; and to foster a caring and peaceful community of learning.

Program focus　Program goals are addressed in a 25-hour teacher's training program, and a program emphasizing peer mediation for children in grades 4–6. Program activities focus on expressing negative feelings; regulating angers in self; and conflict resolution skills. Following are a number of basic themes in the RCCP: curriculum: (a) Cooperation—through a variety of cooperative activities, youngsters learn to value co-operation with peers; (b) Caring—students learn to speak their feelings and actively listen to others through role playing and simulations; (c) Expression of feelings—Students are encouraged to express both their positive and negative feelings through role playing and group exercises; (d) Appreciation of diversity—Students are taught to honor differences and discuss issues of prejudice and discrimination; (e) Responsible decision making—Students are taught the Decision Making Model, such as telling what the problem is; finding as many solutions as possible; deciding which one is good and choose and act on it; (f) Conflict resolution—Students explore negative and possible consequences of different ways of handling conflict, (aggression, collaboration, compromise, appealing to authority). The curriculum focuses on key skills relevant to developing conflict resolution skills: active listening, assertiveness, expression of feeling in appropriate ways, empathy and perspective taking, cooperation, negotiation, and methods for countering bias. Some students are trained as monitors or mediators in order to give children the opportunity to use the conflict resolution skills they have learned outside the classroom. The instructional methods used in the program are diverse, including role-playing, interviewing, and group discussion, brainstorming, teachable moments, and other experiential and affective strategies.

Box 11.1 (continued)

Elements of EI addressed   This program emphasizes a number of components of EI such as: identifying one's own negative feelings in conflict situations; regulating anger in ones self; and taking the perspective of others and empathizing with other's feelings.

Program assessment   The RCCP program was Implemented in New York City in over 100 elementary, middle, and high school among over 40,000 children. The program was evaluated based on 2 waves of developmental data, including 5053 children from grades 2 to 6 from 11 New York elementary schools (Aber, Brown, Henrich, 1999). Those receiving a high number of lessons had a significantly slower growth in self-reported hostile attributions and teacher-reported aggressive behavior, compared to children receiving a low number of lessons (Aber, Brown, Henrich, 1999). Patti and Lantieri (1999) report that an independent evaluation released in May 1990 by Metis Associates found that more than 87% of the teachers said that RCCP was having a positive impact on their students. Teachers and administrators reported the following changes: decreased violence in the classroom; increased used of conflict resolution skills, increased self-esteem and sense of empowerment; enhanced awareness of feelings, more caring behavior, and acceptance of differences. Another study found that participating students showed declining dropout rates and suspension rates. Also, about 92% of the students felt well about themselves and 64% of the teachers reported less physical roles.

Improving Social Awareness, Social Problem Solving Project (ISA/SPSP)

Development   Maurice Elias (Elias & Clabby, 1992; Clabby & Elias 1999; Elias, Gara, Ubriaco, Rothbaum, Clabby & Schuyler, 1986).

Target populations   Grades K-12, with emphasis on elementary and middle school children.

Aims   To improve problem-solving skills; enhance involvement, and increase behavior and interpersonal effectiveness.

Activities   The ISA-SPS curriculum is organized into three phases; readiness for decision making; instructional phase, and application of problem solving thinking. Social decision making and problem solving skills are integrated into everyday academic and interpersonal context in the schools. The program includes well-articulated strategies and activities to help build students' skills during language arts, health, social studies, civics, science, art, gym, or music. The cornerstone of the program is a highly structured classroom instruction of 25–30 hours at each grade level. Three families of EI components are targeted: stress management and impulse control; social problem solving and information processing; and behavioral social skills.

Box 11.1 (continued)

Elements of EI addressed   Students are taught skills in areas loosely over-lapping with EI: awareness of feelings, self-control, anger and stress management, emotion-focused coping, adaptability, and perspective taking. Students are taught to recognize emotions in pictures and facial expressions related to emotions. Emotional lessons merge naturally into reading and writing, health, science, and social studies.

Program assessment   An initial evaluation of the Improving Social Awareness Program (Elias & Clabby, 1992) showed that the program reduced the impact of typical middle-school stressors. Follow-up evaluation 6 years later documented long-term gains in children's prosocial behavior, sense of efficacy and and reduction in pathology and socially disordered behaviors (aggression, vandalism). Program participants showed higher levels of positive prosocial behavior and lower levels of antisocial and self-destructive behavior. Clabby and Elias (1999) reported follow-up evaluation results for a program involving a comparison of 3 cohorts of students who had received social decision making lessons in elementary school. Relative to 9th grade controls, ninth grade students had higher scores in overall social competence, used significantly fewer alcoholic beverages, and reported fewer self-destructive problems. Similarly for 10th and 11th grade students, there was a decrease in property vandalism. Elias, Gar, Ubriaco, Rothbaum, Clabby, and Schuyler (1986) compared children receiving a 1 year or half year preventive social problem solving program in elementary schools with a no-treatment group. One year of training was significantly related to reductions in the severity of a variety of middle-school stressors and a mediating role for social problem solving skills was found. Elias, Gara, Schuyler, Branden-Muller, and Sayette (1991) reported that students who had received a two-year social decision-making program in elementary schools showed higher levels of positive prosocial behavior and lower levels of antisocial self-destructive, and socially disordered behaviors when followed up in high school four to six years later than did the control students who had not received this program.

Seattle Social Development Project

Development   J. David Hawkins (Hawkins, Von Cleve, and Catalano, 1991).

Target populations   Grades 1–9.

Aims   To prevent substance abuse and delinquency.

Program focus   Teaching practices such as proactive class management, interactive teaching, and cooperative learning, is intended to strengthen school bonding. Parents were taught skills in monitoring and supervising children's behavior, in using appropriate rewards and punishments, in using consistent discipline practices, in using effective communication

Box 11.1 (continued)

skills and involving children in family activities. Parents were also encouraged to create age-appropriate family roles for their children and to increase family activities and family time together.

Elements of EI addressed   Unclear.

Program assessment   Experimental parent training by Hawkins, Von Cleve, and Catalano (1991) was offered in seven consecutive weekly sessions to all parents whose children were assigned to experimental classrooms. Reduced rates of delinquency and drug use initiation were reported. Impact increased positive attachment to family and school; less delinquency; less drug-use initiation; and better scores on standardized achievement tests. An evaluation study among fifth grade children showed that the experimental group had stronger home and school attachments than the control group and evidenced lower raters of delinquency and drug use initiation (as reported by Goleman, 1995a, 1995b).

Yale-New Haven Social Competence Promotion Program

Developed   R. Weissberg (Shriver, Schwab-Stone & DeFalco, 1999).

Target populations   Grades 5 to 8.

Aims   To incorporate prevention efforts into a comprehensive strategy sequence that would nurture the development of each child's learning as well as enhance the learning environment. The program has been implemented through broad collaboration among teachers, parents, administration and community leaders who make it possible for children to receive support, guidance, and nurturing that make positive development a reality. Specific goals include: developing a sense of self-worth; fostering socially skilled and positive relations with peers and adults; engage in positive, self-protective behavior practices; feel motivated to contribute responsibly and ethically to their peer group, family, school, and community.

Program focus   The cornerstone of the program is a highly structured classroom instruction of 25–30 hours at each grade. This program used the six-step problem-solving process: (a) stop, calm down, and think before you act, (b) say the problem and how you feel, (c) set a positive goal, (d) think of lots of solutions, (e) Think ahead to the consequences, and (f) go ahead and try the best plan. The combination of curricular materials, schools activities, and school climate, create a comprehensive program to address the needs of the whole child. At each grade level, teachers chose the curriculum from a selection that met the program's criteria in terms of skills, attitudes, and values and content that should be taught. In addition, school and community activities offer school children

Box 11.1 (continued)

educational, recreational, and health-promoting opportunities outside the classroom, which are reinforced by various programs, such as mentoring, outdoor adventure class, peer mediation, and student leadership.

Elements of EI addressed Feelings awareness, emotion-focused coping, and adaptability; self-management (e.g., self-monitoring, self-control, stress management, persistence, emotion-focused coping, adaptability); feeling awareness and perspective taking.

Program assessment The K-12 curriculum was implemented gradually over a 4-period, thus enabling the school district to learn from the implementation. Rather informal surveys were conducted of teachers, parents, administrator and student satisfaction (Shriver, Schwab-Stone & DeFalco, 1999).

Oakland's Child Development Project

Development Eric Schaps (cf. Schaps & Battistich, 1991).

Target populations Grades K-6, particularly high-risk children.

Aims To build a caring and fair school community by nurturing basic values and helping students become caring, fair, and responsible citizens.

Program focus Prepackaged set of curricular materials, which offers increasingly sophisticated contents (e.g., stories) as children go through the elementary and middle-school grades. This gives teachers an entry point to discuss topics such as empathy, perspective taking, and caring. The program also, includes activities that focus on collaborative learning, problem-solving approach to discipline, parent involvement, 'buddy' activities, and tutoring. Students taught how to resist drugs and avoid violent behaviors. The school-wide program was designed to create a general milieu that would support and enhance the classroom program (family events, schoolwide service, and helping activities, buddies activities, tutoring, etc.).

Elements of EI addressed Empathy, impulse control.

Program assessment CDP was evaluated in 3 separate studies (Child Development Project Report, 1999). The first study followed up children from K to 4th grade, with longer-term assessments in 6th, 7th, and 8th grade. The second assessed 2 programs and 2 comparison schools while the third assessment involved 6 districts throughout the U.S. Results in all 3 studies point to the central importance of a caring school community for the development of personal and social qualities (e.g., social competence, concern for others, conflict resolution skills, sense of autonomy) and academic orientations (motivation, liking for school) and qualities that help students avoid the risk of problematic behaviors. No consistent effects of program on student achievement were reported and the impact on

Box 11.1 (continued)

affective parameters was inconsistent. In addition, there were problems in the valid implementation of the program. The authors claim (P. 10): "The data clearly and strongly supported the model for virtually all attitudinal, motivational, and behavioral variables, but not for the achievement measures (Child Development Project Report, 1999). Furthermore, official publications report that the program has been successful in leading to the reduction in alcohol and marijuana, boosting academic motivation, building understanding and appreciation of diversity, and strengthening connections between school and home.

- Problem-solving;
- Awareness and understanding of emotions in self and others;
- Impulse control;
- Emotion regulation;
- Coping with environmental stress and negative emotions;
- Perspective taking and empathy.

EI components can be identified both by examining the program description and curricular materials. However, these components are not always specified as program objectives in the program planning stage nor are they consistently assessed during the program evaluation phase. Some programs have attracted few systematic evaluations (e.g., Seattle Social Development Project, Yale-New Haven Social Competence Promotion Program), whereas others have enjoyed systematic program evaluation efforts (e.g., PATH, RCCP). Some evaluation studies may be construed as one-shot evaluation studies, with no long-term follow-up, while others have conducted follow-ups after five years or more (Elias & Clabby, 1992).

Salovey, Bedell, et al. (2000) conclude that these programs tend to be liked by students and teachers. They are viewed by participating students and teachers as helpful and they may often have an impact on social behavior, especially at school. Goleman (1995b) claims that pooling assessments reveals a widespread benefit for children's emotional and social competence for their behavior in and out of classroom and in improving ability to learn.

In the following section, we discuss a number of basic and methodological problems that appear to plague current EI intervention programs and earmark some desired features and principles for future EI programs.

Basic problems and issues

A major problem in assessing the effectiveness of EI interventions is that very few currently implemented programs were specifically designed to serve as primary prevention or similar programs for promoting, developing, or fostering EI skills. Thus, most of the programs described in appendices D–F in Goleman's 1995 book, cited as evidence in support of the effectiveness of EI interventions, were not, in fact, specifically designed as EI intervention programs. Instead, the majority of these programs were designed for other purposes (e.g., promoting conflict resolution skills, enhancing problem solving skills, reducing drug use, and the like).

Moreover, when examining current programs being touted as "EI interventions," one is puzzled by the meager EI-relevant content of some of these programs. Whereas various facets of EI (e.g., emotional perception and awareness, understanding, emotional regulation) are implicit in models developed to promote emotional and social competencies, these facets have rarely been a central focus of preventive intervention. Thus, a violence reduction or conflict resolution program may include a module focusing on anger expression and management as a means to help participants control violent behavior and reduce aggressive and offending behavior, without making this the focus of the program. A cursory examination of box 11.1 shows that, aside perhaps from the PATH program, none of the others specifically addresses all major facets of EI. In most cases, only one or two facets of emotional competency are actually addressed per program.

A major concern of many current studies is that the size of program effects is often small in absolute terms, so the clinical significance of the changes in the dependent measure is often uncertain. For example, in assessing the effects of the RCCP program, small and inconsistent effects were found (Aber, Jones, Brown, Chaudry & Samples, 1998). The authors claim that this is not surprising, since children's developmental trajectories toward aggression and violence are multiply determined and RCCP targets only some of the many causal factors.

Furthermore, it is quite difficult to compare different EI intervention programs because these programs often have targeted different facets of EI in different age groups (see DeFalco, 1997). Thus, EI programs for younger children tend to focus on building a feelings vocabulary and recognizing facial expressions of emotions. EI programs for middle-school students, on the other hand, often address impulse control and emotion regulation. Finally, programs targeting high-school students generally focus on the role of emotions in helping students resist peer pressure to engage in risky behaviors (e.g., sexual behavior, drug or alcohol use, aggression, and violence).

A further problem with current programs is that they may be misconstrued as teaching students how to feel in a normative sense. It is commonly believed that there is no right way or wrong way of feeling, and feelings are legitimate as long as they are not translated into action. Thus, we need to avoid the mistaken impression that we are teaching people how to feel, and what emotions are acceptable or right in a given context.

A more practical concern is that students may not transfer or apply the skills taught in the course of the program to real life. Thus, one can teach students specific skills like ingredients in baking cake (akin to declarative knowledge) without students actually being able to use them wisely in social situations, e.g., to bake a cake (akin to procedural knowledge). Clearly, the use of skills is a function of knowledge as well as situation-dependent skills. A still further problem in the evaluation of EI programs is that we really don't know *how* they work (Salovey, Bedell, et al., 1999). Even staunch advocates agree that we will only be able to speak to the optimistic claims about EI programs (e.g., reducing drug use, student drop out, or violence) after they been subjected to rigorous, controlled evaluation.

Methodological constraints

Current EI interventions are plagued by a number of methodological problems and flaws that put serious constraints on interpreting the impact and effectiveness of intervention research. To begin with, in some EI interventions, the program intervention model is not clearly spelled-out and the theoretical framework is often tenuous. Furthermore, it is difficult to compare different programs given the same name in the literature (e.g., social-problem solving), because they may not be the same in practice. Even if identical program models or methods were actually deployed, users are likely to find considerable differences between the two reports. These include different specified objectives, different target populations, different geographical or sociocultural settings, differences in the quality of program delivery and monitoring of the implementation, and different measurements used to gauge impact. Furthermore, it is quite difficult to compare different programs since these programs often have targeted different facets of EI in different age groups.

Furthermore, EI intervention programs are vulnerable to conventional threats to the internal and external validity of the research design (Campbell & Stanley, 1963). One worrisome problem is the commonly found nonequivalence of experimental and control groups in EI treatment intervention. Few studies have employed true experimental designs in which experimental units (classrooms or students) are randomly assigned to experimental or control groups, thus assuring the initial equivalence of experimental and control groups. The large majority of EI intervention programs have employed quasi-experimental designs, with intact classrooms serving as experimental units. This is particularly problematic given that it is frequently not possible to obtain pretest scores before the implementation of the intervention.

Furthermore, many descriptions are replete with anecdotal material supporting the effectiveness of these programs, rather than hard data. A case in point: Goleman (1995a, 1995b) presents the testimony of one of the teachers from the New Haven program for inner city children regarding one of the female participants. The claim is "If she hadn't learned to stand up for her right during our Social Development classes, she would almost certainly would have been an unwed mother by now." Goleman (1995a, 1995b) further relates the case of a school principal who reported a steady reduction in suspension from fighting as EI programs phased without clearly specifying how these observations were carried out. Program evaluations (e.g., Lantieri & Patti, 1996) much too frequently tend to rely on the self-reports of student, teachers, or parents, rather than observational or behavioral data. Furthermore, criterion measures of program effects often have unreported psychometric properties and the analyses of empirical data bearing on program effects are often conducted in a simplistic manner.

A common threat to the internal and external validity of the design is that some projects, which appear to have been subjected to more intensive research, yield atypical results. That is, they are especially well resourced or operated by particularly competent or committed teachers or school counselors or psychologists. This source of sampling error may severely limit the generalizability of effects reported in the literature to average real-world settings. Sometimes there are also difficult issues in the assessment of EI such as whether EI can be validly assessed or taught and by which cultural criterion it can be evaluated (Elias et al., 1997).

Another major threat to the internal validity of treatment programs in EI program evaluations is the "Hawthorne effect," which is often responsible for the observed posttest differences between experimental and control groups. Accordingly, experimental teachers rating students on outcome measures may rate students undergoing emotional training in a more positive manner in terms of EI, simply because they know these participants were involved in a special experimental project designed to foster EI.

What constitutes good evidence of program impact is another major question of concern. On the one hand, many studies are plagued by methodological problems, sufficing to track changes in the same students before and after intervention. On the other hand, the randomized controlled trials, which might be useful to evaluate a new drug in medicine, are much more difficult to establish in the more complex and subtle world of education. Moreover, even if possible, these types of trials would have their own difficulties, especially with respect to ecological validity.

Regrettably, most intervention assessment studies have primarily estimated short-term effects, with little known about longer-term effects. As pointed out by Aber, Brown, and Henrich (1999), since policymakers tend to be more convinced by long-term changes in outcome measures, long-term follow up studies are clearly required.

One important concern that should be mentioned is that there are frequently lacunae in the documentation of EI interventions. This is evidenced by information missing on many important items the reader would like to know. For example, when reading the program description, one is often impressed by the fact that the reporting of how the program was actually implemented is frequently absent. Alternatively, the program has not been detailed enough for users to decide how effectively it was actually implemented. Few interventions report information about the generalization to any gains or the maintenance of gains, although both are crucial to estimating practical effectiveness and cost-effectiveness. It is also difficult to find detailed information about real total cost of implementing the program, let alone the calculation of unit cost per participant (Topping et al., 2000).

Desired Features of EI Intervention Programs and Future Research

There would appear common flaws and shortcomings in the design, implementation, and assessment of extant intervention programs. It is not clear that this needs to be the case: even if there is no identifiable, independent concept of EI (see chapter 1), these programs might still have merit. We now briefly present a number of desiderata and considerations when developing and implementing intervention programs of the preceding type (for now, let us call them EI intervention programs) in the future.

Conceptual framework   EI intervention programs should be based on a solid conceptual framework and grounded in a sound intervention model that guides the program implementation and practice (Elias et al, 1997; Zins, Travis III & Freppon, 1997).

Program goals   Program goals should address key facets of EI (e.g., awareness, understanding, expression and regulation of emotions in self and others). Furthermore, program goals need to be specific and well focused and measurable during the program evaluation (Mayer & Salovey, 1997).

Importance of emotional learning   Students, school staff, parents, and the general community, need to perceive emotional competencies as important to cultivate. Elias et al. (1997) goes so far as to argue that EI materials be given as much emphasis as other parts of the academic program. Further, current programs should foster appreciation of diversity and respect for the demands of growing up in a pluralistic society. They should be sensitive, relevant and responsive with regard to the ethnic, gender, and socioeconomic composition of students, as well as that of faculty and staff delivering the instruction and services (Elias et al., 1997).

Comprehensive, multi-component, and systematic program elements (see Zins et al., 2000)   Prior research has shown that traditional prevention models based on single skills (e.g., only social problem-solving, self-control, empathy, etc.) have demonstrated less effectiveness than multi-modal programs that integrate social problem solving, social, and emotional understanding. EI programs need to address multiple facets of emotional competence in order to take advantage of the interdependence of the skills described here (Saarni, 1997). EI intervention programs should simultaneously address students' mental, emotional, social, and physical health, rather than focus on one categorical outcome (Shriver, Schwab-Stone & DeFalco, 1999). Furthermore, programs should strive for multi-level interventions in which peers, parents, the school, and community members create a learning climate and reinforce classroom instruction are most effective in addressing the widespread social problems of children (Shriver, Schwab-Stone & DeFalco, 1999).

Adequate preparation of staff   It is essential to adequately prepare teachers and other professionals prior to implementing EI interventions. The quality of the teacher in emotional literacy classes is essential, perhaps even more so than in other classes (Goleman, 1995a, 1995b). This is so because how a teacher handles her class is in itself a model, a de facto lesson in emotional competence—or the lack thereof. Thus, as stated by Goleman: "Whenever a teacher responds to one student, twenty or thirty others learn a lesson" (1995a, p. 279). However, not every teacher is suited for the job. Specifically, not all teachers are comfortable talking about feelings, nothing in the standard curriculum prepares them for this type of experience, and many teachers are often reluctant to tackle a topic that seems so foreign to their training and routines. In addition, schools will most likely be successful in their efforts when there is strong administrative support and when the program is scheduled appropriately.

Focus on skills   According to Goleman (1995a, 1995b), among the hallmarks of successful EI programs were inculcating a list of key skills, such as competence in self-awareness of feelings, emotion regulation, impulse control, empathy, and perspective taking, cooperation, and settling disputes. These abilities help children resist the pulls towards dangers like substance abuse, pregnancy, and violence.

Full integration into the curriculum   Optimally, emotional literacy programs should not be taught as 'add-ons', but should be fully integrated into the overall school curriculum (Elias et al., 1997; Salovey, Bedell, et al., 1999). Accordingly, an emerging strategy in emotional education is not to create a special class for teaching emotions or emotional skills, but to complement regular academic subjects being taught, perhaps by blending lessons on emotions with other topics (e.g., arts, health, science). Thus, students can learn about how to harness emotions in gym; how to handle stress, anxiety, or frustration in math class; how to empathize with another's plight when reading powerful literature; and how to cope with the experience of envy when getting back their exams or report cards (Salovey et al., 1999). In fact, one would not expect lasting changes to happen unless the program's principles become part of the entire school's culture (Patti & Lantieri, 1999).

Congeniality to the incoming behaviors of the target group   Instructional methods and program content should be developmentally appropriate for the ages (and the grades) at which the program is being delivered (see in particular Elias et al., 1997; Shriver, Schwab-Stone & DeFalco, 1999).

Practice and reinforcing skills   Program skills, attitudes, and beliefs, need to be practiced and frequently reinforced throughout the curriculum (indeed over the entire educational program), including during school, after-school, and during curricular activities (Elias et al., 1997). Furthermore, individuals need to incorporate these emotional skills and strategies into their day-to-day lives. Cultivating emotions involves increasing the awareness of emotional competencies, internalizing these strategies, thinking about how they might be applied, and then practicing the application of these skills in daily life (Salovey, Bedell, et al., 1999). In this respect, the cultivation of emotional competencies is similar to the cultivation of cognitive skills: it is *absolutely* essential to practice what is learned as well as to obtain environmental feedback on one's performance.

Carefully monitoring program implementation   EI programs need to have mechanisms in place to insure high quality program monitoring and implementation (Zins et al., 2000). Thus, it is important to document who participated in the training, what dose of training was provided to the students, the content of the training that was provided, and what mechanisms are in place to determine that the implementers provided the intervention as planned (dosage, content, target population, duration, etc.).

Coordinated effort and partnership between school, family, and community   The family, school, and community should be actively consulted and involved in the planning and implementation of EI intervention programs (see, e.g., Elias et al., 1997; Zins, Travis & Freppon, 1997). Academic support, parent training and involvement in a community have the potential of boosting preventive power by targeting risk factors (Zins, Travis & Freppon, 1997).

Experiential and active methods   EI curricula require teaching methods that ensure active student engagement. Thus, program implementers should strive to use skill-based, experiential, or cognitive approaches to engage learners through methods such as modeling, role playing, performance feedback, expressive arts, play, community-building skills, exhibitions, projects, and individual goal setting (Zins, Travis & Freppon, 1997). Furthermore, it is central to see that these emotional skills are applied in the real world of the playground, lunchroom, and neighborhood.

Long term learning process   Emotional learning needs to be an essential part of children's education over the course of their schooling and the substantive learning is a life-long process. Emotional learning should be delivered regularly and over a sustained period of time, rather than on a one-shot basis. Thus, plans should be made to provide the intervention over multiple years (Zins, Travis & Freppon, 1997). Thus, it is the ongoing process that provides repeated opportunities for students to discover more about themselves and further develop these competencies as they themselves develop (Cohen, 1999a, 1999b, 1999c).

Generalization of program skills to environment   Strategies taught in the course of EI programs need to be generalized to the general school and community environment. This way, a milieu is created that encourages and rewards the use of new skills and promotes their generalization (Elias et al., 1997). Thus, in order for emotional education programs to be effective, the process must be a truly collaborative endeavor between parents and educators. Programs need to involve the entire "village," including educators, parents, administrators and school staff, and community members (Cohen, 1999a, 1999b, 1999c).

Conclusions

We would still appear in the dark, with respect to what we know about the origins of EI. Indeed, present research allows us to make very few substantiated generalizations about the determinants of children's emotional competencies. The influence of key antecedent factors on the development of EI has yet to be systematically mapped out and the contributions of various potential determinants and causal factors are only beginning to be understood. With respect to the heritability of EI, there is little empirical research bearing on the behavioral genetics and heritability of major components thought to make up EI. Future research is needed using behavioral-genetic research paradigms (kinship and twin studies, adoption studies, etc.) to help us tease apart environmental and genetic components of emotional competence.

Overall, progress has been made in our understanding of the origins of children's knowledge of emotional expression and regulation of affect. Our review, as well as those of others, suggests that the direct contributions of specific parental socialization practices on the parameters of emotional competencies (expression, regulation, coping with stress, etc.) are in need of further systematic research. Moreover, at present, little is known about the roles of peers and other socializing agents, as well as of TV and other mass media exposure, in the development of emotions and emotion regulation.

It is important to realize that no real definitive conclusion about origins can be made if we find parents who are emotionally intelligent also tend to have children who are emotionally intelligent. In short, this is consistent with an explanation in terms of either socialization practices and/or genetic factors. It is unclear to what degree the development of emotional competencies reflects developmental changes in cognitive capabilities and social skills rather than the effects of deliberate socialization practices.

Techniques related to the EI construct, particularly to the emotion-perception or emotion-knowledge components, have become part of school-based preventive interventions. Such interventions affect the lives of tens or perhaps hundreds of thousands of children and their families every year (Izard, 2001). Our review of the EI-intervention literature suggests that relatively few EI programs have been systematically assessed. Unfortunately, among those that have been assessed, several suffer from serious methodological flaws (inadequate controls, threats to internal validity, poor measures, assessment of short-term impact alone, etc.). Program evaluations of EI interventions are shown to vary greatly in terms of their availability, scope, and scientific rigor. The rather extensive evaluation of the PATH program, presented above, is more the exception than the rule. Although an increasing number of programs are being evaluated formally, many still have not been subjected to systematic empirical scrutiny.

Furthermore, when examining programs being touted as "EI-intervention programs," one is surprised and puzzled at how sparse the emotional content of these programs actually is. Moreover, in cases in which elements of EI have appeared in the goal statement of the program, measures of the key components of EI have not always been used in the assessment of mediator or outcome variables. One possible reason for this sad state of affairs is that most current programs were initially designed not as EI intervention programs but for other purposes (social-skills or anger-control programs, or drug-abuse-prevention or delinquency-prevention programs). Proponents of EI intervention have vested these existing programs with a minimal dosage of EI content and have enthusiastically embraced them as their own. At present, there is little research showing whether or not programs touted as EI interventions are actually effective in enhancing the kinds of skills included in current models of EI.

The reader should keep in mind that EI interventions are not homogeneous, and one may expect considerable variation in this field. Overall, some current programs may be helpful to "some of the students, some of the time." In effect, we know very little about the effects of school-based teaching and promotion of EI skills and still need to determine to what extent EI programs meaningfully modify EI skills. Even staunch advocates agree that we will only be able to speak to the optimistic claims about EI after they have been subjected to rigorous controlled evaluation (Salovey, Bedell, Detweiler & Mayer, 1999). It appears to us that the field is not entirely ready for a meta-analysis of program effects, especially since a large proportion of the programs do not provide sufficient statistical data to even compute effect sizes! Although in principle there may be efficient ways to educate those who are low in EI at present, we do not know how this is to be accomplished. Moreover, there is little empirical evidence generated by current studies that would recommend particular intervention strategies. In sum, in spite of current theorizing about EI programs, we really do not know that much about how they work, for whom they work, under what conditions they work, or indeed, whether or not they work at all.

12

*Emotional Intelligence, Work, and the
Occupational Environment*

Most people are creative by nature and happy by default. It doesn't seem that
way because modern management is designed to squash those impulses.
Scott Adams

This chapter reviews a number of current issues relating to the claimed
role of emotional intelligence and emotional competencies in the occupational environment. Following a brief overview of how emotions
operate in the workplace, we survey the claimed relevance of different
facets of EI for success and well being in occupational settings. Consideration is then given to the role played by EI in three major areas of
an individual's work life: (a) occupational and career assessment—with
particular emphasis on personnel selection and placement; (b) job performance and satisfaction; and (c) coping with occupational stress. We
conclude by presenting various programs designed to train and develop
emotional competencies in the job environment, with particular emphasis on the management of occupational stress.

Claims about EI have created considerable excitement about the potential of EI both in the business community and in the general public,
although, unfortunately, these claims tend towards the extravagant and
hyperbolic (if not outrageous). Overall, as will be demonstrated in this
chapter, there is precious little evidence to back up these claims, with
the empirical research that allegedly supports many of these claims
pretty thin—if not altogether ephemeral. The reader should keep these
caveats in mind when reading this chapter.

Emotions and the Workplace

An individual's work experience is laced with a wide range of emotions.
Indeed, emotions are a ubiquitous and inseparable part of everyday

life in the workplace (Ashforth & Humphrey, 1995). From moments of boredom, sadness, anger, anxiety, shame, envy, and disgust, to periods of interest and satisfaction, happiness, confidence, pride, and contentment, we confront our own and other's emotions at the workplace on a regular basis (Pekrun & Frese, 1992). Emotions are real-time, on-line indications of how well we think we are coping with occupational affordances, challenges, demands, and threats (Lazarus & Folkman, 1984; Rafaeli & Sutton, 1987). Thus, emotions provide us with invaluable information about our own selves, other people, and the various dynamic transactions that we share inside our organizational environment (Lazarus, 1991). This information filters through to us because our feelings on the job reflect spontaneous emotional responses to the appraisals and interpretations we make of ongoing events in the workplace. By tapping into the rich information that emotions provide us with, we can often alter our thinking and behavior in such a way as to allow us to negotiate organizational challenges in a more adaptive (and productive) manner.

Work and emotions are most plausibly construed to be reciprocally determined. On the one hand, an individual's profession is among the primary determinants of emotional life and a sphere of existence that really matters to most people in Western society (i.e., work → emotions). Work, with its importance for a person's well being, self-esteem, income, and social status, is a major source of both positive and negative emotions. Success (or failure) at work may influence the individual's development and health through the mediation of emotions. On the other hand, emotions are among the primary determinants of behavior and achievement at work, impacting upon individual productivity, satisfaction, well being, and social climate (i.e., emotions → work). Thus, emotions may influence work-related cognitive and motivational processes, which, in turn, affect task and social behavior, and performance outcomes.

Pekrun and Frese (1992) have partitioned the types of emotions exhibited in the workplace along two major dimensions: (a) valence or dominant subjective value system (positive versus negative) and (b) focus (task-related versus social-related). This two-dimensional classification allows further partitioning of the domain of emotions in the workplace into four categories reflecting work-relevant emotions (see table 12.1).

This classification notwithstanding, the role emotions play in the work environment has been relatively neglected in both occupational research and practice, especially in relation to cognition and motivation.

Table 12.1
Four categories of work-relevant emotions (based on Pekrun & Frese, 1992)

	Valence	
Focus	Negative	Positive
Task-related	Boredom	Enjoyment
	Anxiety	Hope
	Despair	Relief
	Sadness	Pride
	Shame/guilt	
	Anger	
Social-related	Social anxiety	Gratitude
	Jealousy	Empathy
	Contempt	Admiration
	Fear	Sympathy

The inferior status afforded to understanding emotions in the workplace is manifested in several ways. For example, low tolerance is given to emotional displays at work, while there is a certain stigma attached to many occupations requiring emotional labor. Moreover, the focus of training programs has historically been on developing intellectual (rather than social or emotional) skills.

One possible explanation for this sad state of affairs is that cognitive, motivational, and performance factors have been viewed as being more urgent for occupational life than emotions. The predominance of *rationality* as the major, all inclusive paradigm for researching occupational environments has led to the neglect of the role of emotions at work (Ashforth & Humphrey, 1995). Furthermore, the common belief that emotion is the antithesis of rationality may have contributed to a somewhat pejorative view of emotion in occupational contexts—partly explaining frequent attempts to control the experience and expression of emotions. Indeed, except for clearly circumscribed conditions (e.g., high-status task member giving negative feedback to subordinates) expressions of negative emotions such as fear, anger, and anxiety tend to be unacceptable in the work setting (Ashforth & Humphrey, 1995). It also transpires that the emotions one portrays on the job may be difficult to classify (Rafaeli & Sutton, 1989). Depending on the perspective adopted, the same emotion can be positive or negative. For example, the friendly smile of a hotel clerk may be construed as friendly by customers, but artificial, negative, and patronizing by the same (or another) hotel clerk.

Pekrun and Frese (1992) lament that the role of emotion has been relatively neglected in occupational research and practice. Presently, relatively little is known about the situational and cognitive antecedents of emotions at work. Furthermore, information on the phenomenology of work-related emotions, the consequences of emotions on the job, or the prevention, optimization, and modification of emotional behavior while performing one's occupational duties is sparse. Research on emotions, in the occupational domain, has generally been confined to a limited set of relatively generalized and stable states. Principally, this research examines stress emotions and work satisfaction or the role of emotions in discrete critical events (e.g., organizational change, role transitions, and intergroup conflict). Regrettably, the potential dysfunction caused by demonstrating emotions, while in an organizational environment, has generally been more salient to researchers and practitioners than the potential positive functions of emotions.

Emotional competencies and the workplace

EI subsumes competencies that are involved in the identification, understanding, and management of emotions. Work-related EI competencies are vital if one is to successfully negotiate the demands, constraints, and opportunities necessary to succeed in the workplace. Plausibly, the learned competencies (or components) of EI may be those that are most readily materialized and translated into on-the-job behaviors. Thus, in order to be able to actually empathize with another's plight, one must have learned the specific empathic skills that translate into caring and compassionate pastoral counseling, bedside nursing, or effective psychotherapy.

A bewildering array of competencies have variously been claimed to be critical for success in occupational settings (see, e.g., Boyatzis, Goleman & Rhee, 2000; Cooper & Sawaf, 1997; Goleman, 1998; Weisinger, 1998). For example, Goleman (1998) lists 25 different competencies necessary for effective performance in the workplace, with different competencies believed to be required in different professions. Thus, confidentiality would presumably be important for loan officers and priests, while trust and empathy appear vital for psychotherapists, social workers, and marriage counselors. Furthermore, of the 180 competence models identified by Goleman (1998), over two thirds of the abilities deemed essential for effective performance were identified as emotional competencies. In fact, based on an unpublished study, commissioned and reported by Goleman (1998), emotional competence has been claimed to count twice as much as IQ and expertise for success in the vast majority of jobs.

We now survey a number of emotional competencies claimed to be of crucial importance in occupational settings. Due to space restrictions, the list of competencies reviewed is selective, rather than exhaustive (the topic in and of itself could fill an entire book). Note also that although we touch upon some constructs emanating from mixed models, the concepts that we focus upon in these passages conform mostly to an ability model of EI (see chapters 1 and 5).

Awareness of emotions Emotional awareness, it should be recalled, involves a number of competencies. These include, accurately identifying the specific emotion one is experiencing; understanding how the emotion is related to one's goals and values; realizing how the emotion is linked to one's thoughts and behaviors; and appreciating how the emotion likely affects accomplishment. Emotional awareness is claimed to serve as a guide in fine-tuning on-the-job performance, including, accurately gauging the feelings of those around us, managing our unruly feelings, keeping ourselves motivated, and developing good work-related emotional skills.

High emotional awareness is commonly held to be the basic building block of EI in the occupational environment (Goleman, 1998; Salovey, Mayer & Caruso, 2000; Weisinger, 1998). The person high in self-awareness is said to be able to monitor themselves, observe themselves in action, to influence actions so they work for their benefit, and so forth. The processes of emotion understanding and regulation can take place, it is claimed, only when affective information is first perceived and then identified by the individual. For example, in order to be able to manage and diminish anger, one needs first to be aware that one is angry (rather than sad or anxious) and pinpoint exactly what environmental event has triggered the specific emotional reaction. Furthermore, in being aware that one is becoming angry with a coworker, supervisor, or client (and that this may be inappropriate), one may defuse one's anger, and respond in a more problem-oriented and adaptive manner.

Goleman (1998) has further claimed that EI is especially important for the regulation of emotions in others at the workplace. Thus, in order to help others help themselves the individual generally needs to be made aware of their own goals, values, and preferences. In a broader sense, self-awareness encompasses several different facets. These facets include, awareness of one's strengths and weaknesses, reflective learning from experience, openness to candid feedback from others, the ability to take things in proportion, the development of positive perspectives, and the capacity to have a sense of humor. It has been argued that because self-aware employees and managers seek out feedback, they also perform better on the job.

Regulation of emotions in the self   The self-regulation of emotions includes a variety of competencies, including restraining and controlling impulses, dampening down distress, effectively channeling negative affect, and intentionally eliciting and sustaining pleasant (e.g., pride) and unpleasant (e.g., anger) emotions, when appropriate. Thus, comedians try to sustain a cheerful disposition, and physicians put themselves in a suitably dour mood when conveying bad news to patients, while bar bouncers may work themselves up to an irritable state (or frenzy) when threatening awkward, unruly clients. In the occupational environment, self-regulation also clearly involves inhibiting personal needs, desires, and emotions in service of organizational needs. In fact, being able to control impulses is commonly viewed as a major prerequisite for successful job performance (Goleman, 1998). The biology of emotional regulation is worth reiterating. The self-regulation of emotions are hypothesized to depend on the working of the emotional centers of the brain (limbic system) in tandem with the brain's executive centers (in the prefrontal areas) (see chapter 6).

A number of specific competencies, such as self-control, stamina, and emotion-focused coping and adaptability, are often subsumed under the concept of emotion regulation. In this section, we focus primarily on self-control, which has been afforded the most attention in the literature. High EI individuals are frequently characterized in the literature as maintaining a high degree of self-control. These individuals can keep disruptive emotions and impulses under check, thus avoiding being impaired cognitively and behaviorally by the negative consequences of these affects. They purportedly stay composed, positive, and unflappable in stressful encounters and are unfazed under threat. They are said to be able to effectively handle a hostile attack without lashing out in return and think clearly and stay focused under pressure. In addition, those with high self-control are claimed to be more likely to make personal sacrifices when an organizational need presents itself. Indeed, self-control is claimed to be essential in order to keep ourselves self-regulated to meet ongoing work requirements, allowing the individual to resist seemingly urgent but actually trivial demands, or the lure of time-wasting distractions (Goleman, 1998).

In contrast, people with poor self-control are supposedly influenced by immediate gratification (or satisfaction) in a self-centered manner. For example, Goleman (1998) claims that individuals with an unsuccessful career record have a problem controlling impulses. They are often reported to crumble under stress, are indiscrete, have little self-restraint in exposing secret or classified company information, manage funds haphazardly, and often succumb to sexual harassment at the workplace. The key circuitry here, according to Goleman (1998), is an array of inhibitory neurons in the prefrontal lobes that can veto the impulsive messages that come from the emotional centers, primarily the amygdala, in moments of rage and temptation (see chapter 6 for a critique). For some, the circuit operates well; for others, it simply does not.

It is important to note that self-control of emotions does not necessarily mean denying or repressing true feelings. In fact, bad moods and negative emotions have important social functions. For example, anger can be an intense source of motivation, particularly when it stems from the urge to right an injustice or inequity. Anger can also help the individual to regulate the behavior of others according to social and organizational norms (Averill, 1982, 1991).

It is worth noting that emotional self-control is not identical to the concept of over-control in the occupational environment, in that there may often be a physical and mental cost to over-control in the workplace (Gross & Levenson, 1997). Thus, people who stifle strong feelings, say anger, with an insubordinate worker, tend to pay a price in terms of increased somatic arousal. When such emotional suppression is chronic, it can impair intellectual performance and interfere with smooth social interactions (see Gross & Levenson, 1997). Furthermore, being emotionally unexpressive often communicates a negative message, a sense of indifference or distance (Goleman, 1998). Research suggests that executives tend to be more controlled emotionally than lower-level managers, with executives giving more consideration to the impact of expressing the wrong feeling in a given situation (Boyatzis, 1982).

Empathizing with and understanding other's emotions   Empathy, it may be recalled, refers to the awareness of other's feelings, needs, and concerns. At the individual level, empathy is a person's ability to sense and understand other people's feelings, concerns, and perspectives (see chapter 9). Empathy also implies taking active interest in other individuals' concerns and feelings, and responding to other individuals' unspoken feelings. In other words, when we are emotionally in tune, we can put aside our own personal agendas for some period, in order to be receptive to other people's signals.

Empathy, it has been claimed, is essential as an emotional guidance system, piloting us in getting along at work (Goleman, 1998). Empathy has been hypothesized to be a meaningful predictor of quality performance in the job environment. Thus, individuals high in empathy are more capable of relating to other group members within a professional organization (Williams & Sternberg, 1988). In addition, the ability to empathize with others and relate to the feelings of others may play a role in the formulation of superior goals, plans, and strategies. Empathic ability is particularly important when the problems to be solved require reconciliation of conflicting opinions in a manner that is acceptable to diverse people working within an organization. People who are not empathic find it difficult to evaluate appropriate responses to socially demanding situations. These individuals also lack the ability to tailor social behavior to the occupational context, thus failing to incorporate other people's needs and feelings into their own conceptualization of socially apt behavior. This follows logically from the fact that being heeded to makes one more receptive in considering another's proposal for change, since a spirit of sharing and equity is established.

Empathy is also claimed to be a motivating factor underlying altruistic behavior (Salovey & Mayer, 1990). Empathy, according to Goleman (1998), also represents the foundation skills for all the social competencies at work. This includes, being attentive to emotional cues, showing sensitivity and understanding of other people's perspectives, and a variety of helping behaviors that are based on understanding other people's needs and feelings. Inside the organizational context, emotional experiencing and empathy refer to qualities of an organization's efforts to identify emotions aroused during radical change, to accept and internalize them, and to act upon them at a deep level of understanding (Huy, 1999). Accordingly, organizational change agents, who are empathetic to the emotions of others in the workplace, tend to be more aware that their change program can threaten the psychological and social defenses of recipients undergoing the change process. Demonstration of concern for one another, at the workplace, constitutes the basis for mutual trust and acceptance and purportedly leads to better work performance. This outcome possibly owes to better coordination and trust among organizational group members under discontinuous conditions (Huy, 1999).

Furthermore, when conceived of as the equivalent of a "social radar," empathy is crucial for success in the business world. This follows from the fact it is important to listen to the customer and competitor's point of view and to see reality from the perspective of both clients and competitors. Furthermore, empathy appears a critical component of conflict resolution. Thus, the best negotiators can sense which points matter most to the other party and gracefully concede them, while pressing for concessions in points that do not carry such emotional valence (Goleman, 1998).

A final point worth mentioning in discussion of empathy is its purported malleability. It is generally assumed that organization members can be trained on the ability to accurately read the subtle social cues and signals given by other members of the organization. In so doing, these individuals can accurately determine the emotions being expressed by their colleagues and learn to understand the perspective taken by others with whom they are required to work. Features such as trainability often give the concept of EI considerable face appeal.

Regulating other people's emotions A work organization is commonly viewed as an integrated system that depends upon the dynamic and complex pattern of interrelationships of the individuals who comprise it. Thus, how each person performs effects the company as a whole. For this reason, the success of the company depends not only on whether employees regulate their own behavior, but also on others being helped to do the same, in order for each individual to maximize their capabilities (Weisinger, 1998). This process involves helping others to, manage their emotions, resolve their conflicts, and be motivated (emotional mentoring). To help others manage their emotions, it is crucial to, keep one's own emotional perspective, know how to calm an out-of-control person, be a supportive listener, and help with goal planning and implementation.

Handling other's emotions is commonly construed to be a basic component of EI. This involves two basic subskills:

• Influencing others. This includes winning people over, fine tuning representations, using complex strategies to build consensus and support, and so forth.

• Effectively communicating with others. This includes having emotional flexibility, dealing with difficult issues directly, listening well, sharing information, and fostering open communication.

   Conflict management is an important related skill that involves handling difficult people and tense situations with tact and diplomacy, spotting potential discord, encouraging debate and open discussion, and orchestrating win-win solutions (Goleman, 1998). To this end, several conflict management strategies may be employed in the workplace. These include, calming both oneself and others down, tuning into one's feelings, showing willingness to work things out, stating one's own point of view in neutral language, and trying to find equitable ways to solve disputes. However, the efficacy of such strategies is somewhat contentious: Should companies spend time and money on long-term conflict management? It may often be more cost-effective to simply relocate or fire the awkward worker.

Further emotional and social competencies   A number of additional emotional and social competencies are claimed to be important for success in the organizational environment. Authors advancing these competencies are clearly advocates of mixed (rather than ability) models of EI (see, e.g., Bar-On, 2000; Boyatzis et al., 2000; Cooper & Sawaf, 1997; Goleman, 1998; Weisinger, 1998). Although competencies, advanced by these various authors, include each of those specified above these additional psychological factors appear all encompassing. Consider, for example, the following (by no means exhaustive) list:

• Personality traits (e.g., conscientiousness, optimism)
• Motivation (e.g., attributions, need for achievement, internal motivation)
• Self-attitudes and concepts (e.g., self-esteem, self-confidence)
• Character (e.g., trust, integrity)
• Cognitive states (e.g., attentional flow)
• Aptitudes (e.g., intuition)
• Social skills (e.g., assertiveness, provision of feedback)
• Social behaviors (e.g., pro-social behaviors)

   Whether placing all such concepts under the EI banner confuses, rather than clarifies, the role of emotional competencies in the workplace would seem to be a contentious point. However, consider the following argument. Because the field of EI remains new, many of the aforementioned concepts, which have been studied in organizational psychology for some time (often with mixed results), are in fact better understood than this fledgling concept. We thus believe that the process of reconceptualizing each of them as forms of emotional intelligence (or competencies) will inevitably lead to obfuscation.

The Role of EI in Career and Occupational Assessment

EI and selection

Recently, the use of EI measures for career selection and placement purposes has become a common practice in many organizations in the Western world. Thus, more and more companies are realizing that EI skills appear a vital component of any organization's management philosophy (and subsequent success). A survey of benchmark practices among major corporations found that four out of five companies are trying to promote EI in their employees through training and development when evaluating performance and hiring (see Goleman, 1998).

It is well established that general ability predicts anywhere from about 10% to 30% of the criterion variance in job performance, leaving about 90% to 70% of the variance in success unaccounted for (see, e.g., Jensen, 1980, 1998). The unexplained percentage of success appears to be, in large part, the consequence of complex (perhaps even chaotic) interactions among hundreds of variables playing out over time. Nevertheless, this well-replicated finding has unleashed a headlong rush by researchers and practitioners alike to predict various parameters of occupational success via noncognitive variables, of which the concept of EI appears a primary candidate.

The concept of EI has even greater appeal since is also claimed to be useful when evaluating ongoing functioning and the well being of employees at critical stages of their careers (i.e., selection, placement, training, and promotion). In addition, as alluded to previously, EI appears valid for gauging the impact and intervention effectiveness of organizational change and restructuring (see also Bar-On, 1997). As one group of writers have argued, "If the driving force of intelligence in twentieth century business has been IQ, then ... in the dawning twenty-first century it will be EQ" (Cooper & Sawaf, 1997, p. xxvii).

A number of rather fantastic and unsubstantiated claims have appeared in the popular literature and the media about the significant role of EI in the workplace. Thus, EI has been claimed to validly predict

IQ   EQ

Figure 12.1
IQ gets you hired—EQ gets you promoted.

a variety of successful behaviors at work, at a level exceeding that of intelligence (see Cooper & Sawaf, 1997; Goleman, 1998; Haygroup, 2000; Weisinger, 1999). In the *Times* article that helped popularize EI, Gibbs wrote, "In the corporate world ... IQ gets you hired but EQ gets you promoted" (1995, p. 59). (We reproduce this sentiment, in all its humorous glory, in figure 12.1.) In no small measure, this argument rests on claims that EI assists people in "teamwork, in co-operation, and in helping others learn how to work together more effectively" (Goleman, 1998, p. 163). Inside conventional wisdom, because each of these factors is thought to impact on an organization's success, EI is given great status. Of note, however, Goleman is unable to cite published empirical data supporting any causal link between EI and any of its supposed positive effects.

Indeed, extravagant claims as to the power of EI to predict success in the workplace appear to fly in the face of existing scientific evidence. Currently, there are no published empirical studies showing that EI meaningfully predicts job success above (and beyond) that predicted by ability and personality measures (see Newsome et al., 2001). Much of the existing evidence bearing on the role of EI in occupational success is either anecdotal or impressionistic. In addition, much of the evidence is based on unpublished or in-house research. Further still, it appears proxy measures of EI are often used in such studies. These tend to focus on emotion-related affective and motivational variables (e.g., attributions, impulse control, or emotional adjustment) rather than the components thought to underlie EI.

Barrick and Mount (1991, 1993) conducted a meta-analysis of 117 criterion-related validity studies of how the Big Five personality dimensions predict job behavior (see also chapter 9). The results from this study may indirectly tell us something about the role of EI-related variables in job success. This assertion follows logically from the fact that the Big Five model overlaps in part with mixed models of EI in its various facets (e.g., trust, altruism, compliance, self-discipline, positive emotions, and so on). Barrick and Mount's meta-analysis demonstrated that conscientiousness, which overlaps with the EI-related traits of competence, order, self-discipline, and so forth, was the best Big Five predictor of job success. However, the overall correlations between this variable and job success, topped out at $r = 0.15$, meaning these facets of EI are unlikely to account for any more than between 2% to 3% of the criterion variance. Extraversion, another Big Five factor, contains mixed-model elements of EI such as warmth, assertiveness, activity, sensation-seeking, and positive emotions. Barrick and Mount found that extraversion was very modestly predictive of success for people in management and sales, although not for those in other professions. These findings notwithstanding, in a large-scale meta-analysis of personality measures Ones, Viswesvaran, and Schmidt (1993) found that integrity tests significantly predict a supervisor's ratings of job performance in a variety of settings (estimated operational validity = 0.41). Integrity tests are composed of facets of the Big Five dimensions of conscientiousness and (low) neuroticism and provide some promise for EI measures, if one allows that EI is a conglomerate of psychological constellations.

There is reason, however, to be extremely skeptical of EI proving itself more useful than intelligence tests in the area of personnel selection. Overall, conventional intelligence tests do a very reasonable job of predicting occupational criteria (especially when compared to personality measures) (see, e.g., Hunter & Schmidt, 1998). A review of the literature by Hunter and Hunter (1984) suggests that cognitive abilities have a mean validity for training success of about 0.55 for all known job families. In addition, recent studies surveyed by Hunter and Hunter show that ability test are valid across all jobs in predicting job proficiency. The validity coefficients vary by both outcome criteria (higher for job training and lower for job performance) and job complexity (higher for greater job complexity). Almost without exception, personalitylike measures are more modestly predictive of job performance than ability measures.

At present, there are no convincing empirical data supporting the use of EI measures for purposes of occupational and career assessment. To the best of our knowledge, there is no replicated research, published in peer-review journals, that has reliably demonstrated that EI measures add meaningful incremental variance to the prediction of occupational criteria. That is, EI does not appear to possess incremental validity above (and beyond) that predicted by conventional ability and personality measures. Furthermore, because there is no hard evidence showing that EI bears a differential pattern of validity for various occupational groupings, there is little psychometric justification for their use in specific occupational contexts.

EI, job performance, and success

Various facets and components of EI have been claimed to contribute to success and productivity in the workplace. Thus, EI is claimed to predict occupational success because it influences one's ability to succeed in coping with environmental demands and pressures (Bar-On, 1997). Workers endowed with high EI are also claimed to be particularly adept at designing projects that involve infusing products with feelings and aesthetics (Mayer & Salovey, 1997). More emotionally intelligent individuals are said to succeed at communicating in interesting and assertive ways, thus making others feel better in the occupational environment (Goleman, 1998). Furthermore, it has been claimed that EI is useful for group development since a large part of effective and smooth team work is knowing each other's strengths and weaknesses and leveraging strengths whenever possible (Bar-On, 1997).

Based on a host of case studies, anecdotal accounts, and evaluation studies, Goleman (1998) concluded that the major qualities differentiating successful from unsuccessful executives were the competencies underlying EI. Failing executives purportedly had poorer emotional competencies and resources, despite strengths in cognitive abilities and technical expertise. In support of this assertion, Goleman (1998) cites a study by Egon Zehnder International (Buenos Aires Office), which compared 227 successful executives with those who failed in their jobs. The study reported: "In every case, their fatal weakness was in EI— arrogance, over reliance on brainpower, inability to adapt to the occasionally disorienting economic shifts in their region, and disdain for collaboration or teamwork" (Goleman, 1998, p. 49). Goleman reports that parallel analyses of successful and failed mangers in Germany and Japan revealed the same pattern. Furthermore, Goleman claims that adaptive competencies are crucial in the workplace and those who fail to adapt and develop flexible skills and social intelligence will simply not succeed. Thus, in a study commissioned by the Center for Creative Leadership at 15 Fortune-500 corporations (Leslie & Van Velson, 1996, in Goleman, 1998), salient differences emerged between successful managers and those who derailed (i.e., were demoted or fired). These differences all related to major dimensions of emotional competence, including self-control, conscientiousness, trustworthiness, responsibility, integrity, social skills, building bonds, and leveraging diversity.

Unfortunately, the aforementioned reports, supporting the efficacy of EI in the workplace, are not easily accessible and the reported conclusions go somewhat beyond the information given. Furthermore, some of the popular claims presented in this literature are misleading: they seem, on face value, to present scientific evidence supporting their claims, but in fact fail to do so (Mayer, Salovey & Caruso, 2000). As a case in point, consider Goleman's (1995, 1998) reference to a study of Bell Laboratory engineers in which the top performers were reportedly more emotionally intelligent than their peers (although not differing in level of general intelligence). A careful reading of the original report shows that this is pure conjecture: the Bell Laboratory engineers were *never* actually tested with any instrument designed to assess EI. Nevertheless, the conclusions of this study in support of the important role of EI in occupational studies have been uncritically accepted. More damaging to the field, perhaps, is the fact that these unsubstantiated claims have been recycled in numerous popular books and articles on EI in the workplace (e.g., Cooper & Sawaf, 1997; Gibbs, 1995; Haygroup, 2000).

A recent paper by Janovics and Christiansen (2001) suggests that self-report measures of EI are virtually of no practical value in predicting performance at work in a sample of 176 employed undergraduate students. Two measures of EI, the TMMS and the Schutte EQ test (see chapter 5), were essentially uncorrelated with job performance. By contrast, performance measures of EI were modestly correlated with job performance, with job performance correlating significantly with the perception ($r = .14$) and understanding ($r = .30$) branches of EI. Curiously, job performance was not significantly correlated with the higher-order facets of the MSCEIT, i.e., the facilitation and managing emotion branches. However, when added to a regression equation, the

MSCEIT did not add significantly to the incremental variance of the job performance criterion when statistically controlling for cognitive ability and the Big-five factor of conscientiousness.

Moreover, a number of studies in the EI literature employ classical motivational, personality, or emotional measures as predictors of EI. One often-cited study by Seligman and Schulman (1986) looked at explanatory style, as a predictor of success, among 94 life-insurance sales representatives. Two field studies provided data demonstrating that insurance agents with optimistic explanatory styles, out survived those agents with more pessimistic explanatory styles, at significantly higher rates. Agents who scored in the optimistic half of the explanatory-style dimension sold 37% more insurance certificates than those agents who scored in the pessimistic half. Further, in a prospective study of 103 newly hired agents, explanatory style predicted first-year survival as well as productivity for the second half of the year. An agent with good explanatory style might persist more and make more sales, and this will make him more optimistic and feed back to an even better explanatory style. Although optimism may be related to EI, it is currently construed as a personality trait (see, e.g., Carver, Scheier & Weintraub, 1989). Thus, it probably should not count as evidence for the predictive validity of EI in occupational settings (see, however, Bar-On, 1997, 2000, and also chapter 5).

The preceding data do not occur in isolation, however. For example, Bar-On (1997) cites a study conducted on a sample of 81 chronically unemployed individuals. These individuals had unusually low EQ-i scores, with the lowest scores on assertiveness, reality testing, and happiness. Similarly, Bar-On (1997) found that individuals from the Young President's Organization (whose membership is dependent on individuals reaching top leadership positions in expanding companies) obtained scores on the EQ-i (on virtually all subscales) exceeding the average by significant amounts. According to Bar-On, this group's success depended on the ability to be independent and to assert their individuality, while being able to withstand various stressors occurring within the job. Nevertheless, the direction of causality in these instances raises some concerns. In particular, low EI scores among the unemployed are likely to be a consequence, rather than a cause, of being chronically unemployed, while those performing well in their job are likely to report high levels of emotional stability.

Constructive thinking refers to a person's ability to think in a manner that solves everyday problems in living at a minimal cost of stress (Katz & Seymour, 1991). A number of studies using constructive thinking, often as a proxy measure of EI, attests to a relationship between EI and job performance, with better constructive thinkers doing better on the job. Thus, constructive thinking has been shown to be related to work performance in a large sample of college students, but not classroom performance. In contrast, general academic intelligence was found to be related to classroom performance but not work performance (Katz & Seymour, 1991). Furthermore, in a study among midshipmen at the Naval Academy, behavioral coping appeared to be the component of constructive thinking most closely associated with success and satisfaction in the organizational environment (Epstein, 1998). Note, however, that the concept of constructive thinking only partially overlaps with the conventional components of ability models of EI (see also chapter 8 for the role of constructive thinking in adaptive processes).

EI has been shown to be related to occupational satisfaction, commitment, and competence. Thus, Bar-On (1997) reported a very modest relationship between total EI scores and job satisfaction in a sample of 314 participants (mainly salespersons, teachers, college students, and nurses). Subscale scores assessing self-regard, social responsibility, and reality testing predicted about 20% of the variance in work satisfaction. However, the nature of that link varies from occupation to occupation. Furthermore, Bar-On (1997) reports that EI predicted a self-report measure of sense of competence on the job (r = about .50). However, it is likely that this reported correlation reflects the influence of extraneous, contaminating variables, including a general sense of positive affectivity, personality factors, response bias (social desirability factors), and method variance (see the critique of Bar-On's EQ-i in chapter 5).

Finally, Carson and Carson (1998) provided data for a sample of 75 nursing department hospital employees showing that EI was positively correlated with career commitment. In this study, EI was operationalized as internal motivation and was found to be positively correlated with the following facets of career: identity, planning, and ability to meet and face obstacles resiliently. A confirmatory factor analysis provided support for a model in which EI, as an antecedent of career commitment, produced organizational-commitment and organizational-citizenship behaviors as outcomes. The authors conclude that those individuals who are most likely to become career-committed tend to be emotionally intelligent.

Guidelines for future development and usage of EI measures in occupational settings

Prior to any widespread use of EI for occupational and career assessment, EI measures need to be systematically constructed, standardized (as well as normed), and validated for use in specific occupational groups and for particular purposes (selection, placement, promotion, and so forth). Up to this point in time, we do not believe that this has been achieved by anyone espousing the utility of measuring, training, or otherwise modifying EI in occupational settings. The following are a series of recommendations for the future development and usage of EI measures for occupational selection and placement purposes. Clearly, any such endeavor rests on the assumption that, in a particular occupational setting, there is a real and genuine need to assess EI factors to predict the kinds of behaviors influenced by emotions in the workplace.

Clarifying the use, purpose, and relevance of EI for specific occupational settings under consideration A first step in constructing EI assessment instruments to meet organizational requirements is to identify precisely the specific contexts, needs, and purposes for which that EI test is being developed. In addition, the potential usefulness of EI measures for prediction of employee performance in specific areas requires justification. Thus, one should distinguish occupations where emotional skills are relevant to successful job performance (e.g., psychotherapist, teacher, member of the clergy) from those in which such skills may be desirable but not crucial (e.g., brain surgeon, mechanical engineer, software programmer). For occupations in which emotional abilities are clearly required, the formal assessment of these skills would appear important.

Furthermore, different jobs appear to call for varying levels of social and emotional involvement and activity. Disparate occupations also require different types of interpersonal interaction. In some jobs (e.g., nursing, psychotherapy, pastoral counseling, elementary school teaching), one interacts emotionally with others during most of one's time on the job. Inside such professions, there is a real need to have frequent interchanges with clients, at an emotional level. Incumbents within these jobs not only need to talk with others face-to-face and exhibit positive, prosaic behavior (e.g., pleasant receptionist), but also assess the reactions of others, and attempt to influence others emotions and motives (e.g., insurance agent). Some jobs require matching one's own behavior to the needs of others (e.g., therapist), creatively influencing others by engaging their emotions, and transforming one's own emotions and also those of others. In other jobs (e.g., college professor), one would interact with people a smaller percentage of time, and the need to be able to recognize and manipulate other's feelings is thus less important. In other occupations (e.g., mathematician, theoretical physicist, pathol-

ogist, or computer technician), there is a very limited on-the-job interaction with people.

*Providing a solid, theoretical rationale for the use of EI in organizational
assessment* A vocational or career-relevant EI measure will ideally be one
with demonstrated theoretical and empirical relevance (see chapter 5).
That is, we need to be able to theoretically account for the proposed relation between the specific EI component(s) assessed and some facet(s)
of job performance. In so doing, we can theoretically justify the inclusion of variables in a test battery that are relevant for career assessment.
Thus, assessment experts need to pay special attention to the theoretical
links between the different facets of EI and the criterion space. One first
needs to identify the specific traits or qualities thought to be associated
with a particular job. For example, in the case of life insurance salespersons, EI-related qualities such as emotional self-regulation and optimism appear vital. The use of EI component sub-tests also needs to be
validated using a large-scale, trait-performance validation design. Unless
this holds, it will be difficult to make valid generalizations to other
tests or adequately specify theoretical relations between traits and work
behavior.

Systematic task analysis A systematic task analysis needs to be conducted in order to derive a network of EI dimensions underlying the
attainment of successful status in different kinds of occupations. Thus, it
is important to determine the specific nature of the emotional abilities
required in a particular career or occupation and to distinguish between
emotional (or social) function and dysfunction. The selection of the relevant emotional competencies to be assessed needs to be matched with
the relevant career components. For example, an analysis of the crimi-
nal justice system may suggest that police officers need to be able to
identify and regulate their aversive emotions. This outcome subsequently
suggests that a measure of emotional regulation needs to be developed
and included in an assessment battery that the researcher might devise
for police officers. This measure, in turn, would need to be validated
against the criterion of regulating emotions at work.

Conducting a cost-benefit analysis Before developing a special measure
of EI, a cost-benefit analysis should be conducted. Thus, for menial low-
level jobs it might not be worth the cost and effort of psychological
screening in pre-employment selection to rule out emotional or social

deficits. However, for a manager working closely with workers in the organization, social and emotional incompetence can have devastating effects on the organization. Thus, the bottom line is that for screening, we need cutoff points on EI scales that flag the type of emotional competence (and incompetence) that can be devastating for a particular role in the organization.

Assembling normative data for specific occupational groups   EI measures used for the purpose of career assessment need to be empirically validated for specific occupational clusters. Thus, EI measures need to provide recent and extensive normative data for different professional groups, with norms based on large and representative samples. Norms must not only be specific to relevant occupational groups but preferably cover a wide range of age groups as well.

Validation process   The process of validating an EI measure requires convincing, empirical evidence that a measure of EI predicts career success. Especially important in this process, is demonstrating that scoring in a positive direction, on a specific EI measure, is associated with predictable occupational consequences. Future research should also test whether the relationship between EI variables and occupational performance is linear throughout the range of responses.

In determining the predictive validity of EI measures, it would appear critical to address the shared variance between EI and other cognitive abilities (especially IQ or general intelligence). Providing that there is only a minimal degree of association between EI and ability measures, the variance contributed by EI to the prediction of job criteria will be expected to be incremental. However, if there is substantial covariance among cognitive ability and EI constructs, the issue of incremental validity requires a more complicated analysis. In order to test the incremental variance contributed by EI measures, it is essential to also include personality measures in the so-called predictor stock (see chapter 5 for further details supporting these arguments).

Furthermore, the discriminant validity of EI measures should be demonstrated. That is, measures should be shown to reliably differentiate between low- and high-performing groups on particular work-related criteria. In the process, one needs to keep in mind the difference between the modal EI characteristics of occupational groups and differences in EI of more and less successful members within a particular group. Thus, EI measures should be able to differentiate between the performance of low (and high) performers within a particular occupational category (e.g., financial analysts) as well as differentiate between different occupational categories (e.g., social workers and financial analysts). It is highly plausible that effective performance in different occupations is likely to involve different emotional (or social) characteristics.

One also needs to be careful in comparing EI measures across incumbents in different occupational categories especially in those instances where the mean EI scores of those in different categories turn out to be similar. Thus, physicians and judges may both score high on EI, yet a person who scores high on EI will not necessarily make a good doctor or judge. On the other hand, scoring low on EI (e.g., low emotional regulation) may constitute grounds for exclusion from certain occupations (e.g., social work, police work, clinicians, and teachers). A caveat here is in order. It needs first to be demonstrated that low EI is meaningfully associated with failure (or poorer performance) in these occupations. One can be high on EI and not be a good lawyer or CEO, since professional success is guided by other variables, such as specific skills and competencies. However, these same individuals are likely to be ineffective on the job if they are not empathetic or have low self-regulation. In such instances, measures of EI may provide exclusionary criteria (rather than criteria allowing inclusion to the group).

Choice of criterion measures   The criterion against which EI predictors in occupational selection and placement are validated should itself be valid and reliable. Typical criteria are productivity measures (e.g., number of items or widgets produced, sales), supervisory ratings (one-time/multiple), absenteeism, or tenure. It is not clear whether these criteria should be recast somewhat to reflect the importance of emotional factors in the workplace. Nevertheless, these criteria should also be uncontaminated. Criterion contamination refers to those situations where the criterion measure itself has been based, at least in part, on predictor measures (see Cohen & Swerdlik, 1999).

Integration of different variables   Clearly, EI is only one factor, along with abilities, interests, motivation, and personality traits, that encompass sets of individual difference variables that are part of a person's career profile (Lowman, 1991). The most sensible approach for integration of multiple measures used in any selection battery involves a sequential model. Accordingly, it is suggested that abilities relevant to the job are assessed at first, followed by assessment of occupational interests, and finally, relevant measures of EI. Thus, if a person has both the ability and interest patterns associated with a particular occupational cluster, than it would make sense to examine EI factors for goodness of fit. Although this is time consuming and expensive it will most likely result in more accurate assessment. It is still an open question whether EI measures should be used together in a multiple-regression prediction equation of relevant job behaviors, along other variables in the predictor stock, or used in a noncompensatory multiple-hurdle framework.

EI and Coping with Occupational Stress

Work can surely be fulfilling, as well as a major source of life satisfaction and well-being, providing a person with a sense of identity and purpose. At the same time, the job environment can also be a source of great personal distress for many people (Cartwright & Cooper, 1996). In fact, occupational stress is rapidly becoming one of the most pressing organizational and health concerns in the Western world today. Widespread concern over the implications of stress in the workplace is attested to by the burgeoning literature on job stress and by the proliferation of stress management and training programs. Moreover, research has demonstrated highly comparable sources of work stress, levels of stress, and personal characteristics that cause workers to be susceptible to stress in various occupational settings across the globe (Mack, Nelson & Quick, 1998).

Occupational organizations have been experiencing rapid and marked changes over the past few decades (Mack et al., 1998). As the so-called information society comes of age, information technology (IT) continues to revolutionize the way that business is conducted, with the work force becoming more diverse and dynamic by the day. During the past two decades, widespread stress has resulted largely from uncertainty and concern for job security consequent to major organizational changes of a radical nature. As a response to struggling economies, the implementation of new technological processes, job obsolescence, and intense foreign and global competition, companies have often met challenges by downsizing, rightsizing, re-engineering, and restructuring on a massive scale. Consequently, even those individuals who have managed to hold onto their jobs no longer take job security for granted. Recent economic and social trends point towards an uncertain future, in which organizations will have to adapt continuously to an ever changing and volatile job market. Lack of effective coping with stress, brought about by rapid changes and transitions and uncertainty in the workplace, may lead to significant decrements in well-being, health, dissatisfaction, job involvement, and job performance. Over three decades, of systematic study in the area of occupational stress, have generated a substantial body of evidence on interacting factors that contribute to stress in the workplace (O'Driscoll & Cooper, 1994). Box 12.1 presents six salient categories of stress in the job environment.

Following the transactional model of stress (see, e.g., Lazarus, 1998; Lazarus & Folkman, 1984), a number of occupational psychologists (Beehr & Newman, 1978; McGrath, 1976) have conceptualized stress in organizations as a dynamic interaction between the person and the environment. Accordingly, job stress arises in an occupational situation that has demands, constraints, and opportunities that are perceived to threaten (or to exceed) a person's personal resources and coping capabilities. This interaction between occupational conditions and the worker's personal resources (beliefs, coping-skills, and dispositions) result in a meaningful change (disruption or enhancement) of the worker's physiological or psychological condition, in that the person is forced to deviate from normal functioning. According to the transactional perspective, to understand the experience of work stress, one must consider both the subjective and objective environment that the individual is encountering. In addition, one needs to consider stable individual differences that influence both the nature and strength of perceived occupational stresses, available and utilized coping resources and responses, and emotional and physical well-being (see figure 12.2).

Individual differences also play a major role in the stress process, with marked variations in a person's potential reaction to organizational stressors. What is a highly distressing event to one individual (e.g., promotion, with new responsibilities), might be viewed as an interesting challenge and opportunity to a person with richer coping resources. Individual-difference factors may determine the needs and desires of individuals, thereby determining perceptions of opportunities, uncertainties of resolution of the dynamic conditions of opportunity, constraints, and demands.

Overall, there is little dispute that stress may have a dysfunctional impact on both the individual and organizational outcomes. Frequently described as the Black Plague of the postindustrial era, stress has become a major problem of everyday life, threatening individual's health, organizational structure, and societal harmony. Indeed, work-related stress appears directly responsible for immense human and financial

Box 12.1
Key categories of work stress (based on Cartwright & Cooper, 1996)

Factors intrinsic to the job, task, or workplace

This category includes physical conditions and task-related sources of stress (Schuler, 1980). Specific sources of stress involving poor physical working conditions surrounding the worker include inadequate lighting, noise, pathogenic agents, physical danger, crowded space, and lack of privacy. Task-related sources of stress include work overload/underload, lack of autonomy, disruption of work patterns (e.g., shift in work load), long and unconventional hours, shift work, extensive travel, high risk, uncertainty, and new technology. French and Caplan (1973) differentiated between quantitative overload, where a worker has too much to do, and qualitative overload, where a task is too difficult for the worker. Research by Cooper and Marshall (1978) suggests that work overload is indeed a major source of stress with important health implications. Both qualitative and quantitative overload produces a variety of different symptoms of psychological strain, such as job dissatisfaction, tension, low self-esteem, threat, high cholesterol levels, and skin resistance. More chronic and serious consequences include coronary heart disease, escapist drinking, and absenteeism.

Role in the organization

Among the key dimensions of perceived role-related stress are ambiguity, conflict, and powerlessness (Katz & Kahn, 1978). Role ambiguity arises when a person has inadequate information about the work role or where there is a lack of clarity about work objectives associated with this role, about work colleague's expectations of the work role, and about scope and responsibilities of the job (Cooper & Marshall, 1978). If employees do not know what their duties are, what authority they possess, how they are to be evaluated, etc., they may hesitate to make decisions and will rely on trial and error in meeting the expectation of the organization. What makes role ambiguity so stressful is that it is related to uncertainty, to an individual's need for security, recognition, and achievement. Role ambiguity has been linked to job stress and high levels of anxiety, along with poor productivity (Kottkamp & Travlos, 1986). Men who suffered from role ambiguity experienced lower job satisfaction and higher job-related stress, and increased futility and lower self-confidence (Katz & Kahn, 1978). Role conflict evolves when behaviors expected by an individual and by others in the organization are inconsistent (Hammer & Tosi, 1974). For example, a novice high-school teacher may perceive incompatible work demands from administrators, fellow teachers, parents, and students. Kahn et al. (1964) reported that role conflict was related to job stress,

Box 12.1 (continued)

high job-related tension, and lower self-esteem. Role conflict exists when an individual in a particular work role is torn by conflicting job demands or is engaged in things she really doesn't want to do (Cooper & Marshall, 1978).

Powerlessness, another major source of job stress, refers to the perception that an individual can't control outcomes. Lack of control over outcomes has been linked to high anxiety, job dissatisfaction, low self-esteem, and poor job performance (Kottkamp & Travlos, 1986). Ashford (1988) found that feelings of personal control and ability to tolerate ambiguity were linked with stress in a sample of 180 AT&T employees who coped with divestiture and transition to an unregulated entity (Ashford, 1988). Newman and Beehr (1979) reported that role conflict and role ambiguity was significantly, but modestly, related to perceived threat on the job in a sample of 61 high-level managers in an executive developmental program. French (1973) demonstrated that role ambiguity, role conflict, role underload, role overload, and role-status incongruency is related to higher stress.

Problematic relationships with others at work

Another source of stress on the job involves the poor relationships between group members, including subordinates, colleagues, and clients (Cooper & Marshall, 1978). This is manifested by low trust, low supportiveness, and low interest in listening to and trying to deal with problems that confront organizational members. Some data suggest those negative interactions with coworkers and employees and clients and supervisors are the most frequently reported source of work-related stress. This is related to a person's need for acceptance and interpersonal recognition. When these interpersonal relations are not satisfactory to an individual, stress is often a result (Schuler, 1980). Poor emotional intelligence would be expected to be a major factor at play in aggravating this source of stress.

Career development

This category includes the threat of job loss, underpromotion, demotion and derailing, having reached a career plateau, early retirement, and unclear career future. A source of fear for many in postindustrial society involves the threat of job security (fear of being redundant, early retirement) and status incongruity (frustration at having reached one's career's ceiling, under- or overpromotion) (Cooper & Marshall, 1978). Transitions and organizational changes are frequently viewed as being extremely disruptive. Indeed, job insecurity and career development have increasingly

Box 12.1 (continued)

become a source of stress during the merger/acquisition boon of the 1980s. Recent sources of stress includes voluntary mergers, corporate takeovers, white-knight rescues, etc. Many experience these stressors as sources of uncertainty and demand for change.

Organizational structure, climate, and culture

This category subsumes stressors related to being in a particular organization and its organizational milieu and culture. This may include lack of a person-role fit, inadequate training and skills, inappropriate management style, lack of feedback from coworkers and superiors, lack of effective consultation, poor communication, and ugly office politics. The mismatch and gap between job demands and requisite knowledge, skills, and abilities will result in high strain for workers in the new service-based economy. Threat to an individual's freedom, autonomy, and identity (e.g., minimal participation in the decision making process, no sense of belonging, lack of effective consultation, poor communication, office politics, restrictions on behavior) is a source of stress for many. Also, personal and sexual harassment have assumed increasing prominence as a source of stress at the worksite. Human service jobs may also pose demands that are different from those of other professions because workers must use themselves as the technology for meeting the needs of clients, who, in turn, do not always express gratitude or appreciation.

Stress associated with organizational climate, including measures of perceived job design, leadership, and relationships with co-workers, have been found to be related to worker satisfaction and alienation in studies of human service workers. A variety of sources of job stress in this category (e.g., workload; role conflict; poor relationships among workers and their peers, supervisors, and subordinates; and lack of subjective fit between person and environment in a number of occupations) have been reported to predict job dissatisfaction, psychological symptoms, and various risk factors in coronary heart disease (French & Caplan, 1973). Career stress is associated with multiple negative outcomes (Ivancevich & Matteson, 1980).

Home-work interface

Managing the interface between work and home is a potential source of stress, particularly for dual career couples or those experiencing financial crises. By providing more flexible work arrangements and adopting family-friendly employment policies, this source of stress may be ameliorated.

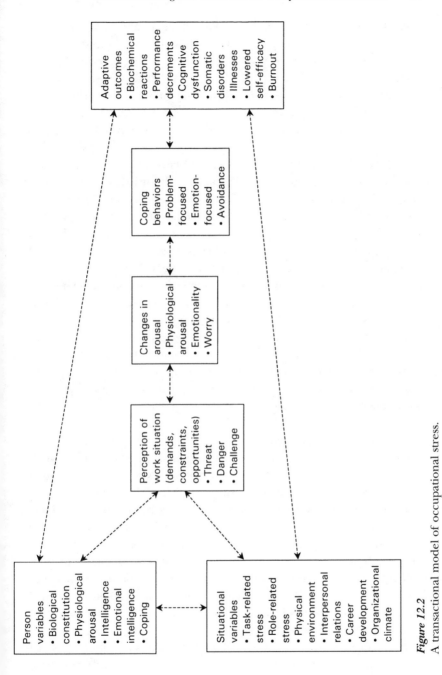

Figure 12.2
A transactional model of occupational stress.

costs (Cartwright & Cooper, 1996). For example, although industry in the United States loses approximately 550 million working days due to absenteeism, it is estimated that 54% of these absences are in some way stress-related (Elkin & Rosch, 1990). The overall total cost of stress to American organizations, as assessed by absenteeism, reduced productivity, compensation claims, health insurance, and direct medical expenses, now adds up to more than $150 billion per annum (Karasek & Theorell, 1990).

Empirical links have been demonstrated between stress and a variety of factors including, poor health behaviors, the incidence of coronary heart disease, certain forms of cancer, peptic ulcers, mental disease and breakdown, family problems, job dissatisfaction, and accidents (Schuler, 1980). The indirect costs of stress are reflected in levels of substance abuse, high divorce rates, mortality rates, and accident statistics. Indeed, stressful encounters at the workplace have been linked to a range of negative outcomes that impair workers effective functioning. Thus, the literature suggests that occupational stress can adversely affect a person's physical and mental health, job satisfaction, performance, and labor turnover. Stress may also result in higher incidences of aggressive behaviors, accidents, and thefts in the occupational environment. Furthermore, work stressors may feed into the family and social environment, becoming a potential source of disturbance that subsequently pervades the whole quality of an individual's life.

Coping with occupational stress

It has been frequently claimed that emotionally intelligent individuals, who can cope flexibly and adaptively with changes in their environment, would be at a major advantage in the changing and dynamic work environments of today (Goleman, 1998). Indeed, adaptability, or flexibility in responding to stress and changes in the organization, has been cited as an important characteristic of emotionally intelligent individuals. This attribute may be a personal resource of crucial importance for surviving in the dynamic and complex workplace of the information age (Boyatzis, 1982). Workers characterized by adaptability are said to smoothly handle multiple and changing demands at the workplace, readily shift priorities, and adapt their responses and tactics to fit fluid circumstances (Goleman, 1998). Adaptable workers and managers, it is claimed, take into account multiple perspectives, seek out or generate fresh ideas, entertain original solutions, relish change and innovation, are open to new information, and can let go of old assumptions (Goleman, 1998). During make-or-break moments in the organization, the ability to be flexible and adaptive to organizational stress, to take in new information without tuning out in self-protection, and to respond nimbly appear crucial. Furthermore, the optimistic disposition of individuals high in EI may influence stress levels by reducing the individual's perception of the uncertainty of resolution of the stressful encounter. Thus, a person with richer emotional competencies should also choose a more appropriate strategy of resolution than the individual with less ability (see chapter 8 for an in-depth discussion of EI and coping processes).

Researchers acknowledge the importance of coping-mechanisms and understanding how such processes operate within the organizational environment. In particular, it has been suggested that coping behaviors can minimize the impact of occupational stress and alleviate its negative consequences. Pearlin and Schooler (1978) have identified three major protective functions of coping:

• Avoiding, eliminating, or modifying conditions giving rise to problems

• Perceptually controlling the meanings of experience in a manner that will neutralize stress levels

• Managing to keep the emotional consequences of the problems one's experiences within acceptable limits

Empirical research on coping with work stress has been problematic, partly because of the complexity of the phenomena and partly because of the methodology that has been commonly employed (see various chapters in Zeidner & Endler, 1996). Thus, as noted by Golembiewski and Munzenrider (1988) whereas coping is a dynamic transactional process, most available measures are static. It is further noted that coping is situation-specific (Zeidner & Saklofske, 1996) and varies with the particular stressors in the job situation and task demands. Thus, an adequate treatment would require a discussion of the specific forms of coping necessary in each occupational setting.

Research further suggests that most people do not cope very well with organizational change and transitions, and consequently suffer long-term adverse mental and physical health. In fact, coping with, and managing, work stress is more complex than dealing with stressful events outside work. This results from inherent constraints within the work environment, which restricts the range of acceptable coping responses and the degree of limited individual control. This further emphasizes the importance of emotional competencies in coping with the stresses of current work environments.

Newman and Beehr (1979) identified four strategies used to cope with work stress: changing one's work environment, changing one's behavior, changing physical conditions (diet, exercise), changing psychological conditions (planning ahead, managing one's life, and so forth). Latack (1986) provided empirical evidence for three dimensions of coping with job stress: *control* (both actions and appraisals), *escape* (actions and thoughts), and *symptom management* (relaxation and exercise).

A review of the literature by Cartwright and Cooper (1996) suggests that work-related stress and routine daily-work hassles elicit more task-oriented or problem-focused strategies than emotion-focused strategies. This phenomena may occur because opportunities to discharge emotions in the workplace are generally restricted. This outcome also resonates with the findings of Lazarus (1991), who observed that individuals used higher levels of problem-focused than emotion-focused coping when negotiating with stressful events on the job. Similarly, Schwartz and Stone (1993) found that work-related problems and stressors are approached via action-oriented and problem-focused coping efforts rather than distraction or other emotion-focused or avoidance strategies. In addition, Pearlin and Schooler (1978) surveyed the effectiveness of coping in four realms: work, marriage, parenting, and household economics. Whereas coping responses were successful in reducing strain in the final three domains, they had relatively little effect on strain resulting from work.

A body of research suggests that whereas individual coping efforts may not be particularly effective in organizational settings, group coping, operationalized as social support, might be particularly effective in group settings (Shinn, Rosario, Morch & Chesnut, 1984). Thus, in the workplace, where many influential stress factors are beyond an individual's control, individual coping strategies may be less potent than higher-level strategies (involving groups of workers or entire organizations). For example, job stressors may be not amenable to individual solutions, but depend on highly organized cooperative efforts that transcend those of the individual, no matter how well developed one's personal resources. La Rocco and Jones (1978) suggest that while the coping strategy of *social support* bears a direct main effect on job-related strains (such as job dissatisfaction), it has a buffering effect on health-related variables, including psychological and somatic outcomes. Furthermore, strain was found to be positively related to emotion-focused coping. These findings suggest either that palliative coping is harmful or that emotion-focused coping is simply a reaction to high levels of job stress (rather than a cause of stress and/or strain). These authors conclude that little is to be gained by exhorting human-service professionals to change their ways of coping, because individual coping has little impact on job strain.

The literature suggests that adaptive coping with occupational stress should lead to positive outcomes, such as heightened job satisfaction, fewer psychosomatic symptoms, and decreased anxiety (Latack, 1986). Hence, if EI is eventually found to be meaningfully related to coping, high-EI individuals should benefit from positive job outcomes.

However, at present we have no direct evidence suggesting that coping moderates the effect of stress on job performance. In a sample 180 AT&T employees, Ashford (1988) found that feelings of personal control and tolerance of ambiguity were among the most useful buffers when coping with divestiture and transition to an unregulated entity. Furthermore, the avoidance of thinking about stress increases stress. Research showed that coping had a minimum effect on the relationship between uncertainty and stress. Active attempts to structure the situation by obtaining information and feedback failed to affect stress or even increased stress. Employees tried to maintain some semblance of orderly work life and career within the firm's changing structure.

Training programs for developing emotional competencies

The past decade has witnessed a proliferation of a variety of training programs designed to promote emotional skills and competencies in the occupational environment. For example, police departments have adopted training designed to help police officers better manage their own reactions and those of others in conflict. Similarly, physicians have been given training on how to be more empathetic towards their patients and to their families (Cherniss et al., 1998).

Proponents of EI programs at the workplace have claimed that the development and training of emotional competencies requires deep changes and the retooling of ingrained habits of thought, feeling, and behavior (see, e.g., Cherniss et al., 1998; Goleman, 1998). Accordingly, there are strong response habits that must be altered in emotional learning and existing neural pathways must be weakened and eventually extinguished before new ones can be established. What this means in practice is that the learning process requires repeated practice over a much longer time. Thus, learners must enter the process with a high degree of motivation, and there must be considerable guidance and support to help them maintain motivation until a new way of thinking becomes second nature (Cherniss et al., 1998). Otherwise, following a short-term training and development program, participants will simply get a short-term buzz of energy that lasts no more than a few days or weeks, after which they fall back into whatever their habitual mode was before. Cherniss and coworkers have delineated several factors contributing to effective social and emotional learning in organizational settings (Cherniss, Goleman, Emmerling, Cowan & Adler, 1998). These are reproduced in box 12.2.

Cherniss et al. review evidence showing that management training programs, focusing on the development of emotional and interpersonal competencies, were generally successful in reaching their program objectives. In addition, self-motivation training (using self-assessment, lecture and discussion, case studies, etc.) can help in fostering creativity and harnessing stronger achievement drive and business performance. A meta-analysis by Burke and Day (1986) found that managerial training programs had an average effect size of over one standard deviation for human relations training and about two thirds of a standard deviation for self-awareness.

Overall, however, few organizations actually test the EI training programs they implement and systematic evaluations of EI programs in organizational frameworks have been rare. Cherniss et al. (1998) reports the results of a recent survey of companies conducted by the American Society for Training and Development. Of the 27 companies claiming to have tried to promote emotional competence through training and development, more than two-thirds did not attempt to evaluate the effect of these efforts. Those who did relied primarily on employee-opinion surveys (American Society for Training and Development, 1997). Evidently, when it comes to EI, hard-nosed companies become soft, and they simply do not insist on hard evidence. Rather than an objective evaluation of the effects of training, the typical evaluation comes in the form of "happy sheets"—feedback from participants about whether trainees liked, or were pleased with, the program.

Because many of the existing programs are designed to help workers and managers cope with stress in the workplace, we present a more detailed discussion of these programs in the section that follows.

Management of occupational stress

Different taxonomies have been offered to classify organizationally based stress management and training intervention programs. One scheme classifies interventions designed to reduce stress at the worksite by the *target* of intervention, namely the individual, the organization, or the

Box 12.2
Proposed guidelines for the development of emotional competence training programs at the worksite (Cherniss et al., 1998)

Preparation of change

Before change can take place, efforts should be made at assuring the motivation, commitment, and self-efficacy of members of the organization. Accordingly, people are likely to be motivated to improve emotional competence if they are convinced that such a change will lead to desirable consequences. Efforts to improve emotional competence should begin with an assessment of the competencies most critical for organizational and individual effectiveness. If employees are ready, motivation and commitment can be strengthened by helping them to set specific meaningful, and realistic goals. Training programs will be more effective if they include activities designed to help learners develop positive expectations for the training and greater self-efficacy.

Doing the work

The next step involves the actual training and development of members of the organization. Emotional and social change needs to occur in a safe and supportive setting, and the relationship between trainers and learners becomes crucial in defining how safe and supportive the learning environment is for the learners. It is assumed that live models that demonstrate the skills and competencies to be mastered are more effective than simply focusing on declarative knowledge or telling the learners what to do and how to do it. Most of the training should involve experiential learning rather than lecture and discussion and there should be ample opportunity for the learners to practice the new skills, both within the training and in as many other domains of life as possible. About a dozen sessions are needed, since deeply embedded neural pathways found in the emotional centers of the brain can only be changed through experiential learning processes that involve repeated modeling, practice, and corrective feedback. Thus, receiving feedback on practice is likely to be particularly invaluable. Furthermore, training materials should encourage the learners to anticipate what barriers and problems they might encounter when they begin to apply what they have learned in their day-to-day lives. Then they learn how these might affect them emotionally and what they might do to deal with these problems. This will inoculate them against potential demoralizing effects.

Box 12.2 (continued)

Evaluation of training efforts

Training efforts should be evaluated to determine just whether people feel good about them but also whether they produce meaningful changes in on-the-job behavior. This is especially important for EI promotion efforts because there is often greater skepticism about whether such work is useful. Even managers who recognize that EI is important for individual and organizational success may question whether a training initiative can bring about significant improvements in these competencies. Evaluation research should be used to help program managers see why and how a training effort works and ways in which it can be improved in the future.

---

individual/organization interface. Interventions that focus on the individual include stress education activities (identifying sources of stress, manifestations of stress, ways of coping with stress, etc.), relaxation programs, and employee skill training (e.g., assertiveness training). Organization-focused interventions involve improving macro-level factors in the organization (improved selection, restructuring, organizational development). Interventions focusing on the organization-individual interface center on improving the personal-organizational interface (e.g., improving emotional or practical skills of employee or management to match job descriptions and requirements).

Cartwright and Cooper (1996) have distinguished three levels of intervention for stress at the worksite (see also Cooper, Liukkonen & Cartwright, 1996; Murphy, 1988). The first level, *primary prevention*, involves stress reduction, including modifying environmental stressors by direct action to eliminate negative impact on the individual. *Secondary prevention* involves mainly stress management, designed to teach employees who are high risk for stress to cope with demands at work in a more adaptive manner. The third level, *tertiary prevention*, involves programs targeting employees who have suffered from high degrees of disabling stress. The programs are generally employee assistance programs, which focus on dealing with outcomes or consequences of the stressful situation. In any case, the latter two levels deal with stress management rather modifying environmental stresses. Ivancevich and Matteson (1987) provide a slightly different classification scheme. These researchers identify three possible areas for intervention in the workplace: reducing intensity and number of stressors, helping the individual modify perception or appraisal of potentially stressful situations, and improving the range of competencies in coping with stress.

Despite a growing volume of studies on occupational stress, relatively few studies have addressed employees' efforts to cope with the stress of the workplace. Indeed, the literature is relatively silent about the ways that employees cope with transitions in the workplace. Furthermore, there are virtually no published studies in the literature that have looked at the relationship between EI, coping, and adaptive outcomes in specific occupational settings. Thus, we are in need of studies that gather systematic information about how persons perceive and report stressful encounters and events that are important at work, how they then cope, and the role of EI in coping with occupational stress.

We now briefly discuss primary and secondary interventions—the two major forms of stress management interventions implemented at the worksite.

Primary interventions   Organizational or macro-level interventions attempt to reduce the stress potential in work situations by reducing the number of environmental stressors affecting workers in the first place. Primary or macro-level interventions focus on shifting the focus from the individual worker to job design, job content, working conditions, and the organizational environment (Mawson, 1993). For sure, identifying and recognizing the problem and taking steps to tackle and solve the problem (i.e., a front-end approach) might arrest the whole stress process. Frequently, the problem and source of stress is often at an organizational level (work overload, toxic work environment, management-worker relations) or at the level of the individual/environment interface (ergonomics, retooling to changing demands, etc.). Although often expensive to implement, these interventions typically require less involvement by management and often do not mandate large-scale structural changes.

Among the many possible organization-directed strategies to reduce stress are the following (Elkin & Rosch, 1990): redesign of the work environment or the task, flexible work schedules, participative management, involving the employee in career development, analyzing work roles and establishing goals, providing social support and feedback, building cohesive teams, establishing fair employment practices, and sharing the rewards. Many of these strategies are directed at increasing employee participation and autonomy.

Burke (1993) reviewed 10 primary or organizational-level interventions. These interventions were reported to have positive effects. Burke concludes that given the limited success of individual level interventions in addressing sources of stress, organization-level interventions should be encouraged. However, in practice, few interventions are actually directed at the organizational level (Cooper & Cartwright, 1994). Thus, most current initiatives have tended to be employee-centered rather than organization-centered, whereby the focus is directed at changing the behavior of employees and improving their lifestyles.

An implicit assumption in the intervention literature is that the organization itself is difficult to change and will continue to be stressful to many workers (overload, rapid pace, pressures and demands, work hours). It follows that the major emphasis should be to improve the adaptability of the individual to the environment. Clearly, organizations prefer to implement secondary (and tertiary) prevention since clinicians feel more comfortable with these and prefer to change individuals than organizations (Cooper, Liukkonen & Cartwright, 1996). These efforts at improving individual coping skills without concomitantly changing environmental work conditions or task-related stressors (overload) have been popularly described as "band-aid" treatments.

Secondary interventions   Secondary or individual level interventions are primarily concerned with the management of experienced stress by increasing awareness of stress antecedents, stress symptoms, and consequences, along with improving the individual's stress management skills through training and educational activities (Cooper, Liukkonen & Cartwright, 1996). The role of secondary prevention is basically damage control, often addressing the consequences rather than the sources of stress inherent in the organization's structure. In particular, these techniques help one deal with stressors in the work environment that cannot be changed and one has to learn to live with. These programs include a wide variety of methods. These include broader participation in decision making, more flexible job and work schedules (core minutes, bandwidth, schedule flexibility, variability, supervisory change approval), greater autonomy, improving person-environment fit, reducing psychological burnout by changing orientation and practice (e.g., work in small groups, supervision, improved training), reducing work-family conflict (e.g., arising from lack of social life, shifts in responsibilities during absences, need for emotional support), and reducing stress of staff reductions, mergers, and acquisitions.

To be effective, interventions must simultaneously address the source of stress or change in the organization, the individual's perception of the stress, moderating variables, the stress response, and behavioral consequences. Thus, a careful diagnosis is required not only of the organization, but also of the employees.

A number of studies suggest that when a stress management program is well designed and implemented, it can produce significant improvements in coping and health outcomes. The most effective programs teach participants a flexible array of techniques, such as muscle relaxation and deep breathing, mental imagery, assertiveness training, lifestyle-modification skills, and cognitive restructuring. Stress reduction techniques include *physical* methods, which aim at putting some emotional distance between person and work, relaxation and meditation, and use of drugs and alcohol. Stress reduction techniques also include *cognitive and psychological* methods, e.g., developing a positive approach to the problem, approaching the job with humor, and separating yourself either physically or cognitively from work (hobbies, travel, social, family, activities, take a walk a few minutes each day). In addition, there are *interpersonal* and *management skills* that can be learned. This category includes activities relating to the utilization of skills, which enhance job effectiveness (team management, communication skills, etc.) (Cartwright & Cooper, 1996).

The EI literature is replete with practical suggestions for coping with occupational stress. Cooper and Sawaf (1997), in their popular book on *Executive EQ*, recommend a three-step strategy for managing emotional energy. These steps are (a) acknowledge and feel—rather than deny or minimize—the emotion experienced, (b) listen to the information or feedback the emotion is giving you (e.g., if one experiences anger or sadness, one should ask what principles, values, assets, resources, or goals are at stake), (c) guide or channel the emotional energy into an appropriate constructive response. The underlying assumption of these authors is that emotions are an energy that is neither good nor bad. What is important is how you respond to it. Presumably, by applying this three-step strategy, one can learn how to better cope with aversive emotions and stress at the worksite and achieve better adaptive outcomes.

Goleman (1998) writes that emotionally intelligent people, best able to handle stress, often have a stress-management technique they call on when needed, whether it's a long bath, a workout, or a yoga session. According to Goleman, regular daily practice of a relaxation method seems to reset the trigger point for the amygdala, making it less easily provoked. The neural resetting gives us the ability to recover more quickly from "amygdala hijacks," while making us less prone to them in the first place. The evidence for this hypothesis is iffy at best (see chapter 6). Additional practical suggestions and tips are presented in box 12.3. Unfortunately, little empirical support is generally offered to back up the suggestions put forth.

A series of recent reviews of the effectiveness of secondary intervention programs suggests that such interventions can make a difference. A recent review shows that stress reduction programs produce significant improvements in measures of well-being and physical symptoms (Cherniss et al., 1998). Similarly, a review of the literature by Burke (1993) suggests that some individual level interventions can make a difference in temporarily reducing adverse responses to perceived stressors. However, there is evidence that such interventions don't have a lasting effect. That is, once individuals encounter demands in the work settings, the benefits of these individual-level interventions disappear. Overall, Burke's (1993) review shows that in the work setting, individual coping responses may be less useful than higher-level strategies involving groups of workers or entire units or organizations. Reynolds, Taylor, and Shapiro (1993) concluded that counseling is successful in treating and rehabilitating employees suffering from stress. However, because these workers are likely to reenter the same work environment they are dissatisfied with, potential productivity gains may not be maximized. Even if symptoms are relieved, this effect may be short-lived if employees return to unchanged work environment and its indigenous stressors. Pearlin and Schooler (1978) conclude that chronic, organizationally generated stressors may be resistant to reduction through individual coping efforts (see also Shinn et al., 1984; Murphy, 1984, 1988). They reviewed the literature on work-site stress management training and concluded that some of this training did have a positive effect, but such effects diminished with the passage of time.

Conclusions

This chapter critically reviewed the theory and evidence for the claimed role of EI and emotional competencies at the worksite. In particular, we critically examined the conceptual basis and empirical evidence for the role of EI in three major facets of organizational life: occupational and career assessment, job performance and satisfaction, and coping with occupational stress. In addition, we looked at the evidence for the effectiveness of training and development programs designed to promote

Box 12.3
Some practical tips in the literature for managing stress

Emotional diary

Cooper and Sawaf (1997) suggest that stress can be managed through an emotional diary or morning notes. According to these authors, a worker should spend two or three minutes every morning clearing away the frustrating, trivial stuff that echoes in their head and plants seed of confusion in their heart. Workers are advised to write whatever they feel and keep the log handy throughout the day. The theoretical and empirical basis for these suggestions is unclear.

Humor

Weisinger (1998) suggests that humor is the best medicine for coping with stress, serving as a distraction to turn us away from whatever distressful emotions we may be having. He suggests it might be helpful to create a humor-filled environment, with silly photographs, jokes, and humorous situations (Weisinger, 1998). Furthermore, the individual can try to look at coworkers and the boss through a "hidden-camera" perspective, observing them in an absurd, whimsical, or silly perspective, rather than in a serious way.

Mental imagery

Weisinger (1998) advances the use of mental imagery as a way to cope with stress. Thus, we can visualize ourselves in almost any situation and can visualize the outcome of a particular situation. Here mental imagery can galvanize us into activity because we visualize ourselves doing the activity. By identifying, refining, and practicing in our mind the steps necessary for successfully staying on course, it is easier for one to be motivated to carry out the steps in real life. Thus, one can imagine oneself relaxing, calling up in minds tasks which one feels are unmotivated, imagine oneself struggling with the task, gaining composure, succeeding, and feeling good.

emotional competencies at the worksite, with particular emphasis on management of occupational stress.

Throughout this chapter, we pointed out a number of problems and flaws in the existing literature on EI in occupational settings. First, the literature is replete with unsubstantiated generalizations regarding the role of EI at the worksite. One case in point is Daniel Goleman's claim "All emotional competencies can be cultivated with the right practice" (1998, p. 284). Unfortunately, there is no evidence to back up this claim. Second, many of the competencies and skills discussed in the literature under the rubric of EI in occupational contexts are not really legitimate and organic components of elements of the EI construct, as currently conceptualized by state-of-the-art ability models of EI. Instead, they may best be characterized as motivational variables (flow, attributions, and self-efficacy), personality variables (anxiety, optimism, self-worth, and conscientiousness), character traits (stamina, trust, integrity), social skills (cooperation, collaboration, building social bonds), or general managerial skills. Third, much of the existing evidence bearing on the role of EI in occupational success is either anecdotal or impressionistic, based on unpublished or in-house research. Much of this line of research uses proxy measures of EI (e.g., constructive thinking) and relies on unpublished commissioned surveys, conducted by the authors themselves (e.g., Goleman, 1998). Despite the important role attributed to a wide array of emotional competencies at the worksite (e.g., emotional awareness, empathy, conflict resolution), there is presently little descriptive, correlational or experimental research, that supports the meaningful role attributed to these competencies in determining occupational success or well-being. Overall, despite the important role attributed to a wide array of emotional competencies at the worksite (e.g., emotional awareness, empathy, conflict resolution), there is presently little descriptive, correlational or experimental research that supports the meaningful role attributed to these competencies in determining occupational success or well-being. Notwithstanding claims by proponents of EI at the worksite with respect to the role of EI in career assessment, EI should probably not be included as part of every standard job selection or classification battery. Instead, EI should be used only where warranted by the job description. Accordingly, when particular emotional skills are part of the job description (e.g., empathy, conflict resolution), it would seem important to assess EI. By contrast, in those jobs where adequate emotional skills are really minimal, there is little sense in assessing EI. At present, there is an urgent need for sound taxonomic research that focuses on determining the EI constructs that are crucial for the performance of particular jobs and identifying the relevant EI measures that best assess these affective constructs.

It is important not to use EI measures in occupational contexts unless they were specifically developed, normed, and validated to that end, and demonstrate adequate occupational relevance. Thus, in occupational contexts it is probably best to avoid using some of the more prevalent broad-brush omnibus EI measures (e.g., MEIS, EQ-i), originally designed for research and general assessment purposes. Most current measures of EI, both self-report and behavioral, fail to satisfy the basic criteria we put forth for developing, validating, and responsibly using measures of EI components in occupational contexts. Thus, current measures are characterized by the following flaws: (a) they often fail to provide an adequate theoretical rationale for their use in a particular occupational setting, (b) they are generally not occupation-specific, (c) they do not provide adequate normative data for different occupational groups, by age, and (d) they fail to provide evidence for predictive and discriminate validity, both within and among occupations. Because there is currently no empirically validated taxonomy of jobs corresponding to separate components of EI, the occupational psychologist will need to exercise clinical or professional judgment to accomplish the task.

Is there any convincing empirical data that would support the valid use of EI measures for purposes of occupational and career assessment? Overall, our review suggests that there is little empirically based evidence, generated from representative samples of respondents in different occupational categories, and published in peer-reviewed journals, to indicate that EI measures do reliably and incrementally predict criteria of job success and well being, above and beyond that predicted by standard ability or personality measures. That is, to the best of our knowledge, there is no valid and replicated research that has reliably demonstrated that EI measures add meaningful unique incremental variance to the prediction of occupational criteria.

Reviews of EI programs at work often include, under the rubric of EI interventions and training programs, worksite programs which have existed in the past (reducing absenteeism or unemployment, increasing self-efficacy and work motivation, sensitivity training, human relations, etc.). The success of these commonplace and longstanding programs is inappropriately taken as effectiveness of EI programs. At present, the effectiveness of EI-based training programs remains unclear.

Furthermore, relatively few studies have addressed employee's efforts to cope with the stress of the workplace and the literature is relatively silent about the ways that employees cope with transitions in the workplace. The implications of current research on coping in occupational settings for the role of EI are complex. On one hand, theory would suggest that individuals high in EI would show a preference for problem-focused over other forms of coping when something can be done to alter the source of stress. However, when little can be done to alter the source of stress, emotion-focused coping should be the most adaptive (see chapter 8). Unfortunately, there is no published research that bears this out, and further research is needed to test these hypotheses. On the other hand, given the research that suggests that individual coping efforts are not very effective in making a difference at the worksheet, it is highly questionable to what extent coping strategies would be helpful to those emotionally intelligent individuals who apply them. Overall, the role of EI in impacting on the effectiveness of macro-level interventions would be expected to be minimal. Furthermore, there are no peer-reviewed studies in the literature, to our knowledge, that systematically looked at the relationship between EI, coping, and adaptive outcomes in specific occupational settings. Thus, we are in urgent need of studies, which enable persons to report events, or stressful encounters that are important to them in specific occupational sites, how they cope with them, and the role of EI in coping with occupational stress.

In sum, it is presently unclear how powerful the links are between EI and outcomes for the organization. A number of basic questions still loom large: Do emotionally intelligent employees produce greater profits for the organization? Does EI enhance well being at the worksite? Can emotional skills at the worksite be effectively taught? Do EI training programs have lasting results? Many of the popular claims presented in the literature regarding the role of EI in determining work success and well-being are rather misleading in that they seem to present scientific studies supporting their claims, while in fact failing to do so. Whereas EI has been reported to be related to performance and affective outcomes (job satisfaction, commitment, and competence), the evidence for performance is very limited and often contradictory. Despite some rather fantastic claims to the contrary, the guiding principle is "Caveat emptor." While EI facets alone, we believe, are unlikely to predict appropriate occupational placement, these variables may provide important dimensions otherwise missing from the conventional batteries assessing ability and interests. However, because there is no hard evidence for the validity of current EI measures, and no validity studies clearly showing differential EI for various occupational groups, there is little psychometric justification for their current use in specific occupational contexts. Our review suggests that that the current excitement surrounding the potential benefits from the use of EI in the workplace may be premature or even misplaced. However, as more empirical data become available, we may soon be able to evaluate to what extent EI contributes unique incremental variance to the prediction of occupational achievement and well being.

IV

Conclusion

13

The Science, the Myth, and the Future of Emotional Intelligence

The great tragedy of Science—the slaying of a beautiful hypothesis by an ugly fact.

Thomas Huxley, 1894

Emotional intelligence has caught the imagination of the general public, the commercial world, and the scientific community. It matches the current zeitgeist of self-awareness and understanding, redressing a perceived imbalance between intellect and emotion in the life of the collective Western mind. Emotional intelligence also connects with several cutting-edge areas of psychological science, including the neuroscience of emotion, self-regulation theory, studies of metacognition, and the search for human cognitive abilities beyond traditional academic intelligence.

The supposed malleability of emotional intelligence has considerable appeal to practitioners tackling personal and social problems. It is perceived as a panacea for clinical patients locked into private misery; obstructive, unproductive employees; and violent, antisocial children. Beyond the more dramatic manifestations of emotional illiteracy, many essentially adjusted people feel their lives would benefit from greater skills in understanding their own emotions and those of other people.

In this final chapter we draw together the various strands of research that address the validity, nature, and practical relevance of emotional intelligence. Our decisive aim is to determine which beliefs about EI are mythical and speculative and which statements have a firm foundation in empirical science. We will first look at some major difficulties with the construct of emotional intelligence. We then turn to address how these difficulties surface in the psychometric properties of EI tests, in theories of the processes underpinning individual differences in emotion regulation, and in the gulf between rhetoric and objective reality that characterize studies of practical applications. We will conclude by separating science from myth and by sketching out some priorities for further research.

Barriers to developing a science of emotional intelligence

Despite the high promise offered by emotional intelligence, we have identified significant impediments to scientific progress related to the following, by no means trivial, issues:

Conceptualizations of EI   Without a clear conception of what "emotional intelligence" means, it is difficult to judge whether existing measures assess EI or perhaps some other constellation of psychological constructs. As we demonstrated throughout, different accounts of EI appear in conflict with one another. Thus, a major disjunction exists between theorists. In the one camp are those who conceptualize EI as a fairly well-defined set of emotion-processing skills (e.g., Mayer, Salovey, et al., 2000). In the other camp are those who adopt a broader definition encompassing multiple aspects of personal functioning that are more loosely related to emotion (e.g., Bar-On, 1997; Goleman, 1995). Unfortunately, as we have seen throughout our exposition, both approaches appear to lack a firm foundation in the existing extensive research literatures on both intelligence and emotion.

In addition, there is a schism between scientific models and popular accounts that tends to make EI an all-encompassing construct, rendering it devoid of much scientific meaning. The trend toward defining EI by exclusion—as all positive qualities that connect to emotion other than cognitive intelligence—is especially disturbing (see Hedlund & Sternberg, 2000). Indeed, there appears a tension between scientific approaches, which are necessarily rational, and the popular zeitgeist, which places more value on personal experience. One might almost see a Zen-like paradox in seeking to understand emotional intelligence via the intellect. In addition, there may be a further tension between the scientific and commercial enterprises. The burgeoning sector of commercial EI products ranges from serious tests, to on-line institutions, to soft, cuddly toys that purport to increase children's EI. Science, with its focus on the limitations and uncertainties surrounding EI, tends to provide a sobering message. Of course, such missives may not be welcome to the salesperson trying to sell the public an ever-extending range of commercially available EI-related products.

Measurement   Moreover, in tune with a zeitgeist that emphasizes *individual* fulfillment, as well as a rapidly developing science of differential psychology, EI has been investigated primarily as a component of individual differences. Thus, a principal focus of empirical research is the development of tests for EI. Certainly, there have been promising developments in EI assessment. Among the myriad of tests developed (or being developed), the MEIS/MSCEIT (e.g., Mayer, Caruso, et al., 1999), EQ-i (e.g., Bar-On, 1997), and SSRI (Schutte et al., 1998) appear as frontrunners in the high-stakes race to develop a definitive instrument. However, psychometrics gives us some well-honed tools for detecting faulty tests, and there are unsettled and unsettling issues associated with the psychometric properties (reliability and validity) of the current crop of EI measures.

Redundancy   The field of differential psychology is already replete with constructs related to different aspects of intelligence and personality. Even a reliable and valid EI test contributes little if it simply measures an existent construct (i.e., it is simply old wine in a new bottle). The issue is also one of predictive validity: does this emerging test tell us anything about the person we could not have discovered from scales that are tried, tested, and true?

Theoretical basis   Psychology is rich in theories of the neural and cognitive processes controlling the mental representation of personally significant events and selection of responses. We can describe adaptive processes in terms of brain systems supporting emotion, in terms of the information-processing software of the mind, and in terms of high-level personal goals and self-knowledge reflecting societal and cultural norms. At this early stage, research on EI has hardly begun to grapple with extant knowledge of these domains. We have aimed in this book to survey research on emotion and adaptation in detail, to determine if there is some master process or set of processes that could be identified with EI.

Practical applications   Contrary to the impression given in some of the more febrile writings on EI, we do not need to hold the front page for the news that emotions are important in everyday life. Emotional problems are a familiar aspect of the psychiatric clinic, the workplace, and the classroom, and there is substantial documentation of practical interventions in these areas. Again, the issue is one of novelty. Does the concept of EI give the practitioner a fresh, and productive, approach to dealing with emotional difficulty, or is the concept too broad and vague to be of practical utility?

Psychometric and Conceptual Issues

Psychometrics, assessment, and emotional intelligence

Measurement is the key to a science of emotional intelligence, and if existing measures fail to pass high (even acceptable) psychometric standards, little remains to the claim that the concept of EI is scientific. In summarizing the state of the art in the psychological assessment of EI, we will first examine conceptual and measurement difficulties inherent in the available tests, which have been developed within self-report and quasi-objective traditions. Thereafter, we will look in more detail at the problem of coherently conceptualizing EI and at how different conceptualizations may suggest different strategies for assessment.

The importance of measurement is recognized in the extensive test development programs of Bar-On (1997, 2000) and Mayer, Salovey, and Caruso (e.g., 2000). These programs have achieved some significant progress. Both the EQ-i and the MEIS/MSCEIT provide an overall assessment of EI that has high internal consistency (reliability). All the EQ-i subscales and several of the MEIS/MSCEIT subscales also have acceptable internal consistency, although we have pointed to the need to improve the reliability of some the performance-test subscales. Other self-report instruments reviewed in chapter 5 also tend to have satisfactory alpha coefficients. Tests of EI predict various other criteria related to emotional function, with self-report scales typically giving higher validity coefficients than the MEIS. Few of the validity studies have used objective measures of criterion performance outside the testing situation, however, and much of the research is simply correlating questionnaires with other questionnaires.

Unfortunately, there is a basic difficulty in accepting these promising results as establishing the reality of emotional intelligence, largely because different tests fail to converge on a common dimension. Self-report (i.e., personalitylike) measures of EI appear to be distinct from performance-based (i.e., abilitylike) measures of EI. In fact, the correlation between the MEIS and the EQ-i is 0.36, indicating the two tests share around 10% of their variation in common (Mayer, Caruso, et al., 2000). In comparison, the MEIS also correlates between 0.30 and 0.40 with measures of cognitive intelligence (Roberts, Zeidner, et al., 2001).

In measurement terms, the MEIS (and presumably the MSCEIT) is as far from whatever the EQ-i measures as it is from IQ. The two scales cannot be measuring the same construct. There may also be different versions of EI within each domain of measurement; for example, the EQ-i and SSRI (Schutte et al., 1998) have somewhat differing personality correlates (see chapter 5), which implies that they represent somewhat different constructs. For now, we must work with the distinct conceptions of EI-as-ability and EI-as-personality. In the passages that follow, we assess the success of measurement of these two conceptions, leaving aside the issue of which is the "true" form of emotional intelligence.

Emotional intelligence and cognitive ability

EI as a cognitive ability   Mayer, Salovey, et al. (2000) advance cogent arguments for treating EI as a type of mental ability, rather than an ability-personality mix. Their approach in developing the MEIS/MSCEIT as an ability test has been partly vindicated in that this instrument avoids redundancy with existing personality measures. Thus, correlations with standard broad personality traits are typically less than 0.30 (Ciarrochi et al., 2000; Roberts, Zeidner et al., 2001). The MEIS also correlates appropriately with cognitive-ability measures (i.e., positively but modestly). Conceptually, the four aspects of emotional intelligence that the MEIS claims to assess—emotion identification, assimilation, understanding, and management—seem meaningful and distinctive. This work is probably the most original in the field, and it certainly merits further attention.

However, we have also found some serious shortcomings to this approach, both at a conceptual level and in terms of research outcomes. Conceptually, there are two unresolved issues. First, the cognitive architecture supporting emotional skills is not well-specified. For example, it is likely that emotion identification has both automatic aspects controlled by innate or highly learned stimulus configurations (e.g., facial expression) and controlled aspects that depend on strategic processing (e.g., factoring in recent events). Put differently, emotional intelligence may depend on both implicit and explicit processes. Either or both processes might contribute to EI, but their roles are not differentiated by Mayer, Salovey, and colleagues (see, e.g., Mayer, Caruso, et al., 2000; Mayer, Salovey, et al., 2000).

Second, research into human cognitive abilities distinguishes practical intelligence from general academic intelligence (Wagner, 2000), as the context-bound cognitive skills needed to solve the often ill-defined problems of real life. For example, there is considerable evidence that tests of one form of practical intelligence, tacit knowledge, are substantially correlated with job performance, even with IQ controlled (Sternberg & Grigorenko, 2000). Recall from chapter 3 that tacit knowledge refers to the informal procedural knowledge required for job performance, or practical know-how. It seems that EI should also have generalized and context-bound aspects, but these components remain poorly differentiated in the Mayer-Salovey-Caruso model. For example, the skills required to judge a work colleague's emotional state, taking into account the background context of workplace practices, conventions, and events, appears different from the skills required to assess emotions in a photograph presented without context. The MEIS/MSCEIT appears to lean towards a generalized assessment, especially in tests requiring understanding of the meanings of emotional words, but such an assessment may not predict context-bound procedural knowledge of emotions.

Third, scoring procedures are questionable (Roberts et al., 2001). There is no definitive, universally accepted body of knowledge about emotional competence that can be used for veridical scoring, in part because of the context- and culture-dependent nature of competence (Zeidner, Matthews, et al., 2001). Tests must be scored using the more debatable methods reviewed in chapter 5, notably expert, consensus, and (sometimes) target scoring. The preferred scoring method must have a satisfactory a priori rationale in order to establish that what is being measured is actually a cognitive ability, as opposed to some preference or cultural value. Both expert and consensus methods have strengths and weaknesses. Expert scoring provides an unequivocal standard, but the rationales for experts' judgments are open to question (not least, by other experts), especially for higher-level aspects of EI, such as emotion management. There are also doubts about the cultural fairness of expert judgments. Consensus scoring substitutes popular standards for the standards of a few individuals, on the assumption that the pooled response of large normative samples is accurate (Legree, 1995). However, there seems to be little direct evidence for this supposition, and consensus may be influenced by culture- or gender-based stereotypes and by beliefs that are popular but false. Roberts et al. (2001) argue that consensus-based scoring may actually assess the individual's conformity to cultural (or social) norms. Being in step with other people's beliefs about emotions may well be advantageous, but it is doubtful that it can be labeled a "true intelligence" according to the criteria described in chapter 3.

One could argue that one or another scoring method is correct, and the others should be discarded. However, it has been claimed that different scoring methods converge (Mayer, Caruso, et al., 2000), supporting the reliability of each one. Despite recent progress (Mayer et al., submitted), there are concerns about the equivalence of different scoring methods for the same test. As discussed in chapter 5, the two forms of scoring the MEIS (expert and consensus) give general factors that correlate at only 0.26, with some subscales cross-correlating higher than this value, and some lower (Roberts et al., 2001). There are similar problems in lack of convergence between consensus and target scoring, which we noted in discussing the Geher et al. (2001) EARS test for emotion perception (see appendix B). Mayer et al. (submitted) report dramatically higher expert-consensus agreement for the MSCEIT, using a larger pool of 21 experts. However, it is unclear what quality is being converged upon: genuine emotional competence, some set of cultural beliefs common to both experts and unselected respondents, or some amalgam of competence and culture (Zeidner, Matthews, et al., 2001). Convergence of scoring is necessary but not sufficient for validity, and whatever scoring system is to be used requires a stronger rationale than is so far apparent (Roberts et al., 2001; Zeidner, Matthews, et al., 2001).

A further challenge to veridical scoring is that Mayer, Caruso, et al. (2000) distinguish different strata of emotional intelligence, ranging from emotion perception to emotion management. Evidently, lower-order components of EI are more readily assessed than higher-order components, and there is some independent psychometric evidence that emotional perception is a psychometrically well-defined factor (see, e.g., Davies et al., 1998). There is perhaps a lesson from intelligence testing too, where chronometric assessments of speed and accuracy of information processing, using relatively simple computerized tasks, are coming back into fashion. Several aspects of emotional function may be assessed in this entirely objective way, using the tasks requiring attention, memory, and verbal processing described in chapter 7.

Assessment of higher-order components of EI is less amenable to such techniques. As the checkered history of attempts to assess social intelligence demonstrates, this aspect of assessment is likely to remain problematic (see chapter 3 and appendix A). As in the case of cognitive intelligence, there may be scope for developing tests of practical or tacit emotional knowledge, linked to specific contexts such as the workplace or the family. However, we anticipate continued difficulties in justifying the scoring of such tests.

Implications from the field of cognitive ability research In chapter 3 we demonstrated a wealth of empirical literature supporting various cognitive ability constructs, and in the context of discussing EI as an ability, it would seem appropriate to comment on the implications they have for emotional intelligence. This discussion is especially pertinent if the intelligence portion of EI is to be taken seriously. As such, research into human cognitive abilities gives us essential guidelines for the quality control of a scientific approach to EI. In short, conditions set by previous research into intelligence establish the delimiting conditions for EI if it is ever to be construed as a form of human ability. This discussion also serves to highlight issues of import for future empirical researchers interested in establishing EI as a form of cognitive ability. Next we speculate the further requirements for progress if these conditions are met.

Establishing dependence required of an intelligence The "positive manifold" principle indicates that intelligence tests lawfully correlate positively with each other, and with each and every newly developed measure that might rightfully be considered an index of human cognitive ability. The implications for new tests of EI have certainly been acknowledged by some commentators, especially those who have developed performance-based measures (see Mayer, Caruso, et al., 1999), but appear to have farther-reaching consequences than some proponents of EI imagine. Not only should EI measures correlate positively among themselves, but each and every new EI test appearing on the commercial market or in scientific circles should be placed within the positive manifold. Moreover, each new EI measure should correlate positively with other established cognitive ability measures; otherwise, it would appear they are not really measuring a true type of intelligence.

Establishing structural independence from other ability concepts It should also be established that EI is structurally independent from concepts like fluid and crystallized intelligence. One of the major problems Guilford encountered was being able to demonstrate that the new, highly novel tests he devised (to measure his myriad primary mental abilities) were not too highly related to those measuring concepts already in existence. Indeed, one of the great strengths of Carroll's (1993) synthesis of ability studies is that he was able to disentangle concepts emanating from disparate laboratories, highlighting redundancies where appropriate. In short, getting the correlational balance right (i.e., an optimal range of correlation coefficients: not too low or high) is a difficult undertaking for EI researchers.

Linking EI to social intelligence is problematic a priori   In the context of the preceding two points, linking EI to social intelligence would appear ill-advised. Over a century of research has left us with more questions than answers about this elusive concept. If anything, though, social intelligence is likely subsumed by crystallized intelligence, and the data already at hand do not rule out a similar fate for the many subscales composing performance-based measures of EI.

Establishing primary emotional abilities   In intelligence research, tests are first developed and then shown to intercorrelate substantially before it is claimed that a new primary mental ability (let alone higher-order constructs like fluid and crystallized intelligence) has been isolated. In the push toward developing commercially available instruments, we wonder whether EI researchers are trying to fly before they can walk. Urgent attention should be directed towards finding primary emotional abilities, a corpus of which, if substantially correlated and still relatively independent of existing constructs, would vindicate the existence of a new broad ability concept: EI.

Analysis of test-item properties   One of the strengths of ability testing is the use of "itemetric" techniques to ensure that items are unbiased (Jensen, 1980). It is axiomatic that the proportion of individuals correctly answering a given item should increase monotonically with their overall test score—a principle that forms the basis for sophisticated test-construction techniques (Lord, 1980). However, even within the ability approach, EI test developers have entirely neglected properties of items. Indeed, as mentioned in chapter 2, consensus-scoring seems to guarantee problems at this level. By definition, if the test item is hard, the consensus will be toward an incorrect answer. Tests require a series of items graduated in difficulty so that they operate with equal reliability when assessing both lower and higher levels of emotional intelligence.

Different cognitive abilities have different construct validities   Our review of the literature on human cognitive abilities suggested that there are many different forms of intelligence and that each makes a unique contribution toward a complete scientific model. It seems that in the clamor to promote general EI (i.e., EQ), researchers have ignored a more intriguing possibility: that the different facets of EI have disparate developmental trajectories, diverse cognitive underpinnings, different responses to training and intervention, and so forth. In short, broad cognitive abilities have different predictive and construct validities. Indeed, we might argue that the proposed generality of EI is contrary to the egalitarian, utopian vision that some have promised. The generality of intelligence, which we believe to be in question, has led to oversimplified accounts, population stereotypes, and questionable policy recommendations, such as those found in *The Bell Curve*. Could it be that EI represents a similarly complex entity? Most frightening, in distilling this complex entity into a single quality, might we not some day soon be reading a book touting the advantages of an emotional elite and the deterioration brought to our society by the emotional underclass?

Establishing biological, psychological, and sociological correlates There is an expansive literature documenting the relationship that human cognitive abilities share with all manner of things, from biological phenomena such as brain activity to mortality rates (high IQ predicts longer life expectancy [see O'Toole & Stankov, 1992]). It might be claimed that EI research is in its infancy and that examining the biological, behavioral, and sociological correlates is perhaps premature. Throughout this book we present data mainly from the first two domains suggesting that charting the correlates of EI is undoubtedly complex. Note, however, that from its inception this is precisely the approach that guided differential psychology in its attempts to measure and subsequently understand intelligence (see, e.g., Galton, 1883). Advances in neuroscience and cognitive psychology have both been applied in more recent times to further our understanding of structural models of intelligence. Research on EI should follow this scientifically productive path. Administratively, at the very least, it would not seem too inconvenient to include information-processing tasks, like the Emotional Stroop, inside multivariate designs aimed at construct validation of tests like the MSCEIT, to improve theoretical understanding of its branches.

Given the zeitgeist value of EI, one candidate sociological correlate of EI, extensively studied by intelligence researchers (see, e.g., Herrnstein & Murray, 1994), stands out: socioeconomic status (SES). If we are wrong in our criticisms and there is sufficient substance to EI for interventions to enhance real-world functioning, expansive commercialization will ensue, and enrollment in top EI institutions is likely to cost big bucks indeed. Somewhat controversially, we suggest a high positive relationship between EI and SES is likely to develop in consequence. That is, socioeconomic status and EI will be related because the opportunities for enhancing it are intimately linked to one's financial standing, just as would appear to be the case with cognitive intelligence, especially crystallized abilities. Indeed, in countries in which educational opportunities appear linked to income, this relationship may already obtain. In any event, if the zeitgeist of emotional intelligence for all is to stand firm, there may be sociological and political questions to be asked about equality of opportunity to emotionally enriching education.

Establishing developmental trajectories   Contrary to what has been claimed by EI researchers, it is a misconception that intelligence increases developmentally (see Mayer, Caruso, et al., 1999), and that this is a necessary condition for EI to qualify as an intelligence. As we saw in discussion of the theory of fluid and crystallized intelligence, studies of cognitive aging represent a fertile ground for cognitive-ability researchers. A most interesting finding inside this theory is that some classes of broad cognitive abilities (like Gf) decline, while others (like Gc) improve. It remains an empirical question as to what the developmental trajectory of EI might look like, simply because no study has yet adequately addressed this issue. Does EI decline over age? Does it remain stable? Does it gradually rise over the life span to decline only in very old age? In fact, each EI construct may have a different developmental trajectory. Note the issue of cognitive aging is no small matter in the standardized scoring of intelligence tests, where allowances are made for changes with age. Ultimately, if changes do occur in EI factors with age, this finding should impact heavily on how performance-based tests are both normed and scored.

Examining group differences   The research on group differences in EI, as we stated in chapter 2, is meager. Intelligence research, on the other hand, has tackled these issues, though unfortunately too often with some degree of political insensitivity. Nevertheless, this is not an issue that can be ignored by EI researchers. If gender differences exist, so be it. This should engage new research aimed at understanding these differences. For example, the differences might be a function of the item content (gender bias may be introduced artifactually by including items slanted towards males or females). Alternatively, these might accrue because of gender differences in motivations and interests (see Graham & Ickes, 1997) or perhaps result from an environmental factor that is possible to change through intervention. Again, it is nonincidental that the zeitgeist value of EI rests on its view of an egalitarian society where we can all have EI in abundance. Demonstrating that group differences are minimal would appear yet another prerequisite if this claim is to have merit.

Emotional intelligence and personality traits

EI as a personality trait   It is generally easier to generate self-assessment tests than ability tests, and so it comes as no surprise that personalitylike tests of EI are mushrooming. Test developers generally claim that their measures are distinct from personality, but item content is typically very similar to standard personality scales. Indeed, as discussed in chapter 9, there already exist personality questionnaires for core components of EI, such as empathy and impulse control. Nevertheless, it is possible that current personality research has neglected some important qualities of the individual. A systematic search for components of EI might reveal dimensions beyond those already mapped by personality researchers. The work of Bar-On (1997, 2000) in developing the EQ-i is notable for its thoroughness in searching for different aspects of EI. Furthermore, research on EI might lead to a reconceptualization of the personality-intelligence interface. Perhaps we have underestimated the extent to which the traits associated with EI represent abilities rather than quali-tative styles of behavior. Perhaps too, EI research can lead us toward fresh perspectives on existing personality models, so that we can rec-onceptualize dimensions such as emotional stability (low neuroticism), agreeableness, and conscientiousness as different aspects of some over-arching factor of EI.

Unfortunately, there is a major and possibly insurmountable road-block to progress of this kind: unlike performance-based measures, self-report scales are highly redundant with existing trait dimensions. As we saw in chapter 5, the correlations between the Bar-On EQ-i and major personality dimensions such as the Big Five are so high as to suggest that "EQ" largely reflects a blend of these traits (especially low neuroticism and trait anxiety). Notably, this finding appears consistent with con-ceptual analysis of the overlaps between EI and the Five Factor Model (FFM) (McCrae, 2000). Furthermore, EI may also be redundant with more specific lower-level "primary" traits, as well as the FFM. As dis-cussed in chapter 5, the EQ-i (Bar-On, 1997) may be reduced to only three constructs: self-esteem, empathy, and impulse control. The issue is then whether residual variance in EI scales adds to the understand-ing of emotional functioning that established personality theory already provides.

In fact, questionnaire studies of EI recapitulate two of the problems of performance-based measures: neglect of the overall psychometric framework and, in predictive studies, low discriminant validity with re-spect to existing scales. Proponents of EI display little awareness of the continuing controversy in personality research over whether it is more useful to assess personality primarily at the level of broad superfactors, such as the Big Five, or at the level of more narrowly defined primary traits. Existing EI research offers little sense of where the construct should be placed within a multistratum model. The problem is compounded by the lack of psychometric coherence of the disparate traits linked to EI. These traits include existing constructs such as alexithymia and empathy, together with new ones empirically derived from factor analysis of EI questionnaires. These include the optimism/mood regulation, appraisal of emotions, social skills, and utilization of emotion factors identified by Petrides and Furnham (2000b) in the SSRI. Researchers on EI seek to stitch together these various constructs into a unified whole, but the evidence from personality research is that this enterprise may be misguided. Within the FFM, for example, alexithymia is linked to neuroticism, empathy to agreeableness, self-control to conscientiousness, and assertiveness to extraversion, and each of these factors is largely independent (see McCrae, 2000). Personality research shows that several traits contribute to emotional functioning, but they do so in different ways that are obscured by lumping them together as EI.

Superficially, questionnaire measures of EI appear to have better predictive validity than ability-based measures (see, e.g., Bar-On, 1997). However, the studies reviewed in chapter 5 suggest that much of this validity is no more than the inevitable consequence of the redundancy of EI scales with existing personality constructs. Saklofske et al. (submitted) found that the SSRI did have some predictive validity over established scales such as the FFM, but the incremental increase in validity was very modest. The EQ-i and similar measures tell us only a little more about the person than could be gauged from a standard personality assessment. A further weakness of questionnaire investigations is their neglect of objective behavioral criteria, although Bar-On (1997) does present some evidence linking the EQ-i to clinical criteria.

Thus, it is highly unlikely that the traits measured by EI scales will ever be as important in theory and practice as the major constructs of personality. Accepted personality scales like the California Personality Inventory (Gough, 1987) and NEO-PI-R (Costa & McCrae, 1992a) have a much greater depth of predictive and construct validation, and this validation continues to grow with further investigations. Nevertheless, EI traits may add to knowledge of personality at the margins. It is understood that primary traits may sometimes be more predictive of criteria than superfactors (e.g., Flett et al., 1995), and so it is not surprising that

EI traits possess modest incremental validity over the FFM (Saklofske et al., submitted). If these traits can be placed within a multistratum model, they may extend existing knowledge usefully. One possibility is that some, but not all, of the traits that contribute to EI may define a distinct primary trait that may be subsumed under the FFM (Petrides & Furnham, in press). In view of the efficacy of existing personality instruments and identified problems in self-report measures of EI, there would appear little reason for the practitioner to use a questionnaire measure of EI routinely. However, such measures may be useful in specific contexts where there is a prior rationale for supposing that the narrow trait or traits is relevant. For example, empathy may be relevant in studies of interpersonal cooperation, and alexithymia in certain clinical settings (see chapter 10). Our general recommendation is that research on emotional intelligence may be most productive when conducted at this more fine-grained level of analysis, matching specific traits to selected contexts or settings.

As a final comment on personality, we have a lingering feeling that EI research fails to separate style from substance adequately. For example, a person claiming to have high emotional sensitivity may be mistaken; as we saw in chapter 9, cognitive intelligence appears to be a better predictor of individual differences in emotion perception than is self-reported empathy (Davis & Kraus, 1997). Furthermore, the relationships between sensitivity and real-world effectiveness are not straightforward; excessive interpersonal sensitivity appears to relate to neurotic traits (McCabe et al., 1999, see also chapter 9). At an anecdotal level, former British premier Margaret Thatcher was notorious for insensitivity to others, and her famous dictum "There is no such thing as society" does not suggest a high level of interpersonal awareness. Although often unpopular with both colleagues and the general public, Mrs. Thatcher was highly successful in winning elections and translating her personal principles into legislation. Clearly, in terms of real-world success, bull-headed insensitivity can sometimes pay off. Indeed, as previously discussed (see chapter 11), traits correlating with EI (e.g., agreeableness and emotional stability) are rather weak predictors of occupational success (Matthews, 1997), and in some contexts may even be disadvantageous. Research on EI overstates the extent to which specific traits are generally desirable or undesirable, and understates the extent to which the costs and benefits of traits are context-dependent.

An open empirical question in urgent need of attention is whether the vast majority of self-report measures of EI reflect impression management and self-deception (notwithstanding Bar-On's, 1997, admirable but limited attempts to assess response bias). The documented tendency for the incompetent to grossly inflate their abilities in self-reports (Kruger & Dunning, 1999) is a particular concern. Given that people may be prone to both egoistic and moralistic self-presentation biases (Paulhus & John, 1998), we also wonder whether the more assertive elements of EI are biased by narcissistic self-aggrandizement, and the more prosocial elements by social conformity. We further speculate as to how the smooth (but superficial) public-relations expert, or the Machiavellian manipulator of others, would perform on a questionnaire measure of EI? As a general conclusion, elevating questionnaire-based EI to the status of a major construct grossly oversimplifies the subtle, multidimensional nature of personality and detracts from understanding human nature.

Reconceptualizing EI

It is an open question whether future research will arrive at a more solid operational definition of emotional intelligence. If not, emotional intelligence will come to be seen as a chimera, a fantastical creature made up by stitching together the parts of several real entities. A major difficulty is that tests of EI may, in fact, be assessing several conceptually different types of construct that should be distinguished (Zeidner, Matthews & Roberts, 2001). Differentiating different constructs may help to explain the lack of psychometric convergence between personalitylike and abilitylike tests, and between different scoring methods. There are at least six possible constructs that may be assessed, in varying proportions, by existing tests, and these should clearly be discriminated:

Basic emotional competencies   Tests of EI purport to measure competencies akin to fluid or crystallized intelligence, perhaps influenced by individual differences in brain function. There is little compelling evidence so far that any of the tests directly assess such competencies. Relatively low-level components of EI, such as emotion identification, should be the most amenable to measurement. Future research in this area might make more use of objective, chronometric testing. Certainly, there is scope for identifying primary abilities for processing emotion stimuli, but whether such abilities would support any higher-order factor is unknown.

Abstract knowledge of emotion   In intelligence research, it has proved useful to distinguish *knowledge* of specific content areas (e.g., of arts and sciences) from the basic competence assessed by IQ tests: over time, competence is invested in acquisition of intellectual knowledge (Acker-man, 1996). Likewise, one aspect of EI may simply be learned knowl-edge of how to interpret cues towards emotion, how to act in emotional situations, and other social skills. Such knowledge would be highly de-pendent on culture. Given that social competence is not a single homo-geneous entity (Topping, Bremner & Holmes, 2000), it is unclear whether any strong general factor would emerge. A feature of emotional knowl-edge is that some elements are abstract and may be expressed in the form of general, culturally shaped beliefs, whereas other knowledge is more context-bound, particular, and linked to personal circumstances.

The MEIS/MSCEIT appears to assess various aspects of abstract knowl-edge, for example, in tests of the understanding branch, which assess emotional vocabulary. Higher-level MEIS/MSCEIT tests for managing emotion may conflate general cultural beliefs with personalized knowl-edge, which factors in contextual influences. As the items include very little context, the respondent may fall back on general cultural stan-dards that do not reveal how the person would deal with a specific inci-dent involving specific persons. One approach to testing would be to assess explicitly the person's level of culture-specific knowledge by ask-ing which response to an item other people (of a given cultural profile) would typically choose. As the mean group response can be assessed independently, the person's knowledge of the group consensus can be objectively assessed. Abstract knowledge should be trainable in the class-room; indeed, undergraduate psychology courses may train this element of EI.

Contextualized knowledge of emotion   The person's knowledge of general cultural beliefs may be important, but it does not encompass the use of detailed contextual information to modulate understanding and re-sponse. Furthermore, much of the knowledge required for handling the somewhat familiar emotional encounters of everyday life is procedural-ized and implicit, and should be distinguished from explicit, declarative knowledge. The travails of social-intelligence research signals the diffi-culties of measuring context-bound interpersonal skills, and this aspect of EI presents the greatest measurement challenge. One might possibly develop measures akin to those of emotional tacit knowledge (see Stern-berg & Grigorenko, 2000) linked to specific contexts. In principle, as-sessment of behavioral response in emotional interpersonal situations would be the best approach to assessment of proceduralized knowledge, but at present, the costs of doing so on a standardized, mass-testing basis would be prohibitive. Perhaps advances in virtual reality and artificial (social) intelligence will eventually support testing of this kind. This form of EI should also be trainable, but through meaningful emotional experiences within specific contexts rather than through intellectual learning.

Personality traits   Empirical data show that much of what is assessed by self-report EI scales constitutes standard personality traits. Although a focus on EI may isolate some hitherto neglected details of personality, for the most part, the scales are redundant. As discussed in chapter 9, personality traits do not index any generalized competence or level of skill (Matthews, 1997, 1999). Instead, personality traits are linked to the major adaptive challenges faced by human beings, such as maintaining personal security (linked to neuroticism) and choosing novel over familiar social environments (extraversion). If personality is organized around these challenges, and not around emotion per se, the person's style of emotion regulation is likely to vary across challenges. A conscientious but neurotic person may successfully handle the demands of building a career through hard work and dedication, but struggle with intimate relationships, for example. People may have multiple social intelligences, depending on the context and what is at stake for the person. As discussed in chapter 9, the biological, information processing, and self-knowledge aspects of personality traits appear to be organized around different contexts for pursuit of adaptive goals. Individual differences in awareness and regulation of emotions may be too weak an influence on contextualized adaptation to appear as an individual difference dimension strongly distinct from existing constructs.

Outcomes of emotional or stressful encounters   As discussed in chapter 4, self-reports may assess the outcomes of emotional encounters. This is best exemplified by Bar-On's (1997) inclusion of general mood as a factor of the EQ-i, and by high correlations between EQ-i scores and overall levels of psychiatric symptoms (Bar-On, 1997). At one level, deconfounding EI from outcome is simply a matter of using greater care in sampling items. However, there is also a more subtle issue concerning the extent to which personal and situational factors interact to produce qualities of emotional intelligence. For example, awareness of the emotions of self and others might reflect not just some basic ability but being in a familiar social environment in which the rules of engagement are understood. It is easier to empathize with like-minded others, than with strangers or people from other cultures. In other words, emotional awareness may reflect not only a basic disposition but also the environment to which the person is exposed. Lack of emotional awareness may reflect not emotional illiteracy but the pressures of dealing with an unfamiliar social environment. Emotional intelligence in this sense may be a consequence of a settled lifestyle rather than a basic competence.

Emotional person-environment fit   An interactionist perspective on outcomes suggests a further conceptualization. Emotional disturbance and disharmony between emotion and cognition reflects a lack of *fit* between person and environment (or more specifically, the adaptive challenge). The concept of person-environment fit is well-known from occupational psychology (e.g., Schneider et al., 1997), in which it refers to the match between the demands of the workplace and the employee's values, goals, and skills. Perhaps the emotionally disturbed person is not the victim of some lack of basic competence, but is a fish out of water, in the sense of being confronted by unfamiliar challenges for which he or she is unprepared by biological predisposition and experience.

In discussing the MEIS/MSCEIT, the leading abilitylike test, we saw that the test developers are moving toward an operational definition of ability based on consensus scoring (Mayer, Caruso et al., 1999). That is, the closer the person is to the population norm, the more intelligent they are. We questioned the rationale for scoring an ability on this basis, but it serves excellently as an index of the fit between the person's beliefs about emotions and the cultural norm. In other words, the consensus-scored test may assess not so much ability, but cultural person-environment fit. It would be expected that a high degree of fit would be associated with better social adjustment, in that congruence between personal and cultural beliefs presumably promotes smoother social interactions and more positive appraisals by others. However, as fit is a relational construct, it is misleading to describe it as an intelligence (chapter 3; see also Roberts, Zeidner, et al., 2001).

Conceptualization and measurement: Conclusions

We have seen that there are serious psychometric weaknesses with all published tests of EI. The most serious problems appear to be redundancy with personality for self-report tests, and the weakness of the rationales for both expert and consensus scoring of abilitylike tests. These weaknesses are not necessarily fatal, and abilitylike tests in particular have considerable potential for further development. However, our closing thought for this section is that progress may require a much more detailed conception of what it means to be emotionally intelligent. As just described, there are at least six different senses of the term, which may be conflated in existing tests.

This is not a problem that can be tackled by blind factor analysis. For example, in intelligence research, we would almost certainly find a general factor within a set of measures including ability tests, grades on schoolwork assignments, and indices of socioeconomic status. However, such a general factor would not be very meaningful, because of its conflation of basic competence, educational attainment, and background environmental factors. What is required in research on EI is a more thorough conceptual analysis, perhaps along the lines suggested, to discriminate conceptually distinct domains and develop coherent measures within each domain. We have made some specific suggestions along these lines, in particular, to assess competence using information-processing tasks, to assess generic cultural knowledge by reference to consensus, and, entailing a greater challenge, to assess context-specific knowledge by tests analogous to those used to assess practical intelligence and tacit knowledge. We may also need to rethink a fundamental conceptual issue. Is EI an underlying competence? Is EI an outcome of more basic psychological factors? Perhaps neither is correct. Rather, EI (if it is anything at all) may be a transactional construct reflecting the degree of match between the person's competence and skills, and the adaptive demands of the environments to which the person is exposed.

Theoretical Issues

Throughout this book we have drawn attention to the limited theoretical basis for emotional intelligence, which, at worst, is often little more than a dating-agency list of desirable qualities. Existing work does indicate (somewhat sketchily) two theoretical perspectives that could be developed in future research. The first is the biological perspective, outlined by Goleman (1995, 2001), that EI represents some kind of interplay between relatively primitive limbic system centers for emotion and control systems in the frontal cortex. There is a rather limited amount of neurological and psychophysiological evidence that can be interpreted within such a framework (Bechara et al., 2000; Lane, 2000). The second perspective is cognitive-psychological and seeks to relate EI to specified information-processing routines. The best example is probably Salovey et al.'s (2000) account of how EI might be linked to coping.

Again, there is very limited evidence, although the EQ-i does appear to correlate with use of more effective coping strategies (Bar-On, 1997).

Both biological and cognitive approaches are potentially valuable, but existing research on EI has hardly begun to tackle the complex task of linking the construct to the huge research literature on emotion, and deriving and testing falsifiable hypotheses. In our analysis of emotion theory, we differentiated two essential steps in such an exercise. First, we need a process-level description of emotional intelligence. When more and less intelligent persons are faced with an emotional challenge, what neural and cognitive processes differ across the two individuals? Multiple levels of processing may be involved, and it is important to distinguish processes at the three levels of the cognitive-science framework (Pylyshyn, 1984) associated with the neural hardware, the information-processing software, and high-level motivations and self-knowledge (system functionality). Second, we need an analysis of how those individual differences in processing may be adaptive or maladaptive in real-world emotional encounters.

In this section, we examine the potential of biological and cognitive accounts of emotion for providing a theoretical basis for EI first at the process level. We follow this with some conclusions on whether individual differences in processing correspond in any simple way to individual differences in adaptation or adaptability.

Biological Bases of Emotional Intelligence

Biological approaches to emotional intelligence (e.g., Bechara et al., 2000) claim that specific brain systems, notably the amygdala and areas of frontal cortex, directly control emotion recognition, emotional conditioning, encoding and retrieval of emotional memories, and real-world decision making. EI may be seen as some overall quality of these several brain systems. There is little doubt that lesions to these brain areas disrupt emotional functioning (although the role of the amygdala in humans seems often to be overstated; see Aggleton & Young, 2000). Biological models have a significant contribution to make to understanding abnormalities of emotional functioning, but we identified various difficulties in linking normal variation in EI directly to brain systems. There are methodological difficulties associated with generalizing animal models to humans, with the distributed and modular nature of brain systems for emotion, with using brain-lesion studies to infer sources of normal variation in emotional functioning, and with the use of emotion as a construct whose existence is inferred (rather than directly measured).

There are also three serious constraints on how successful biological models are ever likely to be, even with improved methods. First, biological models tend to neglect the distinction between hardware and software levels of explanation, although there are some promising developments in using connectionist, neural-net models to interrelate the levels. If some internal program based on abstract representations controls emotional behavior, then localization of emotion provides, at most, only some indirect clues to the nature of the programming. Second, although in animals specific emotions may be tightly coupled to stereotyped responses, such as flight in the case of fear (see Panksepp, 1998), the link between emotion and behavior in humans is much looser. There is no simple isomorphism between emotion and response: studies of emotion and information processing demonstrate finely tuned cognitive control of behavior. Third, biological accounts tend to neglect cognitive control of outputs from the brain systems identified with emotion. No doubt, lower-level brain systems such as the amygdala provide signals that are coded symbolically and processed by higher-level, language-based cognition, but equally, the outputs of cognition feed downward to influence lower-level emotional functioning (e.g., Rolls, 1999).

It follows that purely neurological accounts of emotional intelligence are unlikely to take us very far in understanding individual differences in emotion-regulation. Contrary to claims made in the literature (e.g., Goleman, 1995), there is little evidence that neural processes directly control either irrational emotional outbursts or self-control. For example, panic attacks in part reflect a biologically based oversensitivity to stress (Barlow, 1988). However, research shows that much of the panic-disorder patient's vulnerability derives from cognitive factors: beliefs about the harmfulness of somatic reactions, low perceived control, and a tendency toward catastrophic cognitions (Clark, 1986; Schmidt & Woolaway-Bickel, in press).

On the positive side, the role of the orbitofrontal cortex in emotion-regulation and social-problem solving is worth further exploration (see Bechara et al., 2000; Rolls, 1999). There may be some specialization of frontal cortex into emotional and intellectual executive systems (see Duncan & Owen, 2000). As discussed in chapter 7, we might see EI as a property of an emotional executive. Indeed, if the functional role of such an executive is to interrupt the fixed, innate patterns of response characteristic of animal emotion (Panksepp, 1998), then emotional self-regulation may be a uniquely human quality. Given that localization alone is insufficient for explanation, a research priority is the investigation of the information-processing software supported by frontal systems, i.e., an account of individual differences in the cognitive architecture for processing emotional stimuli. There is considerable scope for applying *cognitive*-neuroscience methods, but animal models are almost certainly inadequate. However, even a cognitive neuroscience of emotion regulation does not address the adaptive significance of individual differences in architecture, for which a knowledge-level analysis is required.

Cognitive bases of emotional intelligence

The more sophisticated theoretical accounts of emotional intelligence (notably, Mayer, Caruso et al., 2000) are rooted in cognitive psychology. It seems plausible that people may differ in the processing routines that evaluate the emotional connotations of events, and select coping responses.

Two of the main attractions of the cognitive-psychological approach are its high degree of engagement with empirical data on emotion and behavior, and its scope for deriving testable predictions about individual differences in behavior. Furthermore, the cognitive psychology of self-regulation, by distinguishing self-referent metacognitive processing from immediate and possibly unconscious stimulus appraisal processes, may serve to differentiate emotional intelligence from emotion itself. Indeed, some evidence links EI to mood regulation (Ciarrochi et al., 2000a, 2001). Perhaps EI relates to some overall self-regulative efficiency that underpins accurate and detailed evaluation of emotions, and selection and control of responses. Concepts related to self-regulation and meta-cognition are at the cutting edge of the cognitive psychology of emotion (e.g., Boekaerts et al., 2000; Wells, 1999), and these are important issues to explore. However, there are various barriers for such a cognitive psychology of EI to overcome.

Some of these barriers reflect misunderstandings of cognitive psychology. Goleman (1995), for example, appears to identify cognition with slow, deliberate reasoning processes. This view is ill informed: cognition refers to the complete array of computational processes performed on abstract data representations, processes that include freewheeling parallel processing and unconscious, implicit processing, as well as step-by-step reasoning.

At a somewhat more sophisticated level, it is similarly erroneous to distinguish an emotional from a rational mind (see Epstein, 1998; Izard, 2001). As Clore and Ortony discuss in their important commentary (2000), both implicit and explicit thinking are equally cognitive (Lazarus, 1984, makes a similar point in rejecting Zajonc's distinction of separate emotion and cognition systems). It may well be productive to differentiate different cognitive systems, such as implicit and explicit cognition. To suppose, however, that there is some mysterious intuitive emotional system that does not operate cognitively is to abandon contact with both the empirical evidence and the conceptual clarity offered by cognitive science.

Cognition is better conceptualized as a complex of many separate but interacting components, regulated in part by a supervisory executive that can itself be split into component parts (Norman & Shallice, 1986). The conscious experience of emotion may be identified with specific key components, such as control signals for self-regulation (e.g., Oatley & Johnson-Laird, 1996). Although we can loosely speak of interaction between cognition and emotion, it is more accurate to refer to interaction between different subsystems of the cognitive architecture, a subset of which control conscious emotional experience. This perspectives support detailed accounts of changes in information-processing during emotional states, referring to cognitive functions such as selective attention (Wells & Matthews, 1994), working memory (Eysenck, 1992), and decision making (Forgas, 1995).

Although we might suppose that some individuals are generally superior in maintaining efficient function while emotional, the distributed, modular nature of cognition raises serious difficulties. Processing emotional stimuli depends on many independent subroutines at different levels of the cognitive architecture, some of which are stimulus-driven and automatic, and others of which are strategy-driven and controlled. Even appraisal itself is probably controlled by multiple mechanisms (Leventhal & Scherer, 1987). Cognitive theories of EI (e.g., Mayer, Caruso et al., 2000a) do not differentiate clearly between these different mechanisms, or link EI to an explicit cognitive architecture. There is little in the available empirical evidence to suggest any general factor for individual differences in the multiple processes that support self-regulation (e.g., conscious and unconscious appraisal processes), although further evidence is undoubtedly required. Furthermore, a description of how more and less emotionally intelligent individuals process information still fails to tackle the key issue of the adaptive value of those processing differences.

Coping and adaptation

Individual differences in neural and cognitive architectures may bias individuals towards more or less efficient emotional functioning. However, understanding how people may be generally more or less adapted to emotional circumstances requires a knowledge-level analysis of EI. The transactional theory of emotion (Lazarus, 1991, 1999) provides an account of emotion and its behavioral consequences in terms of the personal meaning of events and of high-level appraisal and coping processes (i.e., without formal computational specification). This level of analysis may well be the most appropriate one for understanding EI as an index of individual differences in adaptation (or adaptability) to emotional demands. In particular, the emotionally intelligent person should cope more adaptively (see Salovey et al., 1999) than the low-EI person, perhaps in part due to superior abilities to appraise emotions of self and others. There is indeed some research that links EI to individual differences in coping (Bar-On, 1997).

Unfortunately, the existing research literature does not support the notion of a continuum of adaptive competence. It is central to the transactional approach that emotions must be understood within the specific context in which they occur. Nevertheless, there is no necessary connection between how well different events are handled (although there are empirical links established by personality research). It is entirely consistent with the transactional approach that a former president of the United States should appear emotionally intelligent in connecting with the concerns of ordinary people on the campaign trail and emotionally unintelligent in handling romantic encounters. As discussed in chapter 8, there are fundamental difficulties in rating the outcomes of events in terms of adaptive success or failure, due to the many and sometimes conflicting criteria for adaptation that can be applied (Matthews & Zeidner, 2000). Furthermore, the empirical literature on individual differences in coping suggests that particular strategies are only weakly related to coping outcomes (Zeidner & Saklofske, 1996). Although the concept is superficially appealing, we cannot identify EI with emotional adaptivity.

Personality revisited

It is safe to say that nothing resembling EI emerges from the voluminous literature on stress and coping. Perhaps, though, coping researchers have focused too much on specific contexts, and neglected stable individual differences that may only become evident when data are aggregated across studies (see Matthews & Deary, 1998). There is a large personality literature that links traits to general styles of coping (e.g., Deary et al., 1996), although the extent to which these styles control coping within specific situations is moot. The psychometric evidence suggests that personalitylike questionnaires for EI are fatally compromised by their redundancy with existing personality scales, but perhaps we can reconceptualize these existing traits in terms of EI. Perhaps too there may be major adaptive processes for EI that generalize across psychometrically distinct traits.

In chapter 9 we reviewed the empirical data on personality and emotional function, focusing especially on negative emotionality, social competence, prosocial behavior, and self-control. There is extensive evidence that various personality traits, such as those described by the Five Factor model of personality (e.g., Costa & McCrae, 1992a), bias the experience of emotion, appraisal and coping, and behavior within emotional situations. However, the concept of EI adds nothing to existent personality theory. Indeed, to describe those individuals who are emotionally unstable or introverted or disagreeable or unconscientious as "emotionally unintelligent" is confusing on two counts. First, normal personality traits are neither adaptive nor maladaptive in any overall sense. Emotionally instability (neuroticism) confers benefits associated with threat sensitivity, introverts are superior to extroverts at handling monotony and sustaining performance, disagreeable persons may be more resilient in social conflict situations, and lack of conscientiousness relates to creativity and spontaneity. Instead, traits appear to specialize individuals for thriving in certain environments, at the expense of others (Matthews, 1997b; Zeidner & Matthews, 2000). To describe traits as markers for emotional intelligence obscures the subtle balance between dispositional costs and benefits.

Second, at the process level, traits relate to multiple, generally small biases in neural and cognitive architecture, and in self-regulative processes and self-knowledge (Matthews et al., 2000). These biases are in themselves typically adaptively neutral. For example, whether a bias towards selective attention of threat stimuli is adaptive or not depends entirely on the prevalence and nature of threat within a particular context, and upon the person's options for coping. The configurations of processing biases that support the trait obtain meaning from the support they provide to adaptation to particular environments. The major traits of the Five Factor model represent major adaptive challenges such as personal security (neuroticism), influence over others (extraversion), cooperation versus competition (agreeableness) and self-advancement within society (conscientiousness), which represent more fundamental challenges than emotion itself.

Theory: Conclusions

In part II of this book, we reviewed possible theoretical approaches to EI derived from four research areas: affective neuroscience, the cognitive psychology of emotion, coping and stress research, and personality. We can summarize the conclusions of the review as follows:

• To equate EI with neurological properties of brain systems is conceptually naive and of little use in explaining empirical data on human emotional function. The executive role of the orbitofrontal cortex and other frontal systems, such as the cingulate cortex, is a potentially important component of the theory of EI. However, current research does not provide either an adequate account of the emotional information processing that these brain systems support or of biological bases for individual differences in processing.

• EI may potentially be linked to individual differences in the information-processing routines of self-regulation and executive control. However, EI does not appear to map onto the component processes of self-regulation in any coherent way, and the construct offers a highly impoverished view of higher-order emotion regulation, that represents a step backward from existing cognitive models. Much EI work rests on a false separation of conscious reason and unconscious passion, and neglects the key issue of the cognitive architecture supporting different aspects of information-processing related to emotion.

• It appears attractive to link EI to knowledge-level emotional constructs such as the personal meaning of events, appraisal, and coping. However, research in this area provides little conceptual basis or empirical evidence for rank-ordering people in terms of degree of adaptedness or adaptivity. Whether people cope effectively or ineffectively is often dependent on both the context, and on the criteria chosen to define effectiveness.

• The personality traits that overlap with EI as defined by self-report are richly correlated with various subjective and objective indices of emotional functioning, and with neural and cognitive processes supporting adaptation. However, traits such as those of the FFM appear to relate to various adaptive specializations rather than to overall emotional adaptedness. Work on narrow traits sometimes linked to EI, such as empathy and alexithymia (see chapter 10) has been valuable in understanding personality and emotion, but there is no psychometric or theory-based rationale for grouping these traits together under the umbrella of EI.

Overall, our conclusions concerning the prospect for a coherent theory of EI supported by empirical evidence are pessimistic for both ability and mixed (i.e., personalitylike) approaches to the construct. We do not find any clear continuum of emotional competence in brain function, in basic information-processing, in high-level cognitions of person-environment interaction, or by reconceptualizing existing personality traits. Within the normal range of function, it is difficult to link neural and cognitive architectures to adaptive constructs. From the ability perspective, it is certainly worth probing further into individual differences in emotion processes. Perhaps abilities such as emotion perception can be linked to specific brain systems or information-processing routines. Such research is of course at an early stage of development, and no definitive conclusion is possible. So far, there appears little evidence that would suggest that abilities defined in terms of objectively assessed processing efficiencies would prove to be linked either to each other (and hence to some general intelligence) or to real-world adaptive outcomes.

Research on stress and personality deals with adaptive constructs but fails to support the idea that some people are geniuses of adaptation, handling all challenges with equal facility, whereas others struggle to cope regardless of circumstances. Instead, personality traits define multiple and independent patterns of context-dependent strength and weakness, with emotional outcomes primarily representing the person's capabilities for handling the specific demands of the context concerned. For example, neurotic individuals tend to be anxious in stressful social situations because they are cognitively (and, arguably, neurologically) ill equipped to handle specific demands such as handling criticism from others, not because of any generalized deficit in EI. The personalitylike side of EI research appears to be based on fundamental misconceptions about the nature of individual differences in managing emotional encounters.

Applied Issues

In general, the significance of EI for applied psychology is very limited, and largely confined to fine-tuning existing techniques. The root problem is that EI is too generalized a construct to be useful. Successful interventions require a relatively fine-grained understanding of the individual. We saw in chapter 11 that although disturbance of emotional function is a common symptom of clinical disorders, there are various, qualitatively different sources of disturbance, requiring different therapeutic approaches. To label the patient as "emotionally illiterate" simply does not suggest any additional therapeutic direction. In educational and occupational psychology too, there is no evidence to date that some context-free, generic EI may be trained. On the contrary, interventions appear most effective when directed at some specific problem or issue.

The problem is compounded by the conceptual and psychometric limitations of current measures of EI. If, as we have argued, they represent admixtures of genuine abilities, cultural and contextual knowledge, personality, and person-environment fit, scores on the tests are open to too many interpretations to be practically useful. We cannot with confidence, interpret a low test-score as indicating any fundamental lack of competence, and we cannot assume that an increase in test score represents acquisition of competence. It is questionable whether use of test scores for selecting individuals for jobs or training courses would be legally defensible. A job applicant who was unsuccessful because of a low consensus-scored test result might bring a legal case on the basis that the low score primarily represented the person responding differently to other people, rather than the inability to answer the questions correctly. There is a place for existing tests in research, but it is undesirable that test scores should determine real-life decisions concerning individual respondents.

The concept of EI is perhaps least useful in *clinical psychology*, where the principle of taking emotions seriously is already ingrained. Psychological therapies already make use of a rich array of therapeutic techniques directed towards the various abnormal processes that underlie pathology. For example, the various anxiety and mood disorders that require clinical treatment have a number of common sources, such as deep-rooted negative self-beliefs, maladaptive emotion-focused coping, and persevering worry. However, treatment requires a detailed understanding of the cognitive content and process unique to each disorder and, indeed, to the individual patient (e.g., Wells, 1997). In general, emotional disorders require not the enhancement of EI, but the active engagement of the patient in interactions with the outside world that correct faulty beliefs and promote successful coping. On the positive side, there are already some therapeutic techniques that relate to EI, such as targeting the alexithymic patient's skills in recognizing and discussing emotions (Parker, 2000). Similarly, cognitive therapy for PTSD already involves the use of narratives that allow negative emotions and fears to be assimilated (Resick & Schnicke, 1992).

In *educational* settings, the concept of EI has proven itself a catalyst to the thinking and planning of educators and policy makers with respect to training social and emotional skills in the schools. It has also heightened willingness of school policy makers and administrators to implement emotional literacy programs and interventions in the classroom. Proponents of EI have supported and added impetus to the trend of bringing emotional literacy into schools and making emotions and social life themselves key topics for learning and discussion. EI research has recognized the potential for using the school setting as one of the most important contexts for learning and teaching of emotional skills and competencies. The school and community may be used as a means of training emotional competencies for real life and fostering the development of specific skills in these areas (e.g., recognition of emotions in self and others, empathy, conflict resolution). In general, EI research has been consistent with a rising tide of understanding among educators that children's emotional learning is not outside the mandate of the school and indeed should be given serious consideration and promoted in schools.

Despite the role of EI research in strengthening emotional education and life skills training programs, we saw in chapter 11 that, so far, the demonstrable contribution of work on EI has been slight. Indeed, it is hard to see how the contribution of EI could be other than limited, given that we know so little about the development and determinants of EI. There are no published behavioral genetic studies using conventional measures of EI to tease apart biology from environment. Also, we know little about the socialization of EI aside from research on separate competencies (emotional awareness and understanding, empathy, emotion regulation). Research is needed to allow us to make substantiated statements on the environmental and genetic determinants of EI. In contrast to the vast body of developmental literature on general intelligence, empirical research on the development of EI is scant indeed.

In consequence, there is little objective evidence attesting to the useful role of EI as a predictor of school success and adjustment above and beyond that predicted by intelligence and personality factors. There is a plethora of programs seeking to inculcate emotional and social competencies (life-skills training, self science, education for care, social awareness, social-problem solving, social competency, and resolving conflicts creatively) that predates the notion of EI. However, despite the claims that EI skills can be cultivated and improved in the classrooms, the contributions of the numerous existing programs touted as EI interventions are modest. Most were not designed as EI programs and there are very few systematic interventions that meet the canons of internal and external validity in their design. There are serious methodological problems with validation of school-based programs. These include nonequivalence of experimental and control groups, poor documentation of methods, overreliance on self-report criteria of success, poor generalizability of methods, and failure to assess longer-term outcomes. Where evaluation is possible, outcomes tend to be mixed and/or moderate (Topping, Holmes & Bremner, 2000). It has also not been demonstrated that interventions focusing on the core constructs of EI, such as emotional awareness, are more successful than those based on other principles, such as behavior modification.

In *occupational settings,* EI research has increased awareness of the potential role that a wide array of emotional competencies may play at the worksite (e.g., emotional awareness, empathy, conflict resolution, and emotion regulation). EI research has helped increase awareness in top and middle management about the importance of empathy in managers (awareness of other's feelings, needs, and concerns) and the need to be receptive to workers' feelings and needs at the worksite. Conversely, awareness of EI has legitimized the practice among workers of acknowledging and feeling emotions experienced at the worksite, rather than denying or minimizing them. Moreover, it has increased awareness of the importance of listening to the information or feedback the emotion is giving one at the workplace. It is also inspiring research that may shed light on the reciprocal relations between work and emotions, with emotions potentially influencing work-related cognitive and motivational processes, which in turn affect task and social behavior, and performance outcomes.

The limitations of occupational EI research are in some ways similar to the shortcomings of educational research. The ratio of hyperbole to hard evidence is rather high, with overreliance on anecdote and unpublished surveys. EI has been commonly claimed to be useful in occupational assessment, prediction, selection, and on the job performance, with half a dozen books of papers and workshops devoted to describing the usefulness of EI in the occupational environment. However, a review of the empirical evidence provides little justification for such unfettered enthusiasm surrounding the construct in career selection and assessment. In fact, there is not one single study, published in a peer-reviewed journal, that shows that EI predicts occupational success/performance above (and beyond) that predicted by IQ. Initial reports of studies using the current wave of EI measures do not suggest that they will add much predictive power to existing instruments (Janovics & Christiansen, 2001). Furthermore, meta-analyses based on existing personality research (Barrick & Mount, 1991; Tett et al., 1991) show very clearly that personality constructs related to EI such as neuroticism (i.e., stress vulnerability) are only weakly related to job performance. In turn, this finding implies that EI scales are unlikely to be more than modestly predictive of occupational success.

There are clearly benefits to effective training and development programs designed to promote emotional competencies in the workplace. Thus, some promising steps are being taken in program development (Cherniss et al., 1998), although it often seems that changing the organization is more beneficial than changing the worker (Burke, 1993). Again, it is unclear that it is useful to characterize effective interventions as raising EI, when, in fact, programs may variously develop generic social and communication skills, specific job skills, and techniques for coping with stress. Given that different jobs call for different amounts of social and emotional involvement and activity and for different types of interpersonal interaction, a more differentiated conceptualization discriminating different kinds of skills may be more practically valuable.

Applications: Conclusions

The benefits of EI appear to reside mainly in raising awareness of emotional issues and motivating educators and managers to take emotional issues seriously. There is a growing realization that psychological processes considered to be purely cognitive or intellectual in fact depend on a synergy between cognition and emotion (or, strictly, between different modes of cognition). Consequently, it is increasingly seen as legitimate to develop programs for improving emotional skills in the classroom and workplace. Whether or not these programs are actually fostering EI competencies, various useful skills are most likely learned during participation in these programs. These include labeling and describing emotions and enriching linguistic experiences; appraisals of basic emotions in oneself and others; management of emotions; conflict management; taking perspective of others; verbal communication skills; decision-making and problem-solving techniques; cultivating a positive outlook toward life; assertiveness training; effective peer-relation training; promoting health; preventing alcohol, tobacco, and drug use; reducing violence; and developing positive self-esteem. We suspect that such skills are typically specific to the life issue concerned, without building any general set of competencies, or contributing to solving other problems, but future research may show otherwise. Currently, EI mostly serves a cheerleading function, helping to whip up support for potentially (though not always actually) useful interventions focused on a heterogeneous collection of emotional, cognitive, and behavioral skills.

The Science and Myth of Emotional Intelligence

Toward a science of emotional intelligence?

It is uncontroversial to advocate the development of a psychological science of emotion regulation. Indeed, much of the existing research literature on emotion, personality, and self-regulation may be seen exactly in this light. People differ in their processing of emotional information, and the differences between individuals have important consequences for mental health, social functioning, and educational and career success. Research on EI has undoubtedly had heuristic value in focusing the attention of researchers on such issues. The more controversial issue is whether the various existing lines of research can be tied together as facets of emotional intelligence. As we have seen, some of these facets include development of reliable and valid tests for EI, explanations for variation in EI in terms of underlying neural and cognitive processes, integration of EI with the existing differential psychology of intelligence and personality, and practical applications directed explicitly at improving EI.

Research on these topics has some positive features. Both self-report and ability-test scales give reliable overall scores that predict relevant external criteria. We see the ability test approach, exemplified by the MEIS/MSCEIT (e.g., Mayer, Caruso et al., 2000a), as the more promising of the two approaches, given redundancy between self-report EI and existing personality factors. The four branches of emotional intelligence in the Mayer-Salovey-Caruso model provide a focus for future empirical studies that might, for example, examine sources of emotion identification in more detail, and chart their implications for real-world functioning. From the mixed-model, personalitylike perspective, the most promising work appears to be that directed towards relatively narrow constructs such as alexithymia (that predate EI). In general, the development of reliable tests, that can be refined further, creates a starting-point for validation studies. In turn, these may turn out to be informative about the nature and significance of individual differences in emotion-regulation both in the laboratory and in applied settings. There is also considerable scope for construct-validation studies that may link the constructs assessed by the tests to neural and cognitive architectures, and to high-level self-regulation.

Myths of emotional intelligence

We hold that myth is, in its most general and comprehensive nature, the spontaneous and imaginative form in which the human intelligence and human emotions conceive and represent themselves and things in general.

Tito Vignoli, 1882

Despite some promising research developments, we have identified various 'mythical' beliefs about EI that are not scientifically supported. There appear to be four central, defining myths around which the multiple shortcomings we have identified cohere:

Emotional intelligence is a generalized, far-reaching personal quality covering almost all aspects of emotional functioning   Goleman (1995) and, to some extent, Bar-On (1997, 2000) appear to claim that all desirable aspects of emotional function reflect a general factor of EI. Such a factor would be on a par with IQ in bringing together many apparently distinct personal qualities. We seen that tests of EI fail, thus far, to meet psychometric criteria, or even to correlate highly with one another. In addition, the extensive literature on personality shows that qualities such as resilience under stress, self-control, sensitivity to others and social assertiveness are distinct constructs that relate to differing fundamental personality dimensions, and to differing psychological processes. Ability-based approaches to EI generally make more modest claims (e.g., Mayer, Salovey, et al., 2000), though it remains an open question whether there is some general factor for emotional information-processing. Thus far, the search for EI has discovered not some new continent, but what may be a rather minor province of terrain already charted.

Emotional intelligence is directly based on brain systems for emotion   Goleman (1995, 2000) seeks to give EI scientific credibility by linking the construct to brain structures such as amygdala and orbitofrontal cortex. The link is not entirely mythical, in that brain lesions to these structures produce deficits in behaviors related to emotion. Nevertheless, there is no evidence that individual differences, in the normal range, map in any direct way to variation in brain function. The evidence from personality studies is critical here. Certainly, the personality traits that correlate with

EI are substantially heritable, indicating a biological basis for personality. However, psychophysiological studies of personality implicate a wide variety of brain structures (e.g., Zuckerman, 1991), going beyond the traditional emotion centers. In addition, biological models have fared poorly in attempting to explain objective behavioral correlates of personality, and, in general, cognitive-psychological models have greater explanatory power and more predictive success empirically (Matthews & Gillliland, 1999).

Emotional intelligence is critical for real-world success   It is claimed that EI may be the single most important factor predicting job success, especially within a given job category or profession (Goleman, 2001). There is no evidence in peer-reviewed journals to support this claim. The personality literature suggests that the validity of EI measures as predictors of job performance is likely to be modest, and often less than IQ. Similarly, the patterning of adaptive costs and benefits associated with the personality traits linked to EI, suggests that measures of EI cannot be used to index some overall "aptitude for life." The overlap of EI-as-personality with emotional stability (low neuroticism) ensures that tests such as the EQ-i and SSRI will robustly predict happiness and life satisfaction, but this subjective outcome dissociates from objective behavioral indices.

Raising emotional intelligence is essential for countering social disintegration   The preface to Goleman's (1995) book highlights what he perceives as a social crisis, described in flowery phrases such as "the disintegration of civility and safety," "surging rage and despair," and "the rotting of the goodness of our communal lives." The remedy is the teaching of emotion intelligence in schools and, a theme developed in a later book (Goleman, 2000), promoting EI in the workplace. It is questionable whether civilization is falling apart quite so catastrophically. In any case, while it is plausible that school-based programs for EI are beneficial, there is no convincing evidence showing dramatic changes in adaptation, in part because of methodological deficiencies in studies conducted so far. In the occupational and clinical domains, interventions based on EI appear to add little to existing techniques.

In the absence of definitive research findings, we cannot be sure that the myths are entirely false. However, at the least, these sweeping claims are inadequately supported by empirical evidence, and there are solid indications from existing ability and personality research that the claims made are either false or highly overstated. Indeed, while Goleman's (1995) vision has been widely disseminated, much of the empirical research in the area is more sober in its conclusions. It is surprising that exaggerated and very possibly false statements can command such widespread public acceptance. Here, we must point to the deficiencies of the scientific studies conducted to date (while recognizing that these deficiencies are in large measure due to the preliminary nature of the research). As described above, there are major conceptual, psychometric, and theoretical problems to be overcome before EI may be considered a genuine, scientifically validated construct.

Conceptually, there is no agreement among researchers concerning the proper domain for EI and its alignment with intelligence and personality. Psychometric problems include the questionable rationales for scoring abilitylike tests, redundancy with personality for self-report tests, lack of convergence between different tests, and lack of discriminant validity. These are exacerbated by a raft of problems with specific tests, such as poor subscale reliabilities and suspect factor structures. There are also issues related to the culture and gender fairness of the tests, given that scoring method appears to influence group differences (Roberts, Zeidner, et al., 2001). The main theoretical problems (in part reflecting neglect of construct validity) include ambiguity about the processes supporting EI, and failure to develop and test acceptable criteria for individual differences in real-world adaptation. These various problems may or may not be insuperable, but existing research does not yet even show that EI exists as a well-defined psychometric and theoretical construct, let alone that it is critical for adaptation to real-world emotional challenges.

Future prospects for emotional intelligence

This review has identified many weaknesses of research on EI, but it is important not to squash potentially informative research in its early stages. Salovey et al. (2000) have answered critics of EI by drawing a parallel with the decision of the French Academy of Sciences to destroy all meteorites housed in museums because they are "heavenly bodies" and heaven does not exist. Nevertheless, we have seen that there are sufficient problems demonstrated by research for us to take a skeptical line (in the sense of questioning rather than dismissing) in future studies. Roberts, Zeidner, et al. (2001) compared EI to the canals of Mars: even accomplished scientists sometimes see illusory patterns in data.

Test development has advanced to the stage where we can expect conceptually coherent scales for EI that meet normal psychometric standards. By analogy with research on cognitive abilities (e.g., Carroll, 1993),
researchers should search systematically for primary mental abilities of
emotion, perhaps placing them within a multi-stratum model. In addition to measurement issues, there is a pressing need for construct validity research into the neurological and cognitive correlates of EI scales,
using objective criteria. Such research requires a focus on discriminant
validity with respect to existing measures, especially in the case of self-
report. Believers and skeptics alike should address the reliability and
validity issues we have highlighted here, seeking to place the sounder
psychometric constructs within the existing framework of differential
psychology.

Finally, although EI appears to be more myth than science, we should
not underestimate the power of myth. Vignoli (1882), one of the pioneers of positivism, saw myth and science as two fundamental modes of
engaging with the meaning of sensory phenomena. Myths live on in
modern society, as sources of inspiration and motivation and as a device
for translating the unconscious mind into externalized form (Bruner,
1962). Indeed, science itself gives us the myth of the scientist as hero
who, like Galileo and Darwin, struggles against the prejudice of society
but eventually (possibly posthumously) prevails through genius and
dedication. Myths, like those of racial superiority, may also be sinister
and socially harmful. Henry Murray (1962), best known for his work on
personality, listed various properties of myths, including their functions.
This functional analysis provides us with a different perspective on EI, as
a modern myth, or at least a mythic fragment of some myth in the making. The functions of myth, according to Murray (1962), include an
educational function of inspiring effort toward some better way of life.
The EI myth tells us that we should seek self-understanding in order to
further our relationships with others and the common good. It has a
convictional function in maintaining belief and faith, perhaps as a fable
or parable. Through its apparent status as science, the EI myth adds
conviction to the self-help movement in contemporary society. Myth has
a *cynosural* function in that it is "peculiarly and mysteriously attractive
to the senses and imagination" (Murray, 1962, p. 23), inspiring imaginative symbolism. The striking anecdotes in Goleman's (1995) book on
EI serve this function. (The negative view of IQ presented in this book
may serve as what Murray calls a *deterrent* myth that seeks to weaken dis-
valued dispositions). Finally, myths subserve an *integrational* function
that unifies the individual personality or a group of people around a

collective mythic ideology. An important part of the EI agenda appears to be making EI the unifying theme of educational and occupational interventions. In one sense, then, EI may represent a myth of personal and social enlightenment that is best located as a topic for sociological investigation.

Scientists too are not immune to myth. Through examination of nineteenth-century science, Vignoli (1882, pp. 238–239), established that "science itself still nourishes myths within its pale, although unconsciously and in their most rational form." Vignoli rejoiced that experimental psychologists such as Fechner and Wundt had overthrown the myths of their field and created a psychology implying the absence of a soul. A casual glance at the history of psychology in the last century suggests his optimism may have been misplaced; certainly, psychology is more open to mythic infiltration than the physical sciences. The failure of the self-esteem movement in American education illustrates that the vulnerability of the field to inspiring but wrong-headed ideas (see Dweck, 2000; Stout, 2000).

Of course, beliefs that are unsubstantiated by evidence are undesirable and should be exposed, especially if science as being used as a figleaf for dubious real-world applications and claims. Nevertheless, myths may play a positive role even within science. Sometimes in psychology an idea can act as a soupstone, which is falsely believed to be an essential ingredient of theory but nevertheless stimulates research (Navon, 1984). Stankov (2001a) has suggested that EI is a soupstone of this kind. In short, we do not actually need the concept to understand individual differences in emotional function, but both Goleman's (1995) book and scientific studies (see Bar-On & Parker, 2000) have increased interest in this important area of psychology. At a cultural level, science benefits from both consensus and controversy. For example, the suspect science and politics advanced by *The Bell Curve* (Herrnstein & Murray, 1994) spurred the American Psychological Association to issue a more balanced report on intelligence (APA, 1997). In turn, this report drew attention to findings incompatible with the view that IQ is destiny. These include the Flynn effect, the tendency for IQ scores to increase across generations (Flynn, 1998). Similarly, the self-correcting nature of science will, in our view, lead to a deeper understanding of individual differences in emotion regulation. Perhaps the large shadow currently cast by emotional intelligence will appear as the projection of the bright light of publicity on a relatively small, but nonetheless significant, body of evidence.

Appendix A: A Review and Critique of Social Intelligence

In chapter 3 we made passing references to the concept of social intelligence, alluding to overlap with the concept of EI. It is rather curious that many extant conceptualizations of EI grant social intelligence rather brief coverage, perhaps (and this is a rather cynical assertion) because the latter concept remains highly contentious. In the passages that comprise this appendix, we review research conducted into the concept of social intelligence, along the way raising both positive and negative features of its theoretical, empirical, and practical underpinnings.

Origins

As we discussed briefly in chapter 2, psychological investigation of social intelligence has its origins in a paper by Edward Thorndike (1920), which suggested a partitioning of intelligence into three distinct concepts—social, abstract, and mechanical. Thorndike's definition of social intelligence highlighted "the ability to understand and manage men and women, boys and girls—to act wisely in human relations" (1920, p. 227). The concept of social intelligence received rapid acceptance among differential psychologists and spawned a great deal of research during the 1920s and 1930s. However, these pioneering attempts to measure social intelligence were generally unsuccessful. In particular, researchers consistently discovered that tests designed to assess social intelligence loaded on factors defined by existing measures of verbal ability (e.g., Gresvenor, 1927; R. Thorndike & Stein, 1937; Woodrow, 1939). After these early failures, interest in social intelligence waxed and waned considerably. Because this intermittence has become a feature of this field, social intelligence has often been described as a cyclical concept, which drifts in and out of favor as a hot research topic (Walker & Foley, 1973).

By 1960, Cronbach concluded that despite "fifty years of intermittent investigation ... social intelligence remains undefined and unmeasured" (1960/1970, p. 319). Most researchers accepted Cronbach's conclusions that "enough attempts were made to indicate that this line of approach is fruitless," but few considered on what basis these conclusions were drawn.[1] The main basis for Cronbach's pronouncements would appear a study conducted by Robert Thorndike and Stein (1937). Yet, close examination of that article leaves one optimistic that social intelligence might be a viable construct. Robert Thorndike and Stein argued, "Whether there is any unitary trait corresponding to social intelligence remains to be demonstrated" (1937, p. 284), but not that this demonstration would be impossible. In fact, they suggested that with further investigation (using scales with less verbal content than their own and taking a multidimensional view of social intelligence) the construct might ultimately be operationalized.

Guilford's Studies of Behavioral Content

Cronbach's invocation, coupled with the rise of modern cognitive psychology, ensured that little research was conducted into the construct of social intelligence for close to two decades. A notable exception during this period was the work of Guilford and his associates (see Guilford & Hoepfner, 1971; Hendricks, Guilford & Hoepfner, 1969; O'Sullivan & Guilford, 1975; O'Sullivan, Guilford & deMille, 1965; Tenopyr, Guilford & Hoepfner, 1966). Consistent with the central tenets of the structure of intellect model, Guilford, and colleagues, attempted to identify various factors of behavioral cognition. This construct was defined as the "the ability to cognize or understand the thoughts, feelings, or intentions of other people as they are expressed in behavior" (O'Sullivan & Guilford, 1976, p. 2). Tests assessing factors (recall these are defined as the cross of product, content, and operations in Guilford's theory, sometimes referred to as trigrams, and numbering up to 30) include the following:

Expression grouping This test is reportedly a non-verbal measure of social perception involving abstracting common attributes from behavioral or expressive stimuli. Each item of the test consists of three drawings depicting facial expressions, hand gestures, or body postures that show the same thought, feeling, orientation (e.g., happiness, nervousness) (see figure A.1). Participants demonstrate understanding of the underlying behavioral class by selecting from four alternative drawings, the

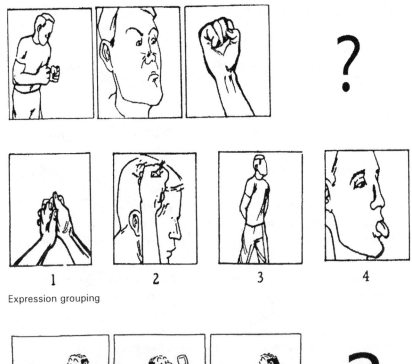

Expression grouping

Missing cartoons

Figure A.1
Two of the social intelligence tests from Guilford's Behavioral Cognition domain. (Select a frame to replace the question mark.)

option belonging with the initial items. The split-half reliability of expression grouping is reported to be only marginally adequate, i.e., 0.61 (see O'Sullivan & Guilford, 1976).

Inflections   In this test, participants are given four pictured facial expressions accompanied by a (prerecorded) spoken word or phrase. The participant's task is to find the picture that matches the auditory stimuli. The reported reliability of this measure is clearly inadequate, i.e., 0.26 (see O'Sullivan et al., 1965), suggesting findings with this test should minimally be treated with caution.

Missing cartoons   In this test, an incomplete cartoon strip is presented (see figure A.1). The participant's task is to choose from four alternatives a cartoon panel that would properly complete the cartoon strip, thus making sense of the feelings and thoughts of the characters. The split-half reliability of missing cartoons is reported to be adequate, i.e., 0.82 (see O'Sullivan & Guilford, 1976).

Facial situations   In this test, the individual is given two pictures of facial expressions and three statements. The participant is required to choose the statement best describing the situation that would go with both pictures. Reported reliabilities, i.e., 0.33 (see O'Sullivan et al., 1965), as for inflections, appear to render the test problematic.

Social translations   O'Sullivan and Guilford (1976) claim that this test measures the ability to assess interpersonal relationships and understand the meaning of verbal and behavioral cues in different contexts. Each of the items comprising this test consists of a short verbal statement (e.g., "Thank you") made between people in a defined relationship (e.g., boss and secretary). Three alternative pairs of relationships are provided (e.g., beggar to stranger, father to son, and chauffeur to boss) and participants are required to identify the two people between whom the statement would have a *different* meaning or intention. Social Translations is unique among behavioral-cognition tests in that it employs printed words only. The split-half reliability of Social Translations is reported to be 0.85 (O'Sullivan & Guilford, 1976).

In the studies conducted with these measures, Guilford and colleagues generally report that hypothesized factors are well defined by their correspondent marker tests. However, as noted above, the reliance by this research group, on subjective factor analytical procedures and single instruments to define constructs, brings each of these findings into question. In his extensive meta-analysis of the psychometric literature Carroll (1993, p. 526–531), contrary to what is claimed by proponents of the structure of intellect model, consistently found evidence for only one factor, which he interpreted as knowledge of behavioral content. Moreover, Carroll found that this factor tends to relate too highly to a higher-order, general intelligence factor. One reason this might not be all that surprising is that several of the tests bear close parallels to established intelligence tests. For example, missing cartoons is not unlike picture arrangement, an established performance IQ subtest of one of the world's most well know cognitive ability measures, the Wechsler Adult Intelligence Scales (see, e.g., Wechsler, 1981). In light of all of this, Carroll recommends that this research domain would profit considerably from "a reasonable taxonomy of behavioral content knowledge, and the construction of measures of different sub-classifications of such a taxonomy" (1993, p. 531).

The Resurgence of Social Intelligence: Recent Findings

After another period of relative dormancy, the 1980s ushered in renewed interest into the concept of social intelligence (see, e.g., Brown & Anthony, 1990; Cantor & Kihlstrom, 1987; Kosmitzki & John, 1993; Legree, 1995; Riggio, Messamer & Throckmorton, 1991; Stricker & Rock, 1990). This trend may be traced, in part, to a move by the prevailing zeitgeist to consider the importance of implicit theories of intellectual functioning, an issue discussed earlier. Also of import was the development (and influence) of both Sternberg's and Gardner's systems theories, both of which, as we have shown, contain concepts that bear more than passing similarities to social intelligence.

A controversial paper by Keating (1978) also appears to have contributed to this resurgent interest in social intelligence. Keating used (a) factor and correlational analysis in the hope of identifying separate academic and social intelligence clusters and (b) multiple regression procedures to predict self-reported social behavior from cognitive measures of social intelligence. His study employed three cognitive tests and three tests assessing behavioral components within a social domain. Neither Keating's attempt to distinguish between intelligences nor his efforts to predict social behavior succeeded. His results imply that social intelligence falls within the realm of intelligence, but not as a separate capability. Keating concluded, "The putative domain of social intelligence lacks empirical coherency, at least as far as it is represented here" (1978, p. 221). Keating attributed this failure, in part, to the possibility that the measures selected to represent the domain of social intelligence were somehow inadequate. He speculates, for instance, that the paper and pencil format (with delimited response options) of many cognitively oriented social intelligence tests bias individuals towards academic styles of reasoning.

Using a similar methodology, but employing different instruments, Ford and Tisak (1983) were able to identify a domain of social intelligence that appears empirically coherent. The success of Ford and Tisak is generally attributed to their use of a behavioral effectiveness definition of social intelligence. These researchers also used multiple measures of relevance to the social intelligence construct (e.g., self, teacher, and peer ratings of social competence and a behavioral observation) (see Carroll, 1993, p. 531). Three sets of analyses similar to those performed by Keating (1978) successfully uncovered and validated a domain of social intelligence. Factor analysis revealed a distinct dimension of social intelligence; correlations also displayed convergent-discriminant validity. A stepwise multiple regression analysis demonstrated that ratings of social competence predicted observed social behavior better than did measures of academic intelligence. Thus, some support for the independence of academic and social intelligence was obtained, although differences in methods used to assess the two forms of intelligence could have contributed to the pattern of results.

Marlowe (1986) tried to provide further evidence that social and academic intelligence could be distinguished. He was also interested in examining the hypothesis that cognitive components of social intelligence formed a complex multidimensional factor structure. Yet Marlowe's positive findings (like those obtained by Ford and Tisak [1983]) must be interpreted with some degree of caution, largely because social and academic intelligence were assessed via notably different methodologies. Academic intelligence was measured by performance, whereas social intelligence was assessed through the use of self-report questionnaires.

Nevertheless, Barnes and Sternberg (1989) found that cognitive aspects of social intelligence (the ability to decode nonverbal cues) and behavioral aspects of social intelligence (self-reported social competence) were moderately correlated with one another. Perhaps more important, Barnes and Sternberg also found that cognitive aspects of social intelligence were not meaningfully correlated with academic intelligence (i.e., traditional tests of mental ability). Thus, evidence exists that academic intelligence can be discriminated from cognitive and behavioral aspects of social intelligence, particularly in those instances in which cognitive notions of social intelligence are defined with reference to complex decoding skills.

A more recent study by Wong, Day, Maxwell, and Meara (1995) used a multitrait-multimethod design, along with confirmatory factor analysis, to find that cognitive and behavioral aspects of social intelligence could be discriminated from academic intelligence. They also demonstrated that some cognitive aspects of social intelligence could be discriminated from one another (in particular, social insight, social perception, and social knowledge). From these findings, Wong et al. (1995) argue that cognitive social intelligence is composed of several related but conceptually independent aspects.

Social Intelligence: A Critique

Overall, research into the conceptual status of social intelligence has provided mixed results. Distilling the findings reviewed above, one of four possibilities emerges:

• Social intelligence is an empirically coherent domain of intelligence, separate from traditional academic intelligence.

• Social intelligence is nothing but a proxy for general, academic intelligence (i.e., psychometric *g* or more correctly, when one examines the tests more closely, crystallized intelligence).

• Social intelligence is closely linked to personality, making it a misnomer to call it a form of intelligence.

• Since implicit theories strongly indicate social intelligence to be a form of cognitive ability then it must similarly be included in explicit theories. The impetus is on the research community to give it greater scope.

That such an equivocal state of affairs should occur in the study of social intelligence requires some additional comment. It certainly seems feasible that the empirical research conducted into social intelligence should be subjected to further analysis. Below we briefly consider some issues that might account for equivocal results, because of their obvious relevance to the related concept of EI.

Cognitive differentiation   Much of the recent research considering the status of the social intelligence construct has used school-aged children as participants. However, it is not clear whether cognitive abilities differentiate before 16 years of age (see, e.g., Horn & Hofer, 1994), which could explain why there are instances in the literature reporting discrepant results. Certainly this issue requires close attention be afforded to the sample characteristics of studies investigating social intelligence (and related concepts).

Questionable analytical techniques and procedures It would appear that a number of papers examining social intelligence are plagued with statistical anomalies. Of course, this feature may, in turn, account for at least some of the inconsistent results reported in the literature. From our review of this literature, these include the following:

• The use of grade point average in exploratory factor analysis to demarcate academic intelligence. Using this index is certainly controversial from the psychometric standpoint, since these are likely to be unreliable. Moreover, the theoretical interpretation of such imprecise measures is open to question.

• Almost without exception, studies examining the construct of social intelligence, within a factor analytic approach, have been based on orthogonal rotations of an initial principal components solution (e.g., Brown & Anthony, 1990; Ford & Tisak, 1983; Marlowe, 1986). However, as Jensen has recently argued, "Varimax [an orthogonal rotation procedure] actually violates the 'simple structure' rationale originally put forward by Thurstone.... Application of Varimax as the end-point solution in a factor analysis of ability measures is just *absolutely wrong*" (1997, p. 8, brackets ours, emphasis his).

• Because behavioral effectiveness criteria are linked to self-reported social intelligence, while cognitive indices of social intelligence are linked to performance-based measures, it remains unclear whether these are in fact two discernible dimensions of social intelligence. Indeed, in a point that is certainly pertinent to measures of EI, it is entirely possible that these two supposedly different conceptual meanings of the construct simply represent something akin to a method factor (see Carroll, 1993).

Atheoretical approaches to the assessment/measurement of relevant constructs
With respect to the operationalization of measures employed in social intelligence research, there are clearly some questionable things going on in the field. None of the newer empirical studies cited above, for example, has (a priori) utilized a theory about personality (or intelligence for that matter) and tried to couch the concept of social intelligence within that framework. Similarly, one or two marker tests have, almost without exception, been employed in research as putative measures of the social intelligence domain, but this leaves the meaning and source of correlation largely uninterpretable (see Carroll, 1993).

The dual nature of social intelligence   A noted difficulty in dealing with social intelligence is that it is not a clearly defined concept with an easily identifiable class of empirical referents. Indeed, the question "What is social intelligence?" tends to invoke a range of conceptualizations. Not surprisingly, various definitions abound in the literature; however, most can be placed into one of two categories:

• Those that stress social cognitive skills (i.e., skills such as the ability to decode social information using verbal and nonverbal cues, the ability to make accurate social inferences, social knowledge, social memory, and so forth).

• Those that stress the social-behavioral skills (i.e., the ability to respond adaptively and perform effectively in social situations). Here social intelligence is defined in terms of behavioral effectiveness.

In their comprehensive review of the social intelligence literature, Walker and Foley (1973, p. 842) note that Edward Thorndike's original definition encompassed both these categories. In particular, Thorndike specified two types of social intelligence, namely, understanding others *and* wise social action. Therefore, Thorndike is interpreted as providing for (a) a cognitive appreciation of others without necessary action on the part of the perceiver and (b) action-orienting coping with others.

Walker and Foley (1973) also note that these two broad categories in themselves demand intensive research so that their various facets can be specified. Furthermore, they suggest that knowing and acting must be evaluated separately before their interaction can be assessed. Too infrequently, it appears that investigators have equated the two aspects of social intelligence or, in dealing with one they have assumed that the other is present. While it is most definitely the case that wise social action presupposes social understanding, social understanding itself is a necessary but not a sufficient cause for wise social behavior. To what extent there are people who know what behavior should be exhibited, because they are capable of reading social cues, but either choose not to act or are unable to act for whatever reason, remains an open empirical question.

Social Intelligence: Implications for the Study of Emotional Intelligence

It has often been suggested by the majority of proponents of EI that it is a subcomponent of, or otherwise closely related to, social intelligence (e.g., Bar-On, 1997; Goleman, 1995; Mayer & Salovey, 1990;

Mayer, Caruso et al., 1999). If we accept this proposition, it might be argued that the prospects for successfully isolating an empirically coherent domain of intelligence that is tied to emotional life are somewhat bleak. For instead of conceiving of this as an area that is relatively new, we are forced to accept that nearly a century of research has left us with little understanding of any of the mechanisms, processes, or structures upon which the very edifice of EI has been erected (namely, social intelligence). Indeed, the equivocal findings in this domain have likely been masked by the so-called "bottom drawer effect," where research providing negative or uninterpretable findings fail to be published in peer-reviewed scientific journals.

Equally critical to increasing our understanding of EI, it would appear that the operationalization and measurement of social intelligence has proven an extremely difficult (some might say arduous) undertaking that is full of pitfalls and problems. In short, there is no gold standard to assess social intelligence. Tests developed by Guilford and his colleagues, for example, appear to suffer from poor reliability and are less factorially distinct than postulated by that theory. This outcome has resulted in the derivation of a narrower factor than most proponents of social intelligence would desire. It also appears that many of these tests have too much conceptual overlap with traditional intelligence (or where self-reported assessment of social intelligence has been attempted, personality) measures. As we have already seen (and take up in chapter 5), this is something not uncommon to extant studies of EI. The situation described by Cronbach about social intelligence in the 1960s ("social intelligence remains undefined and unmeasured" [1960, p. 319]) appears not only true today, but (if history is any guide) may apply to EI fifty years from now (if not for an indefinite period).

One of the aims of this book is to provide the reader with a balanced account of all available data and consistent with this notion it would be inappropriate to end these passages with such a negative statement. Indeed, there do appear some findings in the social intelligence literature, which might hold promise for the concept of EI. Primary among these is the possibility of using the ideas put forward by Guilford and his associates to develop objective indices of individual differences in emotionality. For example, Hendricks, Guilford, and Hoepfner (1969) developed a test known as Alternate Picture Meanings. In this test, individuals are presented with a photograph showing a person making certain facial expressions or gestures. The participant is required to write as many different things that a person might say if she or he felt like the person in the picture. Carroll's (1993) reanalysis of this test indicates that it likely taps individual differences in ideational fluency in the behavioral content domain. This construct may have some relationships to what is now referred to as emotional creativity (e.g., Averill, 2000).

Moreover, it is possible that at least part of the problem with extant measures of social intelligence is that not enough resources have been devoted to test construction (see Carroll, 1993, p. 528). Nor does it appear that any thinking has gone into modern technologies (especially multimedia) and how these might be used to create more psychometrically sound instruments. For example, although not used for purposes of assessing social intelligence (see however, Davies et al., 1998), Archer and colleagues (e.g., Archer, 1988, 1990; Costanzo & Archer, 1993) have developed the Interpersonal Perception Test (IPT). This test involves a series of brief vignettes presented on video that shows people engaging in real-life social interactions. The test appears both reliable and valid, in that it predicts things like social adjustment, self-reported empathy, and the like. Because the design of the IPT is worth considering, arguably as an exemplar by which more objective indices of EI might be constructed, we consider it, along with other performance measures of EI, in some detail in chapter 5.

Concluding Comments

Our review of social intelligence indicates that a concept that shares close parallels with EI, conceptually at the very least, has been at the fore of differential psychology for almost as long as more traditional measures of psychometric intelligence. The resemblance of contemporary EI measures to indices of social intelligence, along with largely negative findings establishing that social intelligence is independent of Gc, might mean that we leave this exposition on a sour, even pessimistic, note. However, equally plausible, is the possibility that with the recent upsurge of interest in EI and commercial investment that this interest has subsequently afforded, valid and reliable assessment of the personal intelligences may be forthcoming. In short, because science is to some extent motivated by sociological forces, with increased funding, the time may be ripe for the zeitgeist that is emotional intelligence. Surely, however, this rests on showing that the science outweighs the myth in the major arguments supporting the existence of emotional intelligence.

Appendix B: A Review of Sundry Other Performance Measures of Emotional Intelligence

In the passages that follow, we provide detailed discussion of several performance measures, mentioned briefly in chapter 5, which might plausibly be used in the future to develop a comprehensive model of EI. These include the following:

• An instrument designed to directly assess the emotion perception facet of the Mayer-Salovey-Caruso model: the Emotional Accuracy Research Scale (EARS)

• Several instruments designed to assess emotional constructs having close ties to contemporary models of EI (e.g., emotional awareness)

• A performance-based measure of social intelligence: the Interpersonal Perception Test—15 (IPT-15)

Emotional Accuracy Research Scale

The Emotional Accuracy Research Scale (EARS) is essentially analogous to the Stories subtest of the branch 1: emotion-perception measure of the MEIS (Geher, Warner & Brown, 2001). Historically, it predates development of the MEIS (see Mayer & Geher, 1996), and may thus lay claim to being the first performance-based emotional intelligence test to employ consensual and target scoring. (The test does not make use of expert scores). Compared to all other performance tests of EI, at 96 items long (i.e., eight emotionally laden vignettes requiring twelve forced-choices between one of two oppositely aligned mood states [e.g., mad—delighted]), it appears the most administratively convenient. Indeed, since Stories from the MEIS consistently shares highest loading on general EI (see discussion above), in a fashion reminiscent of Ravens Matrices, it could be argued that EARS represents the best, single one-off measure of EI available to date. This assertion necessarily depends on demonstrating that EARS has adequate psychometric properties, evaluation of which follows in due course.

Test description
Each of the vignettes and mood items composing EARS were elicited from target individuals (i.e., 'real' people who reported actual events affecting current mood states). Participants completing EARS are required to read each vignette, and then reply to a series of forced-choice items that include pairs of mood-related terms. The participants' task is to determine which item, in each pair, the target likely felt at the time of writing. Two scores are subsequently computed:

Target score   Corresponds to the degree a given participant accurately chooses what the actual person felt, at the time she (or he) wrote the vignette.

Consensus score   As for the MEIS and MSCEIT, represents the degree to which a given participants matches the common consent established from all participants.

Test evaluation and empirical findings
Thus far, two published studies have employed the EARS: Geher et al. (2001), and Mayer and Geher (1996). In the first of these studies, 321 undergraduate students performed the EARS, along with self-report measures of mood, defensiveness, empathy, impression management, and academic aptitude. In the second study, Geher et al. (2001) had forty undergraduate students perform the EARS, five self-report measures of trait empathy, and a laboratory measure of emotion judgment. Because of their scope, these studies allow us to independently assess the psychometric properties and validity of EARS.

Given that the EARS is essentially a measure of Emotion Perception, it is surprising to find that it has (relative to similar tests of the MEIS/MSCEIT) poor reliability: Cronbach $\alpha = 0.24$ (target scoring), 0.53 (consensus scoring) (Mayer & Geher, 1996). Geher et al. (2001) report higher reliabilities, but only after deleting a number of problematic items using item analysis. More vexing perhaps is the fact that the correlation between target and consensus scores is (in a fashion reminiscent of the MEIS) near zero (i.e., 0.14 in Mayer and Geher, 1996; 0.02 in Geher et al., 2001). This low level of correspondence has made the interpretation of relationships between EARS and criterion measures problematic. For example, in the Geher et al. (2001) target score correlates −0.54 with a measure of empathy, while consensus score correlates 0.05 with this same measure!

In terms of validity, the test constructors nonetheless claim to have demonstrated both convergent and divergent validity. In terms of the former, this was purportedly demonstrated in the form of significant correlation with two self-report measures of empathy: Davis' (1983) empathy scale and Mehrabian and Epstein's (1972) empathy scale (which we discuss later in this chapter). Closer inspection of this data reveals particularly weak effects: correlations between EARS and empathy range between −0.06 and 0.24, with target scores consistently yielding lower correlation coefficients. Moreover, these relationships were not replicated in the Geher et al. (2001) investigation. Evidence for divergent validity actually depends on the type of scoring protocol examined and, in any event, rests on flawed logic and a questionable measure. Thus, Geher et al. base their claim for discriminant validation on the fact that "scores on the EARS were found to be negligibly related to SAT scores" (2001, p. 376). Again closer inspection reveals that for target scores this is indeed the case ($r = -0.06$), but that for consensus scores there is moderate correlation ($r = 0.26$) between EARS and *self-reported* SAT scores (see Mayer & Geher, 1996, table 3). Note here the emphasis on the fact that a particularly objective index (SAT) has been self-reported and hence has more questionable psychometric properties than would otherwise appear the case. In addition, it would seem that if EARS is to provide a score that is truly representative of a cognitive ability, moderate positive correlation with the SAT measure is *requisite* as part of *convergent* validity.

Summary

Research with EARS reinforces concerns voiced previously with the MEIS and MSCEIT concerning the absence of scientific standards for determining the accuracy of consensus and expert scores. Indeed, according to psychometric theorizing (Guttman & Levy, 1991), for an item to be considered a true ability item it must be capable of being mapped onto a veridical (rather than sentimental) criterion. This is attainable using some culling or mapping rule, be it logical, semantic, empirical, or normative. We suggest that resolving this issue is prerequisite to advocating further research with the EARS.

Levels of Emotional Awareness Scale

Theoretical framework

Almost a decade prior to the popularization of EI, Lane and Schwartz (1987) proposed that each individual's ability to recognize and describe emotion(s) in their own self and in others was a cognitive skill, which they termed emotional awareness. A central tenet of this model is that individual differences in emotional awareness reflects fundamental variations in degrees of differentiation and integration of cognitive schemata, that are used when processing emotional information (see Karmiloff-Smith, 1992). Under this framework, the importance of emotional awareness to human survival is self-evident. "To the extent that awareness of emotional information is adaptive, it follows that the more information one has about one's emotional state, the greater the potential to use this information in achieving adaptational success" (Lane, 2000, p. 173).

Basing their model closely upon Piaget's stages of cognitive development, Lane and Schwartz (1989) posited five, hierarchically arranged, levels of emotional awareness, which are thought to circumscribe the organization of emotional experience. From the lowest to highest functions, the five levels of emotional awareness are physical sensations, action tendencies, single emotions, blends of emotion, and blends of blends of emotional experience. These levels describe traits, although, they are also used by Lane and his collaborators to refer to statelike phenomenon. Within this model, emotional experiences can be considered a construction consisting of each of the levels of experience up to and including the highest level attained within the hierarchy. In an attempt to measure each of the five levels, Lane, Quinlan, Schwartz, Walker, and Zeitlin (1990) developed (and have subsequently attempted to validate) the Levels of Emotional Awareness Scale (LEAS), which we describe below.

Test description

The LEAS is a paper-and-pencil performance test, in which participants are required to describe their anticipated feelings (and those of a second person) to each of twenty scenes (Lane, 2000). Essentially, it has been constructed to elicit four types of emotion: anger, fear, happiness, and sadness (Lane et al., 1990). Each scene is followed by two questions: "How would you feel?" and "How would the other person (often a friend) feel?" Corresponding to these questions, each person's answer receives two separate scores for each emotion (or emotions) described: one for the self and one for others. A sample scenario, often used by Lane and colleagues in published work, follows:

"You and your best friend are in the same line of work. There is a prize given annually to the best performance of the year. The two of you work hard to win the prize. One night the winner is announced: your friend. How would you feel? How would your friend feel?"

The participant receives a score ranging from 0 to 5 for each scene, corresponding to the five levels of emotional awareness described above. A glossary of words at each level is available to the scorer to guide substantive interpretation and scoring. The lowest level (score = 0) reflects nonemotional responses, often where the word "feel" is used to describe a thought rather than a feeling (e.g., "I don't work hard to win prizes" or "My friend would probably feel the judges knew what they were doing). A level 1 score reflects awareness of physiological cues (e.g., "I'd feel sick about it"). Level 2 consists of words that are typically used in other contexts but are frequently used to convey relatively undifferentiated emotions (e.g., "I'd feel bad") or action tendencies (e.g., "I'd feel like kicking something"). Level 3 responses involve use of one word conveying typical, differentiated emotion (i.e., "happy," "sad," "angry," and so forth). A score of four is given (i.e., level 4), when two or more level 3 words are used to convey greater emotional differentiation than any word alone.

In addition, to receiving a score for the self and the other, participants also receive a total score. This score equals the higher of these two scores, except in those instances where both self and other receive level 4 scores. Under these circumstances, a total score of level 5 is given. An example of a level 5 response for the scenario presented above is as follows:

"I'd feel disappointed that I didn't win but glad that if someone else did, that person was my friend. My friend probably deserved it! My friend would feel happy and proud but slightly worried that my feelings might be hurt" (see, e.g., Lane, 2000, p. 187).

Based on the preceding structural criteria, each participant is thus given a score out of 100 on the LEAS.

Test evaluation and empirical findings

Lane (2000) reports that eight psychometric studies have been undertaken with the LEAS, although at the time of writing, two of these had not been published. Importantly, in each of these studies, acceptable levels of interrater reliability and internal consistency have been obtained (e.g., Lane, Reiman, et al., 1998). To date, test-retest reliability has not been ascertained.

Given that the LEAS depends so heavily upon an individual's ability to articulate emotional responses with increasingly rich vocabulary, a fundamental question to address would appear the extent to which it overlaps with measures of crystallized intelligence (see chapter 3). In their original study, Lane et al. (1990) observed that this relationship was nonincidental since performance on the LEAS correlated moderately ($r = 0.38$) with the Vocabulary subtest of the Wechsler Adult Intelligence Scale, Revised (Wechsler, 1981). These data raise the possibility that the predictive validity of the LEAS derives from its overlap with known intelligence constructs.

A second study (Lane, Kevley, DuBois, Shamasundara & Schwartz, 1995), apparently suggesting otherwise, should be treated with suspicion. In this study, participants ($N = 57$) from the Chicago Medical School were administered the LEAS and the Shipley Institute of Living Scale (SILS). This short-screening test of intelligence, which was originally devised as an index of intellectual deterioration (Shipley, 1940), has a notably low ceiling, i.e., will not result in sufficient spread among high performing individuals (see, e.g., Gregory, 1996). Lane et al. (1995) report a nonsignificant correlation ($r = 0.17$) between the LEAS and SILS. Given the compounded problems of restriction in range (of test scores) and small sample size, definitive statements, concerning overlap between crystallized intelligence and emotional awareness (as measured by the LEAS) are not possible from this study.

While the preceding overlap remains a controversial aspect of the LEAS, promising results have been obtained by Lane and his collaborators in demonstrating another facet of construct validity—the extent that the LEAS captures aspects of a Piagetian cognitive-developmental continuum. Thus, correlations between the LEAS and two instruments subscribing to this Piagetian perspective were moderate ($r = 0.37$ and 0.36, respectively), as expected (Lane, 2000).[1] However, one might query as to why more direct tests of the Piagetian hypothesis (i.e., testing children at various age levels) have yet to be conducted with the LEAS. Moreover, in the case of these measures, one can not rule out the shared influence of crystallized-verbal ability in generating item responses, and that it is this, rather than some cognitive-developmental continuum that accounts for the observed correlation.

Nevertheless, it is certainly the case that the LEAS shares overlap with other measures appearing to form part of the emotional landscape. For example, Lane and colleagues report a correlation of $r = 0.43$ between the LEAS and the Perception of Affect Test. This measure has several subscales (given in different formats) that require participants to detect the presence of basic emotions, which are summed to provide a total score (Rau, 1993). For example, one subtask has stimuli describing an emotional situation without the use of emotive words (e.g., the man looked at the photograph of his recently departed wife). Another subscale uses pictures of faces depicting an individual emotion, with the participants required to match this to another photograph similarly depicting basic emotions (e.g., two people standing next to a grave, with their backs to the camera). The correlation between these tasks has led Lane to conclude that the LEAS is "(1) a measure of the schemata used to process affective information, whether the information is verbal or nonverbal; (2) a measure of the complexity of experience; and (3) not simply a measure of verbal ability" (2000, p. 177).

Discriminant validity has also been demonstrated. According to Lane and colleagues, the LEAS measures the complexity (or structure) of affective experience rather than its intensity. Thus, it should not correlate meaningfully with measures of anxiety, depression, or affective intensity. Across several large-scale studies, Lane (2000) notes that nonsignificant correlations were observed between the LEAS and operational indices of all three of the aforementioned constructs (i.e., Taylor Manifest Anxiety Scale, Beck Depression Inventory, and Affect Intensity Measure, respectively).

Curiously, from our review of the literature, we could not uncover any systematic attempt to ascertain how scores from the LEAS were related to broad personality traits encapsulated under the Big Five Factor framework. Lane and colleagues' insistence on emotional awareness being a trait, the clamor by EI researchers to demonstrate the relative independence of their new constructs from these factors, and theoretical advances such information might bring, render this something of an oversight. It is to be hoped this shortcoming will be rectified some time in the near future.

To assess the usefulness of the LEAS, we turn first to consider recent studies examining its neurological concomitants. In particular, Lane et al. (1998) have used Positron Emission Tomography (PET) to show that, when processing emotional stimuli, people who score high on the

LEAS differ from others in terms of blood flow in particular regions of the brain. This finding suggests that people high in emotional awareness do indeed differ in how they process affective information (relative to those who are low in emotional awareness). Moreover, Lane (1999, 2000) is currently extending this research program, with testable hypotheses formulated concerning the neurological substrata of emotional awareness (see chapter 7).

More recently, Ciarrochi, Chan, and Caputi (2001b) have attempted to evaluate whether the LEAS might be useful in predicting emotionally intelligent behavior. Previous research has found that when people are aware of their mood, they try to prevent that mood from biasing how they think (Schwarz & Clore, 1983). Carriochi et al. (2001b) reasoned that this same effect would occur for people who are chronically, highly aware of their emotions (i.e., those who score high on the LEAS). In one study they measured people's level of emotional awareness and then showed them a video that put them into a positive, neutral, or negative mood. Ciarrochi et al. (2001b) then had participants evaluate their satisfaction with life. People who scored low on the LEAS showed the expected pattern: When in a sad mood, they reported being less happy, whereas when in a happy mood, they reported greater life-satisfaction. In contrast, people high in emotional awareness showed the opposite pattern. When in a sad mood, they reported higher life-satisfaction, whereas in a happy mood, they reported lower life satisfaction. This finding, which constitutes construct validation, is consistent with the idea that people who score high on the LEAS are more aware of their moods and try to prevent those moods from biasing their judgments.

Summary

The LEAS has been shown to relate to emotional processing in particular parts of the brain, to predict the accuracy of emotion recognition in certain circumstances, and to predict how people respond to their moods. These findings provide some evidence for both the validity and utility of this measure, certainly in attempts to understand individual differences in emotional awareness. Of course, emotional awareness is a less broad concept than EI per se, but it is comforting to note that potential factors, other than those based on one school of performance-based approaches are possible. Indeed, a timely experiment would appear one where the relationship between the LEAS and other performance-based indices of EI is examined. Notwithstanding, there is a need to resolve relationships between the LEAS and intelligence constructs inside the context of a multivariate study (with careful attention given to the measures of cognitive ability selected for investigation). Until such time, one can not rule out the rival hypothesis that emotional awareness, like many of the branches of the MEIS (and perhaps MSCEIT), is simply a hitherto neglected primary mental ability of crystallized intelligence.

Measures of emotion expression skill

Researchers have attempted to measure people's skill at expressing emotions, which plausibly is a factor underlying EI. One method asks people to pose basic emotion expressions on cue (e.g., "Now make an angry face"). The expressions are photographed and groups of judges view the expressions and attempt to recognize and categorize them. As the argument goes, an emotionally intelligent person should be capable of expressing basic emotions in a way that judges can easily identify. A second method of measuring expression skill involves examining how people spontaneously express emotions. For example, one study, examined how skilled people were at concealing inappropriate happiness (Friedman & Miller-Herringer, 1991). People were manipulated to believe that they had won a competition and were filmed in the presence (or absence) of the person whom they had beaten. Judges later rated the videos in terms of the emotions they expressed after winning. This type of design allows one to assess the amount of expression (e.g., "How much did the participant smile in general?"). In addition, an indication of a person's skill at making appropriate expressions is possible (e.g., "Did the participant smile at the wrong times, for example, when the defeated peer was in the room?").

There is evidence that emotion expression skill can be measured reliably and that it is moderately related to theoretically meaningful measures such as exhibitionism and the tendency to monitor one's own behavior (Friedman & Riggio, 1999). There is also evidence, consistent with theories of EI, that expressive people are viewed more favorably in social situations (Friedman, Riggio & Casella, 1988). Further research is needed to examine the extent that performance measures of expression are related to intelligence measures, and whether they predict important life outcomes (see Ciarrochi, Chan, Caputi & Roberts, 2001).

Measures of Emotional Competence/Understanding in Children

Research has shown that components appearing to comprise EI (often referred to as "emotional competence" in developmental approaches) can generally be measured reliably and validly in children (Saarni, 1999, 2000). For example, Cassidy, Parke, Butkovsky, and Braungart (1992) measured emotional understanding by showing young children photographs of people experiencing a discrete emotion (e.g., anger or sadness). These children were then asked a series of questions about the pictures, for example, "How do you think this kid is feeling?" Responses are scored for the presence (or absence) of emotional understanding. A highly emotionally intelligent child would be able to identify the emotion, acknowledge experiencing the emotion, understand what caused the emotion, acknowledge expressing the emotion, and reveal understanding of the appropriate responses to others' expression of the emotion. This measure has acceptable interitem reliability and appears related to how well children are accepted by their peers.

In another study, Barth and Bastiani (1997) presented young children with facial expressions of classmates and had them identify the expressed emotion. The researchers then calculated an accuracy score based on the congruence between the judged expression and the expression the classmate was intending to produce. A bias score was also calculated, representing the number of times a child identified a particular type of emotion. For example, some children were biased to see anger in every face. The researchers found that bias scores were reliable across time, whereas accuracy scores were not. Importantly, children who were biased, and saw high levels of anger in faces, also tended to have poorer relationships with their peers. In general, bias scores were better predictors than accuracy scores of peer acceptance. No information was provided in this study about the distinctiveness of the EI measure. However, a study employing similar measures suggests that emotionally perceptive children tend to have moderately higher intelligence test scores (Field & Walden, 1982).

Interpersonal Perception Test—15

Although not necessarily a performance measure of emotional intelligence per se, the Interpersonal Perception Test—15 (IPT-15) is worth considering for several reasons. First, this test measures a closely related construct—social (or interpersonal) intelligence. Second, it may serve to inform future endeavors to construct pragmatic (and theoretically defensible) measures of EI. Finally, researchers subscribing to what we have coined protean conceptions of emotional intelligence might claim that it is justifiable (and valid) measure of their peculiar version of the EI construct. Discussion of the IPT-15, in the passages that follow, provides a cautionary note to this potentially abusive practice.

Test description

Designed by Constanzo and Archer (1993), this task supposedly assesses "social perception" in five areas of human interaction: deception, intimacy, status, kinship, and competition. It is a professional quality, full-color videotape, containing 15 brief scenes. Each scene is paired with a question that has three possible answers—this gives the viewer a chance to decode something important about the scene he/she has just witnessed. The design of the IPT-15 is best-conveyed by briefly describing a few of the scenes.

The first scene shows two adults (a male and a female) having a casual conversation with two young children. The question corresponding to this scene is "Who is the child of the two adults?" Another scene shows a woman first telling her true-life story, and then, after a pause, telling a completely fabricated version of her life history. The question posed to viewers is "Which is the lie and which is the truth?" In a third scene, two men discuss a game of racquetball they have just finished playing between one another. Participants must decide which of the two men has actually won the game.

For every scene, there is an objectively correct answer, which can be verified against an external standard. In the examples just mentioned, one of the children is the child of the two adults; one of the woman's two versions of her life story is a lie; and one of the two men did win the racquetball game.

The IPT has four additional design features that are worth mentioning in the context of the present review. Firstly, in every scene, clues to correct interpretation may be found across a variety of channels. The IPT-15 challenges participants to identify the correct answer to each question by using a broad range of verbal and nonverbal cues present in each scene (such as facial expressions, words, tone of voice, eye movements, gestures, posture, and touching). These cues occur simultaneously in the scenes, just as they do in everyday life. Secondly, all scenes contain unrehearsed, spontaneous interaction, and impromptu conversation. The use of naturalistic behavior represents an attempt to maximize external validity. Finally, twenty-nine different encoders (12 females and 17 males, ranging in age from 18 months to 67 years, and of differing ethnicity) appear in the videotape. None of these encoders are professional actors and the breadth of people represented suggests a good deal of generality.

Test evaluation

The IPT-15 has a test-retest reliability of 0.73 and an internal consistency reliability, determined using the so-called KR-20 formula, of 0.38 (Constanzo & Archer, 1993). Note that the obtained value of KR-20 for this task is reasonably low, perhaps reflecting the diversity of items (i.e., item heterogeneity). Note also reliability is compromised by the fact that the IPT-15 has only 15 items; "effective reliability" is influenced by the number of items in an instrument (Rosenthal, Hall, DiMatteo, Rogers & Archer, 1979). For example, Rosenthal et al. (1979) found an overall KR-20 value of 0.86 using an instrument containing 220 items. A much shorter 20-item subscale, however, only had a median KR-20 value of 0.35.

Despite its obvious relevance to the domain of social intelligence and its potential to clarify the nature of EI, the relation of IPT-15 to other indices of social or emotional intelligence is relatively uncertain. Moreover, until recently, performance on this task, been not been correlated with measures of cognitive ability or personality. Buffier (1997) redressed this imbalance, by having 89 participants perform the IPT-15, along with other psychometric indices. The latter included six putative measures of social intelligence (derived from Guilford's work in the behavioral content domain [see chapter 3]), measures of fluid and crystallized intelligence, and a measure of the Big Five personality factors (i.e., NEO-PIR). Correlations between the IPT-15 and social intelligence measures were moderate (average $r = 0.40$), as were correlations with crystallized intelligence (average $r = 0.32$). The IPT-15, on the other hand, shared near zero correlation with Ravens Progressive Matrices (a marker of fluid intelligence) and all five of the personality factors comprising the NEO-PIR.

Interestingly, Davies et al. (1998, study 3) also included this task in one of their studies into EI, in general replicating these findings for personality and cognitive ability constructs. The IPT-15 was also found to share inconsistent relationships with two self-report measures of factors thought to underlie EI: The Questionnaire Measure of Emotional Empathy ($r = 0.08$) and the Trait Meta-Mood Scale ($r = -0.05$). Moreover, correlations between the IPT-15 and an objective emotional perception test were low and negative in sign (i.e., $r = -0.09$), suggesting poor perception of emotions in photographs is associated with good interpersonal perception.

Summary

Given these inconsistent findings, it is to be hoped future studies will provide more information on the relation between this measure of interpersonal perception and indices of EI. Even so, these data do suggest that if there is a relationship between social and emotional intelligence, it is very weak indeed. Before addressing such issues, however, problems in reliability suggest that this test may be in need of some technical refinements. With the advent of DVD and computer technologies, this may be more cost-effective than in the days the IPT-15 was first developed.

Appendix C: A Review of Sundry Other Self-Report Measures of Emotional Intelligence

In the passages that follow we introduce and critically discuss two commercial self-report instruments, based on rather popular models of EI: Constructive Thinking Inventory (Epstein, 1998) and EQ-Map Test (Cooper, 1996/1997). Because we have not dealt with these models in any great detail in the main body of our book, we also provide the reader with some rather detailed information on conceptual underpinnings. This section closes with a discussion of self-report measures that have served as proxies for emotional intelligence (e.g., Toronto Alexithymia Scale), or of constructs that would appear to overlap conceptually with EI (e.g., self-reported empathy).

Constructive Thinking Inventory

Conceptual background
The Constructive Thinking Inventory (CTI) derives from a major, alternative conceptualization of EI, developed by Seymour Epstein (1998). Because the model is likely to attract some interest, while the measure is relatively benign, we break, in the passages that follow, to discuss its conceptual underpinnings at some length.

Constructive thinking has been heralded by proponents of cognitive-experiential self-theory (CEST) as the key to understanding and fostering psychological adjustment and EI (Epstein, 1998). However, instead of embracing the EI construct, as currently construed and operationalized, CEST proponents suggest that researchers focus on constructive thinking. Constructive thinking refers to the degree to which a person's automatic thinking—the primary form of thinking that occurs intuitively, quickly, and without deliberate intention—facilitates problem solving in everyday life at a minimum cost in stress (Epstein, 1988).

A major centerpiece of CEST is that all behavior is determined by the combined influence of two problem solving modes or 'minds' (i.e., an experiential and a rational mind) (Epstein, 1998). The experiential mind operates preconsciously and automatically (as if seized by one's emotions), experiencing its beliefs as self-evidently valid ("Experiencing is believing"). The experiential mind, learning directly from experience, sees the world in concrete images, metaphors, stories, and other broad categories. This experiential mind thinks quickly, is primed for immediate action, and intimately related to emotions. People can communicate with their experiential mind through fantasy and imagery, the languages it knows best. While at the lowest level of functioning, the experiential mind processes information quickly and crudely, at its highest level, it is a source of intuitive wisdom, inspiration, and creativity.

In contrast, the rational mind is largely analytical, based on abstract representations, oriented towards planning and consideration, and relatively free of emotions. It operates according to logical inference and requires justification of beliefs and assertions by logic and evidence ("Give me proof"). Experience occurs through the conscious and deliberate appraisal of events, with the rational mind learning from abstract representations. Furthermore, the rational mind thinks in terms of fine distinctions and gradations, is highly integrated, striving towards logical consistency.

According to the tenets of this theoretical perspective it is our existential fate to have two selves: an experiential self, derived from our biological past, and a rational self, derived from our cultural and social conditioning. Indeed, several lines of evidence attest to the existence of two minds. These include, insight (as opposed to intellectual knowledge), the desire to do something spontaneous versus consideration of rational utility, the pervasive evidence for irrational fears, superstitious belief, religions, and so forth (Epstein, 1998). The intelligence(s) of the experiential and rational mind are orthogonal (i.e., unrelated). Thus, a person can show high levels of performance on the rational mind but not on the experiential mind, and vise versa. Furthermore, the experiential mind appears to have logic of its own and we can presumably learn from it and the feeling it evokes.

The intelligence of the experiential mind includes emotional intelligence, social intelligence, and practical intelligence. To properly evaluate an emotional reaction and to evaluate to what degree it is an emotionally intelligent response, it is important to attempt to understand the maladaptive, automatic thinking that underlies such emotional reactions. Thus, in order to understand behaviors typically viewed as nonadaptive (e.g., someone that has an anxiety reaction or depressive episode) we need to attempt to understand the maladaptive, automatic thinking that underlies such emotional reactions. In particular, we need to assess whether a person's interpretation of the significance of an event (e.g., failure on a midterm exam, performing poorly on a job interview) is realistic and appropriate to the specific context and person involved.

Components of constructive thinking

The components of emotional and behavioral coping styles represent the two most important elements of constructive thinking. Together they encompass the ability to deal effectively with the outer world of events and the inner world of feelings. Emotional coping consists of the ability to avoid falling into negative self-defeating thoughts and feelings. Individuals with high emotional coping are effective in dealing with negative feelings. They tend to be calm, take things in stride, and do not "sweat the small stuff." They do not take things personally, nor are they overly sensitive to approval, disapproval, or failure, tending not to worry about things that are beyond their control. They are not overly critical of themselves or others, and they do not over-generalize from (or overreact to), unfavorable events. They neither dwell on past misfortunes nor worry endlessly about future ones. Individuals who rely on behavioral-oriented coping, on the other hand, think in ways that promote effective action, focusing their energy in carrying out their plans. They hold a positive disposition towards life and their optimism allows them to take on challenges and risks, as they have the confidence that things will work out well. They circumvent obstacles and compensate quickly for setbacks, in the process regaining momentum and control.

Whereas emotional and behavioral coping contribute directly to constructive thinking, a number of categories of destructive thinking (e.g., categorical thinking, superstitious thinking, esoteric thinking, naive optimism) reflect maladaptive patterns. Categorical thinkers are rigid, judgmental and intolerant thinkers who view issues in black-and-white terms. Categorical thinkers tend to classify people categorically as "good" or "bad," "for" or "against" them. They assume there is only one way to do things and it happens to be their way. Whereas this way of thinking helps simplify thinking, it does not allow the person to see the various gradations and different shades of a complex situation. Superstitious thinking refers to personal superstitions, or the mental games that people play to prepare themselves for disappointment. Esoteric thinkers hold beliefs about unusual and paranormal phenomena and standard superstitions. They believe in traditional superstitions such as omens of bad luck (breaking a mirror, walking under a ladder, having a black cat cross your path) and good luck charms (ghosts, ESP, astrology). Naive optimists tend to jump to conclusions after a positive outcome, as if a single success guaranteed that things would always work out the way one expected or wishes. Although they tend to feel good about themselves and the future, naive optimists hold convictions that are too simpleminded to be a helpful guide in the real world (e.g., "Everyone should love their parents or children"). They fail to think things out too thoroughly and do not plan carefully or take proper precautions for the future.

Test description

Operationalization of the constructive thinking construct is through a test known as the Constructive Thinking Inventory. Each participant provides responses on a five-point rating-scale (ranging from "completely false" [1] to "completely true" [5]) that captures both adaptive and nonadaptive forms of thinking. In particular, constructive thinking is assessed by questions such as the following: "When I am faced with a difficult task, I think encouraging thoughts that help me do my best." Destructive thinking, on the other hand, is measured by items of the following type: "When something good happens to me, I believe it will be balanced by something bad." The CTI contains six subscales measuring core components of the CEST model: emotional coping, behavioral coping, categorical thinking, personal superstitious belief, esoteric thinking, and naive optimism. A global composite, representing overall constructive thinking, may also be obtained.

Empirical findings

Based on research with the CTI, persons who score high on the composite constructive thinking scale, have a positive outlook on life, view their lives as having purpose and direction, and are accepting of themselves and others. Although they are positive thinkers, they temper their optimism with consideration of what is realistic. Good constructive thinkers are flexible and problem-focused thinkers who adapt their thinking to different situations, seeing the dark as well as the lighter sides of the issues. They are also problem-oriented rather than judgmental. Good global thinkers make an effort not to overgeneralize from their experience, whether positive or negative. They generally do not need to resort to magical thinking or other forms of superstition to explain (or control) their environment and they have the self-confidence to face the uncertainties and complexities of reality. Their experiential thinking helps them feel good about themselves (and others), to handle negative stress with minimal disruption, and to take effective actions to resolve everyday conflicts.

Constructive thinking also shares meaningful relationships with a variety of adaptive outcomes. These include, low levels of neuroticism (Hurley, 1996), internal locus of causality (Watson, Morris, Hood, Miller & Waddell, 1999), and "productive load," i.e., productive interactions with the environment (see Epstein & Katz, 1992). Furthermore, constructive thinking scores appear more strongly related than IQ to many criteria considered to represent success in life (specifically, success at work, emotional adjustment, and physical health), with the exception of educational success.

Model evaluation

Despite some positive findings, overall, there appears little that is novel in the constructive thinking model of EI, beyond that represented in existent personality theories. The distinction between the two minds (experiential versus rational) and their attributes, highly overlaps with the Freudian (Freud, 1933) distinction between primary processes (based on preconscious, automatic, and irrational codes) and secondary processes (based on conscious, rational, and symbolic codes). The fact that that these two processes can be in conflict, that the experiential mind conflicts with the rational mind (and overrides it), or that rational thought may control primary automatic forms of thinking, are basic tenets of psychoanalytic thinking. Furthermore, the notion that thought shapes emotions and that one needs to intervene at the cognitive level to impact on emotions is "old hat." Thus, philosophers and theologians as early as 2,500 years ago recognized that thoughts precede emotions and that by training these thoughts, one can reform our emotions. Buddha learned about 2,500 years ago, by carefully observing the mind during meditation, that thought precedes emotions. Five hundred years later the Greek philosopher Epictetus, through logical analysis, came to the conclusion that we react not to events as they objectively occur, but to our thought and interpretations of them. More recently, cognitive therapists such as Aaron Beck, Albert Ellis, and Donald Meichenbaum, have used this insight to develop a very successful psychological treatment for treating many emotional disorders (see chapter 11). Furthermore, most of the elements of destructive thinking (dichotomous thinking, overgeneralization, personalization, and so forth) catalogued by Epstein (1998), appear in the models of Beck and Ellis as irrational forms of thought preceding stressful emotions. In sum, constructive thinking appears to be a new vessel containing old wine.

EQ-Map Test

This self-report measure, devised by Cooper (1996/1997), divides EI into five attributes. These are as follows:

Current environment   Measures life pressures and life satisfactions.

Emotional literacy   Includes items assessing emotional self-awareness, emotional expression, and the awareness of other people's emotions.

EQ competencies   Includes items assessing intentionality, creativity, resilience, interpersonal connections, and constructive discontent.

EQ values and attitudes   Measured by outlook, intuition, compassion, trust, personal power, and integrated self.

Outcomes   Assesses the supposed outcomes of various degrees of EI: general health, quality of life, relationship quotient, and optimal performance.

Test evaluation

Clearly, this instrument measures a wide range of psychological constructs. As such, it may be construed as invoking one of the most protean of all definitions of EI found in the literature. Interestingly, at the time of writing, it had not been subjected to empirical scrutiny by the psychological testing community, which given it is amongst the oldest of the commercially available instruments for assessing EI, is quite surprising. Note, however, with such expansive psychological profiling, it would be extremely unlikely that the test does not have some level of predictive validity. Whether of course this can be attributed to EI per se would appear contentious.

Toronto Alexithymia Scale

Test description

The Toronto Alexithymia Scale (TAS-20) is currently one of the most commonly used EI measures, though in truth, it was not designed explicitly for this purpose, being instead a measure of the clinical syndrome known as alexithymia (see chapter 11). It consists of 20 items, forming three subscales, as well as an overall alexithymia score (Bagby, Parker & Taylor, 1994). The subscales, along with sample items, are these:

Difficulty in identifying feelings   For example, "I am often confused about what emotion I am feeling."

Difficulty describing feelings   For example, "It is difficult for me to find the right words for my feelings."

Externally oriented thinking   For example, "Being in touch with emotions is essential."

Test evaluation

The overall alexithymia score and the first two scale scores tend to be highly reliable. However, the third scale has sometimes been found to be less reliable than is desirable (Bagby, Parker & Taylor, 1994). Importantly, the TAS-20 has been shown to be a valid instrument across disparate cultures and different types of populations (e.g., students and psychiatric patients) (see, e.g., Taylor, 2000).

As predicted by Bagby and his colleagues (1994), the TAS-20 has large overlap with other theoretically relevant scales (e.g., openness to feelings), which suggests that the scale is measuring what it is expected to measure. People who score high on the TAS-20 also tend to score high on measures of negative emotionality and low on positive emotionality, but this overlap is only small to medium in magnitude (Bagby et al., 1994). In addition, the TAS-20 tends not to overlap too highly with either conscientiousness or agreeableness.

The TAS-20 has been shown relate to a number of important life outcomes. For example, people high in alexithymia are more prone to drug addiction, eating disorders, and experiencing physical symptoms (e.g., feeling sick). The scale also predicts the ability to process and manage emotional states and the ability to recognize faces (Taylor & Taylor, 1997). In short, the TAS-20 appears to be a reliable, useful, and distinctive measure. Nevertheless, the fact that the TAS-20 was never intended to explicitly assess EI, renders it suspect as an index of any more broadly based EI construct.

Other Self-Report Measures Related to Emotional Intelligence

There are numerous other self-report measures related to EI, which we might discuss at length. However, due to space constraints, we list them in table C.1, along with their original source, a brief description of task

Table C.1

Test	Source	Brief description	Comment(s)
Affective Communication Test	Friedman, Prince, Riggio & DiMatteo (1980)	Assesses nonverbal expressiveness of emotion	Sample item: "I can easily express emotion over the telephone."
COPE	Carver, Scheier & Weintraub (1989)	Measures coping with stressful events; 13 sub-scales (e.g., active coping, denial, turning to religion)	People's ability to cope with aversive affect may relate to the managing emotions component of EI
Emotional Control Questionnaire	Roger & Najarian (1989)	Measures ability to control emotion in trying circumstances	Consists of four scales: Rehearsal, Benign Control, Emotional Inhibition, and Aggression Control
Emotional Quotient (EQ) Test (available on the Internet)	Goleman (1995)	Measures emotional abilities, general social competencies, and character	Three subscales: Knowing One's Emotions, Motivating Oneself, and Handling Relationships
Monitoring-Blunting Scale	Miller, Brody & Summerton (1988)	Measures the extent that people seek out (or avoid) information when faced with a stressful situation	People's ability to cope with aversive affect may relate to the managing emotions component of EI
Questionnaire Measure of Emotional Empathy	Mehrabian & Epstein (1970)	Measures vicarious aspects of emotional empathy	Sample Item: "I tend to get emotionally involved with a friend's problems."
Repression-Sensitization Scale	Weinberger, Schwarz & Davidson (1979)	Assesses extent to which people defensively avoid aversive emotions and stimuli	Scale has predicted how accurate people are at identifying emotions
Response Styles Questionnaire	Nolen-Hoeksema & Morrow (1991)	Measures the tendency to experience behaviors and thoughts that focus on one's depressive symptoms	Such a focus appears to be emotionally unintelligent in that it increases depressive symptoms

Table C.2
Correlations between selected measures of EI and the Big Five personality factors (from Davies et al., 1998, study 2) ($N = 300$)

Tests	α	O	C	E	A	N
Emotional empathy	0.79	.21	−.11	.08	.28	.23
Affect communication	0.78	.22	−.03	.63	.30	−.08
Goleman's EQ	0.18	.21	−.02	.05	.09	−.08

Notes: We have reanalyzed the data from Davies et al. (1998), study 2. α = internal consistency (from Bar-On, 1997). O = openness; C = conscientiousness; E = extraversion; A = agreeableness; and N = neuroticism.

requirements, and a few critical comments (or sample items). Note that all these measures employ ratings of one form or another, usually a five-point Likert-type scale. The reader is encouraged to consult the primary sources given in this table for more comprehensive details of each respective test.

Evaluation of tests

The vast majority of self-report measures given in table C.1 at best measure one or two components of emotionality that would appear to be related to EI. Indeed, because many of these measures were constructed before the concept of EI came into vogue they will likely serve as instruments by which new tests of EI are validated (rather than define this concept in all its complexity). Nevertheless, given marginal reliabilities, caution is required when using some of these tests. Furthermore, many of tests described in table C.1 show considerable overlap with the Big Five personality factors. In justifying these assertions, we present data from a study conducted by Davies et al. (1998). Here we were able to calculate correlations between the Questionnaire Measure of Emotional Empathy, the Affective Communication Test, the EQ Test,[1] and measures of the Big Five personality factors (see table C.2).

Notes

Chapter 1

1. Http://www.oprah.com/omagazine/200007/omag_200007_iknow.html

Chapter 2

1. The technical manual for the EQ-i refers to a doctoral dissertation that investigated impression management experimentally, attributed to Dowling (1997). However, this work does not appear in the reference list in the manual, and we have been unable to locate it through electronic literature search.

Chapter 3

1. Our discussion of influential figures in the history of intelligence testing is by no means exhaustive and we have, in our own writings on EI, discussed contributions by several other prominent figures (see Zeidner, Matthews & Roberts, 2001). For example, David Wechsler (1983), who is perhaps best remembered for bringing intelligence tests to the attention of clinical psychology, has emphasized the importance of nonintellective factors. Indeed, Wechsler argued that some of these factors may facilitate adaptive behaviors (e.g., drive, will, curiosity, persistence), while others may debilitate (or inhibit) adaptive behaviors. Because of this emphasis, certain commentators have claimed Wechsler hinted at the usefulness of emotional intelligence in his writings (see Kaufman & Kaufman, 2001). We note here, in opposition to such claims, that there is a difference between realizing the importance of nonintellective factors in adaptation to the environment, or personality/intelligence in action, and including an emotional facet in the domain of intelligence.

2. There is even now widespread interest in the entertainment value of consensus scoring inside so-called "reality TV"—witness for example the international popularity of CBS produced *Survivor*.

3. Sternberg et al. define implicit theories as "constructions of people (psychologists or lay persons) that reside in the minds of these individuals" (1981, p. 37).

4. Technically speaking, because specific abilities are unique to any given test, Spearman's model implicitly evokes many intelligence factors (Carroll, 1993).

5. Carroll (1993) provides the following, useful summary definitions of the major principles encapsulated in the terms "eduction of relations" and "education of correlates." "The word *eduction* means the drawing out of some logical abstraction or consequence from two or more stimuli. *Relations* are abstractions like 'similarity' and 'comparison'; *correlates* are the particular attributes of stimuli that are seen as identical, similar, compared, or related in some way" (Carroll, 1993, p. 53).

6. For example, Analogies tests are based on these principles. Consistent with this thought experiment, one could have stimuli portraying the following: happy face is to sad face as angry face is to what?

7. Carroll has suggested that the "literature on individual differences in learning and memory leaves much to be desired" (1993, p. 302). However, from the available evidence he offers a slightly different interpretation to and labeling of the SAR factor, while lamenting that TSR is "in need of further research to clarify its structure" (1993, p. 613). With respect to the former, this ability factor has been replaced by a broader construct, which Carroll labels "General Memory." Note therefore that while the preceding discussion is in keeping with the way these constructs have previously been conceptualized within the psychometric literature, this is (by virtue of the above) less than ideal.

8. In a recent special issue of *Emotion* devoted to the concept of EI, this proposition was strongly advocated by a variety of experts from disparate fields of psychology. Among them Kaufman and Kaufman (2001) who possess extensive expertise in the field of intelligence testing, Izard (2001), who is an eminent, "pure" emotions researcher, and Schaie (2001), a luminary in the field of cognitive aging. We might add that the current research team added their voice to the clamor for EI researchers to be more stringent in their science (Zeidner et al., 2001).

Chapter 4

1. This author, a philosopher, makes some conceptual distinctions not always represented in psychological accounts. First, he distinguishes cognition in the sense of neutral, descriptive beliefs from evaluation of personal significance: most psychologists would classify both as cognition. Second, he distinguishes feeling states from emotions: emotion relates to various categories of conscious experience. Feeling states are one component of the complex emotional experience.

Chapter 5

1. This is not to assert such approaches never attempt to measure EI, for as we shall see shortly, there have been attempts to provide operational indices that seem to adopt this perspective.

2. Because few tests are scored according to target criterion, empirical studies have tended not to focus much on this particular measure (see however, our commentary on the Emotion Accuracy Research Scales [EARS]).

3. Ciarrochi, Chan, and Caputi (2000a) report a two-factor solution of the MEIS, interpreting factor 1 as emotion perception, and factor 2 as understanding and managing emotion. Closer inspection of their analysis reveals a number of problems. For example, their interpretation of factors comprising the MEIS is questionable (factor 1, which they interpreted as emotion perception, also had salient loadings from branch 2 and branch 3 tests). More importantly, Ciarrochi, Chan, and Caputi (2000a) made use of an orthogonal factor rotation procedure. Clearly, because they hypothesized that the two constructs should define a high-order, general EI construct, an oblique rotation should have been performed (see, e.g., Jensen, 1998 for criticisms of such an approach).

4. Recall that the reliabilities of consensus and expert-scores average 0.71 and 0.68 (respectively) for the MSCEIT (Version 2). Performing the requisite mathematics, we might expect correlations approaching 0.70 for the vast majority of subtests, rather than the range of 0.93 to 0.99 reported by Mayer et al. (submitted).

5. This assertion precludes one instance where an Emotional Stroop task was correlated with self-report measures of EI, though the finding was, as we argue, remarkably contradictory (see discussion of the EQ-i). Arguably too, the Ciarrochi et al. (2000) study of mood induction is relevant to judgment and memory processes.

6. The publisher of the EQ-i apparently disagrees with this cautious view. A press release of July 15, 1999 announces that a sample from the United States scored significantly more highly on the test than a Canadian sample, and claims that Americans are superior in expressing their thoughts and feelings, reality testing, and coping skills. Fortunately, the press release sees hope for the unfortunate Canadians, in that these skills can be trained. It is unknown whether tolerance of being patronized is an aspect of emotional intelligence.

7. Note that the complexity of labels, within these response formats, may be a cause for concern (Krause et al., 2001). Unless the respondents are particularly well educated, which may not be so problematic if the instrument is intended only for managers and the like.

Chapter 8

1. Multiple regression methods (Pedhazur, 1997) were used to test for interaction between EI and the experimental conditon, using each of the posttask stress factors listed in table 8.1 as dependent measures. The interaction was significant only for distress: in this case EI appeared to be more strongly associated with lower distress in the control condition than in the experimental conditions.

Chapter 9

1. The traits discussed are all continuous; i.e., there is a spectrum of levels of neuroticism connecting extreme neuroticism and extreme emotional stability. In describing the characteristics of the trait, it is convenient to contrast high N and low N individuals as distinct groups, but they should not be thought of as separate types.

Appendix A

1. Seemingly because of Cronbach's stern rebuke, most structural models of intelligence do not consider social intelligence as forming a viable scientific construct. In addition, no measures of social intelligence were included in the Kit of Reference Factors (French, Ekstrom & Price, 1963) or its revision (Ekstrom, French & Harman, 1976). This psychometric battery is considered by many the primary research tool for cognitive ability assessment (see, e.g., Carroll, 1993; Roberts, Goff, et al., 2001). The inclusion of social intelligence tests in the revised kit was considered and subsequently rejected on the grounds that there was too little evidence to justify this construct's assessment.

Appendix B

1. These tests were the Sentence Completion Test of Ego Development (e.g., Loevinger & Wessler, 1970) and the Cognitive Complexity of the Description of Parents (Blatt, Wein, Chevron & Quinlan, 1979).

Appendix C

1. According to Goleman (2000), the EQ Test was constructed largely in a humorous moment. Given his standing in the field and the fact that many people might have taken it seriously, including researchers (see Davies et al., 1998), we wonder whether this in-joke was judicious.

References

Aber, J. L., Brown, J. L., & Henrich, C. C. (1999). *Teaching conflict resolution: An effective school-based approach to violence prevention.* New York: National Center for Children in Poverty, Colombia University.

Aber, J. L., Jones, S. M., Brown, J. L., Chaudry, N., & Samples, F. (1998). Resolving conflict creatively: Evaluating the developmental effects of a school-based violence prevention program in neighbourhood and classroom context. *Development and Psychopathology, 10,* 187–213.

Abraham, R. (1999). Emotional intelligence in organizations: A conceptualization. *Genetic, Social, and General Psychology Monographs, 125,* 209–224.

Ackerman, P. L. (1988). Determinants of individual differences during skill acquisition: Cognitive abilities and information processing. *Journal of Experimental Psychology: General, 117,* 288–318.

Ackerman, P. L. (1996). A theory of adult intellectual development: Process, personality, interests, and knowledge. *Intelligence, 22,* 227–257.

Ackerman, P. L., & Heggestad, E. D. (1997). Intelligence, personality and interests: evidence for overlapping traits. *Psychological Bulletin, 121,* 219–245.

Adan, A., & Guardia, J. (1993). Circadian variations of self-reported activation: A multidimensional approach. *Chronobiologia, 20,* 233–244.

Aderman, D., & Berkowitz, L. (1970). Observational set, empathy, and helping. *Journal of Personality and Social Psychology, 14,* 125–132.

Adler, S. (1996). Personality and work behavior. *Applied Psychology: An International Review, 45,* 207–224.

Adolphs, R., Cahill, L., Schul, R., & Babinsky, R. (1997). Impaired declarative memory for emotional material following bilateral amygdala damage in humans. *Learning & Memory, 4,* 291–300.

Adolphs, R., Tranel, D., Damasio, H., & Damasio, A. (1994). Impaired recognition of emotion in facial expressions following bilateral damage to the human amygdala. *Nature,* 669–672.

Aggleton, J. P., & Young, A. W. (2000). The enigma of the amygdala: On its contribution to human emotion. In R. D. Lane & L. Nadel (eds.), *Cognitive neuroscience of emotion.* New York: Oxford University Press.

Ainsworth, M. D. S., Blehar, M. C., Waters, E., & Wall, S. (1978). *Patterns of attachment: A psychological study of the strange situation.* Hillsdale, NJ: Lawrence Erlbaum Associates.

Ajzen, I. (1991). The theory of planned behavior. *Organizational Behavior & Human Decision Processes, 50,* 179–211.

Aldwin, C. M., & Revenson, T. T. (1987). Does coping help? A reexamination of the relation between coping and mental health. *Journal of Personality and Social Psychology, 53,* 337–348.

Allik, J., & Realo, A. (1997). Emotional experience and its relation to the five-factor model in Estonian. *Journal of Personality, 65,* 625–647.

Alloy, L. B., & Abramson, L. Y. (1999). The Temple-Wisconsin Cognitive Vulnerability to Depression Project: Conceptual background, design, and methods. *Journal of Cognitive Psychotherapy, 13,* 227–262.

Alloy, L. B., Abramson, L. Y., Whitehouse, W. G., Hogan, M. E., Tashman, N. A., Steinberg, D. L., Rose, D. T., & Donovan, P. (1999). Depressogenic cognitive styles: Predictive validity, information processing and personality characteristics, and developmental origins. *Behaviour Research & Therapy, 37,* 503–531.

Alloy, L. B., & Riskind, J. H. (eds.) (in press). *Cognitive vulnerability to emotional disorders.* Hillsdale, NJ: Lawrence Erlbaum Associates.

Altshuler, J. L., & Ruble, D. N. (1989). Developmental changes in children's awareness of strategies for coping with uncontrollable stress. *Child Development, 60,* 1337–1349.

Amelang, M. (1997). Using personality variables to predict cancer and heart disease. *European Journal of Personality, 11,* 319–342.

American Dialect Society (1999). American Dialect Society: Words of the Year. Available at ⟨http://www.americandialect.org/woty⟩.

American Psychiatric Association (1994). *Diagnostic and statistical manual of mental disorders* (fourth ed.). Washington, DC: American Psychiatric Association. Cited as *DSM-IV*.

American Psychological Association, Public Affairs Office (1997). *Intelligence: Knowns and unknowns.* Washington, DC: American Psychological Association.

American Society for Training and Development (1997). *Benchmarking forum member-to-member survey results.* Alexandria, VA: American Society for Training and Development.

Amirkhan, J. H., Risinger, R. T., & Swickert, R. J. (1995). Extraversion: A "hidden" personality factor in coping? *Journal of Personality, 63,* 189–212.

Anastasi, A., & Urbina, S. (1997). *Psychological testing.* Upper Saddler River, NJ: Simon & Schuster.

Anderson, J. R. (1996). ACT: A simple theory of complex cognition. *American Psychologist, 51,* 355–365.

Anderson, M. (1992). *Intelligence and development: A cognitive theory.* Oxford: Blackwell.

Antonioni, D. (1999). Relationship between the Big Five personality factors and conflict management styles. *International Journal of Conflict Management, 9*, 336–355.

Apfel, R. L., & Sifneos, P. E. (1979). Alexithymia: Concept and measurement. *Psychotherapy and Psychosomatics, 3*, 180–190.

Aranoff, J., Stollack, G. E., & Woike, B. A. (1994). Affect regulation and the breadth of interpersonal engagement. *Journal of Personality and Social Psychology, 67*, 105–114.

Arenson, S., Millikin, M., & Hogan, J. (1993). Validation of personality and cognitive measures for insurance claim examiners. *Journal of Business and Psychology, 7*, 459–473.

Argyle, M., & Lu, L. (1990). The happiness of extroverts. *Personality and Individual Differences, 11*, 1011–1018.

Argyle, M., Martin, M., & Crossland, J. (1989). Happiness as a function of personality and social encounters. In J. P. Forgas & J. M. Innes (eds.), *Recent advances in social psychology: An international perspective*. North Holland: Elsevier.

Aristotle. (1947). On the soul. J. A. Smith, trans. In R. McKeon (ed.), *Introduction to Aristotle* (pp. 145–235). New York: Random House.

Arnold, M. B. (1960). *Emotion and personality* (2 vols). New York: Columbia University Press.

Aronson, E. (2000). *Nobody left to hate: Teaching compassion after Columbine*. New York: A. Worth Publishers.

Artz, S. (1994). *Feeling as a way of knowing: A practical guide for working with emotional experience*. Toronto: Trifolium Books.

Arvey, R. D., Renz, G. L., & Watson, T. W. (1998). Emotionality and job performance: Implications for personnel selection. *Research in Personnel and Human Resource Management, 16*, 103–147.

Asendorpf, J. B. (1998). Personality effects on social relationships. *Journal of Personality & Social Psychology, 74*, 1531–1544.

Ashford, S. J. (1988). Individual strategies for coping with stress. *Journal of Applied Behavioral Science, 24*, 19–36.

Ashford, S. J., & Humphrey, R. H. (1993). Emotional labor in service roles: The influence of identity. *The Academy of Management Review, 18*, 88–115.

Ashforth, B. E., & Humphrey, R. H. (1995). Emotion in the workplace: A reappraisal. *Human Relations, 48*, 97–125.

Aspinwall, L. G., & Taylor, S. E. (1992). Modelling cognitive adaptation: A longitudinal investigation of the impact of individual differences and coping on college adjustment and performance. *Journal of Personality and Social Psychology, 63*, 989–1003.

Asso, D. (1987). Cyclical variations. In M. A. Baker (ed.), *Sex differences in human performance* (pp. 55–80). New York: John Wiley & Sons.

Auerbach, S. M. (1989). Stress management and coping research in the health care setting: An overview and methodological commentary. *Journal of Consulting and Clinical Psychology, 57*, 388–395.

Austin, E. J., & Deary, I. J. (2000). The "four As": A common framework for normal and abnormal personality? *Personality & Individual Differences, 28,* 977–995.

Averill, J. R. (1980). A constructivist view of emotion. In R. Plutchik & H. Kellerman (eds.), *Emotion: Theory, research and experience,* vol. 1: *Theories of emotion* (pp. 305–339). San Diego: Academic Press.

Averill, J. R. (1991). Intellectual emotions. In C. D. Spielberger & I. G. Sarason (eds.), *Stress and emotion: Anxiety, anger, and curiosity* (pp. 3–16). New York: Hemisphere Publishing Corp.

Averill, J. R. (2000). Intelligence, emotion, and creativity. In R. Bar-On & J. D. A. Parker (eds.), *Handbook of emotional intelligence,* pp. 277–298. San Francisco: Jossey-Bass.

Averill, J. R., & Nunley, E. P. (1992). *Voyages of the heart: Living an emotionally creative life.* New York: Free Press.

Averill, J. R., & Thomas-Knowles, C. (1991). Emotional creativity. In K. T. Strongman (ed.), *International review of studies on emotion* (vol. 1, pp. 269–299). London: Wiley.

Averill, L. A. (1982). Recollections of Clark's G. Stanley Hall. *Journal of the History of the Behavioural Sciences, 18,* 341–346.

Avila, C., & Parcet, M. A. (1997). Impulsivity and anxiety differences in cognitive inhibition. *Personality & Individual Differences, 23,* 1055–1064.

Baddeley, A. D. (1986). *Working memory.* Oxford: Oxford University Press.

Bagby, R. M., Parker, J. D. A., & Taylor, G. J. (1994a). The Twenty-Item Toronto Alexithymia Scale. I: Item selection and cross-validation of the factor structure. *Journal of Psychosomatic Research, 38,* 23–32.

Bagby, R. M., Parker, J. D. A., & Taylor, G. J. (1994b). The Twenty-Item Toronto Alexithymia Scale. II: Convergent, discriminant, and concurrent validity. *Journal of Psychosomatic Research, 38,* 33–40.

Bagby, R. M., Parker, J. D. A., Taylor, G. J., & Acklin, M. W. (1993). Alexithymia and the ability to distinguish different emotional states. Poster presentation at the annual meeting of the American Psychosomatic Society, Charleston, SC, March.

Baltes, P., Reese, H., & Lipsitt, L. P. (1980). Life span developmental psychology. *Annual Review of Psychology, 31,* 65–110.

Bandura, A. (1965). Behavioral modification through modeling procedures. In L. Krasner & L. P. Ullmann (eds.), *Research in behavior modification: New developments and implications* (pp. 310–340). New York: Holt, Rinehart & Winston.

Bandura, A. (1976). Social learning theory. In J. T. Spence, R. C. Carson & J. W. Thibaut (eds.), *Behavioral approaches to therapy.* Morristown, NJ: General Learning Press.

Bandura, A. (1986). *Social foundations of thought and action: A social cognitive theory.* Englewood Cliffs, NJ: Prentice-Hall.

Bandura, A. (1990). Perceived self-efficacy in the exercise of control over AIDS infection. *Evaluation & Program Planning, 13,* 9–17.

Bandura, A. (1997). *Self-efficacy: The exercise of control.* New York: W. H. Freeman & Co.

Bandura, A., & Cervone, D. (1983). Self-evaluative and self-efficacy mechanisms governing the motivational effects of goal systems. *Journal of Personality and Social Psychology, 45,* 1017–1028.

Bargh, J. A., & Chartrand, T. L. (1999). The unbearable automaticity of being. *American Psychologist, 54,* 462–479.

Bargh, J. A., Chen, M., & Burrows, L. (1996). Automaticity of social behavior: Direct effects of trait construct and stereotype activation on action. *Journal of Personality & Social Psychology, 71,* 230–244.

Barlow, D. H. (1988). *Anxiety and its disorders: The nature and treatment of anxiety and panic.* New York: Guilford Press.

Barnes, M. L., & Sternberg, R. J. (1989). Social intelligence and decoding of nonverbal cues. *Intelligence, 13,* 263–287.

Barnett, P. A., & Gotlib, I. H. (1988). Dysfunctional attitudes and psychosocial stress: The differential prediction of future psychological symptomatology. *Motivation & Emotion, 12,* 251–270.

Barnhart, C. L., et al. (1974). *The world book dictionary.* Chicago: Field Enterprise Educational Corp.

Baron, R. A. (1990). Countering the effects of destructive criticism. *Journal of Applied Psychology, 75,* 235–245.

Bar-On, R. (1996). *The era of the EQ: Defining and assessing emotional intelligence.* Paper presented at the 100th annual convention of the American Psychological Association, Toronto.

Bar-On, R. (1997). *The Emotional Intelligence Inventory (EQ-i): Technical manual.* Toronto: Multi-Health Systems.

Bar-On, R. (2000). Emotional and social intelligence: Insights from the Emotional Quotient Inventory. In R. Bar-On & J. D. A. Parker (eds.), *The handbook of emotional intelligence* (pp. 363–388). San Francisco: Jossey-Bass.

Bar-On, R., & Parker, J. D. A. (eds.) (2000). *Handbook of emotional intelligence.* San Francisco: Jossey-Bass.

Bar-On, R., Brown, J. M., Kirkcaldy, B. D., & Thome, E. P. (2000). Emotional expression and implications for occupational stress: An application of the Emotional Quotient Inventory (EQ-i). *Personality and Individual Differences, 28,* 1107–1118.

Barret, G. V., & Depinet, R. L. (1991). A reconsideration of testing for competence rather than intelligence. *American Psychologist, 46,* 1012–1024.

Barrett, K. C., & Campos, J. J. (1991). A diacritical function approach to emotions and coping. In E. M. Cummings, A. L. Greene & K. H. Karraker (eds.),

Lifespan developmental psychology: Perspectives on stress and coping (pp. 21–41). Hillsdale, NJ: Lawrence Erlbaum Associates.

Barrett, L. F., & Pietromonaco, P. R. (1997). Accuracy of the five-factor model in predicting perceptions of daily social interactions. *Personality & Social Psychology Bulletin, 23,* 1173–1187.

Barrick, M. R., & Mount, M. K. (1991). The Big-Five personality dimensions and job performance: A metanalysis. *Personnel Psychology, 44,* 1–26.

Barrick, M. R., & Mount, M. K. (1993). Autonomy as a moderator of the relationships between the Big Five personality dimensions and job performance. *Journal of Applied Psychology, 78,* 111–118.

Barrick, M. R., Mount, M. K., & Strauss, J. P. (1993). Conscientiousness and performance of sales representatives: Test of the mediating effects of goal setting. *Journal of Applied Psychology, 78,* 715–722.

Barrick, M. R., Stewart, G. L., Neubert, M. J., & Mount, M. K. (1998). Relating member ability and personality to work-team processes and team effectiveness. *Journal of Applied Psychology, 83,* 377–391.

Barth, J., & Bastiani, A. (1997). A longitudinal study of emotion recognition and preschool children's social behaviour. *Merrill-Palmer Quarterly, 43,* 107–128.

Batson, C. D. (1991). *The altruism question: Toward a social-psychological answer.* Hillsdale, NJ: Lawrence Erlbaum Associates.

Battistich, V. (1988). The measurement of classroom processes and children's prosocial characteristics in the Child Development project. *Moral Education Forum, 14,* 1–11.

Battistich, V., & Solomon, D. (1989). Research on the Child Development Project: Current status and future directions. *Moral Education Forum, 14,* 7–10.

Battistich, V., Solomon, D., Watson, M., Solomon, J., & Schaps, E. (1989). Effects of an elementary school program to enhance prosocial behavior on children's cognitive-social problem-solving skills and strategies. *Journal of Applied Developmental Psychology, 10,* 147–169.

Baum, A., Fleming, R. E., & Singer, J. E. (1983). Coping with technological disaster. *Journal of Social Issues, 39,* 117–138.

Baumeister, R. F., Muraven, M., & Tice, D. M. (2000). Ego depletion: A resource model of volition, self-regulation, and controlled processing. *Social Cognition, 18,* 130–150.

Baumeister, R. F., Smart, L., & Boden, J. M. (1996). Relation of threatened egotism to violence and aggression: The dark side of high self-esteem. *Psychological Review, 103,* 5–33.

Baumrind, D. (1971). Current patterns of parental authority. *Developmental Psychology Monographs, 4,* 99–103.

Bayley, N. (1949). Consistency and variability in the growth of intelligence from birth to eighteen years. *Journal of Genetic Psychology, 75,* 165–196.

Bechara, A., Tranel, D., & Damasio, A. R. (2000). Poor judgment in spite of high intellect: Neurological evidence for emotional intelligence. In R. Bar-On & J. D. A. Parker (eds.), *Handbook of Emotional Intelligence*. San Francisco: Jossey-Bass.

Bechara, A., Tranel, D., Damasio, H., & Adolphs, R., et al. (1995). Double dissociation of conditioning and declarative knowledge relative to the amygdala and hippocampus in humans. *Science, 269,* 1115–1118.

Bechtel, W. (1988). *Philosophy of science: An overview for cognitive science.* Hillsdale, NJ: Lawrence Erlbaum Associates.

Beck, A. T. (1967). *Depression: Causes and treatment.* Philadelphia: University of Pennsylvania Press.

Beck, A. T. (1987). Cognitive models of depression. *Journal of Cognitive Psychotherapy, 1,* 5–37.

Beck, A., Ellis, A., Meichenbaum, D., Seligman, M., & Beck, A. T. (1976). *Cognitive therapy and the emotional disorders.* New York: International Universities Press.

Beckendam, C. C. (1997). *Dimensions of emotional intelligence: Attachment, affect, regulation, alexithymia and empathy.* Doctoral dissertation, Fielding Institute, Santa Barbara, CA.

Beehr, T. A., & Newman, J. E. (1978). Job stress, employee health, and organizational effectiveness: A facet analysis, model, and literature review. *Personnel Psychology, 31,* 665–699.

Bell, R., & Hepper, P. G. (1987). Catecholamines and aggression in animals. *Behavioural Brain Research, 23,* 1–21.

Bellack, J. P., Morjikian R., Barger, S., et al. (2001). Developing BSN leaders for the future: The Fuld Leadership Initiative for Nursing Education (LINE). *Journal of Professional Nursing, 17,* 23–32.

Belmont, J. M., Butterfield, E. C., & Ferretti, R. P. (1982). To secure transfer of training instruct self-management skills. In D. K. Detterman & R. J. Sternberg (eds.), *How and how much can intelligence be increased?* Norwood, NJ: Ablex Publishing Co.

Ben Ze'ev, A. (2000). *The subtlety of emotions.* Cambridge: MIT Press.

Bergin, A. E., & Lambert, M. J. (1979). Counseling the researcher. *Counseling Psychologist, 8,* 53–56.

Berkowitz, L. (1993). *Aggression: Its causes, consequences, and control.* New York: Mcgraw-Hill.

Berry, D. S., Sherman Hansen, J. (2000). Personality, nonverbal behavior, and interaction quality in female dyads. *Personality & Social Psychology Bulletin, 26,* 278–292.

Berry, D. S., Willingham, J. K., & Thayer, C. A. (2000). Affect and personality as predictors of conflict and closeness in young adults' friendships. *Journal of Research in Personality, 34,* 84–107.

Biederman, J., Newcorn, J., & Sprich, S. (1991). Comorbidity of attention deficit hyperactivity disorder with conduct, depressive, anxiety, and other disorders. *American Journal of Psychiatry, 148,* 564–577.

Biehl, M., Matsumoto, D., Ekman, P., Hearn, V., Heider, K., Kudoh, T., & Ton, K. (1997). Matsumoto and Ekman's Japanese and Caucasian Facial Expressions of Emotion (JACFEE): Reliability data and cross-national differences. *Journal of Nonverbal Behavior, 21,* 3–21.

Billings, A. G., & Moos, R. H. (1984). Coping, stress, and social resources among adults with unipolar depression. *Journal of Personality and Social Psychology, 46,* 877–891.

Binet, A., & Simon, T. (1905a). Sur la nécessité d'établir un diagnostic scientifique des états inferieurs de l'intelligence. *L'Année psychologique, 11,* 163–190.

Binet, A., & Simon, T. (1905b). Méthodes nouvelles pour le diagnostic du niveau intellectuel des anormaux (New methods for diagnosing the intellectual level of abnormals). *L'Année psychologique, 11,* 191–244.

Binet, A., & Simon, T. (1916/1983). *The Development of Intelligence in Children.* Salem, NH: Clyer.

Björkqvist, K., Österman, K., & Kaukiainen, A. (2000). "Social intelligence – empathy = aggression?": Erratum. *Aggression & Violent Behavior, 5,* 429.

Blais, M. A. (1997). Clinician ratings of the five-factor model of personality and the *DSM-IV* personality disorders. *Journal of Nervous & Mental Disease, 185,* 388–393.

Blatt, S. J., Wein, S. J., Chevron, E. S., & Quinlan, D. M. (1979). Parental representations and depression in normal young adults. *Journal of Abnormal Psychology, 88,* 388–397.

Blechman, E. A., Prinz, R. J., & Dumas, J. E. (1995). Coping, competence, and aggression prevention. I: Developmental model. *Applied & Preventive Psychology, 4,* 211–232.

Block, J. (1973). Conceptions of sex role: Some cross-cultural and longitudinal perspectives. *American Psychologist, 28,* 512–526.

Block, J. (1995). A contrarian view of the five-factor approach to personality description. *Psychological Bulletin, 117,* 187–215.

Block, J. H., & Block, J. (1980). The role of ego control and ego-resiliency in the organization of behavior. In W. A. Collins (ed.), *Development of cognition, affect, and social relations* (pp. 39–101). Hillsdale, NJ: Lawrence Erlbaum Associates.

Block, J., & Kremen, A. M. (1996). IQ and ego-resiliency: Conceptual and empirical connections and separateness. *Journal of Personality and Social Psychology, 70,* 349–361.

Boekaerts, M., Pintrich, P., & Zeidner, M. (eds.) (2000). *Handbook of self-regulation.* San Diego: Academic Press.

Bolger, E. A., and Schilling, E. A. (1991). Personality and the problems of everyday life: The role of neuroticism in exposure and reactivity to daily stressors. *Journal of Personality, 59,* 335–386.

Bolger, N. (1990). Coping as a personality process: A prospective study. *Journal of Personality and Social Psychology, 59,* 525–537.

Bonnano, G. (1999). Towards an integrative perspective on bereavement. *Psychological Bulletin, 125,* 760–776.

Booysen, A. E., & Erasmus, J. A. (1989). The relationship between some personality factors and accident risk. *South African Journal of Psychology, 19,* 144–152.

Boring, E. G. (1923). Intelligence as the tests test it. *New Republic,* June 6, 1993.

Bornstein, R. F., & Cecero, J. J. (2000). Deconstructing dependency in a five-factor world: A meta-analytic review. *Journal of Personality Assessment, 74,* 324–343.

Botvin, G. J., & Tortu, S. (1988). Preventing substance abuse through life-skills training. In R. H. Price, E. L. Cowen, R. P. Lorion & J. Ramos-McKay (eds.), *14 ounces of prevention: A casebook for practitioners* (pp. 98–110). Washington, DC: American Psychological Association.

Botwin, M. D., Buss, D. M., & Shackelford, T. K. (1997). Personality and mate preferences: Five factors in mate selection and marital satisfaction. *Journal of Personality, 65,* 107–136.

Botwinick, J. (1978). *Aging and behavior.* New York: Springer Publishing Co.

Botzum, W. A. (1951). A factorial study of reasoning and closure factors. *Psychometrika, 16,* 361–386.

Bower, G. H. (1981). Mood and Memory. *American Psychologist, 36,* 129–148.

Bower, G. H., & Cohen, P. R. (1982). Emotional influences in memory and thinking: Data and theory. In S. Fiske & M. Clark (eds.), *Affect and social cognition.* Hillsdale, NJ: Lawrence Erlbaum Associates.

Bowlby, J. (1982). *Attachment and loss.* Vol. 1: *Attachment.* New York: Basic Books.

Bowman, M. L. (1997). *Individual differences in posttraumatic response: Problems with the adversity-distress connection.* Mahwah, NJ: Lawrence Erlbaum Associates.

Boyatzis, R. (1982). *The competent manager.* New York: Wiley & Sons.

Boyatzis, R., Goleman, D., & Rhee, K. (2000). Clustering competence in emotional intelligence: Insights from the emotional competence inventory. In R. Bar-On & J. D. A. Parker (eds.), *Handbook of Emotional Intelligence.* San Francisco: Jossey-Bass.

Boyce, P., & Parker, G. (1989). Development of a scale to measure interpersonal sensitivity. *Australian & New Zealand Journal of Psychiatry, 23,* 341–351.

Boyle, G. J. (1988). Contribution of Cattellian psychometrics to the elucidation of human intellectual structure. *Multivariate Experimental Clinical Research, 8,* 267–273.

Boyle, G. J., Stankov, L., & Cattell, R. B. (1995). Measurement and statistical models in the study of personality and intelligence. In D. Saklofske & M. Zeidner (eds.), *International handbook of personality & intelligence.* New York: Plenum Publishing Corp.

Braden, J. P. (1989). Fact or artefact? An empirical test of Spearman's hypothesis. *Intelligence, 13,* 149–155.

Bradlee, P. M., & Emmons, R. A. (1992). Locating narcissism within the interpersonal circumplex and the Five-Factor model. *Personality & Individual Differences, 13,* 821–830.

Brandstätter, H. (1994). Well-being and motivated person-environment fit: A time-sampling study of emotions. *European Journal of Personality, 8,* 75–94.

Brandt, R. S. (1999). Successful implementation of SEL programs. In J. Cohen (ed.), *Educating minds and hearts* (pp. 173–182). New York: Teachers College Press.

Brantley, P., & Sutker, P. B. (1983). Antisocial personalities. In P. Sutker & H. Adams (eds.), *Comprehensive handbook of psychopathology.* New York: Plenum.

Brebner, J., & Cooper, C. (1986). Personality factors and inspection time. *Personality & Individual Differences, 7,* 709–714.

Brehm, S. S. (1983). La réactance psychologique et la différenciation sociale (Psychological reactance and social differentiation). *Bulletin de psychologie, 37,* 471–474.

Brenner, E. M., & Salovey, P. (1997). Emotion regulation during childhood: Developmental, interpersonal, and individual considerations. In P. Salovey & D. J. Sluyter (eds.), *Emotional development and emotional intelligence: Educational implications.* New York: Basic Books.

Bretherton, I. (1985). Attachment theory: Retrospect and prospect. In I. Bretherton & E. Waters (eds.), *Growing points of attachment theory and research* (pp. 3–35). Chicago: Society for Research in Child Development.

Brief, A. P., & Motowidlo, S. J. (1986). Prosocial organizational behaviors. *Academy of Management Review, 11,* 710–725.

Brody, E. B., & Brody, N. (1976). *Intelligence: Nature, determinants, and consequences.* New York: Academic Press.

Brody, L. R. (1985). Gender differences in emotional development: A review of theories and research. *Journal of Personality, 53,* 102–149.

Brody, N. (1992). *Intelligence* (2nd ed.). New York: Academic Press.

Brotman Band, E., & Weisz, J. R. (1988). How to feel better when it feels bad: Children's perspectives on coping with everyday stress. *Developmental Psychology, 24,* 247–253.

Brown, J. R., & Dunn, J. (1991). "You can cry, Mum": The social and developmental implications of talk about internal states. *British Journal of Developmental Psychology, 9,* 237–256.

Brown, K., Covell, K., & Abramovitch, R. (1991). Time course and control of emotion: Age differences in understanding and recognition. *Merrill-Palmer Quarterly, 37,* 273–287.

Brown, L. T., & Anthony, R. G. (1990). Continuing the search for social intelligence. *Personality and Individual Differences, 11,* 463–470.

Browne-Miller, A. (1995). *Intelligence policy: Its impact on college admissions and other social policies.* New York: Plenum.

Brunas-Wagstaff, J., Bergquist, A., Morgan, K., & Wagstaff, G. F. (1996). Impulsivity, interference on perceptual tasks, and hypothesis testing. *Personality & Individual Differences, 20,* 471–482.

Bruner, J. S. (1962). Myth and identity. In R. M. Ohmann (ed.), *The making of myth* (pp. 159–169). New York: Putnam.

Buck, R. (1984). *The communication of emotion.* New York: Guilford Press.

Buck, R., Miller, R. E., & Caul, D. F. (1974). Sex, personality, and physiological variables in the communication of emotion via facial expression. *Journal of Personality and Social Psychology, 30,* 587–596.

Buffier, F. (1997). Social intelligence, broad cognitive abilities, and the Big Five personality factors. Unpublished honors thesis: Department of Psychology, University of Sydney.

Burger, J. M. (1992). *Desire for control: Personality, social, and clinical perspectives.* New York: Plenum Press.

Burke, M. J., & Day, R. R. (1986). A cumulative study of the effectiveness of managerial training. *Journal of Applied Psychology, 71,* 232–245.

Burke, R. J. (1993). Organizational-level interventions to reduce occupational stressors. *Work and Stress, 7,* 77–87.

Burke, R. J., & Belcourt, M. L. (1974). Managerial role stress and coping responses. *Journal of Business Administration, 5,* 55–68.

Burke, R. J., & Weir, T. (1980). Coping with stress of managerial occupations. In C. L. Cooper & R. L. Payne (eds.), *Current concerns in occupational stress.* New York: Wiley.

Burt, C. R. (1940). *The factors of the mind.* London: University of London Press.

Buss, A. H., & Plomin, R. A. (1984). *Temperament: Early developing personality traits.* Hillsdale, NJ: Lawrence Erlbaum Associates.

Buss, D. M. (1999). Evolutionary psychology: The new science of the mind. Needham Heights, MA: Allyn & Bacon.

Butkovsky, L. L. (1991). Emotional expressiveness in the family: Connection to children's peer relations. Poster presented at the biennial meeting of the Society for Research in Child Development. Seattle, Washington.

Caballo, V. E. (ed.) (1998). *International handbook of cognitive and behavioural treatments for psychological disorders.* Oxford: Pergamon/Elsevier Science.

Caldarella, P., & Merrell, K. (1997). Common dimensions of social skills of children and adolescents: A taxonomy of positive social behaviors. *School Psychology Review, 26,* 265–279.

Calkins, S. D. (1994). Origins and outcomes of individual differences in emotion regulation. *Monographs of the Society for Research in Child Development, 59,* 250–283.

Callister, J. D., King, R. E., Retzlaff, D., & Marsh, R. W. (1999). Revised NEO Personality Inventory profiles of male and female U.S. Air Force pilots. *Military Medicine, 164,* 885–890.

Calvo, M. G., Eysenck, M. W., & Castillo, M. D. (1997). Interpretation bias in test anxiety: The time course of predictive inferences. *Cognition and Emotion, 11,* 43–63.

Campbell, D. T., & Fiske, D. W. (1959). Convergent and discriminant validation by the multitrait-multimethod matrix. *Psychological Bulletin, 56,* 81–105.

Campbell, D. T., & Stanley, J. C. (1963). Experimental and quasi-experimental designs for research on teaching. In N. L. Gage (ed.), *Handbook of research on teaching* (pp. 171–246). Chicago: Rand McNally.

Campbell, K. W., Reeder, G. D., Sedikides, C., & Elliot, A. J. (2000). Narcissism and comparative self-enhancement strategies. *Journal of Research in Personality, 34,* 329–347.

Campos, J. J., & Barrett, K. C. (1984). Toward a new understanding of emotions and their development. In C. E. Izard, J. Kagan & R. B. Zajonc (eds.), *Emotions, cognition, and behavior* (pp. 229–263). Cambridge: Cambridge University Press.

Campos, J. J., Campos, R. G., & Barrett, K. C. (1989). Emergent themes in the study of emotional development and emotion regulation. *Developmental Psychology, 25,* 394–402.

Cantor, N., & Kihlstrom, J. F. (1985). Social intelligence: The cognitive basis of personality. In P. Shaver (ed.), *Review of personality and social psychology* (vol. 6, pp. 15–33). Beverly Hills, CA: Sage.

Cantor, N., & Kihlstrom, J. F. (1987). *Personality and social intelligence.* Englewood Cliffs, NJ: Prentice-Hall.

Caplan, M., Weissberg, R. P., Grober, J. S., Sivo, P. J., Grady, K., & Jacoby, C. (1992). Social competence promotion with inner-city and suburban young adolescents: Effects on social adjustment and alcohol use. *Journal of Consulting and Clinical Psychology, 60,* 56–63.

Caplan, R. D., Cobb, S., French, J., Harrison, R. V., & Pinneau, S. R., Jr. (1975). *Job demands and worker health.* Washington, DC: U.S. Government Printing Office.

Caprara, G. V., Barbaranelli, C., & Zimbardo, P. G. (1996). Understanding the complexity of human aggression: Affective, cognitive, and social dimensions of individual differences in propensity toward aggression. *European Journal of Personality, 10,* 133–155.

Carnavale, A. P., Gainer, L. J., & Meltzer, A. S. (1988). Workplace basics: The skills employers want. *Training and Development Journal, 42,* 22–26.

Carroll, J. B. (1961). The nature of the data, or How to choose a correlation coefficient. *Psychometrika, 26,* 347–372.

Carroll, J. B. (1980). Remarks on Sternberg's "Factor theories of intelligence are all right almost." *Educational Researcher, 9,* 14–18.

Carroll, J. B. (1982). The measurement of intelligence. In R. J. Sternberg (ed.), *Handbook of human intelligence* (pp. 29–120). New York: Cambridge University Press.

Carroll, J. B. (1988). Editorial: Cognitive abilities, factors, and processes. *Intelligence, 12,* 101–109.

Carroll, J. B. (1989). Factor analysis since Spearman: Where do we stand? What do we know? In R. Kanfer, P. L. Ackerman & R. Cudeck (eds.), *Abilities, motivation, and methodology: The Minnesota Symposium on Learning and Individual Differences*. Hillsdale, NJ: Lawrence Erlbaum Associates.

Carroll, J. B. (1992). Cognitive abilities: The state of the art. *Psychological Science, 3*, 266–270.

Carroll, J. B. (1993). *Human cognitive abilities: A survey of factor-analytic studies*. New York: Cambridge University Press.

Carrothers, R. M., Gregory, S. W., & Gallagher, T. J. (2000). Measuring emotional intelligence of medical school applicants. *Academic Medicine, 75*, 456–463.

Carson, A. J., Ringbauer, B., MacKenzie, L., Warlow, C., & Sharpe, M. (2000). Neurological disease, emotional disorder, and disability—they are related: A study of 300 consecutive new referrals to a neurology outpatient department. *Journal of Neurology, Neurosurgery & Psychiatry, 68*, 202–206.

Carson, K. D., & Carson, P. P. (1998). Career commitment, competencies, and citizenship. *Journal of Career Assessment, 6*, 195–208.

Cartwright, S., & Cooper, C. L. (1996). Coping in occupational settings. In M. Zeidner & N. S. Endler (eds.), *Handbook of coping* (pp. 202–220). New York: Wiley.

Carver, C. S., Pozo, C., Harris, S. D., Noriega, V., Scheier, M. F., Robinson, D. S., Ketchan, A. S., Moffat, F. L., Jr. & Clark, K. C. (1993). How coping mediates the effect of optimism on distress: A study of women with early stage breast cancer. *Journal of Personality and Social Psychology, 65*, 375–390.

Carver, C. S., & Scheier, M. F. (1981). *Attention and self-regulation: A control-theory approach to human behavior*. Berlin: Springer-Verlag.

Carver, C. S., & Scheier, M. F. (1998). *On the self-regulation of behavior*. New York: Cambridge University Press.

Carver, C. S., & Scheier, M. F. (2000a). Autonomy and self regulation. *Psychological Inquiry, 11*, 284–291.

Carver, C. S., & Scheier, M. F. (2000b). On the structure of behavioral self-regulation. In M. Boekaerts, P. Pintrich & M. Zeidner (eds.), *Handbook of self-regulation* (pp. 41–84). San Diego: Academic Press.

Carver, C. S., Scheier, M. F., & Pozo, C. (1992). Conceptualizing the process of coping with health problems. In H. S. Friedman (ed.), *Hostility, coping, and health* (pp. 167–199). Washington, DC: American Psychological Association.

Carver, C. S., Scheier, M. F., & Weintraub, J. K. (1989). Assessing coping strategies: A theoretically based approach. *Journal of Personality and Social Psychology, 56*, 267–283.

Cassidy, J. (1994). Emotion regulation: Influences of attachment relationships. In N. A. Fox & J. J. Campos (eds.) *The development of emotion regulation: Behavioral and biological considerations* (pp. 228–249). Chicago: Society for Research in Child Development.

Cassidy, J., Parke, R. D., Butkovsky, L., & Braungart, J. M. (1992). Family peer connections: The roles of emotional expressiveness within the family and children's understanding of emotions. *Child Development, 63,* 603–618.

Cattell, R. B. (1941). Some theoretical issues in adult intelligence testing. *Psychological Bulletin, 38,* 592.

Cattell, R. B. (1944). Interpretation of the twelve primary personality factors. *Character & Personality: A Quarterly for Psychodiagnostic & Allied Studies, 13,* 55–91.

Cattell, R. B. (1963). Theory of fluid and crystallized intelligence: A critical experiment. *Journal of Educational Psychology, 54,* 1–22.

Cattell, R. B. (1971). *Abilities: Their structure, growth, and action.* Boston: Houghton Mifflin.

Cattell, R. B. (1987). *Intelligence: Its structure, growth, and action.* Amsterdam: North-Holland.

Cattell, R. B., & Horn, J. L. (1978). A check on the theory of fluid and crystallized intelligence with description of new test designs. *Journal of Educational Measurement, 15,* 139–164.

Cattell, R. B., Horn, J. L., Sweeney, A. B., & Radcliffe, J. A. (1964). *Motivations Analysis Test.* Champaign, IL: Institute of Personality and Ability Testing.

Ceci, S. J. (1990). *On Intelligence ... more or less: A bio-ecological treatise on intellectual development.* Englewood Cliffs, NJ: Prentice-Hall.

Ceci, S. J. (1990). On the relation between microlevel processing efficiency and macrolevel measures of intelligence. *Intelligence, 14,* 141–150.

Ceci, S. J., & Liker, J. K. (1986). A day at the races: A study of IQ, expertise, and cognitive complexity. *Journal of Experimental Psychology: General, 115,* 255–266.

Ceci, S. J., & Liker, J. K. (1988). Stalking the IQ-experience relationship: When the critics go fishing. *Journal of Experimental Psychology: General, 117,* 96–100.

Center, D. S. (1998). *The Child Development Project: A brief summary of the project and findings from three evaluation studies.* Oakland, CA: Developmental Studies Center.

Chambers, J. A. (1997). *Selected papers from the Eighth National Conference on College Teaching and Learning.* Jacksonville, FL: Florida Community College at Jacksonville.

Chambless, D. L., & Gillis, M. M. (1993). Cognitive Therapy for anxiety disorders. *Journal of Consulting and Clinical Psychology, 61,* 248–260.

Chartrand, T. L., & Bargh, J. A. (1999). The chameleon effect: The perception-behavior link and social interaction. *Journal of Personality & Social Psychology, 76,* 893–910.

Chen, J., & Gardner, H. (1997). Alternative assessment from a multiple intelligences perspective. In D. P. Flanagan, J. L. Genshaft & P. L. Harrison (eds.), *Contemporary intellectual assessment: Theories, tests, and issues* (pp. 105–121). New York: Guilford Press.

Cherniss, C. (2000). Social and emotional competence in the workplace. In R. Bar-On & J. D. A. Parker (eds.), *Handbook of Emotional Intelligence.* New York: Jossey-Bass.

Cherniss, C., Goleman, D., Emmerling, R., Cowan, K., & Adler, M. (1998). *Bringing emotional intelligence in organizations.* New Brunswick, NJ: Consortium for Research on Emotional Intelligence in Organizations, Rutgers University.

Childre, D. L., & Cryer, B. (1999). *From chaos to coherence: Advancing emotional and organizational intelligence through inner quality management.* Boston: Butterworth-Heinemann.

Chlopan, B. E., MacCain, M. L., Carbonell, J. L., & Hagan, R. L. (1985). Empathy: Review of available measures. *Journal of Personality and Social Psychology, 48,* 635–653.

Church, A. T., Katigbak, M. S., Reyes, J. A. S., & Jensen, S. M. (1998). Language and organisation of Filipino emotion concepts: Comparing emotion concepts and dimensions across cultures. *Cognition and Emotion, 12,* 63–92.

Churchland, P. S. (1996). Toward a neurobiology of the mind. In R. R. Llinas & P. S. Churchland (eds.), *The mind-brain continuum: Sensory processes* (pp. 281–303). Cambridge: MIT Press.

Chwelos, G., & Oatley, K. (1994). Appraisal, computational models, and Scherer's expert system. *Cognition and Emotion, 8,* 245–257.

Cialdini, R. B., Brown, S. L., Lewis, B. P., & Luce, C., et al. (1997). Reinterpreting the empathy-altruism relationship: When one into one equals oneness. *Journal of Personality & Social Psychology, 73,* 481–494.

Ciarrochi, J., Chan, A., & Bajgar, J. (2001). Measuring emotional intelligence in adolescents. *Personality & Individual Differences, 31,* 1105–1119.

Ciarrochi, J., Chan, A., & Caputi, P. (2000a). A critical evaluation of the emotional intelligence construct. *Personality and Individual Differences, 28,* 539–561.

Ciarrochi, J., Chan, A., & Caputi, P. (2000b). [Measuring emotional intelligence.] Unpublished data.

Ciarrochi, J., Chan, A., Caputi, P., & Roberts, R. D. (2001). Assessing emotional intelligence (EI): A critical evaluation. To appear in J. Ciarrochi, J. Forgas & J. D. Mayer (eds.), *Emotional intelligence in everyday life: A scientific inquiry.* Washington, DC: American Psychological Association.

Ciarrochi, J., & Deane, F. (2001). The relationship between emotional intelligence and the willingness to seek help from nonprofessional and professional sources. *British Journal of Guidance and Counselling, 29,* 233–246.

Ciarrochi, J., Deane, F., & Anderson, S. (2002). Emotional intelligence moderates the relationship between stress and mental health. *Personality and Individual Differences, 32,* 197–209.

Clabby, J., & Elias, M. (1999). Social decision making/problem solving program. Unpublished research report.

Clark, D. A., & Beck, A. T. (1999). *Scientific foundations of cognitive theory and therapy of depression.* New York: Wiley.

Clark, D. A., Beck, A. T., & Brown, G. (1989). Cognitive mediation in general psychiatric outpatients: A test of the content-specificity hypothesis. *Journal of Personality & Social Psychology, 56,* 958–964.

Clark, D. M. (1986). A cognitive model of panic. *Behaviour Research and Therapy*, 24, 461–470.

Clark, D. M. (1997). Panic disorder and social phobia. In D. M. Clark & C. G. Fairburn (eds.), *Science and practice of cognitive behaviour therapy* (pp. 119–153). New York: Oxford University Press.

Clark, D. M., & Wells, A. (1997). A review of theory and treatment outcome in a range of anxiety disorders (panic, social phobia, hypochondriasis, OCD, GAD, PTSD): Cognitive therapy of anxiety disorders. In L. J., Dickstein, M. B. Riba & J. M. Oldham (eds.), *Review of Psychiatry* (vol. 16, pp. 9–43). Washington, DC: American Psychiatric Press.

Clark, L. A., & Watson, D. (1988). Mood and the mundane: Relations between daily life events and self-reported mood. *Journal of Personality & Social Psychology*, 54, 296–308.

Clark, L. A., & Watson, D. (1991). Tripartite model of anxiety and depression: Psychometric evidence and taxonomic implications. *Journal of Abnormal Psychology*, 100, 316–336.

Clore, G., & Ketelaar, T. (1997). Minding our emotions: On the role of automatic, unconscious affect. In R. S. Wyer Jr. et al. (eds.), *The automaticity of everyday life* (pp. 105–120). Mahwah, NJ: Lawrence Erlbaum Associates.

Clore, G., & Ortony, A. (2000). Cognition in emotion: Sometimes, always, or never? In R. D. Lane & L. Nadel (eds.), *Cognitive neuroscience of emotion*. New York: Oxford University Press.

Cobb, C. D., & Mayer, J. D. (2000). Emotional intelligence. *Educational Leadership*, 58 (3), 14–18.

Cohen, F., & Lazarus, R. (1979). Coping with the stresses of illness. In G. C. Stone, F. Cohen & N. E. Adler (eds.), *Health psychology: A handbook*. San-Francisco: Jossey-Bass.

Cohen, J. (1959). A factor-analytically based rationale of the Wechsler Adult Intelligence Scale. *Journal of Consulting Psychology*, 21, 451–457.

Cohen, J. (1988). *Statistical power analysis for the behavioral sciences* (2nd ed.). Hillsdale, NJ: Lawrence Erlbaum Associates.

Cohen, J. (ed.) (1999a). *Educating minds and hearts: Social emotional learning and the passage into adolescence*. New York: Teachers College Press.

Cohen, J. (1999b). Learning about social and emotional learning: Current themes and future directions. In J. Cohen (ed.), *Educating minds and hearts* (pp. 184–191). New York: Teachers College Press.

Cohen, J. (1999c). Social and emotional learning: Past and present. In J. Cohen (ed.), *Educating minds and hearts: Social emotional learning and the passage into adolescence* (pp. 2–23). New York: Teachers College Press.

Cohen, J. D., Dunbar, K., & McClelland, J. L. (1990). On the control of automatic processes: A parallel distributed processing account of the Stroop effect. *Psychological Review*, 97, 332–361.

Cole, P. M., Michel, M. K., & O'Donnell, L. (1994). The development of emotion regulation and dysregulation: A clinical perspective. In N. A. Fox (ed.), *The development of emotion regulation* (pp. 73–100). Chicago: Society for Research on Child Development.

Colquitt, J. A., & Simmering, M. J. (1998). Conscientiousness, goal orientation, and motivation to learn during the learning process: A longitudinal study. *Journal of Applied Psychology, 83,* 654–665.

Colquitt, J. A., LePine, J. A., & Noe, R. A. (2000). Toward an integrative theory of training motivation: A meta-analytic path analysis of 20 years of research. *Journal of Applied Psychology, 85,* 678–707.

Colvin, C. R., Block, J., & Funder, D. C. (1995). Overly positive self-evaluations and personality: Negative implications for mental health. *Journal of Personality and Social Psychology, 68,* 1152–1162.

Comer, J. P. (1988). Is "parenting" essential to good teaching. *Families and Schools,* 34–40.

Compas, B. E., Malcarne, V. L., & Fondacaro, K. M. (1988). Coping with stressful events in older children and young adolescents. *Journal of Consulting and Clinical Psychology, 56,* 405–411.

Cooper, C. L. (1985). The road to health in American firms. *New Society,* 335–336.

Cooper, C. L., & Cartwright, S. (1994). Healthy mind, healthy organization: A proactive approach to occupational stress. *Human Relations, 4,* 455–471.

Cooper, C. L., & Kelley, M. (1993). Occupational stress in head teachers: A national UK study. *British Journal of Educational Psychology, 63,* 130–143.

Cooper, C. L., Liukkonen, P., & Cartwright, S. (1996). *Stress prevention in the workplace.* Dublin, Ireland: European Foundation for the Improvement of Living and Working Conditions; Lanham, MD: UNIPUB.

Cooper, C. L., & Marshall, J. (1976). Occupational sources of stress: A review of the literature relating to coronary heart disease and mental health. *Journal of Occupational Psychology, 49,* 11–28.

Cooper, C. L., & Marshall, J. (1978a). Sources of managerial and white collar stress. In C. L. Cooper & R. Payne (eds.), *Stress at work* (pp. 81–105). Chichester: Wiley.

Cooper, C. L., & Marshall, J. (1978b). *Understanding executive stress.* London: Macmillan.

Cooper, C. L., & Payne, R. (eds.) (1978). *Stress at work.* Chichester: Wiley.

Cooper, R., & Payne, R. (1967). Extraversion and some aspects of work Behavior. *Personnel Psychology, 20,* 45–57.

Cooper, R. K. (1997). Applying emotional intelligence in the workplace. *Training and Development, 51,* 31–33.

Cooper, R. K., & Sawaf, A. (1997). *Executive EQ: Emotional intelligence in leaders and organizations.* NY: Grosset/Putnam.

Corr, P. J. (2000). Testing problems in J. A. Gray's personality theory: A commentary on Matthews and Gilliland (1999). *Personality & Individual Differences,* *30,* 333–352.

Corr, P. J., Pickering, A. D., & Gray, J. A. (1995). Personality and reinforcement in associative and instrumental learning. *Personality and Individual Differences, 19,* 47–72.

Corter, H. M. (1952). Factor analysis of some reasoning tests. *Psychological Monographs, 66,* 1–31.

Cortina, J. M., Doherty, M. L., Schmitt, N., & Kaufman, G., et al. (1992). The "Big Five" personality factors in the IPI and MMPI: Predictors of police performance. *Personnel Psychology, 45,* 119–140.

Costa, P. T., Jr. (1996). Work and personality: Use of the NEO-PI-R in industrial/organizational psychology. *Applied Psychology: An International Review, 45,* 225–241.

Costa, P. T., Jr. & McCrae, R. R. (1980). Somatic complaints in males as a function of age and neuroticism: A longitudinal analysis. *Journal of Behavioral Medicine, 3,* 245–257.

Costa, P. T., Jr. & McCrae, R. R. (1985). Hypochondriasis, neuroticism, and aging: When are somatic complaints unfounded? *American Psychologist, 40,* 19–28.

Costa, P. T., Jr. & McCrae, R. R. (1986). Personality, coping, and coping effectiveness in an adult sample. *Journal of Personality, 54,* 385–405.

Costa, P. T., Jr. & McCrae, R. R. (1992a). *NEO PI-R professional manual.* Odessa, Florida: Psychological Assessment Resources.

Costa, P. T., Jr. & McCrae, R. R. (1992b). Normal personality assessment in clinical practice: The NEO Personality Inventory. *Psychological Assessment, 4,* 5–13.

Costa, P. T., Jr. & McCrae, R. R. (1992c). Four ways five factors are basic. *Personality and Individual Differences, 13,* 653–665.

Costa, P. T., Jr. & McCrae, R. R. (1994). Set like plaster: Evidence for the stability of adult personality. In T. F. Heatherton, J. L. Weinberger, et al. (eds.), *Can personality change?* (pp. 21–40). Washington, DC: American Psychological Association.

Costa, P. T., Jr., Somerfield, M. R., & McCrae, R. R. (1996). Personality and coping: A reconceptualization. In M. Zeidner, N. S. Endler, et al. (eds.), *Handbook of coping: Theory, research, and applications* (pp. 44–61). New York: John Wiley & Sons.

Costanzo, M., & Archer, D. (1993). *The Interpersonal Perception Task—15 (IPT-15): Videotape and technical manual.* Berkeley: Extension Media Center, University of California.

Cowen, E. L. (1994). The enhancement of psychological wellness: Challenges and opportunities. *American Journal of Community Psychology, 22,* 149–178.

Cox, B. J., Borger, S. C., Asmundson, G. J. G., & Taylor, S. (2000). Dimensions of hypochondriasis and the five-factor model of personality. *Personality & Individual Differences, 29,* 99–108.

Cox, T., & Ferguson, E. (1991). Individual differences, stress, and coping. In C. Cooper & R. Payne (eds.), *Personality and stress* (pp. 7–30). Chichester: Wiley.

Coyne, J. C. (1985). Studying depressed persons' interactions with strangers and spouses. *Journal of Abnormal Psychology, 85,* 186–193.

Coyne, J. C., & Whiffen, V. E. (1995). Issues in personality as diathesis for depression: The case of sociotropy/dependency and autonomy/self-criticism. *Psychological Bulletin, 118,* 358–378.

Cristal, R. E. (1994). Non-cognitive research involving systems of testing and learning. Brooks Air Force Base, TX: Armstrong Laboratory.

Crittenden, P. M. (1994). Peering into the black box: An exploratory treatise on the development of self in young children. In D. Cicchetti & S. L. Toth (eds.), *Disorders and dysfunctions of the self* (pp. 79–48). Rochester, NY: University of Rochester Press.

Crockenberg, S. B. (1981). Infant irritability, mother responsiveness, and social support influences on the security of infant-mother attachment. *Child Development, 52,* 857–880.

Cronbach, L. J. (1957). The two disciplines of scientific psychology. *American Psychologist, 12,* 671–684.

Cronbach, L. J. (1960/1970). *Essentials of psychological testing* (2nd/3rd ed.). New York: Harper & Row.

Cronbach, L. J. (1988). Five perspectives on the validity argument. In H. Wainer & H. I. Braun (eds.), *Test validity*. Hillsdale, NJ: Lawrence Erlbaum Associates.

Cronbach, L. J. (1990). *Essentials of psychological testing* (5th ed.). New York: Harper & Row.

Cronbach, L. J., & Furby, L. (1970). How we should measure "change," or should we? *Psychological Bulletin, 74,* 68–80.

Cronbach, L. J., & Meehl, P. E. (1955). Construct validity in psychological tests. *Psychological Bulletin, 52,* 281–302.

Crowne, D. P., & Marlowe, D. (1964). *The approval motive: Studies in evaluative dependence.* New York: Wiley.

Csikszentmihalyi, M. (1990). *Flow: The psychology of optimal experience.* New York: Harper Collins.

Cummings, E. M., Zahn-Waxler, C., & Radke-Yarrow, M. (1984). Developmental changes in children's reactions to anger in the home. *Journal of Child Psychology and Psychiatry, 25,* 63–74.

Daly, J. W. (1993). Mechanism of action of caffeine. In S. Garattini (ed.), *Caffeine, coffee, and health.* New York: Raven Press.

Damasio, A. R. (1994). The brain binds entities and events by multiregional activation from convergence zones. In H. Gutfreund, G. Toulouse, et al. (eds.), *Biology and computation: A physicist's choice* (pp. 749–758). Singapore: World Scientific Publishing Co.

Damasio, A. R. (1999). *The feeling of what happens: Body and emotion in the making of consciousness.* San Diego, CA: Harcourt.

Danthiir, V., Pallier, G., Roberts, R. D., & Stankov, L. (2001). What the nose knows: Olfaction within the structure of human cognitive abilities. *Intelligence.* In press.

Darwin, C. (1872/1965). *The expression of the emotions in man and animals.* Chicago: University of Chicago Press.

David, C. F., & Kistner, J. A. (2000). Do positive self-perceptions have a "dark side"? Examination of the link between perceptual bias and aggression. *Journal of Abnormal Child Psychology, 28,* 327–337.

David, J. P., & Suls, J. (1999). Coping efforts in daily life: Role of Big Five traits and problem appraisals. *Journal of Personality, 67,* 265–294.

Davidson, D. A., Short, M. A., & Nelson, D. L. (1984). The measurement of empathic ability in normal and atypical five and six year old boys. *Occupational Therapy in Mental Health, 4,* 13–24.

Davies, M., Stankov, L., & Roberts, R. D. (1998). Emotional intelligence: In search of an elusive construct. *Journal of Personality and Social Psychology, 75,* 989–1015.

Davis, M. H. (1983). Measuring individual differences in empathy: Evidence for a multidimensional approach. *Journal of Personality and Social Psychology, 44,* 113–126.

Davis, M. H. (1994). *Empathy: A social psychological approach.* Boulder, CO: Westview Press.

Davis, M. H., & Kraus, L. A. (1997). Personality and empathic accuracy. In W. Ickes, W. John, et al. (eds.), *Empathic accuracy* (pp. 144–168). New York: Guilford Press.

Dawda, D., & Hart, S. D. (2000). Assessing emotional intelligence: Reliability and validity of the Bar-On Emotional Quotient Inventory (EQ-i) in university students. *Personality & Individual Differences, 28,* 797–812.

De Fruyt, F., & Mervielde, I. (1996). Personality and interests as predictors of educational streaming and achievement. *European Journal of Personality, 10,* 405–425.

De Fruyt, F., & Mervielde, I. (1999). RIASEC types and big five traits as predictors of employment status and nature of employment. *Personnel Psychology, 52,* 701–727.

De Raad, B. (2000). *The Big Five personality factors: The psycholexical approach to personality.* Kirkland, WA: Hogrefe & Huber Publishers.

De Raad, B., & Schouwenburg, H. C. (1996). Personality in learning and education: A review. *European Journal of Personality, 10,* 303–336.

Deary, I. J. (2000). Simple information processing and intelligence. In R. J. Sternberg (ed.), *Handbook of intelligence* (pp. 267–284). New York: Cambridge University Press.

Deary, I. J., Agius, R. M., & Sadler, A. (1996). Personality and stress in consultant psychiatrists. *International Journal of Social Psychiatry, 42,* 112–123.

Deary, I. J., Bedford, A., & Fowkes, F. G. R. (1995). The Personality Deviance Scales: Their development, associations, factor structure, and restructuring. *Personality and Individual Differences, 19,* 275–291.

Deary, I. J., Blenkin, H., Agius, R. M., Endler, N. S., Zealley, H., & Wood, R. (1996). Models of job-related stress and personal achievement among consultant doctors. *British Journal of Psychology, 87,* 3–29.

Deary, I. J., Scott, S., & Wilson, J. A. (1997). Neuroticism, alexithymia, and medically unexplained symptoms. *Personality and Individual Differences, 22,* 551–564.

Deary, I. J., Wilson, J. A., & Kelly, S. W. (1995). Globus pharyngis, personality, and psychological distress in the general population. *Psychosomatics, 36,* 570–577.

Decker, P. J. (1982). The enhancement of behavior modeling training of supervisory skills by the inclusion of retention processes. *Personnel Psychology, 35,* 323–332.

DeFalco, K. (1997). Educator's commentary. In P. Salovey & D. J. Sluyter (eds.), *Emotional development and emotional intelligence: Educational implications* (pp. 32–34). New York: Basic Books.

DeFranks, R. S., & Cooper, C. L. (1987). Worksite stress management interventions: Their effectiveness and conceptualization. *Journal of Managerial Psychology, 2,* 4–10.

DeNeve, K. M., & Cooper, H. (1998). The happy personality: A meta-analysis of 137 personality traits and subjective well-being. *Psychological Bulletin, 124,* 197–229.

Denham, S. A. (1986). Social cognition, social behavior, and emotion in preschoolers. *Child Development, 57,* 194–201.

Denham, S. A. (1989). Maternal affect and toddlers' social-emotional competence. *American Journal of Orthopsychiatry, 59,* 368–376.

Denham, S. A. (1998). *Emotional development in young children.* New York: Guilford Press.

Denham, S. A., & Burton, R. (1996). A social-emotional intervention program for at risk four-year-olds. *Journal of School Psychology, 34,* 225–245.

Denham, S. A., & Grout, L. (1993). Socialization of emotion: Pathway to preschooler's emotional and social competence. *Journal of Nonverbal Behavior, 17,* 205–227.

Denham, S. A., McKinley, M., Cuchoud, E. A., & Holt, R. (1990). Emotional and behavioral predictors of peer status in young preschoolers. *Child Development, 61,* 1145–1152.

Denham, S. A., Mitchell-Copeland, J., Strandberg, K., & Highsmith, T. (1994). Parental contributions to preschoolers' emotional competence: Directions and indirect effects. Paper presented at the Dimensions and Consequences of Positive Parenting Symposium at the biennial meeting of the International Society for the Study of Behavioral Development, Amsterdam, Holland.

Denham, S. A., Renwick, S. M., & Holt, R. W. (1991). Working and playing together: Prediction of preschool social-emotional competence from mother-child interaction. *Child Development, 62,* 242–249.

Denham, S. A., Zoller, D., & Couchoud, E. A. (1994). Socialization of preschooler's understanding of emotion. *Developmental Psychology, 30,* 928–936.

Derryberry, D., & Reed, M. A. (1994). Temperament and attention: Orienting toward and away from positive and negative signals. *Journal of Personality and Social Psychology, 66,* 1128–1139.

Derryberry, D., & Reed, M. A. (1997). Motivational and attentional components of personality. In G. Matthews (ed.), *Cognitive science perspectives on personality and emotion.* Amsterdam: Elsevier.

Derryberry, D., & Reed, M. A. (1998). Anxiety and attentional focusing: Trait, state, and hemispheric influences. *Personality & Individual Differences, 25,* 745–761.

Derryberry, D., & Rothbart, M. K. (1988). Arousal, affect, and attention as components of temperament. *Journal of Personality and Social Psychology, 55,* 958–966.

Derryberry, D., & Rothbart, M. K. (1997). Reactive and effortful process in the organization of temperament. *Development and Psychopathology, 9,* 631–650.

Detterman, D. K. (1982). Does *g* exist? *Intelligence, 6,* 99–108.

Detterman, D. K., & Spry, K. M. (1988). Is it smart to play the horses? Comment on "A day at the races: A study of IQ, expertise, and cognitive complexity" (Ceci & Liker, 1986). *Journal of Experimental Psychology: General, 117,* 91–95.

Dewaele, J. M., & Furnham, A. (1999). Extraversion: The unloved variable in applied linguistic research. *Language Learning, 49,* 509–544.

Dickman, S. J. (1990). Functional and dysfunctional impulsivity: Personality and cognitive correlates. *Journal of Personality & Social Psychology, 58,* 95–102.

Dickman, S. J., & Meyer, D. E. (1988). Impulsivity and speed-accuracy tradeoffs in information processing. *Journal of Personality & Social Psychology, 54,* 274–290.

Diener, E. G. S. (1984). Happiness and life satisfaction: A bibliography. *Psychological Documents, 14,* 11.

Diener, E. G. S. (2000). Subjective well-being: The science of happiness and a proposal for a national index. *American Psychologist, 55,* 34–43.

Digman, J. M., & Inouye, J. (1986). Further specification of the five robust factors of personality. *Journal of Personality & Social Psychology, 50,* 116–123.

Dodge, K. A. (1991). The structure and function of reactive and proactive aggression. In D. J. Pepler, K. H. Rubin, et al. (eds.), *The development and treatment of childhood aggression* (pp. 201–218). Hillsdale, NJ: Lawrence Erlbaum Associates.

Dodge, K. A., Pettit, G. S., McClaskey, C. L., & Brown, M. M. (1986). Social competence in children. *Monographs of the Society for Research in Child Development, 51,* 1–85.

Doherty, O., & Matthews, G. (1988). Personality characteristics of opiate addicts. *Personality and Individual Differences, 9,* 171–172.

Dolan, R. J., & Morris, J. S. (2000). The functional anatomy of innate and acquired fear: Perspectives from neuroimaging. In R. D. Lane & L. Nadel (eds.), *Cognitive neuroscience of emotion* (pp. 225–241). New York: Oxford University Press.

Dolgin, K. G., & Azmita, M. (1985). The ability to interpret emotional signals. In G. Zivin (ed.), *The development of expressive behavior* (pp. 319–346). Orlando: Academic Press.

Dorsey, C. M., & Bootzin, R. R. (1997). Subjective and psychophysiologic insomnia: An examination of sleep tendency and personality. *Biological Psychiatry, 41,* 209–216.

Druskat, V. U., & Wolff, S. B. (2001). Building the emotional intelligence of groups. *Harvard Business Review, 79,* 80–87.

DuBois, P. H. (1970). *A history of psychological testing.* Boston: Allyn & Bacon.

Duncan, J., Burgess, P., & Emslie, H. (1995). Fluid intelligence after frontal lobe lesions. *Neuropsychologia, 33,* 261–268.

Duncan, J., Emslie, H., Williams, P., Johnson, R., & Freer, C. (1996). Intelligence and the frontal lobe: The organization of goal-directed behavior. *Cognitive Psychology, 30,* 257–303.

Duncan, J., & Owen, A. M. (2000). Common regions of the human frontal lobe recruited by diverse cognitive demands. *Trends in Neurosciences, 23,* 475–483.

Dunn, J., Brown, J., & Beardsall, L. (1991). Family talk about feeling states and children's later understanding of others' emotions. *Developmental Psychology, 27,* 448–455.

Dunn, L., & Brown, J. (1994). Affect expression in the family, children's understanding of emotions, and their interactions with others. *Merrill-Palmer Quarterly, 40,* 120–137.

Dunn, L., Brown, L., Slomkowski, C., Telsa, C., & Youngblade, L. (1991). Young children's understanding of other people's feelings and beliefs: Individual differences and their antecedents. *Child Development, 62,* 1352–1366.

Dweck, C. S. (2000). *Self-theories: Their role in motivation, personality, and development.* Philadelphia: Psychology Press.

Eden, D., & Aviram, A. (1993). Self-efficacy training to speed re-employment: Helping people to help themselves. *Journal of Applied Psychology, 78,* 353–360.

Edens, J. F. (1999). Aggressive children's self-systems and the quality of their relationships with significant others. *Aggression & Violent Behavior, 42,* 151–177.

Ehlers, A. (1995). A 1-year prospective study of panic attacks: Clinical course and factors associated with maintenance. *Journal of Abnormal Psychology, 104,* 164–172.

Ehlers, A., & Clark, D. M. (2000). A cognitive model of posttraumatic stress disorder. *Behaviour Research & Therapy, 38,* 319–345.

Eich, E. (1995). Searching for mood dependent memory. *Psychological Science, 6,* 67–75.

Eiden, T. C. (1999). Twenty Item Toronto Alexithymia Scale: Construct validity in a college student population. *Dissertation abstracts international*, section B: The sciences and engineering, *60* (2-b), 0869.

Einstein, A. (1973). *Thematic origins of scientific thought.* Cambridge: Harvard University Press.

Eisenberg, N. (1989). Empathy and sympathy. In W. Damon (ed.), *Child development today and tomorrow* (pp. 137–154). San Francisco: Jossey-Bass.

Eisenberg, N., & Fabes, R. (1991). Prosocial behavior and empathy: A multimethod, developmental perspective. In M. Clark (ed.), *Emotion and social behavior* (pp. 119–150). New York: Wiley.

Eisenberg, N., & Fabes, R. A. (1994). Mothers' reactions to children's negative emotions: Relations to children's temperament and anger behavior. *Merrill-Palmer Quarterly, 40,* 138–156.

Eisenberg, N., & Fabes, R. A. (1995). The relation of young children's vicarious emotional responding to social competence, regulation, and emotionality. *Cognition and Emotion, 9,* 203–228.

Eisenberg, N., & Fabes, R. A. (1998). Prosocial development. In N. Eisenberg (ed.), *Handbook of child psychology,* vol. 3: *Social, emotional, and personality development* (pp. 701–778). New York: Wiley.

Eisenberg, N., & Miller, P. A. (1987). The relation of empathy to prosocial and related behaviors. *Psychological Bulletin, 101,* 91–119.

Eisenberg, N., Cumberland, A., & Spinrad, T. L. (1998). Parental socialization of emotion. *Psychological Inquiry, 9,* 241–273.

Eisenberg, N., Fabes, R. A., Bernzweig, J., Karbon, M., Poulin, R., & Hanish, L. (1993). The relations of emotionality and regulation to preschooler's social skills and sociometric status. *Child Development, 64,* 1418–1438.

Eisenberg, N., Fabes, R. A., & Losoya, S. (1997). Emotional responding: Regulation, social correlates, and socialization. In P. Salovey & D. J. Sluyter (eds.), *Emotional development and emotional intelligence: Educational implications* (pp. 129–167). New York: Basic Books.

Eisenberg, N., Fabes, R. A., Murphy, B., Maskz, P., Smith, M., & Karbon, M. (1995). The role of emotionality and regulation in children's social functioning: A longitudinal study. *Child Development, 66,* 1360–1384.

Eisenberg, N., Fabes, R. A., Schaller, M., et al. (1991). The relations of parental characteristics and practices to children's vicarious emotional responding. *Child Development, 62,* 1393–1408.

Eisenberg, N., Wentzel, M., & Harris, J. D. (1998). The role of emotionality and regulation in empathy-related responding. *School Psychology Review, 27,* 506–521.

Ekman, P. (1984). Expression and the nature of emotion. In K. Scherer & P. Ekman (eds.), *Approaches to emotion* (pp. 319–344). Hillsdale, NJ: Lawrence Erlbaum Associates.

Ekman, P. (1989). The argument and evidence about universals in facial expressions of emotions. In H. Wagner & A. Manstead (eds.). *Handbook of Social Psychology*. New York: Wiley & Sons.

Ekman, P. (1993). Facial expression and emotion. *American Psychologist, 48*, 384–389.

Ekman, P. (1994). Strong evidence for universals in facial expressions: A reply to Russell's mistaken critique. *Psychological Bulletin, 15*, 268–287.

Ekman, P. (1999). Facial expressions. In T. Dalgleish & M. J. Power (eds.), *Handbook of cognition and emotion* (pp. 301–320). Chichester: Wiley.

Ekstrom, R. B., French, J. W., & Harman, H. H. (1979). *Cognitive factors: Their identification and replication*. Society of Multivariate Experimental Pschology.

Elias, M. J. (ed.) (1993). *Building decision making and life skills development: Guidelines for middle school educators*. Gaithersburg, MD: Aspen.

Elias, M. J., & Clabby, J. (1992). *Building social problem solving skills: Guidelines from a school-based program*. San Francisco: Jossey-Bass.

Elias, M. J., Bruene-Butler, L., Bum, L., & Schuyler, T. (2000). Voices from the field: Identifying and overcoming roadblocks to carrying out programs in social and emotional learning/emotional intelligence. *Journal of Educational and Psychological Consultation, 11*, 253–272.

Elias, M. J., Gara, M., Ubriaco, M., Rothbaum, P. A., Clabby, J. F., & Schuyler, T. (1986). Impact of a preventive social problem solving intervention on children's coping with middle-school stressors. *American Journal of Community Psychology, 14*, 259–275.

Elias, M. J., Tobias, S. E., & Friedlander, B. S. (1999). *Emotionally intelligent parenting*. New York: Three Rivers Press.

Elias, M. J., Zins, J. E., Weissberg, R. P., Frey, K. S., Greenberg, M. T., Haynes, N. M., Kessler, R., Schwab-Stone, M. E., & Shriver, T. P. (1997). *Promoting social and emotional learning: Guidelines for educators*. Alexandria, VA: Association for Supervision and Curriculum Development.

Elias, M., & Weissberg, R. P. (1990). School-based social competence promotion as a primary prevention strategy: A tale of two projects. *Prevention in Human Services, 7*, 177–200.

Elias, M., Gara, M. A., Schuyler, T. F., Branden-Muller, L. R., & Sayette, M. A. (1991). The promotion of social competence: Longitudinal study of a preventive school-based program. *American Journal of Orthopsychiatry, 61*, 409–417.

Elkin, A. J., & Rosch, P. J. (1990). Promoting mental health at the workplace: The prevention side of stress management. *Occupational Medicine: State of the Art Review, 5*, 739–754.

Ellis, A. (1962). *Reason and emotion in psychotherapy*. New York: Lyle Stuart.

Ellis, A., & Harper, R. A. (1975). *A new guide to rational living*. N. Hollywood, CA: Wilshire.

Elsbach, K. D., & Barr, P. S. (1999). The effects of mood on individual's use of structured decision protocols. *Organization Science, 10*, 181–198.

Emery, N. J., & Amaral, D. G. (2000). The role of the amygdala in primate social cognition. In R. D. Lane & L. Nadel (eds.), *Cognitive neuroscience of emotion.* New York: Oxford University Press.

Emmons, R. A., & Colby, P. M. (1995). Emotional conflict and well being: Relation to perceived availability, daily utilization, and observer reports of social support. *Journal of Personality and Social Psychology, 68,* 947–959.

Endler, N. (1996). Advances in coping research: An international perspective. Paper presented at the symposium Advances in Coping with Stress: International Perspectives, at the International Congress of Psychology, Montreal, August.

Endler, N. (in press). Multidimensional interactionism: Stress, anxiety, and coping. In L. Backman & C. von Hofsen (eds.), *Psychological science 2000: Social, personality, and health perspectives* (vol. 2). Brighton, England: Taylor & Francis/Psychology Press.

Endler, N., Denisoff, E., & Rutherford, A. (1998). Anxiety and depression: Evidence for the differentiation of commonly cooccurring constructs. *Journal of Psychopathology & Behavioral Assessment, 20,* 149–171.

Endler, N., & Parker, J. (1990). Multidimensional assessment of coping: A critical review. *Journal of Personality and Social Psychology, 58,* 844–854.

Endler, N., & Parker, J. (1999). *The Coping Inventory for Stressful Situations (CISS): Manual* (2nd ed.). Toronto: Multi-health System.

Endler, N., Parker, J., Bagby, R. M., & Cox, B. J. (1991). The multidimensionality of state and trait anxiety: The factor structure of the Endler Multidimensional Anxiety Scales. *Journal of Personality and Social Psychology, 60,* 919–926.

Endler, N., Speer, R. L., Johnson, J. M., & Flett, G. (2000). Controllability, coping, efficacy, and distress. *European Journal of Personality, 14,* 245–264.

Engelbrecht, A. S., & Fisher, A. H. (1995). The managerial performance implications of a developmental assessment centre process. *Human Relations, 48,* 387–404.

Epstein, S. (1991). The self-concept, the traumatic neurosis, and the structure of personality. In D. J. Ozer & J. M. Healy Jr. (eds.), *Self and emotion* and *Approaches to understanding lives* (pp. 63–98). Bristol, PA: Jessica Kingsley Publishers.

Epstein, S. (1992). Constructive thinking and mental and physical well-being. In L. Montada, S. H. Filipp & M. J. Lerner (eds.), *Life crises and experiences and loss in adulthood* (pp. 385–409). Hillsdale, NJ: Lawrence Erlbaum Associates.

Epstein, S. (1998). *Constructive thinking: The key to emotional intelligence.* New York: Praeger.

Epstein, S., & Meier, P. (1989). Constructive thinking: A broad coping variable with specific components. *Journal of Personality and Social Psychology, 57,* 332–349.

Erber, R. (1996). The self-regulation of moods. In L. L. Martin & A. Tesser (eds.), *Striving and feeling: Interactions among goals, affect, and self-regulation* (pp. 251–275). Mahwah, NJ: Lawrence Erlbaum Associates.

Ericsson, K. A. (1996). The acquisition of expert performance: An introduction to some of the issues. In K. A. Ericsson et al. (eds.), *The road to excellence: The ac-*

quisition of expert performance in the arts and sciences, sports and games (pp. 1–50). Mahwah, NJ: Lawrence Erlbaum Associates.

Evenden, J. (1999). Impulsivity: A discussion of clinical and experimental findings. *Journal of Psychopharmacology, 13*, 180–192.

Everly, S. E. (1989). *A clinical guide to the treatment of the human stress response.* New York: Plenum.

Eysenck H. J. (1967). *The biological basis of personality.* Springfield, IL: Thomas.

Eysenck, H. J. (1976). *Sex and personality.* London: Open Books.

Eysenck, H. J. (1981). General features of the model. In Eysenck, H. J. (ed.), *A model for personality* (pp. 1–37). New York: Springer.

Eysenck, H. J. (1988). The concept of "intelligence": Useful or useless? *Intelligence, 12*, 1–16.

Eysenck, H. J. (1992). Four ways five factors are not basic. *Personality & Individual Differences, 13*, 667–673.

Eysenck, H. J. (1995). Creativity as a product of intelligence and personality. In D. H. Saklofske & M. Zeidner (eds.), *International handbook of personality and intelligence* (pp. 231–247). New York: Plenum.

Eysenck, H. J. (1997). The learning and theory model of neurosis: A new approach. In S. Rachman et al. (eds.), *Best of behavior research and therapy* (pp. 1–17). New York: Pergamon/Elsevier Science.

Eysenck, H. J., & Eysenck, M. W. (1985). *Personality and individual differences: A natural science approach.* New York: Plenum.

Eysenck, H. J., & Eysenck, S. B. (1977). *Psychoticism as a dimension of personality.* New York: Carne & Russak.

Eysenck, H. J., & Rachman, S. (1965). *The causes and cures of neurosis: An introduction to modern behavior therapy based on learning theory.* San Diego, CA: R. A. Knapp.

Eysenck, H. J., & Wilson, G. D. (1991). *The psychology of sex.* London: Dent.

Eysenck, M. W. (1976). Extraversion, verbal learning, and memory. *Psychological Bulletin, 83*, 389–404.

Eysenck, M. W. (1981). Learning, memory, and personality. In H. J. Eysenck (ed.), *A model for personality.* Berlin: Springer.

Eysenck, M. W. (1992). *Anxiety: The cognitive perspective.* Hove, England: Lawrence Erlbaum Associates.

Eysenck, M. W. (1997). *Anxiety and cognition: A unified theory.* Hove, England: Psychology Press.

Eysenck, M. W., & Calvo, M. G. (1992). Anxiety and performance: The processing efficiency theory. *Cognition and Emotion, 6*, 409–434.

Eysenck, M. W., & Eysenck, M. C. (1979). Memory scanning, introversion-extraversion, and levels of processing. *Journal of Research in Personality, 13*, 305–315.

Eysenck, S. B., & Eysenck, H. J. (1972). The questionnaire measurement of psychoticism. *Medicine*, 2, 50–55.

Eysenck, S. B., & Eysenck, H. J. (1985). A revised version of the psychoticism scale. *Personality & Individual Differences*, 6, 21–29.

Eysenck, S. B., Pearson, P. R., Easting, G., & Allsopp, J. F. (1985). Age norms for impulsiveness, venturesomeness, and empathy in adults. *Personality and Individual Differences*, 6, 613–619.

Fabes, R. A., & Eisenberg, N. (1973). Regulatory control and adults' stress-related responses to daily life events. *Journal of Personality and Social Psychology*, 73, 1107–1117.

Fabes, R. A., Eisenberg, N., Nyman, M., & Michealieu, Q. (1991). Young children's appraisal of others' spontaneous emotional reactions. *Developmental Psychology*, 27, 858–866.

Fancher, R. B. (1985). Spearman's computation of *g*: A model for Burt? *British Journal of Psychology*, 76, 341–352.

Fanning, P. (1994). *Visualization for change* (2nd ed.). Oakland, CA: New Harbinger.

Farmer, A., & McGuffin, P. (1999). Comparing ICD-10 and *DSM-IV*. *British Journal of Psychiatry*, 175, 587–588.

Fedorovich, S., Boyle, C. R., & Hare, R. D. (1994). Wellness as a factor in selection of resident assistants in university student housing. *Journal of College Student Development*, 35, 248–254.

Fehr, B., Samson, D., & Paulhus, D. L. (1992). The construct of Machiavellianism: Twenty years later. In C. D. Spielberger & J. N. Butcher (eds.) *Advances in personality assessment* (vol. 9, pp. 77–116). Hillsdale, NJ: Lawrence Erlbaum Associates.

Feingold, A. (1994). Gender differences in personality: A meta-analysis. *Psychological Bulletin*, 116, 429–456.

Feinman, S., & Lewis, M. (1983). Social referencing and second order effects in ten-month-old infants. *Child Development*, 54, 878–887.

Fenigstein, A., Scheier, M. F., & Buss, A. H. (1975). Public and private self-consciousness: Assessment and theory. *Journal of Consulting and Clinical Psychology*, 43, 522–527.

Ferguson, E., Matthews, G., & Cox, T. (1999). The Appraisal of Life Events (ALE) Scale: Reliability and validity. *British Journal of Health Psychology*, 4, 97–116.

Ferris, G. R., Bergin, T. G., & Gilmore, D. C. (1986). Personality and ability predictors of training performance for flight attendants. *Group and Organizational Studies*, 11, 419–435.

Feshbach, N. (1982). Sex differences in empathy and social behavior in children. In N. Eisenberg (ed.), *The development of prosocial behavior* (pp. 315–338). New York: Publisher Press.

Feshbach, N., & Cohen, S. (1988). Training affects comprehension in young children: An experimental evaluation. *Journal of Applied Developmental Psychology*, 9, 201–210.

Field, K., Cohler, B. J., & Wool, G. (1989). *Learning and education: Psychoanalytic perspectives.* Madison, CT: International Universities Press.

Field, T. M., & Walden, T. A. (1982). Production and discrimination of facial expressions by preschool children. *Child Development, 53,* 1299–1311.

Finnegan, R. A., Hodges, E. V. E., & Perry, D. G. (1994). Preoccupied and avoidant coping during middle childhood. *Child Development, 67,* 1318–1328.

Fischer, K. W., Shaver, P. R., & Carnochan, P. (1990). How emotions develop and how they organize development. *Cognition and Emotion, 4,* 81–127.

Fiske, S. T., & Taylor, S. E. (1991). *Social cognition* (2nd ed.). New York: McGraw-Hill.

Flett, G. L., Hewitt, P. L., Endler, N. S., & Bagby, R. M. (1995). Conceptualization and assessment of personality factors in depression. *European Journal of Personality, 9,* 309–350.

Flett, G. L., Vredenburg, K., & Krames, L. (1997). The continuity of depression in clinical and nonclinical samples. *Psychological Bulletin, 121,* 395–416.

Flynn, J. R. (1987). Massive IQ gains in 14 nations: What IQ tests really measure. *Pyschological Bulletin, 101,* 171–191.

Flynn, J. R. (1999). Searching for justice: The discovery of IQ gains over time. *American Psychologist, 54,* 5–20.

Foa, E. B., Ehlers, A., Clark, D. M., Tolin, D. F., & Orsillo, S. M. (1999). The Posttraumatic Cognitions Inventory (PTCI): Development and validation. *Psychological Assessment, 11,* 303–314.

Foa, E. B., & Kozak, M. J. (1986). Emotional processing and fear: Exposure to corrective information. *Psychological Bulletin, 99,* 20–35.

Foa, E. B., & Riggs, D. S. (1995). Posttraumatic stress disorder following assault: Theoretical considerations and empirical findings. *Current Directions in Psychological Science, 4,* 61–65.

Foa, E. B., & Rothbaum, B. O. (1998). *Treating the trauma of rape: Cognitive-behavioral therapy for PTSD.* New York: Guilford Press.

Fodor, J. A. (1974). Special sciences (Or: Disunity of science as a working hypothesis). *Synthese, 28,* 97–115.

Fogarty, G., & Stankov, L. (1988). Abilities involved in performance on competing tasks. *Personality and Individual Differences, 9,* 35–49.

Folkman, S. (1984). Personal control and coping processes: A theoretical analysis. *Journal of Personality and Social Psychology, 46,* 839–852.

Folkman, S., & Lazarus, R. S. (1980). An analysis of coping in a middle-aged community sample. *Journal of Health and Social Behavior, 21,* 219–239.

Folkman, S., & Lazarus, R. S. (1985). If it changes, it must be a process: Study of emotion and coping during three stages of a college examination. *Journal of Personality and Social Psychology, 48,* 150–170.

Folkman, S., Chesney, M., McKussick, L., Ironson, G., Johnson, D. S., & Coastes, T. J. (1991). Translating coping theory into an intervention. In J. Eckenrode (ed.), *The social context of coping* (pp. 239–260). New York: Plenum.

Folkman, S., Lazarus, R. S., Gruen, R. J., & DeLongis, A. (1986). Appraisal, coping, health status, and psychological symptoms. *Journal of Personality and Social Psychology, 50,* 571–579.

Ford, M. E., & Tisak, M. (1983). A further search for social intelligence. *Journal of Educational Psychology, 75,* 196–206.

Forgas, J. P. (1995). The Affect Infusion Model (AIM): Review and an integrative theory of mood effects on judgment. *Psychological Bulletin, 117,* 39–66.

Forgas, J. P., & Bower, G. H. (1987). Affect in social and personal judgements. In K. Fiedler & J. Forgas (eds.), *Affect, cognition, and social behavior: New evidence and integrative attempts.* Lewiston, NY: Hogrefe.

Fox, N. A. (ed.) (1994). *The development of emotion regulation.* Chicago: Society for Research in Child Development.

Fox, N. A., & Davidson, R. J. (1988). Patterns of brain electrical activity during facial signs of emotion in 10-month-old infants. *Developmental Psychology, 24,* 230–236.

Francis, L. J. (1997). Coopersmith's model of self-esteem: Bias toward the stable extravert? *Journal of Social Psychology, 137,* 139–142.

Frankenhaeuser, M., & Gardell, B. (1976). Underload and overload in working life: Outline of a multidisciplinary approach. *Journal of Human Stress, 2,* 35–45.

Franko, D. L., Powers, T. A., Zuroff, D. C., & Moskowitz, D. S. (1985). Children and affect: Strategies for self-regulation and sex differences in sadness. *American Journal of Orthopsychiatry, 55,* 210–219.

Frayne, C. A., & Latham, G. P. (1987). The application of social learning theory to employee self-management of attendance. *Journal of Applied Psychology, 72,* 387–392.

Fredrickson, B. L. (1998). Cultivated emotions: Parental socialization of positive emotions and self-conscious emotions. *Psychological Inquiry, 9,* 279–280.

Freeman, A., & Oster, C. L. (1988). Cognitive therapy and depression. In V. E. Caballo (ed.), *International handbook of cognitive and behavioural treatments for psychological disorders* (pp. 489–520). Oxford: Pergamon/Elsevier Science.

French, J. R. P. (1976). Job demands and worker health. Paper presented at the American Psychological Association, Washington, DC.

French, J. R. P., & Caplan, R. D. (1973). Organizational stress and individual strain. In A. J. Marrow (ed.), *The failure of success* (pp. 30–36). New York: AMA COM.

French, J. W., Ekstrom, R. B., & Price, L. A. (1963). *Manual for reference tests for cognitive factors.* Princeton, NJ: Educational Testing Service.

Frese, M., & Zapf, D. (1988). Methodological issues in the study of work stress: Objective vs. subjective measurement of work stress and the question of longitudinal studies. In C. L. Cooper & R. Payne (eds.), *Causes, coping, and consequences of stress at work* (pp. 375–411). Chichester, England: John Wiley & Sons.

Freud, S. (1923/1962). *The ego and the id.* J. Strachey, ed. J. Riviere, trans. New York: Norton.

Friedman, H. S., & Miller-Herringer, T. (1991). Nonverbal display of emotion in public and in private: Self-monitoring, personality, and expressive cues. *Journal of Personality and Social Psychology, 61,* 766–775.

Friedman, H. S., & Riggio, R. (1999). Individual differences in the ability to encode complex affects. *Personality and Individual Differences, 27,* 181–194.

Friedman, H. S., Prince, L. M., Riggio, R. E., & DiMatteo, M. R. (1980). Understanding and assessing nonverbal expressiveness: The Affective Communication Test. *Journal of Personality and Social Psychology, 39,* 333–351.

Friedman, H. S., Riggio, R. E., & Casella, D. (1988). Nonverbal skill, personal charisma, and initial attraction. *Personality and Social Psychology Bulletin, 14,* 203–211.

Friedman, H. S., Tucker, J. S., Tomlinson-Keasey, C., & Schwartz, J. E., et al. (1993). Does childhood personality predict longevity? *Journal of Personality & Social Psychology, 65,* 176–185.

Friedman, H., & DiMatteo, R. (1982). *Interpersonal issues in health care.* New York: Academic Press.

Frijda, N. H. (1988). The laws of emotion. *American Psychologist, 43,* 349–358.

Fry, A. F., & Hale, S. (1996). Processing speed, working memory, and fluid intelligence: Evidence for a developmental cascade. *Psychological Science, 7,* 237–241.

Frymier, A. B., Klopf, D. W., & Ishii, S. (1990). Japanese and Americans compared on the affect orientation construct. *Psychological Reports, 66,* 985–986.

Fuchs, D., & Thelen, M. H. (1988). Children's expected interpersonal consequences of communicating their affective state and reported likelihood of expression. *Child Development, 59,* 1314–1322.

Funder, D. C. (1999). *Personality judgment: A realistic approach to person perception.* San Diego: Academic.

Furnham, A. (1981). Personality and activity preference. *British Journal of Social Psychology, 20,* 57–60.

Furnham, A. (1986). Response bias, social desirability, and dissimulation. *Personality & Individual Differences, 7,* 385–400.

Furnham, A. (1992). Personality and learning style: A study of three instruments. *Personality & Individual Differences, 13,* 429–438.

Furnham, A. (1996). Are you smart enough to keep your job? *Fortune, 133,* 34–36.

Furnham, A., & Brewin, C. R. (1990). Personality and happiness. *Personality & Individual Differences, 11,* 1093–1096.

Furnham, A., & Heaven, P. (1999). *Personality and social behaviour.* London: Arnold.

Furnham, A., Jackson, C. J., & Miller, T. (1999). Personality, learning style, and work performance. *Personality & Individual Differences, 27,* 1113–1122.

Furnham, A., & Miller, T. (1997). Personality, absenteeism, and productivity. *Personality & Individual Differences, 23,* 705–707.

Gaensbauer, T. J., & Sands, K. (1979). Distorted affective communications in abused/neglected infants and their potential impact on caretakers. *Journal of the American Academy of Child Psychiatry*, 18, 238–250.

Gal, R., & Lazarus, R. (1975). The role of activity in anticipation and confronting stressful situations. *Journal of Human Stress*, 1, 4–20.

Gallagher, D. J. (1996). Personality, coping, and objective outcomes: Extraversion, neuroticism, coping styles, and academic performance. *Personality & Individual Differences*, 21, 421–429.

Gallois, C. (1993). The language and communication of emotion. *American Behavioral Scientist*, 36, 309–338.

Galton, F. (1869). *Hereditary genius*. London: Macmillan.

Galton, F. (1879). Psychometric experiments. *Brain*, 2, 149–162.

Galton, F. (1883). *Inquiries into human faculty and its development*. London: Macmillan.

Galton, F. (1908). *Memories of my life*. London: Methuen.

Garber, J., & Dodge, K. A. (1991). *The development of emotion regulation and dysregulation*. Cambridge: Cambridge University Press.

Garcia A., & Roberts, R. D. (2000). Emotional "intelligence," cognitive abilities, and personality. Paper presented at the 27th Annual Conference of the Australasian Experimental Psychology Society, Novotel Twin Waters Resort, Queensland, Australia.

Gardner, H. (1983). *Frames of mind: The theory of multiple intelligences*. New York: Basic Books.

Gardner, H. (1993). *Multiple intelligences*. New York: Basic Books.

Gardner, H. (1999). Foreword. In J. Cohen (ed.), *Educating minds and hearts*. New York: Teachers College Press.

Garner, P. W., Jones, D. C., & Miner, J. L. (1994). Social competence among low-income preschoolers: Emotion socialization practices and social cognitive correlates. *Child Development*, 65, 622–637.

Garrett, H. E. (1946). A developmental theory of intelligence. *American Psychologist*, 1, 372–378.

Geer, J. H., & Estupinan, L. A., & Manguno-Mire, G. M. (2000). Empathy, social skills, and other relevant cognitive processes in rapists and child molesters. *Aggression and Violent Behavior*, 5, 99–126.

Geher, G., Warner, R. M., & Brown, A. S. (2001). Predictive validity of the Emotional Accuracy Research Scale. *Intelligence*, 29, 373–388.

Gelb, S. A. (1986). Henry H. Goddard and the immigrants, 1910–1917: The studies and their social context. *Journal of the History of the Behavioral Sciences*, 22, 324–332.

George, J. M., & Bettenhausen, K. (1990). Understanding prosocial behavior, sales performance, and turnover: A group-level analysis in a service context. *Journal of Applied Psychology*, 75, 698–709.

Gergen, K. J. (1995). Metaphor and monophony in the 20th-century psychology of emotions. *History of the Human Sciences, 8,* 1–23.

Gerrig, R. J. (1993). *Experiencing narrative worlds: On the psychological activities of reading.* New Haven: Yale University Press.

Gettler, L. (2000). Just managing. *The Age,* November 3.

Ghiselli, E. E., & Barthol, R. P. (1953). The validity of personality inventories in the selection of employees. *Journal of Applied Psychology, 37,* 18–20.

Gibbs, N. (1995). What's your EQ. *Time,* October 2, pp. 60–68.

Gilbert, P., & Miles, J. N. (2000). Sensitivity to social put-down: Its relationship to perceptions of social rank, shame, social anxiety, depression, anger, and self-other blame. *Personality & Individual Differences, 29,* 757–774.

Giovannini, D., & Ricci, B. P. E. (1981). Culture and sex effect in recognizing emotions by facial and gestural cues. *Italian Journal of Psychology, 8,* 95–102.

Gist, M. E., Stevens, C. K., & Bavetta, A. G. (1991). Effects of self-efficacy and post-training intervention on the acquisition and maintenance of complex interpersonal skills. *Personnel Psychology, 44,* 837–861.

Gmelch, W., Koch, J., Swent, B., & Tung, R. (1982). What stresses school administrators and how they cope. Paper presented at the American Educational Research Association, New York.

Goffman, I. (1969). *Strategic interaction.* Philadelphia: University of Penn Press.

Goh, D. S., & Moore, C. (1978). Personality and academic achievement in three educational levels. *Psychological Reports, 43,* 71–79.

Goldberg, L. R. (1993). The structure of phenotypic personality traits. *American Psychologist, 48,* 26–34.

Goldman, S. L., Kraemer, D. T., & Salovey, P. (1996). Beliefs about mood moderate the relationship of stress to illness and symptom reporting. *Journal of Psychosomatic Research, 41,* 115–128.

Goldner, E. M., Srikameswaran, S., Schroeder, M. L., Livesley, W. J., & Birmingham, C. L. (1999). Dimensional assessment of personality pathology in patients with eating disorders. *Psychiatry Research, 85,* 151–159.

Goldstein, A. P., & Sorcher, M. (1974). *Changing supervisory behavior.* New York: Pergamon.

Goleman, D. (1995a). *Emotional intelligence.* New York: Bantam Books.

Goleman, D. (1995b). EQ: What's your emotional intelligence quotient? *Utne Reader,* 72.

Goleman, D. (1997a). Emotional intelligence in context. In P. Salovey & D. Sluyter (eds.), *Emotional development and emotional intelligence.* New York: Basic Books.

Goleman, D. (1997b). Foreword. In P. Salovey & D. J. Sluyter (eds.), *Emotional development and emotional intelligence.* New York: Basic Books.

Goleman, D. (1998). *Working with emotional intelligence.* New York: Bantam Books.

Goleman, D. (2001). Emotional intelligence: Perspectives on a theory of performance. In press.

Golembiewski, R. T., & Munzenrider, R. F. (1988). *Phases of burnout: Developments in concepts and applications.* New York: Praeger.

Gondoli, D. M., & Braungart-Rieker, J. M. (1998). Constructs and processes in parental socialization of emotion. *Psychological Inquiry, 9,* 283–285.

Gordon, S. L. (1989). The socialization of children's emotion: Emotional culture, competence, and exposure. In C. Saarni & P. L. Harris (eds.), *Children's understanding of emotion.* New York: Cambridge University Press.

Gotlib I. H., Kurtzman H. S., & Blehar M. C. (2000). Cognition and depression: Issues and future directions. *Cognition and Emotion, 11,* 663–673.

Gottman, J. (1996). *The heart of parenting.* New York: Simon & Schuster.

Gottman, J. M. (1997). *Meta-emotion: How families communicate emotionally.* Mahwah, NJ: Lawrence Erlbaum Associates.

Gottman, J. M., & Katz, L. F. (1989). Effects of marital discord on young children's peer interaction and health. *Developmental Psychology, 25,* 373–381.

Gough, H. G. (1987). *California Psychological Inventory manual.* Paolo Alto, CA: Consulting Psychologists Press.

Gould, S. J. (1981). *The mismeasure of man.* New York: Norton.

Gould, S. J. (1997). *The mismeasure of man* (2nd ed.). London: Penguin Books.

Graham, T., & Ickes, W. (1997). When women's intuition isn't greater than men's. In W. Ickes (ed.), *Empathic accuracy* (pp. 117–143). New York: Guilford Press.

Gray, J. A. (1987). *The psychology of fear and stress* (2nd ed.). Cambridge: Cambridge University Press.

Gray, J. A. (1991). Neural systems, emotion and personality. In J. Madden IV (ed.), *Neurobiology of learning, emotion and affect* (pp. 273–306). New York: Raven Press.

Gray, J. A., & McNaughton, N. (1995). The neuropsychology of anxiety: Reprise. In D. A. Hope (ed.), *Nebraska Symposium on Motivation, 1995: Perspectives on anxiety, panic, and fear* (pp. 61–134). Lincoln: University of Nebraska Press.

Graziano, W. G., Hair, E. C., & Finch, J. F. (1997). Competitiveness mediates the link between personality and group performance. *Journal of Personality & Social Psychology, 73,* 1394–1408.

Green, J., Gilchrist, A., Burton, D., & Cox, A. (2000). Social and psychiatric functioning in adolescents with Asperger syndrome compared with conduct disorder. *Journal of Autism & Developmental Disorders, 30,* 279–293.

Green, M. A. (1988). Occupational stress: A study of public school administrators in southeast Massachusetts. Ed.D. dissertation, University of Massachusetts at Amherst.

Greenberg, M. T., Kusche, C. A., Cook, E. T., & Quamma, J. P. (1995). Promoting emotional competence in school-aged children: The effects of the PATHS curriculum. *Development and Psychopathology, 7,* 117–136.

Greenspan, S. I. (1989). Emotional intelligence. In Kay Field, B. J. Cohler & C. G. Wool (eds.), *Learning and education: Psychoanalytic perspectives* (pp. 209–243). Madison, CT: International Universities Press.

Gregory, R. J. (1996). *Psychological testing: History, principles, and applications* (2nd ed.). Boston: Allyn & Bacon.

Greif, E. (1984). *Developmental antecedents of sensitivity to emotions.* Progress report to the National Institute of Mental Health (grant no. 1R01MH39357-01).

Gresvenor, E. L. (1927). A study of the social intelligence of high school pupils. *American Physical Education Review, 32,* 649–657.

Grolnick, W. S., & Ryan, R. M. (1989). Parent styles associated with children's self-regulation and competence in school. *Journal of Educational Psychology, 81,* 143–154.

Gross, A. L., & Bailif, B. (1991). Children's understanding of emotion from facial expressions and situations: A review. *Developmental Review, 11,* 368–398.

Gross, J. J. (1998). The emerging field of emotion regulation: An integrative review. *Review of General Psychology, 2,* 271–299.

Gross, J. J., & John, O. P. (1995). Facets of emotional expressivity: Three self-report factors and their correlates. *Personality and Individual Differences, 19,* 555–568.

Gross, J. J., & Levenson, R. W. (1997). Hiding feelings: The acute effects of inhibiting negative and positive emotions. *Journal of Abnormal Psychology, 106,* 95–103.

Grossman, D. C., Neckerman, H. J., Koepsell, T. D., Liu, P.-Y., Asher, K. N., Beland, K., Frey, K., & Rivara, F. P. (1997). Effectiveness of a violence prevention curriculum among children in elementary school. *Journal of the American Medical Association, 277,* 1605–1611.

Group, C. P. P. R. (1999). Initial impact of the fast track prevention trial for conduct problems. II: Classroom effects. *Journal of Consulting and Clinical Psychology, 67,* 648–657.

Grove, A. S. (1996). *Only the paranoid survive: How to exploit the crisis points that challenge every company and career.* New York: Doubleday.

Gschwandtner, G. (1990). The *Personal Selling Power* superachiever survey report: How superachievers think to reach consistent success. *Personal Selling Power,* May, 11–19.

Gudykunst, W. B., & Ting-Toomey, S. (1988). Culture and affective communication. *American Behavioral Scientist, 31,* 384–400.

Guilford, J. P. (1956). The structure of intellect. *Psychological Bulletin, 53,* 267–293.

Guilford, J. P. (1967). *The nature of human intelligence.* New York: McGraw-Hill.

Guilford, J. P. (1981). Higher-order structure-of-intellect abilities. *Multivariate Behavioral Research, 16,* 411–435.

Guilford, J. P. (1982). Cognitive psychology's ambiguities: Some suggested remedies. *Psychological Review, 89,* 48–59.

Guilford, J. P. (1985). The structure-of-intellect model. In B. B. Wolman (ed.), *Handbook of intelligence: Theories, measurements, and applications.* New York: Wiley.

Guilford, J. P., & Hoepfner, R. (1971). *The Analysis of Intelligence.* New York: McGraw-Hill.

Guion, R. M. (1980). On Trinitarian doctrines of validity. *Professional Psychology, 11,* 385–398.

Guion, R. M., & Gottier, R. F. (1965). Validity of personality measures in personnel selection. *Personnel Psychology, 18,* 135–164.

Gullone, E., & Moore, S. (2000). Adolescent risk-taking and the five-factor model of personality. *Journal of Adolescence, 23,* 393–407.

Gustafsson, J.-E. (1984). A unifying model for the structure of intellectual abilities. *Intelligence, 8,* 179–203.

Gustafsson, J.-E. (1988). Hierarchical models of individual differences in cognitive abilities. In R. J. Sternberg (ed.), *Advances in the psychology of human intelligence* (vol. 4). Hillsdale, NJ: Lawrence Erlbaum Associates.

Gustafsson, J.-E. (1989). Broad and narrow abilities in research on learning and instruction. In R. Kanfer, P. L. Ackerman & R. Cudeck (eds.), *Abilities, motivation and methodology: The Minnesota Symposium on Learning and Individual Differences.* Hillsdale, NJ: Lawrence Erlbaum Associates.

Gustafsson, J.-E. (1992a). The relevance of factor analysis for the study of group differences. *Multivariate Behavioral Research, 27,* 239–248.

Gustafsson, J.-E. (1992b). The "Spearman Hypothesis" is false. *Multivariate Behavioral Research, 27,* 265–267.

Gustafsson, J.-E. (1999). Measuring and understanding G: Experimental and correlational approaches. In P. L. Ackerman, P. C. Kyllonen & R. D. Roberts (eds.), *Learning and individual differences: Process, trait, and content determinants* (pp. 275–291). Washington, DC: American Psychological Association.

Guttman, L. (1965a). Structure of interrelations among intelligence tests. *Proceedings of the Invitational Conference on Testing Problems,* 25–36.

Guttman, L. (1965b). A faceted definition of intelligence. *Cripta Hierosolymitana* (Jerusalem: Hebrew University), *14,* 166–181.

Guttman, L. (1992). The irrelevance of factor analysis for the study of group differences. *Multivariate Behavioral Research, 27,* 175–204.

Guttman, L., & Levy, S. (1991). Two structural laws for intelligence tests. *Intelligence, 15,* 79–103.

Guzzo, R. A., Jette, R. D., & Zatzell, R. A. (1985). The effects of psychologically based intervention programs on worker productivity: A meta-analysis. *Personnel Psychology, 38,* 275–291.

Haan, N. (1977). *Coping and defending: Processes of self-environment organization.* New York: Academic Press.

Haier, R. J., Siegel, B. V., Jr., Nuechterlein, K. H., Hazlett, E., Wu, J. C., Paek, J., Browning, H. L., & Buchsbaum, M. S. (1988). Cortical glucose metabolic rate correlates of abstract reasoning and attention studied with positron emission tomography. *Intelligence, 12,* 199–217.

Haier, R. J., Siegel, B. V., Jr., Tang, C., Abel, L., & Buchsbaum, M. S. (1992). Intelligence and changes in regional cerebral glucose metabolic rate following learning. *Intelligence, 16,* 415–426.

Hakstian, A. R., & Cattell, R. B. (1974). The checking of primary mental ability structure on a broader basis of performances. *British Journal of Educational Psychology, 44,* 140–154.

Hakstian, A. R., & Cattell, R. B. (1978). Higher-stratum ability structures on a basis of twenty primary abilities. *Journal of Educational Psychology, 70,* 657–669.

Halberstadt, A. G. (1991). Socialization of expressiveness: Family influences in particular and a model in general. In R. S. Feldman & S. Rime (eds.), *Fundamental of emotional expressiveness* (pp. 106–162). Cambridge: Cambridge University Press.

Halberstadt, A. G. (1991). Towards an ecology of expressiveness: Family expressiveness in particular and a model in general. In R. S. Feldman & B. Rime' (eds.), *Fundamental of nonverbal behavior* (pp. 106–160). Cambridge: Cambridge University Press.

Halberstadt, A. G. (1998). Of models and mechanisms. *Psychological Inquiry, 9,* 290–294.

Halberstadt, A. G., Denham, S. A., & Dunsmore, J. C. (in press). Affective social competence. *Social Development.*

Hamann, S. B., Stefanacci, L., Squire, L. R., Adolphs, R., Tranel, D., et al. (1996). Recognizing facial emotion. *Nature, 379,* 497.

Hambleton, R. K. (1984). Validating the test scores. In R. A. Berk (ed.), *A guide to criterion-referenced test construction.* Baltimore: Johns Hopkins University Press.

Hammer, M. (1996). *Beyond engineering.* New York: Harper Business.

Hamner, W. C., & Tosi, H. L. (1974). Relationship of role conflict and role ambiguity to job involvement measures. *Journal of Applied Psychology, 59,* 497–499.

Hampson, S. E., Andrews, J. A., Barckley, M., Lichtenstein, E., & Lee, M. E. (2000). Conscientiousness, perceived risk, and risk-reduction behaviors: A preliminary study. *Health Psychology, 19,* 496–500.

Hansen, C. P. (1989). A causal model of the relationship among accidents, biodata, personality, and cognitive factors. *Journal of Applied Psychology, 74,* 81–90.

Hardy, D. F., Power, T. G., & Jaedicke, S. (1993). Examining the relation of parenting to children's coping with everyday stress. *Child Development, 64,* 1829–1841.

Hare, R. D., Hart, S. D., & Harpur, T. J. (1991). Psychopathy and the *DSM-IV* criteria for antisocial personality disorder. *Journal of Abnormal Psychology, 100,* 391–398.

Hargreaves, A. (2000). Mixed emotions: teachers' perceptions of their interactions with students. *Teaching Education, 16,* 811–826.

Harman, H. H. (1976). *Modern factor analysis* (3rd ed.). Chicago: University of Chicago Press.

Harris, P. L., & Lipian, M. S. (1989). Understanding emotion and experiencing emotion. In C. Saarni & P. L. Harris (eds.), *Children's understanding of emotion* (pp. 241–258). New York: Cambridge University Press.

Hatfield, E. E. A. (1994). *Emotional contagion.* New York: Cambridge University Press.

Hawkins, J. D., Cleve, E. V., & Catalano, R. F. (1991). Reducing early childhood aggression: Results of a primary prevention program. *Journal of the American Academy of Child Adolescent Psychiatry, 30,* 208–217.

Hawkins, K. A., & Trobst, K. K. (2000). Frontal lobe dysfunction and aggression: Conceptual issues and research findings. *Aggression & Violent Behavior, 5,* 147–157.

Haygroup (2000). Emotional intelligence: A soft skill with a hard edge. Available at ⟨http://ei.haygroup.com/about_ei/⟩.

Haynes, N. M., & Marans, S. (1999). The cognitive, emotional, and behavioral (CEB) framework for promoting acceptance of diversity. In Jonathan Cohen (ed.), *Educating minds and hearts: Social emotional learning and the passage into adolescence* (pp. 158–170). New York: Columbia University Press.

Heaney, C. A. (1991). Enhancing social support at the workplace: Assessing the effects of the caregiver support program. *Health Education Quarterly, 18,* 477–494.

Heaney, C. A., Price, R. H., & Rafferty, J. (1995). The caregiver support program: An intervention to increase employee coping resources and enhance mental health. In L. R. Murphy, J. J. Hurrell, S. Sauter & G. P. Keita (eds.), *Job Stress Interventions* (pp. 93–108). Washington, DC: American Psychological Association.

Hearnshaw, L. S. (1979). *Cyril Burt: Psychologist.* Ithaca: Cornell University Press.

Heaven, P. C. L. (1996). Personality and self-reported delinquency: A longitudinal analysis. *Journal of Child Psychology & Psychiatry & Allied Disciplines, 37,* 747–751.

Hebb, D. O. (1942). The effects of early and late brain injury upon test scores and the nature of normal adult intelligence. *Proceedings of the American Philosophical Society, 85,* 275–292.

Hebb, D. O. (1949). *The organization of behavior.* New York: Wiley.

Hecaen, H., & Albert, M. L. (1978). *Human neuropsychology.* New York: Wiley.

Hedlund, J., & Sternberg, R. J. (2000). Too many intelligences? Integrating social, emotional, and practical intelligence. In R. Bar-On & J. D. A. Parker (eds.), *The handbook of emotional intelligence* (pp. 171–191). San Francisco: Jossey-Bass.

Heilman, K. M. (2000). Emotional experience: A neurological model. In R. D. Lane & L. Nadel (eds.), *Cognitive neuroscience of emotion* (pp. 328–344). New York: Oxford University Press.

Helmreich, R. L. (2000). Culture and error in space: Implications from analog environments. *Aviation Space & Environmental Medicine, 71,* A133–A139.

Helton, W. S., Dember, W. N., Warm, J. S., & Matthews, G. (1999). Optimism-pessimism and false failure feedback: Effects on vigilance performance. *Current Psychology: Research and Review, 18*, 311–325.

Hendricks, M., Guilford, J. P., & Hoepfner, R. (1969). *Measuring creative social abilities*. Los Angeles: Reports from the Psychological Laboratory, University of Southern California, no. 42.

Hepburn, L., & Eysenck, M. W. (1989). Personality, average mood, and mood variability. *Personality & Individual Differences, 10*, 975–983.

Herrnstein, R. J., & Murray, C. (1994). *The Bell Curve: Intelligence and class structure in American life*. New York: Free Press.

Hetherington, E. M., Cox, M., & Cox, R. (1985). Long-term effects of divorce and remarriage in the adjustment of children. *Journal of the American Academy of Child Psychiatry, 24*, 518–530.

Hilakivi, I., Veilahti, J., Asplund, P., & Sinivuo, J., et al. (1989). A sixteen-factor personality test for predicting automobile driving accidents of young drivers. *Accident Analysis & Prevention, 21*, 413–418.

Hochschild, A. R. (1979). Emotion work, feeling rules, and social structure. *American Journal of Sociology, 85*, 551–575.

Hock, M. (1992). Exchange of aversive communicative acts between mother and child as related to perceived child-rearing practices and anxiety of the child. In K. A. Hagtvet & B. T. Johnsen (eds.), *Advances in test anxiety research* (vol. 7, pp. 156–174). Lisse: Swets and Zeitlinger.

Hoffman, M. L. (1982). The measurement of empathy. In C. E. Izard (ed.), *Measuring emotions in infants and children* (pp. 279–296). Cambridge: Cambridge University Press.

Hogan, J., & Ones, D. S. (1997). Conscientiousness and integrity at work. In R. Hogan & J. A. Johnson (eds.), *Handbook of personality psychology* (pp. 849–870). San Diego, CA: Academic Press.

Hogan, J., Rybicki, S. L., Motowidlo, S. J., & Borman, W. C. (1998). Relations between contextual performance, personality, and occupational advancement. *Human Performance, 11*, 189–207.

Hogan, R. (1987). Personality psychology: Back to basics. In Joel Aronoff, Albert I. Rabin, et al. (eds.), *The emergence of personality* (pp. 79–104). New York: Springer Publishing Co.

Hogan, R., Curphy, G., & Hogan, L. (1994). What we know about leadership effectiveness and personality. *American Psychologist, 49*, 493–504.

Hogan, R., Hogan, J., & Roberts, B. W. (1996). Personality measurements and employment decisions. *American Psychologist, 51*, 469–477.

Hogan, R., Hogan, L., & Murtha, T. (1992). Validation of a personality measure of managerial performance. *Journal of Business and Psychology, 7*, 225–237.

Holbrook, W. L. (1998). A study of the relationships between emotional intelligence and basic writers' skills. *Dissertation abstracts international*, section A: Humanities and social sciences, *58* (7-A), 2631.

Holland, J. (1996). Exploring careers with typology. *American Psychologist,* 51, 397–406.

Hollander, E., & Rosen, J. (2000). Impulsivity. *Journal of Psychopharmacology,* 14, S39–S44.

Hollon, S. D., Shelton, R. C., & Davis, D. D. (1993). Cognitive therapy for depression: Conceptual issues and clinical efficacy. *Journal of Consulting and Clinical Psychology,* 61, 270–275.

Holzinger, K. J. (1938). Relationships between three multiple orthogonal factors and four bifactors. *Journal of Educational Psychology,* 29, 513–519.

Hooven, C., Gottman, J. M., & Katz, L. F. (1995). Parental meta-emotion structure predicts family and child outcomes. *Cognition and Emotion,* 9, 229–264.

Hooven, C., Katz, L., & Gottman, J. M. (1994). The family as a meta-emotion culture. *Cognition and Emotion,* 9, 229–264.

Horn, J. L. (1968). Organization of abilities and the development of intelligence. *Psychological Review,* 75, 242–259.

Horn, J. L. (1970). Organisation of data on life-span development of human abilities. In L. R. Goulet & P. B. Baltes (eds.), *Life-Span Development in Psychology.* New York: Academic Press.

Horn, J. L. (1976). Human abilities: A review of research and theory in the early 1970s. *Annual Review of Psychology,* 27, 437–485.

Horn, J. L. (1979). The rise and fall of human abilities. *Journal of Research and Development in Education,* 12, 59–79.

Horn, J. L. (1980). Concepts of intellect in relation to learning and adult development. *Intelligence,* 4, 285–317.

Horn, J. L. (1982). The aging of human abilities. In B. B. Wolman (ed.), *Handbook of developmental psychology.* New York: Prentice-Hall.

Horn, J. L. (1985). Remodeling old models of intelligence. In B. B. Wolman (ed.), *Handbook of intelligence: Theories, measurements, and applications.* New York: Wiley.

Horn, J. L. (1986). Intellectual ability concepts. In R. J. Sternberg (ed.), *Advances in the psychology of human intelligence.* Hillsdale, NJ: Erlbaum Associates.

Horn, J. L. (1987). A context for understanding information processing studies of human abilities. In P. A. Vernon (ed.), *Speed of information-processing and intelligence.* Norwood, NJ: Ablex.

Horn, J. L. (1988). Thinking about human abilities. In J. R. Nesselroade & R. B. Cattell (eds.), *Handbook of multivariate experimental psychology.* New York: Plenum.

Horn, J. L. (1989). Cognitive diversity: A framework of learning. In P. L. Ackerman, R. J. Sternberg & R. Glaser (eds.), *Learning and individual differences: Advances in theory and research.* New York: W. H. Freeman & Co.

Horn, J. L. (1998). A basis for research on age differences in cognitive capabilities. In J. J. McArdle & R. W. Woodcock (eds.), *Human cognitive abilities in theory and practice* (pp. 57–91). Mahwah, NJ: Lawrence Erlbaum Associates.

Horn, J. L., & Cattell, R. B. (1966). Refinement of the theory of fluid and crystallised general intelligences. *Journal of Educational Psychology, 57,* 253–270.

Horn, J. L., & Donaldson, G. (1980). Cognitive development. II: Adulthood development of human abilities. In O. G. Brim & J. Kagan (eds.) *Constancy and change in human development: A volume of review essays.* Cambridge: Harvard University Press.

Horn, J. L., Donaldson, G., & Engstrom, R. (1981). Apprehension, memory, and fluid intelligence decline in adulthood. *Research on Aging, 3,* 33–84.

Horn, J. L., & Hofer, S. M. (1992). Major abilities and development in the adult period. In R. J. Sternberg & C. Berg (eds.), *Intellectual development.* New York: Cambridge University Press.

Horn, J. L., & Knapp, J. R. (1973). On the subjective character of the empirical base of Guilford's structure-of-intellect model. *Psychological Bulletin, 80,* 33–43.

Horn, J. L., & Knapp, J. R. (1974). Thirty wrongs do not make a right: A reply to Guilford. *Psychological Bulletin, 81,* 502–504.

Horn, J. L., & Noll, J. (1994). System for understanding cognitive capabilities: A theory and the evidence on which it is based. In D. K. Detterman (ed.), *Current topics in human intelligence* (vol. 4). New York: Springer-Verlag.

Horn, J. L., & Stankov, L. (1982). Auditory and visual factors of intelligence. *Intelligence, 6,* 165–185.

Hornak, J., Rolls, E. T., & Wade, D. (1996). Face and voice expression identification in patients with emotional and behavioural changes following ventral frontal lobe damage. *Neuropsychologia, 34,* 247–261.

Hough, L. M. (1992). The "Big Five" personality variables—Construct confusion: description versus prediction. *Human Performance, 5,* 139–155.

House, J. S. (1981). *Work stress and social support.* Reading, MA: Addison-Wesley Publishing Co.

Howard, R. W. (1993). On what intelligence is. *British Journal of Psychology, 84,* 27–37.

Howe, M. J. A. (1988a). Intelligence as an explanation. *British Journal of Psychology, 79,* 349–360.

Howe, M. J. A. (1988b). The hazards of using correlational evidence as a means of identifying the cause of individual ability differences: A rejoinder to Sternberg and a reply to Miles. *British Journal of Psychology, 3,* 490–493.

Howe, M. J. A. (1990a). Does intelligence exist? *Psychologist, 3* (11), 490–493.

Howe, M. J. A. (1990b). Useful word but obsolete concept: A reply to Nettelbeck. *Psychologist, 3* (11), 498–499.

Hui, C. H., & Triandis, H. C. Individualism-collectivism: A study of cross-cultural researchers. *Journal of Cross-Cultural Psychology, 17,* 225–248.

Humphreys, L. G. (1962). The organization of human abilities. *American Psychologist, 17,* 475–483.

Humphreys, L. G. (1967). Critique of Cattell's "Theory of fluid and crystallized intelligence: A critical experiment." *Journal of Educational Psychology, 58,* 129–136.

Humphreys, L. G. (1979). The construct of general intelligence. *Intelligence, 3,* 105–120.

Humphreys, M. S., & Revelle, W. (1984). Personality, motivation, and performance: A theory of the relationship between individual differences and information processing. *Psychological Review, 91,* 153–184.

Hunt, E. (1995). *Will we be smart enough? A cognitive analysis of the coming workforce.* New York: Russell Sage Foundation.

Hunt, E. (2001). Let's hear it for crystallized intelligence. *Learning and Individual Differences.* In press.

Hunter, J. E. (1986). Cognitive ability, cognitive aptitude, job knowledge, and job performance. *Journal of Vocational Behavior, 29,* 340–362.

Hunter, J. E., & Hunter, R. F. (1984). Validity and utility of alternative predictors of job performance. *Psychological Bulletin, 96,* 72–98.

Hunter, J. E., Schmidt, F. L. (1996). Cumulative research knowledge and social policy formulation: The critical role of meta-analysis. *Psychology, Public Policy & Law, 2,* 324–347.

Huntsinger, C. S., Jose, P. E., & Larson, S. L. (1998). Do parent practices to encourage academic competence influence the social adjustment of young European American and Chinese American children? *Developmental Psychology, 34,* 747–756.

Hupka, R. B., Zalesky, Z., Otto, J., Reidl, L., & Tarabrina, N. V. (1997). The colors of anger, envy, fear, and jealousy. *Journal of Cross-Cultural Psychology, 28,* 156–171.

Hurley, J. R. (1998). Agency and communion as related to "Big Five" self-representations and subsequent behavior in small groups. *Journal of Psychology, 32,* 337–351.

Huxley, T. (1894). Biogenesis and abiogenesis. In T. Huxley (ed.), *Collected Essays of Thomas Huxley* (vol. 8). London: Macmillan and Co.

Huy, Q. N. (1999). Emotional capability, emotional intelligence, and radical change. *Academy of Management Review, 24,* 325–345.

Iannotti, R. J., Zahn-Waxler, C., & Cummings, E. M. (1987). The development of empathy and prosocial behavior in early childhood. Paper presented at the Society for Research in Child Development, Kansas City.

Ickes, W. (1993). Empathic accuracy. *Journal of Personality, 61,* 587–610.

Ickes, W., Stinson, L., Bissonette, V., & Garcia, S. (1990). Naturalistic social cognition: Empathic accuracy in mixed-sex dyads. *Journal of Personality and Social Psychology, 54,* 730–742.

Ingram, R. E. (1984). Toward an information-processing analysis of depression. *Cognitive Therapy and Research, 8,* 443–478.

Ingram, R. E., Miranda, J., & Segal, Z. V. (1998). *Cognitive vulnerability to depression.* New York: Guilford Press.

Insead, Q. N. H. (1999). Emotional capability, emotional intelligence, and radical change. *Academy of Management Review, 24,* 325–345.

Isen, A. M. (1999). Positive affect. In T. Dalgleish & M. J. Power (eds.), *Handbook of cognition and emotion* (pp. 521–539). Chichester: Wiley.

Isen, A. M., Daubman, K. A., & Nowicki, G. P. (1987). Positive affect facilitates creative problem solving. *Journal of Personality & Social Psychology, 52,* 1122–1131.

Ivancevich, J. M., & Matteson, M. T. (1987). Organizational level stress management interventions: A review and recommendations. In J. M. Ivancevich & D. C. Ganster (eds.), *Job stress: From theory to suggestion* (pp. 229–248). New York: John Wiley.

Ivancevich, J. M., Matteson, M. T., Freedman, S. M., & Phillips, J. S. (1990). Worksite stress management interventions. *American Psychologist, 45,* 252–261.

Izard, C. (1994). Innate and universal facial expressions: Evidence from developmental and cross-cultural research. *Psychological Bulletin, 115.*

Izard, C. (2001). Emotional intelligence or adaptive emotions? *Emotion, 1,* 249–257.

Izard, C. E., Fine, S. E., Schultz, D., Mostow, A. J., Ackerman, B. P., & Youngstrom, E. A. (2001). Emotion knowledge as a predictor of social behavior and academic competence in children at risk. *Psychological Science, 12,* 18–23.

Izard, C. E., Libero, D. Z., Putnam, P., Haynes, O. (1993). Stability of emotion experiences and their relations to traits of personality. *Maurice Journal of Personality & Social Psychology, 65,* 847–860.

Jackson, S. E., & Schuler, R. S. (1985). A meta-analysis and conceptual critique of research on role ambiguity and role conflict in work settings. *Organizational Behavior and Human Decision Processes, 36,* 66–78.

James, N. (1989). Emotional labor: Skill and work in the social regulation of feelings. *Sociological Review, 37,* 15–42.

James, W. (1890). *The Principles of Psychology.* New York: Henry Holt.

Jang, K. L., Livesley, W. J., & Vernon, P. A. (1999). The relationship between Eysenck's P-E-N model of personality and traits delineating personality disorder. *Personality & Individual Differences, 26,* 121–128.

Janovics, J., & Christiansen, N. D. (2001). Emotional intelligence at the workplace. Paper presented at the 16th Annual Conference of the Society of Industrial and Organizational Psychology, San Diego, April.

Janssens, J. M., Gerris, J. R. M., & Janssen, A. W. H. (1989). Childbearing, empathy, and prosocial behavior. Paper presented at the Society for Research in Child Development, Kansas City, April.

Jenkins, J. M., Oatley, K., & Stein, N. L. (1998). *Human emotions: A reader.* Malden, MA: Blackwell Publishers.

Jensen, A. R. (1970). Hierarchical theories of mental ability. In B. Dockrell (ed.), *On intelligence.* Toronto: Ontario Institute of Education.

Jensen, A. R. (1974). Interaction of Level I and Level II abilities with race and socio-economic status. *Journal of Educational Psychology, 66*, 99–111.

Jensen, A. R. (1979). *g*: Outmoded theory or unconquered frontier? *Creative Science and Technology, 2*, 16–29.

Jensen, A. R. (1980). *Bias in mental testing.* New York: Free Press.

Jensen, A. R. (1982). Reaction time and psychometric *g*. In H. J. Eysenck (ed.), *A model for intelligence.* New York: Springer-Verlag.

Jensen, A. R. (1985a). Methodological and statistical techniques for the chronometric study of mental abilities. In C. R. Reynolds & V. L. Wilson (eds.), *Methodological and statistical advances in the study of individual differences.* New York: Plenum.

Jensen, A. R. (1985b). The nature of black-white differences on various psychometric tests: Spearman's hypothesis. *Behavioral and Brain Sciences, 8*, 193–263.

Jensen, A. R. (1987a). Individual differences in the Hick paradigm. In P. A. Vernon (ed.), *Speed of information-processing and intelligence.* Norwood, NJ: Ablex.

Jensen, A. R. (1987b). Differential psychology: Towards consensus. In S. Modgil & C. Modgil (eds.), *Arthur Jensen: Consensus and controversy.* London: Falmers Press.

Jensen, A. R. (1987c). Psychometric *g* as a focus of concerted research effort. *Intelligence, 11*, 193–198.

Jensen, A. R. (1987d). Process differences and individual differences in some cognitive tasks. *Intelligence, 11*, 107–136.

Jensen, A. R. (1987e). The *g* beyond factor analysis. In J. C. Conoly, J. A. Glover & R. R. Ronning (eds.), *The influence of cognitive psychology on testing and measurement.* Hillsdale, NJ: Lawrence Erlbaum Associates.

Jensen, A. R. (1990). Speed of information processing in a calculating prodigy. *Intelligence, 14*, 259–274.

Jensen, A. R. (1992a). The importance of intraindividual variation in reaction time. *Personality and Individual Differences, 13*, 869–891.

Jensen, A. R. (1992b). Spearman's hypothesis: Methodology and evidence. *Multivariate Behavioral Research, 27*, 225–234.

Jensen, A. R. (1992c). More on psychometric *g* and "Spearman's hypothesis." *Multivariate Behavioral Research, 27*, 257–260.

Jensen, A. R. (1993a). Why is reaction time correlated with psychometric *g*? *Current Directions in Psychological Science, 2*, 53–56.

Jensen, A. R. (1993b). Spearman's hypothesis tested with chronometric information processing tasks. *Intelligence, 17*, 47–77.

Jensen, A. R. (1993c). Reaction times and intelligence: A comparison of Chinese American and Anglo-American children. *Journal of Biosocial Sciences, 25*, 397–410.

Jensen, A. R. (1998). *The g factor: The science of mental ability.* Westport, CT: Praeger Publishers/Greenwood Publishing Group.

Jensen, A. R., & Sinha, S. N. (1992). Physical correlates of human intelligence. In P. A. Vernon (ed.), *Biological approaches to the study of human intelligence.* Norwood, NJ: Ablex.

Jensen, A. R., & Weng, L.-J. (1994). What is a good *g*? *Intelligence, 18,* 231–258.

Jerusalem, M., & Schwarzer, R. (1989). Anxiety and self-concept as antecedents of stress and coping: A longitudinal study with German and Turkish adolescents. *Personality & Individual Differences, 10,* 785–792.

Johnson, A., Johnson, O., & Baksh, M. (1986). The colors of emotions in Machiguenga. *American Anthropologist, 88,* 674–681.

Johnston, W. A., & Dark, V. J. (1986). Selective attention. *Annual Review of Psychology, 37,* 43–75.

Jolley, R. P., Zhi, Z., & Thomas, G. V. (1998). The Development of understanding moods metaphorically expressed in pictures: A cross-cultural comparison. *Journal of Cross-Cultural Psychology, 29,* 358–376.

Jonah, B. A. (1997). Sensation seeking and risky driving: A review and synthesis of the literature. *Accident Analysis & Prevention, 29,* 651–665.

Jones, K., & Day, J. D. (1997). Discrimination of two aspects of cognitive-social intelligence from academic intelligence. *Journal of Education Psychology, 89,* 486–497.

Jones, W. H., Briggs, S. R., & Smith, T. G. (1986). Shyness: Conceptualization and measurement. *Journal of Personality & Social Psychology, 51,* 629–639.

Jones, W. H., Rose, J., & Russell, D. (1990). Loneliness and social anxiety. In H. Leitenberg (ed.), *Handbook of social and evaluation anxiety* (pp. 247–266). New York: Plenum.

Joseph, R. (1996). *Neuropsychiatry, neuropsychology, and clinical neuroscience: Emotion, evolution, cognition, language, memory, brain damage, and abnormal behavior* (2nd ed.). Baltimore, MD: Williams & Wilkins Co.

Joseph, S., & Kuyken, W. (1993). Linking causal attributions and inhibitory processes. *Social Behavior & Personality, 21,* 1–5.

Joshi, M. S., & MacLean, M. (1994). Indian and English children's understanding of the distinction between real and apparent emotion. *Child Development, 65,* 1372–1384.

Judd, T. (1988). The varieties of musical talent. In L. K. Obler & D. Fein (eds.), *The exceptional brain: Neuropsychology of talent and special abilities* (pp. 127–155). New York: Guilford Press.

Kagan, J. (1994). *Galen's prophecy.* New York: Basic Books.

Kagan, J., Reznick, S. J., & Snidman, N. (1987). The physiology and psychology of behavioral inhibition in children. *Child Development, 58,* 1459–1473.

Kagen, N. I., Kagan, H., & Watson, M. G. (1995). Stress reduction in the workplace: The effectiveness of psychoeducational programs. *Journal of Counseling Psychology, 42,* 71–78.

Kahn, R. L., Wolfe, D. M., Quinn, R. P., Snoek, J. D., & Rosenthal, R. A. (1964). *Organizational stress: Studies in role conflict and ambiguity.* New York: Wiley.

Kaplan, R. E., & Palus, C. (1994). *Enhancing 360-degree feedback for senior executives: How to maximize the benefits and minimize the risks.* Greensboro, NC: Center for Creative Leadership.

Kaplan R. M., & Saccuzzo, D. P. (1997). *Psychological testing: Principles, applications, and issues* (4th ed.). Pacific Grove, CA: Brooks-Cole.

Karasek, R. (1989). Control in the workplace and its health related aspects. In S. L. Sauter, J. J. Hurrell & C. L. Cooper (eds.), *Job control and worker health.* Chichester: Wiley.

Karasek, R. A. (1979). Job demands, decision latitude, and mental strain: Implications for job design. *Administration Science Quarterly, 24,* 855–307.

Karasek, R., & Theorell, T. (1990). *Healthy work: Stress productivity and the reconstruction of working life.* New York: Wiley.

Karasek, R., Baker, D., Marker, F., Ahlbom, A., & Theorell, T. (1981). Job decision latitude, job demands, and cardiovascular disease: A prospective study of Swedish men. *American Journal of Public Health, 71,* 694–705.

Karmiloff-Smith, A. (1992). Nature, nurture, and PDP: Preposterous developmental postulates? *Connection Science: Journal of Neural Computing, Artificial Intelligence & Cognitive Research, 4,* 253–269.

Katz, D., & Kahn, R. L. (1978). *The social psychology of organizations.* New York: Wiley.

Katz, L., & Epstein, S. (1991). Constructive thinking and coping with laboratory-induced stress. *Journal of Personality and Social Psychology, 61,* 789–800.

Katz, L., Wilson, B., & Gottman, J. M. (1999). Meta-emotion philosophy and family adjustment: Making an emotional connection. In M. J. Cox & J. Brooks-Gunn (eds.), *Conflict and cohesion in families: Causes and consequences* (pp. 131–165). Mahwah, NJ: Lawrence Erlbaum Associates.

Kaufman, A. S., & Doppelt, J. E. (1976). Analysis of the WISC-R standardization data in terms of the stratification data. *Child Development, 47,* 165–171.

Kaufman, A. S., & Kaufman, J. C. (2001). Emotional intelligence as an aspect of general intelligence: What would David Wechsler say? *Emotion, 1,* 258–264.

Keating, D. P. (1978). A search for social intelligence. *Journal of Educational Psychology, 70,* 218–223.

Keita, G. P., & Sauter, S. L. (eds.) (1992). *Work and well-being.* Washington, DC: American Psychological Association.

Kelderman, H., Mellenbergh, G. J., & Elshout, J. J. (1981). Guilford's facet theory of intelligence: An empirical comparison of models. *Multivariate Behavioral Research, 16,* 37–61.

Kelly, E. L., & Conley, J. J. (1987). Personality and compatibility: A prospective analysis of marital stability and marital satisfaction. *Journal of Personality & Social Psychology, 52,* 27–40.

Kelly, R., & Caplan, J. (1993). How Bell Labs creates star performers. *Harvard Business Review, 71,* 128–139.

Kelman, H. C. (1958). Compliance, identification, and internalization: Three processes of attitude change. *Journal of Conflict Resolution, 2,* 51–60.

Kemper, T. D. (1978). *A social interactional theory of emotions.* New York: John Wiley & Sons.

Kemper, T. D. (1978). Toward a sociology of emotions: Some problems and some solutions. *American Sociologist, 13,* 30–41.

Kendall, P. C. (1993). Cognitive-behavioral therapies with youth: Guiding theory, current status, and emerging developments. *Journal of Consulting & Clinical Psychology, 61,* 235–247.

Kennedy, S. H., Dickens, S. E., Eisfeld, B. S., & Bagby, R. M. (1999). Sexual dysfunction before antidepressant therapy in major depression. *Journal of Affective Disorders, 56,* 201–208.

Ketelaar, T., & Clore, G. L. (1997). Emotion and reason: The proximate effects and ultimate functions of emotions. In G. Matthews (ed.), *Cognitive science perspectives on personality and emotion* (pp. 355–396). Amsterdam: Elsevier.

Kihlstrom, J. F., & Cantor, N. (2000). Social intelligence. In R. J. Sternberg (ed.), *Handbook of intelligence* (pp. 359–379). New York: Cambridge University Press.

Kim, J. A., Szatmari, P., Bryson, S. E., Streiner, D. L., & Wilson, F. J. (2000). The prevalence of anxiety and mood problems among children with autism and Asperger syndrome. *Autism, 4,* 117–132.

King, P. R., & Endler, N. S. (1990). The interaction model of anxiety: A critical appraisal of current research methods. *Personality & Individual Differences, 11,* 233–237.

Kirkcaldy, B., & Furnham, A. (1991). Extraversion, neuroticism, psychoticism, and recreational choice. *Personality & Individual Differences, 12,* 737–745.

Kirmayer, L. J., Robbins, J. M., & Paris, J. (1994). Somatoform disorders: Personality and the social matrix of somatic distress. *Journal of Abnormal Psychology, 103,* 125–136.

Kitayama, S. (1997). Affective influence in perception: Some implications of the amplification model. In G. Matthews (ed.), *Cognitive science perspectives on personality and emotion* (pp. 193–258). Amsterdam: Elsevier Science.

Kline, P. (1998). *The new psychometrics: Science, psychology, and measurement.* New York: Routledge.

Koch, J. L., Tung, R., Gmelch, W., & Swent, B. (1982). Job stress among school administrators: Factorial dimensions and differential effects. *Journal of Applied Psychology, 67,* 493–499.

Kocovski, N. L., & Endler, N. S. (2000). Self-regulation: Social anxiety and depression. *Journal of Applied Biobehavioral Research, 5,* 80–91.

Koelega, H. S. (1992). Extraversion and vigilance performance: 30 years of inconsistencies. *Psychological Bulletin, 112,* 239–258.

Koenig, L. J., Clements, C. M., & Alloy, L. B. (1992). Depression and the illusion of control: The role of esteem maintenance and impression management. *Canadian Journal of Behavioural Science, 24,* 233–252.

Kopp, C. B. (1989). Regulation of distress and negative emotions: A developmental view. *Developmental Psychology, 25*, 343–354.

Kosmitzki, C., & John, O. P. (1993). The implicit use of explicit conceptions of social intelligence. *Personality & Individual Differences, 15*, 11–23.

Kottkamp, R. B., & Travlos, A. L. (1986). Selected job stressors, emotional exhaustion, job satisfaction, and thrust behavior of the high school principal. *Alberta Journal of Educational Research, 32*, 234–248.

Kranzler, J. H., & Jensen, A. R. (1993). Psychometric *g* is still not unitary after eliminating supposed "impurities": Further comment on Carroll. *Intelligence, 17*, 11–14.

Krause, R., Lee, S.-K., Pallier, G., & Stankov, L. (2001). Time management, personality, and individual differences. Submitted.

Kroenke, K., Jackson, J. L., & Chamberlin, J. (1997). Depressive anxiety disorders in patients presenting with physical complaints: Clinical predictors and outcome. *American Journal of Medicine, 103*, 339–347.

Kruger, J., & Dunning, D. (1999). Unskilled and unaware of it: How difficulties in recognizing one's own incompetence lead to inflated self-assessments. *Journal of Personality & Social Psychology, 77*, 1121–1134.

Krystal, H. (1979). Alexithymia and psychotherapy. *American Journal of Psychotherapy, 33*, 17–31.

Krystal, H. (1982/83). Alexithymia and the effectiveness of psychoanalytic treatment. *International Journal of Psychoanalysis and Psychotherapy, 9*, 353–378.

Krystal, H. (1988). *Integration and self-healing: Affect, trauma, alexithymia*. Hillsdale: Analytic Press.

Kyllonen, P. C. (1994). CAM: A theoretical framework for cognitive abilities measurement. In D. K. Detterman (ed.), *Current Topics in Human Intelligence* (vol. 4). New York: Springer-Verlag.

Kyllonen, P. C., & Christal, R. E. (1990). Reasoning ability is (little more than) working memory capacity?! *Intelligence, 14*, 389–433.

La Rocco, J. M., & Jones, A. P. (1978). Co-worker and leader support as moderators of stress-strain relationships in work situations. *Journal of Applied Psychology, 63*, 629–634.

Lajunen, T., & Summala, H. (1995). Driving experience, personality, and skill and safety-motive dimensions in drivers' self-assessments. *Personality & Individual Differences, 19*, 307–318.

Lane, R. D. (1999). Functional neuroanatomy of pleasant and unpleasant emotion. *Dissertation abstracts international*, section B: The sciences and engineering, *60*, 1907.

Lane, R. D. (2000). Levels of emotional awareness: Neurological, psychological, and social perspectives. In R. Bar-On & J. D. A. Parker (eds.), *The handbook of emotional intelligence: Theory, development, assessment, and application at home, school, and in the workplace* (pp. 171–191). San Francisco: Jossey-Bass.

Lane, R. D., Ahern, G. L., Schwartz, G. E., Kasznyak, A. W. (1997). Is alexithymia the emotional equivalent of blindsight? *Biological Psychiatry, 42,* 834–844.

Lane, R. D., Kivley, L. S., Du Bois, M. A., Shamasundara, P., et al. (1995). Levels of emotional awareness and the degree of right hemispheric dominance in the perception of facial emotion. *Neuropsychologia, 33,* 525–538.

Lane, R. D., Quinlan, D. M., Schwartz, G. E., Walker, P. A., & Zeitlin, S. B. (1990). The Levels of Emotional Awareness Scale: A cognitive-development measure of emotion. *Journal of Personality Assessment, 55,* 124–134.

Lane, R. D., Reiman, E. M., Axelrod, B., Yun, L.-S., Holmes, A., & Schwartz, G. E. (1998). Neural correlates of levels of emotional awareness: Evidence of an interaction between emotion and attention in the anterior cingulate cortex. *Journal of Cognitive Neuroscience, 10,* 525–535.

Lane, R. D., & Schwartz, G. E. (1987). Levels of emotional awareness: A cognitive-developmental theory and its application to psychopathology. *American Journal of Psychiatry, 144,* 133–143.

Lane, R. D., Sechrest, L., Riedel, R., Shapiro, D., & Kaszniak, A. (in press). Pervasive emotion recognition deficit common to alexithymia and the repressive coping style. *Psychosomatic Medicine.*

Lane, R. D., Sechrest, L., Reidel, R., Weldon, V., Kaszniak, A. W., & Schwartz, G. (1996). Impaired verbal and nonverbal emotion recognition in alexithymia. *Psychosomatic Medicine, 58,* 203–210.

Lang, P. (1999). Counselling counselling skills and encouraging pupils to talk: Clarifying and addressing confusion. *British Journal of Guidance and Counselling, 27,* 23–33.

Lange, C. G. (1885/1912). The mechanism of the emotions. In Rand, B. (ed.), *The classical psychologists* (pp. 672–684). Boston: Houghton Mifflin.

Lantieri, L., & Patti, J. (1996). *Waging peace in our schools.* Boston: Beacon Press.

Lapides, J. (1980). *Skills for living and working: Tools for personal and career development.* Ann Arbor, MI: LAPID consultants.

Larsen, R. J. (1987). The stability of mood variability: A spectral analytic approach to daily mood assessments. *Journal of Personality & Social Psychology, 52,* 1195–1204.

Larsen, R. J., & Ketelaar, T. (1991). Personality and susceptibility to positive and negative emotional states. *Journal of Personality and Social Psychology, 61,* 132–140.

Larsen, R. J., & Sinnett, L. M. (1991). Meta-analysis of experimental manipulations: Some factors affecting the Velten mood induction procedure. *Personality & Social Psychology Bulletin, 17,* 323–334.

Latack, J. C. (1986). Coping with job stress: Measures and future directions for scale development. *Journal of Applied Psychology, 71,* 377–385.

Latham, G. P., & Frayne, C. A. (1989). Self-management training for increasing job attendance: A follow-up and a replication. *Journal of Applied Psychology, 74,* 411–416.

Latham, G. P., & Lock, E. A. (1991). Self-regulation through goal setting. *Organizational Behavior and Human Decision Processes, 50,* 212–247.

Latham, G. P., & Saarni, L. M. (1979). Application of social-learning theory to training supervisors through behavioral modeling. *Journal of Applied Psychology, 64,* 239–246.

Lawshe, C. H. (1975). A quantitative approach to content validity. *Personnel Psychology, 28,* 563–575.

Lazarus, R. (1991a). *Emotion and adaptation.* New York: Oxford University Press.

Lazarus, R. S. (1991b). Psychological stress in the workplace. In P. L. Parrewe (ed.), *Handbook on job stress* (pp. 1–13). Corte Madeara: Select Press.

Lazarus, R. S. (1993). Coping theory and research: Past, present, and future. *Psychosomatic Medicine, 55,* 237–247.

Lazarus, R. S. (1998a). Coping from the perspective of personality. *Zeitschrift für differentielle und diagnostische Psychologie, 19,* 213–230.

Lazarus, R. S. (1998b). Coping with aging: Individuality as a key to understanding. In I. H. Nordhus, G. R. VandenBos, et al. (eds.), *Clinical geropsychology* (pp. 109–127). Washington, DC: American Psychological Association.

Lazarus, R. S. (1998c). *Fifty years of the research and theory of R. S. Lazarus: An analysis of historical and perennial issues.* Mahwah, NJ: Lawrence Erlbaum Associates.

Lazarus, R. S. (1998d). *The life and work of an eminent psychologist.* New York: Springer.

Lazarus, R. S. (1999). *Stress and emotions: A new synthesis.* New York: Springer.

Lazarus, R., & Folkman, S. (1984). *Stress, appraisal, and coping.* New York: Springer.

Le Pine, J. A., Colquitt, J. A., & Erez, A. (2000). Adaptability to changing task contexts: Effects of general cognitive ability, conscientiousness, and openness to experience. *Personnel Psychology, 53,* 563–593.

LeDoux, J. E. (1995). Emotion: Clues from the brain. *Annual Review of Psychology, 46,* 209–235.

Lee, R. T., & Ashforth, B. E. (1993). A longitudinal study of burnout among supervisors and managers: Comparisons between the Leiter and Maslach (1988) and Golembiewski et al. (1986) models. *Organizational Behavior and Human Decision Processes, 54,* 369–398.

Legree, P. J. (1995). Evidence for an oblique social intelligence factor established with a Likert-based testing procedure. *Intelligence, 21,* 241–247.

Leiter, M. P., & Maslach, C. (1988). The impact of interpersonal environment on burnout and organizational commitment. *Journal of Organizational Behavior, 9,* 297–308.

Lennon, M. C., Dohrenwend, B. P., Zautra, A. J., & Marbach, J. J. (1990). Coping and adaptation to facial pain in contrast to other stressful life events. *Journal of Personality and Social Psychology, 59,* 1040–1050.

Lennon, R., Eisenberg, N., & Carroll, J. (1986). The relation between nonverbal indices of empathy and preschoolers' prosocial behavior. *Journal of Applied Developmental Psychology, 7*, 219–224.

LePage-Lees, P. (1997). Exploring patterns of achievement and intellectual development among academically successful women from disadvantaged backgrounds. *Journal of College Student Development, 38*, 468–478.

Lepore, S. J., & Evans, G. W. (1996). Coping with multiple stressors in the environment. In M. Zeidner & N. S. Endler (eds.), *Handbook of Coping* (pp. 350–377). New York: Wiley.

Leuner, B. (1966). Emotional intelligence and emancipation. *Praxis der Kinderpsychologie und Kinderpsychiatrie, 15*, 196–203.

Levenson, R. W., & Ruef, A. M. (1997). Physiological aspects of emotional knowledge and rapport. In W. Ickes (ed.), *Empathic accuracy*. New York: Guilford Press.

Leventhal, H., & Scherer, K. R. (1987). The relationship of emotion to cognition: A functional approach to a semantic controversy. *Cognition and Emotion, 1*, 3–28.

Levesque, M. J., & Kenny, D. A. (1993). Accuracy of behavioral predictions at zero acquaintance: A social relations analysis. *Journal of Personality & Social Psychology, 65*, 1178–1187.

Levy, P. (1992). Inspection time and its relation to intelligence: Issues of measurement and meaning. *Personality and Individual Differences, 13*, 987–1002.

Lewis, H. B. (1983). *Freud and modern psychology*. New York: Plenum Press.

Lewis, M., & Michalson, L. (1983). *Children's emotions and moods: Developmental theory and measurement*. New York: Plenum.

Lewis, M., & Saarni, C. (1985a). Culture and emotion. In M. Lewis & C. Saarni (eds.), *The socialization of emotions*. New York: Plenum.

Lewis, M., & Saarni, C. (eds.) (1985b). *The socialization of emotions*. New York: Plenum.

Lin, N., Simeone, R. S., Ensel, W. M., & Kuo, W. (1979). Social support, stressful life events, and illness: A model and empirical test. *Journal of Health and Social Behavior*, 108–119.

Lippa, R. A., & Dietz, J. K. (2000). The relation of gender, personality, and intelligence to judges' accuracy in judging strangers' personality from brief video segments. *Journal of Nonverbal Behavior, 24*, 25–43.

Livesley, W. J. (1995b). Past achievements and future directions. In W. J. Livesley (ed.), *The DSM IV Personality Disorders*. New York: Guilford.

Livesley, W. J., & Jang, K. L. (2000). Toward an empirically based classification of personality disorder. *Journal of Personality Disorders, 14*, 137–151.

Livesley, W. J., Jang, K. L., & Vernon, P. A. (1998). Phenotypic and genetic structure of traits delineating personality disorder. *Archives of General Psychiatry, 55*, 941–948.

Livesley, W. J., & Schroeder, M. L. (1990). Dimensions of personality disorder: the *DSM-III-R* cluster A diagnoses. *Journal of Nervous and Mental Disease, 178,* 627–635.

Lochman, J. E., & Dodge, K. A. (1994). Social-cognitive processes of severely violent, moderately aggressive, and non-aggressive boys. *Journal of Consulting & Clinical Psychology, 62,* 366–374.

Lochman, J. E., & Lampron, L. B. (1986). Situational social problem-solving skills and self-esteem of aggressive and nonaggressive boys. *Journal of Abnormal Child Psychology, 14,* 605–617.

Lochman, J. E., Lampron, L. B., & Rabiner, D. L. (1989). Format differences and salience effects in the social problem-solving assessment of aggressive and non-aggressive boys. *Journal of Clinical Child Psychology, 18,* 230–236.

Lochman, J. E., & Lenhart, L. A. (1993). Anger coping intervention for aggressive children: Conceptual models and outcome effects. *Clinical Psychology Review, 13,* 785–805.

Loehlin, J. C. (1992). *Genes and environment in personality development.* Newbury Park, CA: Sage Publications.

Loehlin, J. C. (1992a). Guttman on factor analysis and group differences: A comment. *Multivariate Behavioral Research, 27,* 235–238.

Loehlin, J. C. (1992b). On Schönemann on Guttman on Jensen, via Lewontin. *Multivariate Behavioral Research, 27* (2), 261–264.

Loevinger, J., & Wessler, R. (1970). *Measuring ego development.* Vol. 1: *Construction and use of a sentence completion test.* San Francisco: Jossey-Bass.

Lohman, D. F. (2000). Complex information processing and intelligence. In R. J. Sternberg (ed.), *Handbook of intelligence* (pp. 285–340). New York: Cambridge University Press.

Lohman, M. C., & Finkelstein, M. (2000). Designing groups in problem-based learning to promote problem-solving skill and self-directedness. *Instructional Science, 28,* 291–307.

Lord, F. M. (1960). *Applications of item response theory to practical testing problems.* Hillsdale, NJ: Lawrence Erlbaum Associates.

Lorr, M., & Wunderlich, R. A. (1985). A measure of impulsiveness and its relations to extraversion. *Educational & Psychological Measurement, 45,* 251–257.

Lowman, R. L. (1991). *The clinical practice of career assessment.* Washington, DC: American Psychological Association.

Lusch, R. F., & Serpkenci, R. R. (1990). Personal differences, job tension, job outcomes, and store performance: A study of retail store managers. *Journal of Marketing, 54,* 85–101.

Lyons, C. (1999). The philosophy of cognition and emotion. In T. Dalgleish & M. J. Power (eds.), *Handbook of cognition and emotion* (pp. 21–44). New York: John Wiley & Sons.

Lyubomirsky, S., & Nolen-Hoeksema, S. (1995). Effects of self-focused rumination on negative thinking and interpersonal problem solving. *Journal of Personality and Social Psychology, 69,* 176–190.

Maccoby, E. E., & Martin, J. A. (1983). Socialization in the context of the family: Parent-child interaction. In E. M. Hetherington (ed.), *Handbook of child psychology*, vol. 4: *Socialization, personality, and social behavior*. New York: Wiley.

Mack, D. A., Nelson, D. L., & Quick, J. C. (1998). The stress of organisational change: A dynamic process model. *Applied Psychology: An International Review, 47*, 219–232.

Mackintosh, N. J. (1998). *IQ and human intelligence*. New York: Oxford University Press.

MacLeod, C., & Mathews, A. (1991a). Cognitive-experimental approaches to the emotional disorders. In P. R. Martin (ed.), *Handbook of behaviour therapy and psychological science: An integrative approach*. Oxford: Pergamon.

Maddi, S. R. (1996). *Personality theories: A comparative analysis* (6th ed.). Pacific Grove, CA: Brooks/Cole Publishing Co.

Maddock, R. J., & Buonocore, M. H. (1997). Activation of left posterior cingulate gyrus by the auditory presentation of threat-related words: An fMRI study. *Psychiatry Research: Neuroimaging, 75*, 1–14.

Magai, C., & McFadden, S. H. (1995). *The role of emotions in social and personality development: History, theory, and research*. New York: Plenum Press.

Malatesta, C. Z. (1990). The role of emotions in the development and organization of personality. In R. A. Thompson et al. (eds.), *Socioemotional development* (pp. 1–56). Lincoln: University of Nebraska Press.

Malatesta, C. Z., & Haviland, J. M. (1982). Learning display rules: The socialization of emotion expression in infancy. *Child Development, 53*, 991–1003.

Malatesta-Magai, C. (1991). Development of emotion expression during infancy: General course and pattern of individual differences. In J. Garber & K. A. Dodge (eds.), *The development of emotion regulation and dysregulation*. Cambridge: Cambridge University Press.

Mandal, M. K., Bryden, M. P., & Bulman-Fleming, M. B. (1996). Similarities and variations in facial expressions of emotions: Cross-cultural evidence. *International Journal of Psychology, 31*, 49–58.

Mandler, G. (1984). *Mind and body: Psychology of emotion and stress*. New York: Norton.

Mantzicopoulos, P. Y., & Oh-Hwang, Y. (1998). The relationship of psychosocial maturity to parenting quality and intellectual ability for American and Korean adolescents. *Contemporary Educational Psychology, 23*, 195–206.

Markham, R., & Wang, L. (1996). Recognition of emotion by Chinese and Australian children. *Journal of Cross-Cultural Psychology, 27*, 616–643.

Marlowe, H. A. (1986). Social intelligence: Evidence for multidimensionality and construct independence. *Journal of Educational Psychology, 78*, 52–58.

Marrow, C. C., Jarrett, M. Q., & Rupinski, M. T. (1997). An investigation of the effect and economic utility of corporate-wide training. *Personnel Psychology, 50*, 91–119.

Marsella, A. J., DeVos, G., & Hsu, F. (eds.) (1985). *Culture and self: Asian and Western perspectives.* New York/London: Tavistock.

Marshalek, B., Lohman, D. F., & Snow, R. E. (1983). The complexity continuum in the radex and hierarchical models of intelligence. *Intelligence, 7,* 107–127.

Marshall, C. (2001). Make the most of your emotional intelligence. *Chemical Engineering Progress, 97,* 92–95.

Martin, E. D., & Sher, K. J. (1994). Family history of alcoholism, alcohol use disorders, and the five-factor model of personality. *Journal of Studies on Alcohol, 55,* 81–90.

Martin, L., & Adkins, D. C. (1954). A second-order analysis of reasoning abilities. *Psychometrika, 19,* 71–78.

Martinez-Pons, M. (1997). The relation of emotional intelligence with selected areas of personal functioning. *Imagination, Cognition, and Personality, 17,* 3–13.

Martinez-Pons, M. (1998). Parental inducement of emotional intelligence. *Imagination Cognition and Personality, 18,* 1999.

Martuza, V. R. (1977). *Applying norm-referenced and criterion-referenced measurement in education.* Boston: Allyn & Bacon.

Marx, R. D. (1982). Relapse prevention for managerial training: A model for maintenance of behavior change. *Academy of Management Review, 7,* 433–441.

Mascie-Taylor, C. G., & Gibson, J. B. (1978). Social mobility and IQ components. *Journal of Biosocial Science, 10,* 263–276.

Maslach, C. (1978). How people cope. *Public Welfare, 36,* 56–58.

Matarazzo, J. D. (1972). *Wechsler's measurement and appraisal of adult intelligence* (5th ed.). Baltimore: Williams & Wilkins.

Matsumoto, D. (1990). Cultural similarities and differences in display rules. *Motivation and Emotion, 14,* 195–214.

Matsumoto, D. (1992). American-Japanese cultural differences in the recognition of universal facial expressions. *Journal of Cross-Cultural Psychology, 23,* 72–84.

Matsumoto, D. (1992). More evidence for the universality of a contempt expression. *Motivation and Emotion, 16,* 363–368.

Matthews, G. (1997a). An introduction to the cognitive science of personality and emotion. In G. Matthews (ed.), *Cognitive science perspectives on personality and emotion* (pp. 3–30). Amsterdam: Elsevier.

Matthews, G. (1997b). Extraversion, emotion, and performance: A cognitive-adaptive model. In G. Matthews (ed.), *Cognitive science perspectives on personality and emotion* (pp. 339–442). Amsterdam: Elsevier.

Matthews, G. (1997c). Intelligence, personality, and information-processing: An adaptive perspective. In J. Kingma & W. Tomic (eds.), *Advances in cognition and educational practice: Reflections on the concept of intelligence* (vol. 4, pp. 175–200). Stamford, CT: JAI Press.

Matthews, G. (1999). Personality and skill: A cognitive-adaptive framework. In P. L. Ackerman, P. C. Kyllonen & R. D. Roberts (eds.), *Learning and individual differences: Process, trait, and content determinants* (pp. 251–273). Washington, DC: American Psychological Association.

Matthews, G. (2000). A cognitive science critique of biological theories of personality traits. *History and Philosophy of Psychology, 2,* 1–17.

Matthews, G. (2001a). Levels of transaction: A cognitive science framework for operator stress. In P. A. Hancock & P. A. Desmond (eds.), *Stress, workload, and fatigue* (pp. 5–33). Mahwah, NJ: Lawrence Erlbaum Associates.

Matthews, G. (2001b). A transactional model of driver stress. In P. A. Hancock & P. A. Desmond (eds.), *Stress, workload and fatigue* (pp. 133–163). Mahwah, NJ: Lawrence Erlbaum Associates.

Matthews, G., & Amelang, M. (1993). Extraversion, arousal theory, and performance: A study of individual differences in the EEG. *Personality and Individual Differences, 14,* 347–364.

Matthews, G., & Campbell, S. E. (1998). Task-induced stress and individual differences in coping. *Proceedings of the 42nd Annual Meeting of the Human Factors and Ergonomics Society* (pp. 821–825). Santa Monica, CA: Human Factors and Ergonomics Society.

Matthews, G., Davies, D. R., & Holley, P. J. (1990). Extraversion, arousal, and visual sustained attention: The role of resource availability. *Personality and Individual Differences, 11,* 1159–1173.

Matthews, G., Davies, D. R., & Lees, J. L. (1990). Arousal, extraversion, and individual differences in resource availability. *Journal of Personality and Social Psychology, 59,* 150–168.

Matthews, G., Davies, D. R., Westerman, S. J., & Stammers, R. B. (2000). *Human performance: Cognition, stress, and individual differences.* Hove, England: Psychology Press/Taylor & Francis.

Matthews, G., & Deary, I. J. (1998). *Personality traits.* New York: Cambridge University Press.

Matthews, G., Derryberry, D., & Siegle, G. J. (2000). Personality and emotion: Cognitive science perspectives. In S. E. Hampson et al. (eds.), *Advances in personality psychology* (vol. 1, pp. 199–237). Philadelphia: Psychology Press/Taylor & Francis.

Matthews, G., Desmond, P. A., Joyner, L. A., & Carcary, B. (1997). A comprehensive questionnaire measure of driver stress and affect. In E. Carbonell Vaya & J. A. Rothengatter (eds.), *Traffic and transport psychology: Theory and application* (pp. 317–324). Amsterdam: Pergamon.

Matthews, G., & Dorn, L. (1989). IQ and choice reaction time: An information processing analysis. *Intelligence, 13,* 299–317.

Matthews, G., & Dorn, L. (1995). Cognitive and attentional processes in personality and intelligence. In D. H. Saklofske & M. Zeidner (eds.), *International handbook of personality and intelligence: Perspectives on individual differences* (pp. 367–396). New York: Plenum Press.

Matthews, G., & Falconer, S. (2000). Individual differences in task-induced stress in customer service personnel. In *Proceedings of the Human Factors and Ergonomics Society 44th Annual Meeting*. Santa Monica, CA: Human Factors and Ergonomics Society.

Matthews, G., & Gilliland, K. (1999). The personality theories of H. J. Eysenck and J. A. Gray: A comparative review. *Personality & Individual Differences, 26*, 583–626.

Matthews, G., & Harley, T. A. (1993). Effects of extraversion and self-report arousal on semantic priming: A connectionist approach. *Journal of Personality and Social Psychology, 65*, 735–756.

Matthews, G., & Harley, T. A. (1996). Connectionist models of emotional distress and attentional bias. *Cognition and Emotion, 10*, 561–600.

Matthews, G., Joyner, L., Gilliland, K., Campbell, S. E., Huggins, J., & Falconer, S. (1999). Validation of a comprehensive stress state questionnaire: Towards a state "Big Three"? In I. Mervielde, I. J. Deary, F. De Fruyt & F. Ostendorf (eds.), *Personality psychology in Europe* (vol. 7, pp. 335–350). Tilburg: Tilburg University Press.

Matthews, G., Mohamed, A., & Lochrie, B. (1998). Dispositional self-focus of attention and individual differences in appraisal and coping. In J. Bermúdez, A. M. Perez, A. Sanchez-Elvira & G. L. van Heck (eds.), *Personality psychology in Europe* (vol. 6, pp. 278–285). Tilburg: Tilburg University Press.

Matthews, G., & Oddy, K. (1993). Recovery of major personality dimensions from trait adjective data. *Personality and Individual Differences, 15*, 419–431.

Matthews, G., Pitcaithly, D., & Mann, R. L. E. (1995). Mood, neuroticism, and the encoding of affective words. *Cognitive Therapy and Research, 19*, 563–587.

Matthews, G., Saklofske, D. H., Costa, P. T., Jr., Deary, I. J., & Zeidner, M. (1998). Dimensional models of personality: A framework for systematic clinical assessment. *European Journal of Psychological Assessment, 14*, 35–48.

Matthews, G., Schwean, V. L., Campbell, S. E., Saklofske, D. H., & Mohamed, A. A. R. (2000). Personality, self-regulation, and adaptation: A cognitive-social framework. In M. Boekaerts, P. R. Pintrich & M. Zeidner (eds.), *Handbook of self-regulation* (pp. 171–207). New York: Academic.

Matthews, G., & Stanton, N. (1994). Item and scale factor analyses of the Occupational Personality Questionnaire. *Personality & Individual Differences, 16*, 733–743.

Matthews, G., & Wells, A. (1996). Attentional processes, dysfunctional coping, and clinical intervention. In M. Zeidner & N. S. Endler (eds.), *Handbook of coping: Theory, research, applications* (pp. 573–601). Oxford, England: John Wiley & Sons.

Matthews, G., & Wells, A. (1999). The cognitive science of attention and emotion. In T. Dalgleish & M. J. Power (eds.), *Handbook of cognition and emotion* (pp. 171–192). Brisbane, Australia: John Wiley & Sons.

Matthews, G., & Wells, A. (2000). Attention, automaticity, and affective disorder. *Behavior Modification, 24*, 69–93.

Matthews, G., & Wells, A. (in press). Rumination, depression, and metacognition: The S-REF model. In C. Papageorgiou & A. Wells (eds.), *Rumination: Nature, theory, and treatment of negative thinking in depression*. Chichester: Wiley.

Matthews, G., & Zeidner, M. (2000). Emotional intelligence, adaptation to stressful encounters, and health outcomes. In R. Bar-On & J. D. A. Parker (eds.), *Handbook of emotional intelligence* (pp. 459–489). New York: Jossey-Bass.

Mattlin, J. A., Wethington, E., & Kessler, C. (1990). Situational determinants of coping and coping effectiveness. *Journal of Health and Social Behavior, 31*, 103–122.

Mauro, R. (1992). The role of appraisal in human emotions. *Journal of Personality and Social Psychology, 62*, 301–317.

Mawson, D. L. (1993). Implications for employment interventions and policy. In B. C. Long & S. E. Kahn (eds.), *Woman, work, and coping* (pp. 51–69). Montreal: McGill-Queens University Press.

Mayer, D., & Greenberg, H. M. (1964). What makes a good salesman? *Harvard Business Review, 42*, 119–125.

Mayer, J. D. (1986). How mood influences cognition. In N. E. Sharkey (ed.), *Advances in cognitive psychology* (vol. 1, pp. 290–314). Chichester: John Wiley & Sons.

Mayer, J. D. (1995a). A framework for the classification of personality components. *Journal of Personality, 63*, 819–877.

Mayer, J. D. (1995b). Mood-congruent judgement over time. *Personality and Social Psychology Bulletin, 21*, 237–244.

Mayer, J. D., & Beltz, C. M. (1998). Socialization, society's "emotional contract," and emotional intelligence. *Psychological Inquiry, 9*, 300–306.

Mayer, J. D., & Bremer, D. (1985). Assessing mood with affect sensitive tasks. *Journal of Personality Assessment, 49*, 95–99.

Mayer, J. D., Caruso, D., & Salovey, P. (1999). Emotional intelligence meets traditional standards for an intelligence. *Intelligence, 27*, 267–298.

Mayer, J. D., Caruso, D., & Salovey, P. (2000). Selecting a measure of emotional intelligence: The case of ability scales. In R. Bar-On & J. D. A. Parker (eds.), *The handbook of emotional intelligence* (pp. 320–342). San Francisco: Jossey-Bass.

Mayer, J. D., Caruso, D., Zigler, E., Dreyden, J. I. (1989). Intelligence and intelligence-related personality traits. *Intelligence, 13*, 119–133.

Mayer, J. D., & Cobb, C. D. (2000). Educational policy on emotional intelligence: Does it make sense? *Educational Psychology Review, 12*, 163–183.

Mayer, J. D., DiPaolo, M., & Salovey, P. (1990). Perceiving affective content in ambiguous visual stimuli: A component of emotional intelligence. *Journal of Personality Assessment, 54*, 772–778.

Mayer, J. D., Frasier Chabot, H., & Carlsmith, K. M. (1997). Conation, affect, and cognition in personality. In G. Matthews (ed.), *Cognitive science perspectives on personality and emotion* (pp. 31–63). Amsterdam: Elsevier.

Mayer, J. D., & Gaschke, Y. N. (1988). The experience and meta-experience of mood. *Journal of Personality and Social Psychology, 55*, 102–111.

Mayer, J. D., Gaschke, Y. N., Braverman, D. L., & Evans, T. W. (1992). Mood-congruent judgement is a general effect. *Journal of Personality and Social Psychology, 63,* 119–132.

Mayer, J. D., & Geher, G. (1996). Emotional intelligence and the identification of emotion. *Intelligence, 22,* 89–113.

Mayer, J. D., Gomberg-Kaufman, S., et al. (1991). A broader conception of mood experience. *Journal of Personality and Social Psychology, 60,* 100–111.

Mayer, J. D., & Mitchell, D. C. (1998). Intelligence as a subsystem of personality: From Spearman's *g* to contemporary models of hot processing. In W. Tomic & J. Kingma (eds.), *Advances in cognition and educational practice* (vol. 5, pp. 43–75). Greenwich, CT: JAI Press.

Mayer, J. D., & Salovey, P. (1988). Personality moderates the interaction of mood and cognition. In K. Fiedler & J. Forgas (eds.), *Affect, cognition, and social behavior* (pp. 87–99). Ontario, Canada: C. J. Hogrefe.

Mayer, J. D., & Salovey, P. (1993). The intelligence of emotional intelligence. *Intelligence, 17,* 433–442.

Mayer, J. D., & Salovey, P. (1995). Emotional intelligence and the construction and regulation of feelings. *Applied & Preventive Psychology, 4,* 197–208.

Mayer, J. D., & Salovey, P. (1997). What is emotional intelligence? In P. Salovey & D. J. Sluyter (eds.), *Emotional development and emotional intelligence: Educational implications.* New York: Basic Books.

Mayer, J. D., Salovey, P., & Caruso, D. R. (1997). *Emotional Intelligence Test.* CD ROM version. Needham, MA: Virtual Knowledge.

Mayer, J. D., Salovey, P., & Caruso, D. R. (2000a). Emotional intelligence as *Zeitgeist,* as personality, and as a mental ability. In R. Bar-On & J. D. A. Parker (eds.), *The handbook of emotional intelligence.* San Francisco: Jossey-Bass.

Mayer, J. D., Salovey, P., & Caruso, D. R. (2000b). Competing models of emotional intelligence. In R. J. Sternberg (ed.), *Handbook of human intelligence* (2nd ed.). New York: Cambridge University Press.

Mayer, J. D., Salovey, P., & Caruso, D. R. (in preparation). *The Mayer, Salovey, and Caruso Emotional Intelligence Test: Technical manual.* Toronto: Multi-Health Systems.

Mayer, J. D., Salovey, P., Caruso, D. R., & Sitarenios, G. (2001). Emotional intelligence as a standard intelligence. *Emotion,* submitted.

Mayer, J. D., & Stevens, A. A. (1994). An emerging understanding of the reflective (meta-)experience of mood. *Journal of Research in Personality,* 351–373.

Mayne, T. J. (1999). Negative affect and health: The importance of being earnest. *Cognition and Emotion, 13,* 601–635.

McArdle, J. J., & Horn, J. L. (1983). *Validation by systems modelling of WAIS abilities.* National Institute of Aging.

McCabe, R. E., Blankstein, K. R., & Mills, J. S. (1999). Interpersonal sensitivity and social problem-solving: Relations with academic and social self-esteem, depressive symptoms, and academic performance. *Cognitive Therapy & Research, 23,* 587–604.

McCabe, S. B., Gotlib, I. H., & Martin, R. A. (2000). Cognitive vulnerability for depression: Deployment of attention as a function of history of depression and current mood state. *Cognitive Therapy and Research, 24*, 427–444.

McCallum, M., & Piper, W. E. (2000). Psychological mindedness and emotional intelligence. In R. Bar-On & J. D. A. Parker (eds.), *The handbook of emotional intelligence: Theory, development, assessment, and application at home, school, and in the workplace* (pp. 118–135). San Francisco: Jossey-Bass.

McCauley, R. N. (1996). Explanatory pluralism and the co-evolution of theories in science. In R. N. McCauley (ed.), *The Churchlands and their critics* (pp. 17–48). Oxford: Blackwell.

McClelland, D. C. (1961). *The achieving society.* Princeton, NJ: Van Nostrand.

McClelland, D. C., & Boyatzis, R. E. (1982). Leadership motive pattern and long-term success in management. *Journal of Applied Psychology, 67*, 737–743.

McCoy, C. L., & Masters, J. C. (1996). Children's strategies for the control of emotions in themselves and others. In B. S. Moore & A. M. Isen (eds.), *Affect and social behavior* (pp. 231–268). New York: Cambridge University Press.

McCrae, R. R. (1996). Integrating the levels of personality. *Psychological Inquiry, 7*, 353–356.

McCrae, R. R. (2000). Emotional intelligence from the perspective of the Five-Factor Model of Personality. In R. Bar-On & J. D. A. Parker (eds.), *The handbook of emotional intelligence* (pp. 263–276). New York: Jossey-Bass.

McCrae, R. R., & Costa, P. T. (1986). Personality, coping, and coping effectiveness in an adult sample. *Journal of Personality, 54*, 385–405.

McCrae, R. R., & Costa, P. T. (1989). More reasons to adopt the five-factor model. *American Psychologist, 44*, 451–452.

McCrae, R. R., & Costa, P. T. (1992). Discriminant validity of NEO-PIR facet scales. *Educational & Psychological Measurement, 52*, 229–237.

McCrae, R. R., & Costa, P. T. (1995). Positive and negative valence within the five-factor model. *Journal of Research in Personality, 29*, 443–460.

McCrae R. R., & John, O. P. (1992). An introduction to the five-factor model and its applications. *Journal of Personality, 60*, 175–215.

McCranie, E. W., & Kahan, J. (1986). Personality and multiple divorce: A prospective study. *Journal of Nervous & Mental Disease, 174*, 161–164.

McCraty, R., Atkinson, M., Tiller, W. A., Rein, G., & Watkins, A. (1995). The effects of emotions on heart-rate short-term variability using power spectrum analysis. *American Journal of Cardiology, 76*, 1089–1093.

McCubbin, H. I., McCubbin, M. A., Patterson, J. M., Cabule, A. E., Wilson, L. R., & Warwick, W. (1983). CHIP—Coping Health Inventory for Parents: An assessment of parental coping patterns in the care of the chronically ill child. *Journal of Marriage and the Family, 45*, 359–370.

McDougall, J. (1989). *Theaters of the body: A psychoanalytic approach to psychosomatic illness.* New-York: Norton.

McGrath, J. E. (1976). Stress and behavior in organizations. In M. D. Dunnette (ed.), *Handbook of industrial and organizational psychology* (1st ed.). Chicago: Rand McNally.

McNally, R. J. (1996). Cognitive bias in the anxiety disorders. In Debra A. Hope (ed.). *Nebraska Symposium on Motivation, 1995: Perspectives on anxiety, panic, and fear* (pp. 211–250). Lincoln: University of Nebraska Press.

McNally, R. J., & Shin, L. M. (1995). Association of intelligence with severity of posttraumatic stress disorder symptoms in Vietnam combat veterans. *American Journal of Psychiatry, 152*, 936–938.

McNemar, Q. (1969). *Psychological statistics* (4th ed.). New York: Wiley.

Megargee, E. I. (1997). Internal inhibitions and controls. In R. Hogan, J. A. Johnson, et al. (eds.), *Handbook of personality psychology* (pp. 581–614). San Diego, CA: Academic Press.

Mehrabian, A., & Epstein, S. (1970). A measure of emotional empathy. *Journal of Personality, 40*, 525–543.

Mehta, S. D., Ward, C., & Strongman, K. (1992). Cross-cultural recognition of posed facial expression of emotion. *New Zealand Journal of Psychology, 21*, 74–77.

Meichenbaum, D. H. (ed.) (1975). *Cognitive behavior modification.* Morrison, NJ: General Learning Press.

Menaghan, E. (1982). Measuring coping effectiveness: A panel analysis of marital problems and coping efforts. *Journal of Health and Social Behavior, 23*, 220–234.

Menaghan, E., & Merves, E. (1984). Coping with occupational problem: The limits of individual efforts. *Journal of Health and Social Behavior, 25*, 406–423.

Mesquita, B., & Frijda, N. H. (1992). Cultural variations in emotions: A review. *Psychological Bulletin, 112*, 179–204.

Mesquita, B., Frijda, N. H., & Scherer, K. R. (1997). Culture and emotion. In J. W. Berry, Pierre R. Dasen & T. S. Saraswathi (eds.), *Handbook of cross-cultural psychology* (vol. 2). Sydney: Allyn & Bacon.

Messick, S. (1992). Multiple intelligence or multilevel intelligence? Selective emphasis on distinctive properties of hierarchy: On Gardner's Frames of Mind and Sternberg's Beyond IQ in the context of theory and research on the structure of human abilities. *Psychological Inquiry, 3*, 365–384.

Metcalfe, J. (1998). Cognitive optimism: Self-deception or memory-based processing heuristics? *Personality & Social Psychology Review, 2*, 100–110.

Metz, J. T., Yassillo, N. J., & Cooper, M. (1987). Relationship between cognitive functioning and cerebral metabolism. *Journal of Cerebral Blood Flow and Metabolism, 7* (suppl. 1), S305.

Meyer, G. J., & Shack, J. R. (1989). Structural convergence of mood and personality: Evidence for old and new directions. *Journal of Personality & Social Psychology, 57*, 691–706.

Michalson, L., & Lewis, M. (1985). What do children know about emotions, and when do they know it? In M. Lewis & C. Saarni (eds.), *The socialization of emotions* (pp. 117–139). New York: Plenum.

Michell, J. (1990). *An introduction to the logic of psychological measurement.* Hillsdale, NJ: Lawrence Erlbaum Associates.

Miller, N. E. (1951). Learnable drives and rewards. In S. S. Stevens (ed.), *Handbook of experimental psychology* (pp. 435–472). New York: Wiley.

Miller, P. J., & Sperry, L. L. (1987). The socialization of anger and aggression. *Merrill-Palmer Quarterly, 33,* 1–31.

Miller, P. J., & Sperry, L. L. (1988). The socialization and acquisition of emotional meanings with special reference to language: A reply to Saarni. *Merrill-Palmer Quarterly, 34,* 1–31.

Miller, S. M., & Green, M. L. (1985). Coping with stress and frustration: Origins, nature, and development. In M. Lewis & C. Saarni (eds.), *The socialization of emotions* (pp. 263–314). New York: Plenum.

Miller, S. M., Brody, D. S., & Summerton, J. (1988). Styles of coping with threat: Implications for health. *Journal of Personality and Social Psychology, 34* (1), 142–148.

Mineka, S., Watson, D., & Clark, A. (1998). Comorbidity of anxiety and unipolar mood disorders. *Annual Review of Psychology, 49,* 377–412.

Mintzberg, H. (1977). Planning on the left side and managing on the right. *Harvard Business Review, 54,* 49–58.

Miranda, J., & Persons, J. B. (1988). Dysfunctional attitudes are mood-state dependent. *Journal of Abnormal Psychology, 97,* 76–79.

Miron, D., & McClelland, D. C. (1979). The impact of achievement motivation training on small businesses. *California Management Review, 21,* 13–28.

Mischel, W. (1983). Delay of gratification as process and person variable in development. In D. Magnusson & V. P. Allen (eds.), *Interactions in human development* (pp. 149–165). New York: Academic.

Mize, J., Pettit, G. S., & Meece, D. (2000). Explaining the link between parenting behavior and children's peer competence: A critical examination of the "mediating process" hypothesis. In K. A. Kerns, J. M. Contreras & A. M. Neal-Barnett (eds.), *Family and peers: Linking two social worlds* (pp. 137–167). New York: Praeger.

Moore, B., & Beland, K. (1992). Evaluation of Second Step, Preschool-Kindergarten—A violence-prevention curriculum kit. Unpublished research report.

Morgan, I. A., Matthews, G., & Winton, M. (1995). Coping and personality as predictors of post-traumatic intrusions, numbing, avoidance, and general distress: A study of victims of the Perth flood. *Behavioural and Cognitive Psychotherapy, 23,* 251–264.

Morris, J. A., & Feldman, D. C. (1996). The dimensions, antecedents, and consequences of emotional labor. *Academy of Management Review, 21,* 986–1010.

Morris, J. A., & Feldman, D. C. (1997). Managing emotions in the workplace. *Journal of Managerial Issues, 9,* 257–274.

Morrow, J., & Nolen-Hoeksema, S. (1990). Effects of responses to depression on the remediation of depressive affect. *Journal of Personality and Social Psychology, 100,* 519–527.

Most, B., & Zeidner, M. (1995). Constructing personality and intelligence test instruments: Methods and issues. In D. Saklofske & M. Zeidner (eds.), *International handbook of personality and intelligence* (pp. 475–503). New York: Plenum.

Mowrer, O. H. (1960). *Learning and behavior.* New York: Wiley.

Mughal, S., Walsh, J., & Wilding, J. (1996). Stress and work performance: The role of trait anxiety. *Personality & Individual Differences, 20,* 685–691.

Murphy, K. R., & Davidshofer, C. O. (1998). *Psychological testing: Principles and applications* (4th ed.). Upper Saddle River, NJ: Prentice-Hall.

Murphy, L. R. (1984). Occupational stress management: A review and appraisal. *Journal of Occupational Psychology, 57,* 1–15.

Murphy, L. R. (1988). Workplace interventions for stress reduction and prevention. In C. L. Cooper & R. Payne (eds.), *Causes, coping, and consequences of stress at work* (pp. 301–339). Chichester: Wiley.

Murray, H. A. (1962). Definitions of myth. In R. M. Ohmann (ed.), *The making of myth* (pp. 7–37). New York: Putnam.

Myors, B. (1984). *An investigation of the relationship between attention and intelligence.* Unpublished B.Sc. (with honors) dissertation, University of Sydney, Australia.

Myors, B., Stankov, L., & Oliphant, G. W. (1989). Competing tasks, working memory, and intelligence. *Australian Journal of Psychology, 41,* 1–16.

Navon, D. (1984). Resources: A theoretical soupstone. *Psychological Review, 91,* 216–234.

Neely, J. H. (1991). Semantic priming effects in visual word recognition: A selective review of current findings and theories. In D. E. Besner & G. Humphreys (eds.), *Basic processes in reading* (pp. 264–336). Hillsdale, NJ: Lawrence Erlbaum Associates.

Neisser, U. (1979). The concept of intelligence. *Intelligence, 3,* 217–227.

Nemiah, J. C., Freyberger, H., Sifneos, P. E. (1976). Alexithymia: A view of psychosomatic process. In O. W. Hill (ed.), *Modern trends in psychosomatic medicine* (vol. 3, pp. 430–439). London: Butterworths.

Nemiah, J. C., & Sifneos, P. E. (1970). Affect and fantasy in patients with psychosomatic disorders. In O. W. Hill (ed.), *Modern trends in psychosomatic medicine* (vol. 2, pp. 26–34). London: Butterworths.

Nettelbeck, T. (1990). Intelligence does exist: A rejoinder to M. J. A. Howe. *Psychologist, 3,* 11, 494–497.

Neubauer, A. C. (1997). The mental speed approach to the assessment of intelligence. In J. Kingma, W. Tomic, et al. (eds.), *Advances in cognition and educational practice: Reflections on the concept of intelligence* (vol. 4, pp. 149–173). Greenwich, CT: JAI Press.

Neuman, G. A., & Wright, J. (1999). Team effectiveness: Beyond skills and cognitive ability. *Journal of Applied Psychology, 84,* 376–389.

Newell, A. (1982). The knowledge level. *Artificial Intelligence, 18,* 87–127.

Newman, J. E., & Beehr, T. A. (1979). Personal and organizational strategies for handling job stress: A review of research and opinion. *Personnel Psychology, 32,* 1–43.

Newsome, S., Day, A. L., Catano, V. M. (2000). Assessing the predictive validity of emotional intelligence. *Personality & Individual Differences, 29,* 1005–1016.

Newton, T. (1995). *Managing stress: Emotion and power at work.* London: Sage.

Newton, T. L., & Contrada, R. J. (1994). Alexithymia and repression: Contrasting emotion-focused coping styles. *Psychosomatic Medicine, 56,* 457–462.

Nolen-Hoeksema, S. (1991). Response to depression and their effects on the duration of depressive episodes. *Journal of Abnormal Psychology, 100,* 569–582.

Nolen-Hoeksema, S. (2000). The role of rumination in depressive disorders and mixed anxiety/depressive symptoms. *Journal of Abnormal Psychology, 109,* 504–511.

Nolen-Hoeksema, S., McBride, A., & Larson, J. (1997). Rumination and psychological distress among bereaved partners. *Journal of Personality and Social Psychology, 72,* 855–862.

Nolen-Hoeksema, S., & Morrow, J. (1991). A prospective study of depression and distress following a natural disaster: The 1989 Loma Prieta earthquake. *Journal of Personality and Social Psychology, 61,* 105–121.

Nolen-Hoeksema, S., & Morrow, J. (1993). Effects of rumination and distraction on naturally occurring depressed mood. *Cognition and Emotion, 7,* 561–570.

Nolen-Hoeksema, S., Wolfson, A., Mumme, D., & Fuskin, K. (1995). Helplessness in children of depressed and nondepressed mothers. *Developmental Psychology, 31,* 377–387.

Nordahl, H. M., & Stiles, T. C. (1997). Conceptualization and identification of cognitive schemas in personality disorders. *Nordic Journal of Psychiatry, 51,* 243–250.

Norman, D. A., & Shallice, T. (1986). Attention to action: Willed and automatic control of behaviour. In R. J. Davidson, G. E. Schwartz & D. Shapiro (eds.), *Consciousness and self-regulation: Advances in research* (vol. 4). New York: Plenum.

Nunnally, J. C. (1978). *Psychometric theory* (2nd ed.). New York: McGraw-Hill.

Oatley, K., & Johnson-Laird, P. (1987). Towards a cognitive theory of emotions. *Cognition and Emotion, 1,* 29–50.

Oatley, K., & Johnson-Laird, P. (1996). The communicative theory of emotions: Empirical tests, mental models, and implications for social interaction. In L. L. Martin & A. Tesser (eds.), *Striving and feeling: Interactions among goals, affect, and self-regulation* (pp. 363–393). Hillsdale, NJ: Lawrence Erlbaum Associates.

O'Boyle, M. (1995). *DSM*-III-R and Eysenck personality measures among patients in a substance abuse programme. *Personality and Individual Differences, 18,* 561–565.

O'Driscoll, M. P., & Cooper, C. L. (1994). Coping with work-related stress: A critique of existing measures and proposal for an alternative methodology. *Journal of Occupational and Organizational Psychology, 67,* 343–354.

Olson, B. D., & Evans, D. L. (1999). The role of the Big Five personality dimensions in the direction and affective consequences of everyday social comparisons. *Personality & Social Psychology Bulletin, 25,* 1498–1508.

Omdahl, B. L. (1997). *Cognitive appraisal, emotion, and empathy.* Mahwah, NJ: Lawrence Erlbaum Associates.

O'Neil, R., & Parke, R. D. (2000). Family peer relationships: The role of emotion regulation, cognitive understanding, and attentional processes as mediating processes. In K. A. Kerns, J. M. Contreras & A. M. Neal-Barnett (eds.), *Family and peers: Linking two social worlds* (pp. 195–225). New York: Praeger.

Ones, D. S., Viswesvaran, C., & Schmidt, F. L. (1993). Comprehensive meta-analysis of integrity test validities: Findings and implications for personnel selection and theories of job performance. *Journal of Applied Psychology, 78,* 679–703.

Ormel, J., & Wohlfarth, T. (1991). How neuroticism, long-term difficulties, and life situation change influence psychological distress: A longitudinal model. *Journal of Personality and Social Psychology, 60,* 744–755.

Ormsbee, C. K. (2000). Developing emotional intelligence: A guide to behavior management and conflict resolution in schools. *Intervention School Clinic, 36,* 125–126.

O'Sullivan, M., & Guilford, J. P. (1975). Six factors of behavioral cognition: Understanding other people. *Journal of Educational Measurement, 12,* 255–271.

O'Sullivan, M., & Guilford, J. P. (1976). *Four Factor Tests of Social Intelligence (Behavioral Cognition): Manual of instructions and interpretations.* Palo Alto: Consulting Psychologists Press.

O'Sullivan, M., Guilford, J. P., & deMille, R. (1965). *The measurement of social intelligence.* Los Angeles: Reports from the Psychological Laboratory, University of Southern California, no. 34.

O'Toole, B. I., & Stankov, L. (1992). Ultimate validity of psychological tests. *Personality and Individual Differences, 13,* 699–716.

Ovies, T. M. (1998). An evaluation of two neuropsychological models of alexithymia. *Dissertation abstracts international,* section B: The sciences and engineering, *58* (11-b), 6243.

Paivio, A. (1986). *Mental representations: A dual coding approach.* New York: Oxford University Press.

Pakaslahti, L., & Keltikangas-Jaervinen, L. (1997). The relationships between moral approval of aggression, aggressive problem-solving strategies, and aggressive behavior in 14-yr-old adolescents. *Journal of Social Behavior & Personality, 12,* 905–924.

Palfai, T. P., & Salovey, P. (1992). The influence of affect on self-focused attention: Conceptual and methodological issues. *Consciousness and Cognition, 1,* 306–339.

Palfai, T. P., & Salovey, P. (1993). The influence of depressed and elated mood on deductive and inductive reasoning. *Imagination Cognition and Personality, 13,* 57–71.

Pallant, J. F. (2000). Development and validation of a scale to measure perceived control of internal states. *Journal of Personality Assessment, 75,* 308–337.

Pandey, R., & Mandal, M. K. (1997). Processing of facial expressions of emotion and alexithymia. *British Journal of Clinical Psychology, 36,* 631–633.

Panksepp, J. (1982). Towards a general psychobiological theory of emotions. *Behavioral and Brain Sciences, 5,* 407–467.

Panksepp, J. (1996). Affective neuroscience: A paradigm to study the animate circuits for human emotions. In R. D. Kavanaugh, B. Zimmerberg & S. Fein (eds.), *Emotion: Interdisciplinary perspectives* (pp. 29–60). Mahwah, NJ: Lawrence Erlbaum Associates.

Panksepp, J. (1998). *Affective neuroscience: The foundations of human and animal emotions.* New York: Oxford University Press.

Parasuraman, R. (1998). The attentive brain: Issues and prospects. In R. Parasuraman (ed.), *The attentive brain.* Cambridge: MIT Press.

Parker, J. D. A. (2000). Emotional intelligence: Clinical and therapeutic implications. In R. Bar-On & J. D. A. Parker (eds.), *The handbook of emotional intelligence* (pp. 490–504). San-Francisco: Jossey-Bass.

Parker, J. D. A., & Bagby, R. M. (1997). Impulsivity in adults: A critical review of measurement approaches. In C. D. Webster & M. A. Jackson (eds.), *Impulsivity: Theory, assessment, and treatment* (pp. 142–157). New York: Guilford Press.

Parker, J. D. A., Taylor, G. J., & Bagby, R. M. (1993). Alexithymia and the recognition of facial expressions of emotion. *Psychotherapy and Psychosomatics, 59,* 197–202.

Parker, J. D. A., Taylor, G. J., & Bagby, R. M. (1998). Alexithymia: Relationship with ego defense and coping styles. *Comprehensive Psychiatry, 39,* 91–98.

Parker, J. D. A., Taylor, G. J., & Bagby, R. M. (1998). The alexithymia construct: Relationship with sociodemographic variables and intelligence. *Comprehensive Psychiatry, 30,* 434–441.

Parker, J. D. A., Taylor, G. J., & Bagby, R. M. (2001). The relationship between emotional intelligence and alexithymia. *Personality and Individual Differences, 30,* 107–115.

Parkinson, B. (1996). Emotions are social. *British Journal of Psychology, 87,* 663–683.

Parkinson, B., & Manstead, A. S. R. (1992). Appraisal as a cause of emotion. In M. S. Clark (ed.), *Emotion* (pp. 122–149). Thousand Oaks, CA: Sage Publications.

Pastor, D. L. (1981). The quality of mother-infant attachment and its relation to toddler's initial sociability with peers. *Developmental Psychology, 17,* 326–335.

Patterson, M. L. (1991). A functional approach to nonverbal exchange. In R. S. Feldman & B. Rime (eds.), *Fundamentals of nonverbal behavior* (pp. 458–495). Cambridge: Cambridge University Press.

Patti, J., & Lantieri, L. (1999). Waging peace in our schools: Social and emotional learning through conflict resolution. In J. Cohen (ed.), *Educating minds and hearts* (pp. 126–136). New York: Columbia University Press.

Paulhus, D. L., & John, O. P. (1998). Egoistic and moralistic biases in self-perception: The interplay of self-deceptive styles with basic traits and motives. *Journal of Personality, 66,* 1025–1060.

Paulhus, D. L., Lysy, D. C., & Yik, M. S. M. (1998). Self-report measures of intelligence: Are they useful proxies as IQ tests? *Journal of Personality, 66,* 525–554.

Payne, W. L. (1986). A study of emotion: Developing emotional intelligence, self-integration, relating to fear, pain, and desire. *Dissertation abstracts international, 47,* 203.

Payton, J. W., Wardlaw, D. M., Graczyk, P. A., Bloodworth, M. R., Tompsett, C. J., & Weissberg, R. P. (under review). Social and emotional learning: A framework for quality school-based prevention programs. Unpublished manuscript.

Pearlin, L. I. (1991). The study of coping: An overview of problems and directions. In J. Eckenrode (ed.), *The social context of coping* (pp. 261–276). New York: Plenum.

Pearlin, L. I., & Schooler, C. (1978). The structure of coping. *Journal of Health and Social Behavior, 19,* 2–21.

Pekrun, R., & Frese, M. (1992). Emotions in work and achievement. In C. I. Cooper & I. T. Robertson (eds.), *International Review of Industrial and Organizational Psychology* (vol. 7, pp. 153–200). Chichester: John Wiley.

Pennebaker, J. W. (ed.) (1995). *Emotion, disclosure, and health.* Washington, DC: American Psychological Association.

Pennebaker, J. W. (1997). Writing about emotional experiences as a therapeutic process. *Psychological Science, 8,* 162–166.

Pennebaker, J. W., Rime, B., & Blankenship, V. E. (1996). Stereotypes of emotional expressiveness of Northerners and Southerners: A cross-cultural test of Montesquieu's hypothesis. *Journal of Personality and Social Psychology, 70,* 372–380.

Peterson, C., Seligman, M. E. P., & Vaillant, G. E. (1988). Pessimistic explanatory style is a risk factor for physical illness: A thirty-five year longitudinal study. *Journal of Personality and Social Psychology, 55,* 23–27.

Peterson, D. B. (1996). Executive coaching at work: The art of one-on-one change. *Consulting Psychology Journal, 48,* 78–86.

Petrides, K. V., & Furnham, A. (2000a). Gender differences in measured and self-estimated trait emotional intelligence. *Sex Roles, 42,* 449–461.

Petrides, K. V., & Furnham, A. (2000b). On the dimensional structure of emotional intelligence. *Personality and Individual Differences, 29,* 313–320.

Petrides, K. V., & Furnham, A. (in press). Trait emotional intelligence: Psychometric investigation with reference to established trait taxonomies. *European Journal of Personality.*

Pickering, A. D., Gray, J. A. (1999). The neuroscience of personality. In L. A. Pervin, O. P. John, et al. (eds.), *Handbook of personality: Theory and research* (2nd ed., pp. 277–299). New York: Guilford Press.

Pierloot, R., & Vinck, J. (1977). A pragmatic approach to the concept of alexithymia. *Psychotherapy and Psychosomatics, 28,* 156–166.

Pines, A. M., & Aronson, E. (1981). *Burnout: From tedium to personal growth.* New York: Free Press.

Plotkin, H. M. (1987). What makes a successful salesperson? *Training and Development Journal, 41,* 54–66.

Plutchik, R. (1980). A general psychoevolutionary theory of emotion. In R. Plutchik & H. Kellerman (eds.), *Emotion: Theory, research, and experience,* vol. 1: *Theories of emotion* (pp. 3–33). San Diego: Academic Press.

Plutchik, R. (1984). Emotions: A general psychoevolutionary theory. In K. R. Scherer & P. Ekman (eds.), *Approaches to emotion* (pp. 197–219). Hillsdale, NJ: Lawrence Erlbaum Associates.

Plutchik, R., & Van Praag, H. M. (1995). The nature of impulsivity: Definitions, ontology, genetics, and relations to aggression. In E. Hollander, D. J. Stein, et al. (eds.), *Impulsivity and aggression* (pp. 7–24). Chichester, England: John Wiley & Sons.

Porras, J. I., & Anderson, B. (1981). Improving managerial effectiveness through modeling-based training. *Organizational Dynamics, 9,* 60–77.

Porras, J. L., & Hargis, K. (1982). Precursors of individual change: Responses to a social learning theory based on organizational intervention. *Human Relations, 35,* 973–990.

Posner, M. I., & DiGirolamo, G. J. (1998). Executive attention: Conflict, target detection, and cognitive control. In R. Parasuraman (ed.), *The attentive brain* (pp. 401–423). Cambridge: MIT Press.

Posner, M. I., & Raichle, M. E. (1994). *Images of mind.* New York: Scientific American Library.

Power, T. G., & Manire, S. H. (1992). Child rearing and internalization: A developmental perspective. In J. Janssens & J. Gerris (eds.), *Child rearing: Influence on prosocial and moral development* (pp. 101–123). Amsterdam: Swets & Zeitlinger.

Profyt, L., & Whissel, C. (1991). Children's understanding of facial expression of emotions. I: Voluntary creation of emotion-faces. *Perceptual and Motor Skills, 73,* 199–202.

Putallaz, M. (1987). Maternal behavior and children's sociometric status. *Child Development, 58,* 324–340.

Pylyshyn, Z. W. (1984). *Computation and cognition: Toward a foundation for cognitive science.* Cambridge: MIT Press.

Pylyshyn, Z. W. (1999). What's in your mind? In E. Lepore & Z. W. Pylyshyn (eds.), *What is cognitive science?* Malden, MA: Blackwell.

Quay, H. C. (1993). The psychobiology of undersocialized aggressive conduct disorder: A theoretical perspective. *Development & Psychopathology, 5,* 165–180.

Rabiner, D. L., Lenhart, L., & Lochman, J. E. (1990). Automatic versus reflective social problem solving in relation to children's sociometric status. *Developmental Psychology, 26,* 1010–1016.

Rachman, S. (1993). Obsessions, responsibility, and guilt. *Behaviour Research & Therapy, 31,* 149–154.

Radke-Yarrow, M., Zahn-Waxler, C., & Chapman, M. (1983). Prosocials disposition and behavior. In E. M. Hetherington (ed.), *Manual of child psychology,* vol. 4: *Socialization, personality, and social development* (pp. 469–545). New York: Wiley.

Rafaeli, A. (1989). When clerks meet customers: A test of variables related to emotional expressions on the job. *Journal of Applied Psychology, 74,* 385–393.

Rafaeli, A., & Sutton, R. I. (1987). Expression of emotion as part of the work role. *Academy of Management Review, 12,* 23–37.

Rafaeli, A., & Sutton, R. I. (1989). The expression of emotion in organizational life. *Research in Organizational Behavior, 11,* 1–42.

Rahim, M. A., & Psenicka, C. (1996). A structural equations model of stress, locus of control, social support, psychiatric symptoms, and propensity to leave a job. *Journal of Social Psychology, 136,* 69–84.

Ramirez Basco, M., & Thase, M. E. (1998). *Cognitive-behavioral treatment of bipolar disorder.* In V. E. Caballo (ed.), *International handbook of cognitive and behavioural treatments for psychological disorders* (pp. 521–550). Oxford: Pergamon/Elsevier Science.

Ratner, H., & Stettner, L. (1999). Thinking and feeling: Putting Humpty Dumpty together again. *Merrill-Palmer Quarterly, 37,* 1–26.

Rau, J. C. (1993). Perception of verbal and nonverbal affective stimuli in complex partial seizure disorder. *Dissertation abstracts international,* section B, *54,* 506B.

Raven, J. C. (1938). *Progressive Matrices.* London: H. K. Lewis & Co.

Raven, J. C., Court, J. H., & Raven, J. (1979). *Manual for Raven's Progressive Matrices and Vocabulary Scales.* London: H. K. Lewis & Co.

Raver, C. C. (1996). Relations between social contingency in mother-child interaction and 2-year-olds' social competence. *Developmental Psychology, 32,* 850–859.

Reason, J. T. (1987). The Chernobyl errors. *Bulletin of the British Psychological Society, 40,* 201–206.

Reed, M. A., & Derryberry, D. (1995). Temperament and attention to positive and negative trait information. *Personality & Individual Differences, 18,* 135–147.

Reigeluth, C. M. (ed.) (1999). *Instructional-design theories and models: A new paradigm of instructional theory* (vol. 2). Mahwah, NJ: Lawrence Erlbaum Associates.

Reiss, S., & McNally, R. J. (1985). Expectancy model of fear. In S. Reiss & R. R. Bootzin (eds.), *Theoretical issues in behavior therapy* (pp. 107–121). San Diego, CA: Academic Press.

Resick, P. A., & Schnicke, M. K. (1992). Cognitive processing therapy for sexual assault victims. *Journal of Consulting and Clinical Psychology, 60,* 748–756.

Revelle, W. (1993). Individual differences in personality and motivation: "Noncognitive" determinants of cognitive performance. In A. D. Baddeley, L. Weiskrantz, et al. (eds.), *Attention: Selection, awareness, and control* (pp. 346–373). Oxford: Clarendon Press.

Revelle, W. (1995). Personality processes. *Annual Review of Psychology, 46*, 295–328.

Revelle, W., & Loftus, D. A. (1990). Individual differences and arousal: Implications for the study of mood and memory. *Cognition and Emotion, 4*, 209–237.

Reynolds, C. R., Chastain, R. L., Kaufman, A. S., & McLean, J. E. (1987). Demographic characteristics and IQ among adults: Analysis of the WAIS-R standardization sample as a function of the stratification variables. *Journal of School Psychology, 25*, 323–342.

Reynolds, S., Taylor, E., & Shapiro, P. A. (1993). Session impact in stress management training. *Journal of Occupational and Organizational Psychology, 66*, 99–113.

Richards, A., & French, C. C. (1992). An anxiety-related bias in semantic activation when processing threat/neutral homographs. *Quarterly Journal of Experimental Psychology. A: Human Experimental Psychology, 45*, 503–525.

Riggio, R. E., Messamer, J., & Throckmorton, B. (1991). Social and academic intelligence: Conceptually distinct but overlapping constructs. *Personality & Individual Differences, 12*, 695–702.

Rimoldi, H. J. A. (1948). Study of some factors related to intelligence. *Psychometrika, 13*, 27–46.

Roberts, R. D. (2001). Review of *The handbook of emotional intelligence. Intelligence.* In press.

Roberts, R. D., Goff, G. N., Anjoul, F., Kyllonen, P. C., Pallier, G., & Stankov, L. (2000). The Armed Services Vocational Aptitude Battery: Not much more than acculturated learning (Gc)!? *Learning and Individual Differences, 12*, 81–103.

Roberts, R. D., Pallier, G., & Goff, G. N. (1999). Sensory processes within the structure of human cognitive abilities. In P. L. Ackerman, P. C. Kyllonen & R. D. Roberts (eds.), *Learning and individual differences: Process, trait, and content determinants* (pp. 339–370). Washington, DC: American Psychological Association.

Roberts, R. D., & Stankov, L. (1999). Individual differences in speed of mental processing and human cognitive abilities: Towards a taxonomic model. *Learning and Individual Differences, 11*, 1–120.

Roberts, R. D., Stankov, L., Pallier, G., & Dolph, B. (1997). Charting the cognitive sphere: Tactile and kinesthetic performance within the structure of intelligence. *Intelligence, 25*, 111–148.

Roberts, R. D., Zeidner, M., & Matthews, G. (2001). Does emotional intelligence meet traditional standards for an intelligence? Some new data and conclusions. *Emotions, 1*, 196–231.

Roberts, W. (1986). Nonlinear models of behavior: An example from the socialization of competence. *Child Development, 57*, 1166–1178.

Roberts, W., & Strayer, J. (1987). Parents' responses to the emotional distress of their children: Relations with children's competence. *Developmental Psychology, 23*, 415–422.

Roe, A., & Lunneborg, P. W. (1990). Personality development and career choice. In D. Brown, L. Brooks, et al. (eds.), *Career choice and development: Applying contemporary theories to practice* (2nd ed., pp. 68–101). San Francisco: Jossey-Bass.

Roedema, T. M., Simons, R. F. (1999). Emotion-processing deficit in alexithymia. *Psychophysiology, 36,* 379–387.

Roger, D., & Najarian, B. (1989). The construction and validation of a new scale for measuring emotion control. *Personality and Individual Differences, 10,* 845–853.

Roger, D., Jarvis, G., & Najarian, B. (1993). Detachment and coping: The construction of a new scale for measuring coping strategies. *Personality and Individual Differences, 15,* 619–626.

Rogers, C. R. (1957). The necessary and sufficient conditions of therapeutic personality change. *Journal of Consulting Psychology, 21,* 95–103.

Rolls, E. T. (1999). *The brain and emotion.* New York: Oxford University Press.

Rosenberg, M. L. (1997). Applying science to violence prevention. *Journal of the American Medical Association, 277,* 1641–1642.

Rosenthal, R., Archer, D., Hall, J. A., DiMatteo, M. R., & Rogers, P. L. (1979). Measuring sensitivity to nonverbal communication: The PONS test. In A. Wolfgang (ed.), *Nonverbal behavior: Applications and cultural implications.* New York: Academic Press.

Rosenthal, R., Hall, J. A., MiMatteo, M. R., Rogers, P. L., & Archer, D. (1979). *Sensitivity to nonverbal communication: The PONS test.* Baltimore: Johns Hopkins University Press.

Roskam, E. E., & Ellis, J. (1992a). Commentary on Guttman: The irrelevance of factor analysis for the study of group differences. *Multivariate Behavioral Research, 27,* 205–218.

Roskam, E. E., & Ellis, J. (1992b). Reaction to other commentaries. *Multivariate Behavioral Research, 27,* 249–252.

Ross, A. (1994). Emotion regulation: A theme in optimal self-regulation. In N. A. Fox (ed.), *The development of emotion regulation: Monograph of the Society for Research in Child Development* (pp. 25–52). Chicago: University of Chicago Press.

Rothbart, M. K., & Derryberry, D. (1981). Development of individual difference in temperament. In M. E. Lamb & A. L. Brown (eds.), *Advances in Developmental Psychology.* Hillsdale, NJ: Lawrence Erlbaum Associates.

Rothbart, M. K., & Jones, L. B. (1998). Temperament, self-regulation, and education. *School Psychology Review, 27,* 479–491.

Rothstein, M. G., Paunonen, S. V., & Rush, J. C. (1994). Personality and cognitive ability predictors of performance in graduate business school. *Journal of Educational Psychology, 86,* 516–530.

Rouiller, J. Z., & Goldstein, I. L. (1993). The relationship between organizational transfer climate and positive transfer of training. *Human Resource Development Quarterly, 4,* 377–390.

Royce, J. R., & Powell, A. (1983). *A theory of personality and individual differences: Factors, systems, and processes.* Englewood Cliffs, NJ: Prentice-Hall.

Rubonis, A. V., & Bickman, L. (1991). Psychological impairment in the wake of disaster: The disaster-psychopathology relationship. *Psychological Bulletin, 109,* 384–399.

Ruesch, J. (1948). The infantile personality. *Psychosomatic medicine, 10,* 134–144.

Russell, J. A. (1983). Pancultural aspects of the human conceptual organisation of emotions. *Journal of Personality and Social Psychology, 45,* 1281–1288.

Russell, J. A. (1991). Culture and the categorization of emotions. *Psychological Bulletin, 110,* 426–450.

Russell, J. A. (1994). Is there universal recognition of emotion from facial expression? A review of the cross-cultural studies. *Psychological Bulletin, 115,* 102–141.

Russell, J. A., & Sato, K. (1995). Comparing emotion words between languages. *Journal of Cross-Cultural Psychology, 26,* 384–391.

Russell, J. A., Lewicka, M., et al. (1989). A cross-cultural study of a circumplex model of affect. *Journal of Personality and Social Psychology, 57,* 848–856.

Russell, J. A., Suzuki, N., & Ishida, N. (1993). Canadian Greek and Japanese freely produced emotion labels for facial expressions. *Motivation and Emotion, 17,* 337–351.

Rusting, C. (1999). Interactive effects of personality and mood on emotion-congruent memory and judgment. *Journal of Personality & Social Psychology, 77,* 1073–1086.

Rusting, C., & Larsen, R. (1998). Personality and cognitive processing of affective information. *Personality and Social Psychology Bulletin, 24,* 200–213.

Rusting, C., & Larsen, R. (1999). Clarifying Gray's theory of personality: A response to Pickering, Corr & Gray. *Personality and Individual Differences, 26,* 367–372.

Saarni, C. (1985). Indirect processes in affect socialization. In M. Lewis & C. Saarni (eds.), *The socialization of emotions* (pp. 187–209). New York: Plenum.

Saarni, C. (1987). Cultural rules of emotional experience: A commentary on Miller and Sperry's study. *Merrill-Palmer Quarterly, 33,* 535–540.

Saarni, C. (1988). Emotional competence: How emotions and relationships become integrated. In R. A. Thompson (ed.), *Socioemotional development* (pp. 115–182). Lincoln: University of Nebraska Press.

Saarni, C. (1997). Emotional competence and self-regulation in childhood. In P. Salovey & D. J. Sluster (eds.), *Emotional development and emotional intelligence: Educational implications* (pp. 35–69). New York: Basic Books.

Saarni, C. (1999). *The development of emotional competence.* New York: Guilford Press.

Saarni, C. (2000). Emotional competence: A developmental perspective. In R. Bar-On & J. D. A. Parker (eds.), *The handbook of emotional intelligence* (pp. 68–91). San Francisco: Jossey-Bass.

Safran, J. D., & Wallner, L. K. (1991). The relative predictive validity of two therapeutic alliance measures in cognitive therapy. *Psychological Assessment, 3,* 188–195.

Sagan, C. (1997). *Billions and billions.* New York: Random House.

Saklofske, D. H., Austin, E. J., & Minski, P. S. (in press). Factor structure and validity of a trait emotional intelligence measure. *Personality and Individual Differences.*

Saklofske, D., & Zeidner, M. (eds.) (1995). *International handbook of personality and intelligence* (pp. 299–319). New York: Plenum.

Salkovskis, P. M. (1985). Obsessional-compulsive problems: A cognitive-behavioural analysis. *Behaviour Research and Therapy, 23,* 571–583.

Salovey, P. (1992). Mood-induced self-focused attention. *Journal of Personality and Social Psychology, 62,* 699–707.

Salovey, P., Bedell, B. T., Detweiler, J. B., & Mayer, J. D. (1999). Coping intelligently: Emotional intelligence and the coping process. In C. R. Snyder (ed.), *Coping: The psychology of what works* (pp. 141–164). New York: Oxford University Press.

Salovey, P., Bedell, B. T., Detweiler, J. B., & Mayer, J. D. (2000). Current directions in emotional intelligence research. In M. Lewis & J. M. Haviland-Jones (eds.), *Handbook of emotions.* New York: Guilford Press.

Salovey, P., & Birnbaum, D. (1989). Influence of mood on health-relevant cognitions. *Journal of Personality and Social Psychology, 57,* 539–551.

Salovey, P., Hsee, C. K., & Mayer, J. D. (1993). Emotional intelligence and the self-regulation of affect. In D. M. Wegner & J. W. Pennebaker (eds.), *Handbook of mental control* (pp. 258–277). Englewood, NJ: Prentice-Hall.

Salovey, P., & Mayer, J. D. (1990). Emotional intelligence. *Imagination, Cognition & Personality, 9,* 185–211.

Salovey, P., & Mayer, J. D. (1994). Some final thoughts about personality and intelligence. In R. J. Sternberg & P. Ruzgis (eds.), *Personality and intelligence* (pp. 303–318). New York: Cambridge University Press.

Salovey, P., Mayer, J. D., & Caruso, D. (in press). The positive psychology of emotional intelligence. In C. R. Snyder & S. J. Lopez (eds.), *The handbook of positive psychology.* New York: Oxford University Press.

Salovey, P., Mayer, J. D., Goldman, S., Turvey, C., & Palfai, T. (1995). Emotional attention, clarity, and repair: Exploring emotional intelligence using the Trait Meta-Mood Scale. In J. W. Pennebaker (ed.), *Emotion, disclosure, and health* (pp. 125–154). Washington, DC: American Psychological Association.

Salovey, P., Rothman, A. J., & Rodin, J. (1998). Health behavior. In D. T. Gilbert, S. T. Fiske & L. Gardner (eds.), *The handbook of social psychology* (vol. 2, pp. 633–683). Boston: McGraw-Hill.

Salovey, P., & Sluyter, D. J. (eds.) (1997). *Emotional development and emotional intelligence: Educational implications* (1st ed.). New York: Basic Books.

Salovey, P., Stroud, L. R., Woolery, A., & Epel, E. S. (under review). Perceived emotional intelligence, stress reactivity, and health: Further explorations using the trait meta-mood scale. *Psychology and Health.*

Salovey, P., Woolery, A., & Mayer, J. D. (2001). Emotional intelligence: Conceptualization and measurement. In G. Fletcher & M. S. Clark (eds.), *The Blackwell handbook of social psychology*, vol. 2: *Interpersonal processes.* Oxford, England: Blackwell Publishers.

Salthouse, T. A. (1988). Resource-reduction interpretations of cognitive aging. *Developmental Review, 8,* 238–272.

Sansone, C., Wiebe, D. J., & Morgan, C. (1999). Self-regulating interest: The moderating role of hardiness and conscientiousness. *Journal of Personality, 67,* 701–733.

Sarason, I. G. (1975). Test anxiety and the self-disclosing coping model. *Journal of Consulting & Clinical Psychology, 43,* 148–153.

Sarason, I. G., Sarason, B. R., & Pierce, G. R. (1995). Cognitive interference: At the intelligence-personality crossroads. In D. H. Saklofske & M. Zeidner (eds.), *International handbook of personality and intelligence.* New York: Plenum.

Saucier, G. (1997). Effects of variable selection on the factor structure of person descriptors. *Journal of Personality & Social Psychology, 73,* 1296–1312.

Sauter, S., Murphy, L. R., & Hurrell, J. J. (1990). A national strategy for the prevention of work related psychological disorders. *American Psychologist, 45,* 1146–1158.

Sawyer, K. S. (1996). Sibling contributions to young children's emotional competence. George Masonn University, Fairfax, Virginia.

Sayette, M. A. (1999). Does drinking reduce stress? *Alcohol Research & Health, 23,* 250–255.

Scarrabelotti, M. B., Duck, J. M., & Dickerson, M. M. (1995). Individual differences in obsessive-compulsive behaviour: The role of the Eysenckian dimensions and appraisals of responsibility. *Personality & Individual Differences, 18,* 413–421.

Schacter, D. L. (1996). Searching for memory: The brain, the mind, and the past. New York: Basic Books.

Schaffer, C. E. (1993). *The role of adult attachment in the experience and regulation of affect.* Doctoral dissertation, Yale University.

Schaie, K. W. (2001). Emotional intelligence: Psychometric status and developmental characteristics. *Emotion, 1,* 243–248.

Schaps, E., & Battistich, V. (1991). Promoting health development through school-based prevention: New approaches. In E. Gopelrud (ed.), *Preventing adolescent drug abuse use: From theory to practice.* Rockville, MD: Office of Substance Abuse Prevention, U.S. Dept. of Health and Human Services.

Schaubroeck, J., & Ganster, D. C. (1991). Associations among stress-related individual differences. In C. L. Cooper & R. Payne (eds.), *Personality and stress: Individual differences in the stress process.* Chichester: Wiley.

Schaufeli, W. B., van Dierendonock, D., & van Gorp, K. (1996). Burnout and reciprocity: Towards a dual-level social exchange model. *Work and Stress, 10,* 225–237.

Scherer, K. R. (1984). Emotion as a multicomponent process: A model and some cross-cultural data. *Review of Personality & Social Psychology, 5,* 37–63.

Scherer, K. R. (1997a). The role of culture in emotion-antecedent appraisal. *Journal of Personality and Social Psychology, 73,* 902–922.

Scherer, K. R. (1997b). Profiles of emotion-antecedent appraisal: Testing theoretical predictions across cultures. *Cognition and Emotion, 11,* 113–150.

Scherer, K. R. (1999). On the sequential nature of appraisal processes: Indirect evidence from a recognition task. *Cognition and Emotion, 13,* 763–793.

Scherer, K. R., & Wallbott, H. G. (1994). Evidence for universality and cultural variation of differential emotion response patterning. *Journal of Personality and Social Psychology, 66,* 310–328.

Schilling, D. (1996). *Fifty activities for teaching emotional intelligence: Level I, elementary.* Torrance, CA: Innerchoice Publishing.

Schimmack, U. (1996). Cultural influences on the recognition of emotion by facial expressions: Individualistic or Caucasian cultures. *Journal of Cross-Cultural Psychology, 27,* 37–50.

Schimmack, U., & Grob, A. (2000). Dimensional models of core affect: A quantitative comparison by means of structural equation modeling. *European Journal of Personality, 14,* 325–345.

Schmidt, F. L., & Hunter, J. E. (1998). The validity and utility of selection methods in personnel psychology: Practical and theoretical implications of 85 years of research findings. *Psychological Bulletin, 124,* 262–274.

Schmidt, F. L., Ones, D. S., & Hunter, J. E. (1992). Personnel selection. *Annual Review of Psychology, 43,* 627–670.

Schmidt, N. B., Lerew, D. R., & Joiner, T. E., Jr. (2000). Prospective evaluation of the etiology of anxiety sensitivity: Test of a scar model. *Behaviour Research & Therapy, 38,* 1083–1095.

Schmidt, N. B., & Woolaway-Bickel, K. (in press). Cognitive vulnerability to panic disorder. In L. B. Alloy & J. H. Riskind (eds.), *Cognitive vulnerability to emotional disorders.* Hillsdale, NJ: Lawrence Erlbaum Associates.

Schneider, B., Kristof-Brown, A. L., Goldstein, H. W., & Smith, D. B. (1997). What is this thing called fit? In N. Anderson & P. Herriott (eds.), *International handbook of selection and assessment* (pp. 393–412). Chichester: Wiley.

Schneider, R. J., Ackerman, P. L., & Kanfer, R. (1996). To "act wisely in human relations": Exploring the dimensions of social competence. *Personality and Individual Differences, 21,* 469–481.

Schönemann, P. H. (1992a). Extension of Guttman's result from *g* to PC1. *Multivariate Behavioral Research, 27,* 219–224.

Schönemann, P. H. (1992b). Second round commentary on Guttman. *Multivariate Behavioral Research, 27,* 253–256.

Schore, A. N. (1994). *Affect regulation and the origin of the self: The neurobiology of emotional development.* Hillsdale, NJ: Lawrence Erlbaum Associates.

Schroeder, M. L., Wormsworth, J. A., & Livesley, W. J. (1992). Dimensions of personality disorder and their relationships to the big five dimensions of personality. *Psychological Assessment, 4,* 47–53.

Schuler, R. S. (1980). Definition and conceptualization of stress in organizations. *Organizational Behavior and Human Performance, 25,* 184–215.

Schulman, P. (1995). Explanatory style and achievement in school and work. In G. Buchanan & M. Seligman (eds.), *Explanatory style.* Hillsdale, NJ: Lawrence Erlbaum Associates.

Schutte, N. S., Malouff, J. M., Hall, L. E., Haggerty, D. J., Cooper, J. T., Golden, C. J., & Dornheim, L. (1998). Development and validation of a measure of emotional intelligence. *Personality and Individual Differences, 25,* 167–177.

Schwartz, J. E., & Stone, A. A. (1993). Coping with daily work problems: Contributions of problem content, appraisals, and person factors. *Work and Stress, 7,* 47–62.

Schwarz, N., & Clore, G. L. (1983). Mood, misattribution, and judgments of well being: Informative and directive functions of affective states. *Journal of Personality and Social Psychology, 45,* 513–523.

Schwean, V. L., Saklofske, D. H., Yackulic, R. A., & Quinn, D. (1995). Aggressive and nonaggressive AD/HD boys: Cognitive, intellectual, and behavioral comparisons. *Journal of Psychoeducational Assessment, 14,* 6–21.

Scott, J. (1996). Cognitive therapy of affective disorders: A review. *Journal of Affective Disorders, 37,* 1–11.

Segal, J. (1997). *Raising your emotional intelligence: A practical guide.* New York: Holt.

Segal, Z. V., Gemar, M., Truchon, C., Guirguis, M., & Horowitz, L. (1995). A priming methodology for studying self-representation in major depressive disorder. *Journal of Abnormal Psychology, 104,* 205–213.

Seligman, M. E. P. (1991). *Learned optimism.* New York: Knopf.

Seligman, M. E. P., & Schulman, P. (1986). Explanatory style as a predictor of productivity and quitting among life insurance sales agents. *Journal of Personality and Social Psychology, 50,* 832–838.

Selye, H. (1956). *The stress of life.* New York: McGraw-Hill.

Selye, H. (1976). *The stress of life* (2nd ed.). New York: McGraw-Hill.

Seroczynski, A. D., Bergeman, C. S., & Coccaro, E. F. (1999). Etiology of the impulsivity/aggression relationship: Genes or environment? *Psychiatry Research, 86,* 41–57.

Seyfarth, R. M., & Cheney, D. L. (1997). Behavioural mechanisms underlying vocal communication in nonhuman primates. *Animal Learning and Behavior, 25,* 249–267.

Shafer, A. B. (1999). Factor analysis of Big Five Markers with the Comrey Personality Scales and the Howarth Personality Tests. *Personality & Individual Differences, 26,* 857–872.

Shallice, T., & Burgess, P. (1996). The domain of supervisory processes and the temporal organization of behaviour. In A. C. Roberts & T. W. Robbins (eds.), *The prefrontal cortex: Executive and cognitive functions* (pp. 22–35). New York: Oxford University Press.

Shapiro, L. E. (1997). *How to raise a child with a high EQ: A parent's guide to emotional intelligence.* New York: Harper Collins Publishers.

Shaw, G. K., Waller, S., Latham, C. J., Dunn, G., & Thomson, A. D. (1997). Alcoholism: A long-term follow-up study of participants in an alcohol treatment programme. *Alcohol & Alcoholism, 32,* 527–535.

Shiffrin, R. M., & Schneider, W. (1977). Controlled and automatic human information processing. II: Perceptual learning, automatic attending, and a general theory. *Psychological Review, 84,* 127–190.

Shigehisa, T., & Symons, J. R. (1973). Effects of intensity of visual stimulation on auditory sensitivity in relation to personality. *British Journal of Psychology, 64,* 205–213.

Shinn, M., Rosario, M., Morch, H., & Chesnut, D. E. (1984). Coping with job stress and burnout in the human services. *Journal of Personality and Social Psychology,* 864–876.

Shipley, W. C. (1940). A self-administering scale for measuring intellectual impairment and deterioration. *Journal of Psychology, 9,* 371–377.

Shoda, Y., Mischel, W., & Peake, P. K. (1990). Predicting adolescent cognitive and self-regulatory competencies from preschool delay of gratification. *Developmental Psychology, 26,* 978–986.

Shrauger, J. S., Mariano, E., & Walter, T. J. (1998). Depressive symptoms and accuracy in the prediction of future events. *Personality & Social Psychology Bulletin, 24,* 880–892.

Shriver, T. P., Schwab-Stone, M., & DeFalco, K. (1999). Why SEL is the better way: The New Haven Social Development Program. In J. Cohen (ed.), *Educating minds and hearts: Social emotional learning and the passage into adolescence* (pp. 43–60). New York: Teachers College Press.

Siegle, G. J. (1999). Cognitive and physiological aspects of attention to personally relevant negative information in depression (neural network). *Dissertation abstracts international,* section B: The sciences and engineering, *60,* 2962.

Siegle, G. J., & Ingram, R. E. (1997). Modeling individual differences in negative information processing biases. In G. Matthews (ed.), *Personality and individual differences in psychopathology.* Princeton, NJ: Lawrence Erlbaum Associates.

Sifneos, P. E. (1972). *Short-term psychotherapy and emotional crisis.* Cambridge: Harvard University Press.

Sifneos, P. E. (1975). Problems of psychotherapy of patients with alexithymic characteristics and physical disease. *Psychotherapy and Psychosomatics, 26,* 65–70.

Silver, M. A. (1999). Emotional intelligence and legal education. *Psychology, Public Policy, and Law, 5,* 1173–1203.

Silver, R. L., & Wortman, C. (1980). Coping with undesirable life events. In J. Garber & M. E. P. Seligman (eds.), *Human helplessness* (pp. 279–340). New York: Academic Press.

Simon, H. A. (1967). Motivational and emotional controls of cognition. *Psychological Review, 74,* 29–39.

Simpson, J. A., Ickes, W., & Grich, J. (1999). When accuracy hurts: Reactions of anxious-ambivalent dating partners to a relationship-threatening situation. *Journal of Personality & Social Psychology, 76,* 754–769.

Skinner, B. F. (1978). The ethics of helping people. In L. Wise (ed.), *Altruism, sympathy, and helping: Psychological and sociological principles* (pp. 249–262). New York: Academic Press.

Slade, A., & Aber, J. L. (1992). Attachments, drives, and development: Conflicts and convergences in theory. In J. W. Barron, M. N. Eagle & D. L. Wolitzky (eds.), *Interface of psychoanalysis and psychology* (pp. 154–185). Washington, DC: American Psychological Association.

Sloboda, J. A., Hermelin, B., & O'Connor, N. (1985). An exceptional music memory. *Music Perception, 3,* 155–169.

Smiley, P., & Huttenlocher, J. (1989). Young children's acquisitions of emotion concepts. In P. Harris & C. Saarni (eds.), *Children's understanding of emotion* (pp. 27–79). Cambridge: Cambridge University Press.

Smith, A. C. I., & Kleinman, S. (1989). Managing emotions in medical school: Students' contacts with the living and the dead. *Social Psychology Quarterly, 52,* 56–69.

Smith, C. A., & Ellsworth, P. C. (1985). Patterns of cognitive appraisal in emotion. *Journal of Personality and Social Psychology, 48,* 813–838.

Smith, C. A., & Ellsworth, P. C. (1987). Patterns of appraisal and emotion related to taking an exam. *Journal of Personality and Social Psychology, 52,* 475–488.

Smith, C. A., & Lazarus, R. S. (1993). Appraisal components, core relational themes, and the emotions. *Cognition and Emotion, 7,* 233–269.

Smith, S. M., & Petty, R. E. (1995). Personality moderators of mood congruence effects on cognition: The role of self-esteem and negative mood regulation. *Journal of Personality and Social Psychology, 68,* 1092–1107.

Snow, R. E. (1978). Theory and method for research on aptitude processes. *Intelligence, 2,* 225–278.

Snow, R. E., Kyllonen, P. C., & Marshalek, B. (1984). The topography of ability and learning correlations. In R. J. Sternberg (ed.), *Advances in the psychology of human intelligence* (vol. 2). Hillsdale, NJ: Lawrence Erlbaum Associates.

Snyder, C. R. (1991). The will and the ways: Development and validation of fan individual differences measure of hope. *Journal of Personality and Social Psychology, 60,* 579.

Snyder, C. R. (1999). *Coping: The psychology of what works.* New York: Oxford University Press.

Sokal, M. M. (ed.) (1987). *Psychological testing and American society, 1890–1930.* New Brunswick: Rutgers University Press.

Solomon, D., Watson, M. S., Delucchi, K. L., Schaps, E., & Battistich, V. (1988). Enhancing children's prosocial behavior in the classroom. *American Educational Research Journal, 25,* 527–554.

Solomon, R. C. (1997). Beyond ontology: Ideation, phenomenology, and the cross-cultural study of emotion. *Journal for the Theory of Social Behaviour, 27,* 289–303.

Spearman, C. (1904). General intelligence, objectively determined and measured. *American Journal of Psychology, 15,* 201–293.

Spearman, C. (1923). *The nature of intelligence and the principles of cognition.* London: Macmillan.

Spearman, C. (1927). *The abilities of man.* New York: Macmillan.

Spencer, L. M., McClelland, D., Spencer, L., McClelland, D., & Kelner, S. (1997). Competency assessment methods. In L. J. Bassi & D. F. Russ-Eft (eds.), *What works: Assessment, development, and measurement.* Alexandria, VA: American Society for Training and Development.

Spencer, L. M., & Spencer, S. M. (1993). *Competence at work: Models for superior performance.* New York: John Wiley.

Sperry, R. W. (1993). The impact and promise of the cognitive revolution. *American Psychologist, 48,* 878–885.

Spielberger, C. D. (1972a). *Anxiety: Current trends in theory and research* (vol. 1). New York: Academic Press.

Spielberger, C. D. (1972b). Anxiety as an emotional state. In C. D. Spielberger (ed.), *Anxiety: Current trends in theory and research* (vol. 1). London: Academic Press.

Spielberger, C. D., Jacobs, G. E., Russell, S., & Crane, R. S. (1983). The assessment of anger: The State-Trait Anger Scale. In J. N. Butcher & C. D. Spielberger (eds.), *Advances in personality assessment* (vol. 2, pp. 159–185).

Spielberger, C. D., & Reheiser, E. C. (1994). Job stress in university, corporate, and military personnel. *International Journal of Stress Management, 1,* 19–31.

Spielberger, C. D., Sydeman, S. J., Owen, A. E., & Marsh, B. J. (1999). Measuring anxiety and anger with the State-Trait Anxiety Inventory (STAI) and the State-Trait Anger Expression Inventory (STAXI). In M. E. Maruish (ed.), *The use of psychological testing for treatment planning and outcomes assessment* (2nd ed., pp. 993–1021). Mahwah, NJ: Lawrence Erlbaum Associates.

Sroufe, L. A. (1979). Socioemotional development. In J. Osofsky (ed.), *Handbook of infant development* (pp. 462–516). New York: John Wiley & Sons.

Stankov, L. (1986). Kvashchev's experiment: Can we boost intelligence? *Intelligence, 10,* 209–230.

Stankov, L. (1987). Level I/level II: A theory ready to be archived. In S. Modgil & C. Modgil (eds.), *Arthur Jensen: Consensus and controversy*. London: Falmers Press.

Stankov, L. (1988a). Aging, attention, and intelligence. *Psychology and Aging, 3* (2), 59–74.

Stankov, L. (1988b). Single tests, competing tasks, and their relationship to broad factors of intelligence. *Personality and Individual Differences, 9*, 25–33.

Stankov, L. (1994). The complexity effect phenomenon is an epiphenomenon of age-related fluid intelligence decline. *Personality and Individual Differences, 16*, 265–288.

Stankov, L. (1999). Mining on the "no man's land" between intelligence and personality. In P. L. Ackerman, P. C. Kyllonen & R. D. Roberts (eds.), *Learning and individual differences: Process, trait, and content determinants* (pp. 315–337). Washington, DC: American Psychological Association.

Stankov, L. (2000). Structural extension of a hierarchical view on human cognitive abilities. *Learning and Individual Differences, 12*, 35–51.

Stankov, L. (2001). 'g': A diminutive general. To appear in R. J. Sternberg & E. Grigorenko (eds.), *General factor of intelligence: Fact or fiction?* Los Angeles: Lawrence Erlbaum Associates.

Stankov, L., Boyle, G. J., & Cattell, R. B. (1995). Models and paradigms in personality and intelligence research. In D. Saklofske & M. Zeidner (eds.), *International handbook of personality and intelligence: Perspectives on individual differences* (pp. 15–43). New York: Plenum Press.

Stankov, L., & Chen, K. (1988). Can we boost fluid and crystallized intelligence? A structural modelling approach. *Australian Journal of Psychology, 40*, 363–376.

Stankov, L., & Dunn, S. (1993). Physical substrata of mental energy: The number of neurons and efficient cerebral metabolic processes. *Learning and Individual Differences, 5*, 241–257.

Stankov, L., & Horn, J. L. (1980). Human abilities revealed through auditory tests. *Journal of Educational Psychology, 72*, 21–44.

Stankov, L., Horn, J. L., & Roy, T. (1980). On the relationship between Gf/Gc theory and Jensen's level I/level II theory. *Journal of Educational Psychology, 72*, 21–44.

Stankov, L., & Roberts, R. D. (1997). Mental speed is not the "basic" process of intelligence. *Personality and Individual Differences, 22*, 69–85.

Stankov, L., Roberts, R. D., & Spilsbury, G. (1994). Attention and speed of test-taking in intelligence and aging. *Personality and Individual Differences, 17*, 273–284.

Stankov, L., Seizova-Cajic, T., & Roberts, R. D. (2000). Tactile and kinesthetic perceptual processes within the taxonomy of human cognitive abilities. *Intelligence, 28*, 1–29.

Stansbury, K., & Sigman, M. (1995). Development of behavioral expressions of emotion regulation in normally developing and at-risk preschool children. Manuscript submitted for publication.

Stauffer, J. M., Ree, M. J., & Carretta, T. R. (1996). Cognitive-components tests are not much more than *g*: An extension of Kyllonen's analyses. *Journal of General Psychology, 123*, 193–205.

Steer, R. A., Clark, D. A., Beck, A. T., & Ranieri, W. F. (1995). Common and specific dimensions of self-reported anxiety and depression: A replication. *Journal of Abnormal Psychology, 104*, 542–545.

Steil, R., & Ehlers, A. (2000). Dysfunctional meaning of posttraumatic intrusions in chronic PTSD. *Behaviour Research & Therapy, 38*, 537–558.

Steiner, C., & Perry, P. (1997). *Achieving emotional literacy: A personal program to increase your emotional intelligence.* New York: Avon.

Stelmack, R. M. (1990). Biological bases of extraversion: Psychophysiological evidence. *Journal of Personality, 58*, 293–311.

Stenross, B., & Kleinman, S. (1989). The highs and lows of emotional labor: Detective's encounters with criminals and victims. *Journal of Contemporary Ethnography, 17*, 435–452.

Stephan, W. G., Stephan, C. W., & Vargas, M. C. D. (1996). Emotional expression in Costa Rica and the United States. *Journal of Cross-Cultural Psychology, 27*, 147–160.

Stephenson, R. (1996). Introducing alexithymia: A concept within the psychosomatic process. *Disability and Rehabilitation: An International Multidisciplinary Journal, 18*, 209–214.

Steptoe, A. (1991). Psychological coping, individual differences, and physiological stress responses. In C. L. Cooper & R. Payne (eds.), *Personality and stress: Individual differences in the coping process* (pp. 205–233). Chichester: Wiley.

Sternberg, R. J. (1977). *Intelligence, information processing, and analogical reasoning: The componential analysis of human abilities.* Hillsdale, NJ: Lawrence Erlbaum Associates.

Sternberg, R. J. (1985). *Beyond IQ: A triarchic theory of human intelligence.* Cambridge: Cambridge University Press.

Sternberg, R. J. (1988). Explaining away intelligence: A reply to Howe. *British Journal of Psychology, 79*, 509–533.

Sternberg, R. J. (1993). Sternberg Triarchic Abilities Test. Unpublished manuscript.

Sternberg, R. J. (1996). *Successful intelligence.* New York: Simon and Shuster.

Sternberg, R. J. (2000a). Implicit theories of intelligence as exemplar stories of success: Why intelligence test validity is in the eye of the beholder. *Psychology, Public Policy, and Law, 6*, 159–167.

Sternberg, R. J. (2000b). The concept of intelligence. In R. J. Sternberg (ed.), *Handbook of intelligence* (pp. 3–15). New York: Cambridge University Press.

Sternberg, R. J., & Berg, C. (1986). Quantitative integration: Definitions of intelligence: A comparison of the 1921 and 1986 symposia. In R. J. Sternberg & D. K. Detterman (eds.), *What is intelligence? Contemporary viewpoints on its nature and definition.* Norwood, NJ: Ablex.

Sternberg, R. J., Conway, B. E., Ketron, J. L., & Bernstein, M. (1981). People's conceptions of intelligence. *Journal of Personality and Social Psychology, 41,* 37–55.

Sternberg, R. J., & Detterman, D. K. (eds.) (1986). *What is intelligence? Contemporary viewpoints on its nature and definition.* Norwood, NJ: Ablex.

Sternberg, R. J., & Grigorenko, E. L. (2000). Practical intelligence and its development. In R. Bar-On & J. D. A. Parker (eds.), *The handbook of emotional intelligence* (pp. 215–243). San Francisco: Jossey-Bass.

Sternberg, R. J., & Ruzgis, P. (eds.) (1994). *Personality and intelligence.* New York: Cambridge University Press.

Sternberg, R., & Wagner, R. K. (1986). *Practical intelligence: Nature and origins of competence in the everyday world.* Cambridge: Cambridge University Press.

Sternberg, R. J., Wagner, K., Williams, W. M., & Horvath, J. A. (1995). Testing common sense. *American Psychologist, 50,* 912–927.

Stone, S. V., & Costa, P. T., Jr. (1990). Disease-prone personality or distress-prone personality? In H. S. Friedman (ed.), *Personality and disease.* New York: Wiley.

Stone-McCown, K., Jensen, A. L., Freedman, J. M., & Rideout, M. C. (1998). *Self-science: The emotional intelligence curriculum* (2nd ed.). San Mateo, CA: Six Seconds.

Stone-McCown, K., & McCormick, A. H. (1999). Self-science: Emotional intelligence for children. In C. M. Reigeluth (ed.), *Instructional-design theories and models: A new paradigm of instructional theory* (vol. 2, pp. 537–561). Mahwah, NJ: Lawrence Erlbaum Associates.

Stopa, L., & Clark, D. M. (2000). Social phobia and interpretation of social events. *Behaviour Research & Therapy, 38,* 273–283.

Stout, M. (2000). *The feel-good curriculum: The dumbing down of America's kids in the name of self-esteem.* Cambridge, MA: Perseus Books.

Strayer, J. (1986). Children's attributions regarding the situational determinants of emotion in self and others. *Developmental Psychology, 22,* 649–654.

Stricker, L. J., & Rock, D. A. (1990). Interpersonal competence, social intelligence, and general ability. *Personality & Individual Differences, 11,* 833–839.

Stuller, J. (1997). EQ: Edging toward respectability. *Training, 34,* 43–48.

Suh, E., Diener, E., Oishi, S., & Triandis, H. (1998). The shifting basis of life satisfaction judgements across cultures: Emotions versus norms. *Journal of Personality and Social Psychology, 74,* 482–493.

Suls, J., & Fletcher, B. (1985). The relative efficacy of avoidant and nonavoidant coping strategies: A meta-analysis. *Health Psychology, 4,* 249–288.

Suls, J., Martin, R., & David, J. P. (1998). Person-environment fit and its limits: Agreeableness, neuroticism, and emotional reactivity to interpersonal conflict. *Personality & Social Psychology Bulletin, 24,* 88–98.

Sutton, R. I., & Rafaeli, A. (1988). Untangling the relationship between displayed emotions and organizational scales: The case of convenience stores. *Academy Management Journal, 31,* 461–487.

Sutton, R. L. (1991). Maintaining norms about expressed emotions: The case of bill collectors. *Administrative Science Quarterly, 36,* 245–268.

Svartberg, M., & Stiles, T. C. (1991). Comparative effects of short-term psychodynamic psychotherapy: A meta-analysis. *Journal of Consulting & Clinical Psychology, 59,* 704–714.

Taylor, G. J. (1984). Alexithymia: Concept, measurement, and implications for treatment. *American Journal of Psychiatry, 141,* 725–732.

Taylor, G. J. (1987). *Psychosomatic medicine and contemporary psychoanalysis.* Madison, CT: International Universities Press.

Taylor, G. J. (2000). Recent developments in alexithymia theory and research. *Canadian Journal of Psychiatry, 45,* 234–142.

Taylor, G. J., & Bagby, R. M. (2000). An overview of the alexithymia construct. In R. Bar-On and J. D. A. Parker (eds.). *Handbook of emotional intelligence* (pp. 40–67). San Francisco: Jossey-Bass.

Taylor, G. J., Bagby, R. M., & Luminet, O. (2000). Assessment of alexithymia: Self-report and observer-rated measures. In R. Bar-On & J. D. A. Parker (eds.). *Handbook of emotional intelligence* (pp. 301–319). San Francisco: Jossey-Bass.

Taylor, G. J., Bagby, R. M., & Parker, J. D. A. (1997). *Disorders of affect regulation: Alexithymia in medical and psychiatric illness.* Cambridge: Cambridge University Press.

Taylor, G. J., Parker, J. D. A., & Bagby, R. M. (1999). Emotional intelligence and the emotional brain: Points of convergence and implications for psychoanalysis. *Journal of the American Academy of Psychoanalysis, 27,* 339–354.

Taylor, G. J., Ryan, D., & Bagby, R. M. (1985). Toward the development of a new self-report alexithymia scale. *Psychotherapy and Psychosomatics, 44,* 191–199.

Taylor, G. J., & Taylor, H. L. (1997). Alexithymia. In M. McCallum & W. E. Piper (eds.), *Psychological mindedness: A contemporary understanding* (pp. 77–104). Mahwah, NJ: Lawrence Erlbaum Associates.

Taylor, S. (1996). A meta-analysis of cognitive-behavioural treatments for social phobia. *Journal of Behavior Therapy and Experimental Psychiatry, 27,* 1–9.

Taylor, S. E. (1986). *Health Psychology.* New York: Random House.

Taylor, S. E. (1989). *Positive illusions: Creative self-deception and the healthy mind.* New York: Basic Books.

Terman, L. M., & Merrill, M. A. (1937). *Measuring intelligence: A guide to the administration of the new revised Stanford-Binet tests of intelligence.* New York: Houghton Mifflin.

Tett, R. P., Jackson, D. N., & Rothstein, M. (1991). Personality measures as predictors of job performance: A meta-analytic review. *Personnel Psychology, 44,* 703–742.

Tett, R., Wang, A., Thomas, M., Griebler, J., & Martinez, A. (1997). Development of self-report measures of emotional intelligence. Paper presented at the 1997 Annual Convention of the Southeastern Psychological Association, Atlanta, GA.

Thayer, R. E. (1989). *The biopsychology of mood and arousal.* New York: Oxford University Press.

Thayer, R. E. (1996). *The origin of everyday moods: Managing energy, tension, and stress.* New York: Oxford University Press.

Thompson, R. A. (1990). Emotion and self-regulation. In R. A. Thompson (ed.), *Socioemotional development* (pp. 367–467). Lincoln: University of Nebraska Press.

Thompson, R. A. (1998). Emotional competence and the development of self. *Psychological Inquiry, 9,* 308–309.

Thomson, G. A. (1939/1948). *The factorial analysis of human ability* (1st/3rd ed.). Boston: Houghton-Mifflin.

Thomson, G. H. (1921). The Northumberland Mental Tests. *British Journal of Psychology, 12,* 201–222.

Thorndike, E. L. (1920). Intelligence and its uses. *Harper's Magazine, 140,* 227–235.

Thorndike, E. L., Bregman, E. O., Cobb, M. V., & Woodyard, E. (1926). *The measurement of intelligence.* New York: Bureau of Publications, Teachers College, Columbia University.

Thorndike, E. L., et al. (1921). Intelligence and its measurement: A symposium. *Journal of Educational Psychology, 12,* 123–147, 195–216, 271–275.

Thorndike, R. L., & Stein, S. (1937). An evaluation of the attempts to measure social intelligence. *Psychological Bulletin, 34,* 275–284.

Thorndike, R. L., Hagen, E. P., & Sattler, J. M. (1985). *Stanford-Binet Intelligence Scale* (4th ed.). Chicago: Riverside Publishing.

Thorndike, R. M., & Lohman, D. F. (1990). *A century of ability testing.* Chicago: Riverside Publishing.

Thornton, G. C., & Cleveland, J. N. (1990). Developing managerial talent through simulation. *American Psychologist, 45,* 190–199.

Thurstone, L. L. (1931). Multiple factor analysis. *Psychological Review, 38,* 406–427.

Thurstone, L. L. (1935). *The vectors of the mind.* Chicago: University of Chicago Press.

Thurstone, L. L. (1938). *Primary mental abilities.* Chicago: University of Chicago Press.

Thurstone, L. L. (1944). *A factorial study of perception.* Chicago: University of Chicago Press.

Thurstone, L. L. (1947). *Multiple factor analysis.* Chicago: University of Chicago Press.

Thurstone, L. L., & Thurstone, T. G. (1941). *Factorial studies of intelligence.* Chicago: University of Chicago Press.

Thurstone, T. G., Thurstone, L. L., & Standskov, H. H. (1955). *A psychological study of twins-scores of one hundred and twenty-five pairs of twins on fifty-nine tests.* Psychometric Laboratory, University of North Carolina.

Tice, D. M., & Baumeister, R. F. (1993). Controlling anger: Self-induced emotion change. In D. M. Wegner & J. W. Pennebaker (eds.), *Handbook of mental control* (pp. 393–409). Englewood Cliffs, NJ: Prentice-Hall.

Tokar, D. M., Fischer, Ann R., & Subich, L. M. (1998). Personality and vocational behavior: A selective review of the literature, 1993–1997. *Journal of Vocational Behavior, 53,* 115–153.

Tolich, M. B. (1993). Alienating and liberating emotions at work: Supermarket clerks' performance of customer service. *Journal of Contemporary Ethnography, 22,* 361–381.

Tooby, J., & Cosmides, L. (1992). The psychological foundations of culture. In J. H. Barkow, L. Cosmides & J. Tooby (eds.), *The adapted mind: Evolutionary psychology and the generation of culture* (pp. 19–136). Oxford: Oxford University Press.

Topping, K. J., Holmes, E. A., & Bremner, W. G. (2000). The effectiveness of school-based programs for the promotion of social competence. In R. Bar-On & J. D. A. Parker (eds.), *The handbook of emotional intelligence* (pp. 411–432). San Francisco: Jossey-Bass.

Tranel, D. (1997). Emotional processing and the human amygdala. *Trends in Cognitive Science, 1,* 46–47.

Trapnell, P. D., & Wiggins, J. S. (1990). Extension of the Interpersonal Adjective Scales to include the Big Five dimensions of personality. *Journal of Personality & Social Psychology, 59,* 781–790.

Tross, S. A., Harper, J. P., Osher, L. W., & Kneidinger, L. M. (2000). Not just the usual cast of characteristics: Using personality to predict college performance and retention. *Journal of College Student Development, 41,* 323–334.

Tsuda A., Haraguchi, M., Ozeki, Y., Kurasaki, N., & Tsuda, S. (1993). Animal model of "karoushi" (death from overwork): Characteristics of rats exposed to activity-stress. In *Proceedings of the 1993 International Congress of Health Psychology.* Tokyo: International Congress of Health Psychology.

Tupes, E. C., & Christal, R. E. (1961). *Recurrent personality factors based on trait ratings.* U.S. Air Force, Aeronautical Systems Division, technical report no. 61-97.

Tzeng, O. C. S., Hoosain, R., & Osgood, C. (1987). Cross-cultural componential analysis on affect attribution of emotion terms. *Journal of Psycholinguistic Research, 16,* 443–465.

Ucros, C. G. (1989). Mood-state-dependent memory: A meta-analysis. *Cognition and Emotion, 3,* 139–167.

Underwood, M. K., Coie, J. D., & Herbsman, C. R. (1992). Display rules for anger and aggression in school-age children. *Child Development, 63,* 366–380.

Undheim, J. O., & Horn, J. L. (1977). Critical evaluation of Guilford's structure-of-intellect theory. *Intelligence, 1,* 65–81.

Van der Does, A. J. W., Martin, M., Ehlers, A., & Barsky, A. J. (2000). Heartbeat perception in panic disorder: A reanalysis. *Behaviour Research & Therapy, 38,* 47–62.

Van Reekum, C. M., & Scherer, K. R. (1997). Levels of processing in emotion-antecedent appraisal. In G. Matthews (ed.), *Cognitive science perspectives on personality and emotion* (pp. 259–301). Amsterdam: Elsevier.

Verbeke, W. (1994). Personality characteristics that predict effective performance of salespeople. *Scandinavian Journal of Psychology, 10,* 49–57.

Vernon, P. A., Wickett, J. C., Bazana, P. G., & Stelmack, R. M. (2000). The neuropsychology and psychophysiology of human intelligence. In R. J. Sternberg (ed.), *Handbook of intelligence* (pp. 245–264). New York: Cambridge University Press.

Vernon, P. E. (1950). *The structure of human abilities.* London: Methuen.

Vernon, P. E. (1965). Ability factors and environmental influences. *American Psychologist, 20,* 723–733.

Vignoli, T. (1882). *Myth and science* (2nd ed.). London: Kegan Paul.

Vinokur, A. D., et al. (1991). Long-term follow-up and benefit-cost analysis of the JOBS program: A preventive intervention for the unemployed. *Journal of Applied Psychology, 76,* 213–219.

Vogt, B. A., & Gabriel, M. (eds.) (1993). *Neurobiology of cingulate cortex and limbic thalamus: A comprehensive handbook.* Cambridge, MA: Birkhaeuser.

Vollrath, M., Alnæs, R., & Torgersen, S. (1996). Differential effects of coping in mental disorders: A prospective study in psychiatric outpatients. *Journal of Clinical Psychology, 52,* 125–135.

Vollrath, M., Alnæs, R., & Torgersen, S. (1998). Neuroticism, coping, and change in MCMI-II clinical syndromes: Test of a mediator model. *Scandinavian Journal of Psychology, 39,* 15–24.

Wagner, R. K. (2000). Practical intelligence. In R. J. Sternberg (ed.), *Handbook of human intelligence* (2nd ed., pp. 380–395). New York: Cambridge University Press.

Wagner, R. K., & Sternberg, R. J. (1985). Practical intelligence in real world pursuits. *Journal of Personality and Social Psychology, 49,* 436–458.

Wagner, R. K., & Sternberg, R. J. (1986). Tacit knowledge and intelligence in the everyday world. In R. J. Sternberg & R. K. Wagner (eds.), *Practical intelligence: Nature and origins of competence in the everyday world* (pp. 51–83). New York: Cambridge University Press.

Wagner, R. K., & Sternberg, R. J. (1990). Street smarts. In K. E. Clark & M. B. Clark (eds.), *Measures of leadership* (pp. 493–504). West Orange, NJ: Leadership Library of America.

Walden, T. A. (1991). Infant social referencing. In J. Garber & K. A. Dodge (eds.), *The development of emotion regulation and dysregulation.* Cambridge: Cambridge University Press.

Waldman, I. D., Bouchard, T. J., Jr., Lykken, D. T., & McGue, M. (1993). Special mental abilities in twins reared apart: Competing factor models and genetic and environmental influences. Paper presented at the 28th Annual Behavior Genetics Association Conference, Sydney, Australia, July.

Walker, R. E., & Foley, J. M. (1973). Social intelligence: Its history and measurement. *Psychological Reports, 33*, 839–864.

Wallbott, H. G., & Scherer, K. R. (1986). How universal and specific is emotional experience? Evidence from 27 countries on five continents. *Social Science Information, 25*, 763–795.

Waller, J. H. (1971). Differential reproduction: Its relation to IQ test score, education, and occupation. *Social Biology, 18*, 122–136.

Wallerstein, J. S. (1983). Children of divorce: The psychological tasks of the child. *American Journal of Orthopsychiatry, 53*, 230–243.

Walton, H. J., & Presly, A. S. (1973). Use of a category system in the diagnosis of abnormal personality. *British Journal of Psychiatry, 122*, 259–268.

Watson, D., & Clark, L. A. (1992). On traits and temperament. General and specific factors of emotional experience and their relation to the five-factor model. *Journal of Personality, 60*, 441–476.

Watson, D., & Clark, L. A. (1997). Measurement and mis-measurement of mood: Recurrent and emergent issues. *Journal of Personality Assessment, 68*, 267–296.

Watson, D., & Tellegen, A. (1985). Toward a consensual structure of mood. *Psychological Bulletin, 98*, 219–235.

Watson, M., & Greer, S. (1983). Development of a questionnaire measure of emotional control. *Journal of Psychosomatic Research, 27*, 299–305.

Wechsler, D. (1958). *The measurement and appraisal of adult intelligence* (4th ed.). Baltimore: Williams & Wilkins Co.

Wechsler, D. (1974). The IQ is an intelligent test. In A. J. Edwards (ed.), *Selected papers of David Wechsler.* New York: Academic Press.

Wechsler, D. (1981). *Manual for the Wechsler Adult Intelligence Scale—Revised.* New York: Psychological Corporation.

Wedeck, J. (1947). The relationship between personality and "psychological ability." *British Journal of Psychology, 37*, 133–151.

Wegner, D. M., & Bargh, J. A. (1998). Control and automaticity in social life. In D. T. Gilbert & S. T. Fiske (eds.), *The handbook of social psychology* (4th ed., vol. 1, pp. 446–496). Boston: McGraw-Hill.

Wegner, D. M., & Pennebaker, J. W. (1993). *Handbook of mental control.* Englewood Cliffs, NJ: Prentice-Hall.

Weidner, G., & Collins, R. L. (1992). Gender, coping, and health. In H. W. Krohne (ed.), *Attention and avoidance: Strategies in coping with aversiveness* (pp. 241–265). Toronto, Gottingen: Hogrefe & Huber.

Weinberger, D. A., & Schwartz, G. E. (1990). Distress and restraint as superordinate dimensions of self-reported adjustment: A typological perspective. *Journal of Personality, 58*, 381–417.

Weinberger, D. A., Schwarz, G. E., & Davidson, R. J. (1979). Low-anxious, high-anxious, and repressive coping styles: Psychometric patterns and behavioral and physiological responses to stress. *Journal of Abnormal Psychology, 88*, 369–380.

Weinman, J. (1987). Non-cognitive determinants of perceptual problem-solving strategies. *Personality and Individual Differences, 8,* 53–58.

Weinraub, M., & Wolf, B. M. (1983). Effects of stress and social supports on mother-child interactions in single-and two-parent families. *Child Development, 54,* 1297–1311.

Weisinger, H. (1998). *Emotional intelligence at work: The untapped edge for success.* San Francisco: Jossey-Bass.

Weissberg, R. P., Jackson, A. S., & Shriver, T. P. (1993). Promoting positive social development and health practices in young urban adolescents. In M. Elias (ed.), *Social decision making and life skills development: Guidelines for middle school educators* (pp. 45–77). Gaithersburg, MD: Aspen Publications.

Weissman, A. N., & Beck, A. T. (1978). Development and validation of the Dysfunctional Attitude Scale. Paper presented at the annual meeting of the Association for the Advancement of Behavior Therapy, Chicago.

Wellenkamp, J. (1995). Cultural similarities and differences regarding emotional disclosure: Some examples from Indonesia and the Pacific. In J. W. Pennebaker (ed.), *Emotion, disclosure, and health* (pp. 293–311). Washington, DC: American Psychological Association.

Wellman, H. M., & Woolley, J. D. (1990). From simple desires to ordinary beliefs: The early development of everyday psychology. *Cognition, 35,* 245–275.

Wells, A. (1994). A multi-dimensional measure of worry: Development and preliminary validation of the Anxious Thoughts Inventory. *Anxiety, Stress, and Coping, 6,* 289–299.

Wells, A. (1997). *Cognitive therapy of anxiety disorders: A practice manual and conceptual guide.* Chichester, England: John Wiley & Sons.

Wells, A. (2000). *Emotional disorders and metacognition: Innovative cognitive therapy.* Chichester, England: Wiley.

Wells, A., & Carter, K. (1999). Preliminary tests of a cognitive model of generalized anxiety disorder. *Behaviour Research & Therapy, 37,* 585–594.

Wells, A., & Carter, K. (2001). Further tests of a cognitive model of generalised anxiety disorder: Metacognitions and worry in GAD, panic disorder, social phonia, depression, and nonpatients. *Behavior Therapy, 32,* 85–102.

Wells, A., & Hackmann, A. (1993). Imagery and core beliefs in health anxiety: Content and origins. *Behavioural and Cognitive Psychotherapy, 21,* 265–273.

Wells, A., & Matthews, G. (1994). *Attention and emotion: A clinical perspective.* Hove, England: Lawrence Erlbaum Associates.

Wells, A., & Matthews, G. (1996). Modelling cognition in emotional disorder: The S-REF model. *Behaviour Research & Therapy, 34,* 881–888.

Wells, A., & Matthews, G. (in press). Cognitive vulnerability to anxiety disorders: An integrative approach. In L. B. Alloy & J. H. Riskind (eds.), *Cognitive vulnerability to emotional disorders.* Hillsdale, NJ: Lawrence Erlbaum Associates.

Wenzlaff, R. M., & Eisenberg, A. R. (1998). Parental restrictiveness of negative emotions: Sowing the seeds of thought suppression. *Psychological Inquiry, 9,* 310–313.

Wenzlaff, R. M., & Wegner, D. M. (2000). Thought suppression. *Annual Review of Psychology, 51,* 59–91.

Westman, M., & Eden, D. (1988). Job stress and subsequent objective performance. Working paper no. 963/88.

Wethington, E., & Kessler, R. C. (1991). Situations and processes of coping. In J. Eckenrode (eds.), *The social context of coping* (pp. 13–29). New York: Plenum.

Wexley, K. N., & Baldwin, T. T. (1986). Posttraining strategies for facilitation of positive transfer: An empirical exploration. *Academy of Management Review, 29,* 503–520.

Wharton, A. S. (1993). The affective consequences of service work: Managing emotions on the job. *Work and occupation, 20,* 205–232.

Wharton, A. S., & Erickson, R. J. (1995). The consequences of caring: Exploring the links of women's job and family emotion work. *Sociological Quarterly, 36,* 273–296.

White, J. D. (1999). Personality, temperament, and ADHD: A review of the literature. *Personality & Individual Differences, 27,* 589–598.

White, R. W. (1959). Motivation reconsidered: The concept of competence. *Psychological Review, 66,* 297–333.

Widaman, K. F., & Carlson, J. S. (1989). Procedural effects on performance on the Hick paradigm: Bias in reaction time and movement time parameters. *Intelligence, 13,* 63–85.

Widiger, T. A. (1997). Personality disorders as maladaptive variants of common personality traits: Implications for treatment. *Journal of Contemporary Psychotherapy, 27,* 265–282.

Widiger, T. A., & Clark, L. A. (2000). Toward *DSM*-V and the classification of psychopathology. *Psychological Bulletin, 126,* 946–963.

Widiger, T. A., & Costa, P. T., Jr. (1994). Personality and personality disorders. *Journal of Abnormal Psychology, 103,* 78–91.

Widiger, T., & Shea, T. (1991). Differentiation of Axis I and Axis II disorders. *Journal of Abnormal Psychology, 100,* 399–406.

Widiger, T. A., & Trull, T. J. (1992). Personality and psychopathology: An application of the five-factor model. *Journal of Personality, 60,* 363–393.

Widiger, T. A., Trull, T. J., Hurt, S. W., Clarkin, J., & Frances, A. (1987). A multidimensional scaling of the *DSM*-III personality disorders. *Archives of General Psychiatry, 44,* 557–563.

Wierzbicka, A. (1995). The relevance of language to the study of emotions. *Psychological Inquiry, 6,* 248–252.

Willerman, L. (1991). Commentary on Rushton's Mongoloid-Caucasoid differences in brain size. *Intelligence, 15,* 361–364.

Williams, J. M. G., Watts, F. N., MacLeod, C., & Mathews, A. (1988). *Cognitive psychology and emotional disorders.* Chichester: Wiley.

Williams, W. M., & Sternberg, R. J. (1988). Group intelligence: Why some groups are better than others. *Intelligence, 12,* 351–377.

Wolfgang, A., & Cohen, M. (1988). Sensitivity of Canadians, Latin-Americans, Ethiopians, and Israelis to interracial facial expressions of emotions. *International Journal of Intercultural Relations, 12,* 139–151.

Wong, C. M. T., Day, J. D., Maxwell, S. E., & Meara, N. M. (1995). A multitrait-multimethod study of academic and social intelligence in college students. *Journal of Educational Psychology, 87,* 117–133.

Woodcock, R. W. (1990). Theoretical foundations of the WJ-R measures of cognitive ability. *Journal of Psychoeducational Assessment, 8,* 231–258.

Wortman, C. (1983). Coping with victimization: Conclusions and implications for future research. *Journal of Social Issues, 39,* 195–221.

W. T. Grant Consortium on the School-Based Promotion of Social Competence. (1992). Drug and alcohol prevention curricula. In J. D. Hawkins et al. (eds.), *Communities that care.* San Francisco: Jossey-Bass.

Young, D. P., & Dixon, N. M. (1996). *Helping leaders take effective action: A program evaluation.* Greensboro, NC: Center for Creative Leadership.

Youngblade, L. M., & Dunn, J. (1995). Individual differences in young children's pretend play with mother and sibling: Links to relationships and understanding of other people's feelings and beliefs. *Child Development, 66,* 1472–1492.

Zacker, J., & Bard, M. (1973). Effects of conflict management training on police performance. *Journal of Applied Psychology, 58,* 202–208.

Zahn-Waxler, C. (1991). The case of empathy: A developmental perspective. *Psychological Inquiry, 2,* 155–158.

Zahn-Waxler, C., Cummings, E. M., Mcknew, D., & Radke-Yarrow, M. (1984). Affective arousal and social interactions in young children of manic depressive parents. *Child Development, 55,* 112–122.

Zahn-Waxler, C., Klimes-Dougan, B. K., & Kendziora, K. T. (1998). The study of emotion socialization: Conceptual, methodological, and developmental considerations. *Psychological Inquiry, 9,* 313–316.

Zahn-Waxler, C., & Kochanska, G. (1990). The origins of guilt. In R. A. Thompson (ed.), *Socioemotional development.* Lincoln: University of Nebraska Press. '

Zahn-Waxler, C., Radke-Yarrow, M., & King, R. A. (1979). Child rearing and children's prosocial initiations toward victims of distress. *Child Development, 50,* 319–330.

Zahn-Waxler, C., Robinson, J., & Emde, R. (1992). Development of emphathy in twins. *Developmental Psychology, 28,* 1038–1047.

Zajonc, R. B. (1984). On the primacy of affect. *American Psychologist, 39,* 117–123.

Zak, A., Hunton, L., Kuhn, R., & Parks, J. (1997). Effects of need for control on personal relationships. *Journal of Social Psychology, 137,* 671–672.

Zeidner, M. (1995). Personality trait correlates of intelligence. In D. Saklofske & M. Zeidner (eds.), *International handbook of personality and intelligence* (pp. 299–319). New York: Plenum.

Zeidner, M. (1998). *Test anxiety: The state of the art.* New York: Plenum.

Zeidner, M., & Feitelson, D. (1989). Probing the validity of intelligence tests for preschool children: A smallest space analysis. *Journal of Psychoeducational Assessment, 7*, 175–193.

Zeidner, M., & Hammer, A. (1990). Life events and coping resources as predictors of stress symptoms in adolescents. *Personality and Individual Differences, 11*, 693–703.

Zeidner, M., & Matthews, G. (2000). Personality and intelligence. In R. J. Sternberg (ed.), *Handbook of human intelligence* (2nd ed., pp. 581–610). New York: Cambridge University Press.

Zeidner, M., Matthews, G., & Roberts, R. D. (2001). Slow down, you move too fast: Emotional intelligence remains an "elusive" intelligence. *Emotion, 1*, 265–275.

Zeidner, M., & Saklofske, D. S. (1996). Adaptive and maladaptive coping. In M. Zeidner & N. S. Endler (eds.), *Handbook of coping* (pp. 505–531). New York: John Wiley & Sons.

Zigler, E., & Trickett, P. K. (1979). IQ, social competence, and evaluation of early childhood intervention programs. *Annual Progress in Child Psychiatry and Child Development.*

Zimmerman, B. J. (2000). Self-efficacy: An essential motive to learn. *Contemporary Educational Psychology, 25*, 82–91.

Zinbarg, R., & Revelle, W. (1989). Personality and conditioning: A test of four models. *Journal of Personality & Social Psychology, 57*, 301–314.

Zins, J. E., Elias, M. J., Greenberg, M. T., & Weissberg, R. P. (2000). Promoting social and emotional competence in children. In R. Bar-On & J. D. A. Parker (eds.), *Handbook of social and emotional intelligence.* New York: Jossey-Bass.

Zins, J., Travis, F., III & Freppon, P. A. (1997). Linking research and educational programming to promote social and emotional learning. In P. Salovey & D. J. Sluyter (eds.), *Emotional development and emotional intelligence* (pp. 168–192). New York: Basic Books.

Zuckerman, M. (1991). *Psychobiology of personality.* Cambridge: Cambridge University Press.

Zuckerman, M. (1994). *Behavioral expressions and biosocial bases of sensation seeking.* New York: Cambridge University Press.

Zuckerman, M. (1998). Psychobiological theories of personality. In David F. Barone, Michel Hersen, et al. (eds.), *Advanced personality* (pp. 123–154). New York: Plenum Press.

Zuckerman, M. (1999). *Vulnerability to psychopathology: A biosocial model.* Washington, DC: American Psychological Association.

Zuckerman, M., Kuhlman, D. M., Joireman, J., Teta, P., & Kraft, M. (1993). A comparison of three structural models for personality: The Big Three, the Big Five, and the Alternative Five. *Journal of Personality & Social Psychology, 65,* 757–768.

Zuckerman, M., Kuhlman, D. M., Thornquist, M., & Kiers, H. (1991). Five (or three) robust questionnaire scale factors of personality without culture. *Personality & Individual Differences, 12,* 929–941.

Zuckerman, M., Lipets, M. S., Koivumaki, J. H., & Rosenthal, R. (1975). Encoding and decoding nonverbal cues of emotion. *Journal of Personality and Social Psychology, 32,* 1068–1076.

Index

Abilities, 17–18, 35, 39, 42, 58–61, 64,
  68–69, 72, 81–131, 186, 201–203,
  205, 210, 213, 216–217, 219, 227,
  269, 281, 321–322, 332, 350–351,
  355, 388–389, 421–422, 437, 450,
  456, 516–518, 520, 523, 525, 539,
  544–545, 548. *See also* Intelligence
cognitive, 81–131, 176, 178, 179, 190,
  192, 198, 201, 210, 211, 213, 220,
  269, 351, 482, 486, 517–522
primary mental, 100–101, 521, 527
Abramson, L. Y., 361, 404–405
Absenteeism, 487, 490, 494, 507
Academic achievement, 210, 436, 440,
  444
Achievement motivation, 361–364,
  476
Ackerman, P. L., 12, 67–68, 111, 113,
  267–268, 325, 348
Action tendencies, 252, 313
Adaptation, 15, 26, 43, 54, 59, 71, 80,
  90, 123, 125, 126, 127, 130–131, 133,
  141, 143, 182, 207, 212, 267–270,
  277, 280–281, 284–291, 300–308,
  311–319, 321–330, 368–370, 515
adaptive functions of emotion, 143,
  164–167, 171, 233–234, 248–250,
  266–267
as basis for emotional intelligence,
  7–49, 57, 158–159, 165, 252–253,
  300–301, 303, 311–314, 321, 369–
  370, 426–427, 538–539
as basis for personality, 66, 68, 321–
  370, 529, 537–538, 546–547

and coping, 284–285, 302–308, 311–
  319, 535–536
Adler, M., 497–499, 504, 543
Aggleton, J. P., 241, 532
Aggression, 162, 169, 191, 240, 249,
  251, 313, 341, 354, 356–360, 365,
  380, 384, 423, 448, 452, 494
Aggressiveness, 323, 357
Agreeableness, 41, 46, 64, 66–68, 71,
  128, 190, 212, 213, 217, 219, 221,
  223, 294, 322, 324–325, 344, 351–
  354, 356–357, 359–362, 367–370,
  385–386, 524–526, 537, 583
Alexithymia, 20, 158, 166, 192, 204,
  222, 225, 285, 311, 332, 373–374,
  387–400, 411–412, 417, 525–526,
  538, 544, 582–583
Alloy, L. B., 337, 361, 404–406
Altruism, 324, 351, 354, 359, 361,
  479
Amygdala, 31, 50, 56, 235, 237–242,
  244–247, 252, 279, 281, 357, 425,
  473, 503, 532, 545
Anastasi, A., 32–33, 35, 81, 177, 227
Anger, 55, 141–142, 144–145, 149,
  162, 237, 244, 251, 268, 274, 306,
  313, 323, 356–357, 388, 393, 423,
  429, 431, 434–436, 439–441, 446,
  450–453, 457, 462, 465, 468–469,
  471–473, 481, 490, 503
Antisocial behavior, 169, 325, 350–
  351, 360, 362, 385, 423, 429, 431,
  434–436, 439–441, 446, 450–453,
  457, 462, 465

Antisocial personality, 210, 379, 384–386, 417

Anxiety, 27, 57, 67, 112–113, 140–141, 143–146, 149, 157, 166–170, 223, 239–240, 242, 245, 252, 260–261, 264, 270, 272, 275–276, 283–284, 310, 312, 315, 321–323, 325, 330–339, 341, 347, 374, 380–382, 387, 393, 424, 441, 462, 468–469, 490–491, 497, 506, 524, 540, 569
    disorders, 376–378, 400–402, 405–408, 410–414
    sensitivity to, 406
    social, 287, 378–379
    trait, 148, 152, 210, 212, 330, 332–335, 337, 339, 341, 524

Appraisal, 39, 42, 48–49, 51–52, 57, 61, 111, 148, 152, 154–156, 158, 161, 171, 180–181, 182, 204, 219, 251, 255–259, 264–265, 272, 274–275, 279, 281–282, 284–285, 291–298, 312, 314–316, 318–319, 323–324, 328, 336–339, 341, 352–353, 355, 357–358, 364, 380, 398, 401, 414, 468, 496, 525, 530, 534–538, 543
    primary, 257, 297–298
    secondary, 257, 297–298, 314

Armed Services Vocational Aptitude Battery (ASVAB), 82, 99, 187, 190

Arousal, 144, 151–153, 169, 237, 239, 251, 261, 283, 293, 307, 315, 345–347, 388, 390–392, 406, 423, 429, 431–432, 442, 449–450, 473. *See also* Cerebral cortex, arousal of

Assertiveness, 324, 342, 397, 525, 543, 545
    training, 449, 451, 500, 503

Assessment of emotional intelligence, 15–20, 23, 176–230, 515–517. *See also* Scoring methods
    ability model of, 13, 83, 131, 471, 483, 506, 517–523, 544–545
    conceptual basis for, 9–21
    mixed model of, 12, 321, 471, 479, 517, 524–531, 539, 544
    performance-based and self-report measures contrasted, 18, 39–45, 85, 180, 205, 226–228, 481, 483, 507, 516, 524, 526–527, 529–530, 538, 542, 544, 547–548
    performance-based measures reviewed, 180–205, 563–575
    self-report measures reviewed, 205–223, 577–585

Attachment, 384, 391–392, 396

Attention, 66, 169, 245, 249, 253, 257–258, 261–265, 268, 272, 274–276, 282, 293, 315, 327, 332–339, 341, 346–347, 354, 357, 361, 366–367, 370, 374–375, 391, 401–402, 404, 406, 408–409, 422, 431, 436, 517, 519, 521, 524, 526, 531, 535, 537, 540, 544, 549
    attentional capacity/resources, 168, 170, 237, 239, 241, 249, 266, 275, 288, 315, 336–337, 341, 346, 361, 365, 367, 388–390
    divided, 346
    selective, 168, 253, 261, 357, 366, 370, 391, 401, 535, 537

Attention-Deficit/Hyperactive Disorder (ADHD), 380, 382

Austin, E. J., 219–220, 225, 324, 384, 386, 525–526

Autism, 381–382

Automatic and controlled processing, 259, 273, 338, 402, 517

Autonomic nervous system, 136, 151–154, 168, 237, 242, 283, 421

Averill, J. R., 155–156, 244, 473

Bagby, R. M., 192, 285, 311, 362, 373, 386–393–394, 398–399, 422, 425, 433, 583

Bandura, A., 113, 158, 288, 305, 361, 428, 431

Bar-On, R., 9–11, 15–16, 28, 31, 41–42, 56, 61–62, 67–69, 72, 74, 76, 90, 149, 157–158, 166, 172, 176, 186, 206, 208, 213, 221, 223, 227, 282, 286, 292, 321–324, 330, 351, 356, 359, 476–477, 480, 482–483, 514, 516, 524–525, 527, 529, 532, 536, 545

Barrick, M. R., 168, 330, 343, 351, 362, 479, 543

Bechara, A., 22, 152, 156, 171, 240, 246, 282, 531–533

Beck, A. T., 262, 402–405, 408, 411, 413–414, 581–582

Bell Curve (Herrnstein and Murray), 6–7, 70, 72, 84, 96, 99–100, 114, 522, 549

Ben Ze'ev, A., 36, 47, 52, 137, 139, 155

Big Five (personality factors), 40, 65, 73, 148, 178, 187, 211, 212, 213, 217, 221, 225, 294, 321–322, 324–326, 351, 356, 385–387, 393, 479, 524–526, 537–538, 574, 585

Binet, A., 36, 84–85, 230

Bipolar disorder, 379, 413

Boredom, 350, 468–469

Bower, G. H., 168, 260–263

Boyatzis, R., 12–14, 41, 214–215, 217, 470, 473, 476, 494

Brody, N., 60, 64, 88, 102–103, 110, 123, 421

Burke, R. J., 502, 504, 543

Burnout, 169, 502

Caputi, P., 35, 40, 61, 187–188, 190–192, 210, 223, 228, 268, 292, 517, 534, 570

Career assessment, 76, 467, 477, 480, 483, 485–486, 504, 506–507, 542–543

Carroll, J. B., 19, 22, 25, 43, 59, 61, 63, 82, 84, 93, 95, 97–99, 101, 104, 106–107, 109–110, 115, 122, 127, 130, 196, 200, 520, 548, 554–556, 558, 561

Cartwright, S., 488, 490, 494, 496, 500, 502–503

Caruso, D., 4, 9–10, 12, 14, 16–20, 28, 31, 35, 42–43, 56, 63, 69, 72, 75, 82, 90, 115, 158, 166, 176, 180–183, 186–189, 191, 193, 196–201, 260, 282, 300, 368, 415, 471, 481, 514–520, 523, 530, 534–535, 544, 560

Carver, C. S., 270, 272, 308–310, 312–314, 361, 482, 584

Catano, V. M., 16, 208, 210, 227, 321, 478

Cattell, R. B., 36, 61, 92, 98, 100–102, 104–105, 110, 204, 212, 247

Cerebral cortex, 26, 65–66, 151–152, 235, 241, 279, 425
  arousal of, 65–66, 151–152, 326, 345

Challenge, 57, 147, 239, 242, 249, 252–253, 256, 259, 269–270, 275–276, 281, 294, 298, 317, 321, 326, 328, 332, 348, 355, 358, 370, 402, 415, 519, 524, 528–532, 537, 539–540, 547

Chameleon effect, 353

Chan, A., 35, 40, 61, 187–188, 190–192, 210, 219, 223, 226, 228, 268, 292, 517, 534, 570

Character, 6, 12, 99

Cherniss, C., 497–499, 504, 543

Child-rearing methods, 419, 421, 424, 426, 435

Ciarrochi, J., 35, 40, 61, 99, 115, 187–188, 190–192, 210, 219, 223, 226, 228, 268, 292, 517, 534, 570

Cingulate cortex, 238, 245, 247, 265, 335, 391, 538

Clark, D. A., 403–405, 408, 411

Clark, L. A., 144–145, 148–149, 223, 324, 343–344, 382–383

Clore, G. L., 138, 145, 258–259, 261, 266, 268–269, 278–280, 334, 534

Cognitive architecture, 52, 54, 80, 134, 158, 255, 259, 264–266, 269–270, 280, 282–283, 314, 318, 326–328, 334, 346, 366–367, 369, 403, 517, 534–535, 537–539, 545

Cognitive development, 108–110, 119, 423, 432, 568

Cognitive interference, 146–147

Cognitive-science framework, 50, 54, 56, 63, 80, 130, 138–139, 156, 170, 233, 255, 262, 265, 269, 282, 326, 360, 533
  and explanation at the biological level, 50, 54

Cognitive-science framework (cont.)
  and explanation at the knowledge
    level, 52, 155–157, 170, 270, 272,
    284, 315, 318, 367, 527–529
  and explanation at the level of
    symbolic-information processing,
    50, 53, 315
Cognitive style, 388, 390
Cognitive therapy, 413, 414–415, 540
Cognitive vulnerability, 401, 404–408,
    411
Cohen, J., 78, 443–444, 449, 464
Communication skills, 423, 432, 439,
    446–447, 449–450, 453
Computational models, 136, 256, 259,
    269
Conditioning, 238, 240–241, 246, 250–
    253, 345, 366, 412, 430–431, 532
  operant learning, 430–431
Conflict resolution, 353, 445, 449,
    451–452, 455, 457, 475–476, 506,
    543
Connectionist models, 262–263, 265
Conscientiousness, 46, 64, 66–68, 71,
    178, 190, 212, 213, 214, 215, 216,
    217, 219, 221, 223, 225, 322, 324–
    325, 354, 356, 361, 362–365, 367–
    370, 385, 476, 479, 481–482, 506,
    524–525, 537
Consciousness, 134–136, 138, 233,
    237, 245, 265, 277–279, 314–315,
    414, 583
Consensus scoring, 518, 530
Constructive thinking, 221, 288, 482–
    483, 506, 577–582
Constructivism, 154–155, 162
Control signals, 252–253, 268, 280,
    535
Cooper, C. L., 488, 489, 490–491, 494,
    496, 500, 502–503
Cooper, J. T., 20, 218–220, 225–226,
    321, 323–325, 515, 517
Cooper, R. K., 20, 76–77, 221, 470,
    476–478, 481, 503, 505, 582
Coping, 26, 45, 51, 53–55, 57, 68, 75–
    76, 148, 158, 207, 210, 222, 233–234,
    251, 257, 259, 270, 272, 274–276,

279–280, 282, 283–319, 323, 326,
    328, 332, 336–339, 341, 348, 350,
    353, 357–359, 364, 367, 381, 393–
    394, 400, 402, 405–410, 414–415,
    420, 422, 430, 434, 436–438, 443,
    449–450, 453, 455–456, 467–468,
    472, 480, 483, 488–489, 494–497,
    500–505, 508, 531–532, 534–538,
    540, 543, 579
  avoidance, 147, 250, 275, 284, 290,
    292–294, 298–299, 306, 308–309,
    311–313, 337, 341–342, 363, 369,
    385–386, 393, 407, 430, 496–497
  coping tasks, 306–307
  effectiveness of, 307–316
  emotion-focused, 147, 275, 284, 298–
    299, 304–305, 308, 310–312, 317–
    318, 336, 408, 453, 455, 472, 496,
    498, 540
  palliative, 311, 430
  problem-focused (*see* Coping, task-
    focused)
  task-focused, 147, 284, 298–299, 304–
    305, 308–309, 311–312, 317–318,
    348, 350, 364, 496, 508
Core relational theme, 257
Correlation, definition of, 25, 178–179
Cosmides, L., 48, 249, 252, 268
Costa, P. T., Jr., 41, 64–67, 178, 211,
    213, 224, 294, 294, 323, 328, 330,
    342–343, 348, 381, 384–385, 525,
    537
Cowan, K., 497–499, 504, 543
Creativity, 102, 264, 368–369, 537
Culture, 6, 43–44, 64, 70–72, 164–165,
    187, 199, 210, 235, 247, 250, 254,
    257, 268–269, 306, 318, 327, 361,
    426, 430, 432, 458, 496, 518–519,
    528, 530, 547
Cybernetics, 270–272, 279

Damasio, A. R., 22, 138, 152, 154, 156,
    171, 240, 244, 246, 282, 531–533
Darwin, C., 150–151, 154, 248–249,
    278, 548
Dawda, D., 40, 64, 68, 149, 206, 208,
    211–212, 219, 321, 326

Day, A. L., 16, 208, 210, 227, 321, 478

Deary, I. J., 11, 59, 61, 63, 146, 298, 310, 324, 332, 336, 339, 348, 364, 381, 393, 536

Decision making, 152, 156, 168–169, 237–238, 246, 268–269, 282, 334, 363, 449, 543

Delinquency, 453–454, 465

Denham, S. A., 420, 422, 425, 430–434, 436, 439–441

Dependency, 352

Depression, 139, 144–145, 166, 169, 210, 236, 245, 262–264, 268, 322–323, 325, 330, 335–337, 339, 344, 365, 382–383, 386–387, 393, 434, 569

clinical, 376, 379, 401–406, 408–412, 414

Derryberry, D., 148, 161, 170, 223, 245, 274, 309, 315, 335–336, 366, 402, 408, 422, 440

Descartes, R., 134–135, 141

Deviance, 325, 384

Diagnosis, 375–376, 380, 416

Diagnostic and Statistical Manual of Mental Disorders (4th ed.), 375, 379, 381–384, 414

Diathesis-stressor model of mental disorders, 374, 403

Differential psychology, 21–27, 32, 47, 57, 58–59, 68–69, 71 , 73, 115, 200, 202, 515

Distress, 141, 146–147, 237, 251, 273–276, 293–294, 296, 300, 306–307, 309–310, 313, 330–331, 352, 377–380, 386, 392–395, 400, 408, 410, 414, 421, 424, 430, 434–436, 439, 472, 488–489, 505

Dornheim, L., 20, 218–220, 225–226, 321, 323–325, 515, 517

Driving vehicles, 331, 337, 358

DSM-IV, 375, 379, 381–384, 414

Dundee Stress-State Questionnaire (DSSQ), 146–147, 274, 293–295

Dysfunctional Attitudes Scale (DAS), 403–405

Eating disorders, 381, 387

Effort, 168–169, 257, 266, 270, 272–273, 298, 324, 333, 337–338, 341, 352, 361, 364, 548

Ego resiliency, 68

Electroencephalogram (EEG), 151–152

Elias, M. J., 5, 77–78, 229, 442–444, 447, 452–453, 459, 461–464

Emmerling, R., 497–499, 504, 543

Emotions

assimilation of, 17, 74, 181, 184, 194, 199

basic, 140–146, 148–149, 249, 252, 265–266, 280–281, 543

centralist vs. peripheralist conceptions of, 150–154, 156, 171

dimensional approaches to, 140–149

disclosure of, 75, 289–290, 311, 319, 410–411

expression of, 7–8, 75, 181, 388, 392, 398, 423, 571

facilitation of (*see* Emotions, assimilation of)

identification of (*see* Emotions, perception of)

intensity of, 422

management of, 17, 75, 165, 173, 182, 185, 188, 195, 260, 269, 300, 374, 379, 399, 416, 517–519, 543

perception of, 17–18, 34, 56, 75, 111, 113, 130, 181, 184, 188, 191–194, 196, 199, 202, 204, 218, 233, 246, 258, 260, 263, 268–269, 355, 390, 423, 427, 432, 456, 464, 476, 517, 519, 526–527, 539, 544, 563, 575

philosophy of, 47, 81, 134–135, 139

regulation of, 27, 182, 233–234, 247, 282, 288–289, 292–293, 422, 424, 426–427, 429–431, 433–434, 440–441, 456, 458, 462, 464–465, 471, 475–476, 549

self-report measures of, 136–137, 139–140, 172, 393, 526

understanding, 17, 158, 181, 185, 188, 195–196, 203, 313, 427, 433, 447, 456, 517

Emotional Accuracy Research Scale
(EARS), 519, 563–565
Emotional awareness, 425, 439, 446,
566–571
Emotional coaching, 430
Emotional competence, 35–36, 47, 49,
67–68, 321, 323, 423, 426, 427, 433–
434, 436, 439, 441, 443, 445–446,
448, 456, 461, 462, 464, 470–471,
480–481, 506, 518–519, 539, 572
Emotional Competence Inventory
(ECI), 13–14
Emotional development, 423–424,
435, 441
Emotional disorder, 154–155, 166–
167, 169, 351, 374, 376, 381, 383–
385, 408, 410–412, 417, 540
Emotional education, 442–443, 445,
462, 464
Emotional intelligence
age differences in, 72, 200, 210
ethnicity differences in, 189, 199
gender differences in, 44, 71, 293,
351, 356, 523
group differences in, 32, 69–73, 189,
200, 210, 211, 221, 227, 523, 547
Emotional Intelligence Questionnaire,
222
Emotionality, 9, 58, 63, 241, 246, 278,
323, 330, 334, 342, 354, 393, 422,
424–425, 537, 583
Emotional Quotient Inventory (EQ-i),
15–16, 39, 42, 61, 67, 69, 72, 149,
173, 206–213, 219–220, 221, 227,
292, 321, 323, 325, 341, 351, 356,
399, 482–483, 507, 515–517, 524–
525, 529, 532, 546
description of, 206–208
evaluation of, 208–213
Emotional stability, 323, 331, 342, 354,
368, 482, 524, 526, 546. *See also*
Neuroticism
Emotional Stroop test, 205, 211, 275,
333, 409, 522
Empathy, 56, 67, 166, 169, 209–210,
225, 301–302, 324–325, 351, 353,
354–356, 359, 370, 386, 398, 415,

417, 433, 443, 447–448, 451, 455,
456, 461–462, 469–470, 473–475,
506, 524–526, 538, 541–542, 564–
565, 574
Endler, N. S., 274, 283, 291–293, 298,
305, 310, 312, 323, 330, 332, 336,
386, 495, 525
Energy, 144, 161, 168, 170, 262, 274,
276, 348, 365, 379
Epstein, S., 6, 221, 286–290, 398, 428–
429, 437, 473, 534, 577–578, 581–
582
EQ-Map, 20, 221, 582
Evolutionary psychology, 48, 53–54,
119–120, 123, 143, 164–165, 171,
186, 234, 235, 248–250, 253–354
Executive control, 94, 124, 135, 245–
246, 282, 314, 337, 538
Expert scoring, 518
Explicit and implicit processing, 278–
279, 517, 534
Expressiveness, 424–425, 430, 432,
434, 439
Extraversion, 46, 58, 63–66, 148, 152,
178, 190, 212, 219, 221, 322–323,
326–327, 329, 342–351, 355, 362,
366–370, 385, 479, 525, 529, 537
Eysenck, H. J., 64–66, 88, 322, 325,
334, 344–345, 351, 362, 368, 381,
413
Eysenck, M. W., 65–66, 143, 160, 170,
252, 322, 325, 332–333, 336, 338,
345–346, 351, 362, 535

Facial expressions, 43, 56, 141, 145,
173, 182–183, 225–226, 240–242,
250, 261, 354, 356, 389, 517
Factor analysis, 59–65, 84, 85, 93, 95,
102, 109, 116, 120, 144, 188, 200,
204, 208, 213, 293, 309, 385, 398–
399, 483, 525, 531, 556, 558
Family discourse, 439
Fear, 137, 141–143, 152, 164, 238–242,
247–249, 252, 254, 256, 376, 377,
378, 383–384, 406–407, 409–411,
414–415, 469, 491, 533, 540
Foa, E. B., 164, 406–407, 409–410

Folkman, S., 162–163, 283–285, 296, 298, 300, 303–305, 307–308, 310, 312, 489

Frese, M., 468–470

Frontal lobes, 22, 62, 123, 152, 159, 171, 238, 242, 244, 365
  orbitofrontal cortex, 244–245, 282, 392, 425, 533, 538, 545
  prefrontal cortex, 123, 152, 244–245, 472
  ventromedial frontal cortex, 156, 246

Funder, D. C., 345, 355–356

Furnham, A., 41, 158, 212–213, 219, 225–227, 322–324, 326, 342–343, 346, 348–349, 525–526

Galton, F., 84, 86

Gardner, H., 22, 60, 62–63, 82, 116–123, 301, 398–399

Generalized Anxiety Disorder, 377, 405, 407, 411

Genetics, 48, 60, 64, 95, 145, 236, 362, 390, 419, 421–422, 464–465, 541

Glucose metabolism, 95, 98

Golden, C. J., 20, 218–220, 225–226, 321, 323–325, 515, 517

Goleman, D., 4–5, 7, 10–16, 26–27, 41, 67, 71–72, 76–77, 82, 90, 100, 114, 116, 166, 176, 214–215, 217, 235, 238–239, 242, 246, 267, 269, 275, 277, 279, 287, 297, 317, 319, 323, 325, 327, 341, 359, 361, 411, 420, 422, 444–445, 447, 456–457, 459, 462, 470–474, 476–478, 480–481, 494–495, 497–499, 503–504, 506, 514, 531, 533–534, 543, 545–546, 548–549, 559, 584

Gottman, J., 436, 440

Gray, J. A., 129, 240, 250, 252, 278, 335, 357, 366

Greenberg, M. T., 5, 77–78, 229, 442–444, 446–448, 450, 459, 461–464

Guilford, J. P., 62, 102–104, 203, 520, 552, 554, 560

Guilt, 169, 223, 266–267, 269, 379, 446, 448, 450

Guttman, L., 19, 42, 60, 96, 130, 565

Haggerty, C. J., 20, 218–220, 225–226, 321, 323–325, 515, 517

Hall, L. E., 20, 218–220, 225–226, 321, 323–325, 515, 517

Happiness, 139–140, 157, 173, 191, 223, 257, 262, 317, 342–344, 434, 446, 450, 468, 482, 546

Hardy, D. F., 437–438

Hart, S. D., 40, 64, 68, 149, 206, 208, 211–212, 219, 321, 326

Hawthorne effect, 460

Head size, 95, 98

Health, 161, 165, 170, 284, 289–290, 296, 300–301, 306–309, 313, 317, 330, 338, 363, 378, 381–382, 390, 393–394, 407, 414, 440, 449, 452–453, 455, 461–462, 468, 488–490, 494–496, 503, 543, 544

Hedonic tone, 144, 147

Heritability, 48, 60, 64, 95, 145, 236, 362, 390, 419, 421–422, 464–465, 541

Herrnstein, R. J., 6–7, 70, 82, 86, 93, 96, 100, 115, 190, 522, 549

History of intelligence testing and assessment, 83–86

Horn, J. L., 19, 45, 62, 89, 92, 99, 101–102, 104–105, 108–110, 112, 121

Howe, M. J. A., 87–88, 92

Hunter, J. E., 35, 82, 213, 479

Hypochondriasis, 380–381, 394

Imagination, 368, 393, 513, 548

Impulse control, 12, 207, 208, 209, 210, 302, 437, 447, 450, 452, 455–456, 458, 462, 479

Impulse-control disorders, 381, 413

Impulsivity, 71, 152, 156, 325, 344, 346, 350, 357, 361–363, 365–367, 380, 385–386
  functional vs. dysfunctional, 365–366

Infants, 423–424, 429–430, 432, 435

Ingram, R. E., 53, 263, 335, 401–403

Inhibition, 246, 253, 334, 357, 361, 366, 368, 384, 385

Integrity, 77, 479

Intelligence
  age differences in, 108, 109
  broad factors of, 106–111, 117
  crystallized (Gc), 59, 61, 63, 67, 73,
    93, 99, 105–115, 117, 122, 127–131,
    178, 190, 192, 196, 203–204, 247,
    325, 520–521, 523, 527, 561, 568,
    574
  definitions of, 86–91, 205
  fluid (Gf), 61, 105–115, 117, 122,
    125, 127–131, 247, 520–521, 523,
    527, 574
  general (g), 5–7, 12–13, 20–21 , 23–
    24, 36, 40, 45–46, 58–62, 68–70, 73,
    77, 80, 86–89, 91–100, 105, 110,
    115–116, 119, 123, 125, 191, 205,
    210, 219, 222, 227, 228, 246–247,
    285, 301–302, 316, 327, 356, 421,
    444–445, 471, 477–481, 483, 486,
    516–517, 520, 526–527, 539, 541–
    542, 545–549, 555–557, 571, 581
  implicit theories of, 89–91, 557
  interpersonal, 15, 63, 118, 122, 123,
    301
  intrapersonal, 15, 63, 118, 301, 398
  kinesthetic, 117, 121
  linguistic, 117, 119, 120, 123
  logical-mathematical, 117, 120, 123
  multiple, 60, 62, 116–122
  multistratum models of, 59, 93, 103–
    115, 213, 321, 525–526
  musical, 117, 119, 120, 121, 122
  neo-Spearmanian models of, 94–98
  practical, 6, 60, 128–129, 164, 269,
    517–518, 531
  racial differences in, 96
  structural theories of, 91–115, 129
  Structure-of-Intellect Model of, 62,
    102–104
  systems models of, 115–123, 129
  triarchic theory of, 123–129
Interhemispheric transfer, 390–391
Interpersonal Perception Test—15
  (IPT-15), 180, 203–204, 561, 572–
  575
Interpersonal relationships, 156, 162–
  163, 169–170, 241, 276, 324, 331,
  337–338, 348, 351, 353–354, 359–
  360, 368, 380, 410–411, 420, 442,
  446, 451–452, 484–485, 491, 498,
  503, 530
Interpersonal sensitivity, 323, 339,
  526
Intervention programs, 77–78, 393,
  409, 412–413, 415, 417, 419–421,
  442–464, 469, 472, 477, 497–500,
  502–504, 507–508, 515, 521–523,
  539–544, 546, 549
  educational, 445–464, 541–542
  school-based, 442–445, 542, 546
  workplace-training, 497–500, 542–
  543
Introversion, 46, 58, 63–66, 148, 152,
  178, 190, 212, 219, 221, 322–323,
  326–327, 329, 342–351, 355, 362,
  366–370, 385, 479, 525, 529, 537
IQ, 5–7, 12–13, 20–21 , 23–24, 36, 40,
  45–46, 58–62, 68–70, 73, 77, 80, 86–
  89, 91–100, 105, 110, 115–116, 119,
  123, 125, 191, 205, 210, 219, 222,
  227, 228, 246–247, 285, 301–302,
  316, 327, 356, 421, 444–445, 471,
  477–481, 483, 486, 516–517, 520,
  526–527, 539, 541–542, 545–549,
  555–557, 571, 581
Izard, C. E., 139, 422–423, 432, 465,
  534

Jaedicke, S., 437–438
James, W., 153–154
Jensen, A. R., 84, 87, 92, 94–98, 125,
  421, 445, 477, 521, 558
Job performance, 331, 343, 351, 467,
  471, 472, 475, 477, 479–485, 489,
  491, 497, 504, 518, 542–543, 546
Job satisfaction, 483, 490–492, 494,
  496–497, 508
Job stress, 331, 467, 488–492, 494–498,
  501, 503–504, 506, 508
Johnson-Laird, P. N., 52, 141, 143,
  265–266, 268, 270, 272, 275, 535
Joy, 141, 142, 152–153, 237
Judgment, 256, 262, 334, 355–356,
  368, 401, 439–440, 518

Krystal, H., 395

Lane, R. D., 202–203, 228, 236, 245, 355, 388, 391, 531, 566–570
Lange, C., 153, 251
Language, 238, 242, 244, 253–254, 266, 277, 346, 390, 392, 533
Lazarus, R. S., 13, 48–49, 52–54, 137–141, 148, 154–155, 158–159, 161–163, 172–173, 251, 257, 268, 270, 273–274, 283–285, 296, 298, 300, 303–308, 310–313, 316, 411, 428, 468, 489, 496, 534, 536
LeDoux, J. E., 235, 238–242, 251, 278–279
Levels of control of processing, 258, 314–315, 517
Levels of Emotional Awareness Scale (LEAS), 180, 203, 228, 355, 566–571
Levels of explanation. *See* Cognitive-science framework
Leventhal, H., 257–259, 280, 314, 535
Life events, 160–161, 163–164, 287–288, 313, 330, 332, 375, 382–383, 404, 405, 436, 495–496
Limbic system, 26, 238, 334, 365, 472, 531
Livesley, W. J., 383–385, 387
Lyons, W., 134–135

Machiavellian personality, 324
Mackintosh, N. J., 69–70, 72, 84, 123, 131
Malouf, J. M., 20, 218–220, 225–226, 321, 323–325, 515, 517
Marital dissatisfaction, 331, 436
Marshall, J., 490–491
Matthews, G., 5, 9, 11–12, 18, 19, 26, 37, 40, 43, 47, 49–50, 53, 58–59, 61, 63, 65–66, 68–69, 71–72, 84, 90, 111, 131, 144–148, 157–161, 168–170, 187–190, 198–199, 201, 221, 223, 226–228, 245, 251–252, 259–260, 262–265, 267–268, 272–276, 280, 282, 283–285, 293–295, 298, 300, 307, 309, 311, 314–315, 322–328, 331–333, 335–339, 341, 345–

348, 351, 357–358, 360, 362, 367, 369, 381, 383, 401–403, 405–411, 413, 416, 516–519, 526–527, 529–530, 535–537, 546–547
Maturation, 425
Mayer, J. D., 4, 8–10, 12, 14, 16–20, 28, 31, 35, 40, 42–43, 56, 63, 69, 72, 74–75, 77, 82, 90, 111, 115, 137, 149, 158, 166, 176, 180–183, 186–189, 191, 193, 196–202, 220–221, 228, 260, 282, 286–290, 292–293, 295, 300–301, 311, 313, 316, 319, 368, 388, 410–411, 415, 426–427, 430, 439, 441, 443, 456, 458, 466, 471, 474, 480–481, 514–520, 523, 530–531, 534–536, 544, 547, 559–560, 563–565
Mayer-Salovey-Caruso Emotional Intelligence Test (MSCEIT), 9, 18, 28, 39, 42, 56, 69, 157, 173, 180, 193–202, 293–295, 481, 515–519, 530, 544, 564–565
  description of, 193–197
  evaluation of, 197–200
McCrae, R. R., 40–41, 64–68, 178, 211, 213, 224, 294, 294, 323, 325, 342, 348, 385, 524–525, 537
Measurement of emotional intelligence. *See* Assessment of emotional intelligence
Media, 3–4, 20, 419, 421, 441, 443, 465
Memory, 66, 109, 121, 238, 240, 242, 249, 257–259, 261–262, 263, 268, 282, 327, 333, 336, 346, 391, 401, 403, 409, 411, 519, 535
  long-term, 108, 115, 300, 314
  semantic, 261
  short-term, 68, 106, 109, 327
  working, 61, 68, 108, 160, 205, 293, 336, 346, 535
Metacognition, 56, 115, 124, 127, 244, 272, 276, 300, 314, 319, 332, 337, 338–339, 341, 409, 414, 513
Middle childhood, 437
Minski, P. S., 219–220, 225, 324, 525–526
Modeling, 426–429, 435, 443, 463

Modular systems, 49, 118, 121, 123, 135, 149, 171, 246, 250, 252–253, 260, 281, 403

Mood, 15, 58, 138–139, 144–150, 159–163, 166–170, 172, 191, 200, 223, 262–265, 268–269, 276, 288–290, 295, 302, 319, 323–324, 330–331, 334, 339, 344–345, 350, 352, 369, 374, 376–377, 379–382, 393, 400, 404–408, 412, 417, 472–473, 525, 529–530, 534, 540

assessment of, 144–148

Mood congruence, 148, 168, 262

Mood induction, 22, 161, 168, 191, 264, 292, 344

Mood regulation, 149, 162–163, 219, 228, 268, 269, 288–289, 292–293, 301, 319, 417, 525, 534, 570

Motivation, 22, 99, 112, 129, 131, 137, 141, 146–148, 152, 157, 169–170, 204, 214, 218, 225, 236, 244, 249–250, 252, 266, 269, 270, 273, 275, 280, 326–329, 333, 335, 337, 345, 348, 356–358, 360–364, 366–369, 393, 433, 455–456, 468–469, 473, 476, 478, 482–483, 487, 497–499, 506–507, 523, 532, 542, 545, 548

Motivational Analysis Test (MAT), 112, 204

Mount, M. K., 168, 330, 343, 351, 362, 479, 543

Multifactor Emotional Intelligence Scales (MEIS), 17–21, 28, 181–192, 268, 292, 368, 481, 507, 515–519, 528, 530, 544, 563–565

description of, 182, 184–185

evaluation of, 187–192

Murray, C., 6–7, 70, 82, 86, 93, 96, 100, 115, 190, 522, 549

Murray, H. A., 548

Myth, 513–514, 544–547, 548–549

Narcissism, 344–345, 350, 369

Negative affect, 144–145, 148–149, 162, 168–170, 219, 223–225, 263–264, 266, 272, 274, 276, 298, 322–323, 329, 330–334, 337–339, 355, 369, 376, 381–386, 392–393, 400–401, 405, 408, 411, 423, 427, 429–430, 434–435, 438–441, 448–450, 456, 468–469, 473, 537, 540

Negative automatic thoughts, 414–415

Negative emotion. *See* Negative affect

Neglect, 424–425, 436, 440

Neisser, U., 89–90

Neocortex, 26, 65–66, 151–152, 235, 241, 279, 425

arousal of, 65–66, 151–152, 326, 345

NEO-FFI personality questionnaire, 294

NEO-PI-R personality questionnaire, 213, 385

Network models, 260, 264

of fear, 406–407, 409–410

of semantic memory, 261

Neural-net models, 262–263, 265

Neuroscience, 47–48, 60, 64, 134, 139, 152, 234–236, 253–254, 256, 277–278, 282, 425, 522, 534, 538

Neuroticism, 46, 64–68, 96, 148, 152, 178, 187, 190, 211, 212, 217, 219, 221, 223, 292, 294–295, 318, 322–325, 329, 330–342, 344, 347–348, 352, 354, 356–357, 362, 367–370, 373, 479, 524–525, 529, 537, 543, 546, 581

Newsome, S., 16, 208, 210, 227, 321, 478

Noegenesis, 92, 98–99

Nonverbal behavior, 344, 353, 380

Normative data, 486, 507

Nurturance, 252, 324, 360

Oatley, K., 52, 141, 143, 258, 265–266, 268, 270, 272, 275, 535

Observational learning, 428, 430, 441

Obsessive-compulsive disorder, 269, 364, 377, 383–384, 386, 407, 415

Occupational categories, 487, 507

Occupational stress, 331, 467, 488–492, 494–498, 501, 503–504, 506, 508

Openness, 46, 64–68, 96, 112, 178, 187, 190, 211, 212, 217, 219, 221, 223, 325–326, 354, 385–386

Optimism-pessimism, 14, 152, 157, 208, 219, 225, 332, 476, 482, 485, 506

Organizational change, 470, 474, 477, 488, 491, 495

Organizational climate, 492

Organizational commitment, 483

Organization-focused interventions, 500

Ortony, A., 138, 145, 258–259, 261, 278–280, 534

Panic disorder, 376, 377–378, 388, 393, 406–407, 414

Panksepp, J., 49, 136, 139, 141, 143, 145, 152, 235–237, 249–250, 281, 533

Parental control, 436, 438

Parents, 419, 422–440, 443, 444, 447, 449, 453, 455, 459, 461, 463–465

Parietal cortex, 335

Parker, J. D. A., 158, 192, 274, 285, 292–293, 298, 310–311, 323, 336, 362, 373, 387–391, 393–394, 398–399, 412, 415–416, 422, 425, 433, 540, 583

Pathologically low emotional intelligence (PLEI), 374–376, 381, 383, 387, 400, 410–412, 416

Pearlin, L. I., 307, 309, 311–312, 495, 504

Peers, 423–424, 427, 429, 431, 431, 436, 440–442, 451, 454, 461, 464

Pekrun, R., 468–470

Personality, 12, 14, 16, 40, 160, 178, 210–213, 234, 242, 272, 303, 321–370, 373–376, 379–387, 390, 393–394, 400, 407, 413, 416–417, 424, 436, 439, 478–480, 482–483, 486, 506–507, 515–517, 524–527, 529–530, 536–541, 543–548
cognitive-adaptive model of, 325–330, 369
disorders, 166, 210, 367, 369, 375–376, 379–380, 382–386, 413
Five-Factor Model of, 40, 65, 73, 148, 178, 187, 211, 212, 213, 217, 221, 225, 294, 321–322, 324–326, 351, 356, 385–387, 393, 479, 524–526, 537–538, 574, 585
overlap of, with emotional intelligence, 178, 223–226, 321–326, 368–370, 524–526
traits, 36, 56–58, 63–69, 71, 73, 80, 148, 298, 321–323, 326–327, 329, 336, 348, 350, 355, 362, 368–369, 382, 384, 476, 487, 517, 524–527, 529, 536–539, 545–546

Person-environment fit, 502, 530, 540

Personnel selection, 213, 467, 479

Petrides, K. V., 158, 212–213, 219, 225–227, 322–324, 525–526

Phobia, 143, 252, 376–379, 407, 411–412

Plutchik, R., 137, 141–143

Popular conceptions of emotional intelligence, 10–11, 15, 514

Positive affect, 144–145, 148–149, 162, 168–170, 219, 223–225, 274, 343, 353, 432, 435, 439, 441, 479

Positive emotions. *See* Positive affect

Positive manifold, 92, 94, 96, 99, 129, 520

Post-traumatic stress, 164, 310, 378, 393, 395, 406–407, 410, 540

Power, T. G., 437–438

PPIK theory (process, personality, interests, and knowledge), 111–112

Preschoolers, 423, 434, 436, 446

Primary mental abilities, 520, 548

Problem-focused coping, 147, 284, 298–299, 304–305, 308–309, 311–312, 317–318, 348, 350, 364, 496, 508

Problem solving, 282, 314–315, 339, 346, 358, 363, 409–410, 429–430, 436, 439, 446–447, 449–450, 452, 455–456, 461, 543, 577–578

Procedural knowledge, 267, 282, 315, 405, 458, 518

Processing speed, 61–62, 65, 131

Productivity, 77, 468, 480, 482, 487, 490, 494, 497

Promoting alternative thinking strategies (PATH), 446–450, 457, 465
Prosocial behavior, 169, 269, 324, 329, 350–351, 360–361, 433, 453, 476, 537
Psychoanalysis, 135, 304, 395, 412–413, 416
Psychometrics, 19, 23–24, 32, 46, 58–62, 79–80, 86, 91–100, 114, 127, 129–131, 136, 187–193, 196–200, 208–213, 219–222, 226–228, 322, 362, 459, 515–517, 524–525, 530–531, 545, 561, 564–565, 567–568, 574. *See also* Reliability; Validity
Psychophysiology, 253
Psychosomatic illness, 381
Psychotherapy, 27, 74–76, 79, 374, 393–395, 412–417, 470, 484
Psychoticism, 325, 362, 364, 386
Pylyshyn, Z. W., 50, 52, 138, 255, 532

Radex model, 130
Rationality versus emotionality, 8–9, 33, 34, 37–38, 46, 77, 80, 578
Raven's Progressive Matrices Tests, 92, 97, 99, 109, 196, 574
Reciprocal determinism, 305, 425
Reed, M. A., 245, 335, 366, 402
Relaxation, 284, 496, 500, 503
Reliability, 19, 24, 188, 208, 209, 210, 212, 217, 221, 355, 382, 515–516, 519, 521, 548, 560, 564, 574, 583
Resolving Conflict Creatively Program, 451–452, 456–457
Response bias, 33, 40–41, 80, 483
Reward and punishment systems, 145, 152, 171, 240
Risk taking, 303, 363, 365–368, 458
Roberts, R. D., 9, 12, 16, 18, 35, 37, 40, 43, 45–46, 58–63, 65, 67, 69–72, 84–85, 89–90, 97–101, 104–106, 109, 111, 115, 117–118, 131, 158, 187–191, 198–199, 201, 204–205, 211, 220–221, 223–224, 226–228, 267–268, 294, 326, 398, 516–519, 527, 530, 547, 574, 585

Role ambiguity, 490–491
Rolls, E. T., 48, 152, 240–246, 250, 253–254, 268, 282, 533
Rumination, 26, 221, 267, 290, 295, 311, 314, 317, 335, 339, 384, 386, 408, 410–411

Saarni, C., 5, 70, 229, 420–421, 424, 426–427, 429, 433, 440, 461, 572
Sadness, 141–142, 145, 157, 223, 257, 261, 429, 435–436, 440, 443, 465, 468–469, 503
Saklofske, D. S., 68, 219–220, 225, 284, 302–303, 308–309, 324, 387, 438, 495, 525–526, 536
Salovey, P., 4, 8–10, 12, 14, 16–20, 28, 31, 35, 40, 42–43, 56, 63, 69, 72, 74–75, 82, 90, 111, 115, 149, 158, 166, 176, 180–183, 186–189, 191, 193, 196–202, 220–221, 260, 282, 286–290, 292–293, 295, 300–301, 311, 313, 316, 319, 368, 388, 410–411, 415, 426–427, 430, 435, 439, 441, 443, 456, 458, 466, 471, 474, 480–481, 514–520, 523, 530–531, 534–536, 544, 547, 559–560
Sawaf, A., 76–77, 470, 476–478, 481, 503, 505
Scheier, M. F., 270, 272, 308–310, 314, 361, 482, 584
Schema, 156, 242, 258, 262, 337, 353, 391, 402–406, 408, 414
Scherer, K. R., 22, 257–259, 280, 314, 355, 535
Schizophrenia, 375, 380
Schmidt, F. L., 35, 82, 213, 479
Schooler, C., 307, 309, 312, 495, 504
Schutte, N. S., 20, 218–220, 225–226, 321, 323–325, 515, 517
Schutte Self-Report Inventory (SSRI), 218–220, 225–227, 292, 321, 323–325, 481, 515, 517, 525, 546
description of, 218
evaluation of, 218–220
Scientific method, 31–32, 79–80, 514, 516, 520, 549

Scoring methods, 33, 38–39, 42–46, 80, 186–202, 227, 518–519. *See also* Assessment of emotional intelligence
consensus, 90, 182–183, 187–190, 193, 196–202, 518–519, 521, 530, 563–565
expert, 72, 186, 188–190, 196–200, 202, 518–519, 530
target, 186–187, 192, 518–519, 563–565
Seattle Social Development Project, 449, 453–454, 456
Self, 154–156
Self-awareness, 204, 338–339, 341, 462, 471–472, 498, 513
Self-beliefs, 169, 233, 259, 262, 270, 272, 276, 284, 337, 358, 369, 401–403, 405–406, 409–411, 417, 540
Self-control, 6, 211, 217, 225, 248, 269, 275, 297, 323, 325, 329, 354, 357, 360–362, 364, 367–368, 379, 381, 436, 446–447, 453, 455, 461, 472–473, 481, 525, 533, 537, 545
Self-discrepancy, 270–272
Self-efficacy, 158, 170, 285, 288, 317, 326, 348, 361, 364, 367, 415, 438, 499, 506–507
Self-esteem, 46, 68, 146, 157, 210, 223–225, 323, 326, 339, 345, 348, 352–353, 358, 437, 446, 449–450, 452, 468, 476, 490–491, 524, 543, 549
Self-focus of attention, 146–147, 275–276, 332, 339, 408
Self-knowledge, 134, 150, 165, 272, 275, 315, 326, 334, 337, 348, 360, 367, 369, 402–403, 406, 408–410, 412, 515, 529, 532, 537
Self-Referent Executive Function (S-REF) model, 272–273, 275–276, 314–315, 337–339, 402–403, 408–409, 411
Self-regulation, 135, 149, 155, 159, 163, 165, 172–173, 255, 270, 272, 275, 276–277, 279, 282, 300, 314–316, 323, 328–329, 334, 336, 348,

350, 354, 422, 434, 436, 449–450, 472, 475, 485, 487, 513, 533, 534–535, 538, 544, 545
Selye, H., 151, 283
Sensation seeking, 63, 366, 479
Sensory processes and abilities, 93, 106
Siblings, 423, 427, 441
Siegle, G. J., 53, 148, 161, 170, 223, 245, 263, 274, 309, 315, 335–336, 408
Skills, 233, 267, 270, 275, 281, 314–316, 318, 326–330, 335–336, 351, 356, 358, 360, 367, 380, 487, 489, 492, 502–503, 513–514, 518, 530–531, 543–544, 559
acquisition of, 68, 251, 267–268, 325, 327, 329, 334, 336, 347–348, 369
cognitive, 242, 251, 302, 326–330, 346, 348, 517
emotional, 76–77, 419–420, 422, 426, 431, 436–437, 442–443, 455, 457–458, 461, 463–466, 474–477, 484, 497, 499–500, 506, 508, 541
in emotional disorders, 395, 409–410, 413, 415–416, 540
social, 77, 158, 163, 219, 267, 281, 287–288, 292, 315, 324, 326, 328–329, 338–339, 344–345, 348, 370, 380, 382, 409, 413, 420, 429, 445, 452, 455, 476, 481, 506, 525, 528
Social cognition, 352, 428
Social competence, 27, 113, 123, 215, 324, 329, 427, 432–433, 436–439, 453–456, 528, 537
Social intelligence, 23, 62–63, 73, 90–91, 104, 128, 158, 322, 359–360, 481, 519, 521, 529, 551–561, 574
Social interaction, 156, 162–163, 169–170, 241, 276, 324, 331, 337–338, 348, 351, 353–354, 359–360, 368, 380, 410–411, 420, 442, 446, 451–452, 484–485, 491, 498, 503, 530
Socialization, 419, 422, 424, 426–427, 432–433, 435, 437, 439, 441, 443, 448, 454, 465
Social network, 288, 429

Social problem solving, 78, 445, 447, 452–453, 461

Social support, 75, 162, 225, 276, 288, 292, 310, 319, 406, 409–410, 415, 429, 496, 501

Social withdrawal, 385–386, 417

Socioeconomic status, 522–523, 531

Somatic marker theory, 246

Somatoform disorder, 380–382, 387, 406, 413, 416

Spearman, C., 84, 87–88, 91–94

Speed of processing, 106, 205, 211, 316

Spielberger, C. D., 38, 58, 144–145, 148, 333

Spielberger emotion scales, 136, 144–145, 166

Stanford-Binet Intelligence Scale, 84, 201

Stankov, L., 9, 19, 60–62, 72, 84, 89, 92, 94, 97–98, 100–101, 104–106, 108–111, 113–115, 117, 204, 205, 211, 218, 220, 222, 229, 398, 519, 522, 549, 574, 585

Sternberg, R. J., 22, 59–60, 68, 84, 87–90, 115–116, 123–130, 268, 302, 474, 514, 518, 528, 556

Strategies, 53, 159, 162–163, 169–170, 172, 252, 264–265, 268–269, 288, 321, 334–336, 338, 346–348, 357, 359, 403, 406, 408–409, 430–431, 437–439, 446, 449–452, 463–464, 466, 516–517, 535–536. *See also* Coping

Stress, 15, 27, 53, 56, 113, 144, 151, 165, 169, 182, 191–192, 207–210, 212–213, 222, 226, 234, 274–275, 283–298, 303–308, 312–313, 316–319, 322–324, 326, 328, 330–333, 381, 408, 424, 434–435, 437–438, 456, 462, 464, 467, 488–498, 500–505, 529, 538–539, 543, 545

Stress management, 207, 208, 210, 212, 286, 323, 325, 330, 399, 452–453, 455

Substance abuse, 309, 338, 367, 381, 387, 453–454, 457, 462, 465, 503

Tacit knowledge, 128–129, 518–519, 528, 531

Task engagement, 146–147, 273–275, 276, 293–294, 307, 309, 348

Taylor, G. J., 192, 285, 311, 373, 387–391, 392–395, 398–399, 412, 422, 425, 433, 583

Teachers, 421, 427, 431, 440–444, 452, 454–456, 459–460, 462

Temperament, 421–425, 439

Tension, 144, 146–147, 160, 490–491

Test anxiety, 168–169, 275, 315, 331

Test construction, 92, 102, 201, 258, 323, 507, 515–517, 519, 520–522, 524, 530, 544, 547–548, 561

Thayer, R. E., 58, 139, 144–146, 161–162, 289

Theory of planned behavior, 352

Thought suppression, 409

Threat, 27, 57, 137, 142, 147, 155, 157, 168, 170, 235, 238, 240, 245, 248, 250, 252, 256–257, 259–260, 264, 272, 275, 294, 298, 308–309, 315, 322–323, 332–342, 354, 362, 367, 369, 378, 381, 401, 402–403, 405–406, 409, 410, 411, 468, 472, 474, 489–492, 537

Thurstone, L. L., 100–102

Tooby, J., 48, 249, 252, 268

Toronto Alexithymia Scale (TAS), 192, 388–389, 393, 398–399, 582–583

Training programs, 77–78, 393, 409, 412–413, 415, 417, 419–421, 442–464, 469, 472, 477, 497–500, 502–504, 507–508, 515, 521–523, 539–544, 546, 549

educational, 445–464, 541–542

school-based, 442–445, 542, 546

workplace, 497–500, 542–543

Trait Meta-Mood Scale (TMMS), 220–221, 481, 574

Tranel, D., 22, 152, 156, 171, 240, 246, 282, 531–533

Transactional model of stress, 155, 158, 172, 277, 284, 296–306, 316, 408, 489, 495, 536

Urbina, S., 32–33, 35, 81, 177, 227

Validity, 24, 28, 33–36, 44–46, 65, 69, 80, 95, 177–178, 250, 321, 356, 375, 382, 384, 408, 413, 479–480, 482, 486, 507, 509, 513, 515–516, 519, 524–526, 542, 546, 547–548
  construct, 35–36, 46, 177, 198, 199, 200, 202, 205, 221, 227, 568
  content, 33–34, 46, 177, 182, 226
  convergent, 45–46, 178–179, 565
  discriminant, 145, 179, 191, 217, 219–220, 227–228, 292, 486, 569
  divergent, 46, 228, 565
  ecological, 24, 90
  incremental, 444–445, 480, 486
  predictive, 13, 16, 18–19, 23, 34–35, 46, 97, 128, 129, 177, 196, 201, 219, 226, 227, 228, 423–444, 482, 486, 568
Vigilance, 293, 342, 346–347, 350
Vignoli, T., 545, 548–549

Watson, D., 144–145, 148–149, 223, 225, 324, 343–344, 382–383
Weisinger, H., 76–77, 471, 476, 478, 505
Weissberg, R. P., 5, 77–78, 229, 442–444, 447, 454, 459, 461–464
Wells, A., 169, 221, 268, 272–273, 275–276, 280, 282, 287, 295, 298, 300, 311, 314, 329, 334, 336–339, 345–348, 381, 401–403, 405–414, 416, 534–535, 540
Widiger, T. A., 376, 382–384, 386
Work overload, 490, 501
Work-relevant emotions, 468–469
Work stress, 331, 467, 488–492, 494–498, 501, 503–504, 506, 508
Worry, 112–113, 146–147, 273–276, 290, 293–295, 307, 310–311, 317, 332–333, 335, 337, 338–339, 342, 348, 377–378, 402, 405, 407–410, 540

Yale-New Haven Social Competence Promotion Program, 447, 454, 456
Young, A. W., 241, 532

Zahn-Waxler, C., 421, 433, 435–436
Zeidner, M., 5, 9, 12, 18, 19, 26, 37, 40, 42–43, 47, 49, 58, 60–61, 63, 65–66, 68–69, 71–72, 90, 111–112, 131, 145–146, 158, 168, 187–190, 198–199, 201, 226–228, 252, 267–268, 275, 284–285, 294, 302–303, 305, 308–309, 314–315, 322, 326–327, 331, 333, 336, 362, 369, 413, 438, 495, 516–519, 527, 530, 534, 536–537, 547
Zins, J. E., 5, 77–78, 229, 442–444, 447, 459, 461–464
Zuckerman, M., 65, 152, 159, 242, 245, 325, 357, 362, 365–366, 546